THE
4Os
THE STORY OF
A DECADE

THE
40s
THE *STORY* OF
A DECADE

THE NEW YORKER

Edited by Henry Finder
with Giles Harvey
Introduction by David Remnick

RANDOM HOUSE
New York

Published in the United States by Random House, an imprint and division of
Random House LLC, a Penguin Random House Company, New York.

RANDOM HOUSE and the House colophon are registered trademarks of Random
House LLC.

All pieces in this collection, except as noted, were originally published in
The New Yorker.

The publication dates are given at the beginning or end of each piece.

Letter on page 684 reprinted by permission of The Shirley Jackson Papers,
Manuscript Division, Library of Congress, Washington, D.C.

LIBRARY OF CONGRESS CATALOGING-IN-PUBLICATION DATA
The 40s: the story of a decade / The New Yorker; edited by Henry Finder
with Giles Harvey; introduction by David Remnick.
pages cm
ISBN 978-0-679-64479-8
eBook ISBN 978-0-679-64480-4
1. United States—History—1933–1945. 2. United States—History—1945–1953.
3. United States—Social life and customs—20th century. 4. United States—
Social customs—1933–1945. 5. United States—Social customs—1945–1953.
6. United States—In literature. 7. New Yorker (New York, N.Y.: 1925). I. Finder,
Henry. II. Harvey, Giles. III. New Yorker (New York, N.Y.: 1925). IV. New
Yorker (New York, N.Y.: 1925).
E806.F66 2014
973.917—dc23 2013047082

Printed in the United States of America on acid-free paper

www.atrandom.com

246897531

FIRST EDITION

Book design by Simon M. Sullivan

CONTENTS

PART THREE · POSTWAR

A Note by Louis Menand   231

PART FOUR · CHARACTER STUDIES

A Note by Susan Orlean   321

PART FIVE · THE CRITICS

BOOKS
A Note by Joan Acocella   457

THE CURRENT CINEMA
A Note by David Denby   492

THE THEATRE

A Note by Hilton Als   506

ART & ARCHITECTURE

A Note by Peter Schjeldahl   518

MUSICAL EVENTS

A Note by Alex Ross   534

PART SEVEN · FICTION

A Note by Zadie Smith 585

INTRODUCTION

THE NEW YORKER IN THE FORTIES

David Remnick

G AP-TOOTHED AND SPIKY-HAIRED, Harold Ross arrived in New
York after the Great War and soon became one of the city's most
fantastical characters. He was twenty-seven, an eccentric
searcher shaped by a dropout youth in the American West and a knock-
about start in the news business; before he enlisted, he'd worked for two
dozen papers, some of them for no more than a few weeks. Ross had a
lucky war. He battled the Germans by editing *Stars & Stripes* in Paris.
When he landed in Manhattan, he took up residence in Hell's Kitchen
and went to work for a veterans' publication called *The Home Sector*. He
also worked for a few months, in 1924, for *Judge*, a Republican-funded
humor magazine. In the meantime, he acquired a circle of young Jazz
Age friends (he played softball with Harpo Marx and Billy Rose, shot
ducks with Bernard Baruch) and conceived an idea for a fizzy Manhattan-
centric magazine of his own—a "fifteen-cent comic paper," he called it.
For financial backing, he hit up a baking and yeast scion named Raoul
Fleischmann. Ross never really liked Fleischmann ("The major owner of
The New Yorker is a fool," he once wrote; "the venture therefore is built
on quicksand"), but Fleischmann gave him the wherewithal to lure artists and writers from his accumulating circle of friends, hungry freelanc-
ers, disgruntled newspapermen, and Broadway lights. Harold Ross was
in business.

From the moment he published the first issue of the magazine, in
February 1925, he became one of midtown's most talked-about characters. He was the profane rube who had a mystical obsession with
grammatical punctilio and syntactical clarity. He was the untutored

knucklehead ("Is Moby Dick the man or the whale?" he famously asked) who lived on unfiltered cigarettes, poker chips, and Scotch and yet somehow managed to hire James Thurber and E. B. White, Janet Flanner and Lillian Ross, Edmund Wilson and Vladimir Nabokov, A. J. Liebling and Joseph Mitchell. He could not afford to pay Hemingway's short-story rates, and so—with the guidance of a fiction department led by a cultivated Bryn Mawr graduate named Katharine Angell (later Katharine White)—he went about discovering John O'Hara, John Cheever, J. D. Salinger, and Shirley Jackson. His editorial queries ("Were the Nabokovs a one-nutcracker family?") got to the heart of things.

Ross was in on the joke of his bumpkin persona, and later became its captive, a lonely, twice-divorced workaholic. But he marshaled that persona to lead, to cajole, to set a tone at the magazine that was high-minded in its studied lack of high-mindedness. Ross had the sort of editorial personality that caused his deputies and writers to weep, sometimes in despair, sometimes in gratitude. One day, he would send a note saying "WRITE SOMETHING GOD DAMN IT." And then, on the occasion of good work, he would send a message reading, "I am encouraged to go on." It was all in the service of the weekly cause. He was nothing if not clear. To break up his first marriage, he sent his wife a kind of editorial memo that left no doubt of her faults and his own. Thurber took a crack at portraying the man in *The Years with Ross,* and Wolcott Gibbs wrote a play, *Season in the Sun,* with a directive that the actor playing the Ross character ought to be able to play Caliban or Mr. Hyde "almost without the assistance of makeup."

The richest and funniest portrayal of Ross and the day-to-day affairs of *The New Yorker,* however, resides in his letters, which were edited, expertly, by his biographer, Thomas Kunkel. Those letters reveal the inner life of Ross—the irascibility, the devotion, the single-mindedness—and the evolution of his idea for the New York–based weekly. "Let the other magazines be important," he said throughout the twenties and thirties. Ross was determined to keep things light, to publish fiction, humor, reviews, artwork, and reporting that avoided heaviness, pretension. His models included *Punch,* the British publication known for its cartoons, and *Simplicissimus,* a satirical German weekly. He disdained the quarterlies, academia, and analysis—the genre known to him as "thumb-suckers." He prized shoe-leather reporting, vivid observation, absolute clarity, and conversational tone. He preferred a limited circulation (with expensive ads) to a mass audience. He wanted a magazine that was more stylish than *Life*, more upscale than *Collier's*, more timely than *Vanity Fair*.

Ross was not an especially political man. His racial views were retrograde, even for the times. He tended toward isolationism. When forced, he said, "I'm a liberal, though, by instinct. Human, you might say, and a meliorist by belief." But politics and polemics were not in his early plans for the magazine; he intended to enjoy the Jazz Age, not sing the blues of impending crash. Editorially and commercially, he had conceived *The New Yorker* for the city's "sophisticates," a silvery, elusive sensibility that was defined, particularly in those prewar years, by an aloofness to the troubles of the world. The magazine's dominant visual artist at the time was Peter Arno, an East Coast aristocrat, who, in his covers, portrayed the Depression, when he portrayed it at all, as a mild joke.

Ross's letters, particularly in the magazine's first ten years, show little concern about money and the Depression, except where it concerns the complicated financial arrangements he had with his ex-wife or a drop in ad pages. Two financial subjects do seem to thrill him: the successful investment he made in Chasen's, a smart-set restaurant in Los Angeles built by the vaudevillian Dave Chasen, and the hiring of editorial talent—particularly Katharine Angell, who raised immeasurably the ambitions of the fiction department, and William Shawn, who came to work on "fact" pieces and eventually led the magazine for three and a half decades. On the whole, standards of rectitude and taste, sometimes in the form of puritanical reserve, were more on his mind. In one prolonged letter, he has the energy to debate with E. B. White about the use of the phrase "toilet paper," for instance, which Ross finds "sickening." ("It might easily cause vomiting," he insists. "The fact that we allow toilet paper to be advertised, under the name 'Satin Tissue,' has nothing to do with this matter.") You can read your way through countless letters and think that the Depression did not exist; it hardly cast a shadow on *The New Yorker*. When James Agee and Walker Evans went off to investigate poverty in rural Alabama, it was for *Fortune*.

There were those who noticed *The New Yorker*'s determined detachment. "In the class war *The New Yorker* is ostentatiously neutral," Dwight Macdonald wrote, in a 1937 essay for *Partisan Review* called "Laugh and Lie Down." "It makes fun of subway guards and of men-about-town, of dowagers and laundresses, of shop girls and debutantes. . . . Its neutrality is itself a form of upper class display, since only the economically secure can afford such Jovian aloofness from the common struggle." On September 6, 1940—one year after the Nazi invasion of Poland; six weeks after the magazine finished running St. Clair McKelway's unflattering profile of Walter Winchell—Ross posted a confessional on the bulletin board that seemed to echo Macdonald's point.

MEMO TO *The New Yorker* STAFF
September 6, 1940

In the interests of avoiding possible embarrassment, I would report that I was kicked out of the Stork Club last night, or asked not to come in again (suavely), because the sight of me causes distress to Mr. [Sherman] Billingsley, the proprietor—something I'm doing my best to take in my stride. It's because of the Winchell pieces. I don't know to what extent Mr. Billingsley's aversion extends into this organization, but it certainly includes McKelway.

That's not to say that Ross or his magazine was oblivious to the accumulating catastrophe. Ben Yagoda's fine history of *The New Yorker*, *About Town*, scrupulously points out the signs of belated awareness: in 1939, Rea Irvin published a portfolio of drawings called *A Nazi History of the World*. At the end of the year, Frank Sullivan, in his Christmas verse "Greetings, Friends!," included the couplet "Lebensraum he wants? So! Well, / Let's hope he gets it soon, in hell." The next year, Christina Malman drew a haunting charcoal cover of armed German soldiers watching over a long stream of downtrodden prisoners, many wearing hats, some wearing skullcaps.

Still, the magazine did not figure out how to respond fully to such events until the forties. This anthology represents *The New Yorker*'s great turn, its journalistic, artistic, and political awakening. When the global conflagration began, Ross—to the surprise of his readers and even of some of his staff—proved himself prepared.

In journalism, if not in world events, Ross could be prescient. He told Janet Flanner, as she was about to sail for France, "I don't want to know what you think about what goes on in Paris. I want to know what the French think." In those days of stubbornly dull and ritualistic news reporting, this amounted to revolutionary counsel. Ross was, in effect, asking Flanner to rely on observation and her own intelligence and voice; questions of form were up to her. In January 1940, he told A. J. Liebling, who was cooling his heels in France, waiting impatiently for a battle, "For the time being, I say mark time, and be prepared for excitement if it starts." He gave much the same advice and freedom to many other writers—Mollie Panter-Downes, John Hersey, E. J. Kahn, Jr., John Lardner, and Rebecca West among them—as they set off on their assignments. He put the right players on the field, gave them enormous leeway, begged for copy—and when the time came they produced coverage of the war that was unmatched.

It is hard to overemphasize how fresh *The New Yorker*'s voices in the forties were compared with what was in most other magazines and daily newspapers. The singular "house" voice, E. B. White, wrote with the alarm of his readers. White's Notes and Comment piece on the occasion of the Nazi march on Paris captures the sense that the world was out of synch, the danger not so far from home:

> An hour or two ago, the news came that France had capitulated. The march of the vigorous and the audacious people continues, and the sound is closer, now, and easier to hear.
>
> To many Americans, war started (spiritually) years ago with the torment of the Jews. To millions of others, less sensitive to the overtones of history, war became actual only when Paris became German. We looked at the faces in the street today, and war is at last real, and the remaining step is merely the transformation of fear into resolve.
>
> The feeling, at the pit of every man's stomach, that the fall of France is the end of everything will soon change into the inevitable equivalent human feeling—that perhaps this is the beginning of a lot of things.

(White's were typically the first pieces that readers encountered in each week's issue, and a contribution of his opens each of the sections in this volume.)

Ross was not eager for the United States to enter the war, but his personal views were hardly the point. He dispatched one writer after another into the bottomless story, so much so that there were hardly any staff members left at 25 West Forty-third Street. Ross and Shawn and the rest worked nights and weekends to make their deadlines. They faced paper rationing. Circulation increased, but the circulation department collapsed under the weight of the draft. Ross feared that he would lose Shawn, and was relieved only when Shawn was exempted from service because he and his wife, Cecille, had a son. "*The New Yorker* is a worse madhouse than ever now," White confided to his older brother, "on account of the departure of everybody for the wars, leaving only the senile, the psychoneurotic, the maimed, the halt, and the goofy to get out the magazine."

What built the new reputation of the magazine was a string of pieces including Janet Flanner's Profile of General Pétain, Liebling's dispatches from all over Europe, and Hersey's exclusive about a young officer named John F. Kennedy and his exploits rescuing his crewmates on the PT-109. When the Navy and Kennedy's father, Joseph, tried to get Hersey's piece moved from *The New Yorker* to the larger-circulation *Reader's Digest*, Ross was uncompromising. He wrote to Joseph P. Kennedy, "All of these goings-on led us to believe that we were more or less being chivvied around by a bunch of heavyweights, and since we have long had a feeling here that we *are* kicked around a great deal by the big fellows, or in behalf of the big fellows, we were not disposed to lay down now."

As the journalism deepened, the popularity of the magazine broadened. Between 1941 and the end of the war, in 1945, circulation went from 172,000 to 227,000. Some of that popularity was due to a free, pocket-size "pony" edition of the magazine that was distributed to men and women in the service. It was a marketing boon; many of them bought subscriptions when they came home.

The war made *The New Yorker*. And Ross knew it, even if the knowledge was tinged with regret. He feared pretension and self-importance almost as much as he feared a dropped comma. The second half of the forties was less tumultuous but no less transformative. The American Century, long predicted in jingoistic terms by Henry Luce, Ross's bête noire, took shape. Postwar prosperity infused New York—and *The New Yorker*—with a greater sense of commercial and artistic ambition. The trauma of the war, too, was reflected in the stories of Salinger and Shaw and Nabokov. And despite his fear of pretension, Ross became less self-conscious about the life of the mind; Edmund Wilson was, notably, given the freedom to write about whatever captivated his interest, from the rites of literary culture in postwar London to the customs of the Zuni in New Mexico.

After the war, Ross was so exhausted, so worn down by his editorial struggles and his contentious relations with Fleischmann, that he threatened to resign. And yet, as the country settled into its great boom, he grew accustomed to more ordinary battles over galleys and page proofs and seemed to take a wry and renewed pleasure in them. "There is nothing to be done about [Edmund] Wilson's editing that I know of," he wrote to Katharine White. "He is by far the biggest problem we ever had around here. Fights like a tiger, or holds the line like an elephant, rather."

When there were other battles to be fought, more serious ones, Ross was never fainthearted. Liebling, E. B. White, and Lillian Ross all wrote strong pieces about the more virulent forms of anti-Communism. (The FBI accumulated a file on Liebling, calling him a "careless journalist of the *New Yorker* set" and responsible for "the pinko infiltration of *The New Yorker*.") Ross, without making much of it, stood by them all.

By the end of the decade, *The New Yorker* was flourishing, but Ross was a wreck. He suffered from ulcers, lung ailments, and general exhaustion. He was increasingly ceding authority to Shawn. In 1951, he wrote to his friend the writer Howard Brubaker, "I started to get out a light magazine that wouldn't concern itself with the weighty problems of the universe, and now look at me." By the end of the year, Ross was dead. The fifties at *The New Yorker* were left to the men and women he had nurtured, hectored, cajoled, flattered, berated, agitated, mystified, and, yes, inspired.

PART ONE
THE WAR

A NOTE BY GEORGE PACKER

I N LATE MAY 1940, the writer A. J. Liebling awaited the Second World War in "a little Marseillais restaurant on the Rue Monmartre," dining on "Mediterranean rouget burned in brandy over twigs of fennel." He had returned as a correspondent for *The New Yorker* to the city of his youthful adventures in food and other passions soon after the German invasion of Poland, in the fall of 1939, and he had spent the months of the Phony War in a state of suspended disbelief. Drawing comfort from the "gastronomic normality" of Parisian life, he convinced himself that the Nazis were overrated and the French would put up a tough fight—that this was a replay of the First World War. Even after the Wehrmacht's Blitzkrieg cut through Holland and Belgium "as through butter" and prepared to devour France, Liebling couldn't believe in the coming catastrophe. "The rouget tasted too much as good rouget always had," he wrote; "the black-browed proprietor was too normally solicitous; even in the full bosom and strong legs of the waitress there was the assurance that this life in Paris would never end."

In some ways it was still 1925, the year of *The New Yorker*'s birth. Even after a decade of worldwide depression and rising Fascist power, the magazine remained dedicated to the sophisticated tastes of what its founding editor, Harold Ross, in a letter to prospective investors and subscribers, called "metropolitan life." The main stage was New York, the tone ironic and detached, never passionately engaged, immune to shock. Ross prescribed that the weekly commentary be written "in a manner not too serious"; the magazine prided itself on never taking a political stand. Hitler made a few scattered appearances in its pages during the thirties, as tyrant or buffoon—notably in Janet Flanner's three-part Profile in 1936, based on interviews with the Führer, whose anti-Semitism and race fanaticism received slightly less space than his vegetarianism and celibacy. In 1933, when few people outside Germany understood what Nazism portended, E. B. White, the anonymous voice of the magazine's Comment, wrote, "Thus in a single day's developments in Germany we go back a thousand years into the dark." But two years later, he fell back into characteristic lightheartedness: "We predict that there will be no war in 1936, 1937, 1938, 1939, and 1940. There will be a small war in 1941 between Cambodia and Alberta over a little matter of some Irish Sweepstake tickets, and then there will be no war in 1942, 1943, 1944, 1945, and 1946. Our prophecy is no mere wish-fulfillment—it packs a heap of personal good feelings toward nations." It was as if the magazine knew that the world of witty table talk, society portraits, and Broadway lowlifes was doomed, but, like a character in a Thurber sketch, it couldn't bring itself to wake up from an entertaining dream that had begun to quiver with sinister undertones.

At the end of the summer of 1939, with war apparently imminent, White's Comment finally showed *The New Yorker* to be capable of shock. It sounded the note of a highly civilized sensibility forced to engage with something alien, ugly, and inescapable: "Today is Sunday, August 27th. Perhaps you don't remember that far back, you who presumably now dwell in a world which is either at peace or at war. . . . If war comes, it will be war, and no one wants that. If peace is restored, it will be another arrangement enlarging not simply the German boundary but the Hitler dream. The world knows it can't win."

The war opened *The New Yorker* to the wider world. Without changing beyond recognition, it became a more serious magazine; without sounding like *Time* or *The New Republic*, it became political. It rediscovered places it already knew, perhaps a little too well (London, Paris, Hell's Kitchen), and it discovered places that it had never imagined (Tunisia, the Marianas Islands). The Second World War was total war, involving cities, villages, and much of the world's population, with battlefields in a hotel lobby or an uninhabited island. Partly for this reason, the coverage in *The New Yorker* benefitted from the fact that it was a literary magazine, matching writers to subjects in ways that produced some of the greatest and most original journalism of the war.

Ross deployed much of his available talent to cover the conflict. *The New Yorker*'s war correspondents included the magazine's former managing editor, a movie critic, a sportswriter, humorists, and short-story writers, as well as some of its leading reporters. By happenstance, Mollie Panter-Downes, an English novelist living on a pig farm in Surrey, became the magazine's London correspondent in time for Dunkirk and the

Blitz, and her understated style perfectly captures the British talent for survival through disengagement that Americans learned to admire during the war: "Incidentally, the announcements of the first air-raid deaths are beginning to appear in the obituary columns of the morning papers. No mention is made of the cause of death, but the conventional phrase 'very suddenly' is always used. Thousands of men, women, and children are scheduled to die very suddenly, without any particular notice being taken of them in the obituary columns."

The focus of *The New Yorker*'s war reporting is rarely the big picture. Grand strategy is almost never discussed; the Eastern Front, inaccessible to the magazine's reporters, hardly exists; the names Roosevelt, Churchill, Hitler, and Stalin appear less often than those of ordinary soldiers. The largest event in human history is witnessed in small stories, through details and characters, in what the writer is able to see and hear—an elegant third-floor London drawing room exposed by bombing; a tearful conversation between a major and the sergeant he's casually but deeply offended. The neutrality and omniscience of modern newspaper reporting are not the guiding principle here. The writer's personal relation to the subject is often what gives a piece its insight and power. When the playwright S. N. Behrman visits London for the first time since the start of the war, he finds the nightly blackout terrifyingly total and eerily beautiful. Who would have known that London's Underground shelters blasted American pop tunes all night long, if Behrman hadn't made a point of going down into one?

Liebling—corpulent, witty, and pleasure-loving—becomes an unlikely correspondent with the U.S. Army in North Africa, and later goes on to cover the landings at Normandy and the liberation of Paris. While the memory of his French pleasures occasionally intrudes, like hunger pangs, Liebling's exuberance is restrained, his comic impulses sobered up, his baroque prose style rendered more straightforward and exact by the vast, death-haunted experience in which he plays a small part.

The war consumed *The New Yorker*, along with the rest of the country. Ross begged the War Department for more draft deferments, complaining that he had lost half his editorial staff to military service, and making a case for the magazine's importance to the war effort. In the journalism of the Second World War, the difference between civilian and military dissolved in ways that later became impossible with an all-volunteer army. *New Yorker* correspondents describe the soldiers they meet by their prewar identity ("He was a yacht broker in civilian life and often wrote articles about boats"; "All Riley wanted to do was finish the war and go back to the University of Texas"). A few contributed work to the magazine while still in uniform, while some writers joined the action as if they were members of the unit they were covering. In some of the terse, atmospheric frontline dispatches, it can be hard to tell which was written by a soldier and which by a reporter.

This closeness between observer and participant is accompanied by an open partisanship that became unthinkable after Vietnam. Panter-Downes says of her English countrymen, "The behavior of all classes is so magnificent that no observer here could ever imagine these people following the French into captivity." St. Clair McKelway's series on the strategic bombing of Japan is called "A Reporter with the B-29s," but in fact McKelway was a public-affairs officer with the 21st Bomber Command of the Army Air Force—an official censor. He referred to the enemy as "Japs," never once paused to consider the human cost of the incendiary bombs dropped on Tokyo, and revered the generals who were his direct superiors (including Curtis LeMay), while portraying them with subtlety and humor. In other words, McKelway wrote as a lieutenant colonel whose job was P.R., and who was also a great reporter on the staff of *The New Yorker*—a convergence of roles that would not occur at the magazine today. There's a loss of plausible objectivity in the arrangement, but McKelway wrote about men at war with a frank and knowledgeable love that scarcely appears any longer in American journalism.

When the war was over, Ross realized that the changes in *The New Yorker* would be permanent. "I think our transition to peace, art, amusement, frivolity, etc., will be gradual," he wrote to Flanner, in June 1946, "and probably the magazine will never get back to where it was, on account of having gone heavyweight to a considerable extent during the war." The magazine was about to go even heavier. William Shawn, Ross's deputy (and later his successor), had assigned a young novelist and reporter named John Hersey—the son of missionaries in China—to travel through occupied Japan and write about the effects of the atomic bomb. "Hiroshima" filled the entire issue of August 31, 1946.

Hersey's method of re-creating the destruction of the city through the fate of six individuals produced a daring new form of journalism, modeled on fiction. It portrayed civilians in America's hated enemy, Japan, for the first time as human beings. It rendered the destructive power of nuclear energy all the more terrifying for being brought down to its minute particulars—to the flower patterns seared from women's kimonos onto their skin. The Second World War ended with two radical new shocks to human conscience: the death camps and the bomb. The first received its most eloquent testimony from survivors. The second shock was absorbed in the pages of *The New Yorker*, and transformed into literary art.

NOTES AND COMMENT

E. B. White

SEPTEMBER 2, 1939

THIS WILL BE one of those mute paragraphs written despite the impossible interim of magazine publication, handed over to a linotyper who has already heard later news. Today is Sunday, August 27th. Perhaps you don't remember that far back, you who presumably now dwell in a world which is either at peace or at war. It is three o'clock in the morning. The temperature in New York is 70 degrees, sky overcast. The long vigil at the radio is beginning to tell on us. We have been tuned in, off and on, for forty-eight hours, trying to snare intimations of our destiny, as in a butterfly net. Destiny, between musical transcriptions. We still twitch nervously from the likelihood of war at 86 on the dial to the possibility of peace at 100 on the dial. The hours have induced a stupor; we glide from Paris to London to Berlin to Washington—from supposition to supposition, lightly. (But that wasn't a supposition, that was the Hotel Astor.) The war of nerves, they call it. It is one of those phrases that catch on. Through it all the radio is immense. It is the box we live in. The world seems very close at hand. ("Countless human lives can yet be saved.") We sit with diners at the darkened tables in the French cafés, we pedal with the cyclists weekending in the beautiful English countryside, we march alongside the German troops approaching the Polish border, we are a schoolboy slipping on his gas mask to take shelter underground from the raid that hasn't come, we sit at the elbow of Sir Nevile as he presents the message to the British Cabinet (but what does it say?). Hour after hour we experience the debilitating sensation of knowing everything in the world except what we want to know—as a child who listens endlessly to an adult conversation but cannot get the gist, the one word or phrase that would make all clear. The world, on this Sunday morning, seems pleasingly unreal. We've been reading (between bulletins) that short story of Tomlinson's called "Illusion: 1915," which begins on a summer day in France when the bees were in the limes. But this is Illusion 1939, this radio sandwich on which we chew, two bars of music with an ominous voice in between. And the advertiser, still breaking through: "Have you acquired the safety habit?" Moscow is calling New York. Hello, New York. Let me whisper I love you. They are removing the pictures from the museums. There was a time when the mere nonexistence of war was enough. Not any more. The world is in the odd position of being intellectually opposed to war, spiritually committed to it. That is the leaden note. If war comes, it will be war, and no one wants that. If peace is restored, it will be another arrangement enlarging not simply the German boundary but the Hitler dream. The world knows it can't win. Let me whisper I love you while we are dancing and the lights are low.

PARIS POSTSCRIPT

A. J. Liebling

AUGUST 3/10, 1940 (ON THE FALL OF FRANCE)

O N SATURDAY, MAY IITH, the day after the Germans invaded
Holland and Belgium, I had a letter from Jean-Pierre, a corporal in one of the two French armored divisions, which were
created after the Polish campaign. They were good divisions, and Jean-
Pierre had no way of knowing that the Germans had six times as many.
"The real rough-house is about to begin," he wrote. "So much the better!
It will be like bursting an abscess." Jean-Pierre, whose parents were my
oldest friends in France, was a strong, quiet boy who in civil life had been
a draughtsman in an automobile factory. He liked to play ice hockey and
collect marine algae. He had not wanted a soft job in a factory during the
war because he did not want to be considered a coward.

On the same morning I had a telephone conversation with another
friend of mine, Captain de Sombreuil, who had just arrived from Alsace
on furlough. Upon reaching the Gare de l'Est, he had learned that all
furloughs were cancelled, so he was going back by the next train. He
called me up to say that he wouldn't be able to go to the races at Auteuil
with me as he had planned. "It's good that it's starting at last," he said.
"We can beat the Boches and have it over with by autumn."

In the afternoon I went to Auteuil alone. I watched a horse belonging
to Senator Hennessy, the cognac man, win the Prix Wild Monarch for
three-year-old hurdlers. The track was crowded with people whose main
preoccupations seemed to be the new three-year-olds and the new fashions being worn by the women. That day the Germans were taking Arn-
hem and Maastricht in Holland and attacking Rotterdam with
parachutists. Nobody worried much. Everyone was eager principally to

know whether French troops had yet made contact with the enemy. "The Boches have business with somebody their own size now!" they said pugnaciously. "They will see we are not Poles or Norwegians!" It was conceivable, of course, that the Germans would win a few victories, but it would be a long war, like the last one. All France, hypnotized by 1918, still thought in terms of concentrated artillery preparations, followed by short advances and then, probably, by counterattacks. Even if the Allied troops should fail to save Holland, they would join the Belgians in holding the supposedly magnificent fortified line of the Albert Canal. At worst, the armies could fall back to the Franco-Belgian frontier, where, the newspapers had been proclaiming since September, there was a defensive system practically as strong as the Maginot Line. Confidence was a duty. The advertising department of the Magasins du Louvre discovered another duty for France. The store's slogan was "Madame, it is your duty to be elegant!" "They shall not pass" was considered *vieux jeu* and hysterical. The optimistic do-nothingism of the Chamberlain and Daladier regimes was, for millions of people, the new patriotism. Ten days before the war began in May, Alfred Duff Cooper told the Paris American Club, "We have found a new way to make war—without sacrificing human lives."

• • •

The news of the break-through at Sedan, which reached Paris on the fifth day of the offensive, was, for a few Parisians who were both pessimistic and analytical, the beginning of fear. But it happened so quickly, so casually, as presented in the communiqués, that the unreflective didn't take it seriously. The Belgian refugees began to arrive in Paris a few days after the fighting started. The great, sleek cars of the de-luxe refugees came first. The bicycle refugees arrived soon after. Slick-haired, sullen young men wearing pullover sweaters shot out of the darkness with terrifying, silent speed. They had the air of conquerors rather than of fugitives. Many of them undoubtedly were German spies. Ordinary destitute refugees arrived later by train and as extra riders on trucks. Nothing else happened at first to change the daily life of the town.

• • •

Tuesday evening, May 14th, I climbed the hill of Montmartre to the Rue Gabrielle to visit Jean-Pierre's parents. Henri, Jean-Pierre's father, had long limbs and sad eyes; he combined the frame of a high jumper and the mustaches of a Napoleonic grenadier. He was a good Catholic, and by birth and training he belonged to the wealthier bourgeoisie. By temperament, which he had never been allowed to indulge, he was a bohemian. A long struggle to succeed in business, which he secretly detested, had ended in a defeat just short of total. When war was declared, he was working for a firm of textile stylists whose customers were chiefly foreign mills. Since September, business had fallen off drastically and Henri had had nothing to do except drop in once in a while to keep up the firm's desultory correspondence. Henri spoke English, German, and Dutch in addition to French, and sometimes sang in a deep voice which sounded like a good but slightly flawed 'cello. He often said that he was happy to be living, at last, high on Montmartre, just under Sacré-Cœur. His wife, Eglée, would never have permitted him to live there for any reason less compelling than poverty. Eglée, before her marriage to Henri, had been a buyer in a department store. Recently she had devised a muslin money belt for soldiers to wear under their shirts. She worked an average of sixteen hours a day, making the belts with a frantic dexterity, but about once a fortnight she got so exhausted that she had to stay in bed for two or three days. She had placed the belts in several of the department stores, but her profit was small. Eglée and Henri were both about sixty years old. For thirty-five years Henri had pretended to like trade in order to hold his wife's respect, and Eglée had pretended to loathe trade in order to hold Henri's affection. Neither had succeeded in deceiving the other. He brooded, she scolded, he drank a little, they quarrelled incessantly, and they loved each other more than any two people I have ever known.

As I came into their apartment Tuesday night, Eglée was saying she felt sure Jean-Pierre was dead. Henri said that was nonsense. She said he was an unfeeling parent. Henri became angry and silent. Then he said that often, when he was at Verdun, Eglée had not heard from him for a week at a time. She said that Henri was always talking about Verdun and belittling "Jean-Pierre's war." "To think that after these years of preparing to avoid the old mistakes," Henri said, "the Germans are now eighty miles from us. If they get to Paris, it's all over." Eglée said he was a defeatist to mention such an eventuality. He said, "I am not a defeatist. I am an old soldier and also an old travelling man, and I know how near they are to Paris." I tried to console him by saying that the Dutch, at any rate, were fighting better than anyone had expected. Henri had cousins in Holland. Eglée said the Dutch were Boches and would before long prove it.

The next morning there was a radio announcement that the Dutch had surrendered in Europe but were going to continue the war in the East Indies. In the afternoon, some of the American correspondents, including myself, went to the Netherlands Legation to meet Mynheer Van Kleffens, the Netherlands Minister for Foreign Affairs, who had arrived from London to explain the Dutch decision. Van Kleffens, accompanied by the Netherlands Minister to France and the Netherlands Minister for National Defence, received us and the journalists of other neutral countries in the Legation garden. While we were talking, sadly and quietly, among the trees, the French were losing the war. On that Wednesday, May 15th, the Germans made the deep incision which a few days later was to split the Allied armies. The Foreign Minister, a blond, long-faced man, had a pet phrase which he repeated many times, as a man does when he is too tired to think of new forms for his thought. "The Germans tried this," he would say, recounting some particular method of the German attack, and then he would add, "It failed." "It failed," he would say, and again, "It failed"—until you thought he was talking of a long, victorious Dutch resistance—and then finally, "But to fight longer was hopeless." "We will fight on" was another recurrent phrase. When we asked him whether the Dutch had any planes left to fight with, he said, "No. We had fifty bombers. The last one flew off and dropped its last bomb and never returned."

Holland, with one-tenth the population of Germany but with several times the wealth per capita, had presented fifty bombers against five thousand. It had been comfortable to believe in neutrality, and cheap. Norway, with the fourth largest merchant marine in the world, had not built the few good light cruisers and destroyers which might have barred the weak German navy from its ports. France herself had economized on the Maginot Line, had decided it was too expensive to extend the fortifications from Luxembourg to the sea. The democracies had all been comfortable and fond of money. Thinking of the United States, I was uneasy.

· · ·

The first panic of the war hit Paris Thursday, May 16th. It affected, however, only the most highly sensitized layers of the population: the correspondents, the American and British war-charity workers, and the French politicians. In Paris, because of censorship, news of disaster always arrived unofficially and twenty-four hours late. On the evening of the catastrophic May 15th, even the neurotic clientele of the Ritz and Crillon bars had been calm. But on Thursday people began telling you about Germans at Meaux and south of Soissons, points the Germans didn't actually reach until over three weeks later. There was a run on the Paris branch of the Guaranty Trust Company by American depositors. I lunched in a little restaurant I frequently went to on the Rue Ste.-Anne, and after the meal, M. Bisque, the proprietor, suggested that we go to the Gare du Nord to see the refugees. M. Bisque cried easily. Like most fine cooks, he was emotional and a heavy drinker. He had a long nose like a woodcock and a mustache which had been steamed over cookpots until it hung lifeless from his lip. Since my arrival in France in October he had taken me periodically on his buying trips to the markets so that I could see the Germans weren't starving Paris. On these trips we would carry a number of baskets and, as we filled one after another with oysters, artichokes, or pheasants, we would leave them at a series of bars where we stopped for a drink of apple brandy. The theory was that when we had completed our round of the markets we would circle back on our course, picking up the baskets, and thus avoid a lot of useless carrying. It worked all right when we could remember the bars where we had left the various things, but sometimes we couldn't, and on such occasions M. Bisque would cry that *restauration* was a cursed *métier*, and that if the government would permit he would take up his old rifle and leave for the front. But they would have to let him wear horizon blue; he could not stand the sight of khaki because it reminded him of the English. "They say the English are very brave at sea," he would say, winking slowly, "but who knows? We don't see them, eh?"

The trip to the Gare du Nord was solemn. M. Bisque dragged me to see various mothers sitting on rolls of bedding and surrounded by miauling children; his eyes would water, and he would offer a child a two-franc piece, and then haul me to the buffet, where he would fortify himself with a glass of Beaujolais. At the buffet I remember meeting a red-bearded gnome of a colonial soldier who kept referring to himself as "a real porpoise." "Porpoise" was the traditional Army term for a colonial infantryman. "A real porpoise," the soldier repeated dreamily, "an old porpoise, and believe me, Monsieur, the Germans need *somebody* to bust their snouts for them." He had two complete sets of decorations, one from the old war and one from the new. He was going north to rejoin his regiment and he was full of fight and red wine.

Saturday morning I had another note from Jean-Pierre. He enclosed a bit of steel from a Dornier shot down near him. "How I am still alive I have not time to write to you," he said, "but chance sometimes manages things well." The letter produced the same effect on me as news of a great victory. I called up Henri. He and Eglée had had a letter too.

• • •

On Saturday, May 18th, I went to a press conference held by the Ministry of Information, which had just organized an Anglo-American press section, with quarters in a vast, rococo ballroom at the Hôtel Continental called the Salle des Fêtes. Pierre Comert, chief of the section, held conferences for the correspondents at six every evening, when he would discuss the day's developments from the government's point of view. This evening he announced that Paul Reynaud had taken over the Ministry of National Defence. He also announced that Reynaud had recalled Marshal Pétain from Spain to advise him. General Weygand had already arrived from Syria and it was understood that he would take over the high command in a few days. The two great names, in conjunction, were expected to raise national morale. The two old men, however, were military opposites. Pétain, cautious at sixty, when he had defended Verdun, was at eighty-four incapable of conceiving any operation bolder than an orderly retreat. Weygand believed in unremitting attack. One staff officer later told me, "Weygand's ideas are so old-fashioned that they have become modern again. He is just what we need." Strategically, the two men cancelled each other, but politically they were a perfect team. Both were clericals, royalists, and anti-parliamentarians. There is something about very old soldiers like Hindenburg and Pétain that makes democrats trust them. But Pétain was to serve Laval's purpose as Hindenburg had served Hitler's. However, we were cheerful on the evening we heard about the appointments. The German advance was apparently slowing down, and all of us thought that Weygand might arrange a counterattack soon. A week earlier we had been expecting victories. Now we were cheered by a slightly slower tempo of disaster.

• • •

There was a hot, heavy pause the next few days. I took long walks on the boulevards, and up and down dull, deserted business streets. The wartime population of Paris had slowly increased from late November until April, as evacuated families returned from the provinces, but since the beginning of the offensive the population had again decreased. All the people who remained in town seemed to concentrate on the boulevards. It gave them comfort to look at one another. They were not yet consciously afraid, however. There were long queues in front of the movie houses, especially those that showed double features. You could get a table at a sidewalk café only with difficulty, and the ones that had girl orchestras did particularly well. One girl orchestra, at the Grande Maxeville, was called the Joyous Wings and its bandstand and instruments had been decorated with blue airplanes. There were no young soldiers in the streets, because no furloughs were being issued.

It is simple now to say, "The war on the Continent was lost on May 15th." But as the days in May passed, people in Paris only gradually came to suspect how disastrous that day had been. There was a time lag between every blow and the effect on public morale. I can't remember exactly when I first became frightened, or when I first began to notice that the shapes of people's faces were changing. There was plenty of food in Paris. People got thin worrying. I think I noticed first the thinning faces of the sporting girls in the cafés. Since the same girls came to the same cafés every night, it was easy to keep track. Then I became aware that the cheekbones, the noses, and the jaws of all Paris were becoming more prominent.

There was no immediate danger in Paris unless the Germans bombed it, and when the news was in any degree encouraging I did not think of bombing at all. When the news was bad I thought of bombing with apprehension. It helped me understand why troops in a winning army are frequently brave and on the losing side aren't. We heard anti-aircraft fire every night now, but there were no air-raid alarms, because the planes the guns were firing at were reconnaissance planes. The heaviest shooting would begin in the gray period just before dawn. You wouldn't really settle down to sleep until the morning shooting was over, and you wouldn't wake up until noon.

On the night of May 21st, after Paul Reynaud announced to the Senate that the Germans were at Arras and that France was in danger, I had a *frousse*—a scare—of such extreme character that it amounted to *le trac*, which means a complete funk. It was an oppressively hot night, with thunder as well as anti-aircraft fire, interspersed with noises which sounded like the detonations of bombs in the suburbs. When I lay on my bed face down, I couldn't help thinking of a slave turning his back to the lash, and when I lay on my back I was afraid of seeing the ceiling fall on me. Afterward I talked to dozens of other people about that night and they all said they'd suffered from the same funk. The next morning's papers carried Weygand's opinion that the situation was not hopeless. This cheered everybody. It has since been revealed that May 21st, the day of the great *frousse,* was the day set for the counterattack which might have cracked the Germans. It never came, and by May 22nd, when we were all beginning to feel encouraged, the opportunity had been missed.

Later that day, word got around among the correspondents that negotiations were already on for a separate peace and that if the French didn't sign it the Germans might arrive in Paris in a few days. This counteracted the effect of the Weygand message. Still later, I felt encouraged again as I watched a city gardener weed a bed of petunias in the Square Louvois, the tiny park under my hotel window. Surely, I thought, if the old man believed the Germans were coming in, he would not be bothering with the petunias.

. . .

The greatest encouragement I got during those sad weeks came from Jean-Pierre. Shortly after the Reynaud speech, I went up the hill to Montmartre to take some flowers to Jean-Pierre's mother. For once, Henri and Eglée were smiling at the same time. "You should have been here early this morning for a good surprise!" Henri shouted. "At five there was a knock at our door." "And who do you suppose it was?" his wife cried, taking over the narrative. "Suzette?" I demanded, naming their married daughter, who lived in Grenoble. I was sure that it had been Jean-Pierre, but I wanted to prolong Eglée's pleasure. "No," Eglée announced happily. "It was Jean-Pierre. He was magnificent. He looked like a cowboy." "He came with his *adjudant,*" Henri broke in, "to get engine parts they needed for tanks. The boy has no rest, you know," he said proudly. "When the division goes into action he fights. When they are in reserve and the other fellows rest, he is head of a repair section. He is a magician with engines. And his morale is good! He says that the first days were hard, but that now they know they can beat the Boche." "On the first day of the battle, Jean-Pierre's general was arrested," Eglée said, with a sort of pride. "What *canaille*! Jean said it was fantastic what a traitor the general turned out to be. And there were German spies in French officers' uniforms!" "They met a regiment of artillery without officers," Henri said, "but completely! 'So much the better,' the artillerists said. 'They were traitors anyway. But where in the name of God are we supposed to go?' Fifteen German bombers appeared over Jean-Pierre's unit. 'We're in for it,' he said to himself. But the boy was lucky. The Germans had dropped their bombs elsewhere. Then Jean-Pierre's unit met German tanks. He says our fellows rode right over them. 'There may be a great many of them,' he said, 'but we are better than they are. Our guns penetrate them but they do not penetrate us. As for the spy problem, we have solved that. We simply shoot all officers we do not know.' Jean-Pierre and the *adjudant* stayed for breakfast. Then they had to go away."

Although I knew that an individual soldier had no chance to understand a military situation as a whole, Jean-Pierre's optimism raised my spirits considerably. I believed fully the details of the encounter with the German tanks. Jean-Pierre was of that peculiar race of engine-lovers who cannot lie about the performance of a mechanical thing.

When I returned to my hotel, I passed along Jean-Pierre's confident report to Toutou, the hotel's cashier, with whom I often discussed the war. She was a patriot but a congenital pessimist. All the employees slept on the top floor of the hotel, and as soon as Toutou had read of the German parachutists in Holland she had bought a revolver and cartridges. "If one lands on the roof, I'll pop him!" she had said. "Or perhaps as he descends past my window!"

. . .

In each week of disaster there was an Indian summer of optimism. On the third Sunday after the offensive started, I had dinner with Henri and Eglée. We teased one another about our forebodings a fortnight earlier. "Do you remember how sure you were that the Germans would be here momentarily?" Eglée said to me. "And how you were certain that Jean-Pierre was no longer alive?" Henri asked Eglée. "It seems a year ago," I said sincerely. "I must admit that the French have their heart well hooked on. Any other people would have caved in after such a blow. I wonder where Weygand will make the counterattack." "In Luxembourg, in my opinion," Henri said. "If he made the counterattack too far to the west he would not catch enough Boches. A good wide turning movement, and you will see—the whole band of them will have to scramble off. They will be on the other side of the Albert Canal again in a week."

We talked and listened to the radio, and, as usual, I stayed for tea, then for supper, and then for the final news bulletin broadcast at eleven-thirty. The bulletins earlier in the day had been dull. But something in the speaker's voice this time warned us, as soon as he commenced, that the news was bad. We began to get sad before he had said anything important. Then he said, "Whatever the result of the battle in Flanders, the high command has made provision that the enemy will not profit strategically by its result." "What can he mean?" Eglée asked. "He means that they are preparing to embark that army for England," Henri said. "Unless the enemy captures the army, his victory is tactical but not strategical." "But why must they embark?" Eglée asked. "I do not know," Henri said almost savagely. That was the day—though none of us knew it—that King Leopold told his Ministers he was going to give up. Eglée began to cry. "Now they are coming to Paris," she said, "now they are coming to Paris."

· · ·

As late as Monday, May 27th, people in Paris still believed that the Allies stood a chance of closing the gap between their southern and northern armies. That evening, Pierre Comert, chief of the Anglo-American section of the Ministry of Information, announced at a press conference I went to that operations in the north were "proceeding normally" and that the high command expected the Battle of Flanders to last at least another two weeks. I slept well that night, awakened only a few times by moderate anti-aircraft fire. In the morning, Toutou, the cashier at my hotel, stopped me as I was going out and said, "Did you hear Reynaud on the radio? The King of the Belgians has surrendered his army." She had been crying.

I walked about the streets stupidly the rest of the morning. I had the map well in mind. The Belgians, by their surrender, had laid bare the left flank of the Franco-British armies in Flanders, and I thought the armies would soon be surrounded. Perhaps the French and British in the north would become demoralized and surrender. If they had been seeking an excuse to quit, they had a good one now. People on the streets were saying to each other, "And that isn't the worst of it. All the refugees probably are spies." They did not seem depressed. A fellow wheeling a pushcart loaded with wood stopped and shouted to a colleague on the other side of the street, "Say, old fellow, did you hear the news? Ain't we just taking it on the potato!" In his voice was a note of pride.

I walked around the Place Vendôme a couple of times; the luxury-shop windows had for me a reassuring association of tourists and normal times. Charvet was showing summer ties. I bought a couple from an elegant and hollow-chested salesman. I didn't want to talk to him about the war because he looked sad enough already, but he began to talk about it himself. "We are an indolent people, Monsieur," he said pleasantly. "We need occurrences like this to wake us up." Paris reminded me of that conversational commonplace you hear when someone has died: "Why, I saw him a couple of days ago and he looked perfectly well." Paris looked perfectly well, but I wondered if it might not be better for a city in such danger to show some agitation. Perhaps Paris was dying.

That night, when the shock of the Belgian surrender had begun to wear off, I had a late dinner with two American friends in a little Marseillais restaurant on the Rue Montmartre. We were the only customers. We had Mediterranean rouget burned in brandy over twigs of fennel. Although all three of us knew that the war was lost, we could not believe it. The rouget tasted too much as good rouget always had; the black-browed proprietor was too normally solicitous; even in the full bosom and strong legs of the waitress there was the assurance that this life in Paris would never end. Faith in France was now purely a *mystique;* a good dinner was our profane form of communion.

· · ·

Incredibly, beginning the day after the Belgian surrender, there was a great wave of exhilaration, based on the heroic action of the British and French armies fighting their way out of Flanders. People with relatives in the northern armies had, when they heard of the capitulation, resigned themselves to the capture or death of the trapped men. The German government, in radio broadcasts, had threatened that even if the Allies were able to make a stand at Dunkirk the Germans would sink every boat that tried to embark troops. It was one German threat that didn't come off. People in Paris began to receive telegrams from relatives who had safely arrived in England. Several of my acquaintances received such messages, so we assumed that the number of troops saved was very large.

My old friends Henri and Eglée had not worried about their son Jean-Pierre, because, having seen him on leave since the Germans drove the wedge between the Allied armies, they knew he was south of the Somme. But Henri's brother Paul, who at fifty had been called back into service as a lieutenant of artillery, was with the army in Flanders. One evening shortly after the Belgian surrender, I climbed up to the Rue Gabrielle, just under the crest of Montmartre, to visit Henri and Eglée, and found them in a happy mood, because Paul had reached England. I tried to talk to Eglée about what she and her husband would do if the Germans turned toward Paris after they finished the Dunkirk job. Her answer was simply that she had an order from the Galeries Lafayette for five dozen of the soldiers' muslin money belts she manufactured at home and that after she completed the order she would have to wait eight days for payment, so how could she think of leaving Paris? As for Henri, he said he now constituted the whole office force of the textile-design company he worked for and couldn't leave without giving a month's notice. Peacetime thought patterns were mercifully persistent.

Everyone now was doing his best to forget that the Allied forces had had too few tanks and guns to begin with, and that now the evacuated armies had lost what little they had. We consoled ourselves with stories of individual heroism and with the thought that the Allies, after all, controlled the sea. Only when the evacuation was completed did the enthusiastic French suddenly take cognizance of the fact that there were no more British troops on their side of the Channel. As if spontaneously, the German gibe, "England will fight to the last Frenchman," swam into the popular consciousness and began to seem like a portent.

· · ·

Two kinds of person are consoling in a dangerous time: those who are completely courageous, and those who are more frightened than you are. Fernand, the night porter at my hotel, was completely courageous. "Well, what do you know?" he would ask me when I came home at night. Before I answered, he would say, "We will have them yet, the camels. It takes a few defeats to get our blood up. They poison our lives by provoking the anti-aircraft into making a noise at night. A surprise is preparing itself for those cocos!" It was a pleasure to see him during the frequent early-morning *alertes*. Hearing the sirens, he would go out into the small park in front of the hotel and, shielding his eyes with his hands, search the sky for airplanes. Seeing none, he would shake his head disgustedly and shout up to the female guests at the windows of the hotel, "Do not derange yourselves, Mesdames, it is for nothing again!"

The most frightened man I saw in France was a certain well-known French journalist who wrote under various names in a dozen Parisian newspapers of varying political color. He had a broad, paraffin-textured face which, when he was alarmed, appeared to be on the point of melting. Long before the offensive began in May, he had tried to explain to me why Laval, the appeaser, and Paul Faure, the left-of-Blum Socialist, together with Georges Bonnet, representative of the great banking house of Lazard Frères, were all planning a move to get rid of Paul Reynaud in order to liquidate the war as quickly as possible. They wanted to put Daladier back in Reynaud's place because they knew that as long as Daladier headed the government there would be no effectual war—that eventually the war would die of dry rot, which was what 90 percent of the French politicians and all the French Communists, along with the Germans, wanted. I had asked naïvely why Laval didn't try to become Premier himself. "Because, of course," my journalist friend had said impatiently, "then everybody would *know* he was going to make peace. Then there would be mutiny in the Army." Personally, he used to say, he was a decided partisan of both Reynaud, who wanted to fight, and of Laval, who wanted to make peace. You were always running up against things like that in French politics.

When I met my journalist at lunch one day the first week of June, he was in as spectacular a funk as I have ever observed. "What a terrible mistake to have provoked those people, my dear!" he shrieked. "What madness to concern ourselves with Poland! Laval was so right to have wished to conciliate Mussolini. I am going to give my dog a lethal injection. He could never stand the nervous shock of those bombs that whistle. Working people are so insouciant. They know they have us in their power. I cannot get a man to dig a trench in my garden for me until tomorrow afternoon, and the bombers may be here any minute!" As he stuffed asparagus into his mouth, large tears welled out of his eyes. "Peace, quickly, quickly!" he shouted, after swallowing the asparagus.

. . .

Sunday, June 2nd, I visited the country home of a French newspaper publisher who lived with his large, intelligent family near the town of Melun, thirty miles south of Paris. The countryside, hot and rich and somnolent, and the family, sitting on the lawn after a chicken dinner, made me think of Sundays on Long Island. It was as if no war had ever been. We sat around in lawn chairs, fighting against drowsiness, talking unintently, resisting the efforts of one woman to get up a game like charades. We spoke with no originality whatever of all the mistakes all the appeasers in the world had made, beginning with Ethiopia. We repeated to one another how Italy could have been squelched in 1935, how a friendly Spanish government could have been maintained in power in 1936, how the Germans could have been prevented from fortifying the Rhineland in the same year. We talked of the Skoda tanks, built according to French designs in Czecho-Slovakia, that were now ripping the French army apart. The Germans had never known how to build good tanks until Chamberlain and Daladier presented them with the Skoda plant. These matters had become for every European capable of thought a sort of litany, to be recited almost automatically over and over again.

. . .

Women in the train which took me back to town that evening were talking about the leaflets German planes had dropped, promising to bombard Paris the next day. The word "bombardment" had a terrible sound, evoking pictures of Warsaw and Rotterdam. The train arrived at the Gare de Lyon after eleven. There were no taxis. In the last month they had become increasingly scarce even in the daytime; the drivers simply refused to risk their necks in the pitch-black streets at night. I could not distinguish one street from another. There was a cluster of dim, moving lights at a distance, like a luminous jellyfish seen by another fish at the bottom of the sea. I started toward the lights and tripped over a plank, skinning my knee. When I reached them, I found they came from the electric lanterns of a group of policemen who were stopping pedestrians and examining their papers. They were polite and quiet. One of them told me how to get to my hotel, which took me almost an hour.

The promised bombardment came at about one o'clock the next afternoon, an anticlimax to its advance notices. It was preceded by a tremendous noise of motors in airplanes too high to be seen, and by the angry hammering of anti-aircraft guns. Technically, I was later given to understand, it was, from the German standpoint, a very good bombardment. Two hundred and fifty planes participated, the largest number that had been assembled for a single operation in this war. The bombing, considering the height at which the planes flew—twenty thousand feet—was commendably accurate. However, the results looked nothing like the photographs of Warsaw and Rotterdam, because Paris was reasonably well defended. "The anti-aircraft fire was well nourished," the French said, "so the bombers stayed high." The pursuit squadrons, although they failed to intercept the bombers on their way to Paris, were on their tails so closely that the Germans dropped their bombs quickly and left. If there had been no defending batteries or planes, as at Rotterdam, the bombers would have loafed along a few hundred feet above the main thoroughfares and dropped their high explosives like roach powder. The bombs hit the huge Citroën factory on the Quai de Javel and knocked down a few scattered apartment houses, but the total effect on public morale was tonic. Forty-eight hours after the bombardment, M. Dautry, the Minister of War Industry, took a group of correspondents through the Citroën plant, which had been the chief German objective. There we found a smell of burnt paint, and a great deal of broken glass on the floor, but no serious damage to the great automobile-assembly lines or the part of the plant where shells were made. The women making shells worked on as calmly as girls in an American candy factory.

The day we visited the factory, June 5th, was also the day the Germans began their second attack, the push southward across the Somme that was to carry them to the Spanish frontier. "It is the beginning of the second round," Pierre Comert announced at the press conference that evening. None of us could admit to ourselves that the war might be a two-round knockout. The French would surely be dislodged from the Somme-Aisne line, we conceded, but it would take weeks to do it. Then they would defend Paris and the line of the Seine, then the line of the Loire. By that time, perhaps, the British would be able to do something. Even the United States might begin to understand what was at stake. But this fight was not to have even a decent second round. The rest after the first round had not been long enough; the French were still out on their feet. Unarmed and outnumbered, they were led by two old men who were at loggerheads. As for Reynaud, he had called into his government Ybarnegaray and Marin, two reactionaries whose only surface virtue was a blustering show of war spirit. Raised to power by Socialist votes, Reynaud had turned toward men whom he trusted because they were of his own Rightist background—Pétain, Mandel, Ybarnegaray, Marin. All his Rightist friends except Mandel joined in smothering him. They felt that by making war against Hitler he was betraying his own class.

When I got back to my hotel that night, tired and discouraged, Fernand the porter, looking radiant, said to me, "What they must be digesting now, the Boches!" He showed me a copy of *Le Temps*, which said the German losses were stupefying. All the attacks had been "contained," but the French Army had executed a slight retreat in good order.

· · ·

By now there were perceptible changes in the daily life of Paris. There was no telephone service in the hotels, so you had to make a special trip afoot every time you wanted to tell somebody something. Taxis were harder than ever to find. My hotel, which was typical, had six floors. At the beginning of the war in September the proprietor had closed the fourth, fifth, and sixth floors. Now I was the only guest on the second floor, and there were perhaps a half dozen on the first. The staff, naturally, dwindled like the clientele. Every day somebody said goodbye to me. One by one the waiters left, and then it was the headwaiter, who had been kept on after all of his subordinates had been dismissed. The next day it was Toutou, who left the bookkeeping to the housekeeper. A couple of days later, the housekeeper herself left. Finally, there were only a porter and one chambermaid in the daytime, and Fernand at night. "Perhaps, if the line holds, there will be an upturn in business," the proprietor said.

It was at about this time that my restaurateur friend, M. Bisque, with whom I used to make the rounds of the markets, decided to close his restaurant. It was not that the Germans worried him, he explained to me, but there were no more customers, and also his wine dealer was pressing him to pay his bill. M. Bisque, and his wife, who kept the books, and his daughter Yvette, who possessed the *tour de main* for making a soufflé stand up on a flat plate, and his son, who had been an apprentice in the kitchen of the Café de Paris, and Marie-Louise, the waitress, were all leaving the city to run the canteen in a munitions factory south of Fontainebleau. I wished them Godspeed.

For a few days I had lacked the heart to visit Henri and Eglée. Then Henri had come to my hotel to tell me joyfully they had had another letter from Jean-Pierre, who said he had been working twenty-one hours a day repairing tanks for his division. On Sunday, June 9th, which was a warm and drowsy day, I returned Henri's call. On the way I stopped at a florist shop and bought some fine pink roses. The woman in the shop said that shipments from the provinces were irregular, but that fortunately the crisis came at a season when the Paris suburbs were producing plenty of flowers. "We have more goods than purchasers," she said, laughing. When I arrived at the apartment, I found Eglée busy making her muslin money belts. Henri was amusing himself by reading a 1906 edition of the Encyclopaedia Britannica, one of his favorite possessions, and drinking a *vin ordinaire* in which he professed to find a slight resemblance to Ermitage. "This time I think the line will hold," Henri said. "I served under Pétain at Verdun. He will know how to stop them. Only I don't like that talk of infiltration near Forges-les-Eaux."

"Infiltration" was a grim word in this war. The communiqué never admitted that the Germans had pierced the French line, but invariably announced, "Motorized elements have made an infiltration. They have been surrounded and will be destroyed." Two days later the "infiltration" became a salient, from which new infiltrations radiated. When I left the apartment, Henri walked down as far as the Place des Abbesses with me. He wanted to buy a newspaper. As we stood saying goodbye, we heard a series of reports, too loud and too widely spaced for anti-aircraft. "Those sound like naval guns mounted on railroad cars," Henri said. "The Boches can't be so far away, then." That was the last time I saw Henri.

. . .

At six o'clock that evening, I went to another Anglo-American press conference at the Hôtel Continental. We were told that the Ministry of Information was planning to provide us with safe-conduct passes to use in case we left Paris. That made us suspect that the government would move very soon. Then M. Comert told us that Jean Provoust, who had just been appointed Minister of Information, wanted to talk to all the American correspondents. M. Provoust, the dynamic publisher of *Paris-Soir*, received us in his office with the factitious cordiality of a newspaper owner about to ask his staff to take a pay cut. He said that he didn't want the United States to think the situation was hopeless. "From a military standpoint," he said, "it is improving steadily. Disregard reports of the government quitting Paris. We will have many more chats in this room." John Lloyd, of the Associated Press, who was president of the Anglo-American Press Association, waited to see Provoust after the talk and invited him to be guest of honor at a luncheon the correspondents were having the next Wednesday. The Minister said he would be charmed, and then hurried away.

On my way home I saw a number of garbage trucks parked in the middle of the streets to balk airplane landings. Evidently Paris would be defended. I didn't think, after Provoust's talk, that I would have to leave Paris immediately, but the situation looked so bad that I decided to begin getting my passport in order.

Early the next morning, Monday, June 10th, I set out in a taxi—which the porter had taken two hours to find for me—to go to the Spanish Consulate General to obtain a transit visa. This was easy to get if you already had the Portuguese visa, and luckily I already had one which was good for a year. My taxi-driver came from Lorraine, where, he said, people knew what patriotism meant. He had fought the other war, four years of it. The country needed men like Poincaré, a Lorrainer, now. "The politicians have sold us out," he said. "And that Leopold," he shouted, "there is a fellow they should have got onto long ago!" Now, he expected, the Germans would come to Paris. But it would be defended, like Madrid. "They will come here, the animals," he said, "but they will leave plenty of feathers! Imagine a tank trying to upset the building of the Crédit Lyonnais! Big buildings are the best defence against those machines." He did not know that the real-estate men would never encourage such an unprofitable use of their property. "Even ten centimes on the franc is something," the rich men were already telling one another, "when one has a great many francs."

From the Spanish Consulate I went to the Prefecture of Police, where I asked for a visa which would permit me to leave France. A woman police official, a sort of chief clerk, said, "Leave your passport and come back for it in not less than four days." "But by that time, Madame," I said, "the Germans may be here and the Prefecture may not exist." Naturally, I didn't leave the passport, but I was foolish to question the permanency of the Prefecture. The French civil servants are the one class unaffected by revolution or conquest. The Germans were to come, as it turned out, but the Prefecture was to stay open, its personnel and routine unchanged. Its great accumulation of information about individual Frenchmen, so useful for the apprehension of patriots and the blackmailing of politicians, was to be at the disposal of the Germans as it had been at Philippe-Egalité's and Napoleon the Little's and Stavisky's. The well-fed young *agents* were to continue on the same beats, unaffected by the end of the war they had never had to fight in. Yesterday the Prefecture had obeyed the orders of M. Mandel, who hated Germans. Now it would obey Herr Abetz, who hated Jews. Change of administration. *Tant pis.*

• • •

Afterward I stopped at the Crillon bar, where I met a Canadian general I knew. "The French still have a fine chance," he said. "I am leaving for Tours as soon as I finish this sandwich." I walked over to the Continental to see if M. Comert had any fresh news. As I arrived at the foot of the staircase leading to Comert's office, I met another correspondent on his way out. "If you're going up to the Ministry," he said, "don't bother. The government left Paris this morning." Then he began to chuckle. "You remember when John Lloyd stopped Provoust last night and invited him to the Wednesday luncheon?" he asked. Yes, I remembered. "Well," he said, "Provoust was in a hurry because he was leaving for Tours in a few minutes." I said maybe we had better leave too, and we did.

LETTER FROM LONDON

Mollie Panter-Downes

SEPTEMBER 14, 1940 (ON THE BLITZ)

THE AIR *Blitzkrieg* started in earnest yesterday—Saturday—with the first big raids on London. It is as yet too early to report on the full extent of the damage, which has certainly been considerable, especially in the dwelling-house sections of the East End. Observers of the Spanish War methods of terrorizing civilian populations have frequently remarked that in Spain the heaviest bombardments were directed on working-class districts—structurally more vulnerable and emotionally more prone to panic than less crowded areas of a city. The job of providing homeless and frightened people with shelter and food is one which workers have apparently tackled heroically. They are probably going to have increasingly and tragically frequent opportunities for practice. The figure of four hundred killed, which has just been announced, may well mount higher in future bulletins, in the same way that the figure of raiders brought down was given as five in last evening's reports but by this morning, with fuller information coming in all the time, had totalled eighty-eight.

Those who were weekending in the country guessed the magnitude of the attack from the constant roar of aircraft passing invisibly high up in a cloudless blue sky. At dusk, a red glow could be seen in the direction of London, but it died down as the stars and the searchlights came out, and again waves of bombers passed overhead at intervals of about ten minutes. In between waves, one could hear the distant racket of the anti-aircraft guns picking up the raiders which had just gone by, and at the same time one half heard, half sensed the unmistakable throbbing of the next waves of engines coming nearer over the quiet woods and villages.

This morning it was difficult to get a call through to London, probably because so many anxious people in the country were ringing up to find out what had happened and to try to get in touch with members of their families who were in town. Further big attacks were expected today, but the attitude of those who were returning to the city was sensible and courageous. "Let them send plenty. There will be more for the boys to bring down" was a typical comment.

Up to yesterday, the raids on London had not been developed beyond a point which indicated that they were merely reconnaissance or training flights to accustom enemy pilots to night work over the capital. Sirens had become tiresome interruptions which Londoners learned to expect at fairly regular intervals during the day, roughly coinciding with the morning and evening traffic rush and with the lunch hour. Unless shooting accompanied the alarms, they were ignored, as far as possible, except by especially nervous individuals. The dislocation of office and factory work schedules was more or less remedied by the posting of spotters on rooftops to give the warning when things really become dangerous locally. Until that warning comes, workers have been getting on with the job, sirens or no sirens. No part of the Premier's speech last week was better received, by the way, than his statement that the whole of the air-raid-warning system is to be drastically revised and a new ruling concerning it announced in the near future; what he described as "these prolonged banshee howlings" are apparently more alarming to a great many people than an actual bombardment.

· · ·

Life in a bombed city means adapting oneself in all kinds of ways all the time. Londoners are now learning the lessons, long ago familiar to those living on the much-visited southeast coast, of getting to bed early and shifting their sleeping quarters down to the ground floor. (After recent raids on the suburbs it was noticeable that in all the little houses damaged by anything short of a direct hit people on the upper floors had suffered most, and that in surprisingly many cases those on the ground floor had escaped injury entirely.) Theatres are meeting the threat to their business by starting evening performances earlier, thus giving audiences a chance to get home before the big nighttime show warms up. The actual getting home is likely to be difficult, because the transportation services have not yet worked out a satisfactory formula for carrying on during raids. The busmen's union tells drivers to use their own discretion, and the London transportation board's orders are that buses are to go on running unless a raid develops "in the immediate vicinity." The drivers grumble that it would take a five-hundred-pounder in the immediate vicinity to be heard above the din of their own engines.

The calm behavior of the average individual continues to be amazing. Commuting suburbanites, who up to yesterday had experienced worse bombardments than people living in central London, placidly brag to fellow-passengers on the morning trains about the size of bomb craters in their neighborhoods, as in a more peaceful summer they would have bragged about their roses and squash.

. . .

Earlier in the week, the first anniversary of the declaration of war passed peacefully and found Britons in a state of encouragement which less than three months ago would have seemed downright fantastic. The Anglo-American agreement was a birthday present that was received with tremendous satisfaction. Officially, it was greeted as "the most conspicuous demonstration that has yet been given of the general American desire to afford the utmost help, compatible with neutrality, to a cause now recognized as vital to the future of the United States." Ordinary comment was less solemn, but no less grateful. The successful conclusion of the agreement, combined with the superb work of the R.A.F. and the significant new spirit in the French colonies, has been responsible for a big increase in public confidence which reacted favorably on that sensitive plant, the stock market. In spite of the dark times ahead, it is believed that better things are coming into sight beyond them.

SURVIVAL

John Hersey

JUNE 17, 1944 (ON LIEUTENANT JOHN F. KENNEDY)

OUR MEN IN THE SOUTH PACIFIC fight nature, when they are pitted against her, with a greater fierceness than they could ever expend on a human enemy. Lieutenant John F. Kennedy, the ex-Ambassador's son and lately a PT skipper in the Solomons, came through town the other day and told me the story of his survival in the South Pacific. I asked Kennedy if I might write the story down. He asked me if I wouldn't talk first with some of his crew, so I went up to the Motor Torpedo Boat Training Centre at Melville, Rhode Island, and there, under the curving iron of a Quonset hut, three enlisted men named Johnston, McMahon, and McGuire filled in the gaps.

It seems that Kennedy's PT, the 109, was out one night with a squadron patrolling Blackett Strait, in mid-Solomons. Blackett Strait is a patch of water bounded on the northeast by the volcano called Kolombangara, on the west by the island of Vella Lavella, on the south by the island of Gizo and a string of coral-fringed islets, and on the east by the bulk of New Georgia. The boats were working about forty miles away from their base on the island of Rendova, on the south side of New Georgia. They had entered Blackett Strait, as was their habit, through Ferguson Passage, between the coral islets and New Georgia.

The night was a starless black and Japanese destroyers were around. It was about two-thirty. The 109, with three officers and ten enlisted men aboard, was leading three boats on a sweep for a target. An officer named George Ross was up on the bow, magnifying the void with binoculars. Kennedy was at the wheel and he saw Ross turn and point into the darkness. The man in the forward machine-gun turret shouted, "Ship at two o'clock!" Kennedy saw a shape and spun the wheel to turn for an attack, but the 109 answered sluggishly. She was running slowly on only one of her three engines, so as to make a minimum wake and avoid detection from the air. The shape became a Japanese destroyer, cutting through the night at forty knots and heading straight for the 109. The thirteen men on the PT hardly had time to brace themselves. Those who saw the Japanese ship coming were paralyzed by fear in a curious way: they could move their hands but not their feet. Kennedy whirled the wheel to the left, but again the 109 did not respond. Ross went through the gallant but futile motions of slamming a shell into the breach of the 37-millimetre anti-tank gun which had been temporarily mounted that very day, wheels and all, on the foredeck. The urge to bolt and dive over the side was terribly strong, but still no one was able to move; all hands froze to their battle stations. Then the Japanese crashed into the 109 and cut her right in two. The sharp enemy forefoot struck the PT on the starboard side about fifteen feet from the bow and crunched diagonally across with a racking noise. The PT's wooden hull hardly even delayed the destroyer. Kennedy was thrown hard to the left in the cockpit, and he thought, "This is how it feels to be killed." In a moment he found himself on his back on the deck, looking up at the destroyer as it passed through his boat. There was another loud noise and a huge flash of yellow-red light, and the destroyer glowed. Its peculiar, raked, inverted-Y stack stood out in the brilliant light and, later, in Kennedy's memory.

There was only one man below decks at the moment of collision. That was McMahon, engineer. He had no idea what was up. He was just reaching forward to slam the starboard engine into gear when a ship came into his engine room. He was lifted from the narrow passage between two of the engines and thrown painfully against the starboard bulkhead aft of the boat's auxiliary generator. He landed in a sitting position. A tremendous burst of flame came back at him from the day room, where some of the gas tanks were. He put his hands over his face, drew his legs up tight, and waited to die. But he felt water hit him after the fire, and he was sucked far downward as his half of the PT sank. He began to struggle upward through the water. He had held his breath since the impact, so his lungs were tight and they hurt. He looked up through the water. Over his head he saw a yellow glow—gasoline burning on the water. He broke the surface and was in fire again. He splashed hard to keep a little island of water around him.

Johnston, another engineer, had been asleep on deck when the collision came. It lifted him and dropped him overboard. He saw the flame and the destroyer for a moment. Then a huge propeller pounded by near him and the awful turbulence of the destroyer's wake took him down, turned him over and over, held him down, shook him, and drubbed on his ribs. He hung on and came up in water that was like a river rapids. The next day his body turned black and blue from the beating.

Kennedy's half of the PT stayed afloat. The bulkheads were sealed, so the undamaged watertight compartments up forward kept the half hull floating. The destroyer rushed off into the dark. There was an awful quiet: only the sound of gasoline burning.

Kennedy shouted, "Who's aboard?"

Feeble answers came from three of the enlisted men, McGuire, Mauer, and Albert; and from one of the officers, Thom.

Kennedy saw the fire only ten feet from the boat. He thought it might reach her and explode the remaining gas tanks, so he shouted, "Over the side!"

The five men slid into the water. But the wake of the destroyer swept the fire away from the PT, so after a few minutes, Kennedy and the others crawled back aboard. Kennedy shouted for survivors in the water. One by one they answered: Ross, the third officer; Harris, McMahon, Johnston, Zinsser, Starkey, enlisted men. Two did not answer: Kirksey and Marney, enlisted men. Since the last bombing at base, Kirksey had been sure he would die. He had huddled at his battle station by the fantail gun, with his kapok life jacket tied tight up to his cheeks. No one knows what happened to him or to Marney.

Harris shouted from the darkness, "Mr. Kennedy! Mr. Kennedy! McMahon is badly hurt." Kennedy took his shoes, his shirt, and his sidearms off, told Mauer to blink a light so that the men in the water would know where the half hull was, then dived in and swam toward the voice. The survivors were widely scattered. McMahon and Harris were a hundred yards away.

When Kennedy reached McMahon, he asked, "How are you, Mac?"

McMahon said, "I'm all right. I'm kind of burnt."

Kennedy shouted out, "How are the others?"

Harris said softly, "I hurt my leg."

Kennedy, who had been on the Harvard swimming team five years before, took McMahon in tow and headed for the PT. A gentle breeze kept blowing the boat away from the swimmers. It took forty-five minutes to make what had been an easy hundred yards. On the way in, Harris said, "I can't go any farther." Kennedy, of the Boston Kennedys, said to Harris, of the same home town, "For a guy from Boston, you're certainly putting up a great exhibition out here, Harris." Harris made it all right and didn't complain any more. Then Kennedy swam from man to man, to see how they were doing. All who had survived the crash were able to stay afloat, since they were wearing life preservers—kapok jackets shaped like overstuffed vests, aviators' yellow Mae Wests, or air-filled belts like small inner tubes. But those who couldn't swim had to be towed back to the wreckage by those who could. One of the men screamed for help. When Ross reached him, he found that the screaming man had two life jackets on. Johnston was treading water in a film of gasoline which did not catch fire. The fumes filled his lungs and he fainted. Thom towed him in. The others got in under their own power. It was now after 5 A.M., but still dark. It had taken nearly three hours to get everyone aboard.

The men stretched out on the tilted deck of the PT. Johnston, McMahon, and Ross collapsed into sleep. The men talked about how wonderful it was to be alive and speculated on when the other PT's would come back to rescue them. Mauer kept blinking the light to point their way. But the other boats had no idea of coming back. They had seen a collision, a sheet of flame, and a slow burning on the water. When the skipper of one of the boats saw the sight, he put his hands over his face and sobbed, "My God! My God!" He and the others turned away. Back at the base, after a couple of days, the squadron held services for the souls of the thirteen men, and one of the officers wrote his mother, "George Ross lost his life for a cause that he believed in stronger than any one of us, because he was an idealist in the purest sense. Jack Kennedy, the Ambassador's son, was on the same boat and also lost his life. The man that said the cream of a nation is lost in war can never be accused of making an overstatement of a very cruel fact. . . ."

• • •

When day broke, the men on the remains of the 109 stirred and looked around. To the northeast, three miles off, they saw the monumental cone of Kolombangara; there, the men knew, ten thousand Japanese swarmed. To the west, five miles away, they saw Vella Lavella; more Japs. To the south, only a mile or so away, they actually could see a Japanese camp on

Gizo. Kennedy ordered his men to keep as low as possible, so that no moving silhouettes would show against the sky. The listing hulk was gurgling and gradually settling. Kennedy said, "What do you want to do if the Japs come out? Fight or surrender?" One said, "Fight with what?" So they took an inventory of their armament. The 37-millimetre gun had flopped over the side and was hanging there by a chain. They had one tommy gun, six 45-calibre automatics, and one .38. Not much.

"Well," Kennedy said, "what do you want to do?"

One said, "Anything you say, Mr. Kennedy. You're the boss."

Kennedy said, "There's nothing in the book about a situation like this. Seems to me we're not a military organization any more. Let's just talk this over."

They talked it over, and pretty soon they argued, and Kennedy could see that they would never survive in anarchy. So he took command again.

It was vital that McMahon and Johnston should have room to lie down. McMahon's face, neck, hands, wrists, and feet were horribly burned. Johnston was pale and he coughed continually. There was scarcely space for everyone, so Kennedy ordered the other men into the water to make room, and went in himself. All morning they clung to the hulk and talked about how incredible it was that no one had come to rescue them. All morning they watched for the plane which they thought would be looking for them. They cursed war in general and PT's in particular. At about ten o'clock the hulk heaved a moist sigh and turned turtle. McMahon and Johnston had to hang on as best they could. It was clear that the remains of the 109 would soon sink. When the sun had passed the meridian, Kennedy said, "We will swim to that small island," pointing to one of a group three miles to the southeast. "We have less chance of making it than some of these other islands here, but there'll be less chance of Japs, too." Those who could not swim well grouped themselves around a long two-by-six timber with which carpenters had braced the 37-millimetre cannon on deck and which had been knocked overboard by the force of the collision. They tied several pairs of shoes to the timber, as well as the ship's lantern, wrapped in a life jacket to keep it afloat. Thom took charge of this unwieldy group. Kennedy took McMahon in tow again. He cut loose one end of a long strap on McMahon's Mae West and took the end in his teeth. He swam breast stroke, pulling the helpless McMahon along on his back. It took over five hours to reach the island. Water lapped into Kennedy's mouth through his clenched teeth, and he swallowed a lot. The salt water cut into McMahon's awful burns, but he did not complain. Every few minutes, when Kennedy stopped to rest, taking the strap out of his mouth and holding it in his hand, McMahon would simply say, "How far do we have to go?"

Kennedy would reply, "We're going good." Then he would ask, "How do you feel, Mac?"

McMahon always answered, "I'm O.K., Mr. Kennedy. How about you?"

In spite of his burden, Kennedy beat the other men to the reef that surrounded the island. He left McMahon on the reef and told him to keep low, so as not to be spotted by Japs. Kennedy went ahead and explored the island. It was only a hundred yards in diameter; coconuts on the trees but none on the ground; no visible Japs. Just as the others reached the island, one of them spotted a Japanese barge chugging along close to shore. They all lay low. The barge went on. Johnston, who was very pale and weak and who was still coughing a lot, said, "They wouldn't come here. What'd they be walking around here for? It's too small." Kennedy lay in some bushes, exhausted by his effort, his stomach heavy with the water he had swallowed. He had been in the sea, except for short intervals on the hulk, for fifteen and a half hours. Now he started thinking. Every night for several nights the PT's had cut through Ferguson Passage on their way to action. Ferguson Passage was just beyond the next little island. Maybe . . .

He stood up. He took one of the pairs of shoes. He put one of the rubber life belts around his waist. He hung the .38 around his neck on a lanyard. He took his pants off. He picked up the ship's lantern, a heavy battery affair ten inches by ten inches, still wrapped in the kapok jacket. He said, "If I find a boat, I'll flash the lantern twice. The password will be 'Roger,' the answer will be 'Willco.'" He walked toward the water. After fifteen paces he was dizzy, but in the water he felt all right.

It was early evening. It took half an hour to swim to the reef around the next island. Just as he planted his feet on the reef, which lay about four feet under the surface, he saw the shape of a very big fish in the clear water. He flashed the light at it and splashed hard. The fish went away. Kennedy remembered what one of his men had said a few days before, "These barracuda will come up under a swimming man and eat his testicles." He had many occasions to think of that remark in the next few hours.

Now it was dark. Kennedy blundered along the uneven reef in water up to his waist. Sometimes he would reach forward with his leg and cut one of his shins or ankles on sharp coral. Other times he would step forward onto emptiness. He made his way like a slow-motion drunk, hugging the lantern. At about nine o'clock he came to the end of the reef, alongside Ferguson Passage. He took his shoes off and tied them to the life jacket, then struck out into open water. He swam about an hour, until he felt he was far enough out to intercept the PT's. Treading water, he listened for the muffled roar of motors, getting chilled, waiting, holding the lamp. Once he looked west and saw flares and the false gaiety of an action. The lights were far beyond the little islands, even beyond Gizo, ten miles away. Kennedy realized that the PT boats had chosen, for the first night in many, to go around Gizo instead of through Ferguson Passage. There was no hope. He started back. He made the same painful promenade of the reef and struck out for the tiny island where his friends were. But this swim was different. He was very tired and now the current was running fast, carrying him to the right. He saw that he could not make the island, so he flashed the light once and shouted "Roger! Roger!" to identify himself.

On the beach the men were hopefully vigilant. They saw the light and heard the shouts. They were very happy, because they thought that Kennedy had found a PT. They walked out onto the reef, sometimes up to their waists in water, and waited. It was very painful for those who had no shoes. The men shouted, but not much, because they were afraid of Japanese.

One said, "There's another flash."

A few minutes later a second said, "There's a light over there."

A third said, "We're seeing things in this dark."

They waited a long time, but they saw nothing except phosphorescence and heard nothing but the sound of waves. They went back, very discouraged.

One said despairingly, "We're going to die."

Johnston said, "Aw, shut up. You can't die. Only the good die young."

Kennedy had drifted right by the little island. He thought he had never known such deep trouble, but something he did shows that unconsciously he had not given up hope. He dropped his shoes, but he held onto the heavy lantern, his symbol of contact with his fellows. He stopped trying to swim. He seemed to stop caring. His body drifted through the wet hours, and he was very cold. His mind was a jumble. A few hours before he had wanted desperately to get to the base at Rendova. Now he only wanted to get back to the little island he had left that night, but he didn't try to get there; he just wanted to. His mind seemed to float away from his body. Darkness and time took the place of a mind in his skull. For a long time he slept, or was crazy, or floated in a chill trance.

. . .

The currents of the Solomon Islands are queer. The tide shoves and sucks through the islands and makes the currents curl in odd patterns. It was a fateful pattern into which Jack Kennedy drifted. He drifted in it all night. His mind was blank, but his fist was tightly clenched on the kapok around the lantern. The current moved in a huge circle—west past Gizo, then north and east past Kolombangara, then south into Ferguson Passage. Early in the morning the sky turned from black to gray, and so did Kennedy's mind. Light came to both at about six. Kennedy looked around and saw that he was exactly where he had been the night before when he saw the flares beyond Gizo. For a second time, he started home. He thought for a while that he had lost his mind and that he only imagined that he was repeating his attempt to reach the island. But the chill of the water was real enough, the lantern was real, his progress was measurable. He made the reef, crossed the lagoon, and got to the first island. He lay on the beach awhile. He found that his lantern did not work any more, so he left it and started back to the next island, where his men were. This time the trip along the reef was awful. He had discarded his shoes, and every step on the coral was painful. This time the swim across the gap where the current had caught him the night before seemed endless. But the current had changed; he made the island. He crawled up on the beach. He was vomiting when his men came up to him. He said, "Ross, you try it tonight." Then he passed out.

Ross, seeing Kennedy so sick, did not look forward to the execution of the order. He distracted himself by complaining about his hunger. There were a few coconuts on the trees, but the men were too weak to climb up for them. One of the men thought of sea food, stirred his tired body, and found a snail on the beach. He said, "If we were desperate, we could eat these." Ross said, "Desperate, hell. Give me that. I'll eat that." He took it in his hand and looked at it. The snail put its head out and looked at him. Ross was startled, but he shelled the snail and ate it, making faces because it was bitter.

In the afternoon, Ross swam across to the next island. He took a pistol to signal with, and he spent the night watching Ferguson Passage from the reef around the island. Nothing came through. Kennedy slept badly that night; he was cold and sick.

. . .

The next morning everyone felt wretched. Planes which the men were unable to identify flew overhead and there were dogfights. That meant Japs as well as friends, so the men dragged themselves into the bushes and lay low. Some prayed. Johnston said, "You guys make me sore. You didn't spend ten cents in church in ten years, then all of a sudden you're in trouble and you see the light." Kennedy felt a little better now. When Ross came back, Kennedy decided that the group should move to another, larger island to the southeast, where there seemed to be more coconut trees and where the party would be nearer Ferguson Passage. Again Kennedy took McMahon in tow with the strap in his teeth, and the nine others grouped themselves around the timber.

This swim took three hours. The nine around the timber were caught by the current and barely made the far tip of the island. Kennedy found walking the quarter mile across to them much harder than the three-hour swim. The cuts on his bare feet were festered and looked like small balloons. The men were suffering most from thirst, and they broke open some coconuts lying on the ground and avidly drank the milk. Kennedy and McMahon, the first to drink, were sickened, and Thom told the others to drink sparingly. In the middle of the night it rained, and someone suggested moving into the underbrush and licking water off the leaves. Ross and McMahon kept contact at first by touching feet as they licked. Somehow they got separated, and, being uncertain whether there were any Japs on the island, they became frightened. McMahon, trying to make his way back to the beach, bumped into someone and froze. It turned out to be Johnston, licking leaves on his own. In the morning the group saw that all the leaves were covered with droppings. Bitterly, they named the place Bird Island.

. . .

On this fourth day, the men were low. Even Johnston was low. He had changed his mind about praying. McGuire had a rosary around his neck, and Johnston said, "McGuire, give that necklace a working over." McGuire said quietly, "Yes, I'll take care of all you fellows." Kennedy was still unwilling to admit that things were hopeless. He asked Ross if he would swim with him to an island called Nauru, to the southeast and even nearer Ferguson Passage. They were very weak indeed by now, but after an hour's swim they made it.

They walked painfully across Nauru to the Ferguson Passage side, where they saw a Japanese barge aground on the reef. There were two men by the barge—possibly Japs. They apparently spotted Kennedy and Ross, for they got into a dugout canoe and hurriedly paddled to the other side of the island. Kennedy and Ross moved up the beach. They came upon an unopened rope-bound box and, back in the trees, a little shelter containing a keg of water, a Japanese gas mask, and a crude wooden fetish shaped like a fish. There were Japanese hardtack and candy in the box and the two had a wary feast. Down by the water they found a one-man canoe. They hid from imagined Japs all day. When night fell, Kennedy left Ross and took the canoe, with some hardtack and a can of water from the keg, out into Ferguson Passage. But no PT's came, so he paddled to Bird Island. The men there told him that the two men he had spotted by the barge that morning were natives, who had paddled to Bird Island. The natives had said that there were Japs on Nauru and the men had given Kennedy and Ross up for lost. Then the natives had gone away. Kennedy gave out small rations of crackers and water, and the men went to sleep. During the night, one man, who kept himself awake until the rest were asleep, drank all the water in the can Kennedy had brought back. In the morning the others figured out that he was the guilty one. They swore at him and found it hard to forgive him.

· · ·

Before dawn, Kennedy started out in the canoe to rejoin Ross on Nauru, but when day broke a wind arose and the canoe was swamped. Some natives appeared from nowhere in a canoe, rescued Kennedy, and took him to Nauru. There they showed him where a two-man canoe was cached. Kennedy picked up a coconut with a smooth shell and scratched a message on it with a jackknife: "ELEVEN ALIVE NATIVE KNOWS POSIT AND REEFS NAURU ISLAND KENNEDY." Then he said to the natives, "Rendova, Rendova."

One of the natives seemed to understand. They took the coconut and paddled off.

Ross and Kennedy lay in a sickly daze all day. Toward evening it rained and they crawled under a bush. When it got dark, conscience took hold of Kennedy and he persuaded Ross to go out into Ferguson Passage with him in the two-man canoe. Ross argued against it. Kennedy insisted. The two started out in the canoe. They had shaped paddles from the boards of the Japanese box, and they took a coconut shell to bail with. As they got out into the Passage, the wind rose again and the water became choppy. The canoe began to fill. Ross bailed and Kennedy kept the bow into the wind. The waves grew until they were five or six feet high. Kennedy shouted, "Better turn around and go back!" As soon as the canoe was broadside to the waves, the water poured in and the dugout was swamped. The two clung to it, Kennedy at the bow, Ross at the stern. The tide carried them southward toward the open sea, so they kicked and tugged the canoe, aiming northwest. They struggled that way for two hours, not knowing whether they would hit the small island or drift into the endless open.

The weather got worse; rain poured down and they couldn't see more than ten feet. Kennedy shouted, "Sorry I got you out here, Barney!" Ross shouted back, "This would be a great time to say I told you so, but I won't!"

Soon the two could see a white line ahead and could hear a frightening roar—waves crashing on a reef. They had got out of the tidal current and were approaching the island all right, but now they realized that the wind and the waves were carrying them toward the reef. But it was too late to do anything, now that their canoe was swamped, except hang on and wait.

When they were near the reef, a wave broke Kennedy's hold, ripped him away from the canoe, turned him head over heels, and spun him in a violent rush. His ears roared and his eyes pin-wheeled, and for the third time since the collision he thought he was dying. Somehow he was not thrown against the coral but floated into a kind of eddy. Suddenly he felt the reef under his feet. Steadying himself so that he would not be swept off it, he shouted, "Barney!" There was no reply. Kennedy thought of how he had insisted on going out in the canoe, and he screamed, "Barney!" This time Ross answered. He, too, had been thrown on the reef. He had not been as lucky as Kennedy; his right arm and shoulder had been cruelly lacerated by the coral, and his feet, which were already infected from earlier wounds, were cut some more.

The procession of Kennedy and Ross from reef to beach was a crazy one. Ross's feet hurt so much that Kennedy would hold one paddle on the bottom while Ross put a foot on it, then the other paddle forward for another step, then the first paddle forward again, until they reached sand. They fell on the beach and slept.

Kennedy and Ross were wakened early in the morning by a noise. They looked up and saw four husky natives. One walked up to them and said in an excellent English accent, "I have a letter for you, sir." Kennedy tore the note open. It said, "On His Majesty's Service. To the Senior Officer, Nauru Island. I have just learned of your presence on Nauru Is. I am in command of a New Zealand infantry patrol operating in conjunction with U. S. Army troops on New Georgia. I strongly advise that you come with these natives to me. Meanwhile I shall be in radio communication with your authorities at Rendova, and we can finalize plans to collect balance of your party. Lt. Wincote. P.S. Will warn aviation of your crossing Ferguson Passage."

Everyone shook hands and the four natives took Ross and Kennedy in their war canoe across to Bird Island to tell the others the good news. There the natives broke out a spirit stove and cooked a feast of yams and C ration. Then they built a leanto for McMahon, whose burns had begun to rot and stink, and for Ross, whose arm had swelled to the size of a thigh because of the coral cuts. The natives put Kennedy in the bottom of their canoe and covered him with sacking and palm fronds, in case Japanese planes should buzz them. The long trip was fun for the natives. They stopped once to try to grab a turtle, and laughed at the sport they were having. Thirty Japanese planes went over low toward Rendova, and the natives waved and shouted gaily. They rowed with a strange rhythm, pounding paddles on the gunwales between strokes. At last they reached a censored place. Lieutenant Wincote came to the water's edge and said formally, "How do you do. Leftenant Wincote."

Kennedy said, "Hello. I'm Kennedy."

Wincote said, "Come up to my tent and have a cup of tea."

. . .

In the middle of the night, after several radio conversations between Wincote's outfit and the PT base, Kennedy sat in the war canoe waiting at an arranged rendezvous for a PT. The moon went down at eleven-twenty. Shortly afterward Kennedy heard the signal he was waiting for—four shots. Kennedy fired four answering shots.

A voice shouted to him, "Hey, Jack!"

Kennedy said, "Where the hell you been?"

The voice said, "We got some food for you."

Kennedy said bitterly, "No, thanks, I just had a coconut."

A moment later a PT came alongside. Kennedy jumped onto it and hugged the men aboard—his friends. In the American tradition, Kennedy held under his arm a couple of souvenirs: one of the improvised paddles and the Japanese gas mask.

With the help of the natives, the PT made its way to Bird Island. A skiff went in and picked up the men. In the deep of the night, the PT and its happy cargo roared back toward base. The squadron medic had sent some brandy along to revive the weakened men. Johnston felt the need of a little revival. In fact, he felt he needed quite a bit of revival. After taking care of that, he retired topside and sat with his arms around a couple of roly-poly, mission-trained natives. And in the fresh breeze on the way home they sang together a hymn all three happened to know:

> Jesus loves me, this I know,
> For the Bible tells me so;
> Little ones to him belong,
> They are weak, but He is strong.
> Yes, Jesus loves me; yes, Jesus loves me . . .

CROSS-CHANNEL TRIP

A. J. Liebling

JULY 8, 1944 (ON D DAY)

PEACE OR WAR, the boat trip across the English Channel always begins with the passengers in the same mood: everybody hopes he
won't get seasick. On the whole, this is a favorable morale factor at
the outset of an invasion. A soldier cannot fret about possible attacks by
the Luftwaffe or E-boats while he is preoccupied with himself, and the
vague fear of secret weapons on the far shore is balanced by the fervent
desire to get the far shore under his feet. Few of the hundred and forty
passengers on the LCIL (Landing Craft, Infantry, Large) I was on were
actively sick the night before D Day, but they were all busy thinking
about it. The four officers and twenty-nine men of the United States
Coast Guard who made up her complement were not even queasy, but
they had work to do, which was just as good. The rough weather, about
which the papers have talked so much since D Day and which in fact
interfered with the landing, was not the kind that tosses about transatlantic liners or even Channel packets; it was just a bit too rough for the
smaller types of landing craft we employed. An LCIL, as its name implies, is not one of the smallest, but it's small enough, and aboard our
flat-bottomed, three-hundred-ton job the Channel didn't seem especially bad that night. There was a ground swell for an hour after we left
port, but then the going became better than I had anticipated. LCTs
(Landing Craft, Tanks), built like open troughs a hundred feet long, to
carry armored vehicles, had a much worse time, particularly since, being
slow, they had had to start hours before us. Fifty-foot LCMs (Landing
Craft, Mechanized) and fifty-foot and thirty-six-foot LCVPs (Landing

Craft, Vehicles and Personnel), swarms of which crossed the Channel under their own power, had still more trouble. The setting out of our group of LCILs was unimpressive—just a double file of ships, each a hundred and fifty-five feet long, bound for a rendezvous with a great many other ships at three in the morning ten or fifteen miles off a spot on the coast of lower Normandy. Most of the troops travelled in large transports, from which the smaller craft transferred them to shore. The LCILs carried specially packaged units for early delivery on the Continent doorstep.

Our skipper, Lieutenant Henry Rigg, nicknamed Bunny, turned in early that evening because he wanted to be fresh for a hard day's work by the time we arrived at the rendezvous, which was to take place in what was known as the transport area. So did the commander of a naval beach battalion who was riding with us. The function of this battalion was to organize beach traffic after the Infantry had taken the beach. I stood on deck for a while. As soon as I felt sleepy, I went down into the small compartment in which I had a bunk and went to sleep—with my clothes on, naturally. There didn't seem to be anything else to do. That was at about eight. I woke three hours later and saw a fellow next to me being sick in a paper bag and I went up to the galley and had a cup of coffee. Then I went back to my bunk and slept until a change in motion and in the noise of the motors woke me again.

The ship was wallowing slowly now, and I judged that we had arrived at the transport area and were loafing about. I looked at my wristwatch and saw that we were on time. It was about three. So we hadn't been torpedoed by an E-boat. A good thing. Drowsily, I wondered a little at the fact that the enemy had made no attempt to intercept the fleet and hoped there would be good air cover, because I felt sure that the Luftwaffe couldn't possibly pass up the biggest target of history. My opinion of the Luftwaffe was still strongly influenced by what I remembered from June, 1940, in France, and even from January and February, 1943, in Tunisia. I decided to stay in my bunk until daylight, dozed, woke again, and then decided I couldn't make it. I went up on deck in the gray pre-dawn light sometime before five. I drew myself a cup of coffee from an electric urn in the galley and stood by the door drinking it and looking at the big ships around us. They made me feel proletarian. They would stay out in the Channel and send in their troops in small craft, while working-class vessels like us went right up on the beach. I pictured them inhabited by officers in dress blues and shiny brass buttons, all scented like the World's Most Distinguished After-Shave Club. The admiral's command ship lay nearby. I imagined it to be gaffed with ingenious gimmicks that would record the developments of the operation. I could imagine a terse report coming in of the annihilation of a flotilla of LCILs, including us, and hear some Annapolis man saying, "After all, that sort of thing is to be expected." Then I felt that everything was going to be all right, because it always had been. A boatswain's mate, second class, named Barrett, from Rich Square, North Carolina, stopped next to me to drink his coffee and said, "I bet Findley a pound that we'd be hit this time. We most always is. Even money."

We wouldn't start to move, I knew, until about six-thirty, the time when the very first man was scheduled to walk onto the beach. Then we would leave the transport area so that we could beach and perform our particular chore—landing one platoon of the naval beach battalion and a platoon of Army amphibious engineers—at seven-thirty-five. A preliminary bombardment of the beach defenses by the Navy was due to begin at dawn. "Ought to be hearing the guns soon," I said to Barrett, and climbed the ladder to the upper deck. Rigg was on the bridge drinking coffee, and with him was Long, the ship's engineering officer. It grew lighter and the guns began between us and the shore. The sound made us all cheerful and Long said, "I'd hate to be in under that." Before dawn the transports had begun putting men into small craft that headed for the line of departure, a line nearer shore from which the first assault wave would be launched.

Time didn't drag now. We got under way sooner than I had somehow expected. The first troops were on the beaches. The battleship Arkansas and the French cruisers Montcalm and Georges Leygues were pounding away on our starboard as we moved in. They were firing over the heads of troops, at targets farther inland. Clouds of yellow cordite smoke billowed up. There was something leonine in their tint as well as in the roar that followed, after that lapse of time which never fails to disconcert me. We went on past the big ships, like a little boy with the paternal blessing. In this region the Germans evidently had no long-range coastal guns, like the ones near Calais, for the warships' fire was not returned. This made me feel good. The absence of resistance always increases my confidence. The commander of the naval beach battalion had now come on deck, accoutred like a soldier, in greenish coveralls and tin hat. I said to him cheerfully, "Well, it looks as though the biggest difficulty you're going to have is getting your feet in cold water."

He stood there for a minute and said, "What are you thinking of?"

I said, "I don't know why, but I'm thinking of the garden restaurant behind the Museum of Modern Art in New York." He laughed, and I gave him a pair of binoculars I had, because I knew he didn't have any and that he had important use for them.

Our passengers—the beach-battalion platoon and the amphibious engineers—were now forming two single lines on the main deck, each group facing the ramp by which it would leave the ship. Vaghi and Reich, beach-battalion ensigns, were lining up their men on the port side and Miller, an Army lieutenant with a new beard, was arranging his men on the starboard side. I wished the commander good luck and went up on the bridge, which was small and crowded but afforded the best view.

An LCIL has two ramps, one on each side of her bow, which she lowers and thrusts out ahead of her when she beaches. Each ramp is handled by means of a winch worked by two men; the two winches stand side by side deep in an open-well deck just aft of the bow. If the ramps don't work, the whole operation is fouled up, so an LCIL skipper always assigns reliable men to operate them. Two seamen named Findley and Lechich were on the port winch, and two whom I knew as Rocky and Bill were on the other. Williams, the ship's executive officer, was down in the well deck with the four of them.

. . .

We had been in sight of shore for a long while, and now I could recognize our strip of beach from our intelligence photographs. There was the house with the tower on top of the cliff on our starboard as we went in. We had been warned that preliminary bombardment might remove it, so we should not count too much upon it as a landmark; however, there it was and it gave me the pleasure of recognition. A path was to have been blasted and swept for us through element C (underwater concrete and iron obstacles) and mines, and the entrance to it was to have been marked with colored buoys. The buoys were there, so evidently the operation was going all right. Our LCIL made a turn and headed for the opening like a halfback going into a hole in the line. I don't know whether Rigg suddenly became solicitous for my safety or whether he simply didn't want me underfoot on the bridge, where two officers and two signalmen had trouble getting around even without me. He said, "Mr. Liebling will take his station on the upper deck during action." This was formal language from the young man I had learned to call Bunny, especially since the action did not seem violent as yet, but I climbed down the short ladder from the bridge to the deck, a move which put the wheelhouse between me and the bow. The upper deck was also the station for a pharmacist's mate named Kallam, who was our reserve first-aid man. A landing craft carries no doctor, the theory being that a pharmacist's mate will make temporary repairs until the patient can be transferred to a larger ship. We had two men with this rating aboard. The other, a fellow named Barry, was up in the bow. Kallam was a sallow, long-faced North Carolinian who once told me he had gone into the peacetime Navy as a youth and had never been good for anything else since. This was his first action, except for a couple of landings in Nicaragua around 1930.

The shore curved out toward us on the port side of the ship and when I looked out in that direction I could see a lot of smoke from what appeared to be shells bursting on the beach. There was also an LCT, grounded and burning. "Looks as if there's opposition," I said to Kallam, without much originality. At about the same time something splashed in the water off our starboard quarter, sending up a high spray. We were moving in fast now. I could visualize, from the plan I had seen so often in the last few days, the straight, narrow lane in which we had to stay. "On a straight line—like a rope ferry," I thought. The view on both sides changed rapidly. The LCT which had been on our port bow was now on our port quarter, and another LCT, also grounded, was now visible. A number of men, who had evidently just left her, were in the water, some up to their necks and others up to their armpits, and they didn't look as if they were trying to get ashore. Tracer bullets were skipping around them and they seemed perplexed. What I hate most about tracers is that every time you see one, you know there are four more bullets that you don't see, because only one tracer to five bullets is loaded in a machine-gun belt. Just about then, it seems in retrospect, I felt the ship ground.

I looked down at the main deck, and the beach-battalion men were already moving ahead, so I knew that the ramps must be down. I could hear Long shouting, "Move along now! Move along!," as if he were unloading an excursion boat at Coney Island. But the men needed no urging; they were moving without a sign of flinching. You didn't have to look far for tracers now, and Kallam and I flattened our backs against the pilot house and pulled in our stomachs, as if to give a possible bullet an extra couple of inches clearance. Something tickled the back of my neck. I slapped at it and discovered that I had most of the ship's rigging draped around my neck and shoulders, like a character in an old slapstick movie about a spaghetti factory, or like Captain Horatio Hornblower. The rigging had been cut away by bullets. As Kallam and I looked toward the stern, we could see a tableau that was like a recruiting poster. There was a twenty-millimetre rapid-firing gun on the upper deck. Since it couldn't bear forward because of the pilot house and since there was nothing to shoot at on either side, it was pointed straight up at the sky in readiness for a possible dive-bombing attack. It had a crew of three men, and they were kneeling about it, one on each side and one behind the gun barrel, all looking up at the sky in an extremely earnest manner, and getting all the protection they could out of the gunshield. As a background to the men's heads, an American flag at the ship's stern streamed across the field of vision. It was a new flag, which Rigg had ordered hoisted for the first time for the invasion, and its colors were brilliant in the sun. To make the poster motif perfect, one of the three men was a Negro, William Jackson, from New Orleans, a wardroom steward, who, like everybody else on the LCIL, had multiple duties.

The last passenger was off the ship now, and I could hear the stern anchor cable rattling on the drum as it came up. An LCIL drops a stern anchor just before it grounds, and pays out fifty to a hundred fathoms of chain cable as it slowly slides the last couple of ship's lengths toward shore. To get under way again, it takes up the cable, pulling itself afloat. I had not known until that minute how eager I was to hear the sound of the cable that follows the order "Take in on stern anchor." Almost as the cable began to come in, something hit the ship with the solid clunk of metal against metal—not as hard as a collision or a bomb blast; just "clink." Long yelled down, "Pharmacist's mate go forward. Somebody's hurt." Kallam scrambled down the ladder to the main deck with his kit. Then Long yelled to a man at the stern anchor winch, "Give it hell!" An LCIL has to pull itself out and get the anchor up before it can use its motors, because otherwise the propeller might foul in the cable. The little engine which supplies power for the winch is built by a farm-machinery company in Waukesha, Wisconsin, and every drop of gasoline that went into the one on our ship was filtered through chamois skin first. That engine is the ship's insurance policy. A sailor now came running up the stairway from the cabin. He grabbed me and shouted, "Two casualties in bow!" I passed this information on to the bridge for whatever good it might do; both pharmacist's mates were forward already and there was really nothing else to be done. Our craft had now swung clear, the anchor was up, and the engines went into play. She turned about and shot forward like a destroyer. The chief machinist's mate said afterward that the engines did seven hundred revolutions a minute instead of the six hundred that was normal top speed. Shells were kicking up water-spouts around us as we went; the water they raised looked black. Rigg said afterward, "Funny thing. When I was going in, I had my whole attention fixed on two mines attached to sunken concrete blocks on either side of the place where we went in. I knew they hadn't been cleared away—just a path between them. They were spider mines, those things with a lot of loose cables. Touch one cable and you detonate the mine. When I was going out, I was so excited that I forgot all about the damn mines and didn't think of them until I was two miles past them."

. . .

A sailor came by and Shorty, one of the men in the gun crew, said to him, "Who was it?" The sailor said, "Rocky and Bill. They're all tore up. A shell got the winch and ramps and all." I went forward to the well deck, which was sticky with a mixture of blood and condensed milk. Soldiers had left cases of rations lying all about the ship, and a fragment of the shell that hit the boys had torn into a carton of cans of milk. Rocky and Bill had been moved belowdecks into one of the large forward compartments. Rocky was dead beyond possible doubt, somebody told me, but the pharmacist's mates had given Bill blood plasma and thought he might still be alive. I remembered Bill, a big, baby-faced kid from the District of Columbia, built like a wrestler. He was about twenty, and the other boys used to kid him about a girl he was always writing letters to. A third wounded man, a soldier dressed in khaki, lay on a stretcher on deck breathing hard through his mouth. His long, triangular face looked like a dirty drumhead; his skin was white and drawn tight over his high cheekbones. He wasn't making much noise. There was a shooting-gallery smell over everything, and when we passed close under the Arkansas and she let off a salvo, a couple of our men who had their backs to her quivered and had to be reassured. Long and Kavanaugh, the communications officer, were already going about the ship trying to get things ticking again, but they had little success at first.

Halfway out to the transport area, another LCIL hailed us and asked us to take a wounded man aboard. They had got him from some smaller craft, but they had to complete a mission before they could go back to the big ships. We went alongside and took him over the rail. He was wrapped in khaki blankets and strapped into a wire basket litter. After we had sheered away, a man aboard the other LCIL yelled at us to come back so that he could hand over a half-empty bottle of plasma with a long rubber tube attached. "This goes with him," he said. We went alongside again and he handed the bottle to one of our fellows. It was trouble for nothing, because the man by then had stopped breathing.

We made our way out to a transport called the Dorothea Dix that had a hospital ward fitted out. We went alongside and Rigg yelled that we had four casualties aboard. A young naval doctor climbed down the grapple net hanging on the Dix's side and came aboard. After he had looked at our soldier, he called for a breeches buoy and the soldier was hoisted up sitting in that. He had been hit in one shoulder and one leg, and the doctor said he had a good chance. The three others had to be sent up in wire baskets, vertically, like Indian papooses. A couple of Negroes on the upper deck of the Dix dropped a line which our men made fast to the top of one basket after another. Then the man would be jerked up in the air by the Negroes as if he were going to heaven. Now that we carried no passengers and were lighter, the sea seemed rough. We bobbled under the towering transport and the wounded men swung wildly on the end of the line, a few times almost striking against the ship. A Coastguardsman reached up for the bottom of one basket so that he could steady it on its way up. At least a quart of blood ran down on him, covering his tin hat, his upturned face, and his blue overalls. He stood motionless for an instant, as if he didn't know what had happened, seeing the world through a film of red, because he wore eyeglasses and blood had covered the lenses. The basket, swaying eccentrically, went up the side. After a couple of seconds, the Coastguardsman turned and ran to a sink aft of the galley, where he turned on the water and began washing himself. A couple of minutes after the last litter had been hoisted aboard, an officer on the Dix leaned over her rail and shouted down, "Medical officer in charge says two of these men are dead! He says you should take them back to the beach and bury them." Out there, fifteen miles off shore, they evidently thought that this was just another landing exercise. A sailor on deck said, "The son of a bitch ought to see that beach."

Rigg explained to the officer that it would be impossible to return to the beach and ordered the men to cast off the lines, and we went away from the Dix. Now that the dead and wounded were gone, I saw Kallam sneak to the far rail and be sicker than I have ever seen a man at sea. We passed close by the command ship and signalled that we had completed our mission. We received a signal, "Wait for orders," and for the rest of the day we loafed, while we tried to reconstruct what had happened to us. Almost everybody on the ship had a battle headache.

"What hurts me worst," Lechich said, "is thinking what happened to those poor guys we landed. That beach was hot with Jerries. And they didn't have nothing to fight with—only carbines and rifles. They weren't even supposed to be combat troops."

"I don't think any of them could be alive now," another man said.

As the hours went by and we weren't ordered to do anything, it became evident that our bit of beach wasn't doing well, for we had expected, after delivering our first load on shore, to be employed in ferrying other troops from transports to the beach, which the beach-battalion boys and engineers would in the meantime have been helping to clear. Other LCILs of our flotilla were also lying idle. We saw one of them being towed, and then we saw her capsize. Three others, we heard, were lying up on one strip of beach, burned. Landing craft are reckoned expendable. Rigg came down from the bridge and, seeing me, said, "The beach is closed to LCILs now. Only small boats going in. Wish they'd thought of that earlier. We lost three good men."

"Which three?" I asked. "I know about Rocky and Bill."

"The coxswain is gone," Bunny said. I remembered the coxswain, an earnest young fellow who wanted to be a newspaperman, and who, dressed in swimming trunks, was going to go overboard ahead of everyone else and run a guideline into shore.

"Couldn't he get back?" I asked.

"He couldn't get anywhere," Rigg answered. "He had just stepped off the ramp when he disintegrated. He must have stepped right into an H.E. shell. Cox was a good lad. We'd recommended him for officers' school." Rigg walked away for the inevitable cup of coffee, shaking his big tawny head. I knew he had a battle headache, too.

A while afterward, I asked Rigg what he had been thinking as we neared the coast and he said he had been angry because the men we were going to put ashore hadn't had any coffee. "The poor guys had stayed in the sack as late as they could instead," he said. "Going ashore without any coffee!"

. . .

Long was having a look at the damage the shell had done to our ship, and I joined him in tracing its course. It had entered the starboard bow well above the waterline, about the level of the ship's number, then had hit the forward anchor winch, had been deflected toward the stern of the boat, had torn through the bulkhead and up through the cover of the escape hatch, then had smashed the ramp winch and Rocky and Bill. It had been a seventy-five-millimetre anti-tank shell with a solid-armor-piercing head, which had broken into several pieces after it hit the ramp winch. The boys kept finding chunks of it around, but enough of it stayed in one piece to show what it had been. "They had us crisscrossed with guns in all those pillboxes that were supposed to have been knocked off," Long said. "Something must have gone wrong. We gave them a perfect landing, though," he added with professional pride. "I promised the commander we would land him dry tail and we did." Long has been in the Coast Guard twenty years and nothing surprises him; he has survived prohibition, Miami and Fire Island hurricanes, and three landings. He is a cheerful soul who has an original theory about fear. "I always tell my boys that fear is a passion like any other passion," he had once told me. "Now, if you see a beautiful dame walking down the street, you feel passion but you control it, don't you? Well, if you begin to get frightened, which is natural, just control yourself also, I tell them." Long said that he had seen the commander start off from the ship at a good clip, run well until he got up near the first line of sand dunes, then stagger. "The commander was at the head of the line about to leave the ship when young Vaghi, that big ensign, came up and must have asked him for the honor of going first," Long said. "They went off that way, Vaghi out ahead, running as if he was running out on a field with a football under his arm. Miller led the soldiers off the other ramp, and he stepped out like a little gentleman, too." The space where the starboard ramp had once been gave the same effect as an empty sleeve or eye socket.

It was Frankel, a signalman who had been on the bridge, who told me sometime that afternoon about how the wounded soldier had come to be on board. Frankel, whose family lives on East Eighteenth Street in Brooklyn, was a slender, restless fellow who used to be a cutter in the garment centre. He played in dance bands before he got his garment-union card, he once told me, and on the ship he occasionally played hot licks on the bugle slung on the bridge. "A shell hit just as we were beginning to pull out," Frankel said, "and we had begun to raise the ramps. It cut all but about one strand of the cable that was holding the starboard ramp and the ramp was wobbling in the air when I saw a guy holding on to the end of it. I guess a lot of us saw him at the same time. He was just clutching the ramp with his left arm, because he had been shot in the other shoulder. I'll never forget his eyes. They seemed to say, 'Don't leave me behind.' He must have been hit just as he stepped off the ramp leaving the ship. It was this soldier. So Ryan and Landini went out and got him. Ryan worked along the rail inside the ramp and Landini worked along the outside edge of the ramp and they got him and carried him back into the ship. There was plenty of stuff flying around, too, and the ramp came away almost as soon as they got back. That's one guy saved, anyway." Ryan was a seaman cook who helped Fassy, the commissary steward, in the galley, and Landini was the little First Avenue Italian who had made up a special song for himself—"I'm going over to France and I'm shaking in my pants."

Along about noon, an LCVP, a troughlike fifty-footer, hailed us and asked if we could take care of five soldiers. Rigg said we could. The craft came alongside and passed over five drenched and shivering tank soldiers who had been found floating on a rubber raft. They were the crew of a tank that had been going in on a very small craft and they had been swamped by a wave. The tank had gone to the bottom and the soldiers had just managed to make it to the raft. The pharmacist's mates covered them with piles of blankets and put them to bed in one of our large compartments. By evening they were in the galley drinking coffee with the rest of us. They were to stay on the ship for nearly a week, as it turned out, because nobody would tell us what to do with them. They got to be pretty amphibious themselves. The sergeant in command was a fellow from Cleveland named Angelatti. He was especially happy about being saved, apparently because he liked his wife. He would keep repeating, "Gee, to think it's my second anniversary—I guess it's my lucky day!" But when he heard about what we thought had happened to the men we put ashore, he grew gloomy. The tanks had been headed for that beach and should have helped knock out the pillboxes. It hadn't been the tankmen's fault that the waves had swamped them, but the sergeant said disconsolately, "If we hadn't got bitched up, maybe those other guys wouldn't have been killed." He had a soldier's heart.

THE *SUSPENDED* DRAWING ROOM

S. N. Behrman

JANUARY 27, 1945 (ON POST-BLITZ LONDON)

O ARRIVE IN LONDON in a Saturday twilight late in 1944, after having been away since before the war began, was to experience a sinking of the heart for which even the destruction in the suburbs, visible from the windows of the train, had not prepared me. The suburban wash, hung amply across the gaps made by the bombs in the rows of workers' houses, stirred a quick, sympathetic awareness of human adaptability, and so did the window curtains and flower pots in the truncated dwellings that remained—the persistent, vivid, still-life ameliorations. But these things I somewhat expected, though even here there was a shocking discrepancy between what one has written off as history and what was actually still contemporary. I accepted the neat erasures in the long rows of houses, and even the vestiges of normality in the partially demolished ones. And I wondered about the displaced inhabitants of the houses that were gone. Where, on that darkening afternoon, were they warming their feet and how were they going to kill the unpromising evening?

London was something else again. Nothing in the outworks had quite suggested the lowered atmosphere in the citadel itself. It was not merely the almost deserted railway station. I had arrived late in the day, and the British government official who met me remarked casually that the first V-2s had fallen earlier. They had made deep craters, my host said, but had been far less destructive than had been anticipated. There were no instructions about how to behave if you were out walking when the V-2s came, he said, because there were no alerts. You just strolled along, day-dreaming, till you were hit. The instructions about what to do when you heard the sirens for the V-1s were very simple: fall flat on your face. My host, who was going to give me a lift to Claridge's, where I was to stay, asked me if I'd mind detouring to the Savoy to drop two other visitors who had arrived on the same train. In the curved areaway of the Savoy, off the Strand, I got out for a few minutes while the others went in to register and I walked into the Strand. It was very still. For reassurance, I sought the entrance to the Savoy Grill. Sandbags were piled up against it. I peeped inside. There were a few people sitting around having tea. If, in the old days, there was a vivacious room in Europe, it was the Savoy Grill. It was the nerve center of bohemian and artistic London. I remembered an evening there: Paderewski, Yvonne Printemps, Sacha Guitry; Chaliapin blowing kisses at large. (On the plane coming over, I had heard an anecdote about Guitry. When, recently, he arrived in a French prison for collaborationists, he was told, to cheer him up, that his first wife was there. The effect was the opposite. Guitry threw up his hands. "Everything I can endure," he groaned, "but this!") That evening was millennially far away. What had made me feel that the Savoy Grill would keep up its tempo forever I did not know, but I must have felt that, because I was so struck by the change. My Englishman came back and we resumed our drive to Claridge's. He asked about America. He had been an Oxford debater and had travelled through forty-seven of our states. He was wistful about that forty-eighth state, one of the Dakotas. He wanted me to tell him about it. As I had never been in it either, I couldn't help him much. With a careful detachment, he asked about "the election." In the ensuing eight weeks of my stay, I was to observe that no matter where a conversation started, it always ended up with speculation about the forthcoming election. I may add that I never heard a word against Dewey from any Englishman. That all came from the Americans.

Down the Strand, past the Admiralty Arch, and across Piccadilly Circus, with its boxed-up Eros, I kept my eyes—while I consoled my companion for having missed North or South Dakota—at the windows, watching the familiar streets and the people on the sidewalks. The streets, with distressing elisions, were still there, but they were subdued and very shabby, and so were the pedestrians. There was an air about the buildings and the people of being on the defensive. London, it was apparent at once, had endured unbelievably and was still enduring unbelievably. Thirty-six hours before, I had left an America simmering with the exhilaration of a boom; England was tense in the paroxysm of a death struggle. When I left New York, the end of the war was imminent—"in the bag," as people said—but here it was being fought out.

. . .

An English editor I met on the plane had told me that the day after I arrived would provide one of the biggest news stories of the war: London, for the first time in five years, was to have light. That night, however, the blackout was still to be on, and I deposited my fifty-five pounds of luggage in Claridge's and went for a walk while there was still some daylight. I made for Berkeley Square. Soldiers and sailors, English and American, were walking with their girls in a faint, intermittent drizzle. Most of the women wore no stockings. I had been seeing this all summer in New York. But the American legs were tanned and agreeable, whereas these English ones were muddy and streaked bluish and red with the cold. (A young woman later told me that she was embarrassed at having to go without stockings. "I hate the unusual," she said. As she had been going barelegged for five years, I wondered how long it took for the unusual to become the usual.) The façades of the houses leading into the square have a strangely quiet look; at a casual glance, you might think the houses were shut up for the weekend, but a closer inspection shows you that they have been shut up for longer than that. I peered in through a grimy, narrow, leaded window at the side of a fine oaken street door. Behind it was a great, obscene shambles of shattered brick and mortar and twisted iron. A huge sheet of what had been a fluted ceiling lay against a section of stairway, as if propped up on one elbow. I looked down the row. Several places in the long vista of wreckage had been cleared for the pools—for emergency use against incendiaries—which are now a common feature of the London scene. These dark, liquid oblongs, fine-meshed in the rain, reflected jagged back walls and gargoyles of contorted pipes. I remembered going out to the set in Hollywood where Leslie Howard was making the motion picture of *Berkeley Square*. Those reproductions of eighteenth-century façades had not much less behind them than this one had.

I looked up. On the third story of a house on the corner, following accurately the theatrical convention of the missing fourth wall, was an exquisite, suspended drawing room: delicately tinted blue walls, molded cornices, the curved, rifted ceiling, with a beautifully shaped oval where the center chandelier had been. All but the framework of the rest of the house was gone, but there it hung, this upstairs drawing room, elegant and aloof. I thought of Henry James. Here was his Mayfair, crisply anatomized. What would he have done with that room? With what malevolent ghosts would he have peopled it? What seedlings of social casuistry would have sprouted beneath that non-existent chandelier, simmered along those pastel walls? An acute English critic speaks of James as the harbinger of decay and says that he described the final throes of a society he knew was done with. But James did not, I am sure, anticipate quite this finale. He must have visualized a long, slow inanition—the inhabitants of these drawing rooms giving up eventually because of their inability to sustain their own attitudes, to save face before their own pretensions. Certainly he could not have anticipated such rude visitations as there have been, cutting short the tortuous inhibitions, freezing the slow molds of refinement. Inescapably the Cassandra wails of our prophets, who are fond of reminding us that our civilization, like earlier ones, may disappear, somehow became very plausible. Ordinarily, when we become aware of moral rifts, we believe we can surmount them. Here disintegration was a physical actuality.

Later, I was to have this same feeling in drawing rooms still intact. I visited an august Englishman who has had a career of the highest distinction in English public life. He took me upstairs to show me his books—some of which he had written—and then into his shrouded drawing room. The long salon was musty and denuded. He lifted a linen hood from the head of a lovely statuette of a young girl. The girl smiled ravishingly, as if in sudden relief at her unveiling. He had bought her in Spain years ago. "We cannot, of course," he said, "keep these rooms open any longer." He walked about, uncovering other precious objects. "England," he said in the standard summary, "will never be the same again." He then made a rueful acknowledgment that there would be another England, but he felt that his had vanished. Fashionable London, upper-class London, is a vast, urban Cherry Orchard.

While I was still staring up at the Jamesian drawing room, I was gradually swallowed up by darkness. Before I knew it, the suspended drawing room had disappeared, together with the framework which suspended it. Suddenly there were no buildings, no streets, no squares. There was darkness. I started back to the hotel in something of a panic, knowing that a sense of direction was not my strong point. A few taxis went by and I hailed them, because I had not yet learned that it was no use whatever to hail a taxi in a London street. I was told afterward that in a poll taken to discover what people considered the greatest hardship of the war, the blackout won hands down. I didn't wonder. This blackout was inhuman; it was too literal, it couldn't take a joke. We had had a blackout in New York that gave you a break. I remembered it, on that perilous walk back to Claridge's, as a flaming incandescence, a pillar of fire by night, a civic bonfire. Cars passed by—little points of blue light dragging darkness after them but leaving blackness behind. I made it finally, but I had aged. When I did get to Claridge's, I didn't know it for a minute—not till the doorman flashed his torch to light a guest across the sidewalk. When I got through the swinging door into the lighted lobby, I gasped with relief.

The next night was no better, or any night thereafter. The promised illumination did not come. The government didn't go through with the moderation of the blackout, nor did it make an explanation. About this there was much grumbling. Why, since the bombs that were coming over were pilotless, was the blackout necessary at all? The common explanation, that it was necessary to save fuel, did not silence the grousing, which went on all the time I was in London, as did the blackout—profound, terrifying, impenetrable. The girl at Paddington police station who made out my ration card told me that she hadn't been out in the evening in five years. She would rather stay in than face the blackout. I must say, however, that one night several weeks later the blackout yielded some compensation: for once a full moon overcame it and London lay bathed in silver. Looking back at the Palace from St. James's Street, one saw its turrets against the clear sky as they must have looked at night in the unlit centuries. A companion pointed up to the turret where King Charles had spent his last night before his execution. "He complained," my friend said, "that his feet were cold." I could understand how he felt; it was still nippy. But the walk that night was breathtaking; never had I seen London so unimaginably beautiful. The skeletons of buildings filtered the sky, the ubiquitous pools shimmered, the grayness of the London masonry took kindly to this soft light. I realized that this was the first time I had ever really seen London by moonlight.

Back in my room the first night, I rang for the floor waiter. There he was, my old friend James, flourishing a greatly abbreviated dinner card. He was in tails, as always (the waiters are the only ones left in London who dress for dinner), but he had thinned out a bit and his clothes, quite shiny and threadbare, almost hung on him. Still, he wore them with an air, and his smile of welcome was the only thing in London so far that had not changed. There wasn't much on the menu: a no-man's land of mousses and pilaffs, with nothing really definable. I ventured several choices. "I wouldn't have that, sir," James cautioned each time. Finally I ordered a chicken cutlet, which turned out to have a mealy neutrality. It inexorably filled you up, and that was all that could be said for it. I diverted my attention from it by talking to James.

"Well, James," I began, "quite a lot you've gone through in these five years!"

"Bit rough 'ere and there, sir."

"I'm sure it must have been."

"Worst was in the blitz of '40–'41, when I used to have to walk 'ome at night to Maida Vale, ducking into areaways every second, dodging shrapnel."

"Why did you have to walk?"

"Well, sir, during the worst of the blitz the buses would just draw up at the curb and stay there all night. Had to walk. Pretty thick it was some nights, coming down so fast. Why, sir, would you believe it, one night it took me an hour and a half to walk one hundred yards from this 'otel!"

I was indignant. "Why," I demanded, "wouldn't they let you sleep here, in the hotel?"

James was shocked. "Oh, sir, I wouldn't sleep in this 'otel."

"Why not, James?"

"Far too 'ot. Don't care for the central 'eating. I'm a countryman—like open air, open windows!"

Feeling terribly effete for having proposed sleeping in Claridge's, I finished my dinner quickly and said good night to James. Then I started to go to bed. While I was undressing, the sirens began—a long ululation rising in piercing crescendo. I sat down with a shoe in one hand. There was a deafening crash. A buzz bomb had fallen, and seemingly dreadfully close. I hadn't been so acutely aware, till that moment, that I was in the South of England. I looked at the thick, drawn curtains. Flying glass couldn't very well get through those. Or could it? I put out the light and quickly got under the covers.

• • •

"The next war," said a keen-minded Anglicized Hungarian at a dinner party a few nights later, "will start with someone pressing a push button in some underground electric works in Central Europe, which will send robot bombs to Detroit." It is generally agreed that London escaped complete destruction last summer by only a hair's breadth, that had the invasion not taken place when it did, the enemy installations in France would have sent across twenty-five hundred robots a day. This they were equipped to do. Even allowing for the admitted imprecision of aim, this would have meant the total extinction of the capital. "The robot is a very clever weapon," a distinguished physicist in the British Civil Service told me. "It is, of course, in the early stages of its development, but it has great possibilities." From a Mephistophelean point of view, it has done pretty well already. I arrived after the V-1s had, presumably, done their worst. They were now sporadic but always impending. And when they fell, they and the V-2s, they did something more than show their possibilities. As I was going to dinner one night in Kensington Palace Gardens, the great park flared suddenly into brilliant illumination. The trees became alive with light and dredged from my memory the awful scene in Arthur Machen's novel *The Terror*. For a moment I thought it was a thunderstorm. The air shuddered, as well as the car in which I sat. With the blackness that followed there came the sound of an immense explosion. Then everything was as before, at least where I was. Nothing daunts the London chauffeur. Mine had stopped the car; now he started it again, chuckling to himself. I didn't ask him what he found funny. I arrived at dinner fifteen minutes late. "I thought," said my hostess as she rose to greet me, "that we should have to revise the dinner table." That was the only reference to the explosion. Next day the same chauffeur drove me somewhere else. The London taxi drivers and chauffeurs know everything. Late at night, in some mysterious rendezvous, they check up on every bomb, every explosion. This man was able to give me precise information about last night's bomb. It had killed many people and destroyed or partially demolished several hundred houses.

The nonchalance about bombs is general throughout England. A lady who drives a lorry to blitzed areas told me that she is never in the least frightened, no matter what happens, while she is driving, nor does she flinch no matter what gruesome charges she has to carry. It is only when she is lying in bed at night that she is frightened, and then more at the sirens than at the explosions, because, she imagines, the former are anticipation, the latter *faits accomplis*. If you are alive to hear the explosion, you are all right. On the opening night of John Gielgud's revival of *The Circle*, there was an alert during the last act. The bedraggled and bedizened Lady Kitty was sitting down front on a sofa, admonishing the young Elizabeth to profit by her example and not run away with a married man. The sirens began. In front of the footlights a square transparency lit up to reveal the word "ALERT" in huge black letters—quite unnecessarily, it seemed to me, as the sirens were distinctly audible. Lady Kitty had been describing the shabbier social aspects of life in Monte Carlo. I half expected Yvonne Arnaud, playing Lady Kitty, to say, "My dear Elizabeth, go to the nearest shelter at once." But Lady Kitty didn't. She went on fervently imploring Elizabeth to avoid scandal. No one in the audience stirred, except to strain forward a bit to hear Yvonne Arnaud better.

William Wyler, the director of the motion picture *Mrs. Miniver,* once told me that he wants to do a scene in a film of people having lunch or dinner during an alert, with the conversation proceeding completely undeflected by the bombing. (He says that he'll shoot the scene without telling the actors anything about it and add the sound effects afterward.) In the two months I was in England, I encountered this sort of thing five times. To get a change from the inedible food at Claridge's, I used to go out for the inedible food at several little restaurants I knew. One day I was lunching in one of these with Chaim Weizmann and a number of his friends. Everybody was enchanted with the quietly ironic utterances of this extraordinary man. An alert began, screaming in crescendo over the very roof of the restaurant. Weizmann lifted his voice slightly—the only time I have ever known him to lift it. The conversation went on to its end without a reference to the alert. Not long before, a bomb had fallen on a restaurant in this neighborhood during the lunch hour, killing hundreds of people, but no one said a word about the incident. I never discussed an air raid with anyone in London except taxi drivers and chauffeurs. No one else will talk about them. Three or four lines in the papers will tell you that several bombs fell the day before in Southern England, but that is all. Beyond the casual remark that was made the day I arrived, the V-2s were never spoken of. Presumably it has been different since Churchill's speech about them.

This nonchalance has affected Americans, too. There is the story the Lunts tell. Alfred Lunt was standing in the wings one night ready to make his entrance in the second act of *There Shall Be No Night.* The sirens sounded, and a bomb exploded, quite close. Lynn Fontanne, who was onstage, turned to address the young man playing her son and found him not there. He had obeyed a conditioned reflex and run off the stage to the doubtful shelter of his dressing room. Disregarding this, Lunt made his entrance. His first line was to Miss Fontanne: "Darling, are you all right?" The audience applauded when she said she was all right. "Do you know," Lunt told me, "what Lynn's first remark to me was when we left the stage after the curtain was down? She turned on me accusingly and said, 'That's the first time, Alfred—that's the first time in the years we've been doing this play—that's the very first time you ever read it properly!'" I remarked that I had always suspected that the only really effective director for Lunt was Himmler. This consoled Miss Fontanne.

. . .

The country's absorption in the war is complete, but the peculiar anomalies of English life and English character, political and otherwise, persist. The taxi driver who took me to see Harold Laski knew about him. "Oh, yes, Professor Laski," he said possessively. "I am Labour and I think we'll get in at the next election. Clever man, Professor Laski. Churchill likes him." Laski was amused by this when I told him, as well as by another remark I quoted to him, made by an American when the New York *Times* carried a story that the Laski home had been blitzed during the night. Laski, the *Times* related, had been knocked out of bed, had fallen down several flights of stairs, and waked up. "He must be a light sleeper," said the American.

Then, on a four-hour trip to Cardiff, on a train on which there was no food, no heat, no seats, I stood in a corridor talking to a young instructor in the Home Defense. He was full of gruesome details of the work performed in London by his Home Defense volunteers, one of them a man well over seventy. "Unsparing," he said. "They work sometimes for days with no sleep at all." The most unbearable part of his work, he said, was finding the bodies of children. Only the week before, he had pulled out of the wreckage of a bombed building the body of a little girl about the same age as his own, who was, he thanked God, evacuated to Gloucester and whom he was now on his way to visit. "It isn't all unrelieved gloom, though," he said. "Sometimes funny things happen." I encouraged him to tell me a funny thing. "Well," he said, "one day we were clearing out a badly blitzed house. We found a decapitated man. We looked and looked for his head but couldn't find it. Finally we gave up. As we were carrying the torso through what used to be the garden into the van, we heard a chicken clucking. Hello, I thought, what's that chicken clucking about? There's certainly nothing left for him in the garden. We went back and followed the clucking till we found the chicken. It wasn't in the garden at all but in part of the rubble and it was clucking at the missing head." I was happy to find that there was a lighter side to this man's work.

At the station in Cardiff I was met by Jack Jones, the novelist and playwright and the biographer of Lloyd George. Cardiff, I had been told in London, was hell even in peacetime. Jones took me to a sing in a local tabernacle. A banker in the town had organized a series of Sunday-night sings for service men. The place was packed, the mood warm and informal, and the singing, in Welsh and English, magnificent. The phenomenon of a great crowd spending the evening just singing struck me as extraordinary; in America it wouldn't occur to people to sing en masse without being paid for it. Jones walked me back to my hotel afterward. It was obvious, once we were on the street, that only a few of the American service men in the vicinity had gone to the tabernacle. The rest appeared to be walking the streets with girls, many of them almost children. The atmosphere was high-pitched, like an American college town on a football night. In the few blocks between the tabernacle and the hotel I must have seen twenty pickups. "The girls like the American approach," said Jones. "Your boys dispense with preliminaries. Result: high illegitimacy." It was obvious that the blackout was a help. Long after I went to bed, I could hear the boys and girls tramping the streets, laughing and singing. I heard a boy teaching a Welsh girl "I Can't Give You Anything but Love, Baby." She seemed apt. I was eavesdropping on the active permutation of cultures; I could almost feel the graph of illegitimacy soaring. The process sounded gay.

During a trip to the Valleys, as the mining areas in Wales are called, Jones and I stopped at Merthyr Tydfil, his birthplace and the cradle of the Industrial Revolution. Jones showed me the hut in which he was born. It was one of a whole block of identical huts. He pointed out, at the corner, the privy which served the entire block. Fifty yards from these dwellings is a bronze plaque commemorating the fact that from here the world's first steam locomotive made a run of twenty-seven miles. In the middle of the nineteenth century, Jones told me, Merthyr Tydfil was one of the busiest industrial cities in the world; the products of the surrounding valleys went to every part of the globe. All one can say is that the Industrial Revolution hasn't done well by its birthplace—the eroded hills, the rows of boarded-up buildings, the squalid artifacts left by succeeding generations make one wonder who got the benefits of all this. A few London mansions occupied by absentee mine owners could scarcely compensate for the scars, topographical and human, on the landscape.

These hovels are the shelters of the Industrial Revolution and they are not much better than those of the current one; they're aboveground, and that's about all you can say for them. We went through village after village with shops boarded up, their districts all mined out. The inhabitants go by bus to work in war plants some distance away. What they will do after the war Jones didn't know. It was through one of these villages that the Duke of Windsor made a tour when he was King. As the vistas of misery opened up before him, he muttered, "Something has to be done about this." For this mutter the people are grateful to this day. The Duke is popular in the district. "'E was done in by the 'igher-ups," a taxi driver in Cardiff said to me. There is a decided impression, even in other parts of England, that it was not so much Mrs. Simpson as a program of social improvement, forming slowly in the Duke's conscience, that cost him his crown.

. . .

Having been in London's shelters, I can see readily why most people—at least those who have some alternative—will take their chance on being hit rather than go into them. There are three main types: surface shelters, which look like enlarged Nissen huts; shallow shelters, which vary in size and depth and are only fairly safe; and the deep shelters, of which there are five in London. Each of the last can accommodate eight thousand people. Then, of course, there are the subways, which are still favored by many. On the concrete platforms of the stations are built tiers of steel shelves somewhat like the ones used in American railway stations for checking baggage. On them you see men, women, and small children asleep with their clothes on. As a concession to light sleepers, the trains do not run after eleven-thirty at night, but no alarm clock is needed in the early morning. One morning, while I was waiting in a station for a train, I saw a little boy rather younger than my own, who is seven, lying asleep, his arm curved up over his eyes as if to shield them from the light. The train roared in. Just as I was caught in the crowd that sucked me aboard, quite in the New York fashion, I looked back at this child. The noise of the milling crowd must have penetrated the planes of sleep; he turned abruptly, huddling himself and his blanket against the glazed brick wall behind his bunk.

When I asked why people used the subways when they could use the regular shelters, which at least didn't have trains rushing through them, I was told that the subways appeal to many simply because of their safety;

several of the regular shelters—that is, the surface and shallow ones—have been hit and their occupants killed. What I found most trying in all the shelters, though for the habitués it is probably a solace, was the constant blaring, through loudspeakers, of ancient records of American popular tunes: "Whispering," "Avalon," "Blue Skies." These nostalgic idyls, dinned out in incessant fortissimo, impart an atmosphere of phantasmagoria to scenes that might otherwise be merely abysmally depressing. This public music is a wartime phenomenon; the railway stations, too, have acquired the habit of playing American, or mainly American, jazz records to speed the departing trains. The raucous evocation of the melodies of the seven fat years makes the prevailing dreariness macabre; the orchestrations of "This Side of Paradise" somehow fail in their efforts to diminish the electrified gloom of the urban foxholes.

There are children who have never known any homes but shelters. A pretty young woman sat in one of them beside her baby, which was in a pram. I asked her whether she couldn't be evacuated. She said she had been but hadn't liked the place where they had sent her. "It was the noise," she said. "The place was near a bomber command and I couldn't stand the racket of the bombers making off for France." An apple-cheeked old lady smiled cheerfully at the young woman and me. Someone asked her whether she had had dinner. "Yes," she said, "I went home and cooked it in my own kitchen." "But weren't you bombed out?" "Oh, yes," she said. "The rest of the house is gone, but Jerry didn't get the kitchen." Obviously she was proud of having put one over on Jerry.

The deep shelters are amazing. They are cities hundreds of feet underground. A companion and I timed the descent to one in the lift; it took several minutes. It is planned, after the war, to use them for stations in a projected express subway system. The interminable, brightly lit corridors curving beside the endless shelves of bunks have the antiseptic horror of the German film *Metropolis*. These shelters are really safe. The one we visited has a long bar-canteen which serves cocoa, milk and sandwiches at nominal prices. There is a fully equipped hospital with nurses and doctors in attendance. We walked miles on concrete platforms while the loudspeakers blared "Dardanella" and "Tea for Two." We went to a lower level and visited the power room, which might serve as a sizzling, violet-lit shrine to the God Dynamo. The girl in charge manipulated switches; the immense electric bulb in the heart of an intestinal coil of lighted glass tubing changed its complexion from violet to magenta to lemon. We went to the telephone control. The operator there told us that she could instantly get in communication with the four other deep shelters.

We went up again and walked around the corridors. A good-looking, very neatly dressed man of forty was sitting on a bunk beside a boy who must have been his son, about twelve and also nicely dressed. The boy's hair was brushed smooth and he looked as if he had got himself up to visit a rich aunt. I talked to the man. He said he had lost every possession he had in the world except the clothes he and his son were wearing. They had been living in this shelter for eight months. In the morning he went to his work and the boy went to school. The problem in the shelter was to get up early enough, before six-thirty, because after that hour lift service, except for the aged and crippled, stopped and there were seven hundred stairs.

We finally left the deep shelter. My companion wanted me to see still another type of shelter. I begged off. I simply couldn't stand one more. I was aware that the people in them had been standing them for over five years.

. . .

"Perhaps," an Englishwoman in the Civil Service said to me of the shelter residents, "you would have been less shocked by what you have seen if you were familiar with the peacetime homes of these people." This, of course, is a devastating comment on the civilization which the war is implacably destroying. The transfer of great populations underground has been accomplished, but its accomplishment divides your feelings when you walk the surface of the city. At the end of their day's work, the miners in Wales, emerging with blackened faces, have their cottages to look forward to for the evening, far though they may be from the idyllic interiors of the film version of *How Green Was My Valley*. The Londoners submerge.

The Londoners submerge and sit and listen to the loudspeakers and huddle around the stoves and are patient. Their patience is rather appalling. Nor are they vindictive. They are humorous about "the Jerries." I had been told that the robot raids had changed all that, but I saw nothing to prove it. They have got used to the robots, too. The people I saw do not seem to comprehend that human beings have done this to them. They take it as they might a flood or an earthquake. The bitterness against the Germans is almost entirely confined to the articulate classes, and even among them many think that Vansittart is a crank with a "fixed idea." Compared to the English, we Americans are a very violent people indeed.

It is somehow a misstatement to say that the British are indomitable. It is rather that capitulation is a concept with which they are not equipped. Perhaps it is precisely because they depersonalize the enemy that the idea of a negotiated peace is also foreign to them. After all, you can't negotiate with a flood or an earthquake. The conditions of their life are stringent to an extent which we cannot imagine. For more than five years they have been underfed, underclothed, moving in a darkness lit only by bomb flashes and the venomous streaks of robot bombs. An American congressman from a western state made a hasty trip to England. He stayed four days. He clamored to go to France, where he stayed four more. He went back to New York, bearing the nimbus of one who has stood his ground within the sound of the guns. Upon his return, he gave a statement to the press in which he said that the English were well off, that the shop windows were full of things. One wonders what would have satisfied this congressman, exactly what deprivations he would have liked to see. For myself, I can only say that a case might be made for sending over to England our civilians instead of our soldiers. The war would last longer, but so might the peace.

D DAY, IWO JIMA

John Lardner

MARCH 17, 1945

WO DIVISIONS OF MARINES made the landing on Iwo Jima. These
Marines were frankly apprehensive before the landing. I did not
see a man, either in the staging areas before we boarded ship or on
the journey north to Iwo Jima by transport, who expected anything but
a bloody and disagreeable time of it. Iwo was far closer to the Japanese
mainland than any enemy possession we had attempted to storm before,
and our air observation showed that it was heavily fortified. Moreover, as
officers kept pointing out to one another, Iwo was too small to provide
room for maneuver, being only five miles long and, at the widest point,
two and a half miles wide. Frontal attack was the only possible course,
and the southeast beach, where we planned to land, was the only possible
landing place. "You can't run the ends up there," one major said over and
over again. "Every play is between the tackles." Another officer liked to
say that we would have surprise on our side like a burglar with whooping
cough. This, if it meant anything at all, may have been a reference to the
sinking of some mine sweepers and LCI gunboats of ours which had
gone close to shore during the preliminary naval shelling of Iwo. Even a
Japanese broadcaster had said that we would land on the southeast beach,
but that, as I said, was the only possible landing place. Even so, the Jap
announcer's remarks reinforced the cynical mood of the younger Marine
officers.

The forebodings of these officers—all of which turned out to be perfectly justified except in one or two minor particulars—were uttered humorously, as a rule, but there were also cases of serious gloom among the
officers and many gaudy premonitions among the enlisted men. These

were examples of that detached professional pessimism which is ordinarily confined in war to intelligence officers, whose minds are top-heavy with knowledge of the enemy, his strength, his dispositions, and his potentialities. The Marines bound for Iwo spoke more flatly, and with less whimsical wood-rapping, of the expectation of death than any assault troops I had ever been with before. There were reasons for this apart from the special nature of the Iwo Jima operation. The number of Marine divisions is not large and nearly all of them have been badly mauled in the course of the past three years. Their work calls for it. All but two or three of the Pacific bastions attacked by Marine forces were strongly held and bitterly defended, and even when this was not the case, the mere fundamentals of amphibious landings and assault caused them damage. In the Army, shock troops are a small minority supported by a vast group of artisans, laborers, clerks, and organizers. In the Marines there are practically nothing but shock troops. For such troops, in time, no matter how well trained and competent, a saturation point is bound to come. The Marines in the Pacific point all of this out themselves at the slightest provocation, and it's difficult, in the circumstances, to see what else they could do.

As it happened, the Marine division I went with to Iwo—the Fifth—was a new one, activated about a year ago and now engaged in its first combat mission. Most of its officers and many of its enlisted men, however, were veterans of earlier campaigns with other units. One of its enlisted men, Gunnery Sergeant John Basilone, had won the Congressional Medal of Honor at Guadalcanal. He was killed by mortar fire on Iwo Jima shortly after the division hit the beaches. Officers aboard our transport, especially those with large responsibilities, such as getting artillery ashore or conditioning amtracks and their crews for the first assault landing, stood on deck for two or three days before D Day, succumbing to bleak despair whenever the ocean swells ran high or the wind changed direction. "My God!" said Lieutenant Colonel Rose, a very young man from Toledo. "Imagine if that wind is blowing from the south when we hit!" "I'll tell you a couple of things that can happen to my artillery," said Lieutenant Colonel Duryea, not much older, "if it's rough like this at Iwo." And he did. It was gruesome.

Also unhappy for technical reasons was an officer known in his regiment—our passengers were mainly from the Twenty-seventh Regiment of the Fifth Division—as Purple Heart Louis, a high, broad, hulking man who presented an excellent target and invariably got hit in combat. He anticipated a great deal of bloodshed on Iwo Jima, but aboard the transport he was bothered chiefly by the fact that the cook for the commodore of our transport division fried everything he cooked, and Louis ate at the commodore's table. One of Louis's Purple Hearts had involved the loss of his gall bladder, and fried foods were poison to him. He relieved his misery by looting the junior officers in wardroom poker games at night. Ships in the Pacific are hot at night, with doors and blackened portholes closed and all air shut out, and Louis stripped to his gleaming torso when he played poker, revealing a cicatrix across his belly and abdomen which looked like the mother and father of all Caesarean scars. He was hit in the right arm about an hour and a half after landing on Iwo Jima.

. . .

D Day was Monday, February 19th, and H Hour was 0900. On D-minus-one, the regimental surgeon reported a hundred and twenty-five cases of diarrhea among the men and officers aboard. This had come from something they ate, but that evening the Navy cooks did better and served everyone a turkey dinner with ice cream. At the last meal, breakfast at 0500 the morning of the nineteenth, there was steak and eggs. Everyone had dressed in his green combat blouse and trousers and had strapped on his pistol belt, with a long knife, ammunition, a bandage roll, and one or two canteens attached, and had checked his carbine. After breakfast, everyone put on his helmet, which had a camouflage cover simulating sand, and went out on deck and over to the ladder nets. The sun was just coming up, so Iwo Jima was visible from our line of debarkation, which was several miles out at sea. There the larger transports halted, to keep beyond the range of shore batteries, and put off their cargoes of Marines into small boats. On Suribachi, the volcano at the south end of the island, we could see bursts of fire and smoke from our naval shelling, which continued till H Hour. Some of the men stared at the island. Others remarked that the wind was running in our favor, from the northwest, and that the sea was calmer than it had been, though still difficult. Many could think of nothing but the immediate necessity of climbing the slick, flaccid web of rope down the ship's side without looking silly or getting killed. Even young Marines have been killed on these descents when the sea has been rough, and for those over thirty-five the endless sequence of nets, Jacob's ladders, bouncing gangways, and lurching boats is a hazard and nightmare which can occupy their minds to the exclusion of all other dangers. Admirals and generals can look ridiculous in these circumstances. They are well aware of it, and their tempers during amphibious operations are correspondingly short.

I got into a small boat with Colonel Thomas Wornham, regimental commander, and some of his staff, his messengers, and his radio operators. We chopped and splashed through the ocean swells to Wornham's control ship, which was anchored nearer the shore, at the line at which the first assault troops formed up in their amtracks and began their long, slow, bobbing run for the beach. They went in in ragged waves, which left the departure line at intervals of a few minutes, coached hoarsely by a loudspeaker from the bridge of the control ship. The men in the amtracks were a fierce and stirring sight as they passed us to disappear in the valleys of water between us and the beach. I stood watching them as well as I could from the rail of the control ship beside a regimental messenger, a Navajo Indian named Galeagon, and we spoke of how most of the shock troops we could see, their hands and faces greased dead white for protection against possible flame barriers, sat up very straight and looked intently ahead. The first wave struck the beach approximately at the appointed hour of nine, and simultaneously the Navy shellfire, which had been raking the shoreline, jumped its range to the ridges and pillboxes farther inland. The central ridge was in our sector of the island. We could see the wreckage of Japanese planes piled at one edge of the plateau. We knew that an airfield lay just beyond this junk—one of the two airfields for which the Marines were beginning the dogged battle of Iwo Jima.

After a while, I walked to the cabin of the control ship where the radioman was receiving reports that were coming in to Wornham from the first radios set up on the beach. The first two hours' progress seemed to be good. The Japs had pulled back upland from the shore, leaving few dead behind them, and Wornham's regiment, which was second in the assault line striking north along the beach near Suribachi, had reached high ground, had crossed the southern end of the first airfield, and was beginning a descent to the western shore of the island, a half mile distant from the point where it had landed. I left the wireless room, where the radioman, earphones over his head, was now reading *The Case of the Caretaker's Cat*.

Wornham's Higgins boat, a rectangular little launch with a hinged landing ramp in the bow, pulled up on the starboard quarter of our ship, and those of us who were going ashore with the Colonel climbed down a ladder and jumped in. It was exactly 1100, or two hours after the first landings, and this was the fourteenth wave. I should say that we were the fourteenth wave. As far as I could see, no other boat was moving shoreward at that moment. As we cast off, Galeagon came to the ship's rail and yelled something at us through a megaphone. Wornham, a short, stocky career Marine of about forty, smiling and convivial on our voyage north but now very taut and serious, leaned precariously over the stern of the boat, clutching at the rail, and cupped a hand to one ear. "Red One now under heavy mortar fire!" shouted the messenger. The Fifth Division's share of beaches was Green Beach and Red Beaches One and Two. To the north, the Fourth Division had landed on Yellow One and Two and Blue One and Two. We were fifty feet from the control ship when Galeagon yelled another message. "Red Two under mortar fire," he said, the sound of his voice seeming to bounce across the waves. "Heavy mortar fire on both Red beaches." The others in the boat looked with expressionless faces at Wornham, who smiled wryly. "Head for a point about a hundred feet to the right of the line between Red One and Two," he told the coxswain. Then he turned to the rest of us and said, "All right, be ready to bail out of here goddam fast when we touch that beach."

We all crouched, whether sitting or standing, as the boat moved in. Now and then we wiped spray off our eyes and noses, and we paid no attention to a battleship and a cruiser through whose shadows we passed. I had some trouble crouching, because of my length and because the shelf on which I sat was only a foot or so beneath the stern rail. There was no special need, however, for crouching now, while we were still on water. It was the beaches the Japs were mortaring. We crouched in a sort of instinctive, shrinking alarm at what we were about to meet.

. . .

The Japs burst their mortar and artillery shells up and down the beaches for several days thereafter, but my own sharpest memories of this phase of the Iwo Jima battle are of D Day. That sort of shelling is a procedure someone can always use when he is defending a small area against an enemy who must get his supplies by water. At Iwo, as at Anzio, there quickly developed two fronts—the battle front forward and the shelling front on the beaches, where our supply and reinforcement lines were wholly dependent on boats and amphibious vehicles that were being stalled and pounded by surf and wind. And in the case of Iwo, the Marines depended also on motor or human convoys, which were slowed by drifting volcanic sand. The Japanese were limited only by their ammunition supply. As long as they could stay alive on Iwo Jima and keep their guns intact, they were all right, for they had observation over our supply beaches and we were within the range of their mortars. The mortar shell, a little, bomb-shaped missile, travels in a high, lobbing trajectory and throws its fragments over a wide radius when it explodes. It makes for tearing, disfiguring wounds and for disfigured dead. Since the mortar fire continued steadily for nearly a week on the crowded shoreline, and hasn't stopped on the front lines yet, our casualties have not only been large but tend to be more slashed and mangled than usual.

We saw puffs of smoke—white, gray, and black—pluming from the beach as our boat came closer. Most of the men in the boat, whose first task was to set up a regimental command post somewhere between the beach and the front lines, were burdened with radio equipment. Alwyn Lee, an Australian war correspondent, and I were also fairly cumbrously loaded. A pack in three light pieces is more trouble than a single heavy pack, and I had, in addition to my Army musette bag, a typewriter and a blanket roll containing a poncho and a small spade, or entrenching tool. I also had a sash-type lifebelt buckled around my waist, in conformance a few hours earlier with a transport regulation. This belt dropped off and vanished that day on Iwo Jima, I don't know when or where.

The landing ramp dropped down on the beach and the passengers bustled out with their loads and disappeared behind the first low hummock in the sand. I was on the point of disembarking, second to last, just ahead of the Colonel, when I realized that I had forgotten my gear, and in the moment it took to turn and pick it up piecemeal, Wornham whizzed by me and was gone. I slogged up the beach across one wind-made ridge and trench and then another. Loose, dark sand came up to the tops of my high combat boots at each step, and my breathing was sharp and painful. I made it to the third and deepest trench, some thirty yards in from the shore, and fell to my face there alongside Lee and several men of the command-post detail. When you stopped running or slogging, you became conscious of the whine and bang of mortar shells dropping and bursting near you. All up and down Red Beaches One and Two, men were lying in trenches like ours, listening to shells and digging or pressing their bodies closer into the sand around them.

We were legitimately pinned down for about forty minutes. That is to say, the mortar fire was probably heavy enough and close enough during that time to make it impractical to go further. However, there is such a thing as wishful pinned-down thinking, and it can become a more dangerous state of mind than any other in an area that is being shelled. A man tends to cling to his trench, even if it is in the center of a target, when the sensible thing is to proceed out of the target as quickly as possible, using his own best judgment about when it's prudent to dive for cover again. It seems to take about twenty minutes under shellfire to adjust your nerves and evolve a working formula by which you can make progress and gauge, very roughly, the nearness of hits and the pattern of fire.

Lee and I, by agreement, finally left our gear in a trench near the shore (we planned to salvage it later, if possible) and worked our way up the beach in the wake of Wornham and his men. There were Marines on all sides of us doing the same thing. Each man had a different method of progress. One, carbine in hand, walked along steadily, pausing and dropping to one knee only when something about the sound of the shells seemed to confuse him. Another made a high-hurdling jump into every trench or hole he used. At one point I listened to a frail Nisei interpreter arguing with an officer who wanted to help carry his pack. Again, at a moment when Lee and I were catching our breath, something stirred beside the dune just behind us. A wounded man, his face blackened by sand and powder, had roused himself from the lethargy in which he lay and noticed us. Shell fragments had hit him in one arm, one leg, the buttocks, and one eye. His eye, a red circle in his dark-stained face, worried him most. He wanted to know if there were any medical corpsmen with a litter nearby. He had been so deafened by the explosion of the shell that I had to go very close to make him hear me. There were no corpsmen or litters about. In fact, the enemy fire on the beach made it hard to get help to wounded men for the first two days, and then the process of evacuating them in boats, which had to bump their way through a high surf, was incredibly rough and painful. I promised this man to report him and get him help as soon as possible.

The next Marine we passed was dead, and so were a number of others on our diagonal course over the beach to the upland, but I didn't see a dead Japanese soldier until we got near the edge of the plateau. "That's the third one we've found on Red beaches today so far," said a soldier who sat near the mouth of a Jap concrete pillbox, which gave off a faint, foul smell. This pillbox, with walls three feet thick and built on a frame of metal tubing, was a good specimen of the Jap defenses on Iwo Jima, but in the days that followed I saw others even more substantial, with walls four to five feet thick, revolving gun turrets, and two or more approaches lined with neat stairs.

. . .

By mid-afternoon, Lee and I were ready to send our first dispatches. We decided that the only way to get them off quickly was to make for the flagship, several miles offshore. We did not feel very good about the prospect. The mortar fire on the beaches was as steady as ever and the surf was running higher than it had been in the morning. We reluctantly started down toward the shore, threading our way through a column of silent, apologetic-looking reinforcement troops climbing uphill with boxes of ammunition from the beach. Occasionally a soldier stepped out of line and asked us if we knew where this column was bound. I don't know why the people going downhill inspired more confidence or looked better-informed than the leaders of the column moving uphill, unless it was that the very direction of our progress suggested that we were Iwo Jima tenants of long standing—five or six hours, perhaps—possessed of sweeping oracular powers and the ability to speak words that would restore confidence and banish fear and confusion. This was certainly untrue. Lee and I paused in a hole halfway down the beach to argue about where we had left our packs and typewriters. I thought it was somewhere to the left, but every time I pointed, a shell was dropped on the exact spot I had in mind. Shells were now also chasing amtracks, ducks, and other craft some little way out from the shore.

It seemed clear, by the time we reached Wornham's command post, now at least several minutes old, in a broad shellhole above the beach, that the Japs had quickly abandoned the beaches, after losing a few men, and had taken most of their dead with them. This worried Wornham, because he figured that it meant heavy counterattacks in the next night or two, and he was also worried, as regimental commanders are everywhere in battle, by the problem of keeping his combat battalions in communication with each other and with him. Sitting in his shellhole, along with a couple of dozen staff men, medical officers, messengers, radio operators, and stray visitors who just wanted to be in a hole with other people, we followed, by radio and courier, the adventures of three battalions a few hundred yards away. The battalions were known in Wornham's shellhole by their commanders' names—Robbie, Tony, and Butler. "Tony says he's ready to make his turn up the west beach," Wornham said fretfully, looking at a message in his hand. "I gotta get him."

Now and then he looked around his hole and said plaintively, "Come on, let's break this up. Let's have some room here." At these words, a few of the strays would drift away in one direction or another, and a few minutes later others would take their places. The shells dropped more rarely in that neighborhood, but they were close enough. Tanks began to rumble up from the beach, at long intervals, and angle and stutter their way through a gap at the top of the ridge nearby. Purple Heart Louis came to the edge of the command post and had his right arm bandaged by a doctor to whom we had already reported the position of the wounded Marine on the beach. "I knew Louis would get it again," said a young captain. "Right where he deals the cards, too. I hope it will be a lesson to him."

We heard of death after death of men we had been with on the transport. One divisional surgeon had been killed and another had already had a breakdown from overwork. Visible Japanese dead were still scarce, even though one company had found a nest of Japs and killed a hundred. "Here's a report from FFF Company colonel, sir," said an aide. "He says the presence of a lot of flies in a trench suggests the Japs buried some dead there."

There were live Japs near enough, for whenever the Navy's Grumman fighter planes dived at a point just to our right, near the airfield, they drew machine-gun fire. Looking around, I had the leisure for the first time to think what a miserable piece of real estate Iwo Jima is. Later, when I had seen nearly all the island, I knew that there were no extenuating features. This place where thousands of men of two nations have been killed or wounded in less than three weeks' time has no water, few birds, no butterflies, no discernible animal life—nothing but sand and clay, humpbacked hills, stunted trees, knife-edged kuna grass in which mites who carry scrub typhus live, and a steady, dusty wind.

· · ·

Presently Lee said he thought that if we were going to file our stories we should head toward a place where we could see some boats bunching and where there might be a chance of our getting a ride. We started off, and a few minutes later we tumbled into a trench practically on top of our gear. There were a lot of men in this refuge now. Two Negro soldiers carrying supplies had stopped to give some water to a pair of Marines who were lying quietly at one end. The Marines had been hit by shrapnel and were waiting for litter bearers. After they drank the water, their only movement was a slight, mechanical stirring of their heads each time a shell burst close by. By now almost everyone on the beaches, even those not killed or wounded, had had some sort of direct contact with Japanese shells, if only to the extent of having tiny spent fragments, still burning hot, drop onto their clothing or into the sand right beside them.

By the time we reached a hole by the water's edge, near where we had landed, we had lost our sense of urgency and entered that stage, which comes after a certain amount of time in a shelled area, when you can no longer bring yourself to duck and run constantly, even when you are moving in the open. But the men in the boats along the shoreline immediately re-aroused us. Since they came into the fire zone only at intervals and remained as briefly as possible, they had no time to lose their awareness of danger. It suddenly seemed to us a matter of desperate importance to get out of there at once. An ammunition dump was beginning to grow up around us, and the shelling did not abate.

We went up to a boat whose ramp was slapping the waves a few feet out from the shoreline and whose coxswain was trying to hold her to shore by keeping her engine running. There we encountered a Marine named Connell, who for the next half hour gave the most spectacular demonstration of energy I have ever seen. Though he moved with great speed and fervor, there seemed to be no fear in him. He had been helping moor and unload supply boats all afternoon. He was stripped down to his green Marine shorts, and he spent as much time in the water as out of it, his lank, blond hair plastered to his skull. When he wanted to salvage a piece of equipment from the water, he made a long, flat power dive over the surf. His problem at the moment was to make this boat fast, so that the ammunition aboard her could be unloaded. With the coxswain's permission, we got into the boat and stowed our packs in the stern. It was quickly obvious that the crew of the boat, though they remained calm, were of no help to Connell whatever and considered the odds against unloading at this time overwhelming and the situation irremediable. Connell shouted orders or suggestions at them, but they simply stared at him and then stared up and down the beach at the shellbursts. Connell got hold of a rope, made it fast to the boat, then darted up the beach to tie the other end to a tractor, whose driver surveyed him curiously from the top of the vehicle. Connell persuaded the driver to start his engine and try to pull the boat in. The rope broke. Connell tied it again and it broke again. He swam out to get another rope, but by the time he returned to the beach the driver and tractor had disappeared.

Swimming furiously, he then approached Lee and me, at the stern of the boat, and called out the courteous suggestion that we get ashore. "This is going to take a long time," he shouted over the sound of the surf, "and you fellows will do better somewhere else!" He never once showed the slightest sign of temper or desperation. He appeared to regard the wild scene and his own mighty efforts and constant frustrations as wholly rational and what was to be expected. He was wrong about the boat's being there a long time. A few minutes after Lee and I swam and struggled to shore—Connell made three personal amphibious trips to help us with our gear—the boat withdrew to sea, with its cargo still aboard, possibly to try a landing somewhere else. The last we saw of Connell, he was racing down the beach to grasp a mooring rope on another boat thirty yards away.

. . .

It was getting dark and our clothes and equipment were nearly dry again when we finally boarded an LCT bound for the general neighborhood of the flagship. Five sailors returning from a shore job were grouped in a corner of the hold aft, where the boat's sides rose above their heads. As the vessel pulled out, we saw that four of them were trying vaguely to soothe the fifth, who was in the throes of shock from a near miss by a shell. He was a small young man with an underslung lower jaw. His head lolled back against the bulwark and his eyes rolled violently. "They can't get you here," said one of his colleagues, pointing at the boat's high sides. "Look. They can't even see you." By the time we were a couple of miles out, the sailor had recovered to the point of asking questions about the battle, but these and the answers he himself supplied only had the effect of returning him to a state of shock. The four others stopped looking at him and talked listlessly among themselves.

We made the flagship that night, but my typewriter sank to the bottom of the sea during our transfer from the LCT to a smaller boat that could go alongside the gangplank of the flagship.

. . .

The nature of the Iwo Jima battle did not change much in the days that immediately followed. The Marines made slow and costly gains in ground as they fought northward—gains that struck me then, and still do, as very little short of miraculous. A week or so after D Day, in a little scrub grove halfway across the island, I recognized, behind his whiskers, a staff officer in our transport group who used to surprise me a little by the passion and complete engrossment with which he could discuss for two or three hours at a time such a question as whether or not certain items of battalion equipment should be distributed divisionally, or whether a brother officer of his named Logan, thirty-five hundred miles away, stood eighty-sixth or eighty-seventh on the promotion list. It now seemed to me that such preoccupations were useful indeed if they contributed to the professional doggedness with which this man and the troops of his unit moved forward against such overpowering intimations of mortality. "I hear that the mortar fire is easing up on the beaches," he said seriously. "That's good. There's no reason why everybody on the island should get killed."

LETTER FROM ROME

Philip Hamburger

MAY 19, 1945 (ON V-E DAY)

AVING LIVED FOR A YEAR in a troubled semblance of peace, Rome has accepted the news of peace itself with the helpless and tired shrug of the defeated. My guess is that few cities are sadder today. V-E Day has pointed up an unpleasant fact many people here had tried to forget: that Italy lost the war and can advance no claims for the rewards of peace. To the Italians I've talked with, peace in Europe means at the moment little more than a dreary continuation of their present misery—fantastic prices, black markets, unemployment, the struggle to regain national pride, and the even more difficult struggle to get people to think for themselves after two decades of stupefaction. The German surrender seems to have increased the Roman's capacity for introspection; his comprehension of the situation his country is in is almost morbid, and his personal problems have suddenly loomed larger and become more pressing: how can a young man get to Turin to discover whether his parents survived the German occupation; does the American know someone who will deliver a letter to a lady's husband, a Partisan, in Milan; please, will the United States permit Italians to leave home and settle in America; at the far end of town a wealthy friend has food enough for his friends tonight, but can the American arrange to get them there and back by jeep?

Today, Tuesday, is V-E Day, but the bars and restaurants are deserted, the streets practically empty. No more bells than usual have been rung. To be sure, some flags are out and the sirens have sounded, but something is lacking. Occasional noisy groups of young Italians parade the streets, trying with almost pathetic desperation to crash the gate of victory, but the victory is not theirs and the enthusiasm is hollow. One such procession—fifteen to twenty poorly dressed young men, a boy beating a drum, and another boy carrying a large red flag—straggled down the Via Sistina this afternoon and stopped before a British mess. Through the door they could see men laughing and drinking. *"Finita, finita, la guerra è finita!"* cried the paraders, and a British sergeant, glass in hand, stepped outside, bowed gracefully, and thanked the parade for stopping by. "Good of you to come," he said, and went inside. The procession slowly moved down the street a few doors to a hotel where some Americans live. *"Finita, finita, la guerra è finita!"* the Italians cried. Several Americans stuck their heads out of windows and yelled "Hooray!," and one man with a camera leaned out and said, "Hold it till I get this!" Then everybody stuck his head back in again. The parade disappeared around a corner, the drummer halfheartedly sounding a roll. Of all the troops in town, only the British seem to be in a rejoicing mood. Arm in arm and six or eight abreast, groups of them have been marching through the city, singing. Victory in Europe appears to have accented only the homesickness of the American troops, and, knowing very well that for most of them the end of one war means simply the beginning of another, still farther from home, they have shown little enthusiasm. Tonight I saw hundreds of them sitting alone on curbstones staring into space or ambling along the streets, hands in pockets, looking into shop windows.

• • •

Italy last week was Milan, and, unlike Rome, Milan had its victory, a victory all the more pleasant, perhaps, because it came from within rather than from without. Our troops were greeted there almost with hysteria, but this exhilaration had already been touched off, first by the Partisan uprising in the city and then by the execution of Mussolini and his most infamous henchmen. When the Germans in Italy finally surrendered, the news went almost unnoticed in Milan. The newspapers welcomed the capitulation in modest headlines but continued to devote their biggest ones to Partisan activities. On the whole, the efficiency and triumph of the Partisan tactics seemed to stun even the Partisans, and for the first three or four days after the liberation large groups of them—almost all of whom were dashing around town in captured German cars, rounding up or finishing off lingering Fascists—could be seen embracing one another in the streets.

Because Milan is in the plains and would have been difficult to defend against any reinforcements the Germans might send in to aid the garrison troops, the Committee of National Liberation had to move slowly. Nevertheless, from the beginning of the German occupation, in September, 1943, at least fifteen thousand copies of clandestine newspapers were circulated every week. The newsprint for them was bought on the black market. In March, 1944, the Committee put on a successful eight-day general strike in Milan. In September of that year the Partisans began to attack the Fascists and Germans in the mountains of northern Italy, but they knew that it would be futile to attempt a fight in Milan yet. "Justice and Liberty" squads—one squad to almost every block in the city—were formed and told to provide themselves with arms. The main source of weapons was the garrison of twenty thousand Fascist troops, many of whom were willing to sell their arms if paid high enough prices. Many others were killed at night and robbed of their arms. The acquiring of arms was accelerated last December, when the Allies gave the Committee of National Liberation the task of leading the resistance movement in northern Italy. The Allies not only began to supply arms but also gave a lot of money to a trusted Partisan in Rome, a banker. By intricate financial maneuvering, he was able to transfer the money to the north.

Meanwhile, in Milan, the Partisans shifted their headquarters about once a week, settling now in the office of an obscure razor-blade distributor, now across town in a dismal restaurant. Mussolini, who had a villa on Lake Garda, north of Verona, appeared less and less frequently in Milan. When he did appear, he and his heavily armed cavalcade usually raced through the city, bound for somewhere beyond. By last January, work in the factories making supplies for the Germans had almost entirely stopped because Allied bombing of the Brenner Pass had cut the railway over which coal was sent into the country. In April, the Committee of National Liberation ordered railroad and tramway workers in Milan to strike, snubbed the Fascists when they suggested that everybody let bygones be bygones and that one big brotherly "sacred union" of all Italians might be created, formed a Committee of Revolt, mobilized the Justice and Liberty squads, and finally, on the twenty-fifth, told its ten thousand armed and ten thousand unarmed Partisans to start taking over the city. By noon the following day, a hundred Fascists had been killed and the Committee was in control of Milan. The Germans fought in the suburbs until the twenty-eighth, the day of Mussolini's execution, but those inside the town barricaded themselves in several hotels and refused to come out and fight, preferring to await the arrival of the Allies and to surrender to them.

Although many Romans—and quite a few American correspondents— deplore what went on in the Piazza Loreto on the morning of Sunday, the twenty-ninth, to the Milanese these events will probably always be symbols of the north's liberation. To an outsider like myself, who happened to be on hand to see Mussolini, Clara Petacci, Pavolini, Starace, and some of the other Fascists dangling by their heels from a rusty beam in front of a gas station, the breathless, bloody scene had an air of inevitability. You had the feeling, as you have at the final curtain of a good play, that events could not have been otherwise. In many people's minds, I think, the embellishments of this upheaval—thousands of Partisans firing their machine guns into the air, Fascist bodies lying in a heap alongside the gas station, the enormous, pressing crowd—have been overemphasized and its essential dignity and purpose have been overlooked. This is best illustrated by the execution of Starace—the fanatical killer who was once secretary of the Fascist Party—who was brought into the square in an open truck at about ten-thirty in the morning. The bodies of Mussolini and the others had been hanging for several hours. I had reached the square just before the truck arrived. As it moved slowly ahead, the crowd fell back and became silent. Surrounded by armed guards, Starace stood in the middle of the truck, hands in the air, a lithe, square-jawed, surly figure in a black shirt. The truck stopped for an instant close to the grotesque corpse of his old boss. Starace took one look and started to fall forward, perhaps in a faint, but was pushed back to a standing position by his guards. The truck drove ahead a few feet and stopped. Starace was taken out and placed near a white wall at the rear of the gas station. Beside him were baskets of spring flowers—pink, yellow, purple, and blue—placed there in honor of fifteen anti-Fascists who had been murdered in the same square six months before. A firing squad of Partisans shot Starace in the back, and another Partisan, perched on a beam some twenty feet above the ground, turned toward the crowd in the square and made a broad gesture of finality, much like a highly dramatic umpire calling a man out at the home plate. There were no roars or bloodcurdling yells; there was only silence, and then, suddenly, a sigh—a deep, moaning sound, seemingly expressive of release from something dark and fetid. The people in the square seemed to understand that this was a moment of both ending and beginning. Two minutes later, Starace had been strung up alongside Mussolini and the others. "Look at them now," an old man beside me kept saying. "Just look at them now."

. . .

No city could long remain in the emotional fever of the first days of liberation in Milan, and by the middle of that week there were signs of weariness. Fewer Partisans roamed the streets, and they were less rambunctious. Only isolated shootings took place, and these at night. The slow process of rounding up the twenty-four hundred Fascists in the city continued; they were placed in San Vittoria Jail, in cells recently occupied by their captors. A good many Partisans dropped their clandestine names and resumed their own, which created some confusion among the Partisans themselves, who had never known one another's real names. It suddenly became apparent that the days ahead, like any morning after, meant a slow and complicated readjustment.

As for the city itself, its population has, in a few years, jumped from a million to a million seven hundred thousand. A sixth of Milan's buildings were bombed, a considerable number of them in the center of town. The Duomo, however, has survived; only two of the hundreds of delicate statues along its sides were chipped by bomb fragments, although five of its seven organs were wrecked by the concussions of nearby explosions. On the first day of liberation, a crude sign over the door of La Scala (whose roof had been bombed out) said, "We Want Toscanini," but someone took it down after the entrance of the Allied troops and substituted the American, British, and Russian flags. Most of the church of Santa Maria delle Grazie and all of its cloisters are now rubble, but there are hopes that da Vinci's *Last Supper*, in the refectory, is intact. Before the first bombings of the war, the fresco was lovingly buttressed with heavy wooden scaffolding and bags filled with stones. The framework withstood the bombings and looks sturdy enough from the outside, amid the wreckage, but so far, understandably, no one has had time to begin the painstaking work of removing the wood and the bags of stones to find out whether da Vinci's masterpiece has survived the second World War.

HIROSHIMA

John Hersey

AUGUST 31, 1946

I—A NOISELESS FLASH

AT EXACTLY FIFTEEN MINUTES PAST EIGHT in the morning, on August 6, 1945, Japanese time, at the moment when the atomic bomb flashed above Hiroshima, Miss Toshiko Sasaki, a clerk in the personnel department of the East Asia Tin Works, had just sat down at her place in the plant office and was turning her head to speak to the girl at the next desk. At that same moment, Dr. Masakazu Fujii was settling down cross-legged to read the Osaka *Asahi* on the porch of his private hospital, overhanging one of the seven deltaic rivers which divide Hiroshima; Mrs. Hatsuyo Nakamura, a tailor's widow, stood by the window of her kitchen, watching a neighbor tearing down his house because it lay in the path of an air-raid-defense fire lane; Father Wilhelm Kleinsorge, a German priest of the Society of Jesus, reclined in his underwear on a cot on the top floor of his order's three-story mission house, reading a Jesuit magazine, *Stimmen der Zeit;* Dr. Terufumi Sasaki, a young member of the surgical staff of the city's large, modern Red Cross Hospital, walked along one of the hospital corridors with a blood specimen for a Wassermann test in his hand; and the Reverend Mr. Kiyoshi Tanimoto, pastor of the Hiroshima Methodist Church, paused at the door of a rich man's house in Koi, the city's western suburb, and prepared to unload a handcart full of things he had evacuated from town in fear of the massive B-29 raid which everyone expected Hiroshima to suffer. A hundred thousand people were killed by the atomic bomb, and these six were among the survivors. They still wonder why they lived when so many others died. Each of them counts many small items of chance or volition—a step taken in time, a decision to go indoors, catching one streetcar instead of the next—that spared him. And now each knows that in the act of survival he lived a dozen lives and saw more death than he ever thought he would see. At the time, none of them knew anything.

. . .

The Reverend Mr. Tanimoto got up at five o'clock that morning. He was alone in the parsonage, because for some time his wife had been commuting with their year-old baby to spend nights with a friend in Ushida, a suburb to the north. Of all the important cities of Japan, only two, Kyoto and Hiroshima, had not been visited in strength by *B-san,* or Mr. B, as the Japanese, with a mixture of respect and unhappy familiarity, called the B-29; and Mr. Tanimoto, like all his neighbors and friends, was almost sick with anxiety. He had heard uncomfortably detailed accounts of mass raids on Kure, Iwakuni, Tokuyama, and other nearby towns; he was sure Hiroshima's turn would come soon. He had slept badly the night before, because there had been several air-raid warnings. Hiroshima had been getting such warnings almost every night for weeks, for at that time the B-29s were using Lake Biwa, northeast of Hiroshima, as a rendezvous point, and no matter what city the Americans planned to hit, the Superfortresses streamed in over the coast near Hiroshima. The frequency of the warnings and the continued abstinence of Mr. B with respect to Hiroshima had made its citizens jittery; a rumor was going around that the Americans were saving something special for the city.

Mr. Tanimoto is a small man, quick to talk, laugh, and cry. He wears his black hair parted in the middle and rather long; the prominence of the frontal bones just above his eyebrows and the smallness of his mustache, mouth, and chin give him a strange, old-young look, boyish and yet wise, weak and yet fiery. He moves nervously and fast, but with a restraint which suggests that he is a cautious, thoughtful man. He showed, indeed, just those qualities in the uneasy days before the bomb fell. Besides having his wife spend the nights in Ushida, Mr. Tanimoto had been carrying all the portable things from his church, in the close-packed residential district called Nagaragawa, to a house that belonged to a rayon manufacturer in Koi, two miles from the center of town. The rayon man, a Mr. Matsui, had opened his then unoccupied estate to a large number of his friends and acquaintances, so that they might evacuate whatever they wished to a safe distance from the probable target area. Mr. Tanimoto had had no difficulty in moving chairs, hymnals, Bibles, altar gear, and church records by pushcart himself, but the organ console and an upright piano required some aid. A friend of his named Matsuo had, the day before, helped him get the piano out to Koi; in return, he had promised this day to assist Mr. Matsuo in hauling out a daughter's belongings. That is why he had risen so early.

Mr. Tanimoto cooked his own breakfast. He felt awfully tired. The effort of moving the piano the day before, a sleepless night, weeks of worry and unbalanced diet, the cares of his parish—all combined to make him feel hardly adequate to the new day's work. There was another thing, too: Mr. Tanimoto had studied theology at Emory College, in Atlanta, Georgia; he had graduated in 1940; he spoke excellent English; he dressed in American clothes; he had corresponded with many American friends right up to the time the war began; and among a people obsessed with a fear of being spied upon—perhaps almost obsessed himself—he found himself growing increasingly uneasy. The police had questioned him several times, and just a few days before, he had heard that an influential acquaintance, a Mr. Tanaka, a retired officer of the Toyo Kisen Kaisha steamship line, an anti-Christian, a man famous in Hiroshima for his showy philanthropies and notorious for his personal tyrannies, had been telling people that Tanimoto should not be trusted. In compensation, to show himself publicly a good Japanese, Mr. Tanimoto had taken on the chairmanship of his local *tonarigumi*, or Neighborhood Association, and to his other duties and concerns this position had added the business of organizing air-raid defense for about twenty families.

Before six o'clock that morning, Mr. Tanimoto started for Mr. Matsuo's house. There he found that their burden was to be a *tansu*, a large Japanese cabinet, full of clothing and household goods. The two men set out. The morning was perfectly clear and so warm that the day promised to be uncomfortable. A few minutes after they started, the air-raid siren went off—a minute-long blast that warned of approaching planes but indicated to the people of Hiroshima only a slight degree of danger, since it sounded every morning at this time, when an American weather plane came over. The two men pulled and pushed the handcart through the city streets. Hiroshima was a fan-shaped city, lying mostly on the six islands formed by the seven estuarial rivers that branch out from the Ota River; its main commercial and residential districts, covering about four square miles in the center of the city, contained three-quarters of its population, which had been reduced by several evacuation programs from a wartime peak of 380,000 to about 245,000. Factories and other residential districts, or suburbs, lay compactly around the edges of the city. To the south were the docks, an airport, and the island-studded Inland Sea. A rim of mountains runs around the other three sides of the delta. Mr. Tanimoto and Mr. Matsuo took their way through the shopping center, already full of people, and across two of the rivers to the sloping streets of Koi, and up them to the outskirts and foothills. As they started up a valley away from the tight-ranked houses, the all-clear sounded. (The Japanese radar operators, detecting only three planes, supposed that they comprised a reconnaissance.) Pushing the handcart up to the rayon man's house was tiring, and the men, after they had maneuvered their load into the driveway and to the front steps, paused to rest awhile. They stood with a wing of the house between them and the city. Like most homes in this part of Japan, the house consisted of a wooden frame and wooden walls supporting a heavy tile roof. Its front hall, packed with rolls of bedding and clothing, looked like a cool cave full of fat cushions. Opposite the house, to the right of the front door, there was a large, finicky rock garden. There was no sound of planes. The morning was still; the place was cool and pleasant.

Then a tremendous flash of light cut across the sky. Mr. Tanimoto has a distinct recollection that it travelled from east to west, from the city toward the hills. It seemed a sheet of sun. Both he and Mr. Matsuo reacted in terror—and both had time to react (for they were 3,500 yards, or two miles, from the center of the explosion). Mr. Matsuo dashed up the front steps into the house and dived among the bedrolls and buried himself there. Mr. Tanimoto took four or five steps and threw himself between two big rocks in the garden. He bellied up very hard against one of them. As his face was against the stone, he did not see what happened. He felt a sudden pressure, and then splinters and pieces of board and fragments of tile fell on him. He heard no roar. (Almost no one in Hiroshima recalls hearing any noise of the bomb. But a fisherman in his sampan on the Inland Sea near Tsuzu, the man with whom Mr. Tanimoto's mother-in-law and sister-in-law were living, saw the flash and heard a tremendous explosion; he was nearly twenty miles from Hiroshima, but the thunder was greater than when the B-29s hit Iwakuni, only five miles away.)

When he dared, Mr. Tanimoto raised his head and saw that the rayon man's house had collapsed. He thought a bomb had fallen directly on it. Such clouds of dust had risen that there was a sort of twilight around. In panic, not thinking for the moment of Mr. Matsuo under the ruins, he dashed out into the street. He noticed as he ran that the concrete wall of the estate had fallen over—toward the house rather than away from it. In the street, the first thing he saw was a squad of soldiers who had been burrowing into the hillside opposite, making one of the thousands of dugouts in which the Japanese apparently intended to resist invasion, hill by hill, life for life; the soldiers were coming out of the hole, where they should have been safe, and blood was running from their heads, chests, and backs. They were silent and dazed.

Under what seemed to be a local dust cloud, the day grew darker and darker.

· · ·

At nearly midnight, the night before the bomb was dropped, an announcer on the city's radio station said that about two hundred B-29s were approaching southern Honshu and advised the population of Hiroshima to evacuate to their designated "safe areas." Mrs. Hatsuyo Nakamura, the tailor's widow, who lived in the section called Nobori-cho and who had long had a habit of doing as she was told, got her three children—a ten-year-old boy, Toshio, an eight-year-old girl, Yaeko, and a five-year-old girl, Myeko—out of bed and dressed them and walked with them to the military area known as the East Parade Ground, on the northeast edge of the city. There she unrolled some mats and the children lay down on them. They slept until about two, when they were awakened by the roar of the planes going over Hiroshima.

As soon as the planes had passed, Mrs. Nakamura started back with her children. They reached home a little after two-thirty and she immediately turned on the radio, which, to her distress, was just then broadcasting a fresh warning. When she looked at the children and saw how tired they were, and when she thought of the number of trips they had made in past weeks, all to no purpose, to the East Parade Ground, she decided that in spite of the instructions on the radio, she simply could not face starting out all over again. She put the children in their bedrolls on the floor, lay down herself at three o'clock, and fell asleep at once, so soundly that when planes passed over later, she did not waken to their sound.

The siren jarred her awake at about seven. She arose, dressed quickly, and hurried to the house of Mr. Nakamoto, the head of her Neighborhood Association, and asked him what she should do. He said that she should remain at home unless an urgent warning—a series of intermittent blasts of the siren—was sounded. She returned home, lit the stove in the kitchen, set some rice to cook, and sat down to read that morning's Hiroshima *Chugoku*. To her relief, the all-clear sounded at eight o'clock. She heard the children stirring, so she went and gave each of them a handful of peanuts and told them to stay on their bedrolls, because they were tired from the night's walk. She had hoped that they would go back to sleep, but the man in the house directly to the south began to make a terrible hullabaloo of hammering, wedging, ripping, and splitting. The prefectural government, convinced, as everyone in Hiroshima was, that the city would be attacked soon, had begun to press with threats and warnings for the completion of wide fire lanes, which, it was hoped, might act in conjunction with the rivers to localize any fires started by an incendiary raid; and the neighbor was reluctantly sacrificing his home to the city's safety. Just the day before, the prefecture had ordered all able-bodied girls from the secondary schools to spend a few days helping to clear these lanes, and they started work soon after the all-clear sounded.

Mrs. Nakamura went back to the kitchen, looked at the rice, and began watching the man next door. At first, she was annoyed with him for making so much noise, but then she was moved almost to tears by pity. Her emotion was specifically directed toward her neighbor, tearing down his home, board by board, at a time when there was so much unavoidable destruction, but undoubtedly she also felt a generalized, community pity, to say nothing of self-pity. She had not had an easy time. Her husband, Isawa, had gone into the Army just after Myeko was born, and she had heard nothing from or of him for a long time, until, on March 5, 1942, she received a seven-word telegram: "Isawa died an honorable death at Singapore." She learned later that he had died on February 15th, the day Singapore fell, and that he had been a corporal. Isawa had been a not particularly prosperous tailor, and his only capital was a Sankoku sewing machine. After his death, when his allotments stopped coming, Mrs. Nakamura got out the machine and began to take in piecework herself, and since then had supported the children, but poorly, by sewing.

As Mrs. Nakamura stood watching her neighbor, everything flashed whiter than any white she had ever seen. She did not notice what happened to the man next door; the reflex of a mother set her in motion toward her children. She had taken a single step (the house was 1,350 yards, or three-quarters of a mile, from the center of the explosion) when something picked her up and she seemed to fly into the next room over the raised sleeping platform, pursued by parts of her house.

Timbers fell around her as she landed, and a shower of tiles pommelled her; everything became dark, for she was buried. The debris did not cover her deeply. She rose up and freed herself. She heard a child cry, "Mother, help me!," and saw her youngest—Myeko, the five-year-old—buried up to her breast and unable to move. As Mrs. Nakamura started frantically to claw her way toward the baby, she could see or hear nothing of her other children.

· · ·

In the days right before the bombing, Dr. Masakazu Fujii, being prosperous, hedonistic, and, at the time, not too busy, had been allowing himself the luxury of sleeping until nine or nine-thirty, but fortunately he had to get up early the morning the bomb was dropped to see a house guest off on a train. He rose at six, and half an hour later walked with his friend to the station, not far away, across two of the rivers. He was back home by seven, just as the siren sounded its sustained warning. He ate breakfast and then, because the morning was already hot, undressed down to his underwear and went out on the porch to read the paper. This porch—in fact, the whole building—was curiously constructed. Dr. Fujii was the proprietor of a peculiarly Japanese institution, a private, single-doctor hospital. This building, perched beside and over the water of the Kyo River, and next to the bridge of the same name, contained thirty rooms for thirty patients and their kinfolk—for, according to Japanese custom, when a person falls sick and goes to a hospital, one or more members of his family go and live there with him, to cook for him, bathe, massage, and read to him, and to offer incessant familial sympathy, without which a Japanese patient would be miserable indeed. Dr. Fujii had no beds—only straw mats—for his patients. He did, however, have all sorts of modern equipment: an X-ray machine, diathermy apparatus, and a fine tiled laboratory. The structure rested two-thirds on the land, one-third on piles over the tidal waters of the Kyo. This overhang, the part of the building where Dr. Fujii lived, was queer-looking, but it was cool in summer and from the porch, which faced away from the center of the city, the prospect of the river, with pleasure boats drifting up and down it, was always refreshing. Dr. Fujii had occasionally had anxious moments when the Ota and its mouth branches rose to flood, but the piling was apparently firm enough and the house had always held.

Dr. Fujii had been relatively idle for about a month because in July, as the number of untouched cities in Japan dwindled and as Hiroshima seemed more and more inevitably a target, he began turning patients away, on the ground that in case of a fire raid he would not be able to evacuate them. Now he had only two patients left—a woman from Yano, injured in the shoulder, and a young man of twenty-five recovering from burns he had suffered when the steel factory near Hiroshima in which he worked had been hit. Dr. Fujii had six nurses to tend his patients. His wife and children were safe; his wife and one son were living outside Osaka, and another son and two daughters were in the country on Kyushu. A niece was living with him, and a maid and a manservant. He had little to do and did not mind, for he had saved some money. At fifty, he was healthy, convivial, and calm, and he was pleased to pass the evenings drinking whiskey with friends, always sensibly and for the sake of conversation. Before the war, he had affected brands imported from Scotland and America; now he was perfectly satisfied with the best Japanese brand, Suntory.

Dr. Fujii sat down cross-legged in his underwear on the spotless matting of the porch, put on his glasses, and started reading the Osaka *Asahi*. He liked to read the Osaka news because his wife was there. He saw the flash. To him—faced away from the center and looking at his paper—it seemed a brilliant yellow. Startled, he began to rise to his feet. In that moment (he was 1,550 yards from the center), the hospital leaned behind his rising and, with a terrible ripping noise, toppled into the river. The Doctor, still in the act of getting to his feet, was thrown forward and around and over; he was buffeted and gripped; he lost track of everything, because things were so speeded up; he felt the water.

Dr. Fujii hardly had time to think that he was dying before he realized that he was alive, squeezed tightly by two long timbers in a V across his chest, like a morsel suspended between two huge chopsticks—held upright, so that he could not move, with his head miraculously above water and his torso and legs in it. The remains of his hospital were all around him in a mad assortment of splintered lumber and materials for the relief of pain. His left shoulder hurt terribly. His glasses were gone.

· · ·

Father Wilhelm Kleinsorge, of the Society of Jesus, was, on the morning of the explosion, in rather frail condition. The Japanese wartime diet had not sustained him, and he felt the strain of being a foreigner in an increasingly xenophobic Japan; even a German, since the defeat of the Fatherland, was unpopular. Father Kleinsorge had, at thirty-eight, the look of a boy growing too fast—thin in the face, with a prominent Adam's apple, a hollow chest, dangling hands, big feet. He walked clumsily, leaning forward a little. He was tired all the time. To make matters worse, he had suffered for two days, along with Father Cieslik, a fellow-priest, from a rather painful and urgent diarrhea, which they blamed on the beans and black ration bread they were obliged to eat. Two other priests then living in the mission compound, which was in the Nobori-cho section—Father Superior LaSalle and Father Schiffer—had happily escaped this affliction.

Father Kleinsorge woke up about six the morning the bomb was dropped, and half an hour later—he was a bit tardy because of his sickness—he began to read Mass in the mission chapel, a small Japanese-style wooden building which was without pews, since its worshippers knelt on the usual Japanese matted floor, facing an altar graced with splendid silks, brass, silver, and heavy embroideries. This morning, a Monday, the only worshippers were Mr. Takemoto, a theological student living in the mission house; Mr. Fukai, the secretary of the diocese; Mrs. Murata, the mission's devoutly Christian housekeeper; and his fellow-priests. After Mass, while Father Kleinsorge was reading the Prayers of Thanksgiving, the siren sounded. He stopped the service and the missionaries retired across the compound to the bigger building. There, in his room on the ground floor, to the right of the front door, Father Kleinsorge changed into a military uniform which he had acquired when he was teaching at the Rokko Middle School in Kobe and which he wore during air-raid alerts.

After an alarm, Father Kleinsorge always went out and scanned the sky, and this time, when he stepped outside, he was glad to see only the single weather plane that flew over Hiroshima each day about this time. Satisfied that nothing would happen, he went in and breakfasted with the other Fathers on substitute coffee and ration bread, which, under the circumstances, was especially repugnant to him. The Fathers sat and talked a while, until, at eight, they heard the all-clear. They went then to various parts of the building. Father Schiffer retired to his room to do some writing. Father Cieslik sat in his room in a straight chair with a pillow over his stomach to ease his pain, and read. Father Superior La-Salle stood at the window of his room, thinking. Father Kleinsorge went up to a room on the third floor, took off all his clothes except his underwear, and stretched out on his right side on a cot and began reading his *Stimmen der Zeit*.

After the terrible flash—which, Father Kleinsorge later realized, reminded him of something he had read as a boy about a large meteor colliding with the earth—he had time (since he was 1,400 yards from the center) for one thought: A bomb has fallen directly on us. Then, for a few seconds or minutes, he went out of his mind.

Father Kleinsorge never knew how he got out of the house. The next things he was conscious of were that he was wandering around in the mission's vegetable garden in his underwear, bleeding slightly from small cuts along his left flank; that all the buildings round about had fallen down except the Jesuits' mission house, which had long before been braced and double-braced by a priest named Gropper, who was terrified of earthquakes; that the day had turned dark; and that Murata-*san*, the housekeeper, was nearby, crying over and over, "*Shu Jesusu, awaremi tamai!* Our Lord Jesus, have pity on us!"

· · ·

On the train on the way into Hiroshima from the country, where he lived with his mother, Dr. Terufumi Sasaki, the Red Cross Hospital surgeon, thought over an unpleasant nightmare he had had the night before. His mother's home was in Mukaihara, thirty miles from the city, and it took him two hours by train and tram to reach the hospital. He had slept uneasily all night and had wakened an hour earlier than usual, and, feeling sluggish and slightly feverish, had debated whether to go to the hospital at all; his sense of duty finally forced him to go, and he had started out on an earlier train than he took most mornings. The dream had particularly frightened him because it was so closely associated, on the surface at least, with a disturbing actuality. He was only twenty-five years old and had just completed his training at the Eastern Medical University, in Tsingtao, China. He was something of an idealist and was much distressed by the inadequacy of medical facilities in the country town where his mother lived. Quite on his own, and without a permit, he had begun visiting a few sick people out there in the evenings, after his eight hours at the hospital and four hours' commuting. He had recently learned that the penalty for practicing without a permit was severe; a fellow-doctor whom he had asked about it had given him a serious scolding. Nevertheless, he had continued to practice. In his dream, he had been at the bedside of a country patient when the police and the doctor he had consulted burst into the room, seized him, dragged him outside, and beat him up cruelly. On the train, he just about decided to give up the work in Mukaihara, since he felt it would be impossible to get a permit, because the authorities would hold that it would conflict with his duties at the Red Cross Hospital.

At the terminus, he caught a streetcar at once. (He later calculated that if he had taken his customary train that morning, and if he had had to wait a few minutes for the streetcar, as often happened, he would have been close to the center at the time of the explosion and would surely have perished.) He arrived at the hospital at seven-forty and reported to the chief surgeon. A few minutes later, he went to a room on the first floor and drew blood from the arm of a man in order to perform a Wassermann test. The laboratory containing the incubators for the test was on the third floor. With the blood specimen in his left hand, walking in a kind of distraction he had felt all morning, probably because of the dream and his restless night, he started along the main corridor on his way toward the stairs. He was one step beyond an open window when the light of the bomb was reflected, like a gigantic photographic flash, in the corridor. He ducked down on one knee and said to himself, as only a Japanese would, "Sasaki, *gambare!* Be brave!" Just then (the building was 1,650 yards from the center), the blast ripped through the hospital. The glasses he was wearing flew off his face; the bottle of blood crashed against one wall; his Japanese slippers zipped out from under his feet— but otherwise, thanks to where he stood, he was untouched.

Dr. Sasaki shouted the name of the chief surgeon and rushed around to the man's office and found him terribly cut by glass. The hospital was in horrible confusion: heavy partitions and ceilings had fallen on patients, beds had overturned, windows had blown in and cut people, blood was spattered on the walls and floors, instruments were everywhere, many of the patients were running about screaming, many more lay dead. (A colleague working in the laboratory to which Dr. Sasaki had been walking was dead; Dr. Sasaki's patient, whom he had just left and who a few moments before had been dreadfully afraid of syphilis, was also dead.) Dr. Sasaki found himself the only doctor in the hospital who was unhurt.

Dr. Sasaki, who believed that the enemy had hit only the building he was in, got bandages and began to bind the wounds of those inside the hospital; while outside, all over Hiroshima, maimed and dying citizens turned their unsteady steps toward the Red Cross Hospital to begin an invasion that was to make Dr. Sasaki forget his private nightmare for a long, long time.

. . .

Miss Toshiko Sasaki, the East Asia Tin Works clerk, who is not related to Dr. Sasaki, got up at three o'clock in the morning on the day the bomb fell. There was extra housework to do. Her eleven-month-old brother, Akio, had come down the day before with a serious stomach upset; her mother had taken him to the Tamura Pediatric Hospital and was staying there with him. Miss Sasaki, who was about twenty, had to cook breakfast for her father, a brother, a sister, and herself, and—since the hospital, because of the war, was unable to provide food—to prepare a whole day's meals for her mother and the baby, in time for her father, who worked in a factory making rubber earplugs for artillery crews, to take the food by on his way to the plant. When she had finished and had cleaned and put away the cooking things, it was nearly seven. The family lived in Koi, and she had a forty-five-minute trip to the tin works, in the section of town called Kannon-machi. She was in charge of the personnel records in the factory. She left Koi at seven, and as soon as she reached the plant, she went with some of the other girls from the personnel department to the factory auditorium. A prominent local Navy man, a former employee, had committed suicide the day before by throwing himself under a train—a death considered honorable enough to warrant a memorial service, which was to be held at the tin works at ten o'clock that morning. In the large hall, Miss Sasaki and the others made suitable preparations for the meeting. This work took about twenty minutes.

Miss Sasaki went back to her office and sat down at her desk. She was quite far from the windows, which were off to her left, and behind her were a couple of tall bookcases containing all the books of the factory library, which the personnel department had organized. She settled herself at her desk, put some things in a drawer, and shifted papers. She thought that before she began to make entries in her lists of new employees, discharges, and departures for the Army, she would chat for a moment with the girl at her right. Just as she turned her head away from the windows, the room was filled with a blinding light. She was paralyzed by fear, fixed still in her chair for a long moment (the plant was 1,600 yards from the center).

Everything fell, and Miss Sasaki lost consciousness. The ceiling dropped suddenly and the wooden floor above collapsed in splinters and the people up there came down and the roof above them gave way; but principally and first of all, the bookcases right behind her swooped forward and the contents threw her down, with her left leg horribly twisted and breaking underneath her. There, in the tin factory, in the first moment of the atomic age, a human being was crushed by books.

II—THE FIRE

IMMEDIATELY AFTER THE EXPLOSION, the Reverend Mr. Kiyoshi Tanimoto, having run wildly out of the Matsui estate and having looked in wonderment at the bloody soldiers at the mouth of the dugout they had been digging, attached himself sympathetically to an old lady who was walking along in a daze, holding her head with her left hand, supporting a small boy of three or four on her back with her right, and crying, "I'm hurt! I'm hurt! I'm hurt!" Mr. Tanimoto transferred the child to his own back and led the woman by the hand down the street, which was darkened by what seemed to be a local column of dust. He took the woman to a grammar school not far away that had previously been designated for use as a temporary hospital in case of emergency. By this solicitous behavior, Mr. Tanimoto at once got rid of his terror. At the school, he was much surprised to see glass all over the floor and fifty or sixty injured people already waiting to be treated. He reflected that, although the all-clear had sounded and he had heard no planes, several bombs must have been dropped. He thought of a hillock in the rayon man's garden from which he could get a view of the whole of Koi—of the whole of Hiroshima, for that matter—and he ran back up to the estate.

From the mound, Mr. Tanimoto saw an astonishing panorama. Not just a patch of Koi, as he had expected, but as much of Hiroshima as he could see through the clouded air was giving off a thick, dreadful miasma. Clumps of smoke, near and far, had begun to push up through the general dust. He wondered how such extensive damage could have been dealt out of a silent sky; even a few planes, far up, would have been audible. Houses nearby were burning, and when huge drops of water the size of marbles began to fall, he half thought that they must be coming from the hoses of firemen fighting the blazes. (They were actually drops of condensed moisture falling from the turbulent tower of dust, heat, and fission fragments that had already risen miles into the sky above Hiroshima.)

Mr. Tanimoto turned away from the sight when he heard Mr. Matsuo call out to ask whether he was all right. Mr. Matsuo had been safely cushioned within the falling house by the bedding stored in the front hall and had worked his way out. Mr. Tanimoto scarcely answered. He had thought of his wife and baby, his church, his home, his parishioners, all of them down in that awful murk. Once more he began to run in fear—toward the city.

. . .

Mrs. Hatsuyo Nakamura, the tailor's widow, having struggled up from under the ruins of her house after the explosion, and seeing Myeko, the youngest of her three children, buried breast-deep and unable to move, crawled across the debris, hauled at timbers, and flung tiles aside, in a hurried effort to free the child. Then, from what seemed to be caverns far below, she heard two small voices crying, "*Tasukete! Tasukete!* Help! Help!"

She called the names of her ten-year-old son and eight-year-old daughter: "Toshio! Yaeko!"

The voices from below answered.

Mrs. Nakamura abandoned Myeko, who at least could breathe, and in a frenzy made the wreckage fly above the crying voices. The children had been sleeping nearly ten feet apart, but now their voices seemed to come from the same place. Toshio, the boy, apparently had some freedom to move, because she could feel him undermining the pile of wood and tiles as she worked from above. At least she saw his head, and she hastily pulled him out by it. A mosquito net was wound intricately, as if it had been carefully wrapped, around his feet. He said he had been blown right across the room and had been on top of his sister Yaeko under the wreckage. She now said, from underneath, that she could not move, because there was something on her legs. With a bit more digging, Mrs. Nakamura cleared a hole above the child and began to pull her arm. "*Itai!* It hurts!" Yaeko cried. Mrs. Nakamura shouted, "There's no time now to say whether it hurts or not," and yanked her whimpering daughter up. Then she freed Myeko. The children were filthy and bruised, but none of them had a single cut or scratch.

Mrs. Nakamura took the children out into the street. They had nothing on but underpants, and although the day was very hot, she worried rather confusedly about their being cold, so she went back into the wreckage and burrowed underneath and found a bundle of clothes she had packed for an emergency, and she dressed them in pants, blouses, shoes, padded-cotton air-raid helmets called *bokuzuki,* and even, irrationally, overcoats. The children were silent, except for the five-year-old, Myeko, who kept asking questions: "Why is it night already? Why did our house fall down? What happened?" Mrs. Nakamura, who did not know what had happened (had not the all-clear sounded?), looked around and saw through the darkness that all the houses in her neighborhood had collapsed. The house next door, which its owner had been tearing down to make way for a fire lane, was now very thoroughly, if crudely, torn down; its owner, who had been sacrificing his home for the community's safety, lay dead. Mrs. Nakamoto, wife of the head of the local air-raid-defense Neighborhood Association, came across the street with her head all bloody, and said that her baby was badly cut; did Mrs. Nakamura have any bandage? Mrs. Nakamura did not, but she crawled into the remains of her house again and pulled out some white cloth that she had been using in her work as a seamstress, ripped it into strips, and gave it to Mrs. Nakamoto. While fetching the cloth, she noticed her sewing machine; she went back in for it and dragged it out. Obviously, she could not carry it with her, so she unthinkingly plunged her symbol of livelihood into the receptacle which for weeks had been her symbol of safety—the cement tank of water in front of her house, of the type every household had been ordered to construct against a possible fire raid.

A nervous neighbor, Mrs. Hataya, called to Mrs. Nakamura to run away with her to the woods in Asano Park—an estate, by the Kyo River not far off, belonging to the wealthy Asano family, who once owned the Toyo Kisen Kaisha steamship line. The park had been designated as an evacuation area for their neighborhood. Seeing fire breaking out in a nearby ruin (except at the very center, where the bomb itself ignited some fires, most of Hiroshima's citywide conflagration was caused by inflammable wreckage falling on cook-stoves and live wires), Mrs. Nakamura suggested going over to fight it. Mrs. Hataya said, "Don't be foolish. What if planes come and drop more bombs?" So Mrs. Nakamura started out for Asano Park with her children and Mrs. Hataya, and she carried her rucksack of emergency clothing, a blanket, an umbrella, and a suitcase of things she had cached in her air-raid shelter. Under many ruins, as they hurried along, they heard muffled screams for help. The only building they saw standing on their way to Asano Park was the Jesuit mission house, alongside the Catholic kindergarten to which Mrs. Nakamura had sent Myeko for a time. As they passed it, she saw Father Kleinsorge, in bloody underwear, running out of the house with a small suitcase in his hand.

· · ·

Right after the explosion, while Father Wilhelm Kleinsorge, S.J., was wandering around in his underwear in the vegetable garden, Father Superior LaSalle came around the corner of the building in the darkness. His body, especially his back, was bloody; the flash had made him twist away from his window, and tiny pieces of glass had flown at him. Father Kleinsorge, still bewildered, managed to ask, "Where are the rest?" Just then, the two other priests living in the mission house appeared—Father Cieslik, unhurt, supporting Father Schiffer, who was covered with blood that spurted from a cut above his left ear and who was very pale. Father Cieslik was rather pleased with himself, for after the flash he had dived into a doorway, which he had previously reckoned to be the safest place inside the building, and when the blast came, he was not injured. Father LaSalle told Father Cieslik to take Father Schiffer to a doctor before he bled to death, and suggested either Dr. Kanda, who lived on the next corner, or Dr. Fujii, about six blocks away. The two men went out of the compound and up the street.

The daughter of Mr. Hoshijima, the mission catechist, ran up to Father Kleinsorge and said that her mother and sister were buried under the ruins of their house, which was at the back of the Jesuit compound, and at the same time the priests noticed that the house of the Catholic-kindergarten teacher at the foot of the compound had collapsed on her. While Father LaSalle and Mrs. Murata, the mission housekeeper, dug the teacher out, Father Kleinsorge went to the catechist's fallen house and began lifting things off the top of the pile. There was not a sound underneath; he was sure the Hoshijima women had been killed. At last, under what had been a corner of the kitchen, he saw Mrs. Hoshijima's head. Believing her dead, he began to haul her out by the hair, but suddenly she screamed, "*Itai! Itai!* It hurts! It hurts!" He dug some more and lifted her out. He managed, too, to find her daughter in the rubble and free her. Neither was badly hurt.

A public bath next door to the mission house had caught fire, but since there the wind was southerly, the priests thought their house would be spared. Nevertheless, as a precaution, Father Kleinsorge went inside to fetch some things he wanted to save. He found his room in a state of weird and illogical confusion. A first-aid kit was hanging undisturbed on a hook on the wall, but his clothes, which had been on other hooks nearby, were nowhere to be seen. His desk was in splinters all over the room, but a mere papier-mâché suitcase, which he had hidden under the desk, stood handle-side up, without a scratch on it, in the doorway of the room, where he could not miss it. Father Kleinsorge later came to regard this as a bit of Providential interference, inasmuch as the suitcase contained his breviary, the account books for the whole diocese, and a considerable amount of paper money belonging to the mission, for which he was responsible. He ran out of the house and deposited the suitcase in the mission air-raid shelter.

At about this time, Father Cieslik and Father Schiffer, who was still spurting blood, came back and said that Dr. Kanda's house was ruined and that fire blocked them from getting out of what they supposed to be the local circle of destruction to Dr. Fujii's private hospital, on the bank of the Kyo River.

. . .

Dr. Masakazu Fujii's hospital was no longer on the bank of the Kyo River; it was in the river. After the overturn, Dr. Fujii was so stupefied and so tightly squeezed by the beams gripping his chest that he was unable to move at first, and he hung there about twenty minutes in the darkened morning. Then a thought which came to him—that soon the tide would be running in through the estuaries and his head would be submerged—inspired him to fearful activity; he wriggled and turned and exerted what strength he could (though his left arm, because of the pain in his shoulder, was useless), and before long he had freed himself from the vise. After a few moments' rest, he climbed onto the pile of timbers and, finding a long one that slanted up to the riverbank, he painfully shinnied up it.

Dr. Fujii, who was in his underwear, was now soaking and dirty. His undershirt was torn, and blood ran down it from bad cuts on his chin and back. In this disarray, he walked out onto Kyo Bridge, beside which his hospital had stood. The bridge had not collapsed. He could see only fuzzily without his glasses, but he could see enough to be amazed at the number of houses that were down all around. On the bridge, he encountered a friend, a doctor named Machii, and asked in bewilderment, "What do you think it was?"

Dr. Machii said, "It must have been a *Molotoffano hanakago*"—a Molotov flower basket, the delicate Japanese name for the "bread basket," or self-scattering cluster of bombs.

At first, Dr. Fujii could see only two fires, one across the river from his hospital site and one quite far to the south. But at the same time, he and his friend observed something that puzzled them, and which, as doctors, they discussed: although there were as yet very few fires, wounded people were hurrying across the bridge in an endless parade of misery, and many of them exhibited terrible burns on their faces and arms. "Why do you suppose it is?" Dr. Fujii asked. Even a theory was comforting that day, and Dr. Machii stuck to his. "Perhaps because it was a Molotov flower basket," he said.

There had been no breeze earlier in the morning when Dr. Fujii had walked to the railway station to see a friend off, but now brisk winds were blowing every which way; here on the bridge the wind was easterly. New fires were leaping up, and they spread quickly, and in a very short time terrible blasts of hot air and showers of cinders made it impossible to stand on the bridge any more. Dr. Machii ran to the far side of the river and along a still unkindled street. Dr. Fujii went down into the water under the bridge, where a score of people had already taken refuge, among them his servants, who had extricated themselves from the wreckage. From there, Dr. Fujii saw a nurse hanging in the timbers of his hospital by her legs, and then another painfully pinned across the breast. He enlisted the help of some of the others under the bridge and freed both of them. He thought he heard the voice of his niece for a moment, but he could not find her; he never saw her again. Four of his nurses and the two patients in the hospital died, too. Dr. Fujii went back into the water of the river and waited for the fire to subside.

· · ·

The lot of Drs. Fujii, Kanda, and Machii right after the explosion—and, as these three were typical, that of the majority of the physicians and surgeons of Hiroshima—with their offices and hospitals destroyed, their equipment scattered, their own bodies incapacitated in varying degrees, explained why so many citizens who were hurt went untended and why so many who might have lived died. Of a hundred and fifty doctors in the city, sixty-five were already dead and most of the rest were wounded. Of 1,780 nurses, 1,654 were dead or too badly hurt to work. In the biggest hospital, that of the Red Cross, only six doctors out of thirty were able to function, and only ten nurses out of more than two hundred. The sole uninjured doctor on the Red Cross Hospital staff was Dr. Sasaki. After the explosion, he hurried to a storeroom to fetch bandages. This room, like everything he had seen as he ran through the hospital, was chaotic— bottles of medicines thrown off shelves and broken, salves spattered on the walls, instruments strewn everywhere. He grabbed up some bandages and an unbroken bottle of mercurochrome, hurried back to the chief surgeon, and bandaged his cuts. Then he went out into the corridor and began patching up the wounded patients and the doctors and nurses there. He blundered so without his glasses that he took a pair off the face of a wounded nurse, and although they only approximately compensated for the errors of his vision, they were better than nothing. (He was to depend on them for more than a month.)

Dr. Sasaki worked without method, taking those who were nearest him first, and he noticed soon that the corridor seemed to be getting more and more crowded. Mixed in with the abrasions and lacerations which most people in the hospital had suffered, he began to find dreadful burns. He realized then that casualties were pouring in from outdoors. There were so many that he began to pass up the lightly wounded; he decided that all he could hope to do was to stop people from bleeding to death. Before long, patients lay and crouched on the floors of the wards and the laboratories and all the other rooms, and in the corridors, and on the stairs, and in the front hall, and under the porte-cochère, and on the stone front steps, and in the driveway and courtyard, and for blocks each way in the streets outside. Wounded people supported maimed people; disfigured families leaned together. Many people were vomiting. A tremendous number of schoolgirls—some of those who had been taken from their classrooms to work outdoors, clearing fire lanes— crept into the hospital. In a city of two hundred and forty-five thousand, nearly a hundred thousand people had been killed or doomed at one blow; a hundred thousand more were hurt. At least ten thousand of the wounded made their way to the best hospital in town, which was altogether unequal to such a trampling, since it had only six hundred beds, and they had all been occupied. The people in the suffocating crowd inside the hospital wept and cried, for Dr. Sasaki to hear, "*Sensei!* Doctor!," and the less seriously wounded came and pulled at his sleeve and begged him to come to the aid of the worse wounded. Tugged here and there in his stockinged feet, bewildered by the numbers, staggered by so much raw flesh, Dr. Sasaki lost all sense of profession and stopped working as a skillful surgeon and a sympathetic man; he became an automaton, mechanically wiping, daubing, winding, wiping, daubing, winding.

. . .

Some of the wounded in Hiroshima were unable to enjoy the questionable luxury of hospitalization. In what had been the personnel office of the East Asia Tin Works, Miss Sasaki lay doubled over, unconscious, under the tremendous pile of books and plaster and wood and corrugated iron. She was wholly unconscious (she later estimated) for about three hours. Her first sensation was of dreadful pain in her left leg. It was so black under the books and debris that the borderline between awareness and unconsciousness was fine; she apparently crossed it several times, for the pain seemed to come and go. At the moments when it was sharpest, she felt that her leg had been cut off somewhere below the knee. Later, she heard someone walking on top of the wreckage above her, and anguished voices spoke up, evidently from within the mess around her: "Please help! Get us out!"

. . .

Father Kleinsorge stemmed Father Schiffer's spurting cut as well as he could with some bandage that Dr. Fujii had given the priests a few days before. When he finished, he ran into the mission house again and found the jacket of his military uniform and an old pair of gray trousers. He put them on and went outside. A woman from next door ran up to him and shouted that her husband was buried under her house and the house was on fire; Father Kleinsorge must come and save him.

Father Kleinsorge, already growing apathetic and dazed in the presence of the cumulative distress, said, "We haven't much time." Houses all around were burning, and the wind was now blowing hard. "Do you know exactly which part of the house he is under?" he asked.

"Yes, yes," she said. "Come quickly."

They went around to the house, the remains of which blazed violently, but when they got there, it turned out that the woman had no idea where her husband was. Father Kleinsorge shouted several times, "Is anyone there?" There was no answer. Father Kleinsorge said to the woman, "We must get away or we will all die." He went back to the Catholic compound and told the Father Superior that the fire was coming closer on the wind, which had swung around and was now from the north; it was time for everybody to go.

Just then, the kindergarten teacher pointed out to the priests Mr. Fukai, the secretary of the diocese, who was standing in his window on the second floor of the mission house, facing in the direction of the explosion, weeping. Father Cieslik, because he thought the stairs unusable, ran around to the back of the mission house to look for a ladder. There he heard people crying for help under a nearby fallen roof. He called to passersby running away in the street to help him lift it, but nobody paid any attention, and he had to leave the buried ones to die. Father Kleinsorge ran inside the mission house and scrambled up the stairs, which were awry and piled with plaster and lathing, and called to Mr. Fukai from the doorway of his room.

Mr. Fukai, a very short man of about fifty, turned around slowly, with a queer look, and said, "Leave me here."

Father Kleinsorge went into the room and took Mr. Fukai by the collar of his coat and said, "Come with me or you'll die."

Mr. Fukai said, "Leave me here to die."

Father Kleinsorge began to shove and haul Mr. Fukai out of the room. Then the theological student came up and grabbed Mr. Fukai's feet, and Father Kleinsorge took his shoulders, and together they carried him downstairs and outdoors. "I can't walk!" Mr. Fukai cried. "Leave me here!" Father Kleinsorge got his paper suitcase with the money in it and took Mr. Fukai up pickaback, and the party started for the East Parade Ground, their district's "safe area." As they went out of the gate, Mr. Fukai, quite childlike now, beat on Father Kleinsorge's shoulders and said, "I won't leave. I won't leave." Irrelevantly, Father Kleinsorge turned to Father LaSalle and said, "We have lost all our possessions but not our sense of humor."

The street was cluttered with parts of houses that had slid into it, and with fallen telephone poles and wires. From every second or third house came the voices of people buried and abandoned, who invariably screamed, with formal politeness, *"Tasukete kure!* Help, if you please!" The priests recognized several ruins from which these cries came as the homes of friends, but because of the fire it was too late to help. All the way, Mr. Fukai whimpered, "Let me stay." The party turned right when they came to a block of fallen houses that was one flame. At Sakai Bridge, which would take them across to the East Parade Ground, they saw that the whole community on the opposite side of the river was a sheet of fire; they dared not cross and decided to take refuge in Asano Park, off to their left. Father Kleinsorge, who had been weakened for a couple of days by his bad case of diarrhea, began to stagger under his protesting burden, and as he tried to climb up over the wreckage of several houses that blocked their way to the park, he stumbled, dropped Mr. Fukai, and plunged down, head over heels, to the edge of the river. When he picked himself up, he saw Mr. Fukai running away. Father Kleinsorge shouted to a dozen soldiers, who were standing by the bridge, to stop him. As Father Kleinsorge started back to get Mr. Fukai, Father LaSalle called out, "Hurry! Don't waste time!" So Father Kleinsorge just requested the soldiers to take care of Mr. Fukai. They said they would, but the little, broken man got away from them, and the last the priests could see of him, he was running back toward the fire.

. . .

Mr. Tanimoto, fearful for his family and church, at first ran toward them by the shortest route, along Koi Highway. He was the only person making his way into the city; he met hundreds and hundreds who were fleeing, and every one of them seemed to be hurt in some way. The eyebrows of some were burned off and skin hung from their faces and hands. Others, because of pain, held their arms up as if carrying something in both hands. Some were vomiting as they walked. Many were naked or in shreds of clothing. On some undressed bodies, the burns had made patterns—of undershirt straps and suspenders and, on the skin of some women (since white repelled the heat from the bomb and dark clothes absorbed it and conducted it to the skin), the shapes of flowers they had had on their kimonos. Many, although injured themselves, supported relatives who were worse off. Almost all had their heads bowed, looked straight ahead, were silent, and showed no expression whatever.

After crossing Koi Bridge and Kannon Bridge, having run the whole way, Mr. Tanimoto saw, as he approached the center, that all the houses had been crushed and many were afire. Here the trees were bare and their trunks were charred. He tried at several points to penetrate the ruins, but the flames always stopped him. Under many houses, people screamed for help, but no one helped; in general, survivors that day assisted only their relatives or immediate neighbors, for they could not comprehend or tolerate a wider circle of misery. The wounded limped past the screams, and Mr. Tanimoto ran past them. As a Christian he was filled with compassion for those who were trapped, and as a Japanese he was overwhelmed by the shame of being unhurt, and he prayed as he ran, "God help them and take them out of the fire."

He thought he would skirt the fire, to the left. He ran back to Kannon Bridge and followed for a distance one of the rivers. He tried several cross streets, but all were blocked, so he turned far left and ran out to Yokogawa, a station on a railroad line that detoured the city in a wide semicircle, and he followed the rails until he came to a burning train. So impressed was he by this time by the extent of the damage that he ran north two miles to Gion, a suburb in the foothills. All the way, he overtook dreadfully burned and lacerated people, and in his guilt he turned to right and left as he hurried and said to some of them, "Excuse me for having no burden like yours." Near Gion, he began to meet country people going toward the city to help, and when they saw him, several exclaimed, "Look! There is one who is not wounded." At Gion, he bore toward the right bank of the main river, the Ota, and ran down it until he reached fire again. There was no fire on the other side of the river, so he threw off his shirt and shoes and plunged into it. In midstream, where the current was fairly strong, exhaustion and fear finally caught up with him—he had run nearly seven miles—and he became limp and drifted in the water. He prayed, "Please, God, help me to cross. It would be nonsense for me to be drowned when I am the only uninjured one." He managed a few more strokes and fetched up on a spit downstream.

Mr. Tanimoto climbed up the bank and ran along it until, near a large Shinto shrine, he came to more fire, and as he turned left to get around it, he met, by incredible luck, his wife. She was carrying their infant son. Mr. Tanimoto was now so emotionally worn out that nothing could surprise him. He did not embrace his wife; he simply said, "Oh, you are safe." She told him that she had got home from her night in Ushida just in time for the explosion; she had been buried under the parsonage with the baby in her arms. She told how the wreckage had pressed down on her, how the baby had cried. She saw a chink of light, and by reaching up with a hand, she worked the hole bigger, bit by bit. After about half an hour, she heard the crackling noise of wood burning. At last the opening was big enough for her to push the baby out, and afterward she crawled out herself. She said she was now going out to Ushida again.

Mr. Tanimoto said he wanted to see his church and take care of the people of his Neighborhood Association. They parted as casually—as bewildered—as they had met.

Mr. Tanimoto's way around the fire took him across the East Parade Ground, which, being an evacuation area, was now the scene of a gruesome review: rank on rank of the burned and bleeding. Those who were burned moaned, *"Mizu, mizu!* Water, water!" Mr. Tanimoto found a basin in a nearby street and located a water tap that still worked in the crushed shell of a house, and he began carrying water to the suffering strangers. When he had given drink to about thirty of them, he realized he was taking too much time. "Excuse me," he said loudly to those nearby who were reaching out their hands to him and crying their thirst. "I have many people to take care of." Then he ran away. He went to the river again, the basin in his hand, and jumped down onto a sandspit. There he saw hundreds of people so badly wounded that they could not get up to go farther from the burning city. When they saw a man erect and unhurt, the chant began again: *"Mizu, mizu, mizu."* Mr. Tanimoto could not resist them; he carried them water from the river—a mistake, since it was tidal and brackish. Two or three small boats were ferrying hurt people across the river from Asano Park, and when one touched the spit, Mr. Tanimoto again made his loud, apologetic speech and jumped into the boat. It took him across to the park. There, in the underbrush, he found some of his charges of the Neighborhood Association, who had come there by his previous instructions, and saw many acquaintances, among them Father Kleinsorge and the other Catholics. But he missed Fukai, who had been a close friend. "Where is Fukai-*san*?" he asked.

"He didn't want to come with us," Father Kleinsorge said. "He ran back."

. . .

When Miss Sasaki heard the voices of the people caught along with her in the dilapidation at the tin factory, she began speaking to them. Her nearest neighbor, she discovered, was a high-school girl who had been drafted for factory work, and who said her back was broken. Miss Sasaki replied, "I am lying here and I can't move. My left leg is cut off."

Some time later, she again heard somebody walk overhead and then move off to one side, and whoever it was began burrowing. The digger released several people, and when he had uncovered the high-school girl, she found that her back was not broken, after all, and she crawled out.

Miss Sasaki spoke to the rescuer, and he worked toward her. He pulled away a great number of books, until he had made a tunnel to her. She could see his perspiring face as he said, "Come out, Miss." She tried. "I can't move," she said. The man excavated some more and told her to try with all her strength to get out. But books were heavy on her hips, and the man finally saw that a bookcase was leaning on the books and that a heavy beam pressed down on the bookcase. "Wait," he said. "I'll get a crowbar."

The man was gone a long time, and when he came back, he was ill-tempered, as if her plight were all her fault. "We have no men to help you!" he shouted in through the tunnel. "You'll have to get out by your-self."

"That's impossible," she said. "My left leg . . ." The man went away.

Much later, several men came and dragged Miss Sasaki out. Her left leg was not severed, but it was badly broken and cut and it hung askew below the knee. They took her out into a courtyard. It was raining. She sat on the ground in the rain. When the downpour increased, someone directed all the wounded people to take cover in the factory's air-raid shelters. "Come along," a torn-up woman said to her. "You can hop." But Miss Sasaki could not move, and she just waited in the rain. Then a man propped up a large sheet of corrugated iron as a kind of lean-to, and took her in his arms and carried her to it. She was grateful until he brought two horribly wounded people—a woman with a whole breast sheared off and a man whose face was all raw from a burn—to share the simple shed with her. No one came back. The rain cleared and the cloudy afternoon was hot; before nightfall the three grotesques under the slanting piece of twisted iron began to smell quite bad.

· · ·

The former head of the Nobori-cho Neighborhood Association, to which the Catholic priests belonged, was an energetic man named Yoshida. He had boasted, when he was in charge of the district air-raid defenses, that fire might eat away all of Hiroshima but it would never come to Nobori-cho. The bomb blew down his house, and a joist pinned him by the legs, in full view of the Jesuit mission house across the way and of the people hurrying along the street. In their confusion as they hurried past, Mrs. Nakamura, with her children, and Father Kleinsorge, with Mr. Fukai on his back, hardly saw him; he was just part of the general blur of misery through which they moved. His cries for help brought no response from them; there were so many people shouting for help that they could not hear him separately. They and all the others went along. Nobori-cho became absolutely deserted, and the fire swept through it. Mr. Yoshida saw the wooden mission house—the only erect building in the area—go up in a lick of flame, and the heat was terrific on his face. Then flames came along his side of the street and entered his house. In a paroxysm of terrified strength, he freed himself and ran down the alleys of Nobori-cho, hemmed in by the fire he had said would never come. He began at once to behave like an old man; two months later his hair was white.

. . .

As Dr. Fujii stood in the river up to his neck to avoid the heat of the fire, the wind grew stronger and stronger, and soon, even though the expanse of water was small, the waves grew so high that the people under the bridge could no longer keep their footing. Dr. Fujii went close to the shore, crouched down, and embraced a large stone with his usable arm. Later it became possible to wade along the very edge of the river, and Dr. Fujii and his two surviving nurses moved about two hundred yards upstream, to a sandspit near Asano Park. Many wounded were lying on the sand. Dr. Machii was there with his family; his daughter, who had been outdoors when the bomb burst, was badly burned on her hands and legs but fortunately not on her face. Although Dr. Fujii's shoulder was by now terribly painful, he examined the girl's burns curiously. Then he lay down. In spite of the misery all around, he was ashamed of his appearance, and he remarked to Dr. Machii that he looked like a beggar, dressed as he was in nothing but torn and bloody underwear. Late in the afternoon, when the fire began to subside, he decided to go to his parental house, in the suburb of Nagatsuka. He asked Dr. Machii to join him, but the Doctor answered that he and his family were going to spend the night on the spit, because of his daughter's injuries. Dr. Fujii, together with his nurses, walked first to Ushida, where, in the partially damaged house of some relatives, he found first-aid materials he had stored there. The two nurses bandaged him and he them. They went on. Now not many people walked in the streets, but a great number sat and lay on the pavement, vomited, waited for death, and died. The number of corpses on the way to Nagatsuka was more and more puzzling. The Doctor wondered: Could a Molotov flower basket have done all this?

Dr. Fujii reached his family's house in the evening. It was five miles from the center of town, but its roof had fallen in and the windows were all broken.

. . .

All day, people poured into Asano Park. This private estate was far enough away from the explosion so that its bamboos, pines, laurel, and maples were still alive, and the green place invited refugees—partly because they believed that if the Americans came back, they would bomb only buildings; partly because the foliage seemed a center of coolness and life, and the estate's exquisitely precise rock gardens, with their quiet pools and arching bridges, were very Japanese, normal, secure; and also partly (according to some who were there) because of an irresistible, atavistic urge to hide under leaves. Mrs. Nakamura and her children were among the first to arrive, and they settled in the bamboo grove near the river. They all felt terribly thirsty, and they drank from the river. At once they were nauseated and began vomiting, and they retched the whole day. Others were also nauseated; they all thought (probably because of the strong odor of ionization, an "electric smell" given off by the bomb's fission) that they were sick from a gas the Americans had dropped. When Father Kleinsorge and the other priests came into the park, nodding to their friends as they passed, the Nakamuras were all sick and prostrate. A woman named Iwasaki, who lived in the neighborhood of the mission and who was sitting near the Nakamuras, got up and asked the priests if she should stay where she was or go with them. Father Kleinsorge said, "I hardly know where the safest place is." She stayed there, and later in the day, though she had no visible wounds or burns, she died. The priests went farther along the river and settled down in some underbrush. Father LaSalle lay down and went right to sleep. The theological student, who was wearing slippers, had carried with him a bundle of clothes, in which he had packed two pairs of leather shoes. When he sat down with the others, he found that the bundle had broken open and a couple of shoes had fallen out and now he had only two lefts. He retraced his steps and found one right. When he rejoined the priests, he said, "It's funny, but things don't matter any more. Yesterday, my shoes were my most important possessions. Today, I don't care. One pair is enough."

Father Cieslik said, "I know. I started to bring my books along, and then I thought, 'This is no time for books.'"

When Mr. Tanimoto, with his basin still in his hand, reached the park, it was very crowded, and to distinguish the living from the dead was not easy, for most of the people lay still, with their eyes open. To Father Kleinsorge, an Occidental, the silence in the grove by the river, where hundreds of gruesomely wounded suffered together, was one of the most dreadful and awesome phenomena of his whole experience. The hurt ones were quiet; no one wept, much less screamed in pain; no one complained; none of the many who died did so noisily; not even the children cried; very few people even spoke. And when Father Kleinsorge gave water to some whose faces had been almost blotted out by flash burns, they took their share and then raised themselves a little and bowed to him, in thanks.

Mr. Tanimoto greeted the priests and then looked around for other friends. He saw Mrs. Matsumoto, wife of the director of the Methodist School, and asked her if she was thirsty. She was, so he went to one of the pools in the Asanos' rock gardens and got water for her in his basin. Then he decided to try to get back to his church. He went into Nobori-cho by the way the priests had taken as they escaped, but he did not get far; the fire along the streets was so fierce that he had to turn back. He walked to the riverbank and began to look for a boat in which he might carry some of the most severely injured across the river from Asano Park and away from the spreading fire. Soon he found a good-sized pleasure punt drawn up on the bank, but in and around it was an awful tableau—five dead men, nearly naked, badly burned, who must have expired more or less all at once, for they were in attitudes which suggested that they had been working together to push the boat down into the river. Mr. Tanimoto lifted them away from the boat, and as he did so, he experienced such horror at disturbing the dead—preventing them, he momentarily felt, from launching their craft and going on their ghostly way—that he said out loud, "Please forgive me for taking this boat. I must use it for others, who are alive." The punt was heavy, but he managed to slide it into the water. There were no oars, and all he could find for propulsion was a thick bamboo pole. He worked the boat upstream to the most crowded part of the park and began to ferry the wounded. He could pack ten or twelve into the boat for each crossing, but as the river was too deep in the center to pole his way across, he had to paddle with the bamboo, and consequently each trip took a very long time. He worked several hours that way.

Early in the afternoon, the fire swept into the woods of Asano Park. The first Mr. Tanimoto knew of it was when, returning in his boat, he saw that a great number of people had moved toward the riverside. On touching the bank, he went up to investigate, and when he saw the fire, he shouted, "All the young men who are not badly hurt come with me!" Father Kleinsorge moved Father Schiffer and Father LaSalle close to the edge of the river and asked people there to get them across if the fire came too near, and then joined Tanimoto's volunteers. Mr. Tanimoto sent some to look for buckets and basins and told others to beat the burning underbrush with their clothes; when utensils were at hand, he formed a bucket chain from one of the pools in the rock gardens. The team fought the fire for more than two hours, and gradually defeated the flames. As Mr. Tanimoto's men worked, the frightened people in the park pressed closer and closer to the river, and finally the mob began to force some of the unfortunates who were on the very bank into the water. Among those driven into the river and drowned were Mrs. Matsumoto, of the Methodist School, and her daughter.

When Father Kleinsorge got back after fighting the fire, he found Father Schiffer still bleeding and terribly pale. Some Japanese stood around and stared at him, and Father Schiffer whispered, with a weak smile, "It is as if I were already dead." "Not yet," Father Kleinsorge said. He had brought Dr. Fujii's first-aid kit with him, and he had noticed Dr. Kanda in the crowd, so he sought him out and asked him if he would dress Father Schiffer's bad cuts. Dr. Kanda had seen his wife and daughter dead in the ruins of his hospital; he sat now with his head in his hands. "I can't do anything," he said. Father Kleinsorge bound more bandage around Father Schiffer's head, moved him to a steep place, and settled him so that his head was high, and soon the bleeding diminished.

The roar of approaching planes was heard about this time. Someone in the crowd near the Nakamura family shouted, "It's some Grummans coming to strafe us!" A baker named Nakashima stood up and commanded, "Everyone who is wearing anything white, take it off." Mrs. Nakamura took the blouses off her children, and opened her umbrella and made them get under it. A great number of people, even badly burned ones, crawled into bushes and stayed there until the hum, evidently of a reconnaissance or weather run, died away.

It began to rain. Mrs. Nakamura kept her children under the umbrella. The drops grew abnormally large, and someone shouted, "The Americans are dropping gasoline. They're going to set fire to us!" (This alarm stemmed from one of the theories being passed through the park as to why so much of Hiroshima had burned: it was that a single plane had sprayed gasoline on the city and then somehow set fire to it in one flashing moment.) But the drops were palpably water, and as they fell, the wind grew stronger and stronger, and suddenly—probably because of the tremendous convection set up by the blazing city—a whirlwind ripped through the park. Huge trees crashed down; small ones were uprooted and flew into the air. Higher, a wild array of flat things revolved in the twisting funnel—pieces of iron roofing, papers, doors, strips of matting. Father Kleinsorge put a piece of cloth over Father Schiffer's eyes, so that the feeble man would not think he was going crazy. The gale blew Mrs. Murata, the mission housekeeper, who was sitting close by the river, down the embankment at a shallow, rocky place, and she came out with her bare feet bloody. The vortex moved out onto the river, where it sucked up a waterspout and eventually spent itself.

After the storm, Mr. Tanimoto began ferrying people again, and Father Kleinsorge asked the theological student to go across and make his way out to the Jesuit Novitiate at Nagatsuka, about three miles from the center of town, and to request the priests there to come with help for Fathers Schiffer and LaSalle. The student got into Mr. Tanimoto's boat and went off with him. Father Kleinsorge asked Mrs. Nakamura if she would like to go out to Nagatsuka with the priests when they came. She said she had some luggage and her children were sick—they were still vomiting from time to time, and so, for that matter, was she—and therefore she feared she could not. He said he thought the fathers from the Novitiate could come back the next day with a pushcart to get her.

Late in the afternoon, when he went ashore for a while, Mr. Tanimoto, upon whose energy and initiative many had come to depend, heard people begging for food. He consulted Father Kleinsorge, and they decided to go back into town to get some rice from Mr. Tanimoto's Neighborhood Association shelter and from the mission shelter. Father Cieslik and two or three others went with them. At first, when they got among the rows of prostrate houses, they did not know where they were; the change was too sudden, from a busy city of two hundred and forty-five thousand that morning to a mere pattern of residue in the afternoon. The asphalt of the streets was still so soft and hot from the fires that walking was uncomfortable. They encountered only one person, a woman, who said to them as they passed, "My husband is in those ashes." At the mission, where Mr. Tanimoto left the party, Father Kleinsorge was dismayed to see the building razed. In the garden, on the way to the shelter, he noticed a pumpkin roasted on the vine. He and Father Cieslik tasted it and it was good. They were surprised at their hunger, and they ate quite a bit. They got out several bags of rice and gathered up several other cooked pumpkins and dug up some potatoes that were nicely baked under the ground, and started back. Mr. Tanimoto rejoined them on the way. One of the people with him had some cooking utensils. In the park, Mr. Tanimoto organized the lightly wounded women of his neighborhood to cook. Father Kleinsorge offered the Nakamura family some pumpkin, and they tried it, but they could not keep it on their stomachs. Altogether, the rice was enough to feed nearly a hundred people.

Just before dark, Mr. Tanimoto came across a twenty-year-old girl, Mrs. Kamai, the Tanimotos' next-door neighbor. She was crouching on the ground with the body of her infant daughter in her arms. The baby had evidently been dead all day. Mrs. Kamai jumped up when she saw Mr. Tanimoto and said, "Would you please try to locate my husband?"

Mr. Tanimoto knew that her husband had been inducted into the Army just the day before; he and Mrs. Tanimoto had entertained Mrs. Kamai in the afternoon, to make her forget. Kamai had reported to the Chugoku Regional Army Headquarters—near the ancient castle in the middle of town—where some four thousand troops were stationed. Judging by the many maimed soldiers Mr. Tanimoto had seen during the day, he surmised that the barracks had been badly damaged by whatever it was that had hit Hiroshima. He knew he hadn't a chance of finding Mrs. Kamai's husband, even if he searched, but he wanted to humor her. "I'll try," he said.

"You've got to find him," she said. "He loved our baby so much. I want him to see her once more."

III—DETAILS ARE BEING INVESTIGATED

EARLY IN THE EVENING of the day the bomb exploded, a Japanese naval launch moved slowly up and down the seven rivers of Hiroshima. It stopped here and there to make an announcement—alongside the crowded sandspits, on which hundreds of wounded lay; at the bridges, on which others were crowded; and eventually, as twilight fell, opposite Asano Park. A young officer stood up in the launch and shouted through a megaphone, "Be patient! A naval hospital ship is coming to take care of you!" The sight of the shipshape launch against the background of the havoc across the river; the unruffled young man in his neat uniform; above all, the promise of medical help—the first word of possible succor anyone had heard in nearly twelve awful hours—cheered the people in the park tremendously. Mrs. Nakamura settled her family for the night with the assurance that a doctor would come and stop their retching. Mr. Tanimoto resumed ferrying the wounded across the river. Father Kleinsorge lay down and said the Lord's Prayer and a Hail Mary to himself, and fell right asleep; but no sooner had he dropped off than Mrs. Murata, the conscientious mission housekeeper, shook him and said, "Father Kleinsorge! Did you remember to repeat your evening prayers?" He answered rather grumpily, "Of course," and he tried to go back to sleep but could not. This, apparently, was just what Mrs. Murata wanted. She began to chat with the exhausted priest. One of the questions she raised was when he thought the priests from the Novitiate, for whom he had sent a messenger in midafternoon, would arrive to evacuate Father Superior LaSalle and Father Schiffer.

. . .

The messenger Father Kleinsorge had sent—the theological student who had been living at the mission house—had arrived at the Novitiate, in the hills about three miles out, at half past four. The sixteen priests there had been doing rescue work in the outskirts; they had worried about their colleagues in the city but had not known how or where to look for them. Now they hastily made two litters out of poles and boards, and the student led half a dozen of them back into the devastated area. They worked their way along the Ota above the city; twice the heat of the fire forced them into the river. At Misasa Bridge, they encountered a long line of soldiers making a bizarre forced march away from the Chugoku Regional Army Headquarters in the center of the town. All were grotesquely burned, and they supported themselves with staves or leaned on one another. Sick, burned horses, hanging their heads, stood on the bridge. When the rescue party reached the park, it was after dark, and progress was made extremely difficult by the tangle of fallen trees of all sizes that had been knocked down by the whirlwind that afternoon. At last—not long after Mrs. Murata asked her question—they reached their friends, and gave them wine and strong tea.

The priests discussed how to get Father Schiffer and Father LaSalle out to the Novitiate. They were afraid that blundering through the park with them would jar them too much on the wooden litters, and that the wounded men would lose too much blood. Father Kleinsorge thought of Mr. Tanimoto and his boat, and called out to him on the river. When Mr. Tanimoto reached the bank, he said he would be glad to take the injured priests and their bearers upstream to where they could find a clear roadway. The rescuers put Father Schiffer onto one of the stretchers and lowered it into the boat, and two of them went aboard with it. Mr. Tanimoto, who still had no oars, poled the punt upstream.

About half an hour later, Mr. Tanimoto came back and excitedly asked the remaining priests to help him rescue two children he had seen standing up to their shoulders in the river. A group went out and picked them up—two young girls who had lost their family and were both badly burned. The priests stretched them on the ground next to Father Kleinsorge and then embarked Father LaSalle. Father Cieslik thought he could make it out to the Novitiate on foot, so he went aboard with the others. Father Kleinsorge was too feeble; he decided to wait in the park until the next day. He asked the men to come back with a handcart, so that they could take Mrs. Nakamura and her sick children to the Novitiate.

Mr. Tanimoto shoved off again. As the boatload of priests moved slowly upstream, they heard weak cries for help. A woman's voice stood out especially: "There are people here about to be drowned! Help us! The water is rising!" The sounds came from one of the sandspits, and those in the punt could see, in the reflected light of the still-burning fires, a number of wounded people lying at the edge of the river, already partly covered by the flooding tide. Mr. Tanimoto wanted to help them, but the priests were afraid that Father Schiffer would die if they didn't hurry, and they urged their ferryman along. He dropped them where he had put Father Schiffer down and then started back alone toward the sandspit.

• • •

The night was hot, and it seemed even hotter because of the fires against the sky, but the younger of the two girls Mr. Tanimoto and the priests had rescued complained to Father Kleinsorge that she was cold. He covered her with his jacket. She and her older sister had been in the salt water of the river for a couple of hours before being rescued. The younger one had huge, raw flash burns on her body; the salt water must have been excruciatingly painful to her. She began to shiver heavily, and again said it was cold. Father Kleinsorge borrowed a blanket from someone nearby and wrapped her up, but she shook more and more, and said again, "I am so cold," and then she suddenly stopped shivering and was dead.

• • •

Mr. Tanimoto found about twenty men and women on the sandspit. He drove the boat onto the bank and urged them to get aboard. They did not move and he realized that they were too weak to lift themselves. He reached down and took a woman by the hands, but her skin slipped off in huge, glove-like pieces. He was so sickened by this that he had to sit down for a moment. Then he got out into the water and, though a small man, lifted several of the men and women, who were naked, into his boat. Their backs and breasts were clammy, and he remembered uneasily what the great burns he had seen during the day had been like: yellow at first, then red and swollen, with the skin sloughed off, and finally, in the evening, suppurated and smelly. With the tide risen, his bamboo pole was now too short and he had to paddle most of the way across with it. On the other side, at a higher spit, he lifted the slimy living bodies out and carried them up the slope away from the tide. He had to keep consciously repeating to himself, "These are human beings." It took him three trips to get them all across the river. When he had finished, he decided he had to have a rest, and he went back to the park.

As Mr. Tanimoto stepped up the dark bank, he tripped over someone, and someone else said angrily, "Look out! That's my hand." Mr. Tanimoto, ashamed of hurting wounded people, embarrassed at being able to walk upright, suddenly thought of the naval hospital ship, which had not come (it never did), and he had for a moment a feeling of blind, murderous rage at the crew of the ship, and then at all doctors. Why didn't they come to help these people?

• • •

Dr. Fujii lay in dreadful pain throughout the night on the floor of his family's roofless house on the edge of the city. By the light of a lantern, he had examined himself and found: left clavicle fractured; multiple abrasions and lacerations of face and body, including deep cuts on the chin, back, and legs; extensive contusions on chest and trunk; a couple of ribs possibly fractured. Had he not been so badly hurt, he might have been at Asano Park, assisting the wounded.

• • •

By nightfall, ten thousand victims of the explosion had invaded the Red Cross Hospital, and Dr. Sasaki, worn out, was moving aimlessly and dully up and down the stinking corridors with wads of bandage and bottles of mercurochrome, still wearing the glasses he had taken from the wounded nurse, binding up the worst cuts as he came to them. Other doctors were putting compresses of saline solution on the worst burns. That was all they could do. After dark, they worked by the light of the city's fires and by candles the ten remaining nurses held for them. Dr. Sasaki had not looked outside the hospital all day; the scene inside was so terrible and so compelling that it had not occurred to him to ask any questions about what had happened beyond the windows and doors. Ceilings and partitions had fallen; plaster, dust, blood, and vomit were everywhere. Patients were dying by the hundreds, but there was nobody to carry away the corpses. Some of the hospital staff distributed biscuits and rice balls, but the charnel-house smell was so strong that few were hungry. By three o'clock the next morning, after nineteen straight hours of his gruesome work, Dr. Sasaki was incapable of dressing another wound. He and some other survivors of the hospital staff got straw mats and went outdoors—thousands of patients and hundreds of dead were in the yard and on the driveway—and hurried around behind the hospital and lay down in hiding to snatch some sleep. But within an hour wounded people had found them; a complaining circle formed around them: "Doctors! Help us! How can you sleep?" Dr. Sasaki got up again and went back to work. Early in the day, he thought for the first time of his mother at their country home in Mukaihara, thirty miles from town. He usually went home every night. He was afraid she would think he was dead.

. . .

Near the spot upriver to which Mr. Tanimoto had transported the priests, there sat a large case of rice cakes which a rescue party had evidently brought for the wounded lying thereabouts but hadn't distributed. Before evacuating the wounded priests, the others passed the cakes around and helped themselves. A few minutes later, a band of soldiers came up, and an officer, hearing the priests speaking a foreign language, drew his sword and hysterically asked who they were. One of the priests calmed him down and explained that they were Germans—allies. The officer apologized and said that there were reports going around that American parachutists had landed.

The priests decided that they should take Father Schiffer first. As they prepared to leave, Father Superior LaSalle said he felt awfully cold. One of the Jesuits gave up his coat, another his shirt; they were glad to wear less in the muggy night. The stretcher bearers started out. The theological student led the way and tried to warn the others of obstacles, but one of the priests got a foot tangled in some telephone wire and tripped and dropped his corner of the litter. Father Schiffer rolled off, lost consciousness, came to, and then vomited. The bearers picked him up and went on with him to the edge of the city, where they had arranged to meet a relay of other priests, left him with them, and turned back and got the Father Superior.

The wooden litter must have been terribly painful for Father LaSalle, in whose back scores of tiny particles of window glass were embedded. Near the edge of town, the group had to walk around an automobile burned and squatting on the narrow road, and the bearers on one side, unable to see their way in the darkness, fell into a deep ditch. Father LaSalle was thrown onto the ground and the litter broke in two. One priest went ahead to get a handcart from the Novitiate, but he soon found one beside an empty house and wheeled it back. The priests lifted Father LaSalle into the cart and pushed him over the bumpy road the rest of the way. The rector of the Novitiate, who had been a doctor before he entered the religious order, cleaned the wounds of the two priests and put them to bed between clean sheets, and they thanked God for the care they had received.

. . .

Thousands of people had nobody to help them. Miss Sasaki was one of them. Abandoned and helpless, under the crude lean-to in the courtyard of the tin factory, beside the woman who had lost a breast and the man whose burned face was scarcely a face any more, she suffered awfully that night from the pain in her broken leg. She did not sleep at all; neither did she converse with her sleepless companions.

. . .

In the park, Mrs. Murata kept Father Kleinsorge awake all night by talking to him. None of the Nakamura family were able to sleep, either; the children, in spite of being very sick, were interested in everything that happened. They were delighted when one of the city's gas-storage tanks went up in a tremendous burst of flame. Toshio, the boy, shouted to the others to look at the reflection in the river. Mr. Tanimoto, after his long run and his many hours of rescue work, dozed uneasily. When he awoke, in the first light of dawn, he looked across the river and saw that he had not carried the festered, limp bodies high enough on the sandspit the night before. The tide had risen above where he had put them; they had not had the strength to move; they must have drowned. He saw a number of bodies floating in the river.

. . .

Early that day, August 7th, the Japanese radio broadcast for the first time a succinct announcement that very few, if any, of the people most concerned with its content, the survivors in Hiroshima, happened to hear: "Hiroshima suffered considerable damage as the result of an attack by a few B-29s. It is believed that a new type of bomb was used. The details are being investigated." Nor is it probable that any of the survivors happened to be tuned in on a short-wave rebroadcast of an extraordinary announcement by the President of the United States, which identified the new bomb as atomic: "That bomb had more power than twenty thousand tons of TNT. It had more than two thousand times the blast power of the British Grand Slam, which is the largest bomb ever yet used in the history of warfare." Those victims who were able to worry at all about what had happened thought of it and discussed it in more primitive, childish terms—gasoline sprinkled from an airplane, maybe, or some combustible gas, or a big cluster of incendiaries, or the work of parachutists; but, even if they had known the truth, most of them were too busy or too weary or too badly hurt to care that they were the objects of the first great experiment in the use of atomic power, which (as the voices on the short wave shouted) no country except the United States, with its industrial know-how, its willingness to throw two billion gold dollars into an important wartime gamble, could possibly have developed.

. . .

Mr. Tanimoto was still angry at doctors. He decided that he would personally bring one to Asano Park—by the scruff of the neck, if necessary. He crossed the river, went past the Shinto shrine where he had met his wife for a brief moment the day before, and walked to the East Parade Ground. Since this had long before been designated as an evacuation area, he thought he would find an aid station there. He did find one, operated by an Army medical unit, but he also saw that its doctors were hopelessly overburdened, with thousands of patients sprawled among corpses across the field in front of it. Nevertheless, he went up to one of the Army doctors and said, as reproachfully as he could, "Why have you not come to Asano Park? You are badly needed there."

Without even looking up from his work, the doctor said in a tired voice, "This is my station."

"But there are many dying on the riverbank over there."

"The first duty," the doctor said, "is to take care of the slightly wounded."

"Why—when there are many who are heavily wounded on the riverbank?"

The doctor moved to another patient. "In an emergency like this," he said, as if he were reciting from a manual, "the first task is to help as many as possible—to save as many lives as possible. There is no hope for the heavily wounded. They will die. We can't bother with them."

"That may be right from a medical standpoint—" Mr. Tanimoto began, but then he looked out across the field, where the many dead lay close and intimate with those who were still living, and he turned away without finishing his sentence, angry now with himself. He didn't know what to do; he had promised some of the dying people in the park that he would bring them medical aid. They might die feeling cheated. He saw a ration stand at one side of the field, and he went to it and begged some rice cakes and biscuits, and he took them back, in lieu of doctors, to the people in the park.

. . .

The morning, again, was hot. Father Kleinsorge went to fetch water for the wounded in a bottle and a teapot he had borrowed. He had heard that it was possible to get fresh tap water outside Asano Park. Going through the rock gardens, he had to climb over and crawl under the trunks of fallen pine trees; he found he was weak. There were many dead in the gardens. At a beautiful moon bridge, he passed a naked, living woman who seemed to have been burned from head to toe and was red all over. Near the entrance to the park, an Army doctor was working, but the only medicine he had was iodine, which he painted over cuts, bruises, slimy burns, everything—and by now everything that he painted had pus on it. Outside the gate of the park, Father Kleinsorge found a faucet that still worked—part of the plumbing of a vanished house—and he filled his vessels and returned. When he had given the wounded the water, he made a second trip. This time, the woman by the bridge was dead. On his way back with the water, he got lost on a detour around a fallen tree, and as he looked for his way through the woods, he heard a voice ask from the underbrush, "Have you anything to drink?" He saw a uniform. Thinking there was just one soldier, he approached with the water. When he had penetrated the bushes, he saw there were about twenty men, and they were all in exactly the same nightmarish state: their faces were wholly burned, their eyesockets were hollow, the fluid from their melted eyes had run down their cheeks. (They must have had their faces upturned when the bomb went off; perhaps they were anti-aircraft personnel.) Their mouths were mere swollen, pus-covered wounds, which they could not bear to stretch enough to admit the spout of the teapot. So Father Kleinsorge got a large piece of grass and drew out the stem so as to make a straw, and gave them all water to drink that way. One of them said, "I can't see anything." Father Kleinsorge answered, as cheerfully as he could, "There's a doctor at the entrance to the park. He's busy now, but he'll come soon and fix your eyes, I hope."

Since that day, Father Kleinsorge has thought back to how queasy he had once been at the sight of pain, how someone else's cut finger used to make him turn faint. Yet there in the park he was so benumbed that immediately after leaving this horrible sight he stopped on a path by one of the pools and discussed with a lightly wounded man whether it would be safe to eat the fat, two-foot carp that floated dead on the surface of the water. They decided, after some consideration, that it would be unwise.

Father Kleinsorge filled the containers a third time and went back to the riverbank. There, amid the dead and dying, he saw a young woman with a needle and thread mending her kimono, which had been slightly torn. Father Kleinsorge joshed her. "My, but you're a dandy!" he said. She laughed.

He felt tired and lay down. He began to talk with two engaging children whose acquaintance he had made the afternoon before. He learned that their name was Kataoka; the girl was thirteen, the boy five. The girl had been just about to set out for a barbershop when the bomb fell. As the family started for Asano Park, their mother decided to turn back for some food and extra clothing; they became separated from her in the crowd of fleeing people, and they had not seen her since. Occasionally they stopped suddenly in their perfectly cheerful playing and began to cry for their mother.

It was difficult for all the children in the park to sustain the sense of tragedy. Toshio Nakamura got quite excited when he saw his friend Seichi Sato riding up the river in a boat with his family, and he ran to the bank and waved and shouted, "Sato! Sato!"

The boy turned his head and shouted, "Who's that?"

"Nakamura."

"Hello, Toshio!"

"Are you all safe?"

"Yes. What about you?"

"Yes, we're all right. My sisters are vomiting, but I'm fine."

Father Kleinsorge began to be thirsty in the dreadful heat, and he did not feel strong enough to go for water again. A little before noon, he saw a Japanese woman handing something out. Soon she came to him and said in a kindly voice, "These are tea leaves. Chew them, young man, and you won't feel thirsty." The woman's gentleness made Father Kleinsorge suddenly want to cry. For weeks, he had been feeling oppressed by the hatred of foreigners that the Japanese seemed increasingly to show, and he had been uneasy even with his Japanese friends. This stranger's gesture made him a little hysterical.

Around noon, the priests arrived from the Novitiate with the handcart. They had been to the site of the mission house in the city and had retrieved some suitcases that had been stored in the air-raid shelter and had also picked up the remains of melted holy vessels in the ashes of the chapel. They now packed Father Kleinsorge's papier-mâché suitcase and the things belonging to Mrs. Murata and the Nakamuras into the cart, put the two Nakamura girls aboard, and prepared to start out. Then one of the Jesuits who had a practical turn of mind remembered that they had been notified some time before that if they suffered property damage at the hands of the enemy, they could enter a claim for compensation with the prefectural police. The holy men discussed this matter there in the park, with the wounded as silent as the dead around them, and decided that Father Kleinsorge, as a former resident of the destroyed mission, was the one to enter the claim. So, as the others went off with the handcart, Father Kleinsorge said goodbye to the Kataoka children and trudged to a police station. Fresh, clean-uniformed policemen from another town were in charge, and a crowd of dirty and disarrayed citizens crowded around them, mostly asking after lost relatives. Father Kleinsorge filled out a claim form and started walking through the center of town on his way to Nagatsuka. It was then that he first realized the extent of the damage; he passed block after block of ruins, and even after all he had seen in the park, his breath was taken away. By the time he reached the Novitiate, he was sick with exhaustion. The last thing he did as he fell into bed was request that someone go back for the motherless Kataoka children.

. . .

Altogether, Miss Sasaki was left two days and two nights under the piece of propped-up roofing with her crushed leg and her two unpleasant comrades. Her only diversion was when men came to the factory air-raid shelters, which she could see from under one corner of her shelter, and hauled corpses up out of them with ropes. Her leg became discolored, swollen, and putrid. All that time, she went without food and water. On the third day, August 8th, some friends who supposed she was dead came to look for her body and found her. They told her that her mother, father, and baby brother, who at the time of the explosion were in the Tamura Pediatric Hospital, where the baby was a patient, had all been given up as certainly dead, since the hospital was totally destroyed. Her friends then left her to think that piece of news over. Later, some men picked her up by the arms and legs and carried her quite a distance to a truck. For about an hour, the truck moved over a bumpy road, and Miss Sasaki, who had become convinced that she was dulled to pain, discovered that she was not. The men lifted her out at a relief station in the section of Inokuchi, where two Army doctors looked at her. The moment one of them touched her wound, she fainted. She came to in time to hear them discuss whether or not to cut off her leg; one said there was gas gangrene in the lips of the wound and predicted she would die unless they amputated, and the other said that was too bad, because they had no equipment with which to do the job. She fainted again. When she recovered consciousness, she was being carried somewhere on a stretcher. She was put aboard a launch, which went to the nearby island of Ninoshima, and she was taken to a military hospital there. Another doctor examined her and said that she did not have gas gangrene, though she did have a fairly ugly compound fracture. He said quite coldly that he was sorry, but this was a hospital for operative surgical cases only, and because she had no gangrene, she would have to return to Hiroshima that night. But then the doctor took her temperature, and what he saw on the thermometer made him decide to let her stay.

. . .

That day, August 8th, Father Cieslik went into the city to look for Mr. Fukai, the Japanese secretary of the diocese, who had ridden unwillingly out of the flaming city on Father Kleinsorge's back and then had run back crazily into it. Father Cieslik started hunting in the neighborhood of Sakai Bridge, where the Jesuits had last seen Mr. Fukai; he went to the East Parade Ground, the evacuation area to which the secretary might have gone, and looked for him among the wounded and dead there; he went to the prefectural police and made inquiries. He could not find any trace of the man. Back at the Novitiate that evening, the theological student, who had been rooming with Mr. Fukai at the mission house, told the priests that the secretary had remarked to him, during an air-raid alarm one day not long before the bombing, "Japan is dying. If there is a real air raid here in Hiroshima, I want to die with our country." The priests concluded that Mr. Fukai had run back to immolate himself in the flames. They never saw him again.

. . .

At the Red Cross Hospital, Dr. Sasaki worked for three straight days with only one hour's sleep. On the second day, he began to sew up the worst cuts, and right through the following night and all the next day he stitched. Many of the wounds were festered. Fortunately, someone had found intact a supply of *narucopon*, a Japanese sedative, and he gave it to many who were in pain. Word went around among the staff that there must have been something peculiar about the great bomb, because on the second day the vice-chief of the hospital went down in the basement to the vault where the X-ray plates were stored and found the whole stock exposed as they lay. That day, a fresh doctor and ten nurses came in from the city of Yamaguchi with extra bandages and antiseptics, and the third day another physician and a dozen more nurses arrived from Matsue— yet there were still only eight doctors for ten thousand patients. In the afternoon of the third day, exhausted from his foul tailoring, Dr. Sasaki became obsessed with the idea that his mother thought he was dead. He got permission to go to Mukaihara. He walked out to the first suburbs, beyond which the electric train service was still functioning, and reached home late in the evening. His mother said she had known he was all right all along; a wounded nurse had stopped by to tell her. He went to bed and slept for seventeen hours.

. . .

Before dawn on August 8th, someone entered the room at the Novitiate where Father Kleinsorge was in bed, reached up to the hanging light bulb, and switched it on. The sudden flood of light, pouring in on Father Kleinsorge's half sleep, brought him leaping out of bed, braced for a new concussion. When he realized what had happened, he laughed confusedly and went back to bed. He stayed there all day.

On August 9th, Father Kleinsorge was still tired. The rector looked at his cuts and said they were not even worth dressing, and if Father Kleinsorge kept them clean, they would heal in three or four days. Father Kleinsorge felt uneasy; he could not yet comprehend what he had been through; as if he were guilty of something awful, he felt he had to go back to the scene of the violence he had experienced. He got up out of bed and walked into the city. He scratched for a while in the ruins of the mission house, but he found nothing. He went to the sites of a couple of schools and asked after people he knew. He looked for some of the city's Japanese Catholics, but he found only fallen houses. He walked back to the Novitiate, stupefied and without any new understanding.

. . .

At two minutes after eleven o'clock on the morning of August 9th, the second atomic bomb was dropped, on Nagasaki. It was several days before the survivors of Hiroshima knew they had company, because the Japanese radio and newspapers were being extremely cautious on the subject of the strange weapon.

. . .

On August 9th, Mr. Tanimoto was still working in the park. He went to the suburb of Ushida, where his wife was staying with friends, and got a tent which he had stored there before the bombing. He now took it to the park and set it up as a shelter for some of the wounded who could not move or be moved. Whatever he did in the park, he felt he was being watched by the twenty-year-old girl, Mrs. Kamai, his former neighbor, whom he had seen on the day the bomb exploded, with her dead baby daughter in her arms. She kept the small corpse in her arms for four days, even though it began smelling bad on the second day. Once, Mr. Tanimoto sat with her for a while, and she told him that the bomb had buried her under their house with the baby strapped to her back, and that when she had dug herself free, she had discovered that the baby was choking, its mouth full of dirt. With her little finger, she had carefully cleaned out the infant's mouth, and for a time the child had breathed normally and seemed all right; then suddenly it had died. Mrs. Kamai also talked about what a fine man her husband was, and again urged Mr. Tanimoto to search for him. Since Mr. Tanimoto had been all through the city the first day and had seen terribly burned soldiers from Kamai's post, the Chugoku Regional Army Headquarters, everywhere, he knew it would be impossible to find Kamai, even if he were living, but of course he didn't tell her that. Every time she saw Mr. Tanimoto, she asked whether he had found her husband. Once, he tried to suggest that perhaps it was time to cremate the baby, but Mrs. Kamai only held it tighter. He began to keep away from her, but whenever he looked at her, she was staring at him and her eyes asked the same question. He tried to escape her glance by keeping his back turned to her as much as possible.

• • •

The Jesuits took about fifty refugees into the exquisite chapel of the Novitiate. The rector gave them what medical care he could—mostly just the cleaning away of pus. Each of the Nakamuras was provided with a blanket and a mosquito net. Mrs. Nakamura and her younger daughter had no appetite and ate nothing; her son and other daughter ate, and lost, each meal they were offered. On August 10th, a friend, Mrs. Osaki, came to see them and told them that her son Hideo had been burned alive in the factory where he worked. This Hideo had been a kind of hero to Toshio, who had often gone to the plant to watch him run his machine. That night, Toshio woke up screaming. He had dreamed that he had seen Mrs. Osaki coming out of an opening in the ground with her family, and then he saw Hideo at his machine, a big one with a revolving belt, and he himself was standing beside Hideo, and for some reason this was terrifying.

• • •

On August 10th, Father Kleinsorge, having heard from someone that Dr. Fujii had been injured and that he had eventually gone to the summer house of a friend of his named Okuma, in the village of Fukawa, asked Father Cieslik if he would go and see how Dr. Fujii was. Father Cieslik went to Misasa station, outside Hiroshima, rode for twenty minutes on an electric train, and then walked for an hour and a half in a terribly hot sun to Mr. Okuma's house, which was beside the Ota River at the foot of a mountain. He found Dr. Fujii sitting in a chair in a kimono, applying compresses to his broken collarbone. The Doctor told Father Cieslik about having lost his glasses and said that his eyes bothered him. He showed the priest huge blue and green stripes where beams had bruised him. He offered the Jesuit first a cigarette and then whiskey, though it was only eleven in the morning. Father Cieslik thought it would please Dr. Fujii if he took a little, so he said yes. A servant brought some Suntory whiskey, and the Jesuit, the Doctor, and the host had a very pleasant chat. Mr. Okuma had lived in Hawaii, and he told some things about Americans. Dr. Fujii talked a bit about the disaster. He said that Mr. Okuma and a nurse had gone into the ruins of his hospital and brought back a small safe which he had moved into his air-raid shelter. This contained some surgical instruments, and Dr. Fujii gave Father Cieslik a few pairs of scissors and tweezers for the rector at the Novitiate. Father Cieslik was bursting with some inside dope he had, but he waited until the conversation turned naturally to the mystery of the bomb. Then he said he knew what kind of bomb it was; he had the secret on the best authority—that of a Japanese newspaperman who had dropped in at the Novitiate. The bomb was not a bomb at all; it was a kind of fine magnesium powder sprayed over the whole city by a single plane, and it exploded when it came into contact with the live wires of the city power system. "That means," said Dr. Fujii, perfectly satisfied, since after all the information came from a newspaperman, "that it can only be dropped on big cities and only in the daytime, when the tram lines and so forth are in operation."

. . .

After five days of ministering to the wounded in the park, Mr. Tanimoto returned, on August 11th, to his parsonage and dug around in the ruins. He retrieved some diaries and church records that had been kept in books and were only charred around the edges, as well as some cooking utensils and pottery. While he was at work, a Miss Tanaka came and said that her father had been asking for him. Mr. Tanimoto had reason to hate her father, the retired shipping-company official who, though he made a great show of his charity, was notoriously selfish and cruel, and who, just a few days before the bombing, had said openly to several people that Mr. Tanimoto was a spy for the Americans. Several times he had derided Christianity and called it un-Japanese. At the moment of the bombing, Mr. Tanaka had been walking in the street in front of the city's radio station. He received serious flash burns, but he was able to walk home. He took refuge in his Neighborhood Association shelter and from there tried hard to get medical aid. He expected all the doctors of Hiroshima to come to him, because he was so rich and so famous for giving his money away. When none of them came, he angrily set out to look for them; leaning on his daughter's arm, he walked from private hospital to private hospital, but all were in ruins, and he went back and lay down in the shelter again. Now he was very weak and knew he was going to die. He was willing to be comforted by any religion.

Mr. Tanimoto went to help him. He descended into the tomblike shelter and, when his eyes were adjusted to the darkness, saw Mr. Tanaka, his face and arms puffed up and covered with pus and blood, and his eyes swollen shut. The old man smelled very bad, and he moaned constantly. He seemed to recognize Mr. Tanimoto's voice. Standing at the shelter stairway to get light, Mr. Tanimoto read loudly from a Japanese-language pocket Bible: "For a thousand years in Thy sight are but as yesterday when it is past, and as a watch in the night. Thou carriest the children of men away as with a flood; they are as a sleep; in the morning they are like grass which groweth up. In the morning it flourisheth and groweth up; in the evening it is cut down, and withereth. For we are consumed by Thine anger and by Thy wrath are we troubled. Thou has set our iniquities before Thee, our secret sins in the light of Thy countenance. For all our days are passed away in Thy wrath: we spend our years as a tale that is told. . . ."

Mr. Tanaka died as Mr. Tanimoto read the psalm.

. . .

On August 11th, word came to the Ninoshima Military Hospital that a large number of military casualties from the Chugoku Regional Army Headquarters were to arrive on the island that day, and it was deemed necessary to evacuate all civilian patients. Miss Sasaki, still running an alarmingly high fever, was put on a large ship. She lay out on deck, with a pillow under her leg. There were awnings over the deck, but the vessel's course put her in the sunlight. She felt as if she were under a magnifying glass in the sun. Pus oozed out of her wound, and soon the whole pillow was covered with it. She was taken ashore at Hatsukaichi, a town several miles to the southwest of Hiroshima, and put in the Goddess of Mercy Primary School, which had been turned into a hospital. She lay there for several days before a specialist on fractures came from Kobe. By then her leg was red and swollen up to her hip. The doctor decided he could not set the breaks. He made an incision and put in a rubber pipe to drain off the putrescence.

. . .

At the Novitiate, the motherless Kataoka children were inconsolable. Father Cieslik worked hard to keep them distracted. He put riddles to them. He asked, "What is the cleverest animal in the world?," and after the thirteen-year-old girl had guessed the ape, the elephant, the horse, he said, "No, it must be the hippopotamus," because in Japanese that animal is *kaba,* the reverse of *baka,* stupid. He told Bible stories, beginning, in the order of things, with the Creation. He showed them a scrapbook of snapshots taken in Europe. Nevertheless, they cried most of the time for their mother.

Several days later, Father Cieslik started hunting for the children's family. First, he learned through the police that an uncle had been to the authorities in Kure, a city not far away, to inquire for the children. After that, he heard that an older brother had been trying to trace them through the post office in Ujina, a suburb of Hiroshima. Still later, he heard that the mother was alive and was on Goto Island, off Nagasaki. And at last, by keeping a check on the Ujina post office, he got in touch with the brother and returned the children to their mother.

. . .

About a week after the bomb dropped, a vague, incomprehensible rumor reached Hiroshima—that the city had been destroyed by the energy released when atoms were somehow split in two. The weapon was referred to in this word-of-mouth report as *genshi bakudan*—the root characters of which can be translated as "original child bomb." No one understood the idea or put any more credence in it than in the powdered magnesium and such things. Newspapers were being brought in from other cities, but they were still confining themselves to extremely general statements, such as Domei's assertion on August 12th: "There is nothing to do but admit the tremendous power of this inhuman bomb." Already, Japanese physicists had entered the city with Lauritsen electroscopes and Neher electrometers; they understood the idea all too well.

. . .

On August 12th, the Nakamuras, all of them still rather sick, went to the nearby town of Kabe and moved in with Mrs. Nakamura's sister-in-law. The next day, Mrs. Nakamura, although she was too ill to walk much, returned to Hiroshima alone, by electric car to the outskirts, by foot from there. All week, at the Novitiate, she had worried about her mother, brother, and older sister, who had lived in the part of town called Fukuro, and besides, she felt drawn by some fascination, just as Father Kleinsorge had been. She discovered that her family were all dead. She went back to Kabe so amazed and depressed by what she had seen and learned in the city that she could not speak that evening.

. . .

A comparative orderliness, at least, began to be established at the Red Cross Hospital. Dr. Sasaki, back from his rest, undertook to classify his patients (who were still scattered everywhere, even on the stairways). The staff gradually swept up the debris. Best of all, the nurses and attendants started to remove the corpses. Disposal of the dead, by decent cremation and enshrinement, is a greater moral responsibility to the Japanese than adequate care of the living. Relatives identified most of the first day's dead in and around the hospital. Beginning on the second day, whenever a patient appeared to be moribund, a piece of paper with his name on it was fastened to his clothing. The corpse detail carried the bodies to a clearing outside, placed them on pyres of wood from ruined houses, burned them, put some of the ashes in envelopes intended for exposed X-ray plates, marked the envelopes with the names of the deceased, and piled them, neatly and respectfully, in stacks in the main office. In a few days, the envelopes filled one whole side of the impromptu shrine.

. . .

In Kabe, on the morning of August 15th, ten-year-old Toshio Nakamura heard an airplane overhead. He ran outdoors and identified it with a professional eye as a B-29. "There goes Mr. B!" he shouted.

One of his relatives called out to him, "Haven't you had enough of Mr. B?"

The question had a kind of symbolism. At almost that very moment, the dull, dispirited voice of Hirohito, the Emperor Tenno, was speaking for the first time in history over the radio: "After pondering deeply the general trends of the world and the actual conditions obtaining in Our Empire today, We have decided to effect a settlement of the present situation by resorting to an extraordinary measure. . . ."

Mrs. Nakamura had gone to the city again, to dig up some rice she had buried in her Neighborhood Association air-raid shelter. She got it and started back for Kabe. On the electric car, quite by chance, she ran into her younger sister, who had not been in Hiroshima the day of the bombing. "Have you heard the news?" her sister asked.

"What news?"

"The war is over."

"Don't say such a foolish thing, sister."

"But I heard it over the radio myself." And then, in a whisper, "It was the Emperor's voice."

"Oh," Mrs. Nakamura said (she needed nothing more to make her give up thinking, in spite of the atomic bomb, that Japan still had a chance to win the war), "in that case . . ."

. . .

Some time later, in a letter to an American, Mr. Tanimoto described the events of that morning. "At the time of the Post-War, the marvelous thing in our history happened. Our Emperor broadcasted his own voice through radio directly to us, common people of Japan. Aug. 15th we were told that some news of great importance could be heard & all of us should hear it. So I went to Hiroshima railway station. There set a loudspeaker in the ruins of the station. Many civilians, all of them were in boundage, some being helped by shoulder of their daughters, some sustaining their injured feet by sticks, they listened to the broadcast and when they came to realize the fact that it was the Emperor, they cried with full tears in their eyes, 'What a wonderful blessing it is that Tenno himself call on us and we can hear his own voice in person. We are thoroughly satisfied in such a great sacrifice.' When they came to know the war was ended—that is, Japan was defeated, they, of course, were deeply disappointed, but followed after their Emperor's commandment in calm spirit, making whole-hearted sacrifice for the everlasting peace of the world—and Japan started her new way."

IV—PANIC GRASS AND FEVERFEW

On August 18th, twelve days after the bomb burst, Father Kleinsorge set out on foot for Hiroshima from the Novitiate with his papier-mâché suitcase in his hand. He had begun to think that this bag, in which he kept his valuables, had a talismanic quality, because of the way he had found it after the explosion, standing handle-side up in the doorway of his room, while the desk under which he had previously hidden it was in splinters all over the floor. Now he was using it to carry the yen belonging to the Society of Jesus to the Hiroshima branch of the Yokohama Specie Bank, already reopened in its half-ruined building. On the whole, he felt quite well that morning. It is true that the minor cuts he had received had not healed in three or four days, as the rector of the Novitiate, who had examined them, had positively promised they would, but Father Kleinsorge had rested well for a week and considered that he was again ready for hard work. By now he was accustomed to the terrible scene through which he walked on his way into the city: the large rice field near the Novitiate, streaked with brown; the houses on the outskirts of the city, standing but decrepit, with broken windows and dishevelled tiles; and then, quite suddenly, the beginning of the four square miles of reddish-brown scar, where nearly everything had been buffeted down and burned; range on range of collapsed city blocks, with here and there a crude sign erected on a pile of ashes and tiles ("Sister, where are you?" or "All safe and we live at Toyosaka"); naked trees and canted telephone poles; the few standing, gutted buildings only accentuating the horizontality of everything else (the Museum of Science and Industry, with its dome stripped to its steel frame, as if for an autopsy; the modern Chamber of Commerce Building, its tower as cold, rigid, and unassailable after the blow as before; the huge, low-lying, camouflaged city hall; the row of dowdy banks, caricaturing a shaken economic system); and in the streets a macabre traffic—hundreds of crumpled bicycles, shells of streetcars and automobiles, all halted in mid-motion. The whole way, Father Kleinsorge was oppressed by the thought that all the damage he saw had been done in one instant by one bomb. By the time he reached the center of town, the day had become very hot. He walked to the Yokohama Bank, which was doing business in a temporary wooden stall on the ground floor of its building, deposited the money, went by the mission compound just to have another look at the wreckage, and then started back to the Novitiate. About halfway there, he began to have peculiar sensations. The more or less magical suitcase, now empty, suddenly seemed terribly heavy. His knees grew weak. He felt excruciatingly tired. With a considerable expenditure of spirit, he managed to reach the Novitiate. He did not think his weakness was worth mentioning to the other Jesuits. But a couple of days later, while attempting to say Mass, he had an onset of faintness and even after three attempts was unable to go through with the service, and the next morning the rector, who had examined Father Kleinsorge's apparently negligible but unhealed cuts daily, asked in surprise, "What have you done to your wounds?" They had suddenly opened wider and were swollen and inflamed.

As she dressed on the morning of August 20th, in the home of her sister-in-law in Kabe, not far from Nagatsuka, Mrs. Nakamura, who had suffered no cuts or burns at all, though she had been rather nauseated all through the week she and her children had spent as guests of Father Kleinsorge and the other Catholics at the Novitiate, began fixing her hair and noticed, after one stroke, that her comb carried with it a whole handful of hair; the second time, the same thing happened, so she stopped combing at once. But in the next three or four days, her hair kept falling out of its own accord, until she was quite bald. She began living indoors, practically in hiding. On August 26th, both she and her younger daughter, Myeko, woke up feeling extremely weak and tired, and they stayed on their bedrolls. Her son and other daughter, who had shared every experience with her during and after the bombing, felt fine.

At about the same time—he lost track of the days, so hard was he working to set up a temporary place of worship in a private house he had rented in the outskirts—Mr. Tanimoto fell suddenly ill with a general malaise, weariness, and feverishness, and he, too, took to his bedroll on the floor of the half-wrecked house of a friend in the suburb of Ushida.

These four did not realize it, but they were coming down with the strange, capricious disease which came later to be known as radiation sickness.

• • •

Miss Sasaki lay in steady pain in the Goddess of Mercy Primary School, at Hatsukaichi, the fourth station to the southwest of Hiroshima on the electric train. An internal infection still prevented the proper setting of the compound fracture of her lower left leg. A young man who was in the same hospital and who seemed to have grown fond of her in spite of her unremitting preoccupation with her suffering, or else just pitied her because of it, lent her a Japanese translation of de Maupassant, and she tried to read the stories, but she could concentrate for only four or five minutes at a time.

The hospitals and aid stations around Hiroshima were so crowded in the first weeks after the bombing, and their staffs were so variable, depending on their health and on the unpredictable arrival of outside help, that patients had to be constantly shifted from place to place. Miss Sasaki, who had already been moved three times, twice by ship, was taken at the end of August to an engineering school, also at Hatsukaichi. Because her leg did not improve but swelled more and more, the doctors at the school bound it with crude splints and took her by car, on September 9th, to the Red Cross Hospital in Hiroshima. This was the first chance she had had to look at the ruins of Hiroshima; the last time she had been carried through the city's streets, she had been hovering on the edge of unconsciousness. Even though the wreckage had been described to her, and though she was still in pain, the sight horrified and amazed her, and there was something she noticed about it that particularly gave her the creeps. Over everything—up through the wreckage of the city, in gutters, along the riverbanks, tangled among tiles and tin roofing, climbing on charred tree trunks—was a blanket of fresh, vivid, lush, optimistic green; the verdancy rose even from the foundations of ruined houses. Weeds already hid the ashes, and wild flowers were in bloom among the city's bones. The bomb had not only left the underground organs of plants intact; it had stimulated them. Everywhere were bluets and Spanish bayonets, goose-foot, morning glories and day lilies, the hairy-fruited bean, purslane and clotbur and sesame and panic grass and feverfew. Especially in a circle at the center, sickle senna grew in extraordinary regeneration, not only standing among the charred remnants of the same plant but pushing up in new places, among bricks and through cracks in the asphalt. It actually seemed as if a load of sickle-senna seed had been dropped along with the bomb.

At the Red Cross Hospital, Miss Sasaki was put under the care of Dr. Sasaki. Now, a month after the explosion, something like order had been reestablished in the hospital; which is to say that the patients who still lay in the corridors at least had mats to sleep on and that the supply of medicines, which had given out in the first few days, had been replaced, though inadequately, by contributions from other cities. Dr. Sasaki, who had had one seventeen-hour sleep at his home on the third night, had ever since then rested only about six hours a night, on a mat at the hospital; he had lost twenty pounds from his very small body; he still wore the ill-fitting glasses he had borrowed from an injured nurse.

Since Miss Sasaki was a woman and was so sick (and perhaps, he afterward admitted, just a little bit because she was named Sasaki), Dr. Sasaki put her on a mat in a semi-private room, which at that time had only eight people in it. He questioned her and put down on her record card, in the correct, scrunched-up German in which he wrote all his records: *"Mittelgrosse Patientin in gutem Ernährungszustand. Fraktur am linken Unterschenkelknochen mit Wunde; Anschwellung in der linken Unterschenkelgegend. Haut und sichtbare Schleimhäute mässig durchblutet und kein Oedema,"* noting that she was a medium-sized female patient in good general health; that she had a compound fracture of the left tibia, with swelling of the left lower leg; that her skin and visible mucous membranes were heavily spotted with *petechiae*, which are hemorrhages about the size of grains of rice, or even as big as soybeans; and, in addition, that her head, eyes, throat, lungs, and heart were apparently normal; and that she had a fever. He wanted to set her fracture and put her leg in a cast, but he had run out of plaster of Paris long since, so he just stretched her out on a mat and prescribed aspirin for her fever, and glucose intravenously and diastase orally for her undernourishment (which he had not entered on her record because everyone suffered from it). She exhibited only one of the queer symptoms so many of his patients were just then beginning to show—the spot hemorrhages.

. . .

Dr. Fujii was still pursued by bad luck, which still was connected with rivers. Now he was living in the summer house of Mr. Okuma, in Fukawa. This house clung to the steep banks of the Ota River. Here his injuries seemed to make good progress, and he even began to treat refugees who came to him from the neighborhood, using medical supplies he had retrieved from a cache in the suburbs. He noticed in some of his patients a curious syndrome of symptoms that cropped out in the third and fourth weeks, but he was not able to do much more than swathe cuts and burns. Early in September, it began to rain, steadily and heavily. The river rose. On September 17th, there came a cloudburst and then a typhoon, and the water crept higher and higher up the bank. Mr. Okuma and Dr. Fujii became alarmed and scrambled up the mountain to a peasant's house. (Down in Hiroshima, the flood took up where the bomb had left off—swept away bridges that had survived the blast, washed out streets, undermined foundations of buildings that still stood—and ten miles to the west, the Ono Army Hospital, where a team of experts from Kyoto Imperial University was studying the delayed affliction of the patients, suddenly slid down a beautiful, pine-dark mountainside into the Inland Sea and drowned most of the investigators and their mysteriously diseased patients alike.) After the storm, Dr. Fujii and Mr. Okuma went down to the river and found that the Okuma house had been washed altogether away.

. . .

Because so many people were suddenly feeling sick nearly a month after the atomic bomb was dropped, an unpleasant rumor began to move around, and eventually it made its way to the house in Kabe where Mrs. Nakamura lay bald and ill. It was that the atomic bomb had deposited some sort of poison on Hiroshima which would give off deadly emanations for seven years; nobody could go there all that time. This especially upset Mrs. Nakamura, who remembered that in a moment of confusion on the morning of the explosion she had literally sunk her entire means of livelihood, her Sankoku sewing machine, in the small cement water tank in front of what was left of her house; now no one would be able to go and fish it out. Up to this time, Mrs. Nakamura and her relatives had been quite resigned and passive about the moral issue of the atomic bomb, but this rumor suddenly aroused them to more hatred and resentment of America than they had felt all through the war.

Japanese physicists, who knew a great deal about atomic fission (one of them owned a cyclotron), worried about lingering radiation at Hiroshima, and in mid-August, not many days after President Truman's disclosure of the type of bomb that had been dropped, they entered the city to make investigations. The first thing they did was roughly to determine a center by observing the side on which telephone poles all around the heart of the town were scorched; they settled on the torii gateway of the Gokoku Shrine, right next to the parade ground of the Chugoku Regional Army Headquarters. From there, they worked north and south with Lauritsen electroscopes, which are sensitive to both beta rays and gamma rays. These indicated that the highest intensity of radioactivity, near the torii, was 4.2 times the average natural "leak" of ultra-short waves for the earth of that area. The scientists noticed that the flash of the bomb had discolored concrete to a light reddish tint, had scaled off the surface of granite, and had scorched certain other types of building material, and that consequently the bomb had, in some places, left prints of the shadows that had been cast by its light. The experts found, for instance, a permanent shadow thrown on the roof of the Chamber of Commerce Building (220 yards from the rough center) by the structure's rectangular tower; several others in the lookout post on top of the Hypothec Bank (2,050 yards); another in the tower of the Chugoku Electric Supply Building (800 yards); another projected by the handle of a gas pump (2,630 yards); and several on granite tombstones in the Gokoku Shrine (385 yards). By triangulating these and other such shadows with the objects that formed them, the scientists determined that the exact center was a spot a hundred and fifty yards south of the torii and a few yards southeast of the pile of ruins that had once been the Shima Hospital. (A few vague human silhouettes were found, and these gave rise to stories that eventually included fancy and precise details. One story told how a painter on a ladder was monumentalized in a kind of bas-relief on the stone façade of a bank building on which he was at work, in the act of dipping his brush into his paint can; another, how a man and his cart on the bridge near the Museum of Science and Industry, almost under the center of the explosion, were cast down in an embossed shadow which made it clear that the man was about to whip his horse.) Starting east and west from the actual center, the scientists, in early September, made new measurements, and the highest radiation they found this time was 3.9 times the natural "leak." Since radiation of at least a thousand times the natural "leak" would be required to cause serious effects on the human body, the scientists announced that people could enter Hiroshima without any peril at all.

As soon as this reassurance reached the household in which Mrs. Nakamura was concealing herself—or, at any rate, within a short time after her hair had started growing back again—her whole family relaxed their extreme hatred of America, and Mrs. Nakamura sent her brother-in-law to look for the sewing machine. It was still submerged in the water tank, and when he brought it home, she saw, to her dismay, that it was all rusted and useless.

. . .

By the end of the first week in September, Father Kleinsorge was in bed at the Novitiate with a fever of 102.2, and since he seemed to be getting worse, his colleagues decided to send him to the Catholic International Hospital in Tokyo. Father Cieslik and the rector took him as far as Kobe and a Jesuit from that city took him the rest of the way, with a message from a Kobe doctor to the Mother Superior of the International Hospital: "Think twice before you give this man blood transfusions, because with atomic-bomb patients we aren't at all sure that if you stick needles in them, they'll stop bleeding."

When Father Kleinsorge arrived at the hospital, he was terribly pale and very shaky. He complained that the bomb had upset his digestion and given him abdominal pains. His white blood count was three thousand (five to seven thousand is normal), he was seriously anemic, and his temperature was 104. A doctor who did not know much about these strange manifestations—Father Kleinsorge was one of a handful of atomic patients who had reached Tokyo—came to see him, and to the patient's face he was most encouraging. "You'll be out of here in two weeks," he said. But when the doctor got out in the corridor, he said to the Mother Superior, "He'll die. All these bomb people die—you'll see. They go along for a couple of weeks and then they die."

The doctor prescribed suralimentation for Father Kleinsorge. Every three hours, they forced some eggs or beef juice into him, and they fed him all the sugar he could stand. They gave him vitamins, and iron pills and arsenic (in Fowler's solution) for his anemia. He confounded both the doctor's predictions; he neither died nor got up in a fortnight. Despite the fact that the message from the Kobe doctor deprived him of transfusions, which would have been the most useful therapy of all, his fever and his digestive troubles cleared up fairly quickly. His white count went up for a while, but early in October it dropped again, to 3,600; then, in ten days, it suddenly climbed above normal, to 8,800; and it finally settled at 5,800. His ridiculous scratches puzzled everyone. For a few days, they would mend, and then, when he moved around, they would open up again. As soon as he began to feel well, he enjoyed himself tremendously. In Hiroshima he had been one of thousands of sufferers; in Tokyo he was a curiosity. Young American Army doctors came by the dozen to observe him. Japanese experts questioned him. A newspaper interviewed him. And once, the confused doctor came and shook his head and said, "Baffling cases, these atomic-bomb people."

. . .

Mrs. Nakamura lay indoors with Myeko. They both continued sick, and though Mrs. Nakamura vaguely sensed that their trouble was caused by the bomb, she was too poor to see a doctor and so never knew exactly what the matter was. Without any treatment at all, but merely resting, they began gradually to feel better. Some of Myeko's hair fell out, and she had a tiny burn on her arm which took months to heal. The boy, Toshio, and the older girl, Yaeko, seemed well enough, though they, too, lost some hair and occasionally had bad headaches. Toshio was still having nightmares, always about the nineteen-year-old mechanic, Hideo Osaki, his hero, who had been killed by the bomb.

. . .

On his back with a fever of 104, Mr. Tanimoto worried about all the funerals he ought to be conducting for the deceased of his church. He thought he was just overtired from the hard work he had done since the bombing, but after the fever had persisted for a few days, he sent for a doctor. The doctor was too busy to visit him in Ushida, but he dispatched a nurse, who recognized his symptoms as those of mild radiation disease and came back from time to time to give him injections of Vitamin B_1. A Buddhist priest with whom Mr. Tanimoto was acquainted called on him and suggested that moxibustion might give him relief; the priest showed the pastor how to give himself the ancient Japanese treatment, by setting fire to a twist of the stimulant herb moxa placed on the wrist pulse. Mr. Tanimoto found that each moxa treatment temporarily reduced his fever one degree. The nurse had told him to eat as much as possible, and every few days his mother-in-law brought him vegetables and fish from Tsuzu, twenty miles away, where she lived. He spent a month in bed, and then went ten hours by train to his father's home in Shikoku. There he rested another month.

. . .

Dr. Sasaki and his colleagues at the Red Cross Hospital watched the unprecedented disease unfold and at last evolved a theory about its nature. It had, they decided, three stages. The first stage had been all over before the doctors even knew they were dealing with a new sickness; it was the direct reaction to the bombardment of the body, at the moment when the bomb went off, by neutrons, beta particles, and gamma rays. The apparently uninjured people who had died so mysteriously in the first few hours or days had succumbed in this first stage. It killed 95 percent of the people within a half mile of the center, and many thousands who were farther away. The doctors realized in retrospect that even though most of these dead had also suffered from burns and blast effects, they had absorbed enough radiation to kill them. The rays simply destroyed body cells—caused their nuclei to degenerate and broke their walls. Many people who did not die right away came down with nausea, headache, diarrhea, malaise, and fever, which lasted several days. Doctors could not be certain whether some of these symptoms were the result of radiation or nervous shock. The second stage set in ten or fifteen days after the bombing. The main symptom was falling hair. Diarrhea and fever, which in some cases went as high as 106, came next. Twenty-five to thirty days after the explosion, blood disorders appeared: gums bled, the white-blood-cell count dropped sharply, and *petechiae* appeared on the skin and mucous membranes. The drop in the number of white blood corpuscles reduced the patient's capacity to resist infection, so open wounds were unusually slow in healing and many of the sick developed sore throats and mouths. The two key symptoms, on which the doctors came to base their prognosis, were fever and the lowered white-corpuscle count. If fever remained steady and high, the patient's chances for survival were poor. The white count almost always dropped below four thousand; a patient whose count fell below one thousand had little hope of living. Toward the end of the second stage, if the patient survived, anemia, or a drop in the red blood count, also set in. The third stage was the reaction that came when the body struggled to compensate for its ills—when, for instance, the white count not only returned to normal but increased to much higher than normal levels. In this stage, many patients died of complications, such as infections in the chest cavity. Most burns healed with deep layers of pink, rubbery scar tissue, known as keloid tumors. The duration of the disease varied, depending on the patient's constitution and the amount of radiation he had received. Some victims recovered in a week; with others the disease dragged on for months.

As the symptoms revealed themselves, it became clear that many of them resembled the effects of overdoses of X-ray, and the doctors based their therapy on that likeness. They gave victims liver extract, blood transfusions, and vitamins, especially B_1. The shortage of supplies and instruments hampered them. Allied doctors who came in after the surrender found plasma and penicillin very effective. Since the blood disorders were, in the long run, the predominant factor in the disease, some of the Japanese doctors evolved a theory as to the seat of the delayed sickness. They thought that perhaps gamma rays, entering the body at the time of the explosion, made the phosphorus in the victims' bones radioactive, and that they in turn emitted beta particles, which, though they could not penetrate far through flesh, could enter the bone marrow, where blood is manufactured, and gradually tear it down. Whatever its source, the disease had some baffling quirks. Not all the patients exhibited all the main symptoms. People who suffered flash burns were protected, to a considerable extent, from radiation sickness. Those who had lain quietly for days or even hours after the bombing were much less liable to get sick than those who had been active. Gray hair seldom fell out. And, as if nature were protecting man against his own ingenuity, the reproductive processes were affected for a time; men became sterile, women had miscarriages, menstruation stopped.

. . .

For ten days after the flood, Dr. Fujii lived in the peasant's house on the mountain above the Ota. Then he heard about a vacant private clinic in Kaitaichi, a suburb to the east of Hiroshima. He bought it at once, moved there, and hung out a sign inscribed in English, in honor of the conquerors:

M. FUJII, M.D.
MEDICAL & VENEREAL

Quite recovered from his wounds, he soon built up a strong practice, and he was delighted, in the evenings, to receive members of the occupying forces, on whom he lavished whiskey and practiced English.

. . .

Giving Miss Sasaki a local anaesthetic of procaine, Dr. Sasaki made an incision in her leg on October 23rd, to drain the infection, which still lingered on eleven weeks after the injury. In the following days, so much pus formed that he had to dress the opening each morning and evening.

A week later, she complained of great pain, so he made another incision; he cut still a third, on November 9th, and enlarged it on the twenty-sixth. All this time, Miss Sasaki grew weaker and weaker, and her spirits fell low. One day, the young man who had lent her his translation of de Maupassant at Hatsukaichi came to visit her; he told her that he was going to Kyushu but that when he came back, he would like to see her again. She didn't care. Her leg had been so swollen and painful all along that the doctor had not even tried to set the fractures, and though an X-ray taken in November showed that the bones were mending, she could see under the sheet that her left leg was nearly three inches shorter than her right and that her left foot was turning inward. She thought often of the man to whom she had been engaged. Someone told her he was back from overseas. She wondered what he had heard about her injuries that made him stay away.

. . .

Father Kleinsorge was discharged from the hospital in Tokyo on December 19th and took a train home. On the way, two days later, at Yokogawa, a stop just before Hiroshima, Dr. Fujii boarded the train. It was the first time the two men had met since before the bombing. They sat together. Dr. Fujii said he was going to the annual gathering of his family, on the anniversary of his father's death. When they started talking about their experiences, the Doctor was quite entertaining as he told how his places of residence kept falling into rivers. Then he asked Father Kleinsorge how he was, and the Jesuit talked about his stay in the hospital. "The doctors told me to be cautious," he said. "They ordered me to have a two-hour nap every afternoon."

Dr. Fujii said, "It's hard to be cautious in Hiroshima these days. Everyone seems to be so busy."

. . .

A new municipal government, set up under Allied Military Government direction, had gone to work at last in the city hall. Citizens who had recovered from various degrees of radiation sickness were coming back by the thousand—by November 1st, the population, mostly crowded into the outskirts, was already 137,000, more than a third of the wartime peak—and the government set in motion all kinds of projects to put them to work rebuilding the city. It hired men to clear the streets, and others to gather scrap iron, which they sorted and piled in mountains opposite the city hall. Some returning residents were putting up their own shanties and huts, and planting small squares of winter wheat beside them, but the city also authorized and built four hundred one-family "barracks." Utilities were repaired—electric lights shone again, trams started running, and employees of the waterworks fixed seventy thousand leaks in mains and plumbing. A Planning Conference, with an enthusiastic young Military Government officer, Lieutenant John D. Montgomery, of Kalamazoo, as its adviser, began to consider what sort of city the new Hiroshima should be. The ruined city had flourished—and had been an inviting target—mainly because it had been one of the most important military-command and communications centers in Japan, and would have become the Imperial headquarters had the islands been invaded and Tokyo been captured. Now there would be no huge military establishments to help revive the city. The Planning Conference, at a loss as to just what importance Hiroshima could have, fell back on rather vague cultural and paving projects. It drew maps with avenues a hundred yards wide and thought seriously of preserving the half-ruined Museum of Science and Industry more or less as it was, as a monument to the disaster, and naming it the Institute of International Amity. Statistical workers gathered what figures they could on the effects of the bomb. They reported that 78,150 people had been killed, 13,983 were missing, and 37,425 had been injured. No one in the city government pretended that these figures were accurate—though the Americans accepted them as official—and as the months went by and more and more hundreds of corpses were dug up from the ruins, and as the number of unclaimed urns of ashes at the Zempoji Temple in Koi rose into the thousands, the statisticians began to say that at least a hundred thousand people had lost their lives in the bombing. Since many people died of a combination of causes, it was impossible to figure exactly how many were killed by each cause, but the statisticians calculated that about 25 percent had died of direct burns from the bomb, about 50 percent from other injuries, and about 20 percent as a result of radiation effects. The statisticians' figures on property damage were more reliable: sixty-two thousand out of ninety thousand buildings destroyed, and six thousand more damaged beyond repair. In the heart of the city, they found only five modern buildings that could be used again without major repairs. This small number was by no means the fault of flimsy Japanese construction. In fact, since the 1923 earthquake, Japanese building regulations had required that the roof of each large building be able to bear a minimum load of seventy pounds per square foot, whereas American regulations do not normally specify more than forty pounds per square foot.

Scientists swarmed into the city. Some of them measured the force that had been necessary to shift marble gravestones in the cemeteries, to knock over twenty-two of the forty-seven railroad cars in the yards at Hiroshima station, to lift and move the concrete roadway on one of the bridges, and to perform other noteworthy acts of strength, and concluded that the pressure exerted by the explosion varied from 5.3 to 8.0 tons per square yard. Others found that mica, of which the melting point is 900° C., had fused on granite gravestones three hundred and eighty yards from the center; that telephone poles of *Cryptomeria japonica,* whose carbonization temperature is 240° C., had been charred at forty-four hundred yards from the center; and that the surface of gray clay tiles of the type used in Hiroshima, whose melting point is 1,300° C., had dissolved at six hundred yards; and, after examining other significant ashes and melted bits, they concluded that the bomb's heat on the ground at the center must have been 6,000° C. And from further measurements of radiation, which involved, among other things, the scraping up of fission fragments from roof troughs and drainpipes as far away as the suburb of Takasu, thirty-three hundred yards from the center, they learned some far more important facts about the nature of the bomb. General MacArthur's headquarters systematically censored all mention of the bomb in Japanese scientific publications, but soon the fruit of the scientists' calculations became common knowledge among Japanese physicists, doctors, chemists, journalists, professors, and, no doubt, those statesmen and military men who were still in circulation. Long before the American public had been told, most of the scientists and lots of non-scientists in Japan knew—from the calculations of Japanese nuclear physicists—that a uranium bomb had exploded at Hiroshima and a more powerful one, of plutonium, at Nagasaki. They also knew that theoretically one ten times as powerful—or twenty—could be developed. The Japanese scientists thought they knew the exact height at which the bomb at Hiroshima was exploded and the approximate weight of the uranium used. They estimated that, even with the primitive bomb used at Hiroshima, it would require a shelter of concrete fifty inches thick to protect a human being entirely from radiation sickness. The scientists had these and other details which remained subject to security in the United States printed and mimeographed and bound into little books. The Americans knew of the existence of these, but tracing them and seeing that they did not fall into the wrong hands would have obliged the occupying authorities to set up, for this one purpose alone, an enormous police system in Japan. Altogether, the Japanese scientists were somewhat amused at the efforts of their conquerors to keep security on atomic fission.

. . .

Late in February, 1946, a friend of Miss Sasaki's called on Father Kleinsorge and asked him to visit her in the hospital. She had been growing more and more depressed and morbid; she seemed little interested in living. Father Kleinsorge went to see her several times. On his first visit, he kept the conversation general, formal, and yet vaguely sympathetic, and did not mention religion. Miss Sasaki herself brought it up the second time he dropped in on her. Evidently she had had some talks with a Catholic. She asked bluntly, "If your God is so good and kind, how can he let people suffer like this?" She made a gesture which took in her shrunken leg, the other patients in her room, and Hiroshima as a whole.

"My child," Father Kleinsorge said, "man is not now in the condition God intended. He has fallen from grace through sin." And he went on to explain all the reasons for everything.

. . .

It came to Mrs. Nakamura's attention that a carpenter from Kabe was building a number of wooden shanties in Hiroshima which he rented for fifty yen a month—$3.33, at the fixed rate of exchange. Mrs. Nakamura had lost the certificates for her bonds and other wartime savings, but fortunately she had copied off all the numbers just a few days before the bombing and had taken the list to Kabe, and so, when her hair had grown in enough for her to be presentable, she went to her bank in Hiroshima, and a clerk there told her that after checking her numbers against the records the bank would give her her money. As soon as she got it, she rented one of the carpenter's shacks. It was in Nobori-cho, near the site of her former house, and though its floor was dirt and it was dark inside, it was at least a home in Hiroshima, and she was no longer dependent on the charity of her in-laws. During the spring, she cleared away some nearby wreckage and planted a vegetable garden. She cooked with utensils and ate off plates she scavenged from the debris. She sent Myeko to the kindergarten which the Jesuits reopened, and the two older children attended Nobori-cho Primary School, which, for want of buildings, held classes out of doors. Toshio wanted to study to be a mechanic, like his hero, Hideo Osaki. Prices were high; by midsummer Mrs. Nakamura's savings were gone. She sold some of her clothes to get food. She had once had several expensive kimonos, but during the war one had been stolen, she had given one to a sister who had been bombed out in Tokuyama, she had lost a couple in the Hiroshima bombing, and now she sold her last one. It brought only a hundred yen, which did not last long. In June, she went to Father Kleinsorge for advice about how to get along, and in early August, she was still considering the two alternatives he suggested—taking work as a domestic for some of the Allied occupation forces, or borrowing from her relatives enough money, about five hundred yen, or a bit more than thirty dollars, to repair her rusty sewing machine and resume the work of a seamstress.

• • •

When Mr. Tanimoto returned from Shikoku, he draped a tent he owned over the roof of the badly damaged house he had rented in Ushida. The roof still leaked, but he conducted services in the damp living room. He began thinking about raising money to restore his church in the city. He became quite friendly with Father Kleinsorge and saw the Jesuits often. He envied them their Church's wealth; they seemed to be able to do anything they wanted. He had nothing to work with except his own energy, and that was not what it had been.

• • •

The Society of Jesus had been the first institution to build a relatively permanent shanty in the ruins of Hiroshima. That had been while Father Kleinsorge was in the hospital. As soon as he got back, he began living in the shack, and he and another priest, Father Laderman, who had joined him in the mission, arranged for the purchase of three of the standardized "barracks," which the city was selling at seven thousand yen apiece. They put two together, end to end, and made a pretty chapel of them; they ate in the third. When materials were available, they commissioned a contractor to build a three-story mission house exactly like the one that had been destroyed in the fire. In the compound, carpenters cut timbers, gouged mortises, shaped tenons, whittled scores of wooden pegs and bored holes for them, until all the parts for the house were in a neat pile; then, in three days, they put the whole thing together, like an Oriental puzzle, without any nails at all. Father Kleinsorge was finding it hard, as Dr. Fujii had suggested he would, to be cautious and to take his naps. He went out every day on foot to call on Japanese Catholics and prospective converts. As the months went by, he grew more and more tired. In June, he read an article in the Hiroshima *Chugoku* warning survivors against working too hard—but what could he do? By July, he was worn out, and early in August, almost exactly on the anniversary of the bombing, he went back to the Catholic International Hospital, in Tokyo, for a month's rest.

. . .

Whether or not Father Kleinsorge's answers to Miss Sasaki's questions about life were final and absolute truths, she seemed quickly to draw physical strength from them. Dr. Sasaki noticed it and congratulated Father Kleinsorge. By April 15th, her temperature and white count were normal and the infection in the wound was beginning to clear up. On the twentieth, there was almost no pus, and for the first time she jerked along a corridor on crutches. Five days later, the wound had begun to heal, and on the last day of the month she was discharged.

During the early summer, she prepared herself for conversion to Catholicism. In that period she had ups and downs. Her depressions were deep. She knew she would always be a cripple. Her fiancé never came to see her. There was nothing for her to do except read and look out, from her house on a hillside in Koi, across the ruins of the city where her parents and brother died. She was nervous, and any sudden noise made her put her hands quickly to her throat. Her leg still hurt; she rubbed it often and patted it, as if to console it.

. . .

It took six months for the Red Cross Hospital, and even longer for Dr. Sasaki, to get back to normal. Until the city restored electric power, the hospital had to limp along with the aid of a Japanese Army generator in its back yard. Operating tables, X-ray machines, dentist chairs, everything complicated and essential came in a trickle of charity from other cities. In Japan, face is important even to institutions, and long before the Red Cross Hospital was back to par on basic medical equipment, its directors put up a new yellow brick veneer façade, so the hospital became the handsomest building in Hiroshima—from the street. For the first four months, Dr. Sasaki was the only surgeon on the staff and he almost never left the building; then, gradually, he began to take an interest in his own life again. He got married in March. He gained back some of the weight he lost, but his appetite remained only fair; before the bombing, he used to eat four rice balls at every meal, but a year after it he could manage only two. He felt tired all the time. "But I have to realize," he said, "that the whole community is tired."

· · ·

A year after the bomb was dropped, Miss Sasaki was a cripple; Mrs. Nakamura was destitute; Father Kleinsorge was back in the hospital; Dr. Sasaki was not capable of the work he once could do; Dr. Fujii had lost the thirty-room hospital it took him many years to acquire, and had no prospects of rebuilding it; Mr. Tanimoto's church had been ruined and he no longer had his exceptional vitality. The lives of these six people, who were among the luckiest in Hiroshima, would never be the same. What they thought of their experiences and of the use of the atomic bomb was, of course, not unanimous. One feeling they did seem to share, however, was a curious kind of elated community spirit, something like that of the Londoners after their blitz—a pride in the way they and their fellow-survivors had stood up to a dreadful ordeal. Just before the anniversary, Mr. Tanimoto wrote in a letter to an American some words which expressed this feeling: "What a heartbreaking scene this was the first night! About midnight I landed on the riverbank. So many injured people lied on the ground that I made my way by striding over them. Repeating 'Excuse me,' I forwarded and carried a tub of water with me and gave a cup of water to each one of them. They raised their upper bodies slowly and accepted a cup of water with a bow and drunk quietly and, spilling any remnant, gave back a cup with hearty expression of their thankfulness, and said, 'I couldn't help my sister, who was buried under the house, because I had to take care of my mother who got a deep wound on her eye and our house soon set fire and we hardly escaped. Look, I lost my home, my family, and at last my-self bitterly injured. But now I have gotted my mind to dedicate what I have and to complete the war for our country's sake.' Thus they pledged to me, even women and children did the same. Being entirely tired I lied down on the ground among them, but couldn't sleep at all. Next morning I found many men and women dead, whom I gave water last night. But, to my great surprise, I never heard any one cried in disorder, even though they suffered in great agony. They died in silence, with no grudge, setting their teeth to bear it. All for the country!

"Dr. Y. Hiraiwa, professor of Hiroshima University of Literature and

Science, and one of my church members, was buried by the bomb under the two storied house with his son, a student of Tokyo University. Both of them could not move an inch under tremendously heavy pressure. And the house already caught fire. His son said, 'Father, we can do nothing except make our mind up to consecrate our lives for the country. Let us give *Banzai* to our Emperor.' Then the father followed after his son, *'Tenno-heika, Banzai, Banzai, Banzai!'* In the result, Dr. Hiraiwa said, 'Strange to say, I felt calm and bright and peaceful spirit in my heart, when I chanted *Banzai* to Tenno.' Afterward his son got out and digged down and pulled out his father and thus they were saved. In thinking of their experience of that time Dr. Hiraiwa repeated, 'What a fortunate that we are Japanese! It was my first time I ever tasted such a beautiful spirit when I decided to die for our Emperor.'

"Miss Kayoko Nobutoki, a student of girl's high school, Hiroshima Jazabuin, and a daughter of my church member, was taking rest with her friends beside the heavy fence of the Buddhist Temple. At the moment the atomic bomb was dropped, the fence fell upon them. They could not move a bit under such a heavy fence and then smoke entered into even a crack and choked their breath. One of the girls begun to sing *Kimi ga yo*, national anthem, and others followed in chorus and died. Meanwhile one of them found a crack and struggled hard to get out. When she was taken in the Red Cross Hospital she told how her friends died, tracing back in her memory to singing in chorus our national anthem. They were just 13 years old.

"Yes, people of Hiroshima died manly in the atomic bombing, believing that it was for Emperor's sake."

A surprising number of the people of Hiroshima remained more or less indifferent about the ethics of using the bomb. Possibly they were too terrified by it to want to think about it at all. Not many of them even bothered to find out much about what it was like. Mrs. Nakamura's conception of it—and awe of it—was typical. "The atom bomb," she would say when asked about it, "is the size of a matchbox. The heat of it was six thousand times that of the sun. It exploded in the air. There is some radium in it. I don't know just how it works, but when the radium is put together, it explodes." As for the use of the bomb, she would say, "It was war and we had to expect it." And then she would add, *"Shikata ga nai,"* a Japanese expression as common as, and corresponding to, the Russian word *"nichevo"*: "It can't be helped. Oh, well. Too bad." Dr. Fujii said approximately the same thing about the use of the bomb to Father Kleinsorge one evening, in German: "*Da ist nichts zu machen.* There's nothing to be done about it."

Many citizens of Hiroshima, however, continued to feel a hatred for Americans which nothing could possibly erase. "I see," Dr. Sasaki once said, "that they are holding a trial for war criminals in Tokyo just now. I think they ought to try the men who decided to use the bomb and they should hang them all."

Father Kleinsorge and the other German Jesuit priests, who, as foreigners, could be expected to take a relatively detached view, often discussed the ethics of using the bomb. One of them, Father Siemes, who was out at Nagatsuka at the time of the attack, wrote in a report to the Holy See in Rome, "Some of us consider the bomb in the same category as poison gas and were against its use on a civilian population. Others were of the opinion that in total war, as carried on in Japan, there was no difference between civilians and soldiers, and that the bomb itself was an effective force tending to end the bloodshed, warning Japan to surrender and thus to avoid total destruction. It seems logical that he who supports total war in principle cannot complain of a war against civilians. The crux of the matter is whether total war in its present form is justifiable, even when it serves a just purpose. Does it not have material and spiritual evil as its consequences which far exceed whatever good might result? When will our moralists give us a clear answer to this question?"

It would be impossible to say what horrors were embedded in the minds of the children who lived through the day of the bombing in Hiroshima. On the surface their recollections, months after the disaster, were of an exhilarating adventure. Toshio Nakamura, who was ten at the time of the bombing, was soon able to talk freely, even gaily, about the experience, and a few weeks before the anniversary he wrote the following matter-of-fact essay for his teacher at Nobori-cho Primary School: "The day before the bomb, I went for a swim. In the morning, I was eating peanuts. I saw a light. I was knocked to little sister's sleeping place. When we were saved, I could only see as far as the tram. My mother and I started to pack our things. The neighbors were walking around burned and bleeding. Hataya-*san* told me to run away with her. I said I wanted to wait for my mother. We went to the park. A whirlwind came. At night a gas tank burned and I saw the reflection in the river. We stayed in the park one night. Next day I went to Taiko Bridge and met my girl friends Kikuki and Murakami. They were looking for their mothers. But Kikuki's mother was wounded and Murakami's mother, alas, was dead."

A NOTE BY JILL LEPORE

O NE SUMMER EVENING in 1943, Orson Welles performed a *New Yorker* piece by E. B. White on CBS Radio, reading with a double bass what White had written with a clarinet. White had been asked by the Writers' War Board to explain the meaning of democracy. "Surely the Board knows what democracy is," he began. "Democracy is a letter to the editor. Democracy is the score at the beginning of the ninth." Living on a farm in Maine, White had been mailing his pieces to *The New Yorker,* pitching in, more than he wanted to pitch in, because Harold Ross had lost much of his staff to the war and also because White believed that the magazine had sometimes failed to say "things that seem to need saying." (Ross said he was glad to have him, even "if only by the thimble-full.") What needed saying White usually knew how to say. "Democracy," he closed, "is a request from a War Board, in the middle of a morning in the middle of a war, wanting to know what democracy is."

Every war cleaves time. Before the war, *The New Yorker* was one kind of magazine; after, it was another. In the late thirties and into the forties, Ross's reluctance to take an editorial position about the relationship between the United States and the Allied Forces had made the magazine seem muffled and aloof. "Tilley's hat and butterfly return to plague us all," White wrote, bitterly. If, in the end, the war brought the world into *The New Yorker* and carried *The New Yorker* to the world, it also changed how the magazine reported on Americans at home. The clock in McSorley's seems hardly to have ticked between 1854, when the saloon opened, and 1940, when *The New Yorker* published Joseph Mitchell's profile of it, but in an article by Mitchell that appeared in 1949, Caughnawaga Mohawks living in Brooklyn build bridges and skyscrapers out of iron and steel; on weekends, they watch television. "MARRIAGE BLAMED AS DIVORCE CAUSE," a headline from the Memphis *Commercial*

Appeal, was one of only a handful of bottom-of-column notices posted in the Ho Hum Department in a decade. As Ross explained to White in the summer of 1946, "These are not Ho Hum times."

. . .

Most of the following essays about the American scene offer one answer or another to the question the War Board asked in 1943: What is democracy? The answers in these essays are darker than White's, and for one reason: in peacetime, the wartime defense of American democracy yielded to criticism of its failures. Democracy might be the score at the top of the ninth, but one suspects the game's been rigged.

In "Letter from a Campaign Train," Richard Rovere reports on the contest between Thomas Dewey's 1948 presidential campaign, with its "junior-executive briskness," and the "general dowdiness and good-natured slovenliness" of Truman's. The difference between the two campaigns, Rovere writes, "is the difference between horsehair and foam rubber, between the coal-stove griddle and the pop-up toaster. Dewey is the pop-up toaster." Lopsidedness is also the theme of the story Lillian Ross tells in "Symbol of All We Possess," in which Ross rides to Atlantic City in a 1948 Pontiac sedan with Wanda Nalepa, a twenty-two-year-old registered nurse from the Bronx. She is competing in the Miss America Pageant. Miss New York State doesn't stand a chance. She's too short, she's too skinny, and she can't dance. Ross writes about her with a searing affection:

> The contestants would be judged on four counts: appearance in a bathing suit, appearance in an evening gown, personality, and talent. Miss Nalepa was wondering about her talent. Her act, as she planned it, was going to consist of getting up in her nurse's uniform and making a little speech about her nursing experience.
>
> "I don't know what else I can do to show I've got talent," she said. "All I know how to do is give a good back rub."

Rebecca West's "Opera in Greenville," the story of a trial held in South Carolina in 1947, ran to over thirty pages in the magazine. It is a masterpiece of restraint. Thirty-one white men stood trial for lynching Willie Earle, a young black man accused of robbing and stabbing to death a white man. In the courtroom, the judge allows the defendants to sit with their families; West writes, of one man with his children,

"During the recess, he spread his legs wide apart, picked up one or the other of the little girls under her armpits, and swung her back and forth between his knees." The city's blacks sit in the balcony. West peers at them: "Every day there went into court a number of colored men and women who were conspicuously handsome and fashionably dressed, and had resentment and the proud intention not to express it written all over them." West starts her piece with a stream, ends it with a fever, and issues a verdict of her own about what the court's ruling has done to every living soul in Greenville County, South Carolina, population 137,000: "These wretched people have been utterly betrayed."

The war changed *The New Yorker* by making it more accountable to world affairs, but also by making it differently accountable to what was happening in the United States, including in places like a singularly hideous courthouse in South Carolina. Ross edited "Opera in Greenville" himself, something he didn't often do. In January 1948, he wrote to West that there had been not a single lynching reported in the South in the six months since her piece had appeared. "We made the best of that one," he told her. Democracy is a reporter in a courtroom, eyeing the balcony. Democracy is a terrible, terrible fight.

NOTES AND COMMENT

E. B. White

JULY 3, 1943

WE RECEIVED A LETTER from the Writers' War Board the other day asking for a statement on "The Meaning of Democracy." It presumably is our duty to comply with such a request, and it is certainly our pleasure.

Surely the Board knows what democracy is. It is the line that forms on the right. It is the don't in don't shove. It is the hole in the stuffed shirt through which the sawdust slowly trickles; it is the dent in the high hat. Democracy is the recurrent suspicion that more than half of the people are right more than half of the time. It is the feeling of privacy in the voting booths, the feeling of communion in the libraries, the feeling of vitality everywhere. Democracy is a letter to the editor. Democracy is the score at the beginning of the ninth. It is an idea which hasn't been disproved yet, a song the words of which have not gone bad. It's the mustard on the hot dog and the cream in the rationed coffee. Democracy is a request from a War Board, in the middle of a morning in the middle of a war, wanting to know what democracy is.

THE OLD HOUSE AT HOME

Joseph Mitchell

APRIL 13, 1940 (ON MCSORLEY'S OLD ALE HOUSE)

MCSORLEY'S OCCUPIES THE GROUND FLOOR of a red brick tenement at 15 Seventh Street, just off Cooper Square, where the Bowery ends. It was opened in 1854 and is the oldest saloon in the city. In eighty-six years it has had four owners—an Irish immigrant, his son, a retired policeman, and his daughter—and all of them have been opposed to change. It is equipped with electricity, but the bar is stubbornly illuminated with a pair of gas lamps, which flicker fitfully and throw shadows on the low, cobwebby ceiling each time someone opens the street door. There is no cash register. Coins are dropped in soup bowls—one for nickels, one for dimes, one for quarters, and one for halves—and bills are kept in a rosewood cashbox. It is a drowsy place; the bartenders never make a needless move, the customers nurse their mugs of ale, and the three clocks on the walls have not been in agreement for many years. The clientele is motley. It includes mechanics from the many garages in the neighborhood, salesmen from the restaurant-supply houses on Cooper Square, truck-drivers from Wanamaker's, internes from Bellevue, students from Cooper Union, clerks from the row of secondhand bookshops north of Astor Place, and men with tiny pensions who live in hotels on the Bowery but are above drinking in the bars on that street. The backbone of the clientele, however, is a rapidly thinning group of crusty old men, predominantly Irish, who have been drinking there since they were youths and now have a proprietary feeling toward the place. Some of these veterans clearly remember John McSorley, the founder, who died in 1910 at the age of eighty-seven. They refer to him as Old John, and they like to sit in rickety armchairs around the big belly stove which heats the place, gnaw on the stems of their pipes, and talk about him.

. . .

Old John was quirky. He was normally affable but was subject to spells of unaccountable surliness during which he would refuse to answer when spoken to. He went bald in early manhood and began wearing scraggly, patriarchal sideburns before he was forty. Many photographs of him are in existence, and it is obvious that he had a lot of unassumed dignity. He patterned his saloon after a public house he had known in Ireland and originally called it the Old House at Home; around 1908 the signboard blew down, and when he ordered a new one he changed the name to McSorley's Old Ale House. That is still the official name; customers never have called it anything but McSorley's. Old John believed it impossible for men to drink with tranquillity in the presence of women; there is a fine back room in the saloon, but for many years a sign was nailed on the street door, saying, "Notice. No Back Room in Here for Ladies." In McSorley's entire history, in fact, the only woman customer ever willingly admitted was an addled old peddler called Mother Fresh-Roasted, who claimed her husband died from the bite of a lizard in Cuba during the Spanish-American War and who went from saloon to saloon on the lower East Side for a couple of generations hawking peanuts, which she carried in her apron. On warm days, Old John would sell her an ale, and her esteem for him was such that she embroidered him a little American flag and gave it to him one Fourth of July; he had it framed and placed it on the wall above his brass-bound ale pump, and it is still there. When other women came in, Old John would hurry forward, make a bow, and say, "Madam, I'm sorry, but we don't serve ladies." This technique is still used.

In his time, Old John catered to the Irish and German workingmen—carpenters, tanners, bricklayers, slaughterhouse butchers, teamsters, and brewers—who populated the Seventh Street neighborhood, selling ale in pewter mugs at five cents a mug and putting out a free lunch inflexibly consisting of soda crackers, raw onions, and cheese; present-day customers are wont to complain that some of the cheese Old John laid out on opening night in 1854 is still there. Adjacent to the free lunch he kept a quart crock of tobacco and a rack of clay and corncob pipes—the purchase of an ale entitled a man to a smoke on the house; the rack still holds a few of the communal pipes. Old John was thrifty and was able to buy the tenement—it is five stories high and holds eight families—about ten years after he opened the saloon in it. He distrusted banks and always kept his money in a cast-iron safe; it still stands in the back room, but its doors are loose on their hinges and there is nothing in it but an accumulation of expired saloon licences and several McSorley heirlooms, including Old John's straight razor. He lived with his family in a flat directly over the saloon and got up every morning at five; he walked to the Battery and back before breakfast, no matter what the weather. He unlocked the saloon at seven, swept it out himself, and spread sawdust on the floor. Until he became too feeble to manage a racing sulky, he always kept a horse and a nanny goat in a stable around the corner on St. Mark's Place. He kept both animals in the same stall, believing, like many horse-lovers, that horses should have company at night. During the lull in the afternoon a stable-hand would lead the horse around to a hitching block in front of the saloon, and Old John, wearing his bar apron, would stand on the curb and groom the animal. A customer who wanted service would tap on the window and Old John would drop his currycomb, step inside, draw an ale, and return at once to the horse. On Sundays he entered sulky races on uptown highways.

From the time he was twenty until he was fifty-five, Old John drank steadily, but throughout the last thirty-two years of his life he did not take a drop, saying, "I've had my share." Except for a few experimental months in 1905 or 1906, no spirits ever have been sold in McSorley's; Old John maintained that the man never lived who needed a stronger drink than a mug of stock ale warmed on the hob of a stove. He was a big eater. Customarily, just before locking up for the night, he would grill himself a three-pound T-bone, placing it on a coal shovel and holding it over a bed of oak coals in the back-room fireplace. He liked to fit a whole onion into the hollowed-out heel of a loaf of French bread and eat it as if it were an apple. He had an extraordinary appetite for onions, the stronger the better, and said that "Good ale, raw onions, and no ladies" was the motto of his saloon. About once a month during the winter he presided over an on-the-house beefsteak party in the back room, and late in life he was president of an organization of gluttons called the Honorable John McSorley Pickle, Baseball Nine, and Chowder Club, which held hot-rock clambakes in a picnic grove on North Brother Island in the East River. On the walls are a number of photographs taken at outings of the club, and in most of them the members are squatting around hogsheads of ale; except for the president, they all have drunken, slack-mouthed grins and their eyes look dazed. Old John had a bullfrog bass and enjoyed harmonizing with a choir of drunks. His favorite songs were "Muldoon, the Solid Man," "Swim Out, You're Over Your Head," "Maggie Murphy's Home," and "Since the Soup House Moved Away." These songs were by Harrigan and Hart, who were then called "the Gilbert and Sullivan of the U.S.A." He had great respect for them and was pleased exceedingly when, in 1882, they made his saloon the scene of one of their slum comedies; it was called *McSorley's Inflation*.

Although by no means a handshaker, Old John knew many prominent men. One of his closest friends was Peter Cooper, president of the North American Telegraph Company and founder of Cooper Union, which is a half-block west of the saloon. Mr. Cooper, in his declining years, spent so many afternoons in the back room philosophizing with the workingmen that he was given a chair of his own; it was equipped with an inflated rubber cushion. (The chair is still there; each April 4th for a number of years after Mr. Cooper's death, on April 4, 1883, it was draped with black cloth.) Also, like other steadfast customers, Mr. Cooper had a pewter mug on which his name had been engraved with an icepick. He gave the saloon a life-sized portrait of himself, which hangs over the mantel in the back room. It is a rather appropriate decoration, because, since the beginning of prohibition, McSorley's has been the official saloon of Cooper Union students. Sometimes a sentimental student will stand beneath the portrait and drink a toast to Mr. Cooper.

Old John had a remarkable passion for memorabilia. For years he saved the wishbones of Thanksgiving and Christmas turkeys and strung them on a rod connecting the pair of gas lamps over the bar; the dusty bones are invariably the first thing a new customer gets inquisitive about. Not long ago, a Johnny-come-lately infuriated one of the bartenders by remarking, "Maybe the old boy believed in voodoo." Old John decorated the partition between barroom and back room with banquet menus, autographs, starfish shells, theatre programs, political posters, and worndown shoes taken off the hoofs of various race and brewery horses. Above the entrance to the back room he hung a shillelagh and a sign: "BE GOOD OR BEGONE." On one wall of the barroom he placed portraits of horses, steamboats, Tammany bosses, jockeys, actors, singers, and assassinated statesmen; there are many excellent portraits of Lincoln, Garfield, and McKinley. On the same wall he hung framed front pages of old newspapers; one, from the London *Times* for June 22, 1815, contains a paragraph on the beginning of the battle of Waterloo, in the lower right-hand corner, and another, from the New York *Herald* of April 15, 1865, has a single-column story on the shooting of Lincoln. He blanketed another wall with lithographs and steel engravings. One depicts Garfield's deathbed. Another is entitled "The Great Fight." It was between Tom Hyer and Yankee Sullivan, both bare-knuckled, at Still Pond Heights, Maryland, in 1849. It was won by Hyer in sixteen rounds, and the prize was $10,000. The judges wore top hats. The brass title tag on another engraving reads, "Rescue of Colonel Thomas J. Kelly and Captain Timothy Deacy by Members of the Irish Revolutionary Brotherhood from the English Government at Manchester, England, September 18, 1867." A copy of the Emancipation Proclamation is on this wall; so, almost inevitably, is a facsimile of Lincoln's saloon licence. An engraving of Washington and his generals hangs next to an engraving of a session of the Great Parliament of Ireland. Eventually Old John covered practically every square inch of wall space between wainscot and ceiling with pictures and souvenirs. They are still in good condition, although spiders have strung webs across many of them. New customers get up on chairs and spend hours studying them.

. . .

Although Old John did not consider himself retired until just a few years before he died, he gave up day-in-and-day-out duty back of the bar around 1890 and made his son, William, head bartender. Bill McSorley was the kind of person who minds his own business vigorously. He inherited every bit of his father's surliness and not much of his affability. The father was by no means a lush, but the son carried temperance to an extreme; he drank nothing but tap water and tea, and bragged about it. He did dip a little snuff. He was so solemn that before he was thirty several customers had settled into the habit of calling him Old Bill. He worshipped his father, but no one was aware of the profundity of his worship until Old John died. After the funeral, Bill locked the saloon, went upstairs to the family flat, pulled the shutters to, and did not come out for almost a week. Finally, on a Sunday morning, gaunt and silent, he came downstairs with a hammer and a screwdriver and spent the day painstakingly securing his father's pictures and souvenirs to the walls; they had been hung hit or miss on wires, and customers had a habit of taking them down. Subsequently he commissioned a Cooper Union art teacher to make a small painting of Old John from a photograph. Bill placed it on the wall back of the bar and thereafter kept a hooded electric light burning above it, a pious custom that is still observed.

Throughout his life Bill's principal concern was to keep McSorley's exactly as it had been in his father's time. When anything had to be changed or repaired, it appeared to pain him physically. For twenty years the bar sagged in the middle like a plough mule's back. A carpenter warned him repeatedly that it was about to collapse; finally, in 1933, he told the carpenter to go ahead and prop it up. While the work was in progress he sat at a table in the back room with his head in his hands and got so upset he could not eat for several days. In the same year the smoke- and cobweb-encrusted paint on the ceiling began to flake off and float to the floor. After customers complained that they were afraid the flakes they found in their ale might strangle them to death, he grudgingly had the ceiling repainted. In 1925 he had to switch to earthenware mugs; most of the pewter ones had been stolen by souvenir hunters. In the same year a coin-box telephone, which he would never answer himself, was installed in the back room. These were about the only major changes he ever allowed. Occasionally one of the pictures his father had hung would fall off the wall and the glass would break, and he would fill in the gap. His contributions include a set of portraits of the wives of Presidents through the first Mrs. Woodrow Wilson, a poster of Barney Oldfield in a red racing car, and a poem called "The Man Behind the Bar." He knew this poem by heart and particularly liked the last verse:

When St. Peter sees him coming he will leave the gates ajar,
For he knows he's had his hell on earth, has the man behind the bar.

As a businessman, Bill was anachronous; he hated banks, cash registers, bookkeeping, and salesmen. If the saloon became crowded, he would close up early, saying, "I'm getting too confounded much trade in here." Agents for the brewery from which he bought his ale often tried to get him to open a checking account; he stubbornly continued to pay his ale bills with currency, largely silver. He would count out the money four or five times and hand it to the driver in a paper bag. Bill was an able bartender. He understood ale; he knew how to draw it and how to keep it, and his bar pipes were always clean. In warm weather he made a practice of chilling the mugs in a tub of ice; even though a customer nursed an ale a long time, the chilled earthenware mug kept it cool. Except during prohibition, the rich, wax-colored ale sold in McSorley's always has come from the Fidelio Brewery on First Avenue; the brewery was founded two years before the saloon. In 1934, Bill sold this brewery the right to call its ale McSorley's Cream Stock and gave it permission to use Old John's picture on the label; around the picture is the legend "As brewed for McSorley's Old Ale House." During prohibition McSorley's ale was produced mysteriously in a row of washtubs in the cellar by a retired brewer named Barney Kelly, who would come down three times a week from his home in the Bronx. On these days the smell of malt and wet hops would be strong in the place. Kelly's product was raw and extraordinarily emphatic, and Bill made a practice of weakening it with near beer. In fact, throughout prohibition Bill referred to his ale as near beer, a euphemism which greatly amused the customers. One night a policeman who knew Bill stuck his head in the door and said, "I seen a old man up at the corner wrestling with a truck horse. I asked him what he'd been drinking and he said, 'Near beer in McSorley's.'" The prohibition ale cost fifteen cents, or two mugs for a quarter. Ale now costs a dime a mug.

· · ·

Bill was big and thick-shouldered, but he did not look strong; he had a shambling walk and a haggard face and always appeared to be convalescing from something. He wore rusty-black suits and black bow ties; his shirts, however, were surprisingly fancy—they were silk, with candy stripes. He was nearsighted, the saloon was always dimly lit, and his most rigid conviction was that drink should not be sold to minors; consequently he would sometimes peer across the bar at a small-sized adult and say, "Won't sell you nothing, bud. Get along home, where you belong." Once he stared for a long time at a corner of the saloon and suddenly shouted, "Take your foot off that table!" Evidently he had been staring at a shadow; no one was sitting in the corner. Bill was tyrannical. Reading a newspaper, he would completely disregard a line of customers waiting to be served. If a man became impatient and demanded a drink, Bill would look up angrily and shout obscene remarks at him in a high, nasal voice. Such treatment did not annoy customers but made them snicker; they thought he was funny. In fact, despite Bill's bad disposition, many customers were fond of him. They had known him since they were young men together and had grown accustomed to his quirks. They even took a wry sort of pride in him, and when they said he was the gloomiest, or the stingiest, man in the Western Hemisphere there was boastfulness in their voices; the more eccentric he became, the more they respected him. Sometimes, for the benefit of a newcomer, one of these customers would show Bill off, shouting, "Hey, Bill, lend me fifty dollars!" or "Hey, Bill, there ain't no pockets in a shroud!" Such remarks usually provoked an outburst of gamy epithets. Then the customer would turn proudly to the newcomer and say, "See?" When prohibition came, Bill simply disregarded it. He ran wide open. He did not have a peephole door, nor did he pay protection, but McSorley's was never raided; the fact that it was patronized by a number of Tammany politicians and minor police officials probably gave it immunity.

Bill never had a fixed closing hour but locked up as soon as he began to feel sleepy, which was usually around ten o'clock. Just before closing he would summon everybody to the bar and buy a round. This had been his father's custom and he faithfully carried it on, even though it seemed to hurt him to do so. If the customers were slow about finishing the final drink, he would cough fretfully once or twice, then drum on the bar with both fists and say, "Now, see here, gents! I'm under no obligoddamnation to stand here all night while you baby them drinks." Whenever Bill completely lost his temper he would jump up and down and moan piteously. One night in the winter of 1924 a feminist from Greenwich Village put on trousers, a man's topcoat, and a cap, stuck a cigar in her mouth, and entered McSorley's. She bought an ale, drank it, removed her cap, and shook her long hair down on her shoulders. Then she called Bill a male chauvinist, yelled something about the equality of the sexes, and ran out. When Bill realized he had sold a drink to a woman, he let out a cross between a moan and a bellow and began to jump up and down as if his heels were on fire. "She was a woman!" he yelled. "She was a goddamn woman!"

Bill was deaf, or pretended to be; even so, ordinary noises seemed to bother him unduly. The method he devised to keep the saloon tranquil was characteristic of him. He bought a fire-alarm gong similar to those used in schools and factories and screwed it to the seven-foot-tall icebox behind the bar. If someone started a song, or if the old men sitting around the stove began to yell at each other, he would shuffle over to the gong and give the rope a series of savage jerks. The gong is there yet and is customarily sounded at a quarter to midnight as a warning that closing time is imminent; the customers grab their ears when it goes off. Bill was consistent in his aversion to noise; he didn't even like the sound of his own voice. He was able to go for days without speaking, answering all questions with a snort or a grunt. A man who drank in McSorley's steadily for sixteen years once said that in that time Bill spoke exactly four intelligible words to him. They were "Curiosity killed the cat." The man had politely asked Bill to tell him the history of a pair of rusty convict shackles on the wall. He learned later that a customer who had fought in the Civil War had brought them back from a Confederate prison in Andersonville, Georgia, and had given them to Old John as a souvenir.

Bill would sometimes take an inexplicable liking to a customer. Around 1911 a number of painters began hanging out in McSorley's. Among them were John Sloan, George Luks, Glenn O. Coleman, and Stuart Davis, the abstractionist. They were all good painters, they did not put on airs, and the workingmen in the saloon accepted them as equals. One night, Hippolyte Havel, the anarchist, came in with the painters. Havel was a long-haired, myopic, gentle-mannered Czech whose speeches often got him in trouble with the police. Even Bill was curious about him. "What's that crazy-looking feller do for a living?" he asked one of the painters. Playing safe, the painter said Havel was a politician, more or less. Havel liked the place and became a steady customer. Most nights, after making a fiery speech in Union Square, he would hurry down to McSorley's. To the amazement of the old-timers, a strong friendship grew up between him and Bill, who was a Tammany Democrat and an utter reactionary; no one was ever able to figure out the basis of the friendship. Bill called the anarchist Hippo and would let him have credit up to two dollars; other customers were not allowed to charge so much as a nickle cigar. Bill had an extremely vague idea about Havel's politics. Charles Francis Murphy, the Tammany boss, occasionally dropped in, and once Bill told Havel he was going to speak a good word to the boss for him. "Maybe he'll put you in line for something," Bill said. The anarchist, who thought no man was as foul as a Tammany boss, smiled and thanked him. A police captain once took it upon himself to warn Bill against Havel. "You better keep your eyes on that long-haired nut," he said. "Why?" asked Bill. The question annoyed the police captain. "Hell fire, man," he said, "Havel's an anarchist! He's in favor of blowing up every bank in the country." "So am I," said Bill. Bill's friendship for Havel was extraordinary in every way. As a rule, he reserved his kindness for cats. He owned as many as eighteen at once and they had the run of the saloon. He fed them on bull livers put through a sausage grinder and they became enormous. When it came time to feed them, he would leave the bar, no matter how brisk business was, and bang on the bottom of a tin pan; the fat cats would come loping up, like leopards, from all corners of the saloon.

Bill had been married but was childless, and he used to say, "When I go, this place goes with me." In March, 1936, however, he changed his mind—why, no one knows—and, to the surprise of the veteran customers, sold both saloon and tenement to Daniel O'Connell, an old policeman, who, since 1900, had spent most of his leisure at a table in the back room. O'Connell retired from the Department two days before he purchased the saloon. He was the kind of man of whom people say, "If he can't speak a good word about you, he won't speak a bad one." He was almost as proud of the saloon's traditions as Bill and willingly promised he would make no changes; that was one of the conditions of the sale. Almost from the day Bill sold out, his health began to fail. He took a room in the house of a relative in Queens. Sometimes, in the afternoon, if the weather was good, he would shuffle into the bar, a sallow, disenchanted old man, and sit in the Peter Cooper chair with his knotty hands limp in his lap. For hours he would sit and stare at the painting of Old John. The customers were sure he was getting ready to die, but when he came in they would say, "You looking chipper today, Billy boy," or something like that. He seemed grateful for such remarks. He rarely spoke, but once he turned to a man he had known for forty years and said, "Times have changed, McNally." "You said it, Bill," McNally replied. Then, as if afraid he had been sentimental, Bill coughed, spat, and said, irrelevantly, "The bread you get these days, it ain't fit to feed a dog." On the night of September 21, 1938, barely thirty-one months after he quit drawing ale, he died in his sleep. As close as his friends could figure it, his age was seventy-six.

. . .

The retired policeman made a gentle saloonkeeper. Unlike Bill, he would never throw a quarrelsome drunk into the street but would try to sober him up with soup. "If a man gets crazy on stuff I sold him, I can't kick him out," he said one day. "That would be evading my responsibility." He was proprietor for less than four years. He died last December 8th and left the property to a daughter, Mrs. Dorothy O'Connell Kirwan. A young woman with great respect for tradition, Mrs. Kirwan has chosen to remain completely in the background. At first customers feared that she would renovate the place, but they now realize that this fear was groundless. "I know exactly how my father felt about McSorley's," Mrs. Kirwan said recently, "and no changes will be made. So long as I am owner, the rule against women customers will remain in force." She herself has visited the saloon only twice, and then on Sunday nights after hours. She appointed a brother-in-law, Joe Nida, manager and retained the old bartenders, Eddie Mullins and Joe Martoccio. Mike, the cook, a Ukrainian, was also retained. The most important member of the staff of McSorley's, however, is not actually an employee. His name is Tommy Kelly, and he is called Kelly the Floorwalker. He is not related to Barney Kelly, the prohibition brewer. Since around 1904, Kelly has acted as a sort of volunteer potboy and master of ceremonies. During prohibition, Bill had him on the payroll, but most of the time he has worked for the pleasure of it. When business is brisk, he totes mugs from the bar to the tables; also, he makes an occasional trip to the butcher for Mike. In the winter he keeps a fire going. When he shows up, around 8:30 A.M., he is just an average, sad-eyed little man with a hangover, but by noon lukewarm ale has given him a certain stateliness; by six he is in such a good humor that he stands near the door and shakes hands with incoming customers just as if he were the proprietor. Strangers think he is the proprietor and call him Mr. McSorley. Technically, Kelly is a truckdriver, but he always says business is slow in his line. Once, for a brief period, he took a job as night clerk in a funeral parlor in Brooklyn, quitting because a corpse spoke to him. "This dead guy told me to take my hat off indoors," Kelly says. In one way or another, death pops up repeatedly in Kelly's talk. Each morning, Mullins, the bartender, asks him how he feels. If he doesn't feel so good, he says, "I'm dead, but I just won't lie still." Otherwise he says, "For a old drunk with one leg in the grave and not a penny to his name, I can't complain."

. . .

To a steady McSorley customer, most other New York saloons seem feminine and fit only for college boys and women; the atmosphere in them is so tense and disquieting that he has to drink himself into a coma in order to stand it. In McSorley's, the customers are self-sufficient; they never try to impress each other. Also, they are not competitive. In other saloons if a man tells a story, good or bad, the man next to him laughs perfunctorily and immediately tries to tell a better one. It is possible to relax in McSorley's. For one thing, it is dark and gloomy, and repose comes easy in a gloomy place. Also, there is a thick, musty smell that acts as a balm to jerky nerves; it is really a rich compound of the smells of pine sawdust, tap drippings, pipe tobacco, coal smoke, and onions. A Bellevue interne once said that for many mental disturbances the smell in McSorley's is more beneficial than psychoanalysis. It is an utterly democratic place. A mechanic in greasy overalls gets as much attention as an executive from Wanamaker's. The only customer the bartenders brag about is Police Inspector Matthew J. McGrath, who was a shot- and hammer-thrower in four Olympics and is called Mighty Matt.

At midday, McSorley's is crowded. The afternoon is quiet. At six, it fills up with men who work in the neighborhood. Most nights there are a few curiosity-seekers in the place. If they behave themselves and don't ask too many questions, they are tolerated. The majority of them have learned about the saloon through John Sloan's paintings. Between 1912 and 1930, Sloan did five paintings, filled with detail, of the saloon— *McSorley's Bar,* which shows Bill presiding majestically over the tap and which hangs in the Detroit Institute of Arts; *McSorley's Back Room,* a painting of an old workingman sitting at the window at dusk with his hands in his lap, his pewter mug on the table; *McSorley's at Home,* which shows a group of argumentative old-timers around the stove; *McSorley's Cats,* in which Bill is preparing to feed his drove of cats; and *McSorley's, Saturday Night,* which was painted during prohibition and shows Bill passing out mugs to a crowd of rollicking customers. Every time one of these appears in an exhibition or in a newspaper or magazine, there is a rush of strangers to the saloon. *McSorley's Bar* was reproduced in Thomas Craven's *A Treasury of Art Masterpieces,* which came out last winter, and there have been many strangers in the saloon since. Last November there was a retrospective exhibition of Sloan's work in Wanamaker's art department, and a number of McSorley patrons attended it in a body. One asked a clerk for the price of *McSorley's Cats.* "Three thousand dollars," he was told. He believed the clerk was kidding him and is still indignant. Kelly likes the Sloan paintings but prefers a golden, corpulent nude which Old John hung in the back room many years ago, right beside Peter Cooper's portrait. To a stranger, attracted to the saloon by a Sloan painting, Kelly will say, "Hey, Mac, if you want to see some real art, go look at the naked lady in the back room." The nude is stretched out on a couch and is playing with a parrot; the painting is a copy, probably done by a Cooper Union student, of Gustave Courbet's *La Femme au Perro-quet*. Kelly always translates this for strangers. "It's French," he says learnedly. "It means 'Duh Goil and duh Polly.'"

. . .

McSorley's bar is short, accommodating approximately ten elbows, and is shored up with iron pipes. It is to the right as you enter. To the left is a row of armchairs with their stiff backs against the wainscoting. The chairs are rickety; when a fat man is sitting in one, it squeaks like new shoes every time he takes a breath. The customers believe in sitting down; if there are vacant chairs, no one ever stands at the bar. Down the middle of the room is a row of battered tables. Their tops are always sticky with spilled ale. In the centre of the room stands the belly stove, which has an isinglass door and is exactly like the stoves in Elevated stations. All winter Kelly keeps it red hot. "Warmer you get, drunker you get," he says. Some customers prefer mulled ale. They keep their mugs on the hob until the ale gets hot as coffee. A sluggish cat named Minnie sleeps in a scuttle beside the stove. The floor boards are warped, and here and there a hole has been patched with a flattened-out soup can. The back room looks out on a blind tenement court. In this room are three big, round dining-room tables. The kitchen is in one corner of the room; Mike keeps a folding boudoir screen around the gas range, and pots, pans, and paper bags of groceries are stored on the mantelpiece. While he peels potatoes, he sits with early customers at a table out front, holding a dishpan in his lap and talking as he peels. The fare in McSorley's is plain, cheap, and well cooked. Mike's specialties are goulash, frankfurters and sauerkraut, and hamburgers blanketed with fried onions. He scribbles his menu in chalk on a slate which hangs in the barroom and consistently misspells four dishes out of five. There is no waiter. During the lunch hour, if Mike is too busy to wait on the customers, they grab plates and help themselves out of the pots on the range. They eat with their hats on and they use toothpicks. Mike refers to food as "she." For example, if a customer complains that the goulash is not as good as it was last Wednesday, he says, "No matter how not as good she is, she's good enough for you."

The saloon opens at eight. Mike gives the floor a lick and a promise and throws on clean sawdust. He replenishes the free-lunch platters with cheese and onions and fills a bowl with cold, hard-boiled eggs, five cents each. Kelly shows up. The ale truck makes its delivery. Then, in the middle of the morning, the old men begin shuffling in. Kelly calls them "the steadies." The majority are retired laborers and small businessmen. They prefer McSorley's to their homes. A few live in the neighborhood, but many come from a distance. One, a retired operator of a chain of Bowery flop-houses, comes in from Sheepshead Bay practically every day. On the day of his retirement, this man said, "If my savings hold out, I'll never draw another sober breath." He says he drinks in order to forget the misery he saw in his flop-houses; he undoubtedly saw a lot of it, because he often drinks twenty-five mugs a day, and McSorley's ale is by no means weak. Kelly brings the old men their drinks. To save him a trip, they usually order two mugs at a time. Most of them are quiet and dignified; a few are eccentrics. About twelve years ago one had to leap out of the path of a speeding automobile on Third Avenue; he is still furious. He mutters to himself constantly. Once, asked what he was muttering about, he said, "Going to buy a shotgun and stand on Third Avenue and shoot at automobiles." "Are you going to aim at the tires?" he was asked. "Why, hell no!" he said. "At the drivers. Figure I could kill four or five before they arrested me. Might kill more if I could reload fast enough."

Only a few of the old men have enough interest in the present to read newspapers. These patrons sit up front, to get the light that comes through the grimy street windows. When they grow tired of reading, they stare for hours into the street. There is always something worth looking at on Seventh Street. It is one of those East Side streets completely under the domination of kids. While playing stickball, they keep great packing-box fires going in the gutter; sometimes they roast mickies in the gutter fires. Drunks reel over from the Bowery and go to sleep in doorways, and the kids give them hotfoots with kitchen matches. In McSorley's the free-lunch platters are kept at the end of the bar nearer the street door, and several times every afternoon kids sidle in, snatch handfuls of cheese and slices of onion, and dash out, slamming the door. This never fails to amuse the old men.

The stove overheats the place and some of the old men are able to sleep in their chairs for long periods. Occasionally one will snore, and Kelly will rouse him, saying, "You making enough racket to wake the dead." Once Kelly got interested in a sleeper and clocked him. Two hours and forty minutes after the man dozed off, Kelly became uneasy— "Maybe he died," he said—and shook him awake. "How long did I sleep?" the man asked. "Since the parade," Kelly said. The man rubbed his eyes and asked, "Which parade?" "The Paddy's Day parade, two years ago," Kelly said scornfully. "Jeez!" the man said. Then he yawned and went back to sleep. Kelly makes jokes about the regularity of the old men. "Hey, Eddie," he said one morning, "old man Ryan must be dead!" "Why?" Mullins asked. "Well," Kelly said, "he ain't been in all week." In summer they sit in the back room, which is as cool as a cellar. In winter they grab the chairs nearest the stove and sit in them, as motionless as barnacles, until around six, when they yawn, stretch, and start for home, insulated with ale against the dreadful loneliness of the old. "God be wit' yez," Kelly says as they go out the door.

OPERA IN GREENVILLE

Rebecca West

JUNE 14, 1947 (ON A LYNCHING TRIAL)

THE NOTE of Greenville, South Carolina, is rhetorical. Among the stores and offices on Main Street there is a vacant lot that suddenly pretends to be a mountain glade, with a stream purling over a neatly assembled rockfall; and in the foreground there is staked a plaque bearing the words "Greenville City Water Works. 1939. The water supply of Greenville, South Carolina, pure, sparkling, life's most vital element, flows by gravity from an uncontaminated mountain watershed of nine thousand acres, delivered through duplicated pipe lines, fourteen million gallons capacity, a perfect water for domestic and industrial uses." Not in such exuberant terms would the existence of a town water supply be celebrated in the North or in my native England, and no deduction can be drawn from this that is damaging to the South. The exuberance of the inscription is actually a sober allusion to reality. Here one remembers that water is a vital element, as it is not in the North or in England. One is always thinking about water, for one is always wanting to have a drink or take a shower or get some clothes washed. The heat of the South is an astonishment to the stranger. When the lynching trial in Greenville came to its end, late in May, it was full summer there, and the huge, pale bush roses that grow around the porches were a little dusty. Greenville was as hot as the cities that lie on the Spanish plains, as Seville and Córdoba. But in those cities the people do not live a modern life, they do not work too grimly, and they sleep in the afternoons; here they keep the same commercial hours as in New York, and practice the hard efficiency that is the price this age asks for money. In fact, the lynching for which thirty-one men were being tried in the Court House was committed not, as might be imagined by an interested person who was trying to size the matter up by looking at a map and gazetter, in a backward small town, but in a large, modern city.

To sustain the life of a large, modern city in this cloying, clinging heat is an amazing achievement. It is no wonder that the white men and women in Greenville walk with a slow, dragging pride, as if they had taken up a challenge and intended to defy it without end. These people would deny that it is the climate that has challenged them. They speak of the coolness of the nights almost before the stranger has mentioned the heat of the day. When they name the antagonist against whom they have to pit themselves, they simply and passionately and frequently name the North, with the same hatred, the profounder because it is insolently unrequited, that the Irish feel for the English. But the stranger will obstinately continue to admire them for living and working in this land over which the sun seems to be bending low, and for doing more than live and work: for luxuriating in rhetoric, and topping rhetoric with opera.

Near the center of Greenville there stands an old white church, with a delicate spire and handsome steps leading down from a colonnade— the kind of building that makes an illusion of space around itself. This is the First Baptist Church. In there, on Sunday evenings, there is opera. The lovely girls with their rich hair curling around their shoulders and their flowered dresses showing their finely molded throats and arms sit beside the tall young men, whose pale shirts show the squareness of their shoulders and the slimness of their waists, and they join in coloratura hymns with their parents and their grandparents, who sing, like their children, with hope and vehemence, having learned to take things calmly no more than the older characters in opera. As they sing, the women's dresses become crumpled wraps, the men's shirts cling to them, although the service does not begin till eight o'clock at night. But, undistracted by the heat, they listen, still and yet soaring, to the anthems sung by an ecstatic choir and to a sermon that is like a bass recitative, ending in an aria of faith, mounting to cadenzas of adoration. In no other place are Baptists likely to remind a stranger of Verdi.

· · ·

In the Court House, also, there was opera. This is a singularly hideous building, faced with yellow washroom tiles, standing in Main Street, next the principal hotel, which, it should be noted for those who want to understand the character of Greenville, is cleaner and more comfortable and kinder to the appetite than most of the great New York hotels at this moment. The courtroom is about the size of the famous court at the Old Bailey, in London. In the body of the courtroom there were chairs for about three hundred white persons. The front rows were occupied by the thirty-one defendants who were being tried for lynching a Negro early on the morning of February 17th of this year. With the exception of three young men, one a member of a wealthy mill-owning family, one a salesman, and one a restaurant proprietor, these defendants were all Greenville taxi-drivers. Some were quite good-looking and alert young men; most were carefully and cleanly dressed; some were manifest eccentrics. The most curious in aspect was a young man of twenty-five who must have weighed about three hundred pounds. The contours of his buttocks and stomach suggested that they were molded in some ductile substance like butter, and his face, which was smiling and playful, was pressed upward, till it turned toward the ceiling, by an enormous accumulation of fat under the chin and jaws. His name was Joy, and he was known as Fat Joy. The most conspicuous by reason of character was Roosevelt Carlos Hurd, Sr., who was a taxi-driver also working as a taxi dispatcher, a man of forty-five with hair that stood up like a badger's coat, eyes set close together and staring out under glum brows through strong glasses, and a mouth that was unremitting in its compression. He looked like an itinerant preacher devoted to the worship of a tetchy and uncooperative God. Several of the statements made by other defendants alleged that Mr. Hurd was the actual trigger man of the lynching, the man who fired the shot that killed the Negro.

Nearly all these defendants were exercising a right their state permits to all persons accused of a capital offense. They had brought their families to sit with them in court. Many had their wives beside them, young women, for the most part very young women, in bright cotton and rayon dresses, their curled hair wild about them. A number of these women had brought their children with them; one had five scrambling over her. Mr. Hurd, though married and a father, was accompanied only by his own father, a thin and sharp-nosed man, his eyes censorious behind gold-rimmed spectacles, the whole of him blanched and shrivelled by austerity as by immersion in a caustic fluid. It was altogether plain that at any moment he and his son might become possessed by the idea that they were appointed God's arm and instrument, and that their conception of God would render the consequence of this conviction far from reasonably bland.

Behind the defendants and their families sat something under two hundred of such white citizens of Greenville as could find the time to attend the trial, which was held during working hours. Some were drawn from the men of the town who are too old or too sick to work, or who do not enjoy work and use the Court House as a club, sitting on the steps, chewing and smoking and looking down on Main Street through the hot, dancing air, when the weather is right for that, and going inside when it is better there. They were joined by a certain number of men and women who did not like the idea of people being taken out of jail and murdered, and by others who liked the idea quite well. There were also a number of the defendants' friends. Upstairs, in the deep gallery, sat about a hundred and fifty Negroes, under the care of two white bailiffs. Many of them, too, were court spectators by habit. It is said that very few members of the advanced group of colored people in the town were present. There were reasons, reticently guarded but strongly felt, that they did not want to make an issue of the case. They thought it best to sit back and let the white man settle whether or not he liked mob rule. But every day there went into court a number of colored men and women who were conspicuously handsome and fashionably dressed, and had resentment and the proud intention not to express it written all over them. They might be put down as Negroes who feel the humiliation of their race so deeply that they will not even join in the orthodox movements for its emancipation, because these are, to their raw sensitiveness, tainted with the assumption that Negroes have to behave like good children to win a favorable report from the white people. In the shadows of the balcony the dark faces of these people could not be seen.

. . .

The taxi-drivers of Greenville are drawn from the type of men who drive taxis anywhere. They are people who dislike steady work in a store or a factory or an office, or have not the aptitude for it, have a certain degree of mechanic intelligence, have no desire to rise very far in the world, enjoy driving for its own sake, and are not afraid of the dangers that threaten those who are on the road at night. They are, in fact, tough guys, untainted by intellectualism, and their detachment from the stable life of the community around them gives them a clan spirit that degenerates at times into the gang spirit. The local conditions in Greenville encourage this clan spirit. In every big town, the dangers that threaten taxi-drivers as they go about their work are formidable and shameful to society, and they increase year by year. In Greenville, they are very formidable indeed. A great many people are likely to hire taxis, for there are relatively few automobiles in the region; two-thirds of the people who are likely to hire a Greenville taxi live in small communities or isolated homes; it is so hot for the greater part of the year that people prefer to drive by night. Hence the taxi-drivers spend a great part of their time making journeys out of town after dark. In consequence, a large number of taxi-drivers have during the last few years been robbed and assaulted, sometimes seriously, by their fares.

On February 15, 1947, an incident occurred that drew the taxi-drivers of Greenville very close together. A driver named Brown picked up a Negro fare, a boy of twenty-four called Willie Earle, who asked him to drive to his mother's home in Pickens County, about eighteen miles from Greenville. Mrs. Earle, by the way, had given birth to Willie when she was fourteen. Both Willie Earle and Brown had been the victims of tragedy. Willie Earle had been a truck driver and had greatly enjoyed his occupation. But he was an epileptic, and though his mates conspired with him to conceal this fact from his employer, there came a day when he fell from the truck in a fit and injured himself. His employer, therefore, quite properly decided that he could not employ him on a job in which he was so likely to come to harm, and dismissed him. He could not get any other employment as a truck driver and was forced to work as a construction laborer, an occupation that he did not like so well and that brought him less money. He became extremely depressed, and began to drink heavily. His fits became more frequent, and he developed a great hostility to white men. He got into trouble, for the first time in his life, for a sudden and unprovoked assault on a contractor who employed him, and was sent to the penitentiary, from which he had not been long released when he made his journey with Brown. Brown's tragedy was also physical. He had been wounded in the first World War and had become a taxi-driver, although he was not of the usual type, because his state of health obliged him to take up work that he could leave when he needed rest. He was a man of thoughtful and kindly character. A Greenville resident who could be trusted told me that in the course of some social-service work he had come across a taxi-driver and his wife who had suffered exceptional misfortune, and that he had been most impressed by the part that Brown had played in helping them to get on their feet again. "You could quite fairly say," this resident told me, "that Brown was an outstanding man, who was a good influence on these taxi boys, and always tried to keep them out of trouble. Lynching is just the sort of thing he wouldn't have let them get into."

Willie Earle reached his home that night on foot. Brown was found bleeding from deep knife wounds beside his taxi a mile or two away and was taken to a hospital, where he sank rapidly. Willie was arrested, and put in Pickens County Jail. Late on the night of February 16th, the melancholy and passionate Mr. Roosevelt Carlos Hurd was, it was said, about certain business. Later, the jailer of the Pickens County Jail telephoned to the sheriff's office in Greenville to say that a mob of about fifty men had come to the jail in taxicabs and forced him to give Willie Earle over to them. A little later still, somebody telephoned to the Negro undertaker in the town of Pickens to tell him that there was a dead nigger in need of his offices by the slaughter-pen in a byroad off the main road from Greenville to Pickens. He then telephoned the coroner of Greenville County, whose men found Willie Earle's mutilated body lying at that place. He had been beaten and stabbed and shot in the body and the head. The bushes around him were splashed with his brain tissue. His own people sorrowed over his death with a grief that was the converse of the grief Brown's friends felt for him. They mourned Brown because he had looked after them; Willie Earle's friends mourned him because they had looked after him. He had made a number of respectable friends before he became morose and intractable.

. . .

Thirty-six hours after Willie Earle's body had been found, no arrest had been made. This was remarkable, because the lynching expedition—if there was a lynching expedition—had been planned in a café and a taxi-cab office that face each other across the parking lot at the back of the Court House. On the ground floor of the Court House is the sheriff's office, which has large windows looking on the parking lot. A staff sits in that office all night long. But either nobody noticed a number of taxi-drivers passing to and fro at hours when they would normally be going off duty or nobody remembered whom he had seen when he heard of a jail break by taxi-drivers the next day. When the thirty-six hours had elapsed, Attorney General Tom C. Clark sent in a number of F.B.I. men to look hard for the murderers of Willie Earle. This step evoked, of course, the automatic resentment against federal action which is characteristic of the South; but it should have been remembered that the murderers were believed to number about fifty, and Greenville had nothing like a big enough police staff to cope with such an extensive search. Very soon the F.B.I. had taken statements from twenty-six men, who, along with five others whom they had mentioned in their statements, were arrested and charged with committing murder, being accessories before or after the fact of murder, and conspiring to murder. It is hard to say, now that all these defendants have been acquitted of all these charges, how the statements are to be regarded. They consist largely of confessions that the defendants were concerned in the murder of Willie Earle. But the law has pronounced that they had no more to do with the murder than you or I or President Truman. The statements must, therefore, be works of fiction, romances that these inhabitants of Greenville were oddly inspired to weave around the tragic happenings in their midst. Here is what one romancer invented about the beginnings of that evil:

Between ten and eleven P.M. on February 16, 1947, I was at the Blue Bird Cab Office and heard some fellows, whose identities I do not know, say that the nigger ought to be taken out and lynched. I continued to work until about two A.M. February 17, 1947, at which time I returned to the Blue Bird Taxi Office where R. C. Hurd was working on the switchboard. After I had been at the office for a few minutes, Hurd made several telephone calls to other taxicab companies in Greenville, including the Yellow Cab Company, the Commercial Cab Company, and the Checker Cab Company. He asked each company to see how many men it wanted to go to Pickens. Each time he called he told them who he was. When he finished making the calls, he asked me to drive my cab, a '39 Ford coach which is number twenty-nine (29), and carry a load of men to Pickens. I told him that he was "the boss." He then got a telephone call from one of the taxicab companies and he told them he would not be able to go until Earl Humphries, night dispatcher, got back from supper. After Earl Humphries returned from supper, Hurd, myself, Ernest Stokes, and Henry Culberson and Shephard, all Blue Bird drivers, got in Culberson's cab, which was a '41 Ford colored blue. We rode to the Yellow Cab Company on West Court Street followed by Albert Sims in his cab. At the Yellow Cab Company, we met all the other cab drivers from the cab companies. After all got organized, the orders given me by R. C. Hurd were to go back and pick up my cab at the Blue Bird Office. I would like to say here that Hurd had already made arrangements for everybody to meet at the Yellow Cab Company.

These sentences touch on the feature that disquiets many citizens of Greenville: A great deal was going on, at an hour when the city is dead, right under the sheriff's windows, where a staff was passing the night hours without, presumably, many distractions. They also touch on the chief peril of humanity. Man, born simple, bravely faces complication and essays it. He makes his mind into a fine wire that can pry into the interstices between appearances and extract the secret of the structural intricacy of the universe; he uses the faculty of imitation he inherits from the ape to create on terms approximating this intricacy of creation; so there arrive such miracles as the telephone and the internal-combustion engine, which become the servants of the terrible simplicity of Mr. Hurd, and there we are back at the beginning again.

A string of about fifteen automobiles lined up for the expedition. All but one of these were taxicabs. In their statements, the taxi-drivers spoke of the one that was not a taxi as a "civilian" automobile and of the people who were not taxi-drivers as "civilians." When they got to Pickens County Jail, which lies on the corner of a highway and a side road, about twenty miles from Greenville, some of them parked on the highway and some on the side road. A taxi shone its spotlight on the front door, and they called the jailer down. When they told him they had come for the Negro, he said, "I guess you boys know what you're doing," and got the jail keys for them. The only protest that he seems to have uttered was a request that the men should not use profanity, in case his wife should hear it. He also, with a thoughtfulness of which nobody can complain, pointed out that there were two Negroes in the jail, and indicated which of the two had been guilty of nothing worse than passing a bad check.

· · ·

The men who took Willie Earle away were in a state of mind not accurately to be defined as blood lust. They were moved by an emotion that is held high in repute everywhere and especially high in this community. All over the world friendship is regarded a sacred bond, and in South Carolina it is held that it should override nearly all other considerations. The romances in statement form throw a light on the state of mind of those who later told of getting Willie Earle into a taxi and driving him to a quiet place where he was to be killed. One says that a taxi-driver sat beside him and "talked nice to him." He does not mean that he talked in a way that Willie Earle enjoyed but that the taxi-drivers thought that what he was saying was elevating. Mr. Hurd described how Willie Earle sat in the back seat of a Yellow Cab and a taxi-driver knelt on the front seat and exhorted him, "Now you have confessed to cutting Mr. Brown, now we want to know who was the other Negro with you." Willie Earle answered that he did not know; and it appears to be doubtful that there was another Negro with him. The taxi-driver continued, in the accents of complacent pietism, "You know we brought you out here to kill you. You don't want to die with a lie in your heart and on your tongue."

. . .

The leader for the prosecution was nominally Robert T. Ashmore, the Greenville County solicitor, a gentle and courteous person. But the leading prosecuting attorney was Sam Watt, who comes from the neighboring town of Spartanburg, a lawyer of high reputation throughout the South. He was assigned to the case by the Attorney General of the State of South Carolina at the suggestion of the Governor, about ten days after the F.B.I. men had gone in. When he arrived, the preliminaries of the case were over; and they had been conducted in a disastrous fashion. The statements, which were not sworn, might have been supplemented when the defendants applied to be released under bond, for it was perfectly possible to demand that the applicants should again recite their connection with the crime in the form of sworn affidavits prepared by their own attorneys. This had not been done. The defendants had been turned loose unconditionally, and most of them, by the time Sam Watt came into the case, had returned to their duties as taxi-drivers. A prosecutor who introduced these statements in court would be a very lucky man if he could support them by strong corroborative evidence, and a very unlucky one if he could not.

It cannot be said, therefore, that the prosecution had put together a valid argument for a conviction. The trial had not the pleasing pattern, the agreeable harmony and counterpoint, of good legal process, however much the Judge tried to redeem it. But whether the jury returned their verdict of not guilty because they recognized the weakness of the State's case, it was hard to guess. It was the habit of certain people connected with the case to refer to the jury with deep contempt, as a parcel of boobs who could be seduced into swallowing anything by anybody who knew how to tickle them up by the right mixture of brutish prejudice and corny sentimentality; and it was odd to notice that the people who most despised the jury were those who most despised the Negroes. To me, the jurymen looked well built and well groomed; and they stayed awake, which is the first and most difficult task of a juror, although they, like the attorneys, kept their coats on when the heat was a damp, embracing fever. I marvelled at nothing about this jury except its constitution.

. . .

Of the prosecuting attorneys, Mr. Ashmore made a speech that was not very spirited but was conscientious and accepted the moral values common to civilized people without making any compromise. Sam Watt, who has a deep and passionate loathing of violence and disorder, and who is such a good attorney that the imperfections of the case must have vexed him to his soul, handled the situation in his own way by using the statements to build up a picture of the lynching in all its vileness. It was a great, if highly local, speech, and it is possible that some of its effect will survive, though the close of the case cancelled it for the moment. That cancellation was due to the remarkable freedom of two of the defense attorneys from the moral values accepted by Mr. Ashmore and Mr. Watt. The two other defense attorneys accepted them; one wholly, the other partly. Mr. Bradley Morrah, Jr., accepted them wholly, Mr. Ben Bolt partly.

Both Mr. Marchant and Mr. Morrah gave the impression that they were stranded in the wrong century, like people locked in a train that has been shunted onto a siding. Mr. Morrah was as old-fashioned in appearance as Governor Dewey; he looked like a dandy of 1890. He was very likable, being small and delicately made yet obviously courageous; and there was nothing unlikable in his oratory. He told the court that he had known his cousin for twenty-five years and knew that he had never had a vicious thought, and he wished that it was possible for him to take John Marchant's heart out of his breast and turn it over in his hand so that the jury could see that there was not an evil impulse in it.

Mr. Ben Bolt is a slow-moving, soft-voiced, gray-haired person of noble appearance, who is said to make many speeches about the common man. . . . He pointed out that the Bible condemns conviction without several witnesses. It was not necessary to bring in the Bible to explain that, but Mr. Bolt was certainly going about his proper business when he proceeded to demonstrate the insufficiency of the evidence against the defendants. Representing the lynching as an episode that nobody but the meddlesome federal authorities would ever have thought of making a fuss over, he said, "Why, you would have thought someone had found a new atomic bomb," but "all it was was a dead nigger boy." This is not a specifically Southern attitude. All over the world there are people who may use the atomic bomb because they have forgotten that it is our duty to regard all lives, however alien and even repellent, as equally sacred.

Mr. John Bolt Culbertson's speeches were untainted by any regard for the values of civilization. He went all the way over to the dead-nigger-boy school of thought. Mr. Culbertson is a slender, narrow-chested man with a narrow head. His sparse hair is prematurely white, his nose is sharp, and his face is colorless except for his very pink lips. He wears rimless spectacles and his lashes are white. The backs of his hands are thickly covered with fine white hairs. In certain lights, he gives the impression of being covered with frost. He has a great reputation in the South as a liberal. He is the local attorney for the C.I.O. and has worked actively for it. He has also been a friend to the emancipation of the Negroes and has supported their demands for better education and the extension of civil rights. He recently made an address to Negro veterans, which took courage on his part and gave them great happiness. He is one of the very few white men in these parts who shake hands with Negroes and give them the prefix of Mr. or Mrs. or Miss. Many young people in Greenville who wish to play a part in the development of the New South look to him as an inspiring teacher, and many Negroes feel a peculiar devotion to him. Mr. Culbertson belongs to the school of oratory that walks up and down in front of the jury box. At the climactic points of his speeches, he adopts a crouching stance, puts his hands out in front of him, parallel to one another, and moves them in a rapid spin, as if he were a juggler and they were plates. Mr. Culbertson pandered to every folly that the jurors might be nursing in their bosoms. He spoke of the defendants as "these So'th'n boys." Only two or three could be considered boys. The ages of the others ranged from the late twenties to the fifties. It was interesting, by the way, to note how all the attorneys spoke with a much thicker Southern accent when they addressed the jury than when they were talking with their friends. Mr. Culbertson attacked the F.B.I. agents in terms that either meant nothing or meant that it was far less important to punish a murder than to keep out the federal authorities. He made the remark, strange to hear in a court of law, "If a Demo-cratic administration could do that to us, what would a Republican administration do to us down here?"

The thread on which these pearls were strung appeared to be the ar-gument that the murder of Willie Earle was of very slight importance except for its remote political consequences. Mr. Culbertson was to prove that he did not give this impression inadvertently. He went into his crouching stance, his hands were spinning, he shone with frosty glee, exultantly he cried, "Willie Earle is dead, and I wish more like him was dead." There was a delighted, giggling, almost coquettish response from the defendants and some of the spectators. Thunderously, the Judge called him to order. Culbertson, smiling at the defendants, almost wink-ing at them, said, "I didn't refer to Willie Earle as a Negro." When the Judge bade him be careful, he continued, still flirting with his audience, "There's a law against shooting a dog, but if a mad dog were loose in my community, I would shoot the dog and let them prosecute me." A more disgusting incident cannot have happened in any court of law in any time.

The attitude of Greenville toward this speech was disconcerting. Prosperous Greenville did not like it, but it likes very little that Mr. Cul-bertson does, and it explained that one could expect nothing better from him, because he is a liberal. If it was objected that this was precisely not the kind of speech that could be expected from a liberal, this Greenville answered that it was a horrid speech, and that liberals are horrid, an ar-gument that cannot be pursued very far.

It was for the speech made by the fourth defense attorney, Mr. Thomas Wofford, that Greenville apologized most unhappily, though most la-conically. Mr. Wofford is a person whom the town likes, or, to put it more accurately, for whom it feels an uneasy emotional concern. He is a man in his late thirties, red-haired, lightly built, and quick on his feet, intelligent, nerve-ridden, well mannered, with a look in his eyes like a kicking horse. In the preliminary stages of the case, when the Judge was compiling a list of questions to be put to the veniremen to determine their suitability as jurors in this case, Sam Watt desired that they should be asked if they were members of any "secret organization, lodge, or as-sociation." Mr. Wofford objected, on the ground that such a question might be "embarrassing."

All the defense attorneys exaggerated their Southern accents and as-sumed a false ingenuousness when they addressed the jury, but none more so than Mr. Wofford. This elegantly attired and accomplished person talked as if he had but the moment before taken his hands off the plow; and he was careful to mop the sweat from his brow, because it is well known that the simple admire an orator who gives out even from the pores. He excelled his colleagues not only in this play acting but in his contempt for the jury. He assumed that they hated strangers, as the stupid do. Like Mr. Culbertson, he disregarded the Judge's ruling that no alleged action of Willie Earle was to be mentioned as affording "justification, mitigation, or excuse" for the lynching. He said, "Mr. Watt argues, 'Thou shalt not kill.' I wonder if Willie Earle had ever read that statement." This was as flagrant a defense of the lynching as Mr. Culbertson's remark "Willie Earle is dead, and I wish more like him was dead" and the allusion to the mad dog. But it was much more dangerous, because it was not obviously disgusting. "We people get along pretty well," he said, "until they start interfering with us in Washington and points North," and he spoke of the Northern armies that had laid waste the South in the Civil War. He abused the "Northern agitators, radio commentators, and certain publications" for interfering in this case. He said that "they refer to us as 'a sleepy little town.' They say we are a backward state and poor—and we are. But this state is ours. To the historian, the South is the Old South. To the poet, it is the Sunny South. To the prophet, it is the New South. But to us, it is *our* South. I wish to God they'd leave us alone." This would be an attitude that one would respect in the case of the ordinary citizen of Greenville. But in view of Mr. Wofford's desire not to embarrass secret organizations, his hostility to all law-enforcement agencies, and his attitude toward murder, it would be interesting to know what he wanted to be left alone to do.

· · ·

Shortly after three o'clock, the jury went out to consider their verdict and the Judge left the bench. He had directed that the defendants need not be taken out, and might sit in court and visit with their families and friends. So now the court turned into a not enjoyable party, at which one was able to observe more closely certain personalities of the trial. There was Mrs. Brown, the widow of the murdered taxi-driver, a spare, spectacled woman of the same austere type as the Hurds. She was dressed in heavy but smart mourning, with a veiled hat tipped sharply on one side, and she was chewing gum. So, too, was the professional bondsman who was the animating spirit of the committee that had raised funds for the defense of the defendants, a vast, blond, baldish man with the face of a brooding giant baby; but he was not genteel, as she was—he opened his mouth so wide at every chew that his gum became a matter of public interest. It had been noticeable during the trial that whenever the Judge showed hostility to the introduction of race hatred into the proceedings, this man's chewing became particularly wide and vulpine. A judge from another local court, and various other Greenville citizens, drifted up to the press table and engaged the strangers in defensive conversation. The Southern inferiority complex took charge. They supposed that an English visitor would be shocked by the lynching, but it was impossible for anybody to understand who had always lived in a peaceable community where there was no race problem. . . . I said what I had been saying constantly since my arrival: that lately Europe had not been really what one could call a peaceable community, and that my standards of violence were quite high, and that the lynching party did not seem very important to me as an outbreak of violence but that it was important as an indication of misery; that we English had a very complex and massive race problem in South Africa, where one of the indubitably great men of the British Empire, General Smuts, professed views on the color bar which would strike Greenville as fairly reactionary; and that my Northern friends, on hearing that I was going to the lynching party, had remarked that while Southern lawlessness has a pardonable origin in a tragic past, Northern lawlessness has none and is therefore far more disgraceful. What I said brought no response. We might have been sitting each in a glass case built by history.

. . .

At a little after half past eight, it was known that the jury had sounded its buzzer, which meant that they had made up their minds. This certainly meant that the accused persons had been acquitted of all charges. The jurymen had been out only five hours and a quarter, and they would have had to stay out much longer than that before all of them would have consented to a conviction; and they would have had to stay out much longer before they could have announced that they had failed to agree. The press knew what the verdict was and knew there was still an hour till the Judge would return. Yet we knew too that it is not what happens that matters so much as how it happens. Up in the gallery, thirteen Negroes were sitting in attitudes of fatigue and despair. Behind them, three windows looked on a night whitened by the lights of Main Street.

This had been a miserable case for these Negroes. They had not even been able to have the same emotional release that would have been granted them if Willie Earle had been an innocent victim, a sainted martyr. It happened that the only constructive proposal concerning this morass of misery stretching out to infinity round this case that I heard during my stay at Greenville came from a Negro. That, oddly enough, was a plea for the extension of the Jim Crow system. "There is nothing I wish for more," he said, "than a law that would prohibit Negroes from riding in taxicabs driven by white men. They love to do it. We all love to do it. Can't you guess why? Because it is the only time we can pay a white man to act as a servant to us. And that does something to me, even though I can check up on myself and see what's happening. I say to myself, 'This is fine! I'm hiring this white man! He's doing a chore for me!'" He threw his head back and breathed deeply and patted his chest, to show how he felt. "If riding in a white taxicab does that to me, what do you think it does to Negroes who haven't been raised right or are full of liquor? Then queer things happen, mighty queer things. Killing is only one of them."

. . .

At length, the Judge was seen standing at the open door of his chambers, and the defendants were brought into court. They were all very frightened. Mr. Hurd, though he was still confused, seemed to be asking himself if he had not been greatly deceived. Fat Joy was shifting along, wearing sadness as incongruously as fat men do. As they sat down, their wives clasped them in their arms, and they clung together, melting in the weakness of their common fear. The Judge came onto the bench and took some measures for the preservation of order in the court. The jury entered. One juror was smiling; one was looking desperately ashamed; the others looked stolid and secretive, as they had done all through the trial. They handed the slips on which they had recorded their verdicts to the clerk of the court, who handed them to the Judge. He read them through to himself, and a flush spread over his face.

As soon as the clerk had read the verdicts aloud and the Judge had left the bench and the courtroom, which he did without thanking the jury, the courtroom became, in a flash, something else. It might have been a honky-tonk. The Greenville citizens who had come as spectators were filing out quietly and thoughtfully. Whatever their opinions were, they were not to recover their usual spirits for some days. As they went, they looked over their shoulders at the knot of orgiastic joy that had instantly been formed by the defendants and their supporters. Mr. Hurd and his father did not give such spectacular signs of relief as the others. They gripped each other tightly for a moment, then shook hands stiffly, but in wide, benedictory movements, with the friends who gathered around them with the ardent feeling that among the defendants Mr. Hurd especially was to be congratulated. The father and son were grinning shyly, but in their eyes was a terrible light. They knew again that they were the chosen vessels of the Lord. Later, Mr. Hurd, asked for a statement, was to say, "Justice has been done . . . both ways." Meanwhile, the other defendants were kissing and clasping their wives, their wives were laying their heads on their husbands' chests and nuzzling in an ecstasy of animal affection, while the laughing men stretched out their hands to their friends, who sawed them up and down. They shouted, they whistled, they laughed, they cried; above all, they shone with self-satisfaction. In fact, make no mistake, these people interpreted the verdict as a vote of confidence passed by the community. They interpreted it as a kind of election to authority.

· · ·

There could be no more pathetic scene than these taxi-drivers and their wives, the deprived children of difficult history, who were rejoicing at a salvation that was actually a deliverance to danger. They had been saved from the electric chair and from prison by men who had conducted their defense without taking a minute off to state or imply that even if a man is a murderer one must not murder him and that murder is foul. These people had been plunged back into chaos. It is to be remembered that in their statements these men fully inculpated each other. At present they are unified by the trial, but when the tension is over, there will come into their minds that they were not so well treated as they might have been by their friends. Then the propaganda for murder which was so freely dished out to them during their trial may bear its fruit.

It was impossible to watch this scene of delirium, which had been conjured up by a mixture of clownishness, ambition, and sullen malice, without feeling a desire for action. Supposing that one lived in a town, decent but tragic, which had been trodden into the dust and had risen again, and that there were men in that town who threatened every force in that town which raised it up and encouraged every force which dragged it back into the dust; then lynching would be a joy. It would be, indeed, a very great delight to go through the night to the home of such a man, with a few loyal friends, and walk in so softly that he was surprised and say to him, "You meant to have your secret bands to steal in on your friends and take them out into the darkness, but it is not right that you should murder what we love without paying the price, and the law is not punishing you as it should." And when we had driven him to some place where we would not be disturbed, we would make him confess his treacheries and the ruses by which he had turned the people's misfortunes to his profit. It would be only right that he should purge himself of his sins. Then we would kill him, but not quickly, for there would be no reason that a man who had caused such pain should himself be allowed to flee quickly to the shelter of death. The program would have seemed superb had it not been for two decent Greenville people, a man and a woman, who stopped as they went out of the courtroom and spoke to me, because they were so miserable that they had to speak to someone. "This is only the beginning," the man said. He was right. It was the beginning of a number of odd things. Irrational events breed irrational events. The next day I was to see a Negro porter at the parking place of a resort hotel near Greenville insult white guests as I have never seen a white hotel employee insult guests; there were to be minor assaults all over the state; there was to be the lynching party in North Carolina. "It is like a fever," said the woman, tears standing in her eyes behind her glasses. "It spreads, it's an infection, it's just like a fever." I was prepared to admit that she, too, was right.

LETTER FROM A CAMPAIGN TRAIN

Richard Rovere

OCTOBER 16, 1948 (ON THE 1948 PRESIDENTIAL CAMPAIGN)

CANDIDATES NOTORIOUSLY PROMISE better than they ever perform, but if Governor Dewey manages the Presidency half as well as he is managing his campaign for it, we are about to have four, eight, twelve, sixteen years of cool, sleek efficiency in government. I venture upon this prophecy after quite a spell of riding aboard the Dewey Victory Special, the train that has been hauling the Republican candidate, his wife, and his entourage of advisers, well-wishers, favor-curriers, and newspapermen up and down the country since mid-September. Before I looked in on the Dewey campaign, I had acquired some seasoning and a basis for comparison by serving a correspondent's hitch on the train that took President Truman and his similar, but far smaller, group of fellow-passengers over much the same route. As far as the arts and techniques, as distinct from the political content, of the campaigns are concerned, the difference between the Democratic and Republican operation is, I calculate, thirty or forty years. It is the difference between horsehair and foam rubber, between the coal-stove griddle and the pop-up toaster. Dewey is the pop-up toaster.

Everything I've seen of the Dewey campaign is slick and snappy. This is in strong contrast to the general dowdiness and good-natured slovenliness of the Truman campaign, at least when and where I observed it. Truman's mass meetings were all old-style political rallies, brightened up, on occasion, by some droopy bunting and by Department of Sanitation brass bands. In San Francisco, the Democrats contracted a most unfortunate alliance with a musical branch of the local parent-teacher association, which called itself the Mother Singers of America. The Mother Singers were authentic mothers—and grandmothers—who wrapped themselves in yards of brown monk's cloth and sang the kind of songs you would expect them to. The Dewey group favors professional musicians, professional decorators, and professionals in everything else. All the way down the line, his effects are more dramatic and more electrifying. At a Truman meeting, the President, as a rule, takes his seat on the platform and sits quietly, a slender and almost pathetic figure surrounded by florid police commissioners and senators of heroic bulk, through all the preliminaries. When his turn finally comes to speak, his advance toward the microphone hardly takes the multitude by storm. Dewey's entrances are delayed. He remains in the wings until all the invocations and endorsements are over. Sometimes he stays away from the meeting hall until the last moment. Then, with a great whining of motorcycle-escort sirens to hush the crowd and build up suspense, he arrives. The instant his name is spoken, he comes onstage, seemingly from nowhere, arms outstretched to embrace the crowd and gather in the applause that breaks the hush. It is an uncannily effective piece of business. Dewey doesn't seem to walk; he coasts out like a man who has been mounted on casters and given a tremendous shove from behind. However it is done, he rouses the crowd to a peak of excitement and enthusiasm, and he has to wait an agreeably long while for the racket to die down.

Dewey likes drama, but he has an obvious distaste for the horseplay side of politics. He accepts honorary memberships in sheriffs' posses and fraternal organizations, but he is uncomfortable during the installation ceremonies. On his first transcontinental tour after his nomination, he collected some fifteen cowpuncher hats, but he refused to try on any of them in public. The only time he got into the spirit of things was at his rally in the Hollywood Bowl. For this gathering, his local managers, mainly movie people, arranged a first-class variety show. In addition to assembling a lot of stars who endorsed the candidate in short, pithy, gag-laden speeches, they hired a marimba band and a chorus line for the preliminary entertainment. For the invocations, they recruited a minister, a priest, and a rabbi all of whom could have played romantic leads themselves. At the end of Dewey's speech, the marimba band struck up "God Bless America," as a recessional. Dewey was still standing at the microphone, and Mrs. Dewey, as she always does after he finishes, came forward to join him. Perhaps the pageantry finally overcame him, for suddenly he breathed deep and took aboard a full load of the fine night air of Hollywood. Then he gave vent to the rich baritone he spent so many years developing. ". . . land that I love," he sang, and, slipping an arm around Mrs. Dewey's waist, looked encouragingly at her. Mrs. Dewey came in on the next line, and together they went all the way through the rest of the Irving Berlin anthem.

· · ·

It is one of the paradoxes of 1948 that the man in office is a much less experienced campaigner than the man who is seeking to win the office. Truman was on the public payroll when Dewey was still a college boy in Michigan, but his serious campaigning has been limited to two tries for the United States Senate and one for the Vice-Presidency. It wasn't bush-league stuff, but it wasn't big-league, either. Dewey, on the other hand, is entitled to wear service stripes for three major campaigns. In 1940, he sought the Republican nomination as vigorously as he sought the main prize in 1944 and is seeking it now. The effects are apparent in the organization and planning of every phase of his campaign travels. There is far more foresight and far better timing and scheduling than in the President's tour. Dewey's staff work is superior, too. For example, correspondents with Truman were forced, while I was aboard his train, to miss deadline after deadline because they had to wait too long for advance copies of the President's speeches. Presumably his ghost-writers, some of whom were on the train and some of whom were back in Washington, were agonizing up to the zero hour, trying to make their sentences come out right. And then the sentences didn't come out right anyway. The rhetoric that Truman was given to deliver was coarse, gritty, old-fashioned political stuff, with about as much flow as oatmeal. Dewey's speeches, which reporters can put on the telegraph wires twelve to twenty-four hours before delivery time, are as smooth and glossy as chromium. It may be that, on analysis, their cliché content would turn out to be neither much lower nor much higher than that of Truman's speeches, but, as one man on the challenger's train put it, they are written and spoken in such a manner that they give one the feeling Dewey has not borrowed his clichés from the masters but has minted them all by himself.

A conscientious search for the literary antecedents of Dewey's speeches might show that the strongest influence is the *Reader's Digest*. They are full of the good cheer, the defiant optimism, the inspirational tone, and the breathtaking simplification that have made that magazine so popular. If Dewey's speeches are not consciously modelled on the *Digest*, there are few of them that would not seem at home in its pages. "Your future lies ahead of you," a catchy line that turned up in several of the speeches, would make a splendid *Digest* title. Moreover, in sound *Digest* fashion, Dewey is promising to start, when he gets to Washington, "the greatest pruning and weeding operation in American history." When the thought first occurred to me that Dewey or his advisers might have picked up a few tricks from the *Digest*, I asked James C. Hagerty, the candidate's press secretary, if he had any idea whether or not this was the case. "I hardly think so," Hagerty said. "The Governor has a style all his own that he's been working on for years." Even so, it is worth noting that one of the important personages aboard the Dewey train is Stanley High, a Roving Editor of the *Digest* and the author of some of the most celebrated articles it has published in recent years. The dope on Mr. High, as I got it from Hagerty, is that he is travelling with Dewey not as an author but as a former clergyman. His function, I was told, is to advise Dewey on the religious implications of political issues and on the political implications of religious issues. Still, it might be that, unknown to Hagerty, Mr. High finds time, in between issues, to make a phrase here and condense a line of argument there.

Dewey's effect on his audience is unquestionably greater than Truman's. He does not, so far as I am able to judge, draw larger crowds. The business of estimating the size of crowds is, by the way, probably one of the most nonsensical and misleading aspects of political reporting. Some correspondents make a hobby of it, and conceivably their technique improves with practice, but most of them rely on police officials for their figures. Suspecting that a policeman can be as wrong as the next man, I made a simple test at one Dewey meeting. I asked the ranking police official for his estimate and then asked the manager of the auditorium for his. The policeman's count, which turned up in a number of newspapers, was 50 percent higher. Since the manager's standard of living is directly related to the size of the audiences in his auditorium, I imagine it would be safer to string along with him. Then, there is always an element of fortuitousness in the size of the street crowds that watch the candidates ride through the big cities. There is no way of telling how many people have come out of their way to see the distinguished visitor and how many just happen to be around. It is customary for campaign managers to take advantage of the fortuitous element. Campaign trains have an oddly predictable way of arriving for afternoon meetings just before the lunch hour and for evening meetings just before the stores and offices close. A candidate's procession never goes directly from the depot to its destination in town. The Civic Center may be only three or four blocks up State Street from the Union Station, but the motorcade is certain to follow a route that covers at least thirty blocks, and thereby catches a lot more innocent bystanders. Possibly the best way to calculate the turnout of admirers would be to estimate the number of onlookers carrying bundles and then subtract them from the total.

For judging crowds, the ear is probably a more reliable instrument than the eye. Its verdict, I would say, favored Dewey almost everywhere. No Truman crowd that I heard responded with more than elementary courtesy and occasionally mild and rather weary approval. Partly, no doubt, this was because the President has a lamentable way of swallowing the very lines he ought to bellow or snarl, and partly, I think, it was because he simply didn't have his audience with him. Dewey's ovations are never, as the phrase goes, thundering, but his applause is not mere politeness. Dewey is not an orator in the classic sense, but he is a first-class elocutionist, and when he fixes his eyes on the crowd and says that the way to avoid having Communists in the government is to avoid appointing them in the first place, as he plans to do, he gets what he wants from the customers, which means, naturally, that they are getting what they want from him.

• • •

The junior-executive briskness in the running of the Dewey campaign extends, quite mysteriously, to many phases of life aboard the train. Campaign trains become, in their few weeks of existence, compact social organizations. They develop their own mores and their own institutions. One of the most remarkable—indeed, almost weird—features of life on them is the way the spirit of the leading passenger, riding in the last car, seems to dominate and mold the spirit of the entourage. It is understandable that this should happen to the staff of the candidate, but it actually affects even the newspapermen. Candidates have nothing to do with the selection of the reporters who accompany them. In some cases, to be sure, the reporters select candidates, and it is conceivable that psychological affinity may have influenced their choices. But the effect of that affinity would be, at best, a small one, and it would govern only a few journalists. Yet I am prepared to testify under oath that the atmosphere even in the press section of the Truman train is pure Harry Truman, and the atmosphere in the press section of the Dewey train is pure Tom Dewey. One is like life in the back rooms at District Headquarters, the other like life in the Greenwich Country Club. The favorite beverage in the club cars on the Truman train, when I was on it, was the Kentucky bourbon highball, before, during, and after meals. I don't recall seeing a single cocktail served. Highballs are often seen on the Dewey train, but Martinis and Manhattans are more in vogue. The principal diversion on the Truman train was poker, generally seven-card stud. At least two games were always in progress. If any poker is played on the Dewey train, it is played behind closed compartment doors. There are, however, several spirited bridge games going on all the time.

It may be that the correspondents with Truman took to the more rugged forms of recreation because their life was more rugged. Life with Truman was not exactly primitive but, compared to life with Dewey, it was hard. If you wanted anything laundered, you did it yourself, in a Pullman basin. When you detrained anywhere for an overnight stay, it was every man for himself. You carried your duffel and scrabbled for your food. If a man was such a slave to duty that he felt obliged to hear what the President said in his back-platform addresses, he had to climb down off the train, run to the rear end, mingle with the crowd, and listen. Often, this was a hazardous undertaking, for the President was given to speaking late at night to crowds precariously assembled on sections of roadbed built up fifteen or twenty feet above the surrounding land. The natives knew the contours of the ground, but the reporters did not, and more than one of them tumbled down a cindery embankment. The Dewey organization sees that none of these inconveniences trouble the life of anyone on the Governor's train. Whenever the Dewey train stops overnight, luggage vanishes from your berth and is waiting for you in the hotel room you have been assigned. Good Republican caterers have hot coffee and thick roast-beef sandwiches waiting in the press rooms at every stopover. Laundries are alerted a thousand miles ahead to be ready to turn out heavy loads in a few hours. There is really no need for anyone to bestir himself and risk his life to hear the whistle-stop speeches, since almost the entire train is wired for sound and the words of the Governor are carried over the public-address system.

· · ·

Truman and Dewey are contrasting types, but in many fundamental ways they act on roughly the same principles and proceed toward roughly the same ends. Office-seeking is a great leveller. Most men who engage in it are sooner or later forced to abandon themselves to the ancient practices of audience-flattering, enemy-vilifying, name-remembering, moon-promising, and the like. In these matters, the 1948 candidates are just about neck and neck. Offhand, I would say that Truman is working a little harder at enemy-vilifying and name-remembering, while Dewey looks a little stronger in audience-flattering and also has a slight edge in the scope and beauty of his promises. This last is a natural consequence of the relative positions of the two men. Truman, being in office, can hardly claim the ability to deliver in a second term what he has manifestly been unable to deliver in his first. There is no one, however, to gainsay Dewey when he asserts that under his leadership "every American will walk forward side by side with every other American." Some drillmasters might quibble over the difficulty of achieving such a formation, but no one pays any attention to logic in this season of the quadrennium.

It is probably a good thing for the sanity of the Republic that we do have this suspension of logic during campaigns, for the fact is that reason is outraged not only by the speeches of the candidates but by the very idea of this travelling up and down the country to make them. I have been unable to find, on the Dewey train, the Truman train, or anywhere else, a single impartial and responsible observer of national affairs who is willing to defend the thesis that this tearing around will affect the electoral vote in even one state. There are, no doubt, some people in every community who will vote for the man who says the pleasantest things about the local crop and the local rainfall, but their number is probably balanced by the number of intelligent citizens who will decide, the next morning, to vote *against* the man who disturbed their children's rest by roaring through the night, surrounded by a hundred motorcycle cops with a hundred sirens, so that he could deliver an address pointing out that the Republicans invented the depression or that the Democrats invented Communism. Nobody knows exactly why or when people switch political allegiances, but it is known that an insignificant number of them do during a campaign. Jim Farley said, in the early Roosevelt days, that every vote in the country was frozen by October 1st, and the work done by Mr. Roper and Dr. Gallup indicates that the results are settled long before that.

In theory, the institution of the travelling campaign is educational as well as political. It gives the voters a chance to hear the candidates and learn their views first-hand. No doubt the theory had great merit a century ago, but today it is possible for any citizen to hear the candidates' voices and to learn their views in his own home, where the acoustics are a good deal better than in a stadium or auditorium. If an appraisal of views is the important goal, the conscientious citizen must attend to that matter between campaigns, not during them, for what he gets around election time is not a candidate's idea of things but his own, as nearly as the candidate is able to figure it out and reproduce it. One could also argue that it is a healthy thing in a democracy for the people to see their Presidents and Presidents-to-be, to give them the once-over and observe what psychologists call their "expressive movements." This notion has some measure of plausibility, but it will be harder to find it four years from now, when, they tell us, television will be installed in every American home that today has radio. There will be no reason then for not chopping the observation platform from some obsolete Pullman, setting it up in a television studio, and hiring a few extras to lug aboard the baskets of apples, the Stetsons, and the bouquets.

One feature of the old ritual, however, will be beyond the grasp of science for quite a while yet. That is handshaking. "Hell's bells!" a political adviser on one of the trains said to me. "Everybody knows that we don't go through all this business to win friends or influence people. We go through it to keep the friends we've already got. The only important thing that happens on this train is the handshaking and hello-there-Jacking that go on back in the caboose. We've got a party organization to keep going, and the best way to keep it going is to have the big men in the party get out and say nice things to the little men. I don't care which party it is. It means everything to the strangers you see in the club cars to go back home and tell how they rode down to the state line with the big wheel and how, when they went into his private car, he remembered them well from his last swing around the country. If you think party organizations are not a good and necessary thing in a democracy, then you can write all this off as a lot of nonsense. If you think they're important, then you can't deny the usefulness of these trips." Stated in those terms, the question is a weighty one.

SYMBOL OF ALL WE POSSESS

Lillian Ross

OCTOBER 22, 1949 (ON THE MISS AMERICA PAGEANT)

THERE ARE THIRTEEN MILLION WOMEN in the United States between the ages of eighteen and twenty-eight. All of them were eligible to compete for the title of Miss America in the annual contest staged in Atlantic City last month if they were high-school graduates, were not and had never been married, and were not Negroes. Ten thousand of them participated in preliminary contests held in all but three of the forty-eight states. Then, one cool September day, a Miss from each of these states, together with a Miss New York City, a Miss Greater Philadelphia, a Miss Chicago, a Miss District of Columbia, a Miss Canada, a Miss Puerto Rico, and a Miss Hawaii, arrived in Atlantic City to display her beauty, poise, grace, physique, personality, and talent. The primary, and most obvious, stake in the contest was a twenty-five-thousand-dollar scholarship fund—a five-thousand-dollar scholarship for the winner and lesser ones for fourteen runners-up—which had been established by the makers of Nash automobiles, Catalina swim suits, and a cotton fabric known as Everglaze. The winner would also get a new four-door Nash sedan, a dozen Catalina swim suits, and a wardrobe of sixty Everglaze garments. The contest was called the Miss America Pageant. The fifty-two competitors went into it seeking, beyond the prizes, great decisions. Exactly what was decided, they are still trying to find out.

Miss New York State was a twenty-two-year-old registered nurse named Wanda Nalepa, who lives in the Bronx. She has honey-blond hair, green eyes, and a light complexion, and is five feet three. Some other statistics gathered by Miss America Pageant officials are: weight, 108; bust, 34; waist, 23; thigh, 19; hips, 34; calf, 12¼; ankle, 7½; shoe size, 5; dress size, 10. She was asked in an official questionnaire why she had entered the Atlantic City contest. She answered that her friends had urged her to. The day before the contest was to start, I telephoned Miss Nalepa at her home to ask when she was leaving for Atlantic City. She said that she was driving down the next morning and invited me to go along.

Miss Nalepa lives in a second-floor walkup apartment in a building near 164th Street on Sherman Avenue, a couple of blocks from the Grand Concourse. At eight the following morning, I was greeted at the door of the Nalepa flat by a thin young man in his late twenties wearing rimless glasses. "Come right in, Miss," he said. "I'm Teddy, Wanda's brother. Wanda's getting dressed." He led me into a small, dim living room, and I sat down in a chair next to a table. On the table were two trophies—a silver loving cup saying "Miss Sullivan County 1949" and a plastic statuette saying "Miss New York State 1949"—and a two-panel picture folder showing, on one side, Miss Nalepa in a bathing suit and, on the other, Miss Nalepa in a nurse's uniform. Teddy sat on the edge of a couch and stared self-consciously at a crucifix and a holy picture on the wall across the room. I asked him if he was going to Atlantic City. He said that he was a tool-and-die maker and had to work. "Bob—that's Wanda's boy friend—he's driving you down," he said. "Bob can get more time off. He's assistant manager for a finance company."

One by one, the family wandered into the room—Mr. Nalepa, a short, tired-looking man who resembles Teddy and who works in a factory making rattan furniture; Mrs. Nalepa, a small, shy woman with gray hair; and Wanda's younger sister, Helen, a high-school senior. Each of them nodded to me or said hello, but nobody said anything much after that. Then a pair of French doors opened and Wanda came in and said hello to me. Everybody studied her. She wore an eggshell straw sailor hat set back on her head, a navy-blue dotted-swiss dress, blue stockings, and high-heeled navy-blue pumps. For jewelry, she wore only a sturdy wristwatch with a leather strap and her nursing-school graduation ring.

"I hope this looks all right," Miss Nalepa said in a thin, uncertain voice. "I didn't know what to wear."

"Looks all right," her father said.

The doorbell rang. Teddy said that it must be Bob. It was Bob—a tall, gaunt man of about thirty with a worried face. He nodded to everybody, picked up Miss Nalepa's luggage and threw several evening gowns over one arm, said that we ought to get going, and started downstairs.

"Well, goodbye," said Miss Nalepa.

"Don't forget to stand up straight," her sister said.

"What about breakfast?" her mother asked mildly.

"I don't feel like eating," Miss Nalepa said.

"Good luck, Wanda," said Teddy.

"Well, goodbye," Miss Nalepa said again, looking at her father.

"All right, all right, goodbye," her father said.

Miss Nalepa was about to walk out the door when her mother stepped up timidly and gave her a peck on the cheek. As we were going downstairs together, Miss Nalepa clutched at my wrist. Her hand was cold. "That's the second time I ever remember my mother kissed me," she said, with a nervous laugh. "The first time was when I graduated from high school. I looked around to see if anybody was watching us, I was so embarrassed."

We found Bob and a pudgy, bald-headed man named Frank stowing the bags in the luggage compartment of a 1948 Pontiac sedan. I learned that Frank, a friend of Bob's, was going along, too. Women neighbors in housecoats were leaning out of windows to watch the departure. Frank told Miss Nalepa that a photograph of her taken from the rear had come out fine. "Wanda has a perfect back," he said to me. "I'm getting this picture printed in the *National Chiropractic Journal*. I'm a chiropractor."

I got in front, with Bob and Miss Nalepa. Frank got in back. On our way downtown, Miss Nalepa told me that we were to stop at Grand Central to pick up her chaperone, a Miss Neville. Miss Neville represented WKBW, the radio station in Buffalo that, with the blessings of the Miss America Pageant people but without any official blessings from Albany, had sponsored the New York State contest. A couple of weeks before competing in that one, which was held at the Crystal Beach Amusement Park, near Buffalo, Miss Nalepa had won the title of Miss Sullivan County in a contest held in the town of Monticello, thus qualifying for the state contest, and a week or so before that she had won the title of Miss White Roe Inn, the inn being situated outside the town of Livingston Manor, in Sullivan County. She had gone to the inn for a short vacation at the insistence of a friend who thought she could win the beauty contest there. Miss Nalepa had heard of such contests and of others held at local theatres but hadn't ever entered one before. "I never had the nerve," she told me. "I always knew I was pretty, but it always made me feel uncomfortable. When I was six, I remember a little boy in the first grade who used to watch me. I was terrified. I used to run home from school every day. At parties, when I was older, the boys paid a lot of attention to me, and I didn't like it. I wanted the other girls to get attention, too." Miss Nalepa went to a vocational high school, to study dressmaking; worked in a five-and-ten-cent store for a while after graduation; considered taking singing lessons but dropped the idea after her two sisters told her she had no singing ability; and went to the Rhodes School, in New York City, for a pre-nursing course and then to Mount Sinai Hospital, where she got her R.N. degree in 1948. She didn't like to go out on dates with the hospital doctors. "Doctors are too forward," she said.

• • •

At Grand Central, Miss Neville, a pleasant, gray-haired lady, who said she had not been in Atlantic City for twenty years and was very enthusiastic about going there now, got in the back seat with Frank, and they began talking about chiropractic. As we headed for the Holland Tunnel, the three of us in the front seat discussed the contest. "Don't expect much and you won't be disappointed," Miss Nalepa said, clutching Bob's arm. She thought it would be nice to have some scholarship money and said that if she won any, she might use it to learn to play some musical instrument. No money had come with the Miss White Roe Inn title. She had received seventy-five dollars from the Sullivan County Resort Association for becoming Miss Sullivan County, and a picture of her in a bathing suit had appeared in the New York *Daily News* captioned "Having Wandaful Time." When she was named Miss New York State, she was given three evening gowns and two pieces of luggage. She earned ten dollars a day nursing, but she hadn't worked for more than a month— not since she started entering beauty contests—and she had had to borrow three hundred dollars from members of her family for clothes, cosmetics, jewelry, a quick, $67.50 course in modelling, and other things designed to enhance beauty, poise, and personality. She was worried about being only five feet three. The Miss Americas of the preceding six years had all been five feet seven or more. The contestants would be judged on four counts: appearance in a bathing suit, appearance in an evening gown, personality, and talent. Miss Nalepa was wondering about her talent. Her act, as she planned it, was going to consist of getting up in her nurse's uniform and making a little speech about her nursing experience.

"I don't know what else I can do to show I've got talent," she said. "All I know how to do is give a good back rub."

"Listen, what you need right now is a good meal," Bob said.

Miss Nalepa said she wasn't hungry.

"You've got to eat," Bob said. "You're too skinny."

"You've got to eat," Frank repeated. "You're too skinny."

We stopped for breakfast at a roadside restaurant. Miss Nalepa had only half a cheeseburger and a few sips of tea.

· · ·

In Atlantic City, Miss Nalepa and her chaperone headed for the hotel they had been assigned to, the Marlborough-Blenheim, where they were to share a double room. I said I was going to check in at the Claridge, across the street, and Bob offered to take my bag over. As the two of us walked over, he said that he and Frank were going to hang around for a short while and then go back to New York. "She's not going to win," he said. "I told her she's not going to win. That nursing isn't the right kind of talent. They'll want singing or dancing or something like that."

In the lobby there were large photographs of Miss America of 1948, and of the current Miss Arizona, Miss Florida, Miss Chicago, and Miss District of Columbia, all of whom, I learned from my bellhop, had been assigned to that hotel. "Big crowd comes down every year to see the crowning of Miss America," he said. "This is America's Bagdad-by-the-Sea. The only place on the ocean where you'll find a big crowd relaxing at recreations in the fall."

On my bureau was a small paper cutout doll labelled "Miss America, Be Be Shopp, in her official gown of Everglaze moire for the Miss America Pageant, September 6–11, 1949."

"You seen Be Be yet?" an elevator boy with round shoulders and watery eyes asked me as I was going back down. "Be Be's staying with us. Be Be looks real good. Better than last year. You seen Miss Florida yet?" I shook my head. "She's something!" he said.

I went out to the boardwalk, where booths for the sale of tickets to the Pageant had been set up in a line running down the middle, between two rows of Bingo Temples, billboard pictures of horses diving into the ocean from the Steel Pier, and places named Jewelry Riot, Ptomaine

Tavern, and the Grecian Temple. The roller chairs were rolling in and out among the ticket booths. "Get your ticket now to see the beauties at the parade!" a middle-aged lady called to me from one of them. "Bleacher seats are twenty-five cents cheaper than last year!"

The contestants were registering for the Pageant at the Traymore, so I went over there. A couple of dozen policemen were standing outside the registration room. I asked one of them if Miss New York State had arrived. "Not yet, sister," he said. "Stick around. I got my eye on all of them."

A white-haired gentleman wearing a green-and-purple checked jacket asked him how the registration was going.

"You want to see the beauties, buy a ticket to the Pageant," the policeman said.

"They got any tall ones?" asked the gentleman.

"Yeah, they got some tall ones," the policeman said. "Utah is five, ten. She comes from Bountiful—Bountiful, Utah."

"Hope it won't rain for the parade tomorrow," said the gentleman.

"It don't look too promising," observed the policeman.

Miss Nalepa and her chaperone turned up, and I went inside with them. The contestants were standing in an uneven line, looking unhappily at each other, before a table presided over by a middle-aged woman with a Southern accent. She was Miss Lenora Slaughter, the executive director of the Pageant. The atmosphere was hushed and edgy, but Miss Slaughter was extravagantly cheerful as she handed out badges and ribbons to the contestants. When Miss Nalepa's turn came to register, Miss Slaughter gave her a vigorous hug, called her darling, handed her a ribbon reading "New York State," and told her to wear it on her bathing suit, from the right shoulder to the left hip. I introduced myself to Miss Slaughter, and she shook my hand fervently. "You'll want to follow our working schedule," she said, giving me a booklet. "All the girls are going upstairs now to be fitted with their Catalina bathing suits, and then they get their pictures taken, and tonight we're having a nice meeting with all the girls, to tell them what's what. The Queen—Miss America of 1948; we call Miss America the Queen—will be there. You're welcome to come. . . . Miss California!" she cried. I moved on and Miss California took my place. Miss New York State clutched at my arm again and nodded toward Miss California, who had a large, square face, long blond hair, and large blue eyes. (Height, 5'6¼; weight, 124; bust, 36; waist, 24¼; thigh, 20; hips, 36; shoe size, 6½-AA; dress size, 12; age, 19. Reason for entering the contest: "To gain poise and develop my personality.") Miss New York State stood still, staring at her. "Come on, Wanda," said her chaperone. "We've got to get you that bathing suit."

The bathing suits were being handed out and fitted in a two-room suite upstairs. The contestants put on their suits in one room while the chaperones waited in the other. The fitting room was very quiet; the other was filled with noisy, nervous chatter.

Miss Alabama's chaperone was saying, "I'm grooming one now. She'll be ready in two years. She's sure to be Miss America of 1951."

"Have you seen Nebraska? She's a definite threat," said Miss New Jersey's chaperone to Miss Arkansas's chaperone.

"What's her talent?" asked Miss Arkansas's chaperone.

"Dramatic recitation," said Miss N.J.'s.

"She'll never make the first fifteen," said Miss Ark.'s.

"Confidentially," said one chaperone to another, "confidentially, I wouldn't pick *any* of the girls I've seen to be Miss America."

"Some years you get a better-looking crop than others," her companion said. "At the moment, what I've got my mind on is how I can get me a good, stiff drink, and maybe two more after it."

I went into the other room, where Miss New York State was having trouble with her suit. She did not like Catalina suits, she told me; they didn't fit her, and she wished the Pageant officials would let her wear her own. Another contestant paused in her struggle with her suit and said it was very important to like the official Pageant suits. "There just wouldn't *be* a little old Pageant without Catalina," she said severely.

. . .

That night, Mr. Haverstick acted as chairman of the meeting of the contestants in Convention Hall, the world's largest auditorium. He is a solid, elderly gentleman with a large, bald head. He introduced the first speaker of the evening, Miss Slaughter, describing her as a friend they all knew and loved, the friend who had been working for the Pageant since 1935. Miss New York State and most of the other contestants were wearing suits and hats. They sat attentively, their hands folded in their laps, as Miss Slaughter stood up and shook her head unbelievingly at them. "I see your faces and I see a dream of fifty-one weeks come true," she said. "Now, I want you all to listen to me. I'm going to ask you girls to keep one thought in mind during this great week. Think to yourself 'There are fifty-one other talented, beautiful girls in this contest besides myself.' Get out of your head the title of Miss America. You're already a winner, a queen in your own right." She announced that a special prize— a thousand-dollar scholarship—would be awarded to the contestant elected Miss Congeniality by her competitors.

An elderly, heavyset woman with a high-pitched, martyred voice, Mrs. Malcolm Shermer, chairman of a group of local hostesses who would escort the contestants from their hotels to the Pageant activities and back again, stood up and said that she would personally watch over the girls in their dressing room. "When I wake up on Pageant morning, it's like another Christmas Day to me," she said, and went on to list some rules of decorum the contestants would have to follow. The girls were not to make dates with any man, or even have dinner with their fathers, because the public had no way of knowing whether or not a man was a contestant's father; they were not to enter a cocktail lounge or night club; they were to stick to their chaperones or their hostesses. "You have reached the top of the Miss America mountain," Mrs. Shermer said in a complaining tone, "so we're making you almost inaccessible, because all good businessmen put their most valuable belongings in a safe place." The contestants looked impressed. Miss New York State sighed. "They don't take any chances," she remarked to me. "This is just like school."

Miss America of 1948, clad in a suit of Everglaze (I later discovered that she had driven over faithfully in a Nash), then welcomed the fifty-two contestants. She smiled and told the contestants to keep smiling from the moment they woke up every day to the moment they fell asleep. Mr. Haverstick nodded solemnly. "Always have that smile on your face," she said. "Your smiles make people feel happy, and that's what we need— happier people in the world." The contestants all managed a smile. They continued to smile as Mr. Bob Russell was introduced as the master of ceremonies of the Pageant. He came forward with that lively skip characteristic of night-club M.C.s and said, "Girls, this week you're performers, you're actresses, you're models, you're singers and entertainers. Girls, show this great city that you're happy American girls, happy to be in Atlantic City, the city of beautiful girls!" Mr. Haverstick blushed and managed a small smile of his own. The contestants were instructed to wear evening gowns, but not their best ones, in the parade that was going to take place the next day. Still conscientiously smiling, they filed out of the hall. Miss New York State let go of her smile for a moment and told me that she was returning to her room. She would lie down and elevate her feet for twenty minutes, put pads soaked with witch hazel over her eyes, take two sleeping pills, and go to sleep.

On the way out, Miss Slaughter stopped me and said that I was going to see the best contest in the Pageant's history. It had come a long way, she said, from the first one, in 1921, when it was called the Bathers' Revue. The first winner, given the title of the Golden Mermaid, was Margaret Gorman, of Washington, D.C., who briefly considered a theatrical career and then went home and married a real-estate man. "In those years, we offered nothing but promises and a cup," Miss Slaughter said. "Now we get real big bookings for our girls, where they can get started on a real big career. This is not a leg show and we don't call the beauties bathing beauties any more. The bathing part went out in 1945, when we started giving big scholarships." Miss America of 1945—Bess Myerson, of the Bronx—the first winner to be awarded much more than promises and a cup, won a five-thousand-dollar scholarship and bookings worth ten thousand dollars. "Bess went right out and capitalized," Miss Slaughter said. "She went to Columbia and studied music, got married, and had an adorable baby girl, and now she runs a music school and does modelling, too." The next winner—Marilyn Buferd, of Los Angeles—wanted to get into the movies. She got a two-hundred-and-fifty-dollar-a-week job as a starlet with Metro-Goldwyn-Mayer. She is now in Italy, under contract to Roberto Rossellini. Miss America of 1947—Barbara Jo Walker, of Memphis—caused the Pageant officials considerable worry. "She upped and announced she wanted to get married; she didn't want to go out and make money and get publicity," Miss Slaughter said. "Well, there was nothing we could do but let her get married to this medical student of hers, and now we've brought her back this year to be a judge." Be Be Shopp, whose term would run out in five days, had been the biggest money-maker as Miss America. "She just never stopped working at it," Miss Slaughter said. "She set a real good example for our girls." Miss Shopp travelled across three continents, appearing at conventions and similar gatherings with a vibraharp, the instrument with which she had demonstrated her talent at last year's contest by playing "Trees." Miss America of 1944 went back to her home in Kentucky and married a farmer. Miss America of 1943 is singing in a night club in Paris. Miss America of 1942 married Phil Silvers, the comedian. Most of the Miss Americas back to 1921 got married soon after winning their titles. Miss America of 1937, however, has neither married nor embarked on a career. "Miss America of 1937 got crowned, and the next morning she just vanished," Miss Slaughter said, looking pained. "Why, she ran right home, someplace in New Jersey, and when we found her, she refused to come out—no explanation or *any*thing. Just the other day, she decided she wanted to be a model or actress or something, but maybe it's too late now."

· · ·

The following morning, the contestants were photographed again in their Catalina swim suits. After lunch they were assembled in the ballroom of a hotel near one end of the boardwalk for the American Beauty Parade, which would wind up near the other end, a distance of four and a half miles. Roller chairs and beach chairs were lined up along the route; the supply had been sold out (at $6.15 and $2, respectively) three weeks before. State police had been brought in to help keep order. It was a fine day for a parade—clear, sunny, and brisk. The business streets back of the boardwalk were almost deserted. The boardwalk was packed. Every roller chair was occupied, occasionally by as many as six people. Along the parade route a shabby, eager, excited crowd of men, women, and children stood six and eight deep or sat in bleachers. Some carried small American flags, and others waved the paper-doll replicas of Be Be Shopp. Miss Arizona stood near the door of the ballroom. She would be one of the first to leave. She wore a long skirt of red suède, slit at one side, and a multicolored blouse of Indian design. Miss New York State, looking rested and wearing an aquamarine-colored satin gown, was off in a corner, watching Miss America of 1948, who was wearing a slip and contemplating the original of the dress she was pictured in on the paper doll. The dress lay across the backs of two chairs. It had a large hoop skirt and was decorated on the front with the official flowers, appliquéd, of the forty-eight states. She announced that she had to wear the gown in the parade and every night of the Pageant. "It weighs thirty pounds," she said. "How am I ever going to play my vibraharp in it?"

Miss New York State shook her head in speechless marvel. "Will you play every night, Miss Shopp?" she asked.

"Call me Be Be, please," Miss America said, showing a dimpled smile. "Everybody calls me Be Be. I play my vibraharp every place I go. I've made two hundred and sixty-one appearances with it, opening stores and things. The vibraharp weighs a hundred and fifty pounds, and a man usually carries it for me. They were the only men I got close to all year. I worked so hard I didn't have a chance to have any real dates."

Miss Florida, who was standing nearby, shook her head sadly. "Mah goodness, no dates!" she said.

Two women attendants climbed up on chairs and held the thirty-pound gown aloft while the Queen crawled under it. "Is it in the center of me?" she asked as her head and shoulders emerged. Everybody said that it was in the center of her and that she looked glorious. Miss America was now ready to lead the parade. I went outside and found a place on the boardwalk near a mobile radio-broadcasting unit, where Miss America's father, who is physical-education director at the Cream of Wheat Corporation in Minneapolis, was being interviewed. "I'm just as excited this year as last year," he was saying. "I'm just starting to realize she's Miss America."

The parade took two hours. Each contestant sat on a float pushed by a couple of men. Not one contestant let Atlantic City down by failing to keep a smile on her face. Miss New York State, preceded by Hap Brander's string band and a float proclaiming the merits of Fralinger's Salt Water Taffy, got a big hand from the audience. Most of the other contestants merely sat and smiled, but she stood and waved and laughed and shouted and seemed to be having the time of her life.

· · ·

The contestants were to rehearse that night with Bob Russell in Convention Hall, and I decided to go over there. Going through the lobby of my hotel, I ran into Miss Florida with her mother.

"Don't forget to smile, honey," her mother said, smiling.

"Ah don't have *any* trouble smilin', Mama," said Miss Florida.

"That's a good girl, honey," her mother said.

The statistics on Miss Florida showed that at eighteen she was already a veteran beauty. She was Citrus Queen of Florida in 1947, Railroad Exposition Queen in Chicago in 1948, Miss Holiday of Florida of 1949, and Miss Tampa of 1949. (Reason for entering the Atlantic City contest: "Because the Chamber of Commerce of Tampa asked me to compete.")

At Convention Hall, Mr. Russell, standing on the stage surrounded by weary-looking contestants, was outlining the procedure for the next three nights. A long ramp ran out into the auditorium at right angles to the stage, and a few of the contestants squatted on it, as though they were too exhausted to move back to the stage with the others. Miss New York State seemed fairly fresh. Her face was flushed, but she appeared to smile without effort. She wanted to know whether I had seen her in the parade. "That was *fun*," she said. "I was standing and yelling things, and people were yelling things to me. That was really a lot of *fun*. I never thought that people would be so *friendly*."

"Please, girls," said the M.C. "I need your attention."

"I'm used to a long, hard day from nursing," Miss New York State whispered. "Some of these girls look all done in." Smiling, she gave the M.C. her attention. He explained that the contestants would be divided into three groups. Each night, one group would compete for points on their appearance in evening dress, another in bathing suits, and the members of the third would demonstrate their talents. The girls would be judged on personality at two breakfasts, when the judges would meet and talk with them. Every girl would be scored in these four categories, and the fifteen girls with the highest total number of points would compete in the semifinals of the contest, at which time the judges would reappraise them and choose the queen and the four other finalists. Miss New York State was assigned to a group that included Miss Florida, Miss California, and Miss Arizona; they would appear the first night in bathing suits, the second in evening gowns, and on the third they would demonstrate their talents. The winners of the bathing-suit and talent competitions would be announced each night, but not the runners-up, and neither the winners nor the runners-up in the evening-gown competition. In this way, it would not be known who the semifinalists were until they were named on the fourth, and last, night of competition. Each day, Mr. Russell said, he would rehearse the girls in whatever they had prepared to do to show their talent that night. He then made the contestants line up in alphabetical order and parade together from the wings onto the stage and off it down the long ramp—the same ramp each would eventually be required to walk alone. The parade would wind up on each of the first three nights with the appearance of Miss America of 1948 in her thirty-pound gown. The other girls would raise empty water glasses in a toast to her while Mr. Russell sang the Miss America Pageant song, which goes:

> Let's drink a toast to Miss America,
> Let's raise our glasses on high
> From Coast to Coast in this America,

As the Sweetheart of the U.S.A. is passing by.
To a girl, to a girl.
To a symbol of happiness.
To the one, to the one
Who's the symbol of all we possess.

. . .

Miss New York State took only an hour to get dressed for the opening night. I stopped by her room before dinner. She was studying herself in a mirror. She wore an ice-blue satin evening gown, her hair was shining, she had on very little makeup, and her face was smooth and pale. She put on a rhinestone necklace, looked hard at herself, wiped a bit of lipstick from a front tooth, and shrugged. "I'm so vain," she said.

"We'd better go down to dinner," Miss Neville said. "You're due at Convention Hall at eight."

The hotel dining room was filled, mostly with elderly ladies in high lace collars, canes hanging from the backs of their chairs. Several of them applauded as Miss New York State made her entrance, and one later sent her a note wishing her good luck. Miss New York State ordered onion soup, filet of sole, a caramel-nut sundae, and tea with lemon. After she had finished her fish, she waited placidly for her sundae, which was not served until almost eight.

I found a seat at the press table at Convention Hall, abreast of the ramp, as Mr. Russell, wearing a dinner jacket, skipped out and announced that the parade was going to begin. Miss Alabama and the fifty-one others came onto the ramp, smiling but shaking with nervousness. My seat was not far from where Miss New York State stood on the ramp, and I could see her trembling with a kind of sick, forced laughter. The judges, all in evening dress, were introduced: Vyvyan Donner, women's editor of Twentieth Century–Fox Movietone News; Ceil Chapman, dress designer; Clifford D. Cooper, president of the United States Junior Chamber of Commerce; Guy E. Snavely, Jr., who was described as a husband, father, and executive secretary of Pickett & Hatcher, an educational foundation in Birmingham, Alabama; Paul R. Anderson, president of Pennsylvania College for Women, in Pittsburgh; Mrs. Barbara Walker Hummell, Miss America of 1947; Conrad Thibault, baritone; Vincent Trotta, art director of the National Screen Service, a company that makes posters and billboards for motion pictures; Coby Whitmore, commercial artist; Hal Phyfe, photographer; and Earl Wilson, columnist. Voting was by ballot, with two certified public accountants acting as tellers of the ballots. From the press table I picked up a brochure about Convention Hall and read that it is 488 feet long, 288 feet wide, and 137 feet high, and that it could be transformed in a few hours into a full-size football field or into the world's largest indoor fight arena. "The place dwarfs," a gentleman seated next to me said with finality.

After the parade, the group competing in evening gowns that night came onstage one by one, modelled before the judges, and walked down the ramp. Then they came out in a group and lined up in front of the judges, who sat in their enclosure, which adjoined the ramp. Miss Illinois, a pert girl with green eyes and blond hair, fixed in a Maggie (Jiggs' Maggie) hair-do, winked saucily at the judges. She wore a strapless white gown with a rhinestone-trimmed bodice. (Height, 5'6¼; weight, 118; bust, 35; hips, 35½; age, 19. Reason for entering the Pageant: "I entered with the sincere hope of furthering my career.") Mr. Russell urged the girls to give big smiles and urged the judges to pay attention to coiffure, grooming, and symmetry of form. The contestants faced front, turned to show their profiles, turned to show their backs, turned to show their other profiles, then faced front again, and retired. The tellers collected the ballots. Next, a group in bathing suits came out, led by Miss Arizona. Miss California, the tall blonde, came next. Miss Florida followed, and, after a few other contestants, Miss New York State. As they stood before the judges, the M.C. asked them to examine the girls' figures carefully for any flaws. For example, he asked, did the thighs and the calves meet at the right place. Miss New York State stood rigidly, once grasping at the hand of Miss North Dakota. The audience of nine thousand, who had paid from $1.25 to $6.15 for their tickets, sat patiently and stared. The bathing-suiters retired, and Mr. Russell announced that he would do impersonations of Al Jolson, Bing Crosby, Eddie Cantor, and Enrico Caruso. After this demonstration of versatility, he said that the curtains were about to open on "our beautiful old-fashioned Southern garden." The curtains parted. All the girls, in evening gowns, were seated in chairs on simulated grass. Here and there were potted palms. For some reason, Miss New York State sat behind one of them.

The talent competition began. Miss Alabama, a mezzo-soprano, led off by singing "'Neath the Southern Moon," accompanied, more or less, by a pit orchestra. Miss Nevada's talent, it seemed, was raising purebred Herefords; she had wanted to bring one of her cows, she said in a brief

speech, but the officials wouldn't let her. Miss Colorado gave a monologue from *Dinner at Eight*. Miss Hawaii danced a hula. Miss Indiana
showed a movie demonstrating her talent in swimming. Miss New Jersey
sang "Mighty Lak' a Rose." Miss Minnesota, a small version of Be Be
Shopp, played some gypsy airs on a violin. While the judges marked
their ballots, Miss Shopp entertained by playing "Smoke Gets in Your
Eyes" on her vibraharp, evidently not handicapped by the thirty-pound
gown. Then the preliminary winners were announced: Bathing Suit, a
tie between Miss Arizona and Miss California; Talent, Miss Minnesota.

The contestants got back to their hotels late, because Miss Michigan
was given a party backstage in honor of her nineteenth birthday. This
had come about because she had decided early in the evening that she
wanted to drop out of the Pageant and go home at once. I had been advised of the circumstance by an official of the Pageant. "This little brat
wants to run out on us," he had said, stuffing some chewing tobacco into
his mouth. "We're taking a gamble and blowing a sawbuck on a cake for
her. It better work." It worked. Miss Michigan decided to stay in Atlantic City. Everybody appeared to enjoy the party, and everybody made a
determined effort to be Miss Congeniality. Miss New York State showed
no disappointment at not having won first place in the swim-suit competition. "California is so *tall*," she said to me.

. . .

At my hotel the next afternoon, I ran into Miss Arizona's chaperone in
the elevator. "I thought I would die last night before they announced that
my girl had won," she said. "I've been with her ever since she won her
first contest, three years ago, but I've never been through anything like
that before." Three years ago, she told me, Miss Arizona had won a teen-
age beauty contest sponsored by Aldens, a mail-order house in Chicago;
she had then attended a modelling school and had modelled teen-age
clothes for Aldens catalogue. The business people of Arizona (Arizona
has the largest man-made lake in North America and the largest open-
pit copper mine in the world, and it is great to live in Arizona, a brochure
entitled "Miss Arizona, 1949—Jacque Mercer," put out by the contestant's sponsor, the Phoenix Junior Chamber of Commerce, and handed
to me by the contestant's chaperone, said) had given her twenty-five
hundred dollars to prepare for the Atlantic City contest. The chaperone
invited me to come up to her room to look at Miss Arizona's wardrobe.
It was a spectacular wardrobe, put together with taste. Miss Arizona was

an only child. Her mother had married at fifteen and had named her daughter Jacque after a doll she had had. "Jackie's parents are here, but I'm making them stay away from her," the chaperone said. "They're schoolteachers. Schoolteachers don't know what to do with children." Miss Arizona came into the room.

"The Pageant asked Jackie what kind of car she likes and I said to put down Nash," said the chaperone.

"I like Cadillacs," Miss Arizona said. She opened a shoe box and stared at a pair of high-heeled button-strap shoes.

"Your mother went right out and bought a pair just like them," the chaperone said to her.

I told Miss Arizona and her chaperone that I had to get along, in order to look in on Miss New York State. Miss Arizona immediately said she liked Miss New York State. "*She* doesn't giggle, the way some of the others do," she explained. "I don't care for girls who giggle." She flicked a speck of dust off one of her new shoes. "I'll be glad when this is over and I can frown at people if I feel like it," she said. "I sometimes feel as though my face is going to crack. But I keep that bi-ig smile on my face." She laughed.

When I joined Miss New York State, she was wearing her nurse's uniform—white dress, white stockings, and white shoes. She was going, she said, to the Atlantic City Hospital. Two photographers covering the Pageant had heard that she had no way of demonstrating her talent, and had arranged to make a movie short showing her in professional action. She looked crisp and efficient. She had had a busy morning, she said, having been examined for personality at the first of the two breakfasts with the judges. The contestants sat at small tables, with a couple of judges at each. After each course, a bell rang and the judges changed tables, which gave them an opportunity to talk with all the contestants. Miss New York State said that most of the girls had trouble getting their breakfast down but that she had had orange juice, bacon and eggs, toast, marmalade, and tea. "I wasn't going to sit there and let all that good food go," she said. She didn't know whether she had made a favorable impression on the judges. "I told Conrad Thibault I had never heard of him," she said. "He didn't seem to like that."

• • •

Before the Pageant's second-evening program began, some of the judges wandered about Convention Hall, presumably judging the new Nash waiting in the lobby for the winner and judging the audience, which was approximately the same size it had been the first night. Earl Wilson stopped at the press table and said he had been reading an essay on beauty by Edmund Burke. "He says that an object of beauty should be comparatively small and delicate, bright and clear, with one section melting neatly into the other," he said. "The essay didn't affect me any. I like 'em big." He was joined by a gentleman from Omaha, who listened to him impatiently for a while. "I tell you what you're gonna pick, Earl," he finally broke in. "You're gonna pick the kind of girl *I* would pick for my own wife or daughter. That's what we got this contest for." Mr. Wilson nodded respectfully and moved on.

In front of the dressing room, Miss Florida was taking leave of her mother.

"Smile, now, honey," said her mother.

"Ah *am* smilin', Mama," said Miss Florida.

Inside, Miss New York State was standing with her back right up against an ironing board while a lady attendant pressed the skirt of the gown she was wearing for the evening's competition. It had a white net skirt and a white satin bodice. She had bought it at a New York wholesale house for $29.75. She looked around admiringly and objectively at the dresses of the other girls. "What beautiful *gowns*," she said.

Miss Florida was smiling at no one in particular. The city of Tampa had given her her gown—ruffled champagne-colored lace (a hundred and fifty yards)—and matching elbow-length gloves. Miss California sat gravely before a mirror in a dress of blue satin trimmed with black lace on the bodice and a black lace bow at the waist. Miss Arizona stood in a corner, a tense smile on her face, in a gown with a hoop skirt of ruffles of white organdie eyelet (a hundred and sixty yards) with a bouquet of red carnations at one side.

Miss Missouri came in, and Miss New York State waved to her. "Missouri is going to dance tonight," she told me. "I like dancing. It always makes me feel good. You know," she went on rapidly, "I found out today I'm photogenic. One of those photographers told me I could be a model, and my picture is in all the papers. One of the papers said I was *outstanding*." She grabbed my arm. "Nobody ever called me *outstanding* before."

Mrs. Shermer, the chief hostess, called out that the girls were to line up in the wings, and that they should be careful not to step on each other's dresses. Miss New York State took her place in line and the contestants started to move onto the stage, big smiles on their faces.

"Mind my horse!" Miss Montana said cheerily to her hostess.

"I *would* get the one with the horse," the hostess said to me.

I went out front and again sat down at the press table, next to a man whose badge said he was Arthur K. Willi, of R.K.O. Radio Pictures. Throughout the evening-gown and bathing-suit parades, he held a pair of opera glasses to his eyes, then he put them down with a groan. "I look and I look and I look, and what do I see?" he said. "If Clark Gable walked out on that stage right now, he would fill it up, or Maggie Sullavan, or Dorothy Maguire. There's nothing here, nothing—not even when I look at these kids with the eyes of the masses."

The M.C. brought out two platinum blondes and introduced them as Miss Atlanta of 1947 and Miss Omaha of 1947. They did a tap dance to "I Got Rhythm." "Those poor kids," Willi said. "Those poor, poor kids. Look at them. They look as though they had been knocking around Broadway for fifteen years." When the talent session began, he put the glasses back to his eyes. Miss Kansas, who was twenty-two, sang "September Song" with a deliberately husky voice. Miss Canada sang "Sempre Libera" from *La Traviata*. Miss Connecticut recited "Jackie, the Son of the Hard-Boiled Cop." Miss Montana, wearing a conventional riding coat and frontier pants, rode her horse, a nine-year-old mare named Victory Belle, out onto the stage. Miss Illinois grinned confidently at the judges, and in a strong soprano sang "Ouvre Ton Cœur" as though she meant it. Miss Wisconsin wound up with a baton-twirling act. The winners: Bathing Suit, Miss Colorado; Talent, Miss Canada.

"The Pageant wants publicity in the Canadian papers," a newspaperman near me said.

Willi put his opera glasses in his coat pocket. "They've all lost their youth already," he said. "They come down here for what? To lose their youth!"

· · ·

Miss New York State's picture was in the New York, Philadelphia, and Atlantic City newspapers the next morning. She was shown at the Atlantic City Hospital, wearing her uniform and holding a two-year-old girl who had just had her tonsils out. Photographers from the wire services had accompanied the moviemakers to the hospital, and pictures of her had been sent out across the country. Miss Arizona had dark circles under her eyes when I encountered her in our hotel lobby after lunch, and she said that she was going to spend the afternoon thinking about

Shakespeare and listening to a recording of Tchaikovsky's *Romeo and Juliet* overture, to get in the mood for her talent demonstration that night—Juliet's potion scene. She had stayed up all the night before talking about it and other Pageant matters with her chaperone. Miss Arizona had played Juliet at Phoenix Junior College, having been chosen from five hundred girls who had tried out for the part. She wanted to be an actress; she wouldn't go to Hollywood until she had attended drama school and spent several years in the theatre. "Hollywood would try to make me be something *they* wanted me to be," she said. "I won't do that. My grandfather always said that you can have anything you want in the world, any way you want it, if you want it enough to work hard enough for it."

That night, Miss Arizona came out in a wispy white nightgown and, in the auditorium that could be transformed in a few hours into a full-size football field, called up the faint, cold fear thrilling through her veins that almost freezes up the heat of life. The audience was restless and noisy as she expressed her fear that she would die ere her Romeo came. She was followed by Miss Greater Philadelphia, playing "I'm in the Mood for Love" on an electric guitar. Miss Mississippi did Hagar berating Abraham, in a dramatic reading popular with elocution teachers. Miss California acted the part of a girl who had been wronged by a man, in a reading even more popular with elocution teachers. Miss Florida sang "Put Your Shoes On, Lucy," which was announced in a release to the press as "Put Your Shoes on Lucy." Miss New York State, wearing her ice-blue evening gown, gave a short talk on nursing. She spoke without any expression at all, as though she were reciting something she had memorized with difficulty. "Ever since I was a little girl, I was taught that people were here for the purpose of serving others," she said. The audience shifted unsympathetically in their seats. Somebody muttered that Miss Illinois ought to stop flirting with the judges. Miss New York State said she had decided to become a nurse when she visited a friend who was a patient in a veterans' hospital during the war. She had been shocked by the men's helplessness. She would now show a film of herself going about her usual duties. While the film was being run, she made flat, realistic comments on it. She was pictured in the children's ward, in the maternity ward, and assisting a surgeon at an operation. At the end of the picture, the audience applauded halfheartedly. The winners: Bathing Suit, Miss Illinois; Talent, Miss Arizona.

I met Miss New York State as she was going back to her hotel. She felt pretty good, she said. She had enjoyed standing before all those people and telling them about nursing, and she had liked watching the talent of the others. "Wasn't Miss Arizona *good*?" she said. "She got hysterical so *easily*."

. . .

I was awakened at seven by the sound of gunfire. Some former Seabees had arrived in the city for a convention, and the Navy was welcoming them with a mock assault landing on the beach. It was the last day of the Pageant, and the boardwalk seemed to sag with the crowds.

The auditorium that night had a capacity audience, including stand-ees, of twenty thousand. The Seabees came en masse. Most of the police at the hall felt that Miss California would be the winner, but the captain in charge of the detail was indifferent. "All you can do is look, and you get tired looking," he said. "I been guarding the beauties since 1921. An old lady come up to me during the parade the other day and says hello. I must of looked at her strange, because she says she was Miss Maryland of 1924. She was a grandmother! That kind of thing don't make me feel no better."

The contestants arrived and were counted. No one was missing; no one had walked out on the Pageant. The girls had had breakfast that morning with the judges again and then had voted for Miss Congeniality; Miss Montana and Miss New Jersey had tied for the honor and split the thousand-dollar scholarship. An only fairly congenial Miss wanted to know what kind of education you could get with a five-hundred-dollar scholarship. "Why, same as you can do with a bigger one," said Miss New Jersey. "Take voice lessons, or go to tap-dance school, or even go to Europe and learn something." Miss Slaughter nodded staunchly in approval. Also at the breakfast, Miss America of 1948 had made all fifty-two Misses members of the Pageant sorority—Mu Alpha Sigma, whose letters stand for Modesty, Ambition, and Success—and each girl had been given a gold-filled pin. "The most thrilling thing a girl could have," Miss America had said. "It means that all of you are queens. Remember that when the fifteen semifinalists are named tonight, *all* of you are queens." Miss New York State had asked if the sorority high sign was a big smile, a remark that didn't get much of a laugh. "Well," said Miss New York State to me that evening, looking at her sorority pin, "I finally belong to a sorority." She had voted for Miss Montana as Miss Congeniality. "I knew that I would never be elected," she told me. "In nursing, I got to know too much about human nature to be able to *act* congenial."

Mrs. Shermer was looking very pleased. She told Earl Wilson she had a hot item for his column—she had discovered some contestants putting on false eyelashes. Mr. Wilson looked pleased, too. He had spent the afternoon autographing copies of his latest book at a department store in town. Miss Arizona had received a wire from her father (who was staying at a nearby hotel) saying that she had made first base, second base, and third base and concluding, "Now slide into home!" Miss Arizona was excited, and so was her chaperone. Miss New York State was unusually high-spirited and talkative; another photographer had called her photogenic, she said.

Mr. Russell was in tails for the big night. The curtains opened on the "beautiful old-fashioned Southern garden" again. One by one, the fifteen semifinalists stood up as their names were called: Miss Arizona, Miss Arkansas, Miss California, Miss Canada, Miss Chicago, Miss Colorado, Miss Hawaii, Miss Illinois, Miss Kansas, Miss Michigan, Miss Minnesota, Miss Mississippi, Miss New Jersey, Miss New York City, and Miss Wisconsin. Each of them was now sure of at least a thousand-dollar scholarship. The losers sat motionless in the Southern garden, some smiling, some in tears, others trying unsuccessfully to look indifferent. Out front, Miss Florida's mother cried softly, but Miss Florida was still smiling. Miss New York State, this time only half hidden behind a potted plant, looked puzzled but interested in what was going on.

The semifinalists paraded before the judges once again, then withdrew to change into bathing suits. Mr. Russell asked the losers to walk the ramp, one by one, for the last time. "Give the valiant losers a hand, folks," he said. "They've got what it takes. They are your future wives and mothers of the nation." The valiant losers got a big hand. Miss New York State walked very gracefully—better than she had walked in competition. She waved cheerfully as she passed me and with her lips silently said, "Bob—is—here." She received more applause than any of the other losers and quite a few whistles from the gallery. Then Miss Omaha of 1947 and Miss Atlanta of 1947 did their tap dance. Miss New York State watched them with a look of resigned but genuine appreciation.

The semifinalists paraded in bathing suits, and then demonstrated their talent all over again. While the judges marked their ballots, a six-year-old girl named Zola May played Chopin's "Minute Waltz" on a piano. The M.C. then spoke glowingly of the three donors of the prizes, and introduced the president of the company that makes Everglaze, the president of Catalina, and a delegation of three stout men in white linen suits from Nash. They all took bows. Then the M.C. asked Eddie Cantor to come out of the audience and up on the stage. Cantor did, and said hoarsely and passionately, "Communism hasn't got a chance when twenty thousand people gather to applaud culture and beauty."

Then the five big-prize finalists were announced: Miss Arizona, Miss California, Miss Colorado, Miss Illinois, and Miss Mississippi. Mr. Russell interviewed them, and their manner in replying was supposed to help the judges measure them for poise and personality. Each girl was asked three questions: "How do you plan to use your scholarship?" "Do your future plans include marriage, a career, or what?" "What did you get out of the Pageant?" Miss New York State peeked attentively around the potted plant as Miss Arizona, leading off in alphabetical order, replied tersely but politely that she planned to study dramatics at Stanford University, that she wanted marriage first and a career second, and that the Pageant had given her a chance to test herself before a new audience in a new part of the country. Miss California wanted to study interior decorating at the University of California and then go into the furniture business with her father; she wanted a career, so that she could help whomever she married; she was grateful to the Pageant for giving her the opportunity to meet so many wonderful girls from all over the country. Miss Illinois said that music was her first ambition. Mr. Russell, breaking the routine, asked her if she had ever been in love. She replied that she *was* in love but that music was still her first ambition. Miss New York State watched and listened carefully. No entertainment was at hand while the judges were voting again, so Mr. Russell asked the audience to sing "Smiles" until the ballots were counted, and he waved at the valiant losers to join in.

The winners were announced in reverse order: Fifth place, Miss California ($1,500); fourth place, Miss Colorado ($2,000); third place, Miss Illinois ($2,500); second place, Miss Mississippi ($3,000); first place, Miss Arizona ($5,000, plus the new four-door Nash sedan, the dozen Catalina swim suits, and the wardrobe of sixty Everglaze garments), now Miss America of 1949. There were hoots and boos, as well as cheers, from the audience. The Governor of New Jersey, who had arrived after Miss Arizona had done her Juliet scene, awarded her a gilt statue, half as high as she was, of a winged Miss and said, "The world needs the kind of beauty and talent you have." Most of the losers then straggled out of the Southern garden into the wings, and a number of chaperones, hostesses, parents, and press people crowded onto the stage. I went along. Miss New York State came forward to watch Miss America of 1948 crown her successor. Miss America of 1948 wept, and her mother, standing nearby, wept with her. The new Miss America, tremulous but happy, said, "I only hope you'll be half as proud of me as I am of the title Miss America." *Her* mother, who had suddenly been surrounded by a group of admiring strangers, was much too occupied with her own emotions to notice her daughter coming slowly down the ramp, crown on her head, purple robe over her shoulders, and sceptre in her hand. The orchestra (the violinist holding a cigar in a corner of his mouth) played "Pomp and Circumstance," and Miss America of 1949 walked the length of the ramp, smiling graciously.

"This is the beginning," a reporter said to me. "She's going to spend the rest of her life looking for something. They *all* are."

"She is now the most desirable girl in the United States," another said.

When the Queen got back to the stage, Miss New York State offered her her solemn congratulations. "I'm glad you won, kid," she said. "I was rooting for you."

Then the new Miss America was engulfed by still photographers, newsreel men, and interviewers. Miss New York State stood beside me on the fringe of the crowd and watched.

"Everybody wants my autograph because I'm her father," Miss America's father was saying.

Her mother wanted to know whether the parents were to get a badge or ribbon, too.

"We rehearsed what she would say for hours," Miss America's chaperone was saying.

"We got to get her in the Nash!" one of the Nash triumvirate in white suits was saying.

A group of people were asking Miss Slaughter about the new queen's plans. "She's going to have breakfast with all the newspaper people in New York," Miss Slaughter said. "Then she gets outfitted with a whole new wardrobe by Everglaze, and she wears Everglaze whenever she goes out in public—it's in her contract. She's got to fly to California to preside at the Catalina swim-suit show, and after that she's got to make a couple of screen tests in Hollywood. I've been going mad arranging for those screen tests." A perspiring gentleman said that the winner of the recent

Mrs. America contest at Asbury Park had invited the new Miss America to compete in a contest with her and he wanted to know how the Queen felt about this. "She says no comment because I say she says no comment," the head of the Pageant public relations said firmly.

Miss New York State shook her head at the wonder of it all. "Going to Hollywood!" she said. "She'll probably be in the movies."

The two of us walked back to the dressing room, where we found Miss Missouri tearfully folding up her Catalina swim suit. Miss New York State looked puzzled at her tears and said that *she* hadn't cried, because when you don't expect very much, you're never disappointed. She was returning to New York with Bob the next morning. She had the name of a photographer who wanted to take a lot of pictures of her to sell to magazines, and another man wanted to talk to her about becoming a model. She was not going back to nursing if she could help it. "You *get* more when you're a model," she said.

PART THREE

POSTWAR

A NOTE BY LOUIS MENAND

————————

THE WORD FINALLY CAME at 7:03 P.M., Eastern War Time, on Tuesday, August 14, 1945. That's when the message went up on the ticker in Times Square: "Official—Truman announces Japanese surrender." Rumors and false alarms had been circulating since the bombing of Nagasaki, five days before, and by the time the news flashed, there were half a million people in Times Square. "The victory roar that greeted the announcement beat upon the eardrums until it numbed the senses," the *Times* reported. "For twenty minutes wave after wave of that joyous roar surged forth."

Hats and flags were flung in the air; confetti and paper streamers were thrown from the windows of office buildings. Strangers embraced. People wept. By 10 P.M., there were two million men and women jammed into the area from Fortieth to Fifty-second streets between Sixth and Eighth avenues. The celebration went on until after 3 A.M., and continued the next day. Wednesday and Thursday were national holidays. More than nine million men and women under arms were on their way home. The war was over.

The war turned the United States into a world power and New York City into a world capital. Paris had been occupied by the Germans for four years; London, Rome, Berlin, Tokyo, and Leningrad (St. Petersburg) had been devastated by bombs. Hundreds of European scientists, writers, artists, and intellectuals had fled to America, many of them ending up New Yorkers. Apart from a few Japanese fire balloons and inconsequential shellings, the mainland United States had never been attacked. Of the more than fifty million people who had died in the fighting, only some four hundred thousand of them were Americans.

France, Italy, Germany, and Britain were broke: after four hundred years, the age of European empire was coming to an end. The United

States found itself nearly the only healthy economy in a world of damaged states. In the late 1940s, with 7 percent of the world's population, the United States had 42 percent of the world's income; produced 57 percent of the world's steel, 62 percent of the world's oil, and 80 percent of the world's automobiles; and owned three-quarters of the world's gold. Per-capita income was almost double the incomes in the next most well-off nations, and Americans consumed 50 percent more calories a day than most people in Western Europe did. The war economy had pulled the country out of a long depression: unemployment was less than 4 percent. And, as everyone knows, one way Americans found to express their faith in the future was to start having lots of babies.

Harold Ross, who was hypochondriacal about the magazine under the best of circumstances, had worried that the war would ruin *The New Yorker*. Instead, it transformed it. As Brendan Gill put it, many years later, "From a publication deliberately parochial in range and tone, consisting of a few funny drawings, some funny short pieces, an occasional serious short story, and the Profiles, limited enough in both length and intentions to deserve to be called profiles, it became a publication in which it was natural to look for the highest quality of reporting in almost any field of activity, from almost anywhere on earth."

Among the writers whom Ross brought in to replenish his staff, many of whom had joined the military or been sent overseas to report, was E. J. Kahn, Jr., who did both: he fought in the Pacific while contributing a column, The Army Life. A specialist in detail, he went on to write more than three million words for the magazine. His typically pointillist account of the Berlin airlift of 1948, the first major postwar confrontation between the United States and the Soviets, is included here. Edmund Wilson, Lillian Ross, Richard Rovere, Rebecca West, and John Hersey all joined the magazine's staff during the war, and all became exemplars of the more serious and sophisticated journalism that characterized the postwar *New Yorker*.

Wilson became the magazine's book critic in 1944, when he was forty-eight. He was hired to replace Clifton Fadiman, and he was one of the greatest book critics of his time, but he had many other talents as a writer. One was reporting. This was surprising to people who knew him. Wilson was a physically unprepossessing and mechanically challenged man. He did not know, for instance, how to drive a car. When Isaiah Berlin met him for the first time, in 1946, he was startled to find "a thick-set, red-faced, pot-bellied figure not unlike President Hoover." And Gill wondered, "This short, fat, breathless, diffident man—how did he so quickly gain the confidence of strangers?"

Yet Wilson was a marvelous reporter. His reporting has the same quality that we find in his criticism: he simply saw things more clearly than other people did. In 1945, he embarked on a tour of Europe to assess the state of a ruined continent. (The pieces were collected in his book *Europe Without Baedeker,* published in 1947.) His dispatches from Greece and Crete, in 1946, are masterpieces of the steady, patiently cumulative, slightly understated journalistic style that came to flourish at the magazine under the editorship of William Shawn. The Greeks had been brutalized by the Nazis; they were about to be abandoned by Britain, their Big Power ally; they were facing a civil war involving an indigenous Communist Party—and Wilson begins one report with a long description of the color differences between the Italian and the Greek landscapes.

Yet, in the end, it's all there: the sharply observed distinction between the Socialist enthusiast and the Communist fellow traveler; the portrait of the deafness and decadence of the British imperial mentality; the sketch of the opportunistic American businessman whose kind will soon replace the British; a verbal picture of the vague, widespread, probably hopeless hope in a democratic and egalitarian future. Not long after Wilson left, fears of the Communist threat in Greece, along with anxieties about Soviet intentions in Turkey, became the justification for the announcement of the Truman Doctrine—in effect, the declaration of the Cold War.

The idea of women reporters made Ross uncomfortable, but, like many people trying to run a business during the war, he was obliged to find women to fill positions that had been vacated by men who left to join the war effort. In 1945, he (or, rather, Shawn, his deputy) hired Lillian Ross. She began as a Talk of the Town reporter, but quickly discovered what became her most famous beat, Hollywood. In common with *New Yorker* artists like Helen Hokinson and Peter Arno, Ross was brilliant at taking the air out of stuffed shirts, a species of which Hollywood has its share. Her method was just to let self-important people talk. All she usually had to do was write down what they said. Her story on the industry's reaction to the House Un-American Activities Committee's investigation into Communist influence is funny and lacerating, as is "Picture," her celebrated anatomy of the making of a John Huston movie, published in the magazine, in five parts, in 1952.

Lillian Ross's writing has some of the insouciance that had character-ized the tone of the prewar magazine. In 1948, a little insouciance was still possible. As it was in France and even in Russia, the immediate postwar period in America was a giddy time. The world seemed ready to begin anew; anything seemed possible. After a world war, it was hard to take congressional witch-hunting (as in Ross's piece) or subversive-tracking G-men (as in Richard Rovere's report on a tour of the F.B.I. headquarters, in Washington) entirely seriously. They must have seemed slightly farcical remnants of wartime anxieties, rather than what they turned out to be: the official face of Cold War America, the dark cloud that accompanied postwar prosperity.

Rovere, too, was a Shawn hire. He joined the magazine in 1944, when he was twenty-nine. Harold Ross had little interest in Washington, D.C.; he thought it was a boring city. Although he ran Janet Flanner's Letter from Paris and Mollie Panter-Downes's Letter from London every two weeks, he could bring himself to publish a Letter from Wash-ington only once a month. Rovere began filing his column in December 1948, and he quickly grasped the importance of anti-Communist hyste-ria. He was one of the first journalists to take on Joseph McCarthy, and he wrote the Letter from Washington until 1978, the year before he died.

The magazine as a whole soon took politics, national and interna-tional, seriously enough. But the war also changed national psychology: it deprovincialized the millions of men and women who had gone over-seas. A magazine that was identified by its name and its tone with Amer-ica's most cosmopolitan city, a place that, more than any other with the possible exception of Hollywood, had flourished thanks to the influx of European artists and thinkers in the 1930s and '40s, was nicely positioned to reflect back to its readers their new sense of themselves as citizens of the world.

NOTES AND COMMENT

E. B. White

THIS MAGAZINE TRAFFICS with all sorts of questionable characters, some of them, no doubt, infiltrating. Our procedure so far has been to examine the manuscript, not the writer; the picture, not the artist. We have not required a statement of political belief or a blood count. This still seems like a sensible approach to the publishing problem, although falling short of Representative J. Parnell Thomas's standard. One thing we have always enjoyed about our organization is the splashy, rainbow effect of the workers: Red blending into Orange, Orange blending into Yellow, and so on, right across the spectrum to Violet. (Hi, Violet!) We sit among as quietly seething a mass of reactionaries, revolutionaries, worn-out robber barons, tawny pipits, liberals, Marxists in funny hats, and Taftists in pin stripes as ever gathered under one roof in a common enterprise. The group seems healthy enough, in a messy sort of way, and everybody finally meets everybody else at the water cooler, like beasts at the water hole in the jungle. There is one man here who believes that the solution to everything is proper mulching—the deep mulch. Russia to him is just another mulch problem. We have them all. Our creative activity, whether un- or non-un-American, is properly not on a loyalty basis but merely on a literacy basis—a dreamy concept. If this should change, and we should go over to loyalty, the meaning of "un-American activity" would change, too, since the America designated in the phrase would not be the same country we have long lived in and admired.

. . .

PART THREE: POSTWAR · 235

We ran smack into the loyalty question the other day when we got a phone call from another magazine, asking us what we knew about a man they had just hired. He was a man whose pieces we had published, from time to time, and they wanted to know about him. "What's his political slant?" our inquisitor asked. We replied that we didn't have any idea, and that the matter had never come up. This surprised our questioner greatly, but not as much as his phone call surprised us. When he hung up, we dialled Weather and listened to the rising wind.

. . .

Louis B. Mayer told the House Committee he wouldn't know a Communist if he saw one. Later he testified that three writers in his employ had been mentioned to him as Communists, and he named them. The newspaper accounts added that among the movies written by one of them, Lester Cole, was *The Romance of Rosy Ridge,* and when we learned that this picture was currently playing at Loew's Forty-second Street, we sent our man Stanley over to see it, with instructions to watch especially for subversive propaganda and to report back. Lest we inadvertently distort the sense of Stanley's notes in attempting to rephrase them, here they are, just as he turned them in:

"Wish I knew shorthand. This a post–Civil War costume-&-dialect picture, & what with everybody in cast mumbling & me taking notes in dark, can't guarantee accuracy my version dialogue. Anyhow, picture begins with M-G-M lion & 'Ars gratia artis.' Un-American phrase? Lester Cole did screen play all right—said so on screen. Most pictures have either Guy Kibbee or Thomas Mitchell, & this one has both. Van Johnson is star. How much more American can you get? Plot involves Confederate-minded family with old man (Mitchell) unwilling forgive & forget. Van Johnson is Union vet. Wanders along playing mouth organ, moves in with family, falls in love with daughter (Janet Leigh—cute). Masked night riders burning barns, stirring up trouble between Union & Confederate sympathizers in Missouri. Nobody dares help neighbors harvest crops, because have to protect own barns. Van finally breaks down ill will. Also shoots four men & horse with five bullets; beats up fifth guy barehanded, thus disposing of barn-burners; gets girl; rides off toward horizon with her at end, like close of FitzPatrick Traveltalk. Elapsed time: 1 hr., 45 mins. This not entire story, but hard to keep awake. At least I absorbed more of movie than fellow next to me, who fell asleep moment Van started in on that mouth organ.

"As to possible propaganda lines, near start of picture somebody says, 'Peace is achieved by the good will of people & not by flourishing strokes of a pen.' Might be Senator Taft line. There's little boy (guess you couldn't make picture like this without little boy), who says he always carries a fishing rod with him, in case he happens to run across any fish. Would say too frivolous & opportunistic an attitude toward life's grim realities to be politically harmful. Guy Kibbee flatly disapproves of barn-burning, believes in property rights. Somebody asks Van explain difference between right & wrong. He says, 'To me, right is lots o' things, like plantin' your fields an' havin' rain fall on 'em, like havin' songs to sing when your heart is right.' He said more along that line, but I got lost. Also said, 'Rain water tastes better'n sassprilla.' Statement allowed to go unanswered. Point debatable, I should say. Twice during picture, Kibbee, trying to get arguments settled, urges everyone present to be democratic & to take a vote. This accepted American way for resolving squabbles? Possible un-American note when two women are discussing what to wear to party & one says, 'Shucks, Maw, dressin' purty ain't everythin'.' Possible current allusion when Van says, 'The war's over, but some people, 'stead o' lookin' for friends, are lookin' for trouble.' Crack at somebody here? Twice during picture, Van, barefooted & carrying shoes over shoulder, explains that they're good-wearing shoes, and so he wants to preserve them. Honest toil, neighborly love, thrift stressed throughout. Van says of dead soldier buddy & himself, 'We both wanted to make this country a free country, for folks—all folks—to live in.' Pinko sentiment, maybe? Noticed one thing. Communists supposed to be exploiting plight of Negroes in South nowadays. Well, this about Civil War issues & not a single Negro in it, not even one in background strummin' on ol' banjo. I'd give it clean bill of health but wouldn't want anyone to think I recommend seeing it."

GREEK DIARY: COMMUNISTS, SOCIALISTS, AND ROYALISTS

Edmund Wilson

OCTOBER 20, 1945

HAD INTERVIEWS, in Athens, with two remarkable professors who have become political figures: George Georgalas and Alexander Svolos. Both are middle-aged men of top standing in their fields, and they are typical of the Greek intellectuals who have been driven by the needs of their country to take an active part in the E.A.M. movement, the National Liberation Front, which organized the resistance to the Germans and which controlled most of the countryside of Greece before the Papandreou government, a creation of the British, took over. They present the best possible proof that that movement has not been the creation either of professional radicals or of cutthroats from the mountains. Svolos, an authority on constitutional law, was the president and spokesman of E.A.M. through the period of crisis last winter; Georgalas, formerly the head of the government geological service, is now the director of E.P.O.N., the United Panhellenic Organization of Youth, which is the junior branch of E.A.M.

Georgalas I saw in his office, just off his geology classroom in the Polytechnic School. He showed me the statistics on Greek education with the enthusiasm and energy of a man who was fighting for reforms that were obviously needed and that inevitably had to come: the rudiments of democratic education. The state of Greek education seems really, to an American, incredible. The figures for the school year 1937–38 show how bad the situation was before the general wreck brought by the war. At the beginning of that year, out of a population of seven and a half millions, there were 987,000 children attending the primary schools, and before the year was done, 80,000 had dropped out. Of 231,000 children who had entered the first grade in these schools, only 82,000 were surviving in the sixth grade, so that only about a third of the ordinary Greeks (who did not go to private schools) got even a complete primary education. The teaching, too, was quite inadequate: one teacher had sometimes a hundred pupils. In 1937, 3,700 villages had no school of any kind. In the same year there were graduated from the high schools only 94,920 students. Of these high schools there were five hundred to educate the less than 9 percent of the population who practiced the liberal professions, and only two to give agricultural training to the more than 58 percent engaged in agriculture. The education in the high schools was mainly based on the reading of the ancient Greek authors in a purely philological way and the study of the physical sciences in a purely theoretical way and with no direct contact with nature. "Here you Americans," Georgalas said, "are inventing an atomic bomb, while our physicists in Greece have hardly come to grips with any practical problem!" Among the graduates of the two universities, Athens and Salonika, in 1937–38, 45 percent became lawyers, 33 percent doctors, 7 percent philologists, 5 percent chemists, and of the remaining 10 percent, 8 percent had gone in for the physical sciences. The men from these schools and colleges that equipped them with a classical education did not want to return to the towns: they almost invariably remained in Athens to find or look for government jobs and become "parasites on the bourgeoisie." There had, in 1937–38, been 11,140 graduates of the regular universities, while at the two small agricultural schools nineteen students had been graduated, of whom only two were of working-class origin. The principal school of agriculture, founded in 1920, had been closed in 1939 by the dictator Metaxas and its faculty obliged to become part of the University of Salonika, where they had been working ever since with no laboratories.

What E.A.M. was aiming at was to provide instruction in agricultural chemistry and other technical subjects which would make it possible for the peasants to develop their barren country and raise their meagre standard of living. The reactionaries had never wanted this, because they did not want the common people strengthened. There would be no real education in Greece till the monarchists were removed from power.

E.P.O.N. itself, he told me, had taken in children under fourteen from all sorts of political backgrounds, and had once had five hundred thousand members. It had organized two hundred stations, where the children were fed and given playgrounds; but all this work had been undone when the public activities of E.A.M. had been stopped.

. . .

With Svolos I talked mainly about politics, and I put to him certain questions to which he was in a position to know the answers. I had in my mind a fairly clear version of the incidents that had led up to the civil war. The British, in their anxiety to bring back the King and to defeat the activities of the Communists, had been alarmed by the Left tendencies of E.A.M. and by the formidable proportions it had attained, and they had attempted to disarm E.L.A.S., its army. They had announced that they were disarming all units, of the Right as well as of the Left, in order to create a true national army; but when E.L.A.S. in good faith had laid down its arms, the Royalist troops—the Mountain Brigade and the Sacred Battalion—were allowed to retain theirs. On December 3rd of last year, E.A.M. held a demonstration in Constitution Square, in Athens, to protest against the policy of the British. They were unarmed, and many of the women had brought their small children. The British had given a permit for this meeting, but they had revoked it at three o'clock that morning in such a way that it had been impossible to call off the demonstration. Nobody seems to know precisely what started the trouble: the Royalists claimed that the crowd were trying to rush the guard at the government's headquarters in the Grande Bretagne Hotel; but there is no question that the majority of the demonstrators went on quietly marching while the Royalist police fired into them and killed and wounded about a hundred people. Funerals were held the next day, and a procession passed through the streets. The Royalists fired on the procession from the windows of hotels and killed or wounded between a hundred and fifty and two hundred people.

I asked Svolos now whether it were true, as had been said and as might seem to be indicated by the British revocation of the permit at that impossible time of night, that the whole thing had been a British provocation intended to provide them with a pretext for crushing E.A.M. before it grew stronger. He answered that he did not necessarily believe that the British role in the drama had been so simple or so conscious as this. They had perhaps not provoked the insurrection that followed these attacks by the Royalists, but they "had not been sorry" to have it happen. It was an example of the familiar British practice of half allowing, half stimulating actions which, though carried out by other people, would be advantageous to British interests. He said that the responsibility had to be shared, in various proportions, by the Royalists, the British, and the Communists. Was it true, as I had been told by an American who said that he had been in a position to know, that at the time of the Lebanon conference of May, 1944, stage-managed by the British, when Svolos had wired to E.A.M. for advice as to how to proceed in regard to a proposed program for a "government of National Unity," and E.A.M. had directed him to make certain reservations, the telegraphed answer from E.A.M. had been suppressed by British Ambassador Leeper? He replied that it was impossible to say that the telegram had been suppressed but that it had certainly been sent and had never arrived. Was the impression I had got correct that, at the time of the crisis last winter, the Greek Communists in E.A.M. had been acting without the approval or knowledge of Moscow—Stalin perhaps having agreed at Yalta, in return for a free hand elsewhere, not to interfere with the British in the Mediterranean? Svolos said that he believed this to be true—that the Greek Communists had at that time sent a delegate to Russia but that Moscow had refused to see him and dispatched him straight back to Athens, and that, throughout this period, the Moscow radio had made no mention of events in Greece. I asked him about the atrocities alleged to have been committed by E.A.M.—mass executions of civilians murdered with knives and axes, men and women hostages marched barefoot for days in the snow, till many died of exhaustion—of which so much was made by Ambassador Leeper in his reports to Anthony Eden. Svolos did not deny that such things had happened, but said that they were not, as had been declared, mere outrages by ruffians from the mountains but a part of a long and bitter history of private revenges and political reprisals that had begun under the Metaxas regime and gone on through the German occupation, during both of which periods the Greek Fascists had been committing most of the atrocities. After the liberation, the British, who controlled the news from Greece, had succeeded in forestalling or suppressing reports of what the reactionaries were doing to the liberals. At present, as everybody knew, the jails were full of political prisoners, and every day the agents of the government were arresting more people without warrant, shooting them and beating them up on the street, and torturing them to extort information. He was worried by Bevin's speech on British policy, which had been delivered the day before. They had been hoping for an amnesty, but now Bevin, it seemed, had announced that this might be difficult, since, according to him, there were "violent criminals" mixed up with the political prisoners, and there was a problem of sorting these out.

I asked Svolos what sort of following he thought E.A.M. could now command if it were free to function politically. It seemed to be generally admitted that at the time of the civil war it had been backed by about 80 percent of the Greeks. He replied that the Socialists had now split off from E.A.M., but that the Socialists and the Communists between them could still, he thought, command a following of 75 percent of the people. And he pointed out that when these Left elements asked the British to allow the Greeks to form what was described as "a representative government," they had proposed a combination which did not at all reflect these proportions but gave undue importance to the Right—the formula being one third Royalist, one third democratic and center, and only one third Socialists and Communists.

I asked him why he had split with the Communists. Because their methods were so unscrupulous, he said. Nobody else could get on with people who made a practice of double-dealing; nor could they accomplish their own aims in that way. He himself had always been a Socialist—he had been removed by Metaxas from his university chair; and now, dissociating himself from E.A.M., he had organized last April a new Socialist Party by the fusion of three other parties. Georgalas, he told me, belonged to a small Socialist group that was still a part of E.A.M. and that he believed to consist of camouflaged Communists. During my interview with Georgalas, I had had a very definite impression that I was talking to a convinced fellow-traveller, and I was interested by Svolos' confirmation. Later I tried to put my finger on the indications which had made me feel this. It seemed to me that I was able to identify them in a peculiar extreme cheerfulness and certainty with which he had talked about everything. The middle-class C.P. member or sympathizer is transported into a kind of substratosphere where, like the aviator who goes too high, he falls victim to a treacherous euphoria. There is no question in his mind that he has picked the winning side and is about to cash in on the stakes, and he does not need to argue about it any more than a Rosicrucian is obliged to defend his esoteric doctrine. Georgalas, no doubt by temperament a sanguine and self-confident man, had, I felt, succumbed a little to that mood of Communist blitheness which is not entirely reassuring. He had talked to me at length and with feeling about the soul-destroying pedantry with which the ancient Greek authors were taught: "Why we love Homer and Sophocles," he said, "they would never find out from their teachers! A little niece of mine was terribly proud because she knew about a verb form which only occurs about once in the whole of Greek literature and which, as I told her, I had taught Greek for years without ever knowing about. But that was what our education aimed at!" I demurred that this might not be entirely the fault of the reactionary powers who presided over education in Greece, that, even in democratic America, Shakespeare was often taught just like that—that this was a tendency of the academic profession at all times and everywhere. But he smilingly shook his head, brushed my interruption off, and went on; and it seemed to me that, in his Marxist optimism, he was sure that these stupidities would disappear so soon as the Communists should come to power.

With Svolos it was quite different. You could talk to him as to anyone else. He lived in the same world as I did, where there were difficulties, doubts, confused issues, conflicts between expediency and principle. He reminded me a little of Silone, in Rome, who was engaged in a similar task: the attempt to build up, out of the Socialist tradition and the survivors from the old Socialist groups, a movement that would be strong enough to resist the Russians and avert the kind of paralyzing dictatorship which Russian Communism has always brought with it. Such people are anxious and intent; they are never unnaturally cheerful. The only time, during a long stay in Rome, when I ever saw Silone look happy was at the time of the Socialist Congress last July, when I met him on the street, beaming, and he told me that he believed that the pro-Stalinist Socialists were certain to be outvoted on the issue of a merger with the Communists.

• • •

I had made, on a trip to Delphi, the acquaintance of a young Greek woman, who was acting as interpreter for U.N.R.R.A., and I saw something of her and her family. They belonged to the well-to-do Greek bourgeoisie—that is, they had once been well-to-do, for few people in Greece have much money or can buy much with what they have. The V.s lived in a well-furnished apartment on the Odos Vasilissis Sophias, among the palaces, the fine houses, and the embassies of the fashionable quarter of Athens; but three generations and two branches of the family were obliged to share half a dozen rooms, so that their life was rather hampered and constricted. There were Eleni and her husband, their two children, her mother-in-law, her brother-in-law, and his wife. And they got water only, I think, twice a week and had to save it in buckets and heat it themselves.

Yet this was, for them, a period of relative security. Eleni's husband had worked against the Germans and had had to escape to Egypt, and Eleni had had to spend a couple of years alone with the children in Athens. Their persistence through it all in the habits and the attitudes of comfortable people made rather an odd impression—especially when one remembered how completely they had been cut off from the rest of their kind in Europe. It was as if they had preserved in a vacuum an abstraction of the bourgeoisie, an essence which had never been troubled by the social upheavals going on in the world or by the ordeals of their native country. Their culture was at least as much French as Greek. Eleni's husband had studied law in Paris, and Eleni spoke French with her children. Her mother and her stepfather, whom I met there one day, spoke French, they told me, even between themselves. But the effect was not to place the V.s in a larger international world: it was rather to make the French language seem like something nonconductive and insipid, a medium of intercourse that did not imply any real relation either with actual, present-day Athens or with present-day, distant Paris.

On the occasion of one of my calls, I found Eleni's mother-in-law reading an old back number of *Les Œuvres Libres,* and she explained that they had not been able, in Greece, to get any new French books since before the war. I walked up to the large, glass-doored bookcase and looked in at the paperbacks, which seemed to exhale a peculiar staleness. They were the biographies, the novels, and the poetry, including much that was second-rate, of the early 1900s and the twenties. I had already been conscious in Italy of the extent to which the war and Mussolini had kept the Italians cut off from the main currents of contemporary thought; but there the crop of brilliant white and colored covers with titles in vivid type that had come out last spring, like flowers, in the shop windows and the sidewalk newsstands—the translations of contemporary books, the new editions of French and Italian classics, the first Italian printings of outlawed Italian authors, and the innumerable new reviews—had been rapidly making up for this. In Greece there was no similar revival. To go into Kauffman's, the headquarters for foreign books, was almost like exploring an attic; and in Eleutheroudakis', the Athenian Brentano's, you were shocked to see how rare and how precious modern books on technical subjects, such as medicine and engineering, had become. A look into the V.s' bookcase was a contact, from which one drew back, with a cultural day-before-yesterday that was somehow still a part of the present world. And near the bookcase hung a small oil painting which seemed to me in key with the books, for it depicted not a person or a landscape but what appeared to be a room in a museum—perhaps one of the great chambers of the Vatican—with indistinct paintings on the walls and something in a case, that one could not see. It was, I thought, characteristic of the household. Eleni's husband knew an extraordinary amount about an extraordinary variety of things—the history and culture of Greece, and European philosophy and music, as well as his profession of law—and wrote more or less on all these subjects; but his opinions (I do not say it invidiously of so agreeable and learned a man) made sometimes as dry eating as must have been the legendary steaks supposed to have been cut by the Russians from the mammoth found frozen in Siberia. He was a Royalist, and, as with all such people whose position had been thus reduced, I could not but feel that his politics were founded—however subtly he might justify them—on an identification with his remnants of property and with the social prestige he enjoyed of the cultural interests and intellectual standards which were unquestionably what he most valued. Nor do I mean to sneer at this. How many similar people in the United States, deprived of social standing and financial independence—which is what the Greek bourgeoisie seem menaced with as no group in America is—could be sure of being able to uphold or defend the things they have been taught to admire?

Eleni, who was younger than her husband, did not, I thought, though loyal to Church and King, quite follow all the bourgeois prejudices, for she told us that some friend of hers was taking her to meet the Soviet Ambassador. She had the special sort of elegance and fineness that is not monied or aristocratic in the usual European sense but a part of some old kind of nobility, at once primitive and civilized, that still thrives in the Greek islands. I used to go swimming with them in the afternoons, and it depressed me to contrast with the beach reserved for the military Americans the *"plage"* at Gliphada, which had once, I was told, been the gayest and smartest of Athens. We U.N.R.R.A. men and soldiers on leave and engineers and war correspondents had a fine row of clean little houses that seemed to have been newly built, with various kinds of service, such as a woman who splashed you with water to wash the sand off your feet, and a bar where they opened your PX beer and supplied you with glasses to drink it. But at Gliphada the old casino had been completely dismantled by the Germans, and there was nothing but a sordid little place where you had to take turns in the bathhouses, rather sickening with the smell of the muddy sand with which the floors were caked and of the fish which was always being fried right next to the wet bathing suits. Eleni, against this background, in a faded pink bathing costume that brought out the tan of her arms and legs and showed her slender and sinuous body, all the more attracted one's attention by her naturalness and poise and grace; and two glimpses of her still stay in my mind as if I had brought them home engraved on Minoan seals: one of her figure going quickly up the stairs, obliquely so that I saw her in profile, pressing firmly but lightly on each of the steps with her rather long feet, showing none of the self-consciousness or vanity of a pretty woman at the beach; and the other of her standing in the water and playing with her little girl, smiling so that she made her eyes slits as she splashed with her palm tipped back at the wrist, at every splash thrusting her face forward and hissing, as if she had been some elemental creature—some siren that resembled a water snake. When I asked her what she was supposed to be, she answered that it wasn't anything.

· · ·

The V.s invited me to dinner one evening to celebrate Eleni's birthday. It was then that I met her mother and her stepfather, and I was amazed at her mother's youth, as I had been when I discovered that Eleni had children of ten and thirteen. Eleni had been married at sixteen, and her mother when she was not much older. The stepfather was a cosmopolitan man who apologized with dignity for the Greeks: they had recently been led to misbehave themselves by certain lawless and alien elements, and it was regrettable that this should have given the world a poor opinion of them. We went for dinner to one of the very best night clubs: a place such as, for gaiety and glamour, I had not seen, since the war, in Europe. It was also the first full-length meal under completely clean and attractive conditions that I had had since I had been in Greece, and evidently also a treat for the V. s. You got just the same dishes as elsewhere: sliced tomatoes, rice pilaff, and fish, but you got enough instead of too little. The place was full of well-groomed British officers with Athenian "society" girls, some of them very pretty with their blond hair in two rolls over their temples, so that their faces looked like valentines. Eleni and her mother enjoyed themselves recognizing people and gossiping about them. Some of these Greek girls were engaged to Englishmen.

There was with us a youngish journalist who wrote for a Royalist paper: he was a tall man of the world, very lively and rather dapper, with mustaches in the style of George II—as Eleni said to me later, "always perfectly delighted with himself." He was an old friend of Eleni's husband, who loved to talk politics with him. I had the impression that the combinations and projects which these two were always discussing were among the least realistic of the many schools of café-table politics with which Athens so abounds; but it had to be admitted this evening that their hopes, from an unexpected quarter, were getting the most heartening encouragement. The journalist had just heard over the radio the news of Bevin's speech on British foreign policy, and he relayed it to us with unrestrained glee and much gloating over the chagrin of the Left: "He said that the Labour Government would continue to follow the policy that England had already supported, that they could see no good reason for a change in Greece before the Greek elections took place, and that they would make every effort in the meantime to see that law and order were preserved—that they would send a police mission." He described to us at length a visit to England, from which he had just returned. He had been gratified unspeakably, at a party, to see a fashionable English lady recognize, by a glance at his insignia, an officer of the Greek Air Force. And he went on to tell us a story about another party, at which he had had *un succès foudroyant avec trois compliments—trois seulement, mais très méditerranéens.* The first compliment I cannot remember, but the second had been detonated at the time when they were playing a game of "What famous person would you most like to be?" The lady whom he hoped to impress had, in his turn, put this question to him, and he had answered, *"La ville de Hiroshima." "'Pourquoi?' J'ai répondu, 'Je voudrais être la ville de Hiroshima, si vous étiez la bombe atomique pour me tomber dessus!'"* Later she had returned and said, smiling, *"Dîtes-moi, qu'est-ce que vous voudriez être encore?" "Cette fois je lui ai répondu—toujours très méditerranéen, 'Je voudrais être une cigarette.' 'Pourquoi?' 'Pour brûler entre vos lèvres!' Le prochain après midi, à cinq heures, elle m'a téléphoné,"* etc.

The floor show seemed to me absolutely marvellous. I had forgotten how good such things could be, had hardly realized they were still going on. There were a girl who did an Oriental tumbling dance; a girl who sang in Greek and English; a couple who did a folk dance from one of the islands, fresh and animated and gone in a flash; and the great feature: a famous woman dancer who was also a romantic legend. I learned about her from Eleni and her mother. The Germans had had her on the carpet, the elder but far-from-old lady explained to me, for her well-known association with the English. But she had stood up to them with perfect sang-froid: *"Que j'ai eu un amant anglais—même deux, trois, quatre,"* she was supposed to have replied, *"qu'est-ce que ça fait?"* She had had German lovers, too, Eleni thought; she had run through all the nationalities and always remained herself—and Eleni added with admiration: *"Elle ment avec une facilité inouïe."* I saw that the myth of this performer, the great dancer who is also a great courtesan, had come to mean a good deal in Athens, which had been so much without the luxuries and so much at the mercy of the war. She was the devotee of art and love who had endured through all the hardship and conflict, and she was almost a sacred figure.

And she *was* extremely good: very beautiful, quick, sure, and dashing, and able to get into everything she did a personality of enchanting insolence. Before one knew it, she would have leapt on a chair, and would be bending down and kissing one of the diners, and then would hit him over the head with her tambourine. I had avoided such black-market places: one night at one of the too well-supplied restaurants in Rome, where we had been dining at outdoor tables, a small mob had gathered behind us and begun reaching in for the food, and we had seen them dispelled with brutality—an old woman knocked down in the street—by the strong-arm men from the restaurant. But I succumbed to the brilliance of this night club, and, since I had been there without my long-distance glasses and we had been sitting in a corner a long way to the rear of the show, I decided to go again and see it better. I got up another party the next night with a man I knew in U.N.R.R.A. and two of the U.N.R.R.A. girls, and this time we had an excellent table in the middle and on the edge of the floor. The girls, who had been there often, said we were right in the spot to be kissed. This time some of the acts, seen distinctly, turned out rather disappointing; but the fascinating dancer was wonderful. Her first appearance was a ballroom number, which had its climax in a piece of business—an ecstatic start and smile as her partner, kneeling, kissed her midriff—that, for daring, style, naturalness, and timing, took your breath away. When she came out for the second time, she seemed to be some sort of priestess or idol—possibly Javanese; and, exhilarated as I was by the excellent white wine—well cooled and non-resinated—I was preparing to fall under her spell when she abruptly disappeared from the stage. The music went on playing, but she did not come back. "Did you see what happened then?" the U.N.R.R.A. man asked the girls. "Yes: the thing that held her dress behind broke." "Somebody's catching hell back there!" he said.

It was two evenings before I left Athens, and this image was to remain in my mind as my last memory of the world of the Greek bourgeoisie.

THE BIRCH LEAVES FALLING

Rebecca West

OCTOBER 26, 1946 (ON THE NUREMBERG TRIALS)

I T WAS THE LAST TWO DAYS of the Nuremberg trial that I went abroad to see. Those men who had wanted to kill me and my kind and who had nearly had their wish were to be told whether I and my kind were to kill them and why. Quite an occasion. But for most of the time my mind was distracted from it by bright, sharp, smaller things. Consider the marvels of air travel. It was necessary, and really necessary, that a large number of important persons, including the heads of the armed and civil services, should go to Nuremberg and hear the reading of the judgment, because in no other conceivable way could they gather what the trial had been about. Long, long ago, the minds of all busy people who did not happen to be lawyers had lost touch with the proceedings. The daily reports inevitably concentrated on the sensational moments when the defendants sassed authority back. To follow the faint obtusions of the legal issues in the press took the type of mind that reads its daily portion and never misses, and, indeed, even a tougher type of mind than that, since this duty had to be discharged without the fear of hell as inspiration. That kind of integrity carries one irresistibly to the top of the grocery store, and almost no further. The high positions fall to people with pliant minds, who drop every habit if it is not agreeable or immediately serviceable. These were all at sea about Nuremberg, and it was a pity, for English public opinion had gone silly about it. There had surged up a wave of masochist malaise, akin to the Keynesian scorn for Versailles after the last war, which spread and split over any attempt to cope with the situation of victory. There was need for the influential to talk some sense on the subject. It was unfortunate that these responsible persons, as well as the newspaper correspondents, had to travel to Nuremberg by air. This amounted to a retrogression to the very early days of railway transport; planes carry so few passengers, and so many pilots have been demobilized. Nuremberg is between three and four hours' flight from London, but to attend a sitting of the court that began on Monday, September 30th, I had to leave on the previous Tuesday.

I was bidden by the authorities, the day before, to wait for my papers in a block of offices built on a site which, up to a few years ago, was occupied by the town house of a ducal family. I frequented it in those days, though not to visit the duke and duchess. I used to pass, on another errand, through their halls, where gold and lacquer and crystal reflections swam in the depths, a little sadder than still water, of mirrors some centuries old, and go across a patch of sour grass where lean London cats, masterless and therefore as God made them, mocked and bullied the plump ducal cats, who, as the price of love and regular meals, had suffered a certain misfortune, and finally enter a sort of outhouse, in which an old gentleman sat among an uncontrollable spilth of papers, such a spilth as would have sent one, had it been of water, telephoning right and left for plumbers. The duke was Roman Catholic; this man had been an Anglican clergyman in a village on his estates, and had been converted to the ancient faith; to provide for him, he had been given the task of putting in order the family archives. It was kindly meant, but the poor old gentleman, who was a scholar, was in the state of one who has been turned out in a forest during the autumn and been told that each fallen leaf bears a message and he must piece the leaves together. In panic, he complained to every visitor that in these papers he found chains of evidence running all through modern history to this and that event, and he could not keep them in order or deliver any neat whole to the historians. Now there were no mirrors and no cats, and no old gentleman lost among an excess of significance, but a bright civil servant in a bright office, who brightly handed me some papers. When I saw that they were my Army orders, in triplicate, I knew that I was entering a man's world, in the pejorative sense. It was decreed that I should fly from an airport half an hour from my home in the country, and I applauded that. Nothing, I said, could be more convenient. I was checked and chilled. I must, it seemed, report at an office in the heart of London, and that at six in the morning. But why? It had to be. I looked into the face of something as immutable as the will of God but not as sensible as that. Well, could I leave my bag in that office overnight? No, I could not. How was I to get a bag, at an hour when there are no taxis and no buses, to an office no-where near a subway? They did not know. It is true that I have a husband who can wake at any hour at will, and that we had our automobile in town. But how did authority know that? How did authority know that I am the kind of woman who, finding that neither my club nor any hotel could give me a room, would spend the night on the sofa of my club cardroom? That was not my original intention. People play bridge so late. I had hoped to use the sofa in the ladies' rest room, but I found someone else was there already. She said she had just got off a train from Milan. Gloomily, I went and waited till hearts and diamonds permitted me to wind a rug around me on the other, narrower sofa. It was hard to sleep there. I looked at the gilt pilasters of the room and remembered that this club had once been the town house of the fifth Marquess of Lansdowne, who had embarrassed the government in the middle of the last war by starting a movement in favor of peace negotiations. He was impelled to this unconventional and unpopular action, some said, be-cause of his grief at the death of a son in battle; others said he had done it because, the bluest of Conservatives, he had seen that a prolonged war would bring down the old order in ruins. I was glad not to be visited by his ghost. Yes, the death of a young man in that abortive war has seemed, in each successive year, more tragic. Yes, the old order is in ruins; a club has trespassed on your family's house; I have trespassed on that club. But to stop fighting would not have been the answer. And what is the an-swer? Excuse me! I am going to Nuremberg tomorrow morning! Very early!

A motorbus took the planeload of us out of London night into country dawn, passing, in the ghostly twilight, a corner where, one breezy April afternoon when I was in my twenties, I had helped Joseph Conrad chase his bowler hat across the road. He had seemed to me then an exciting exotic, writing of such unusual things as danger. Now, as the plane rose into the leaden sky, we looked down on a land that was recording, after this worst of summers, a disaster that restored one's self-respect because it was not made by statesmen or soldiers or any men at all but by nature. In the fields, sheaves that should have stood in harvest time like stocky golden girls and then been gathered in were crouched and drab, like old scrubwomen, and would never know the honor of a barn. Half-finished ricks heeled over on their narrow bases. The pastures looked quite lus-treless. Across the North Sea, in Belgium and Holland, the ditches that should have scored fine, silver lines were broad, gross troughs of sullen water. There would be much less milk this winter, fewer eggs, less meat, perhaps less bread. There would be financial disaster in these little, sodden villages, these farms standing in black smears of mud. Worse than that, there would be mental misery, a sense of guilt. I had seen on my own farm how men who had overworked throughout the war years could not stand up to this wet summer. The bombs that fell in our valley, by reason of its likeness to another, where an important research station was hidden, were realized to be the work of an enemy and taken as fair enough. But even those who did not believe in God believed that this summer was a judgment of God, a sign that they had not found favor with a force which might have been kind, which had decided to withhold, which perhaps knew something wrong in the heart and was therefore just and irrevocable. The wet summer, which showed that God was disagreeable, the lack of shoes, which showed that governments, of whatever color, were inefficient—that is what everybody would be grumbling about in the sulky land below us. Here someone would be putting a hand in the bed of wheat spread in the barn and groaning because it was hot, hot as a hot-water bottle, and so no good for seed; and here someone would be raising his foot across his knee and twisting his neck to see the sole of his boot and groaning because there was another hole and the sock inside was soaking wet. The plane seemed a fortunate molecule, immune from the dowdy sorrows beneath. It was an illusion. Nearly all the passengers except myself and another correspondent were industrialists and technicians on their way to Hamburg on important business. The airport at Hamburg was under water.

. . .

A man's world, a man's world. I was in it, all right. When I got to Berlin, grave young men said impatiently that I must get on the next plane going back to London, because they had no idea how to send me to Nuremberg. I laid my Army orders down on the table, but nobody would look at them. Nobody ever did, then or afterward. When the young men turned the other way, I got into an automobile that had been sent to fetch another correspondent, and the pair of us went to a hotel in the Kurfürstendam which is used as a press camp, and there they knew all about me. Yes, of course I could go to Nuremberg. Either I could go by American plane from the Tempelhof airport, which was doubtful, as there was such a competition for seats, or I could go by train by way of Frankfurt, which would take about eighteen hours.

Easy in my mind, I spent the afternoon walking incredulously about the city. I had always been a social failure in Berlin. Except in a few Jewish homes, I had been considered light-minded and flimsily dressed. At a villa in Dahlem, a banker had wrestled publicly for my soul. "At the beginning of the inflation," he told me, "I was on holiday in Switzerland. When I came back, I found that my wife had sold our dog for a sack of potatoes."

"How terrible," I said.

"Terrible?" he said. "What are you calling terrible?"

"Why," I answered weakly, "terrible that you should have had to sell your dog for a sack of potatoes."

"No, no, it was not terrible," he said huffily. "Naturally, I loved my family more than I loved my dog. How fortunate it was that I was able to sell my dog and gain in exchange nourishment for my dear wife and children. It is easy to see that you in England have no real experience of national misfortune when you call it terrible that I had to sell a dog for the sake of my family."

These lumbering creatures had blown away like smoke; only a few of them now walked in the streets of their town, and they were lean and did not bellow and kept their elbows by their sides. They had had houses as coarse as themselves, gross in design and ornamented with gross sculptures. These were now austere shells. Piranesi, he who loved to draw the well-fleshed architecture of the Romans and their Renaissance descendants, was smitten in his latter years with madness and drew only buildings stripped to the bare brick and dedicated to the harsh necessity of being prisons. Berlin is like page after page of his *Carceri*. Different towns have different modes of desolation. There is no rubble in Berlin, few waste lots, but mile after mile of purged houses scoured by the wind and rain, mere diagrams of habitation.

A man's world, a man's world. The bright civil servant had fitted me out with a letter of credit for forty pounds. Authority sent me next morning on a drive to a little villa, cozily red with Virginia creeper, seven miles out in the suburbs, where there was a pay office which could cash it. It couldn't. Some new currency regulations had come into being that prevented one's cashing anything anywhere. I needed dollars to pay for my passage to Nuremberg. I could not buy them legitimately. I had to go to another part of Berlin and buy British scrip, a kind that is valid only in the British zone, where I was not going. My instinct then told me to go and sit in a bar. When the link between alcohol and the currency regulations had declared itself and I had acquired my dollars, I realized that I was, so far as authority was concerned, going to stay in Germany for the rest of my life. It was obvious that my fares and my keep would far exceed the sum of money I had been allowed to export. I rang up the English newspaper which had sent me abroad. They told me to draw on their resident correspondent at Nuremberg. This gave me confidence for about a quarter of an hour, at the end of which time I discovered that the same new currency regulations had forbidden any correspondent to draw more than fifteen dollars a week, which is less than he could conceivably live upon. During this time of financial perturbation, I was continually being told that I would never succeed in getting on a plane to Nuremberg but would have to reconcile myself to the long train journey. In the morning, I left Berlin by a plane with five empty seats. The others were occupied by a number of currency experts, who, I gathered, were going to Nuremberg to discuss the fact that some of the new regulations—not those which had affected me—meant nothing at all. During the journey, they made the same discovery about several other regulations, which they had apparently thought till then were all right.

It is the fate of works of art to be extraordinarily poignant because they cannot be blamed. I cannot weep for the citizens of Berlin, because I always suspected that they did not know enough to come in out of the rain, even when it turned into blood, but nobody expects a statue to know when to come in out of the rain, so I can be very sorry for the statues of Berlin. They seemed, when I first knew them, to be considerably more stable than I was ever likely to be. Opposite the Brandenburger Tor, down by the Reichstag, there was a vast column commemorating the three victorious wars of nineteenth-century Germany—the war against Denmark, the war against Austria, the Franco-Prussian War. Nearby was a statue of von Moltke, and another, of a German general named von Roon, and a whale of a statue of Bismarck with, around the base, a lot of allegorical women with breasts like artillery pieces. In the Tiergarten, that pleasant expanse of woodland stretching away from the Brandenburger Tor, there was the Sieges-Allee, the gorgeous chaplet of dynastic piety in which, sculptured in marble as white as wedding-cake icing, in curious enclosures like marble opera loges, stood the Margraves of Brandenburg and their modern descendants among the Hohenzollerns. Among its glades there was also a rose garden, presided over by a statue of the Empress Victoria, wearing not only a marble hat but a marble veil. There was also a statue of a nude girl riding a horse, very pleasant to come upon in a walk under the tall trees, naturalistic but quite good.

All but these two women, the Empress with the marble hat and the girl with none, were picked up and moved in the middle thirties. Hitler did not want anything to remind the people of the Hohenzollerns or their servants or their victories. He moved the vast column almost a mile down the avenue, he distributed the statues of Bismarck and von Moltke and von Roon around it, and he put the Sieges-Allee in an unfrequented area of the park. This was an act of extravagance and folly which should have convinced everybody that if Hitler fought a war, he would probably lose it, but the statues gained by it; they were set deeper among the trees, they lost their smugness, they looked as if they were part of the setting of a romantic drama. They have since undergone another change, which has lifted them to the heights of memorability. The trees of the Tiergarten have nearly all been destroyed. Some were burned in the raids; some were hit by Russian artillery during the battle for the city; most of the rest were cut down by the freezing population last winter. Now the great park is nothing but a vast potato patch, with here and there a row of other vegetables, and from this rise the statues, in an inappropriate prominence that is to marble what embarrassed nakedness is to humanity. Above them, the column of the three victorious wars is surmounted by the French flag, and their horizon is bounded by riddled cliffs that were once splendid villas and apartment houses. But as well as this appalling, landscape-wide humiliation, they have suffered more private troubles. The pedestals of von Moltke and von Roon, the bellies of the women who were symbolizing some forgotten thesis around Bismarck, are scrawled with the names and addresses of Russian soldiers. The Empress Victoria has lost her marble veil, her marble hat, her marble head. Decapitated, she stands among the amazed pergolas. The Sieges-Allee has suffered a peculiar loss of the same sort. Its statues and busts have been left intact; they belong to a kind of realistic art that would be greatly admired by the Russians. But each of the marble opera loges is supported on each side by a Hohenzollern eagle, and each of these has been decapitated, very neatly, and evidently by a suitable instrument. Only the naked girl on the horse is as she was, but there are marks of attempts to get her off the horse, and a friend who lives in Berlin tells me that one morning he found, under the horse, three champagne bottles, all full and unopened and of an excellent brand. There is now no statuary at all at the Brandenburger Tor, except a new memorial to the Russian troops, which is surmounted by a realistic figure that, fantastically, resembles Mussolini. The sentry who guarded it was, like so many of the Russian soldiers in Berlin, a ravishing small boy with pink cheeks and a nose that turned up to heaven with the gravity of prayer. I quite understood why they had made the statue on the memorial look like Mussolini; that nose would not have gone well in marble or bronze.

. . .

In Nuremberg, the press camp was another example of the poignancy of works of art under conquest. The camp was the *Schloss* belonging to the Fabers, the pencil manufacturers, and, according to the old-fashioned custom, which persisted in Germany long after it had been abandoned in England and in the United States, it was built beside the factory from which the family fortune was derived. It lay a mile or two outside the town, and as one drove toward it, its romantic absurdity loomed above flat fields. It stank of wealth, like the palaces of Pittsburgh, but it was twice the size of any of them, and it had a superior, more allusive fantasy. It had spires and turrets as fussy as lobster claws, winding staircases that wound not like staircases but with the unnecessary ambition of the larger intestine, a marble entrance hall that was like a fusion of a fish shop and a bathroom, and somehow one knew that the architect and the man who had commissioned him had both been thinking of the Nibelungenlied and the Meistersingers. In its heyday, it must have been intolerable, particularly if one had a sense of the Fabers as human beings. A clue to them could be found in the immense grounds, which were laid out in what is known in Germany as an English park, though actually no park in England is closely planted with shrubs and trees. This was dotted with various pavilions, and the heavy cedar door of one, which was built like a temple, had been battered open. The interior was panelled with carefully chosen marbles, some the color of meat, some of gravy, and in an alcove, on a pedestal bearing the family arms, was a statue of the founder of the firm playing with a little girl and boy. On his beard, the little girl's ringlets, everybody's buttons and boots, the sculptor had worked with particularly excited care. Two chilly orange marble benches were provided for his descendants to sit on to contemplate the image and the memory of their progenitor. He looked a self-respecting old gentleman. There was nothing about him to suggest that the fruit of his loins would presently fantasticate his prudently acquired acres with a mansion drop-sical in its inflated whimsy. Nor was there anything in that mansion which threatened just how bad things were to be before the night fell.

Now this mansion was punished by the presence of a crowd of corre-spondents, which on physical grounds alone was an offense to the genius of the mansion. The protocol of its hospitality must once have been stu-pendous. Only members of certain families would have been invited, and they would have arrived with valets and ladies' maids, and after a recep-tion by the host and hostess would have been passed along the colossal corridors by clusters of servants to suites where beds banked with super-fluous pillows shone with the highlights of fine linen. In the room where I slept, there were nine hospital beds. On one side of me was a French correspondent, a lovely girl the color of cambric tea, with crenellated hair that spoke of North Africa and with the bold and gracious manners of a wild princess. And on the other was another French correspondent, a girl pale and fairish, and eager but always a little tired, as is often the case with those who spent their adolescence in the Resistance movement. Nothing can have been so offensive to the mansion as the French women correspondents. The most conspicuous of them was Madeleine Jacob, with her superb, haggard Jewish face, her long black locks, so oddly springing from a circle of white hair on the center of her scalp, her tum-bled white waist and pleated skirt of a tartan that was not only non-Scottish but almost anti-Scottish, her air of contentious intellectual gaiety, as of one who has been dragged backward through a hedge of ideas and has enjoyed every minute of it. She was always the first to catch the eye of the living observer in the crowded dining room; she must have been the first and the worst to any ghostly observer. The women for whom this mansion was built lived inside their corsets as inside towers; their coiffures were almost as architectural; all their contours had to be preserved by an iron poise. They would have refused to believe that these ink-stained gypsies had, in fact, invaded their halls because they had been on the side of order against disorder, stability against incoherence.

. . .

How much easier would we journalists have found our task at Nurem-berg if only the universe had been less fluid, if anything had been abso-lute, even so simple a thing as the sight we had gone to see—the end of the trial. And we saw it. With observation whetted by practice and our sense of the historic importance of the occasion, we let nothing that happened in the court go by us. We formed opinions about it with edges sharp as honed razors. We knew, when the judges issued a decree that the defendants were not to be photographed while they were being sentenced, that it was a silly and sentimental interference with the rights of the press. Yet about that our opinions were perhaps not so definite as appeared in the talk of the bar. The correspondents who had been at Nuremberg a long time were not so sure about this decree as those who had come for just these last two days. The correspondents who had been in Germany a long time did not appear to like to talk about it very much. It seemed that when one has never seen a man, one does not find anything offensive about the idea of photographing him while he is being sentenced to death, but that if one has seen him often, the idea becomes unattractive. It is not exactly pity that takes one. One would not alter the sentence of death. The future must be protected. The ovens where the innocent were baked alive must remain cold forever; the willing stokers, so oddly numerous, it appears, must be discouraged from lighting them again. But when one sees a man day after day, the knowledge of his approaching death becomes, in the real sense of the word, wonderful. One wonders at it every time one thinks of it. I remembered that I did not care at all the first time I heard William Joyce sentenced to death, but that the second time I was stirred and astonished, and that the third time I knew awe. The day he was hanged, I found myself looking at my hand and thinking in perplexity that someday it would not move because I willed it, and that on that day I would have no will, I would not be there; and Joyce was a kind of partner in my thought, not an object for pity. It is an intensification of the feeling we have in the fall, when the leaves drop. The leaves are nothing to us, but the melancholy, the apprehension grows.

It was like that in other parts of Nuremberg, where the lawyers lived who had seen every session of the court. They had all been waiting for this day when the judgment would be delivered and the defendants sentenced, for it meant that they would turn their backs on the moldy aftermath of murder and get back to the business of living. But now that this day had come, they were not enjoying it. All automobiles were stopped now on the main roads for search and scrutiny of the occupants by the military police. At one barrier, two automobiles were halted at the same time, and a visitor travelling in one saw that in the other was the engaging wife of one of the English judges, a tall Scandinavian with that awkwardness which is more graceful than grace, that shyness which is more winning than any direct welcome. They exchanged greetings and the visitor said, "I shall be seeing you in court tomorrow." The other looked as if she had been slapped across the high cheekbones. "Oh, no," she said. "Oh, no. I shall not be in court tomorrow." She had attended almost all other sessions of the court. Around the house of another judge, a line of automobiles waited all through the evening of the day before the judgment session, and passersby knew that the judiciary was having its last conference. The judge's wife came to the window and looked out over the automobiles and the passerby and far into the suburban woods that ring the house. She has kept into maturity the delicate and self-possessed good looks of a spirited girl, and ordinarily she refuses to let her appearance betray what she is thinking or feeling. But as she stared out into the darkening woods, it could be seen that the boredom she was suffering had something ghastly about it, and that she was living through a patch of time comparable to the interval between a death in the house and a funeral.

There was another house, still further away from Nuremberg, where this aversion to the consequences of the trial which was not disapproval of it could be experienced. This, like the press camp, was a villa an industrialist had built beside his factory, but it was smaller and not so gross and had been the scene of a war of taste in which some of the victories had fallen to the right side. The industrialist who had built it, and furnished it in the style of a Nord-Amerika liner, had had two sons, and one had married a wife who was still in the house and who silently acted as a butler to the conquerors who had requisitioned it. She was, in fact, though she told no one for a very long time, half Lorrainer and half French, and she had a deep love and knowledge of Greek art. So here and there in the rooms, along with the family busts and the whacking great Japanese bronzes, realistically mustachioed, that all German bourgeois households cherished, were torsos and heads that, in the Greek way, presented the whole truth about certain moments of physical existence. There was a torso which showed how it is with a boy's body, cut clean with training, when the ribs rise to a deep and enjoyed breath. There was the coifed head of a girl who knew she was being looked at by the world and, innocent and proud, let it look. In this room, parties of people concerned with the trial held glasses of good wine in their hands, talked generously of pleasant things and not of the judgment and the sentences, and every now and then looked at these sculptures as if they were earnests of another and better life. About this house, and all the houses where the legal personnel lived, armed guards paced through the night, and searchlights shone into the woods, falling fiercely on the piebald trunks of the birch trees, the compactly contorted pines, the great pottery jars, overflowing with red nasturtiums, that marked the course of the avenues. Down through the strong brightness there slowly drifted the yellow birch leaves, all night long.

. . .

There came the day of the judgment and the day of the sentences, and I was again aware that I was in a man's world. Life in Nuremberg was difficult in any case, because of transport. The city is so devastated that the buildings used by the authorities are a vast distance apart, and one cannot walk. Cars are old and rapidly falling to pieces, and the drivers have been out there too long and care about nothing except going home. But when the great day came, there was added a new exasperation in the extreme congestion of the Palace of Justice. It was obviously possible that some Nazi sympathizers would try to get into the court and assassinate the counsel and the judges, and it was obvious that the authorities would have to take special care in scrutinizing the passes of the correspondents and the visitors. I had seen myself having to stop at the entrance of the court and show my pass, whereupon a trained scrutineer would examine it under a strong light. Nothing so simple happened. Authority jammed the corridors with a solid mass of military policemen, who again and again demanded passes and peered at them in a half light. These confused male children would have been quite incapable of detecting a forged pass if they had been able to see it, but in this deep shadow it was difficult to read print, much less inspect a watermark. This congestion of pass-demanding military policemen occurred at every point where it was necessary for correspondents to move freely, to look around and find their seats, to get in touch with their colleagues. At the actual entrance to the gallery, there was posted a new official, to whom I took a savage dislike because he infringed on a feminine patent. Although he was male and a colonel, he had the drooping bosom and careworn expression of a nursing mother, and he stared at my quite obviously valid pass minute after minute with the moonish look of a woman trying to memorize the pattern of a baby's bootee. Was I irritable? Yes. I and all England, all Europe, are irritable because we are controlled by and sick of organization. And perhaps he was slow and awkward because all people in organization not of the scheming and tyrannic sort are sick of exercising control on resentful subjects.

What did we see in the courtroom? Everybody knows by now. It is no longer worth telling: it was not worth telling if you knew too little; it could not be told if you knew too much. The door at the back of the dock shut on the last of the prisoners, who had worked their final confusion by showing a heroism to which they had no moral right, who had proved that it is not true that the bully is always a coward and that not even in that respect is life simple.

Then the court rose, rose up into the air, rose as if it were going to fly out of the window. People hurried along the corridors into each other's offices, saying goodbye—goodbye to each other, goodbye to the trial, goodbye to the feeling that was like fall. That was if they were the great, of course, for only the great could get out of Nuremberg. The lesser would have to wait at the airport or the railway stations for days as the fog took a hand in the congestion and the planes could not leave the ground safely in the mornings, and more and more people tried to go home by train. On the floor of every office there were packing cases: the typewriters had to go home, the stationery had to go home, the files had to go home. The greater bent down to say goodbye to the lesser, on their knees beside the packing cases; the lesser beamed up at the greater. It was a party; it was like going off for a cruise, only instead of leaving home you were going home; it was grand, it was happy, it was as positively good as things seem only in childhood, when nobody doubts that it is good when the school term comes to an end. Yet if one could not leave Nuremberg, this gaiety did not last intact after the sun went down. Then one heard words that brought back what one felt about the end of the trial, when one did not turn one's mind away from it. A man said, "Damn it all. I have looked at those men for ten months. I know them as I know the furniture in my room. Oh, damn it all. . . ."

• • •

That vague, visceral mournfulness, that sympathy felt for the doomed flesh as for the frosted flower, settled on the mind steadily during the days that passed after the return from Nuremberg, as the executions drew nearer. It was dispersed suddenly by the news of Göring's suicide. A dozen emotions surprised me by their strength. The enormous clown, the sexual quiddity with the smile that was perhaps too wooden for mockery and perhaps not, had kicked the tray out of the hands of the servant who was carrying it; the glasses had flown into the air and splintered, the wine of humiliation we had intended him to drink had spilled on the floor. It was disconcerting to realize that the man's world in which Nuremberg had had its being had in effect been just as crazy as it had looked. All to no purpose had the military police fallen over my feet and had I fallen over theirs, all to no purpose had the colonel with the bosom brooded pendulously over my pass. The cyanide had freely flowed. I felt fear. Whether this romantic gesture would revive Nazism depended on the degree to which the people in the waterlogged Europe I had seen from the plane were preoccupied with the spoiled harvest and their lack of shoes. If their preoccupation was slight or desperate, they might equally play with the idea of restoring the Nazi regime. I remembered the incidental obscenities of Nuremberg, such as the slight smell that hung round the door of the room that housed the atrocity exhibits—the shrunken head of the Polish prisoner, the soap made from concentration-camp corpses, and the like; I remembered the vigor of some of the defendants, and the passivity of the German people in the streets, blank paper on which anything could be written. But also there came a vague, visceral cheerfulness, applause for the flesh that had not accepted its doom but had changed it to something else that made a last proof of its strength, such as one might have felt for a beast that has been caught in a trap and that, when its captors come, arches its back and makes a last stand. All the people I had seen fleeing from Nuremberg, who would be halfway across the world now, trying to forget the place, would be straightening up from whatever they had been doing and saying with a laugh, before they could check themselves, "Oh, that one! We always knew he would get the better of us yet."

THE BEAUTIFUL SPOILS: MONUMENTS MEN

Janet Flanner

MARCH 8, 1947 (ON NAZI ART THEFT)

'T THE HEIGHT OF ITS WAR EFFORT, the United States had almost three million men under arms in the European Theatre of Operations. A dozen men out of these millions were functioning, under G-5, Operations Branch, SHAEF, as a *rarissimo* group known as Monuments, Fine Arts, and Archives. Up to almost the end of the war, it was the modest job of these few American Monuments men, and their two or three British colleagues, to try to check on and protect, over an area of thousands of square miles, what was left of the Continent's art and historic monuments. And when peace came in Europe, it was the aim of this group, then swollen to some twenty-five members (officers, sergeants, and pfc.s, mostly Americans), to collect a few hundred thousand items of displaced art—French, Dutch, Belgian, Czech, Russian, Polish, and even German—to be returned to or held in trust for the proper people in whichever country they had been owned before 1939.

In 1942, the American Defense–Harvard Group and the Committee of the American Council of Learned Societies, two groups interested in the protection of works of art in the war zones, had drawn President Roosevelt's attention to the probability that Europe's beauty would suffer badly if the Allies invaded the Continent. As a result, he created, in 1943, the American Commission for the Protection and Salvage of Artistic and Historic Monuments in War Areas, more conveniently known as the Roberts Commission, because Justice Owen J. Roberts, of the Supreme Court, was its chairman. The Roberts body acted as intermediary between the War Department and scholars from Columbia, Harvard's Fogg Art Museum, the Metropolitan Museum, the Frick Art Reference Library, and other erudite centers that supplied the Army with information for what was called the Supreme Headquarters Official Lists of Protected Monuments, a vast, military guidebook of historic lay buildings, churches, and museums that were to be saved, if possible; that is, they were not to be targets, or be slept in, or be looted. Monuments, Fine Arts, and Archives, operating in the field, took up where the Roberts Commission left off. The optimistic prospectus set forth early in 1944 for the M.F.A. & A. envisaged a bang-up Allied advisory staff, topped by a lieutenant colonel, with sixteen majors, more than half to be American, aided by a number of predominantly American field outfits, each containing a minimum of twelve junior officers; plus an officer attached to the H.Q. G-5 of each Army, and three more officers under him at the front, assisted by six enlisted men. All of them were to be kept scurrying around in trucks and jeeps, with cameras and typewriters, so they could send to the rear "a constant flow of reports and information," under fifteen subheadings. That, at any rate, was the dream.

Eleven days before the Normandy invasion, General Eisenhower issued a letter to field commanders that began, "Shortly we will be fighting our way across the Continent of Europe. . . . Inevitably, in the path of our advance will be found historical monuments and cultural centers which symbolize to the world all that we are fighting to preserve. It is the responsibility of every commander to protect and respect these symbols whenever possible." On June 6th, however, art preservation must have been the last thing the field commanders thought about as they battled for an invader's toehold in the Atlantic Wall, blasting Gothic spires and billeting their tired, dirty men in any Norman château, full of art or not, they were lucky enough to find intact. In any case, no Monuments men were present to make suggestions. About a fortnight later, two American Monuments officers, Captain (afterward Major) Bancel LaFarge, A.U.S., and Lieutenant George Stout, U.S. N.R., and one Englishman, Squadron Leader J. E. Dixon-Spain, R.A.F., arrived in Normandy—without typewriters, cameras, or trucks—and were turned loose to hitchhike toward their goal, the salvation of art. The situation the trio found themselves in was novel: they had to explain, practically in the heat of battle, who they were, what they were trying to do, and why. Their task was to give first aid to badly injured art (though they had no

supplies to repair with), to prevent improper billeting in historic buildings (though the field commanders were supposed to have the Protected
Monuments Lists with them, even if they didn't read them), and to inspect and report on the state of the monuments to be protected (though
they had no machines to inspect in or to type with). Whether the whole
Monuments project was to continue or be scrapped—the latter was
greatly favored by some brass hats before the scheme was even tried—
depended on the kind of show these three (and three other Americans
and two other British, who were added before the summer's end) were
able to put up. The amazing accomplishments of these eight men, who at
first had to make their way by riding on anything from regimental laun-
dry trucks to liberated bicycles, resulted in the piecemeal arrival of the
Allies' full wartime art group, which—the early ambitious plans
forgotten—was maintained at an average strength of fifteen, and which,
up to the end of hostilities, scoured France, Belgium, the Netherlands,
Luxembourg, and Germany and actually inspected 3,145 monuments
and archives, or what was left of them.

· · ·

The M.F.A. & A. was among the smallest outfits, and was certainly the
most recherché one, in the Allied armies. Once, in the autumn of 1945,
shortly after the German capitulation, it swelled to eighty-four officers
and men, but while the fighting was on, no such number, it was felt,
could be spared for art. About half of the Americans in the M.F.A. & A.
had been recommended by the Roberts Commission for transfer to
Monuments on the basis of their civilian backgrounds. They were largely
youngish art professors, museum curators, sculptors, painters, and architects, and occasionally talented dilettantes. Their chief adviser to
SHAEF was the Slade Professor of Fine Art from Cambridge University, Lieutenant Colonel Geoffrey Webb. Some of the luminaries among
the earlier American Monuments men were—in addition to LaFarge,
who had been a New York architect, and Stout, who had been an expert
on conservation at the Fogg Art Museum—Lieutenant Lamont Moore,
National Gallery, Washington; Lieutenant Sheldon Keck, Brooklyn
Museum; Lieutenant Calvin Hathaway, Cooper Union Museum for the
Arts of Decoration; Captain Everett Lesley, Art Professor, University of
Minnesota; Pfc. Lincoln Kirstein, art patron; Captain Robert Posey, ar-
chitect; Captain Walker Hancock, Prix de Rome sculptor; Lieutenant
James Rorimer, Metropolitan Museum; Captain Walter Huchthausen,

Art and Architecture Professor, University of Michigan; and Captain Ralph Hammett, architect.

The first of these professional art experts were sent off to their Normandy-invasion jobs carrying directives sprinkled with such helpful hints as "A castle is usually defined as a large fortified building and a palace as an unfortified stately mansion or residence of royalty," of which republican France has none. The Monuments men's own definition of a palace was, according to one of them, "the local honey on the Supreme H.Q. protected list, where the blasted colonels will certainly billet their troops unless a wandering Monuments man gets there first with an 'Off Limits' sign and his neck stuck out." In their billeting-overseeing job, the Monuments men were like frantic boarding-house keepers, trying to put thousands of lodgers into the right rooms and out of the wrong ones and, above all, trying to prevent them from pocketing everything pretty that belonged to the house. "Off Limits" signs were tried and didn't work, so "Protected Monument" signs were stuck up to discourage our uniformed souvenir hunters from liberating art items to send home to Mom. And the cynical Monuments men marked off really attractive debris and important buildings with white tape, falsely indicating the presence of unexploded mines. It was the worry of our State Department, especially after the Liberation idyll began to fade, that the prestige of the United States Army and the American idea would decline still further if our troops and officers manhandled or lawlessly occupied the western democracies' historic properties. As long as our armies remained in Europe, "the greatest single" M.F.A. & A. problem, an official report declared, was saving the Continent's art "from spoliation and damage by the U.S. Armed Forces." A great deal of minor damage was, it seems, done to châteaux by billeted Americans who nailed pinup girls to highly valued, highly carved antique *boiseries*. This was, however, literally only a pinprick among all the wounds art suffered.

The worst billeting jam occurred in the autumn of 1944, while the war was still on, in the Paris sector—the part of France that is richest in palaces and châteaux—when American troops were pouring toward the front. Improper billeting became almost as big an M.F.A. & A. pain as the unwarranted demands for fancier billets by outfits that were already billeted. One colonel of a replacement group aspired to billet his fifty officers in Mme. de Pompadour's historic mansion at Fontainebleau— a demand that was easy to refuse because another outfit had accidentally just set fire to the Henri IV wing of Fontainebleau Palace. The Monuments people also received endless intimate requests from the French: that a Quartermaster trucking battalion billeted in the Château de Celle please respect the collection of stag antlers belonging to its owner, the Duc de Brissac; that the room in which Cardinal Richelieu once slept in the Château Fleury-en-Bière be marked "Off Limits"; that an Air Forces unit near Chantilly abandon its project to practice-bomb a camouflaged hunting lodge on an island where the Vollard art collection was hidden. There was a claim that all the furniture of the Château Voisenon had disappeared with a certain distinguished bombardment group, famous also for liking comfort. There was a protest that American troops billeted in the Château de Frémigny, built for a friend of Napoleon, had done more harm in the two months they were in residence than the Germans billeted there had done in four years. However, the M.F.A. & A. report on the gutted Château de Chamerolles, where Germans had also been billeted for four years, noted the owners' complaint that the Boches had carted off seven hundred valuable paintings and drawings, a hundred and forty-seven sixteenth- and seventeenth-century Oriental rugs, some seventeenth-century tapestries, and masses of rare silver—the most Herculean cleaning out accomplished by any unit in Europe in the entire war.

The Battle of the Bulge produced a great number of front-line billeting disasters. Surprise, confusion, danger, and bitter cold drove our men into any shelter, no matter how artistic; those who weren't freezing in foxholes were sweating it out in Belgian châteaux almost as fine as those in Touraine. The Château de Pailhe, the finest Louis XV structure in Belgium, was burned to the ground when the Americans used gasoline cookers on a parquet floor. Chimney fires and ruined marble mantelpieces were frequent. Most of our men had had no experience with elegant, ancestral open fireplaces; they had been brought up on comfortable steam heat.

An unexpected secondary war duty of the Monuments men consisted of acting as an ambulant lost-and-found department for art. In 1940, as the Germans started invading, western Europe frantically began hiding the treasures it loved, burying them in gardens the way dogs cache bones, hiding them in haylofts, in church steeples, in slaughterhouses, in bank basements or lunatic asylums, in any place of concealment that seemed logically safe or so absurd that it was unlikely to be discovered. City people sent their valuables to the country for safety and country people carted their stuff to town. The first reaction of the populace in the Liberation, after the cheers, was to hunt for their things. As the Monuments men moved around, they made lists of lost-and-found art, sent reports to one another, dispatched inquiries, and filed good news of discoveries and clues.

They also took notes on the gigantic, yawning destruction of the architectural face of war-struck Europe—of those now lost features of beauty, art, and picturesqueness, of housed history or charm, whose disappearance makes the profile of the Continent unrecognizable and will necessitate the rewriting of all the Baedekers. The first handful of Monuments officers, by thumbing rides and not standing on professional dignity, covered a tremendous amount of territory and compiled, often on borrowed typewriters, reams of notes that could serve the guidebook editors well. They didn't see everything, but they saw a lot. In the twelve weeks before Christmas of 1944, one man travelled thirteen thousand miles in France and inspected two hundred and twenty-four monuments. The M.F.A. & A. notes showed that in the most badly injured regions of the occupied countries, damage ran to about 45 percent. In Germany, inventor of the blitz, 45 percent of the great historical monuments were struck and 60 percent were blitzed to nothingness. The Monuments men also observed a fact that would have gratified the medieval building trades: the fragile-looking Gothic constructions, with their airy, resilient flying buttresses and broken surfaces, resisted the shock of bomb concussion better than the solid, unbroken surfaces of the Renaissance constructions, which—being built on the modern, four-square principle—were bashed flat by modern blast.

The Monuments reports were brief and melancholy. Of Boulogne, after Patton's Third Armored had fought its way in, the summarizing note read, "On M.F.A. & A. requests, engineers scraped 14th-century cathedral ruins from street functioning as Red Ball highway between Omaha and Utah beaches." A British note read, "Antwerp, Musée Plantin-Moretus, world's most famous printing museum, 18th century façade struck by buzz bomb." Major the Lord Methuen, Royal Scots Guards, the M.F.A. & A. officer in the Brussels region, kept a diary in the best travelling-Englishman manner, with appreciative observations on art ("Aerschot, inspected Béguinage, pleasant building dated 1636, badly damaged by bombing. Thielt, inspected charming Renaissance Belfry with tower and spire shot up in '44") as well as notes on whom he'd lunched with and the latest difficulties with his sinus, which was troubling him in the Lowlands climate. In Holland, the notes of Major Ronald Balfour, Fine Arts Officer for the Canadian First Army and former Fellow at King's College, Cambridge, were also personal, but they had a severer tone: "To appoint an officer for a whole area and to expect him to cadge lifts is not only faintly ludicrous but gives the Netherlands authorities a clear and perhaps accurate impression that we are not interested in their monuments at all."

The M.F.A. & A. men who followed the Allies into Aachen and the Rhineland became simply obituary writers, since dead art lay in every direction: "Cologne, circa 80 percent of monuments and churches destroyed, including St. Maria im Capitol, famous Romanesque landmark . . ." "Kleve, Stitskirche, mid 14th century, air bombed Oct. '44, again Feb. '45, an eliminating operation. Church shattered." After completing his mortuary report on Kleve, including a two-page epitaph on architectural details of the church alone, Major Balfour, the Canadian First Army Monuments officer, was killed by Nazi shellfire. From the town of Xanten came this note: "St. Victor's cathedral, rated most beautiful Gothic complex of buildings in the Rhineland, is wrecked. Shot, shell, blast." Another note recorded: "Münster, remarkable for assembly of fine buildings 14–18th century, is gone for good. Aerial bombardment Sunday March 25, 1945." A Münster postscript, written by an M.F.A. & A. archivist, said, "Münster city records on methods of Nazi treatment of Jews as well as future plans in that regard reported intact in Schloss Nordkirchen." From Trier: "Dom, 11th century, oldest church in Germany, heavily bombed Xmas week, '44. Karl Marx House, birthplace, used as Nazi newspaper H.Q., direct bomb hit, destroyed." Near the Ruhr pocket, Captain Huchthausen, the peacetime Professor of Art and Architecture at the University of Michigan, was killed by machine-gun fire on an *Autobahn*. Like all Monuments men, he felt that his job was concerned not only with the death of art but occasionally with its resuscitation. He was killed in a borrowed jeep while answering a hurry call to come inspect a newly found art cache.

• • •

It was the discovery of one underground art cache after another and the unexaggerated reports that they were worth millions of dollars that presently gave European art its place on the front page, along with the battles, and made it unnecessary for the Monuments men to go on being apologetic about their work. The first underground cache our armies encountered was a specially constructed art air-raid shelter in a deep subterranean sandstone chamber outside the Dutch town of Maastricht. There the Dutch had stored their most valuable museum pictures, with Nazi approval. The fact that the art had been hidden by our Allies decreased the excitement of the discovery for our men, though they took sightseeing tours underground to stare at some Rembrandts—once it had been explained who and how important Rembrandt was. For the next fortnight, every Dutch daub found in a farmhouse attic was called a Rembrandt, and the nearest Monuments officer was sent for, posthaste, to authenticate it.

Then, in April, 1945, in the mountains of Germany and Austria, our armies made the first of a series of spectacular, melodramatic discoveries of enemy-hidden subterranean treasure troves, which turned out to be the most dazzling, rich, compact underground depots of art in history. The first buried cache was found on April 2nd by elements of the Eighth Infantry Division, in the Westphalian copper mine at Siegen. As a matter of fact, Lieutenant Stout had already discovered it, at long distance (and had tipped off Headquarters to be on the lookout for it), while studying an annotated Nazi art catalogue he had come on in Aachen, whose rich cathedral treasures had been hidden at Siegen. He had also borrowed the cathedral's curate as a sort of guide. When the Monuments men finally entered the mine with the curate, its corridors were without light and reeked of the mine's sulphur and the stench of a vast, departed German civilian population, which had hidden there in semi-suffocation for two weeks, first from the *Amerikaner* bombs and then from the incoming *Amerikaner* soldiers, who butchered children, the German radio had warned. Deep in the mine, behind a locked door, the Monuments men found the German caretakers and the art they took care of—among other things, more than four hundred great pictures.

Later, when the Eighth Infantry turned the mine into an exhibition place, it posted at the mouth a sign, bearing its insigne (a golden arrow), that read, "Golden Arrow ART MUSEUM (Siegen Copper Mine). Europe's Art Treasures RESTORED. Paintings of the OLD MASTERS, Rembrandt, Rubens, Van Dyck, Delacroix, Van Gogh, Holbein. Bones and Crown of CHARLEMAGNE. Original Music of BEETHOVEN. Discovered and Guarded by the 8th INFANTRY DIVISION." The manuscript of Beethoven's Sixth Symphony, taken from the Beethoven House in Bonn, was indeed in the mine; the Charlemagne crown there was only a modern exhibition copy, which our officers and troops tried on as happily as if it had been the real thing; Charlemagne's bones were merely a part of his skull, imbedded in a silver, jewelled, life-size bust. The mine had been equipped with a dehydrating plant, but our bombs had wrecked it in January, and in the interim some of the damp pictures had become encrusted with a green, plush-like mold that made the people in them look as though they were suffering from a novel skin disease. The art—much of it still carefully packed in boxes sitting comfortably on floor boards, since the Nazis never spared labor in fitting up their underground art repositories—was again somewhat disappointing to our soldiers, because it hadn't been stolen from one of our Allies: it was merely Kraut riches, which included the Aachen Cathedral's tenth-century gemmed cross and twelfth-century crosier and enamelled gold shrine; canvases by Stephan Lochner; church and museum treasures from Münster and Alsatian Metz (which the Germans had always rated German); and the best of the contents of the Rhineland's wealthy museums, including the Essen Volkwang Museum's collection of French moderns, which was among the finest in Europe.

On April 6th, four days after the Siegen find, the American Army uncovered its second German cache—the Kaiseroda salt mine, at Merkers, in Thuringia. This discovery satisfied everybody and definitely put art on the war map. The Merkers art got a high ranking because it was mixed up with the colorful personality of General Patton and with a new type of treasure that really made sense—millions of dollars' worth of gleaming, solid gold. The Merkers mine was a lucky discovery of the 347th Infantry of Patton's Third Army. An M.P., Private Mootz by name, was told by a couple of French deportee women that what looked like a sawmill on yonder hill was the entrance to a salt mine filled with gold and other treasures so vast that when, a few weeks before, they had arrived from Berlin, it had taken scores of slave laborers seventy hours to carry the stuff into the place of hiding, seven hundred metres underground. The first visit by one of the M.P.'s officers disclosed that the mine also contained a Prussian State Collections curator and a British war prisoner, who had helped to tote the gold and knew exactly where it was. Before many hours had passed, the mine was bristling with extra M.P.s, a tank battalion to guard the mine head, a reinforced rifle company thrown around its four other entrances, and jeeps everywhere, armed with machine guns. The area also boiled with excited reconnaissance parties, special details, and Intelligence and Counterintelligence. When a number of officers, accompanied by an American banker, a gold expert who had been hastily flown in from Paris, descended into the mine and reached the cache, they saw a breathtaking sight: five hundred and fifty canvas bags, each containing a million reichsmarks in gold; four hundred smaller bags, containing brick gold; and, to one side, sordid boxes of gold fillings from Jews' teeth and their gold wedding rings, which the Nazis had thoughtfully saved from the concentration camps at Auschwitz and Buchenwald. On second glance, the officers also noticed some art. According to German bankers, with which Army Intelligence seemed to find the countryside teeming, Patton's Third had discovered the entire gold reserve of the Nazi State's Reichsbank. This was the first instance in modern military annals of a belligerent's capturing his enemy's every red cent. The American banker appraised the gold at $250,000,000. It was known that Germany started the war with a gold reserve of $50,000,000, so the Nazi conquests had really paid. Part of the Merkers bullion was identified as belonging to Belgium, which in panic had passed it to France in 1940, which had later passed it to Dakar, from which Vichy later ordered it passed to the insistent Germans.

The Army's first report—an unofficial one, since no Monuments men had yet been invited in to have a peek—said that the Merkers art treasures were not masterpieces. Actually, the Merkers art was so masterly that it was worth at least twice as much as the Merkers gold. Two hundred and two of its German pictures, once the pride of Berlin's now wrecked Kaiser Friedrich Museum and at present cached in the Washington National Gallery, were alone valued at $80,000,000. The lovely polychrome head of the Egyptian Queen Nofretete, found in a wooden box labelled *"Dic Bunte Königin"* ("The Multicolored Queen"), was only one extremely valuable item in the Merkers trove of art from fifteen Berlin state museums. On the sixth day after the discovery came the distinguished visitors—Generals Eisenhower, Bradley, Eddy, and Patton. All fourteen stars, representing the top brains and valor of our Army in Europe, descended into the mine in the same elevator, operated by a grim German. Soon after that, the gold was removed—rapidly. Protected by fighter planes, ack-ack guns, and anti-tank guns, the gold was trucked to Frankfurt and its rather less bombed Reichsbank vaults, where, at last official reports, it remains, the most heavily guarded cache in Europe. For nine months before the Merkers find, Monuments men had been disparagingly known in the Army as "those guys with their goddam art." The Merkers gold and Patton's personality had made art itself important. An art cache was thereafter known as an "art target," and all Patton's rivals itched to strike one too. Clearly, art finds meant publicity to any outfit's Public Relations officer. Capturing towns was valorous and still the aim of the war, but capturing art was a glamorous new idea.

Patton's lucky Third made the next strike, too, with the discovery, in May, just before the European war's end, of the art cache in the salt mine of Alt Aussee, up in the mountains near Salzburg. Among its sixty-seven hundred paintings was the great Hitler Collection for the museum he planned to set up in memory of his mother at Linz, in Austria, plus the art stolen in Italy by the Hermann Göring Division as a present for its chief's 1944 birthday. To two of the Third's Monuments men, Captain Posey and Pfc. Kirstein, Alt Aussee's cache was far from a surprise. Months before, in Trier, they had squeezed a tip about it from a German who had been connected with the French headquarters of E.R.R., *der Einsatzstab Reichsleiter Rosenberg für die Besetzten Gebiete,* or the Reich Leader Rosenberg Task Force for Occupied Territories, the official German art-looting organization. The two Monuments men had been impatiently waiting ever since for their outfit to fight its way to the mine. Once the Allies entered Germany, there was a steady trickle of tips about art in the Allied Intelligence reports. These were assembled in England by British and American Monuments officers and passed back to the proper authorities on the Continent. German prisoners also added tidbits of news, and from interrogations of the German population, then anxious to please, came an incoherent but informative mass of facts, clues, and rumors about hundreds of German art hideouts. There had been, to start with, a list, filched from the E.R.R. offices in Paris, of the six German aboveground hideouts, at Neuschwanstein, Chiemsee, Kögl, Seisenegg, Nickolsburg, and Kloster Buxheim. This list had been stolen by the French in 1942, when our Monuments men were still miles and years away from their goal. The major art, however, had been moved by the time the Monuments men caught up, in 1945. The terrible success of the Allied bombing had driven art, considered by the Nazis more valuable than their people, to safety in new hideouts, often unknown to the Allies, underground.

. . .

The fourth big German cache was discovered by the United States First Army in the twenty-four kilometres of underground passages of a salt mine at Bernterode, in the Thuringia Forest. At first view, it was perhaps the most startling of all. It featured the caskets of Feldmarschall von Hindenburg and his wife; of Kaiser Friedrich Wilhelm I, his bier decorated by a wreath and red ribbon bearing the name of his admirer, Adolf Hitler; and of Prussia's most revered king, Frederick the Great. Using Scotch tape, the methodical Germans had attached to each coffin lid a paper label bearing the name of the occupant scribbled in red crayon. The effect of this morbid scene was enhanced by an array of two hundred and twenty-five German battle banners, the relics of centuries of Prussian campaigns. Around Frederick the Great's coffin lay those of his Sans Souci Palace treasures that he had loved most—dozens of his paintings by Watteau, Chardin, Lancret, and Boucher, and boxes containing his library, most of the books in French and all of them bound in scarlet leather. Mixed in with swastika-marked flags were the sparkling insignia of earlier German greatness—the Hohenzollern crowns fabricated for Friedrich Wilhelm I and Sophia Dorothea in 1713 (with the jewels missing, these having been "removed for honorable sale," as an accompanying German note stated); a gold *Totenhelm*, or death helmet, dated 1688, for dead kings lying in state; a blue enamel royal orb, or *Reichsapfel;* two magnificent royal swords, dated 1460 and 1540; and an 1801 Hohenzollern sword and scabbard, the latter a terrific, yard-long, tawdry blaze of diamonds and rubies.

The French, Italian, and Russian slave laborers milling about the neighborhood when the liberating troops arrived said that the caskets had been hauled in a few weeks before under the supervision of the highest German military men and had been walled up in such secrecy and so quickly that they hadn't known what was being hidden away. It was the presence of fresh mortar in the main mine corridor that had led four sergeants and two corporals of the 330th Ordnance Depot Company, an art target hopefully in mind, to start digging through five feet of still damp masonry. What they had discovered was the sacred elements of Germanic revivalism—in readiness if and when Hitler failed. Bernterode was the most important political repository in all the Reich. By coincidence, our Monuments men brought the caskets out of the mine on V-E Day, while their radio was dialled to the Armed Forces' network, over which London's celebration of the great event was being broadcast. To the tune of "The Star-Spangled Banner," Frederick the Great, in a bronze coffin so vast that there was only a half inch to spare, rose majestically on the mine elevator, and just as he reached the free air, there sounded the monarchial strains of "God Save the King."

In a brick kiln in the town of Hungen was the most insultingly housed cache of all. Here were hidden the most precious Jewish archives, tomes, and synagogue vessels from all over Europe, including the Rosenthalian collection from Amsterdam and that of the Frankfurt Rothschilds. In the kiln, the repository for the Jewish material Rosenberg planned to use in his projected postwar academy, where anti-Semitism was to be taught as an exact science, priceless illuminated parchment torahs were found cut into covers for Nazi stenographers' typewriters or made up into shoes. Here, too, were thousands of Jewish identity cards, marked with a yellow "J," all that remained of Jews who had perished in Nazi crematories.

. . .

Having found thousands of items of looted art, far from home, and of German-owned art, displaced from its bombed-out museum habitat, the Monuments men, after V-E Day, were faced with the final two problems of their arduous war-and-peace job. The first was the physical act of removing this art—either heaving it up, sometimes heavy and sometimes light, but always valuable and breakable, from the bowels of the earth or from the castles in which it had been stored and transporting it along ruined roads and across streams without bridges. The second problem was to find safe places to put the art in. The first was the harder. The terrible technical difficulties were made quite clear in a rhetorical question one Monuments officer put to a friend: "How would *you* go about hauling up a close-to-life-size Michelangelo marble statue of the Virgin and Child from the bottom of a salt mine, in a foreign country, with the mine machinery *kaput* from our bombs, with nearly no help from our Army, since it was authorized to give nearly none, without proper tools, without trained handlers, and without even the tattered bed coverlets of the moving man's trade to use as padding?" Monuments men used what they found in German military stores for padding. Gasproof Nazi boots were cut into wedges to use as buffers between paintings; gasproof capes made ideal waterproofings; the full-length German sheepskin coats, tailored for the disastrous Russian campaign, were perfect to wrap around sculpture. For labor, the Monuments men, in their desperation, used any willing human being they could find—Polish, French, Russian, Belgian, Dutch, and Baltic slave workers, male and female, all grimly delighted to help pry loose Germany's loot, and minor German jailbirds, in the jug for stealing our Army rations and lent by petty German officials eager to curry favor with the conquerors. Some of the newer Monuments men were young curators from rich American museums who had never moved anything heavier than a Degas pastel. During the first summer, autumn, and winter following the peace, the Monuments men—under the supervision of Lieutenant Stout, the Fogg Art Museum expert, as Monuments chief for all the evacuations in the 12th Army Group area, which comprised the German-Austrian mountains and took in six hundred big and little depositories—spent months in red-tape-bound, wearying, exciting, maddening, and often incoherent work, and by the time they were through they had removed a large percentage of the Nazi-hidden art, much of it with their own hands.

After viewing Germany's ruins in their search for dependable receptacles, the Monuments men chose the Verwaltungsbau, in Munich, for the central collecting point for looted E.R.R. art, for the Hitler and Göring thefts and purchases, and for any other art from the occupied countries. This had been the Nazi Party's administration building for South Germany, one of a solid, tasteless, white-stone pair of Party edifices—the other being Hitler's headquarters building, the Führerbau, next door—which oddly escaped destruction in the ruination of Munich and which, in all their dual, matching ugliness, now dominate the Königsplatz, of whose earlier architectural charm little but the battered façade of the Glyptothek Museum remains. The central collecting point, soon known as the Bau to the Monuments men, was set up and run by Lieutenant Craig Smythe, U.S. N.R., of the National Gallery; Lieutenant Commander Hamilton Coulter, U.S. N.R., a New York architect; and Captain Edwin Rae, art instructor, University of Illinois. The Verwaltungsbau had been partially gutted, and its tons of secret, sacred Nazi documents—including lists of Party members as well as of anti-Nazis scheduled to be shot—had been scattered by post–V-E Day German mobs. The huge building had to be repaired, cleaned, lighted, staffed, and guarded at a time when a broom was a rarity, when coal was lacking, and glass for smashed windows and skylights had to be scrounged. Then, anti-Nazis had to be discovered among the German curators to aid in the colossal task. Finally, the Army, with the war over, with half a country to patrol, and with the art-target game only a memory, was naturally indifferent about lending good, strong G.I. guards to sit up night and day eying pretty pictures.

The Verwaltungsbau actually served not only as a collecting point but as a repatriation point; Allied art arrived in bulk and was then carefully parcelled out, on signed receipt, to the Allied countries to whom it had belonged before the Germans got hold of it. To facilitate the work, representatives of the Allied governments also functioned at the Bau. As art items were tentatively identified, through catalogues or often by the Nazis' own tags, they were placed in storerooms—each nation had its own—for further checking of ownership. When the identification was verified, the art was trucked off home, at the concerned nation's expense, after a receipt had been signed releasing the Allied authorities from further responsibility. Art that had actually been bought by the Nazis from private owners was, as a rule, simply put into government custody, when it got home, on the principle that unless the former owner could prove that the property had been sold under duress, it should become the property of the state. The wrangling over ownership is still going on.

To complete their knowledge of the Nazi looting, it was necessary for the Monuments men to do considerable detective work, establishing—by interrogation and by locating and studying Nazi, collaborationist, and other documents all over occupied Europe—exactly how, by whom, and for which Nazi bigwigs this massive spoliation of art had been organized. On this complicated information was based one phase of the "crimes against civilization" with which some of the Nazi war criminals—especially Göring, Rosenberg, and Frank—were charged at the Nuremberg trials. Lieutenants Theodore Rousseau, of the National Gallery, and James Plaut, of Boston's Institute of Modern Art, both of the Navy and both speaking fluent German and French, and Navy Lieutenant S. L. Faison, art professor of Williams College, made up a roving secret service for the Art Looting Investigation Unit of the Office of Strategic Services, which worked with the Monuments men. The only full-time Monuments detective was Lieutenant Walter Horn, a Hamburg-born anti-Nazi who for years had been art professor at the University of California. By the repeated use of his most effective phrase, in German, "If you are not telling me the truth, you will pay for it with your head," he got Germans to tell him the truth. It was by this method that he obtained from a Nuremberg city councillor information as to the whereabouts of five of the greatest insignia of the Holy Roman Empire, including the real eleventh-century crown of Charlemagne, pipped with raw sapphires, emeralds, rubies, and amethysts and tipped with a jewelled cross, and the St. Mauritius thirteenth-century sword. Nazi propaganda had carefully spread the rumor, after V-E Day, that a certain S.S. officer had sunk these relics in the Zell-am-See. Actually, on highest Nazi Party orders, the insignia had been secreted in an aperture in a false wall, eight stories underground, in the bottom basement of an apartment house built on the rocky slope of the Nuremberg Paniersplatz. Today, the interested visitor walks down (and later up) eight flights of stairs, accompanied by a slovenly janitor, to see the visible evidence of this ingenuous-looking, completely unsuspected hideaway—a jagged hole, such as any plumber might have made, leading into what appears to be a flue, such as any furnace might possess, just large enough to contain the five sacred relics, each fitted into its own beautiful locked, sealed, engraved, rust-proof copper box. This cache of Holy Roman Empire relics was second in national sentimental and political value only to the royal and martial caskets at Bernterode. Ideologically, these two were the most important of all the German caches, laid by in a desperate hour against the Germanic comeback.

· · ·

While the Bau was functioning as the collecting point for looted art, a collecting point for the E.R.R. loot from Jewish libraries, synagogues, and private documentary collections was set up at Offenbach in an unbombed I.G. Farben building. Some German-owned art, mainly from the Rhineland, was installed in still another collecting point, at Marburg, in the Staatsarchiv building. The major collecting point for German-owned art, including that from the great Berlin museums, was settled at Wiesbaden, in the old Landesmuseum. Captain Walter Farmer, of the M.F.A. & A., took over the building, considerably the worse for wear, from the Army service troops, who had been using it as a joint clothing and D.P. center. Here, after he had overcome the customary difficulties of getting brooms, soap, and window glass, seventy-five rooms were filled with Germany's most valuable art, usually still packed in the carefully labelled boxes in which the Germans had embarked it toward safety and hiding. There were hundreds of boxes, containing pictures by Cimabue, Mantegna, Dürer, Hieronymus Bosch, Bellini, and all the other great artists of Europe for centuries back. The Landesmuseum also housed hundreds of neat, sliding-panelled, annotated cases containing the German museums' fine print and engraving collections—all packed as carefully as if they were food, awaiting the great day when the Reich would be victorious and could once again savor its art publicly, in its huge museums. The Landesmuseum's so-called Treasure Room, kept under special guard, looked like the delirious dream of a private collector. Crowded into it was every kind of particularly precious art, piled in corners from floor to ceiling, spread on tables, ranged from the locked doors to the barred windows—objects in gold, in silver, studded with diamonds, festooned with pearls, bloody with rubies; objects once held by kings, worn or collected by dukes, or revered by bishops, and all finally become the public property of the wealthy, powerful German State, under its Kaisers. An important part of the Landesmuseum job was to demonstrate to the Germans the Monuments–War Department idea that art has nothing to do with war or race; that it belongs first to everybody and second to the people who legally owned it; and that German art was simply being held by the Monuments unit in trust until responsible German authority could offer the guards and the housing such treasures required. As illustration of this theory, the Landesmuseum staged two exhibitions for the Germans of their own magnificent property—a superb painting show of early gems, including some by van der Goes and Bouts; and a fine engraving show, with the catalogues in both German and English.

Unfortunately, it was also at the Landesmuseum that the Monuments ideal was, in the opinion of the Monuments men themselves, betrayed. The two hundred and two German-owned pictures now cached in our National Gallery came from the Landesmuseum collection. In December, 1945, the Monuments officers, acting on orders received in November from Berlin to select—which they conscientiously did—a representative collection of German art, finished the job of packing it for transportation and sent a Monuments officer to accompany it on its hegira to our national capital. All this was unanimously disapproved of by Major LaFarge, then chief of M.F.A. & A. in the U.S. Military Government for Germany, the section's other officers, and its men, as well as by most museum officials in the United States. Ironically enough, some of the pictures selected—paintings by Botticelli, Rubens, Rembrandt, and van Eyck—had, in June, 1941, been reproduced in an article in the Nazi Paris propaganda magazine *Signal* contemptuously denying an alleged Allied report that fourteen of Germany's museum masterpieces had gone out to the vulgarian United States in exchange for millions of dollars in cash to aid in financing the Nazi war. The facts about what the Monuments men bitterly called the Westward Ho Plan for sending this collection of German art to the States are still obscure. What is known, however, is that, as far as Europe was concerned, the idea was first heard of in Berlin in July of that year, when President Truman was attending the Big Three Potsdam Conference. In a private meeting with certain chiefs of our American Military Government, in Potsdam, the suggestion to send the art was made, reputedly by General Clay, Deputy Military Governor of the United States Zone. It is further reported that President Truman, perhaps thinking he was doing art a good turn, agreed to the suggestion. On the other hand, it has also been reported that the idea originated in the minds of non-museum men back in Washington, who decided not to identify themselves when the plan was bitterly criticized by the American press and museum people everywhere.

The protest by the Monuments men themselves did not carry any weight. In November, twenty-eight of the Monuments men operating in Germany sent a letter to their chief, Major LaFarge, deploring the fact that the United States was violating its concept, unique in military history, that the conquerors would leave conquered art untouched. What was even worse, they argued, was our government's adopting the Nazis' hypocritical line that the art was merely being taken into "protective custody." Some of the Monuments men asked to be transferred out of their jobs, because they did not want to have anything to do with carrying out the order. They were cautioned that anyone who attempted to impede the shipment would be court-martialled. The official end of the Westward Ho squabble came when the office of Secretary of State Byrnes, in answer to all the criticism, told the press that the decision to transport the German art to Washington had been arrived at "on the basis of a statement made by General Clay that he did not have adequate facilities and personnel to safeguard German art treasures and that he could not undertake the responsibilities of their proper care." The White House also told the press that the pictures would be returned to Germany "as soon as possible." So far, they have at least been kept in dignified hiding in the National Gallery.

Since the pictures, valued at $80,000,000, were taken without our having consulted our three Allies in occupied Germany, it was feared that the United States had set a precedent for the removal of valuables, but England and France, at any rate, have not imitated us yet. The Russian Fine Arts officer in Berlin has, at last report, not given to our Monuments chief there any statement of his government's attitude toward the disposition of German-owned art in the Russian zone, but it is known that some masterpieces from the Dresden Gemäldegalerie, including the Raphael Sistine Madonna (and its pensive little cherubs), are now on view in a Moscow museum, in a newly furnished room called the Dresden Art Room, or words to that effect.

• • •

Today the M.F.A. & A., aside from its offices in Berlin, is practically inoperative in Europe. The work of returning the looted art from the Verwaltungsbau, which it was estimated would take six months from V-E Day, was finally completed, except for snag ends, last summer. The Wiesbaden Landesmuseum is now in the hands of a civilian representative of the U.S. Military Government. A few of the museum aesthetes of the old guard are polishing off final Monuments details in Munich, Wiesbaden, Stuttgart, and Berlin.

The Führerbau, twin of the Verwaltungsbau, also stands useless and empty today. Between these paired, pompous buildings once stood the two little Greco-Nazi Honor Temples, where the bodies of those who died in Hitler's Munich *Putsch* reposed as public heroes of the Nazi State. The bodies were removed by the American Army after that State fell, and given a more modest burial elsewhere, and a few weeks ago the Army demolished the temples themselves. Inside the stripped Führerbau, Hitler's workroom still contains recognizable elements of its former impersonal, tasteless luxury: the brown carpet on which he used to pace, now stained and torn, still covers the lengthy floor; the green marble mantelpiece before which his impressive desk stood, like an altar before the sacred fire, is intact; the sear wall covering retains its autumnal tint. The rest of the building is a void. This is the place where, eight and a half years ago, Prime Ministers Chamberlain and Daladier accepted from the exulting Führer and his Reichsmarschall the terms of Munich. The only furnishing left in the Führerbau's long, once elegantly filled marble foyer, at the bottom of the grandiose staircase—which those two visiting plenipotentiaries climbed and descended between stiff lines of Nazi guards, while the democracies everywhere waited in suspense—is a large tattered globe of the world, slashed by the knives of passing G.I.s.

COME IN, LASSIE!

Lillian Ross

FEBRUARY 21, 1948 (ON THE RED SCARE IN HOLLYWOOD)

HOLLYWOOD IS BAFFLED by the question of what the Committee on un-American Activities wants from it. People here are wondering, with some dismay and anxiety, what kind of strange, brooding alienism the Committee is trying to eliminate from their midst and, in fact, whether it was ever here. They are waiting hopefully for Chairman J. Parnell Thomas, or Congress, or God, to tell them. They have been waiting in vain ever since last November, when eight writers, a producer, and a director—often collectively referred to these days as "the ten writers"—were blacklisted by the studios because they had been charged with contempt of Congress for refusing to tell the Thomas Committee what political party, if any, they belong to. In the meantime, business, bad as it is, goes on. The place is more nervous than usual, but it is doing the same old simple things in the same old simple ways. The simplicities of life in Hollywood are not, of course, like those anywhere else. This is still a special area where you get remarkable results simply by pushing buttons; where taxi-drivers jump out of their cabs, open their doors, and politely bow you inside; where you can buy, in "the world's largest drugstore," a good-looking clock for $735; where all the lakes in the countryside are labelled either "For Sale" or "Not for Sale"; and where guests at parties are chosen from lists based on their weekly income brackets—low ($200–$500), middle ($500–$1,250), and upper ($1,250–$20,000). During the last few months, party guests have tended to be politically self-conscious, whatever their brackets, but this is not especially embarrassing in Hollywood, where it is possible to take an impregnable position on both sides of any controversy. At an upper-bracket party not long ago, a Selznick man introduced to me as Merve told me that he was appalled and outraged by the blacklisting of the ten writers. "It's a damn shame," Merve said, beaming at me. "Those human beings got a right to think or believe anything without letting Washington in on their ideas. They can't put their ideas into Hollywood pictures. Nobody can."

Just then, we were approached by Sam Wood, the producer, who was feeling grumpy, according to Merve, because his latest picture, *Ivy*, had cost $2,000,000 to make and was expected to gross only $1,500,000.

"Glad to see you, Sam," said Merve. "Listen, Sam, I want you to tell this young lady what you think of the way Congress investigated us here in Hollywood."

"I say Congress ought to make everybody stand up publicly and be counted!" Mr. Wood shouted. "I say make every damn Communist stand up and be counted. They're a danger and a discredit to the industry!"

Merve continued to beam. "Make *every* radical, every Communist, every Socialist, and every Anarchist stand up and be counted," he said expansively. "We ought to get every one of them out of the industry."

The political self-consciousness at parties is, on the whole, rather cheerful. "I never cut anybody before this," one actress remarked happily to me. "Now I don't go anywhere without cutting at least half a dozen former friends." At some parties, the bracketed guests break up into subgroups, each eying the others with rather friendly suspicion and discussing who was or was not a guest at the White House when Roosevelt was President—one of the few criteria people in the film industry have set up for judging whether a person is or is not a Communist—and how to avoid *becoming* a Communist. Some of the stars were investigated several years ago, when the un-American Activities Committee was headed by Martin Dies, and the advice and point of view of these veterans are greatly sought after. One actor who is especially in demand at social gatherings is Fredric March, who suddenly discovered, when called to account by Mr. Dies, that he was a Communist because he had given an ambulance to Loyalist Spain. Dies rebuked him, and it then turned out that Mr. March had also given an ambulance to Finland when she was at war with Russia. "I was just a big ambulance-giver," Mr. March said to his sub-group at a recent party, loudly enough for other sub-groups to hear. "That's what I told Dies. 'I just like to give ambulances,' I told him, and he said, 'Well, then, Mr. March, before you give any more ambulances away, you go out and consult your local Chamber of Commerce or the American Legion, and they'll tell you whether it's all right.'"

Some groups play it safe at parties by refusing to engage in any conversation at all. They just sit on the floor and listen to anyone who goes by with a late rumor. There are all sorts of rumors in Hollywood right now. One late rumor is that the newest black-market commodity in town is the labor of the ten writers, who are reported to be secretly turning out scripts for all the major studios. Another is that one producer is founding a film company and will have all ten of the blacklisted men on his staff. Rumors that the F.B.I. is going to take over casting operations at the studios are discounted by those who have lived in Hollywood for more than fifteen years. The casting director at Metro-Goldwyn-Mayer, a fidgety, cynical, sharply dressed, red-cheeked man named Billy Grady, Sr., who has worked in Hollywood for nearly twenty years, thinks that it would serve J. Edgar Hoover right if the casting of actors were handed over to the F.B.I. "Hoover thinks *he's* got worries!" Grady shouted at me in a Hollywood restaurant. "What does a G-man do? A G-man sends guys to Alcatraz! Ha! I'd like to see a G-man find a script about Abraham Lincoln's doctor in which we could work in a part for Lassie. What do you find inside of Alcatraz? Picture stars? Directors? Cameramen? No! The goddam place is full of doctors, lawyers, and politicians. This is the fourth biggest industry in the country, and only three men in this industry ever went to jail. There are fifty thousand people in this industry, and all they want is the right to take up hobbies. Spencer Tracy takes up painting. Clark Gable takes up Idaho. Dalton Trumbo, who got the sack, takes up deep thinking. Take away their hobbies and they're unhappy. When they're unhappy, I'm unhappy. For God's sake, Tracy doesn't paint when he's acting. Gable doesn't shoot ducks. Trumbo doesn't think when he's writing for pictures. I say let them keep their goddam hobbies. They're all a bunch of capitalists anyway."

. . .

The order of creation in Hollywood still works backward, and not only in the matter of filming the end or middle of a picture before the beginning. A man who recently had the job of working up advance interest in a yet-to-be-made picture based on *The Robe* managed to commit the biggest Bible publisher in the country to putting out an edition of the New Testament containing color photographs from the film. "I get this plug in the Bible," he said to me. "Then I hear we need someone of the calibre of Tyrone Power to play the hero. We get Power, see? Then we put him in the Bible. *Then* we put him in the picture. Only trouble is we can't make the picture yet. Ty is too busy." Evidently, Communism is also responsible for this trouble. Power, returning from a trip abroad lately, announced that he had seen so much suffering in Europe that he had come back determined to spend his time fighting Communism. This, as interpreted by Louella Parsons, meant that he had given up Lana Turner for the cause.

Hollywood, for the most part, is waiting earnestly for the Thomas Committee to define Communism, to name at least one film it considers Communistic, and to set down rules about what should and should not be thought about by a good American. Until the Committee offers something helpful, however, Hollywood feels it has no choice but to pay close attention to the counsel of Louella Parsons, Hedda Hopper, and Jimmy Fidler, whose guidance to date has consisted of warnings that the public will not be satisfied with the blacklisting of only ten men, that the public wants Congress to complete its investigation of Communism in the industry, and that all writers, actors, producers, directors, and agents who have ever contributed so much as a nickel to the League of Women Shoppers had better announce their political views if they know what's good for them. Those who fear the thunder on the Right say they are going to leave Hollywood. "I'm a dead duck!" one sad-eyed misanthrope exclaimed to me. "All I can do now is go someplace and raise chickens. Been thinking of doing it for nine years anyway." Some say they will go back to Broadway or write novels, projects they too have been considering for nine years, more or less. A number of actors and producers, including Charlie Chaplin, are planning to go to England, France, or Italy, where they believe that they will be free to make the kind of pictures they like. Jack L. Warner, busiest of the Brothers, is genially inclined to bolster up the courage of those who are ready to throw in the towel. "Don't worry!" he roars, slapping the backs of the lesser men around him. "Congress can't last forever!"

· · ·

Some people in Hollywood like to think of it as still a place for pioneers. "We're the modern covered-wagon folks," I was told by Ruth Hussey, the actress, who returned here not long ago from an appearance on Broadway. "We are, we're the modern covered-wagon folks. Pioneers come out here broke, and within a few years they're earning fifty thousand a year." In a way, Miss Hussey is exceptional. Everybody else seems eager to complain about the difficulty of making or keeping money. Studios complain about their telephone bills. Drivers of studio cars complain that they are now being paid by the trip instead of by the week. Santa Anita race-track officials complain that betting has fallen off. Informal statisticians complain that only seventy-five million people a week went to the movies in 1947 and that maybe only sixty million will go in 1948. Producers complain about bankers' reluctance to lend them money. Bankers complain that the revenue from American films shown overseas in 1947 was only $100,000,000, which is $38,000,000 less than the revenue from American films shown overseas in 1946, and that the revenue in 1948 may be as low as $50,000,000. Both Anglophiles and Anglophobes complain about the British import tax, imposed last August, which would confiscate 75 percent of the English earnings of any American film imported since then. Studio executives complain about production costs and overhead, and studio workers complain about being laid off to cut down on production costs and overhead. The employment of actors and writers is said to be the lowest in twenty years. As of the first of the year, twenty-three feature pictures were in production, as against twice that number in January of last year. "Hollywood is girding its loins," a representative of the Motion Picture Association of America said to me. "Hollywood is pulling in its belt. Hollywood is pinching its pennies, taking stock of its cupboards, buckling down, putting its shoulder to the wheel and its nose to the grindstone, and looking deep within itself. Hollywood is *worrying about the box office.*"

Almost the only motion-picture star who is taking conditions in his stride is Lassie, a reddish-haired male collie, who is probably too mixed up emotionally over being called by a girl's name to worry about the box office. Lassie is working more steadily, not only in films but on the radio, than anyone else in Hollywood. He is a star at M-G-M, the leading studio in Hollywood, which is fondly referred to out here as the Rock of Gibraltar. Visitors there are politely and desperately requested not to discuss politics or any other controversial matters with anyone on the lot. Louis B. Mayer, production chief of M-G-M, recently took personal command of the making of all pictures, of the purchase of all scripts, and of the writing of all scripts and commissary menus. The luncheon menu starts off with the announcement that meat will not be served on Tuesdays. "President Truman has appealed to Americans to conserve food, an appeal all of us will gladly heed, of course," it says. Patrons are politely and desperately encouraged to eat apple pancakes or broiled sweetbreads for lunch. Lassie eats apple pancakes for lunch. Visitors are politely and desperately introduced to Lassie, who ignores them. "We'd be in a hole if we didn't have Lassie," I heard an M-G-M man say. "We like Lassie. We're sure of Lassie. Lassie can't go out and embarrass the studio. Katharine Hepburn goes out and makes a speech for Henry Wallace. Bang! We're in trouble. Lassie doesn't make speeches. Not Lassie, thank God." At the moment, Lassie is making a picture with Edmund Gwenn about a country doctor in Scotland. Originally, the script called for a country doctor in Scotland who hated dogs, but a part has been written in for Lassie, the plot has been changed, and the picture is to be called *Master of Lassie*. "It will help at the box office," Lassie's director says. Only three other pictures are in production at M-G-M, the biggest of them being a musical comedy called *Easter Parade,* starring Fred Astaire and having to do with Easter on Fifth Avenue at the beginning of the century. One of Lassie's many champions at M-G-M told me that he had favored writing in a part for Lassie in *Easter Parade* but that he had dropped the idea. "I couldn't find a good Lassie angle," he explained.

. . .

The most noticeable effect on Hollywood of the Thomas Committee investigation is, perhaps, an atmosphere of uncertainty. A man I know named Luther Greene, who belongs to what he calls the C.I.S. ("the cheap international set," he says. "I just get passed around from party to party"), took me one evening to a small gathering at the Beverly Hills home of N. Peter Rathvon, a former New York attorney and investment banker who is now president of R.K.O. Greene and Rathvon, it seemed, thought that I might find an evening in the Rathvon household instructive. Rathvon is a mannerly, mild, yet stubborn little man, with the unwavering enthusiasm of a film-magazine fan for the movies. He has been converted, he says, to Hollywood's suburban family life. "People enjoy having babies out here," he says. "They enjoy inviting each other to dinner and sitting in the sunshine. That's life." Rathvon has two daughters and a son, rarely dines in a restaurant, and takes a sun bath at least once a week. Two of the ten men who were cited with contempt by Congress— Adrian Scott and Edward Dmytryk—worked at his studio, and it was he who had to inform them that they had brought disgrace upon R.K.O. and to dismiss them, a task he did not relish. After dinner, there was, as there is every evening the Rathvons are at home, a movie. That evening it was *Good News,* which deals with college life. After the showing, one of Rathvon's daughters, who goes to the Westlake School for Girls, denounced it as positively silly. Rathvon posted himself behind a small bar and made drinks for everybody. Then he offered to show Greene and me around his house. "Charles Boyer used to live here," he said. "It's an odd sensation, very odd, to live in a house Charles Boyer used to live in." He led us up a narrow spiral staircase, like those in lighthouses, to a bedroom with blond, primavera-panelled walls and another small bar. "This was Charles Boyer's bedroom," he said. "It's my bedroom now." Greene told Rathvon that I had heard a lot about the movable glass roof over the patio of the house, and asked him to show me how it worked. Our host took us downstairs, pushed a button in the patio, and then seemed to stop breathing. The glass roof overhead slid back, exposing the heavens. He pushed another button and watched anxiously as the roof moved back into place. "I used to be fond of playing with this," he said. "These days, I never know whether it's going to come back."

Later, after a prolonged discussion of Charles Boyer's acting, Charles Boyer's reading habits, and Charles Boyer's intelligence, someone said that Charles Boyer, together with several hundred other stars, had signed a statement protesting that the Thomas Committee investigation was unfair and prejudiced.

"What about that, Peter?" Greene asked. "A lot of people in your business feel that a man's politics has nothing to do with his work in pictures. Why, Scott and Dmytryk made *Crossfire* for you on a shoestring—five hundred and ninety-five thousand dollars. Took them twenty-two days. You'll gross three million on that picture. For heaven's sakes, why *fire* the men?"

"I sure hated to lose those boys," Rathvon said miserably. "Brilliant craftsmen, both of them. It's just that their usefulness to the studio is at an end. Would you like to go out on the terrace and look down on the lights of Hollywood?" Everyone said yes, and we all went out on the terrace to look down on the lights of Hollywood.

On our way home, Greene said that his social evenings were becoming more and more of a strain. "Everyone spends the night looking at those goddam lights," he said unhappily. "I think I'll go to Lady Mendl's tomorrow."

. . .

The Screen Writers Guild a while back voted to intervene as *amicus curiae* in the civil suits that five of the ten blacklisted men have brought against their studios for breaking their contracts. It also decided to decline an invitation of the Association of Motion Picture Producers to cooperate in eliminating subversives from the studios. The Guild agreed, in addition, to oppose the blacklisting of writers because of their political views, as long as those views do not violate the law. On the other hand, the Guild turned down a proposal by some of its members to give financial and public-relations support to the ten men in their trials for contempt. The Motion Picture Association of America, which voted with the Producers' Association to blacklist the ten men and not to employ or re-employ any one of them until he is acquitted of contempt of Congress or swears that he is not a Communist, not long ago addressed a communication to Adrian Scott, one of the ten. From it, Scott, who had then been out of work about two weeks, learned that the 1947 Humanitarian Award of the Golden Slipper Square Club, a philanthropic organization in Philadelphia, had been given to Dore Schary, R.K.O.'s executive vice-president in charge of production, for having made, among other pictures, *Crossfire,* which Scott produced and Dmytryk directed. According to an inscription on the award, it was made for Schary's "contribution to good citizenship and understanding among men of all religions, races, creeds, and national origins." The award was accepted for Schary by Eric Johnston, president of the Motion Picture Association, who told the Philadelphians, "In Hollywood, it's ability that counts. . . . Hollywood has held open the door of opportunity to every man and woman who could meet its technical and artistic standards, regardless of racial background or religious belief." "We're not supposed to be useful any more because they say the public has lost confidence in us," one of the ten blacklisted men said to me. "But they're not withdrawing any of the pictures we worked on. Ring Lardner's name is thrown on the screen in front of the public seeing *Forever Amber.* Lester Cole's name is up there on *High Wall.* If the public has confidence in these pictures, the public still has confidence in us."

An exceedingly active Hollywood agent, a woman, claims that since the start of the Congressional investigation the studios have been calling for light domestic comedies and have been turning down scripts with serious themes. "You might say the popular phrase out here now is 'Nothing on the downbeat,'" she said. "Up until a few months ago, it was 'Nothing sordid.'" The difference between "Nothing sordid" and "Nothing on the downbeat," she explained, is like the difference between light domestic comedy and *lighter* domestic comedy. After the investigation got under way, the industry called in Dr. George Gallup to take a public poll for the studios. Dr. Gallup has now submitted figures showing that 71 percent of the nation's moviegoers have heard of the Congressional investigation, and that of this number 51 percent think it was a good idea, 27 percent think not, and 22 percent have no opinion. Three percent of the 51 percent approving of the investigation feel that Hollywood is overrun with Communism. The studio executives are now preparing a campaign to convince this splinter 3 percent, and the almost as bothersome 97 percent of the 51 percent, that there is no Communism in the industry. There is some disagreement about whether the industry should tackle the unopinionated 22 percent or leave it alone.

In the midst of the current preoccupation with public opinion, many stars are afraid that the public may have got a very wrong impression about them because of having seen them portray, say, a legendary hero who stole from the rich to give to the poor, or an honest, crusading district attorney, or a lonely, poetic, antisocial gangster. "We've got to resolve any conflicts between what we are and what the public has been led to believe we are," one actor told me. "We can't afford to have people think we're a bunch of strong men or crusaders." At the Warner Brothers studio, some time ago, I accepted a publicity representative's invitation to watch the shooting of a scene in *Don Juan*, a Technicolor reworking of the *Don Juan* made in 1926 with John Barrymore. Filming of the production has since been called off, owing to the illness of the star, Errol Flynn, but he was still in good health the day I was there. "I want you to meet Errol," said the publicity representative. "Just don't discuss anything serious with him—politics, I mean." Being a publicity man out here seems to have taken on some of the aspects of a lawyer's and an intelligence agent's duties and responsibilities. Studio visitors who are suspected of having ways of communicating with the public are always accompanied by a publicity man, or even two publicity men. The present-day importance of the publicity man is indicated by the fact that a member of the trade at M-G-M now occupies the office of the late Irving Thalberg, Thalberg still being to Hollywood what Peter the Great still is to Russia. I asked Flynn, who stood glittering in royal-blue tights and jerkin, golden boots, and a golden sword, how his version of *Don Juan* compared with Barrymore's. "That's like comparing two grades of cheese," he said moodily. "The older is probably the better. But I'm trying to make my Don Juan as human as possible. Jack's was a tough Don Juan. Mine is human. The script calls for one of the Spanish nobles to tell me that Spain is going to war. 'You're not afraid?' he asks me. 'Yes, I am afraid!' I reply. I added that line to the script myself. I don't want to be heroic. This picture is definitely non-subversive."

A Paramount man informed me that he had the perfect solution for both the split-personality problem and the Thomas Committee problem. "Make your pictures more of a mish-mosh than ever!" he said, glowing all over with health, well-being, and the resolution of a man who has at last found inner calmness. "*Confuse* the enemy—that's my technique. Confuse them all!" He has apparently confided his formula to Ray Milland, a Paramount actor whom I came across while he was working on *Sealed Verdict*. "My picture is politically significant," Mr. Milland said to me. (Paramount publicity men, like the Warner men, warn visitors not to discuss politics with stars, but Mr. Milland brought up the subject himself.) "This is a picture about political justice," Milland went on. "I play Major Robert Lawson, a brilliant young American prosecutor in the American-occupied zone of Germany, where I am closing my case against six Nazi war criminals, including General Otto Steigmann, whose war crimes against humanity were most revolting. I get Steigmann condemned to death by hanging, and then I am visited by a beautiful French model named Themis Delisle, and I fall in love with her. No, first Themis Delisle tells me that Steigmann is innocent, *then* I fall in love with her. My young aide, Private Clay Hockland, has been having an affair with a seventeen-year-old German girl, who is pregnant and shoots Private Hockland and then becomes seriously ill, although Private Hockland is also seriously ill after the *Fräulein* shoots him." Milland was interrupted by a man who wanted to comb his hair. "Later," Milland said to him, and firmly continued telling me about Private Hockland's death, the assorted difficulties of the ladies in the cast, and the problem of getting penicillin in the black market for the *Fräulein*. He was interrupted periodically by the man who wanted to comb his hair, but he proceeded unswervingly to a castle, for the hanging of General Steigmann. "I tell the General his mother has snitched on him," Milland said, "but he boasts that Hitlerite Germany will rise again. I knock him to the floor and take a vial of poison from a scar on his cheek, for Themis Delisle has revealed his last and most dramatic secret. Steigmann confesses his guilt, and Themis returns to France to defend herself, but she leaves with the promise that a certain brilliant young American lawyer— me—will be fighting on her team." Milland beckoned to the man with the comb. "Now," he concluded belligerently, "I'd like to see the Thomas Committee find anything in *that*."

Walter Wanger, head of Walter Wanger Pictures, Inc., maintains that the public has an unjustifiably poor opinion of Hollywood, and one day, trailing the inevitable publicity man, he took me to his studio commissary to tell me about the progress the industry has made since he got into it, twenty-five years ago. "In those days, we couldn't even have an unhappy ending," he said. "Today, pictures are different. Pictures have made great and wonderful contributions to the country and to the world." Wanger ordered coffee. Then he said that pictures had helped raise our standard of living, had encouraged understanding among men, and had, because of their merit and integrity, contributed to social progress. Wanger drank his coffee. I mentioned the last two Wanger pictures I had seen—*Arabian Nights* (love in a Bagdad harem) and *Canyon Passage* (Technicolor on the prairie). "I made those pictures because I wanted to be a success," Wanger replied. "If you want to stay in this business, if you want to make pictures that contribute to the country's welfare, you've got to make pictures that make money."

Some producers express the interesting point of view that there are no Communistic pictures, that there are only good pictures and bad pictures, and that most bad pictures are bad because writers write bad stories. "Writers don't apply themselves," I was informed by Jerry Wald, a thirty-six-year-old Warner Brothers producer, customarily described as a dynamo, who boasts that he makes twelve times as many pictures as the average producer in Hollywood. "Anatole France never sat down and said, 'Now, what did a guy write last year that I can copy this year?'" Wald assured me. "The trouble with pictures is they're cold. Pictures got to have emotion. You get emotion by doing stories on the temper of the times." The Congressional investigation, he said, would have no effect on his plans for this year's pictures on the temper of the times. These will include one on good government (with Ronald Reagan), another about underpaid schoolteachers (with Joan Crawford), and an adaptation and modernization of Maxwell Anderson's *Key Largo* (with Humphrey Bogart, Lauren Bacall, Edward G. Robinson, and Lionel Barrymore). "Bogart plays an ejected liberal," Wald said, "a disillusioned soldier who says nothing is worth fighting for, until he learns there's a point where every guy must fight against evil." Bogart, who two or three months before had announced that his trip to Washington to protest against the methods of the Thomas Committee hearings had been a mistake, was very eager, Wald said, to play the part of an ejected liberal.

At Wald's suggestion, I had lunch one day with several members of the *Key Largo* cast, its director, John Huston, and a publicity representative at the Lakeside Golf Club, a favorite buffet-style eating place of stars on the nearby Warner lot. The actors were in a gay mood. They had just finished rehearsing a scene (one of the new economies at Warner is to have a week of rehearsals before starting to film a picture) in which Bogart is taunted by Robinson, a gangster representing evil, for his cowardice, but is comforted by the gangster's moll, who tells Bogart, "Never mind. It's better to be a live coward than a dead hero." Bogart had not yet reached the point where a guy learns he must fight against evil. Huston was feeling particularly good, because he had just won a battle with the studio to keep in the film some lines from Franklin Roosevelt's message to the Seventy-seventh Congress on January 6, 1942: "But we of the United Nations are not making all this sacrifice of human effort and human lives to return to the kind of world we had after the last world war."

"The big shots wanted Bogie to say this in his own words," Huston explained, "but I insisted that Roosevelt's words were better."

Bogart nodded. "Roosevelt was a good politician," he said. "He could handle those babies in Washington, but they're too smart for guys like me. Hell, I'm no politician. That's what I meant when I said our Washington trip was a mistake."

"Bogie has succeeded in not being a politician," said Huston, who went to Washington with him. "Bogie owns a fifty-four-foot yawl. When you own a fifty-four-foot yawl, you've got to provide for her upkeep."

"The Great Chief died and everybody's guts died with him," Robinson said, looking stern.

"How would you like to see *your* picture on the front page of the Communist paper of Italy?" asked Bogart.

"Nyah," Robinson said, sneering.

"The *Daily Worker* runs Bogie's picture and right away he's a dangerous Communist," said Miss Bacall, who is, as everybody must know, Bogart's wife. "What will happen if the American Legion and the Legion of Decency boycott all his pictures?"

"It's just that my picture in the *Daily Worker* offends me, Baby," said Bogart.

"Nyah," said Robinson.

"Let's eat," said Huston.

After a while, Bogart began to complain about the iron curtain that separates the stars from the public. "There's only four rips," he said glumly, "four outlets through the iron curtain—Louella, Hedda, Jimmy, and Sheilah Graham. What can a guy do with only four rips?"

"Nyah," said Robinson.

Hollywood has various ideas about what the iron curtain is and where it is. Twentieth Century–Fox is making a picture called *The Iron Curtain*—about Communist spies' stealing atomic-bomb secrets in Canada—around which there is an iron curtain keeping visitors from everyone and everything connected with the picture. A Los Angeles newspaperman tried, unsuccessfully, to penetrate it. He was investigated by a man from Twentieth Century–Fox. A lady named Margaret Ettinger, who is generally credited with being "everybody's press agent" and who handles vaseline, diamonds, and Atwater Kent as well as many movie and radio stars, says there is an iron curtain around Louella Parsons. "Louella is my cousin, but I have a tougher time breaking into her column than into Hedda's," she says. Sheilah Graham, whose syndicated column appears locally in the Hollywood *Citizen-News,* in writing a few weeks ago about a certain star's red sweater and a certain singer's flashy red car, remarked that the color was still popular in Hollywood. The newspaper received a lot of letters calling Miss Graham a Communist. One of them suggested that an iron curtain be set up around *her.*

· · ·

A few weeks ago, many people in Hollywood received through the mails a booklet called "Screen Guide for Americans," published by the Motion Picture Alliance for the Preservation of American Ideals and containing a list of "Do"s and "Don't"s. "This is the raw iron from which a new curtain around Hollywood will be fashioned," one man assured me solemnly. "This is the first step—not to fire people, not to get publicity, not to clean Communism out of motion pictures but to rigidly control all the contents of all pictures for Right Wing political purposes." The Motion Picture Association of America has not yet publicly adopted the "Screen Guide for Americans" in place of its own "A Code to Govern the Making of Motion and Talking Pictures," which advances such tenets as "The just rights, history, and feelings of any nation are entitled to consideration and respectful treatment" and "The treatment of bedrooms must be governed by good taste and delicacy." Although it is by no means certain that the industry has got around to following these old rules, either to the letter or in the spirit, there is a suspicion that it may have already begun at least to paraphrase some of the "Screen Guide's" pronouncements, which appear under such headings as "Don't Smear the Free Enterprise System," "Don't Deify the 'Common Man,'" "Don't Glorify the Collective," "Don't Glorify Failure," "Don't Smear Success," and "Don't Smear Industrialists." "All too often, industrialists, bankers, and businessmen are presented on the screen as villains, crooks, chiselers, or exploiters," the "Guide" observes. "It is the *moral* (no, not just political but *moral*) duty of every decent man in the motion picture industry to throw into the ashcan, where it belongs, every story that smears industrialists as such." Another admonition reads, "Don't give to your characters—as a sign of villainy, as a damning characteristic—a desire to make money." And another, "Don't permit any disparagement or defamation of personal success. It is the Communists' intention to make people think that personal success is somehow achieved at the expense of others and that every successful man has hurt somebody by becoming successful." The booklet warns, "Don't tell people that man is a helpless, twisted, drooling, sniveling, neurotic weakling. Show the world an *American* kind of man, for a change." The "Guide" instructs people in the industry, "Don't let yourself be fooled when the Reds tell you that what they want to destroy are men like Hitler and Mussolini. What they want to destroy are men like Shakespeare, Chopin, and Edison." Still another of the "Don't"s says, "Don't ever use any lines about 'the common man' or 'the little people.' It is not the American idea to be either 'common' or 'little.'" This despite the fact that Eric Johnston, testifying before the Thomas Committee, said, "Most of us in America are just little people, and loose charges can hurt little people." And one powerful man here has said to me, "We're not going to pay any attention to the Motion Picture Alliance for the Preservation of American Ideals. We *like* to talk about 'the little people' in this business."

I was given a copy of "Screen Guide for Americans" by Mrs. Lela Rogers, one of the founders of the Motion Picture Alliance for the Preservation of American Ideals. Mrs. Rogers, the mother of Ginger, is a pretty, blond-haired lady with a vibrant, birdlike manner. "A lot of people who work in pictures wouldn't know Communism if they saw it," she said to me. "You think that a Communist is a man with a bushy beard. He's not. He's an American, and he's pretty, too." The Congressional investigation of Hollywood, Mrs. Rogers thinks, will result in better pictures and the victory of the Republican Party in the next election. "Last month, I spoke about Communism at a ten-dollar-a-plate dinner given by the Republican Party," she said. "My goodness, I amassed a lot of money for the campaign. Now I have more speaking engagements than I can possibly fulfill." Mrs. Rogers is also writing screen plays. I wanted to know if she was following the "Do"s and "Don't"s of the "Screen Guide for Americans." "You just bet I am," she said. "My friend Ayn Rand wrote it, and sticking to it is easy as pie. I've just finished a shooting script about a man who learns how to live after he is dead."

Other people in the industry admit that they are following the "Guide" in scripts about the living. One man who is doing that assured me that he nevertheless doesn't need it, that it offers him nothing he didn't already know. "This is new only to the youngsters out here," he said. "They haven't had their profound intentions knocked out of them yet, or else they're still earning under five hundred a week. As soon as you become adjusted in this business, you don't need the 'Screen Guide' to tell you what to do." A studio executive in charge of reading scripts believes that Hollywood has a new kind of self-censorship. "It's automatic, like shifting gears," he explained. "I now read scripts through the eyes of the D.A.R., whereas formerly I read them through the eyes of my boss. Why, I suddenly find myself beating my breast and proclaiming my patriotism and exclaiming that I love my wife and kids, of which I have four, with a fifth on the way. I'm all loused up. I'm scared to death, and nobody can tell me it isn't because I'm afraid of being investigated."

William Wyler, who directed the Academy Award picture *The Best Years of Our Lives*, told me he is convinced that he could not make that picture today and that Hollywood will produce no more films like *The Grapes of Wrath* and *Crossfire*. "In a few months, we won't be able to have a heavy who is an American," he said. The scarcity of roles for villains has become a serious problem, particularly at studios specializing in Western pictures, where writers are being harried for not thinking up any new ones. "Can I help it if we're running out of villains?" a writer at one of these studios asked me. "For years I've been writing scripts about a Boy Scout–type cowboy in love with a girl. Their fortune and happiness are threatened by a banker holding a mortgage over their heads, or by a big landowner, or by a crooked sheriff. Now they tell me that bankers are out. Anyone holding a mortgage is out. Crooked public officials are out. All I've got left is a cattle rustler. What the hell am I going to do with a cattle rustler?"

Hollywood's current hypersensitivity has created problems more subtle than the shortage of heavies. *Treasure of Sierra Madre,* a film about prospecting for gold, was to have begun and ended with the subtitle "Gold, Mister, is worth what it is because of the human labor that goes into the finding and getting of it." The line is spoken by Walter Huston in the course of the picture. John Huston, who directed it, says that he couldn't persuade the studio to let the line appear on the screen. "It was all on account of the word 'labor,'" he told me. "That word looks dangerous in print, I guess." He paused, then added thoughtfully, "You can sneak it onto the sound track now and then, though." At a preview, in Hartford, Connecticut, of *Arch of Triumph,* attended by its director, Lewis Milestone, and by Charles Einfield, president of Enterprise Productions, which brought it out, the manager of the theatre asked Einfield whether it was necessary to use the word "refugees" so often in the picture. "All the way back to New York," says Milestone, "Charlie kept muttering, 'Maybe we mention the word "refugees" too many times?' 'But the picture is *about* refugees,' I told him. 'What can we do now? Make a new picture?'"

A Msgr. Devlin, the Western representative of the Legion of Decency, has been on the set of *Joan of Arc,* which is being produced by Walter Wanger and stars Ingrid Bergman, since production started, and the services of a Father Doncoeur, of France, were enlisted shortly afterward. The director, Victor Fleming, who directed *Gone with the Wind,* said to me, "We've worked very closely with the Catholic Church, doing it the way they want it done. We want to be sure all these artists don't get a bum steer." I watched the shooting of a scene in which Miss Bergman, supposedly dying, lay on a prison bed of straw. The Bishop and the Earl of Warwick, her captors, leaned over her, and the Earl said, "She must not be allowed to die. Our King has paid too much for this sorceress to allow her to slip through our fingers." "Cut!" Fleming shouted. "Say that as if you *mean* it," he went on frantically. "She's *valuable property*! She must not be allowed to *die*! We have to finish the picture with her! This picture is costing three million dollars! Put more *feeling* into it! She must not be allowed to *die,* goddammit!" Just before the cameras were started up again, Fleming remarked, "*Gone with the Wind* was more fun than this. It cost about a million and a half more than *Joan.*" Everything, apparently, used to be more fun.

· · ·

Most producers stick firmly to the line that there is no Communism whatever in the industry and that there are no Communistic pictures. "We're going to make any kind of pictures we like, and nobody is going to tell us what to do," I was informed by Dore Schary, the R.K.O. vice-president and winner of the Golden Slipper Square Club's Humanitarian Award. He is a soft-spoken, unpretentious, troubled-looking man in his early forties, who might be regarded as one of Miss Hussey's "modern covered-wagon folks." In sixteen years, Schary pioneered from a $100-a-week job as a junior writer to his present position, which brings him around $500,000 a year. When he testified before the Thomas Committee, he said that R.K.O. would hire anyone it chose, solely on the basis of his talent, who had not been proved to be subversive. The R.K.O. Board of Directors met soon afterward and voted not to hire any known Communists. Schary then voted, like the other producers, to blacklist the ten men because they had been cited for contempt. He is talked about a good deal in Hollywood. Many of his colleagues are frequently critical of the course he has taken, and yet they understand why he has done what he's done. "I was faced with the alternative of supporting the stand taken by my company or of quitting my job," Schary told me. "I don't believe you should quit under fire. Anyway, I like making pictures. I want to stay in the industry. I like it." Schary is one of the few Hollywood executives who will talk to visitors without having a publicity man sit in on the conversation. "The great issue would have been joined if the ten men had only stood up and said whether or not they were Communists," he continued. "That's all they had to do. As it is, ten men have been hurt and nobody can be happy. We haven't done any work in weeks. Now is the time for all of us to go back to the business of making pictures, good pictures, in favor of anything we please." I asked Schary what he was planning to make this year. "I will assemble a list," he said. He assembled the following out of his memory, and I wrote them down: *Honored Glory* (in favor of honoring nine unknown soldiers), *Weep No More* (in favor of law and order), *Evening in Modesto* (also in favor of law and order), *The Boy with Green Hair* (in favor of peace), *Education of a Heart* (in favor of professional football), *Mr. Blandings Builds His Dream House* (in favor of Cary Grant), *The Captain Was a Lady* (in favor of Yankee clipper ships), *Baltimore Escapade* (in favor of a Protestant minister and his family having fun).

"Committee or no Committee," Schary said, "we're going to make all these pictures exactly the way we made pictures before."

LETTER FROM WASHINGTON

Richard Rovere

THE NORTH ATLANTIC PACT WAS SIGNED almost a month ago, but it isn't in effect yet, and there is a chance that it never will be. That chance was somewhat reduced, however, late last week, when Dean Acheson announced a clearance-sale price on the lend-lease program for Western Europe. He said he thought that in the year coming up, the job could be done for $1,130,000,000, and that a good part of that sum would not be an immediate cash outlay, since we have a lot of spare parts in our military establishment that could be shipped abroad and be replaced here at our leisure. Up to the time of this statement, which was made in a closed session of the Senate Foreign Relations Committee, unofficial and semi-official quotations on the cost of the program had become more and more fanciful—fanciful, that is, if we assume that Mr. Acheson's figure stands for the true cost. The earliest figures cited, when the speculation started a few months ago, were fairly close to the one named by Mr. Acheson, but in the meantime they had jumped a couple of hundred million every few days, and every time they jumped, another senator came down with a bad case of the shakes and declared that he was thinking of voting against the whole program, treaty and all, because we haven't the money. One of the first to be affected by the bullish talk was Senator Walter F. George, of Georgia, a man whose devotion to the administration's foreign policy has been equalled only by his devotion to hard money and double-entry bookkeeping. After hearing Mr. Acheson, the Senator authorized reporters to say that he was beginning to see things in a different light. Still, a number of people in Washington are wondering why we got all those high estimates in the first place. Were they really miscalculations? Or could it be that the highest ones, which were double Mr. Acheson's estimate, represented the whole loaf, and that the administration, mindful of a certain proverb, is settling for half a loaf, in order to push the treaty through? If this is the case, the consequences, naturally, could be tragic, for a lot of grief has come to the world because of too great a reliance on this proverb. There is a third way of accounting for the disparity; the fact that the State Department waited until the figures kicking around the Capitol were running above two billion dollars before it put out its "All Prices Slashed 50 Percent" sign could lead one to suspect that it was playing the old trick of marking the goods way up in order to make the reduced price look like an irresistible bargain.

If that was the game, it was a very foxy one, and up to now the administration has been just the opposite of foxy in the way it has gone about selling the Pact to the Senate. First off, it forgot Congress's touchiness about its Constitutional responsibility for the declaration of war, and let the word get around that under the treaty we would be honor-bound to start shooting the moment Luxembourg, Iceland, Portugal, or anyone else ran up distress signals. Next, the State Department's protocol people invited only a handful of senators to witness the signing of the Pact—an inexcusable oversight, for which only partial amends were made when, at the last minute, some of the more understanding guests were asked to shove over and provide room for the men who have the power to make the North Atlantic entente about as effective as the Alliance of the Three Emperors. Shortly after that, President Truman, apparently without realizing what he was doing, approved the proposal of Dr. Edwin G. Nourse, of the Council of Economic Advisers, that the money to rehabilitate the European armies be got in part by whittling down our own military budget—an idea that wasn't at all what the President, to say nothing of the generals and admirals, had in mind. Dr. Nourse's speech raised the hope in the Senate that the lend-lease deal could be worked not just cheaply but without cost, and it was up to the administration to dash this hope. Destroying pleasant illusions is a good way to lose friends, and the administration lost plenty. There were other blunders, too, and they came in such profusion that the belief was expressed in some quarters that the Pact would not be ratified, because it couldn't get to the Senate floor in less than ten weeks, and within that time the administration would make enough blunders to insure its defeat.

The outlook has improved during the past week, but not many people here would be rash enough to go on record with the statement that the

Pact is now certain to be ratified. The general feeling, I think, is that if a rollcall were taken this week or next, there would be not more than ten or twelve votes against ratification. In the present atmosphere, the lend-lease proposals, which, of course, involve the House as well as the Senate, would probably carry, too, though the fight would be tougher and the margin of victory slimmer. But there won't be a rollcall this week or next, and since nowadays epochal events can occur in the time it takes to finish an average Senate committee hearing, it would be unwise to predict that the current Congressional attitude will last into the approaching summer. Two or three new people's democracies could spring into being by then; Stalin could apprehensively come to terms with the West, or even take Winston Churchill's advice and die. (However, Ex-Ambassador Smith has returned from Moscow with the news that nonagenarians are common in the Dzhugashvili family and with the opinion, based on observation, that the Generalissimo is feeling tiptop and has many years of rich, full living ahead of him.) Developments of this sort could drastically affect sentiment in Congress, and so could a number of less dramatic ones at home—an increase of troubles in the domestic economy, for example, or a realignment in Congress because of an issue with no bearing on the Pact. If a lot could happen while the Pact is in committee, a lot more could happen before it comes to a vote. The Pact will probably get to the Senate floor fairly soon after it has been approved in committee, which means about a month from now, but it's going to stay there a long time. The party leaders plan to allow every member of the Senate to speak on the Pact; this will be what is known as a Historic Debate, so no one is likely to forgo his chance to be heard, and heard at length. The supporters of the Pact are doubtless at work now dusting off ancient pieties to put into the record, and the opponents are doubtless improving the delaying tactics with which they held up the authorization of more Marshall Plan funds for several days beyond the deadline. There isn't any deadline on this one, and the betting here is that we'll still be at it on the Fourth of July or even, some wise money says, Labor Day. Historic Debates are interesting, but one disadvantage is that they give some people the idea of running out and making a little history while the debating is going on.

• • •

It isn't news to anyone that J. Edgar Hoover, who will this year celebrate his completion of a quarter century as director of the Federal Bureau of

Investigation, is a superb showman and a master politician. He has served under four Presidents—two Republicans and two Democrats—and has had seven Attorneys General shot out from over him in the course of achieving an endurance record unequalled by anyone else in high appointive office today. Somehow surmounting nature, which endowed him with a rather moist and commonplace personality, he has become for millions of Americans one of the most vivid and exciting figures in our public life. His career has been so replete with accomplishments that many of them have not received half the attention they merit. This was borne in upon me a few days ago when, in the agreeable company of some out-of-town high-school boys and girls, I went on a conducted tour of the F.B.I. headquarters, in the Department of Justice Building. This student group was one of the many that have come to Washington, from all over the East and the Middle West, this spring—as others have come in other springs—to spend a few days watching democracy at work and having themselves a good time. They make extensive tours in rubberneck buses, shake hands with their congressman and listen patiently as he tries to justify his ways to the teen-age mind, sit for a while in the House and Senate galleries, peer at historic documents in the National Archives, get some lessons in applied physics at the Bureau of Standards, watch paper money being made at the Bureau of Engraving and Printing, and, invariably, tour the F.B.I. headquarters. I had been told that by far the most popular feature of these junkets is the F.B.I. tour, so I decided to go along with a group and see what the show was like.

The F.B.I. has its own entrance to the Department of Justice Building, and its own handsome lobby. Our group assembled at noon in this lobby, where a sign announces that there are free tours every half hour from nine to four, Monday through Friday. On this day, though, which was at the height of the student-pilgrimage season, they must have been starting out every seven or eight minutes, for our cluster of forty or so was one of five in the lobby. In a few minutes, a brisk, neatly dressed, sandy-haired man in his early twenties came out of an elevator, introduced himself to us as our guide, and apologized for keeping us waiting and for the poor condition of his throat, which he had to clear about every half sentence. He said that it had been an unusually busy day; he and his fellow-guides had already escorted more than three thousand people through the building, and the strain on their voices was telling. He gave us a brief verbal preview and then said, "And now, folks, if there are any particular questions at all, please don't heztate." This was the line with which he ended every one of his set speeches along the way. Since he had said nothing this time to provoke questions, none were asked. Our guide broke us up into groups small enough for the elevators and instructed us to go to a room on the fifth floor, where he would shortly rejoin us. This room, a lounge, is a tempering tank for tourists; on its walls are many photographs and brightly colored charts and diagrams explaining the F.B.I. and its operations. Moreover, it is right across the corridor from the office of J. Edgar Hoover himself. "The Chief works just the other side of that door," our guide told us when he arrived. (It was a superfluous remark, for the famous occupant's name and title are emblazoned on the door in lettering worthy of a California chain dentist.) "Don't know whether he's in or not right now. Lots of times, when he's in, he likes to step outside and shake hands with all you folks." We gaped hopefully at the door, but it didn't open, and the guide herded us down a hall. A short distance away is the law library of the Department of Justice. It is necessary for sightseers to troop the entire length of the library to get to the great laboratories where human hairs are split and human blood is analyzed practically to the point of identifying the person from whom it leaked. "You're now passing through the second-largest law liberry in the United States," our guide said, "and I'm sure you'll all understand what I mean when I say that we'll appreciate it very much if you'll be just as quiet as you can possibly be. You see, we've got a lot of our attorneys in here studying up on the books so they can present the government's case on a lot of the spy and murder trials you've been reading about in your home-town papers, and we don't like to disturb them." It was a thoughtful request but an idle one to make of several dozen high-school students on vacation, and the most that can be said for our group is that it clattered along at a smart clip and didn't stop to examine any of the books. Just as I thought it a remarkable fact that J. Edgar Hoover manages to get his important work done in an office across the hall from a public gathering place that is refilled every half hour, or less, I was deeply impressed by the knowledge that the government's case is represented in the courts by men who do their legal research in a library in which traffic is as heavy as it is in the lobby of a large hotel.

Only a swinging door separates the library from the laboratories. "In here, folks," our guide said, pointing down a corridor with a series of rooms opening onto it from both sides, "you will see millions of dollars' worth of scientific crime-detecting equipment. These are the most up-to-date crime laboratories in the entire world." I must confess that although I never doubted the claims being made by the guide for all this equipment, I found the equipment itself rather unstimulating. It looked like what one sees, in smaller quantity, in any doctor's office or in the high-school physics and chemistry laboratories with which my companions were unquestionably familiar. I gathered, though, that not many of the students shared my disappointment. The glamour the equipment lacked in appearance seemed more than made up for by the glamour imparted to it by the setting and by the rhetoric of our guide. "Here, on your right, now," he was saying, "is where we can identify a murderer or a sabatoor beyond the shadow of a doubt, with only a drop or two of his saliva. The police department in your home town could send us a sample of saliva, and it wouldn't take us hardly any time to let them know whether they'd got their man." The guide proceeded learnedly on the subject of saliva analysis before asking if there were any particular questions at all. Naturally, there were several, all of them highly technical, except for one from a youngster who wanted to know how the police would locate the drops of incriminating saliva. The guide thought for a moment and then said that saliva might be found on an envelope recently licked by the killer. The boy asked where they'd get the envelope, but by that time we had moved along to the hair-splitting apparatus: "One little piece of hair, and we can substanchewate right off whether it's animal hair and, if so, what kind of animal, or, if it's human hair, what race it came off of—Mongoloid, Niggroid, or Caucasian. The Bureau does this free of charge for any law-enforcement agency in the United States. You see, folks, every hair on your head is made up of tiny cells you can only see in these high-power machines, and the cells on everyone's head are different, so that . . ."

Thus we progressed, down through the Serology Section, the Toxicology Section ("just a little piece of brain or kidney . . ."), the Adhesive Tape Section ("samples here of every kind of adhesive tape ever manufactured in the United States and many from foreign lands"), the Tire-Tread Section, the Rubber-Heel Section, the Typewriter Section, the Reference Firearms Collection, and the rest. The trip through the laboratories makes one feel certain that our struggle against crime, espionage, and subversion is in good hands, and that whenever Mr. Hoover's bloodhounds latch onto an old envelope or a heelprint, a couple more enemies of society are gone geese. What stirred me most, however, was not so much the proof of the F.B.I.'s efficiency—of that I had already been persuaded by news stories, gossip columns, and comic books—as the wonderful ingenuity with which the laboratories, and most of the rest of the F.B.I. headquarters, are laid out. The laboratories may or may not be arranged in the most utilitarian fashion, but from the broader standpoint of the public interest they are very nearly perfect. Not even Norman Bel Geddes could improve on the job. The microscopes, the spectrographs, and all the other scopes and graphs in the various rooms, handsomely framed in large picture windows that extend almost from floor to ceiling, are arrayed along both sides of the corridor. The charts and specimen collections, such as the Reference Firearms Collection, face outward toward the public rather than inward toward the technicians, and so does almost everything else, including the better-looking filing cabinets. This way, everything serves a double purpose; it plays its part in the war on crime and it helps to build up confidence in our form of government. Unfortunately, on the day of our visit we couldn't see how this policy works out when the equipment has to be used, for, crime apparently being at a low ebb, none of the instruments we were shown was actually being put to any use by anyone.

Here and there we encountered brief delays, waiting for groups ahead of us to move on. At one point, we were held up for quite a while because a boy from a grammar-school group, a child of seven or eight, took violently ill, possibly because of the heat, during the brain-and-kidney lecture. The traffic finally got so dense that our guide and two others decided to merge their three groups. We proceeded from the laboratories to a large exhibit room, the riches of which are so numerous and so varied that it would be impossible to describe all of them. If you can imagine a combination of the most exciting features of Mme. Tussaud's, the entrance to the Rialto Theatre, and the cleverest advertising devices of, say, the Champion Spark Plug display at the Automobile Show in Grand Central Palace, you will have an idea of what the room is like. There is, for instance, a giant register on one of the walls that looks like a mileage recorder on a speedometer; its last digit changes every time a new set of fingerprints is received into the F.B.I. files. It clicked about twenty times while we were within sight, and the last figure we saw was 111,453,482. The walls of the room are covered with strikingly colored photographs, most of them life-size, of famous G-men and their victims. The photographs are pasted on heavy cardboard, and are cut out, silhouette style, and glued to the walls. One set of photographs is of a criminal named

Roscoe Pitts, who tried to alter his fingerprints by having skin from his torso grafted onto his fingertips. There is a stunning life-size picture of his mutilated midsection. The place has no dummies, as a waxworks has, but it is really better than Mme. Tussaud's, because many of the properties are not reproductions but genuine relics. John Dillinger's bullet-ridden straw hat, his bloodstained shirt collar, and the cigar he was about to light when the G-men plugged him are all on display. So is his death mask. Then, there is a collection of Guns Used by Notorious Gangs and Gangsters, and the Dead File, which contains the F.B.I.'s records on a number of spectacular public enemies who won't be troubling the Bureau any more. It seemed to me that the exhibit room was an even greater triumph of the F.B.I.'s educational program than the laboratories were, and I gathered that the boys and girls with me felt the same way about it.

All things considered, we had been well prepared for the pièce de résistance of the tour, a visit to the F.B.I. shooting gallery, in the basement. This range is used by the G-men, each of whom is required to brush up on his marksmanship at least once a month. The man who was shooting when we got there didn't need much brushing-up. His target, made of paper, was a life-size black-and-white drawing of an ugly customer in a snap-brim hat, pulling a rod. We stood directly behind this G-man while he gave us a short lecture on the three guns he was about to use: the .38 police revolver; the Magnum revolver, the most powerful hand weapon ever made; and the Thompson sub-machine gun. After his talk, the lights went out, except for one bright light on the target, and for a few seconds there was an almost unbearable racket as the G-man, whose ears were plugged with cotton wadding, let go with the three weapons. After he had finished, he pressed a button, the other lights went on, and the target, suspended on wires by pulleys, came rushing toward us. The paper man had been hit twice in each arm and about eight times in the chest and stomach, and there was an almost continuous slit straight across his neck, just above the collar line. After a great deal of gee-whizzing and holy-smoking, our guide spoke up. "And now, folks," he said, for the last time, "if there are any particular questions at all, please don't heztate." "How do we get out of here?" one of the girls asked in a quavering voice.

DIE LUFTBRÜCKE

E. J. Kahn, Jr.

MAY 14, 1949 (ON THE BERLIN AIRLIFT)

FTER THE BLOCKADE IS ENDED next week, the Berlin airlift will probably continue for a while, on a gradually reduced scale, but for all practical purposes this prodigious operation at last appears to be over, and the score can be added up. Nothing quite like the airlift has ever happened before. For the first time in history, a community of a couple of million people, cut off from its sources of supply, as far as land and water transport are concerned, has been kept alive for months with supplies brought in by air. Specifically, the nearly two and a quarter million residents of the three Western-power sectors of Berlin have been sustained by the lift economically, and perhaps ideologically, since June 26, 1948. The fourth occupying power has, not unexpectedly, taken a disparaging view of this extraordinary delivery service. One of the Left Wing propaganda lines thrown hopefully toward West Berliners went, in effect: "Don't let those Americans, British, and French kid you into thinking that they're exerting themselves on your behalf. Have you forgotten so quickly that during the war, when they bombed your homes and killed your children, they never seemed to have any trouble sending four or five hundred planes to Berlin at once? So why should you get excited over this vaunted airlift of theirs? What does it consist of, anyway? Just one measly plane at a time." Arithmetically, such an argument was unassailable. Unlike a fleet of bombers, the airlift has not filled the sky, either visually or aurally. However, the argument ignored both the obvious fact that the wartime bombers did not have to land inside Berlin to deliver their cargoes and the fact that while there have not been many aircraft over the city at any one time since last June, there has almost always been at least one. Twenty-four hours a day, as a rule, and seven days a week, no matter where a person happened to be in the three hundred and forty-four square miles that comprise the shattered city of Berlin—an area twenty-four square miles larger than that of the five boroughs of New York—he has been able to hear the steady, patient drone of an airlift plane overhead. An instant after the sound of its engines ebbed away, the purposeful hum of another plane would come within earshot. Just as a trickle of water can, if sufficiently prolonged, wear down the stoutest rock, so the airlift, with its unostentatious but ceaseless trickle of flights, carved a large hole in the Soviet blockade of Berlin, if, indeed, it was not in large measure responsible for the Russians' decision to lift the blockade.

The airlift has been unimpressive to the Berlin eye and its planes have averaged only seven or eight short tons apiece per trip, but it has provided the inhabitants of West Berlin with a million and a half short tons of supplies. The French have played only a modest, earth-bound role in the airlift operation. The Americans and the British have done all the flying and between them worked out so precise and smooth a procedure that, unless hampered by weather, they have been able matter-of-factly to deliver to West Berlin, from eight outlying airbases, around eight thousand short tons of airborne cargo every twenty-four hours. One day in mid-April, when ideal flying conditions prevailed and everybody worked extra hard, the airlift ferried in 12,940.9 tons of cargo. Just ten days after that performance, by what may have been pure coincidence, the American State Department announced that the Soviet Union seemed disposed to sit down with the Western powers and discuss doing away with the Russian blockade, the Western counter-blockade, and the muddled dual-currency situation here that had prompted an admirer of Samuel L. Clemens to declare that the main intention of the occupying powers in Berlin seemed to be that never the twain marks should meet.

The American and British personnel engaged in the operation call it the airlift, the literal German version of which is *"Luftversorgung,"* but the Germans themselves, uncharacteristically, prefer the shorter word *"Luftbrücke,"* which means "air-bridge." To its direct beneficiaries, the lift is almost invariably *"die Luftbrücke."* During the summer of 1948, the Americans and the British worked independently. In mid-October, they set up a joint organization, called the Combined Airlift Task Force, with headquarters at Wiesbaden, in the United States Occupation Zone, two hundred and eighty miles southwest of Berlin. The United States Air Force and the Royal Air Force still have separate titles for their respective assignments. The Americans call theirs Operation Vittles. The British call theirs Operation Plainfare. They had decided on "Planefare," to stress the manner of transport of Berlin's supplies rather than their austerity. Shortly after the airlift began, however, an R.A.F. man inadvertently used "Plainfare" in an official document, and that spelling became official. There is no evidence that any American airman has thought of switching to "Operation Victuals."

The names "Vittles" and "Plainfare" were invented when the airlift was starting and when its sole objective was to keep West Berlin from running short of food. Both names, once the airlift was an apparently permanent phenomenon, became metonymical misnomers. Only 30 percent of the tonnage ferried to Berlin has been edible; such is the complexity of modern urban civilization that in Berlin coal, not bread, has proved to be the staff of municipal life. It has taken only fifteen hundred tons of foodstuffs a day, or a little more than a pound per person, to provide West Berliners with an adequately nourishing, if not notably fancy, diet. But it has taken two pounds of coal per person per day to provide even the subnormal quantities of heat, electric power, gas, and other utility services they have been getting since they began living in a blockaded community. Three out of every five tons of cargo carried on the airlift have consisted of coal. Quite a bit of this has been for Berlin's manufacturing industries, which have also been receiving a small but steady flow of raw materials, for without industrial activity there would have been even more unemployment in the Western sectors than there is now, and unemployed residents of those sectors have trouble, naturally, buying their daily allotment of food. (The Americans and British haven't been giving the food away; they have just fetched it in.) Some of the industrial plants that have received airlift coal are below the flight paths that all airlift planes have had to follow, and now and then the smoke from the flown-in coal, as it billowed from the factories' stacks, has obscured the vision of the airlift pilots. Among the products manufactured by the West sectors' still-struggling factories are small locomotives, which have been exported, in airlift planes, to the coal mines of the Ruhr, where they have expedited the production of coal to be airlifted to the plants in Berlin that have created the smoke that has annoyed the pilots who have flown in the coal. The Berlin airlift has been a complicated business.

· · ·

At the Postdam Conference, in July, 1945, Germany was cut up into four zones of occupation, and Berlin, deep within the Soviet Zone, into four sectors. A belt of Russian-occupied territory, nowhere less than seventy-five miles wide and at some points twice that wide, separates the Western zones of Germany from the Western sectors of Berlin. In November, 1945, the members of the Allied Control Council, the four-power agency then supervising the Occupation, wrote down a set of rules covering air traffic to and from the quadripartite city. Straight lines were drawn, on a map, from the Allied Control Authority building, in the heart of Berlin, to three westerly cities—Frankfurt am Main, in the American Zone, and Bückeburg and Hamburg, in the British. Each line represented a twenty-mile-wide corridor, through which all non-Russian air traffic from the Western zones to Berlin would thereafter have to be routed. The Bückeburg corridor, crossing a hundred miles of Russian-occupied Germany, is the central one. The Hamburg corridor, to the north, also crossing a hundred Russian-occupied miles, and the Frankfurt corridor, to the south, crossing a hundred and eighty, converge on the Bückeburg corridor as it nears Berlin, like the outer edges of an enormous arrowhead. Each of the occupying powers, including the Soviet Union, has the right to send planes along all three corridors at any time. In 1945, there were four landing fields inside Berlin. The sectors assigned at the Potsdam Conference to the United States and Great Britain included two of them—Tempelhof, the city's most elegant airdrome before the war, and Gatow, which had been a training center for Luftwaffe fighter pilots. The Soviet Union got the other two. It also had eight fields in its own zone, just beyond the city limits. When, on June 24, 1948, the Russians stopped all land traffic to Berlin from the west (water traffic was not halted until two days later), the Western powers had good reason to be grateful for that formal agreement about the corridors. Without them, and without the two fields in Berlin, there couldn't have been any airlift.

On June 25th, two B-17s, based in Wiesbaden and ordinarily used on passenger runs, each delivered five tons of food and medical supplies to West Berlin. The day after that, General Lucius D. Clay, the American military governor in Germany, telephoned from his headquarters here to the headquarters of the U.S. Air Forces in Europe, in Wiesbaden, an order that an all-out cargo airlift to Berlin be created immediately. (The

British hurriedly took similar steps.) Before the day was over, twenty-five C-47s—the military designation for the two-engine transport known to civilians as the DC-3—had ferried eighty tons of food and medicine to Tempelhof. The airlift was under way. It was estimated that forty-five hundred tons was the minimum amount of supplies required daily—once the reserve supplies on hand were exhausted—to keep the inhabitants of that area alive, reasonably healthy, and unreceptive to whatever advances might be made to them from the east. That minimum was attained in a little over six weeks.

. . .

A little less than two-thirds of the freight delivered by the airlift has been coal, and a little less than one-third food; the rest, amounting to 7 percent of the total, has been industrial raw materials, liquid fuel, and whatnot—all intended to help, in one way or another, to convince the people of West Berlin that, considering their peculiarly isolated position, they were faring quite handsomely, and to give the million-odd folk in East Berlin something to think about, too. The Combined Airlift Task Force has brought West Berlin, among other things, pig iron, X-ray film, vitamin tablets, newsprint, pencils, stationery, snowplows, hand tools, machine tools, surgical instruments, combs, window glass, cement, nails, chemicals, police uniforms, matches, candles, ladies' underwear, TNT, and detonators, the last two (for removing rubble) in separate shipments. Berlin is a big radio-manufacturing center, and the radio industry has to have magnets for loudspeakers; the airlift has furnished them, but because magnetized magnets throw airplane compasses out of whack, the magnets had to be demagnetized before they were shipped and remagnetized afterward. The list also includes bicycle parts, sheet steel, needles, thread, typewriter keys, asbestos, buttons, quicksilver, insulating tape, paints, lacquers, medicine bottles, roofing felt, and a thousand other items, among them five and a half pounds of dried-banana flakes that the airlift has ferried in every week for each of three German infants who have a rare digestive ailment and are unable to assimilate any other food.

Once a month, the Task Force's planning experts have got together at their headquarters, in Wiesbaden, and, with frequent recourse to the slide rules that have invariably decorated their desks, made an informed guess at the amount of tonnage they expected to be able to fly to Berlin the following month. Their estimate has been passed along to the Bipartite Economic Commission, which is a mammoth agency in Frankfurt, generally known as Bico; the information has then been sent on to a Bico subsidiary called the Berlin Airlift Coordinating Committee, or Bealcom. Meanwhile, Bealcom has obtained from German and Western officials in Berlin an estimate of the Western sectors' requirements for the month. Bealcom, the chairman of which has been suffering from stomach ulcers, has then had to decide how much of what kind of commodities would be shipped to Berlin from each base in the Western zones. It has established priorities among commodities, so that if the Task Force should prove unable to do as well as it hoped to, the most essential items could be carried in—newsprint, say, on the eve of an election. The Task Force has nearly always done better than its announced expectations, and this has made people in some small-minded non-aviation circles suspect that the air people have set their quotas a mite low, so that they could point with pride to the regularity with which they exceeded them. Whenever there has been space to handle more than the assigned cargo, it has been given over to coal. The procedure of assembling cargoes has been little different from what it was before the blockade. Food, coal, and other commodities have simply been sent by the dealers who handle them to airbases, instead of to railway freight houses, barge piers, or truck depots. When the commodities have reached Berlin, they have been turned over to the German distributors who handled supplies before the blockade.

· · ·

Tempelhof, the airfield in the United States sector, was among the Nazis' most splendid ornaments before the war. Its hangars and administrative offices—quite a few of them later damaged by bombs and Russian artillery—form a continuous, curving, half-mile-long structure, with only 20 percent less floor space than the Pentagon. Surmounting the edifice is a twenty-foot eagle, clutching the earth in its talons. In the customary Nazi fashion, a swastika shield was once appended to the globe. Soon after the Americans took over the premises, they denazified the bird with a speed and ingenuity they have been accused of not always applying to livelier holdovers from the old regime. They slapped some white paint on the eagle's head and some gold paint on its beak and then superimposed the Stars and Stripes on the swastika. They ended up with a very presentable American eagle. Tempelhof, for all its splendor, is poorly situated. A seven-story apartment house stands near the approach to the field, and a number of industrial plants, some with tall smoke-stacks, are nearby. One of the plants, a brewery, had a chimney almost five hundred feet high. After the owner had ignored a few oral complaints by the pilots, some American engineers came around one day and made a few exploratory nicks at the base of the offending tower— the kind of nicks designed for the insertion of charges of dynamite. The brewer soon clipped a couple of hundred feet off his chimney. The French have been more forthright in dealing with navigational hazards. A couple of hundred yards from Tegel, the airfield in their sector, there stood the two towers of Radio Berlin, a station under Soviet control. Some French engineers blew them up one day, and not only didn't give the Russians a hint of their intentions but didn't even tell the Americans, who were in charge of airlift flight operations at the field.

The principal drawback of Tempelhof last June was that it had only the one runway, and that was in indifferent shape. Two weeks after the airlift got going, engineers began to repair the runway and construct a second one there. By mid-September, it was finished, and in October a third was completed. Meanwhile, the British improved the runway at Gatow, and meanwhile, too, the Americans were building the field at Tegel, with one runway. Bulldozers, graders, rock-crushers, dump trucks, asphalt, and steel matting were flown in for the work; several of the larger pieces of machinery had to be cut apart with acetylene torches in the Western zones, and then welded together here. The engineers had nowhere near as much equipment as they wanted, however, and they were obliged to follow the example set by other engineers during the Hump operation. At that time, Indians and Chinese built airfields practically by hand. Almost the same thing happened in Berlin. Six hundred thousand cubic yards of brick rubble were converted into runway foundations by Germans working with hand tools and wheelbarrows. At Tegel, twenty thousand Germans were employed, in round-the-clock shifts. Women made up 40 percent of this labor force. A Hearst man took a photograph of some of them on the job and sent it to the United States, where a Hearst paper tacked on a caption identifying the subjects as slave laborers toiling under the lash of the Reds. The runway at the Tegel airfield was completed in just under three months, and the field was officially dedicated last November, when an American airlift plane flew in with twenty thousand pounds of cheese and two Air Force generals.

The Germans in West Berlin at first reacted to *die Luftbrücke* with a mixture of enthusiasm and skepticism. Most of them were certain that the venture was ill-starred, but many of them felt that it nonetheless deserved a thumping round of applause, for effort. Accordingly, they turned up at the airfields in large numbers and showered pilots, along with a few passersby in uniform, with tokens of their gratitude and esteem—bouquets, old coins and stamps, books, stickpins, souvenir plaques, songs about the airlift, and, in one instance, a pair of dogs. The Germans also spent a lot of time looking up, wide-eyed and open-mouthed, at the sky, even though there wasn't much to see. During October, to commemorate the completion of the airlift's first hundred days of operations, the West Berlin post offices cancelled all outgoing mail with a *Luftbrücke* postmark. In recent months, the airlift has been taken as a matter of course, and a freight-carrying plane has attracted no more attention here than a United Parcel Service truck does in Westchester. West Berliners lately have gazed at the sky only when there wasn't an airplane in sight. In three years, they switched from being apprehensive at hearing an alien plane to being apprehensive at not hearing one.

. . .

Before the blockade, the American, British, and French sectors got a total of some fifteen thousand tons of cargo a day, by railroad, barge, truck, and plane. The eight thousand tons a day that have been delivered by the airlift have had a somewhat greater utility per ton. In the pre-blockade days, West Berliners got fresh potatoes. During the blockade, they have got dehydrated ones, which weigh and bulk less and which, though inferior in taste, provide equal nourishment. In addition to potatoes, their airborne bounty has included frozen and canned beef, frozen and canned pork, frozen and smoked fish, flour, processed and natural cheeses, dehydrated vegetables (mostly carrots, onions, and cabbage), lard, suet, margarine, butter, sugar, honey, salt, rolled oats, rice, grits, macaroni, spaghetti, noodles, pudding powder, yeast, cake flour, coffee, tea, cocoa, powdered eggs, soup powder, dried skim and dried whole milk, dried fruits, chocolate, and assorted baby foods. A little more than half of this has been produced in West Germany and the rest has been imported—vegetables and potatoes from England, the Netherlands, Italy, and Hungary; cheese from Switzerland and Denmark; wheat and flour, oats, dried peas and beans, meat, powdered eggs, and dehydrated potatoes from the United States. The frozen meat, the cheese, and the chocolate have had the highest shipping priority. They have been regarded as the most perishable of the foods and also the most pilferable, and the longer it has taken to get them on a plane, the more tempting they have become to the occasional weak-willed German or displaced person doing the loading.

In recent months, no loader has had a chance to be tempted for very long. The usual elapsed time between removing meat from refrigerated freight cars at a siding at the Rhein-Main airbase, trucking it to a plane, loading it, flying it two hundred and eighty miles to Berlin, unloading it, and trucking it to a cold-storage warehouse has come down to four hours. Salt, a commodity carried exclusively by the British, was a problem of another sort, early in the airlift, because it corrodes the metal parts of aircraft. The British got around that for a while by moving it in flying boats that commuted between a lake in Hamburg and a lake in Berlin and that had already been treated to make them impervious to salt water. When winter came along, it was feared that the lakes would freeze over, and the flying boats were grounded—or, rather, docked. By then, though, somebody had come up with one of the many ingenious ideas that the airlift has inspired. Noncorrodible copper panniers were suspended from the bomb bays of several old British bombers, and the delivery of salt without harm to the delivery wagons was thus triumphantly assured.

The American, British, and French colonies in Berlin add up to less than 1 percent of the population of the West sectors, and it has not been difficult to keep them reasonably well provided with delicacies peculiar to their tastes—kippered herring for British breakfasts, wines for French lunches, and olives for American Martinis. (The wives of some United States military-government officials in Berlin put out a cookbook entitled "Operation Vittles" during the winter, the proceeds going to charity. The recipes dealt with such unaustere concoctions as beef Stroganoff, cherries *à l'eau de vie,* eggnog chiffon pie, and crêpes Suzette. Only one entry, a punch called Block-ade, seemed at all indigenous. Its ingredients are two cans fruit cocktail, one cup sugar, two bottles cognac, six bottles red wine, six bottles white wine, six bottles champagne. Serves seventy-five.) All the food brought in for the Germans in the Western sectors has been rationed. The amount allotted has varied according to how strenuous the recipient's occupation was. The average German has been authorized to buy enough food in each of a dozen major food categories—meat, potatoes, bread, sugar, salt, and so on—to give him about two thousand calories a day, which, though slightly below the amount recommended by our National Research Council for a sedentary man (twenty-four hundred), has been more than enough to sustain life. Many Berliners have amplified their food allotment by growing produce, and then there has always been the black market, for those who could afford it. The Western occupation authorities, eager to stimulate husbandry, have brought in, via the airlift, garden implements, vegetable seeds, and fertilizer, and, on one occasion a few weeks ago, a three-ton shipment of young fruit trees. West Berliners have occasionally complained, ever since the success of the airlift has made them feel secure enough to complain, that they don't care for the taste of dehydrated potatoes, but from a strictly medical point of view, they are believed to have thrived during the blockade.

Before the war, Berlin manufactured more than half the electrical products used in Germany, and it was a flourishing industrial center generally. Not long after the blockade began, when it became evident to the Western military governors that unless the city was to become a giant poorhouse, its economic life would have to be kept functioning, they began to permit manufacturers to import raw materials. (German manufacturers have been required to pay delivery charges, at the pre-blockade rail rate, for whatever goods they have received by airlift.) Lately, two hundred and sixty tons of raw materials have been flown in daily, and—what is equally important—a hundred tons of manufactured goods have been flown out. The value of the radio tubes, light bulbs, lathes, milling machines, telephone and telegraph equipment, and other precision instruments shipped out has been a quarter of a million dollars a day. In addition, the airlift has flown fifty thousand Germans out of Berlin. The British, who have taken care of nearly all the native passenger traffic (though there are several American Overseas Airlines flights between Berlin and Frankfurt every week, and the United States Army runs still another passenger service for its own people), decided, a few months ago, in order to demonstrate that blockaded Berlin was getting along all right not only economically but also culturally, to fly the Berlin Symphony Orchestra, seventy strong, to London for a concert. Two handsomely outfitted passenger planes, dispatched from London to pick up the musicians, stopped en route at Wunstorf, one of the airlift bases in the British Zone. To the R.A.F. men it was unthinkable that any plane should fly into Berlin without adding its mite to the airlift's daily tonnage, so they had a hundred-pound sack of flour deposited on every seat in both ships. Each sack was tied down with a safety belt. It was undoubtedly the most stylish delivery of flour ever made.

PART FOUR

CHARACTER STUDIES

A NOTE BY SUSAN ORLEAN

O NE THING WILL NEVER CHANGE: people are interested in other people. Empires crumble, traditions shatter, formats explode, trends wither, boundaries are perforated; what endures is our curiosity to know what's going on inside the other guy. Magazines thrive because the articles they publish are the bound and printed satisfaction of that curiosity. From the start, *The New Yorker* devoted lots of its prime real estate to what it called Profiles. I'd even argue that Profiles are the single essential unit of *The New Yorker*'s identity, the one element that is indispensable to the magazine.

In the forties, Profiles were different, and maybe even had greater consequence than they do today. We did not know each other back then the way we know each other now. These days, Barack Obama sends us emails; the Pope tweets; celebrity divorces are posted in real time. We know, or, at least, we *feel* that we know, a great deal about people of power and prominence in the world, thanks to the nonstop digital gush of information—personal, professional, significant, ridiculous. In the forties, by contrast, the informational distance between celebrated people and regular people was vast. The people the magazine profiled were usually well recognized, but, for most of the public, they were well out of reach, and they kept tight control over their images. A Profile written at the length and with the intimacy encouraged by *The New Yorker* offered a rare chance to get close.

The magazine in the forties was staffed by giants of the form: E. J. Kahn, Jr., Lillian Ross, Janet Flanner, St. Clair McKelway, Joseph Mitchell. These writers didn't invent the Profile, but sometimes it feels as if they had. Each had a distinct voice, but their writing had in common a tone of familiarity and authority—qualities that became the mark of a *New Yorker* Profile. Their pieces move at a majestic, leisurely pace. (So leisurely, in fact, that you could probably injure someone if you rolled up all three installments of Richard O. Boyer's Duke Ellington Profile and swatted him with it.) There is no paragraph up top announcing the purpose of the Profile or what the subject happens to be selling at the moment. There is no grand summing up at the end of the piece. There is never that self-conscious moment in which the writer makes a plea for taking the story seriously, even when the subject is obscure. A wonderful confidence underpins every one of these stories; it seems that the writers simply believed that their interest in any subject was justification enough for writing about it. As a reader, you notice only the writer's decisions—what to include, what to examine closely, what to describe. You never feel that the story has been stage-managed by the subject or by a publicist or, for that matter, by an editor with an agenda. Readers sense that the story is authentic, and that it grew out of a genuine interest on the part of the writer, rather than out of a press release. Having grown up in the age of celebrity journalism, I was used to reading articles that were very obviously directed by some interested party. The first time I read these pioneering *New Yorker* pieces, I remember being amazed; I couldn't believe you could really find stories like this, in which the writer, and not the subject, set the pace.

In many ways, the stories of this period are very external. The war—the hovering, hungry, uninvited guest of the era—is a constant, and so is the tail end of the Depression. Context, in these pieces, is everything; inner life, not so much. After all, this was a decade before psychotherapy got a popular foothold, and many decades before the advent of confessional journalism and the rehab memoir. The classic *New Yorker* Profile rarely speculates on psychology—a predisposition that continues to this day. Instead, clues to the makeup of the subject's soul are scattered for readers to gather and analyze for themselves. The stuff that would set many writers on fire—scandal, for instance—is handled matter-of-factly and then set in context. For instance, in Janet Flanner's Profile of Marshal Pétain, she notes that the elderly Pétain manages to preside over Vichy France with remarkable vigor. She then adds, almost casually, that his secret is the regular use of stimulants, probably Benzedrine or ephedrine, and that he valued his doctor so highly that he named him to a government post so he could accompany Pétain to high-level meetings. Marshal Pétain—a drug addict! This shocker would have been front and center in a typical story, and would have undoubtedly been followed by much armchair analysis on Pétain's psychological wiring. But that's not the *New Yorker* style and definitely not Flanner's style, which is to carefully layer facts around her subject and observe coolly as he or she goes about daily life. The result is more like a complex diorama built around an individual than like a tight-focus portrait against a blank background. Each of these Profiles, then, becomes much more than a sketch of a personality: each is a piece of time and history, channeled through one individual's life.

The Profiles of this period are so good and so definitive that it seems petty to pick a favorite. But, if I had to choose, I would pick Lillian Ross's "El Único Matador," the Profile of the matador Sidney Franklin. There are so many things I love about this piece: Ross's perfect ear for Franklin's self-importance ("I am A Number One," Franklin says. "I am the best in the business, bar none"); her comfortable mastery of the facts of the sport; her humor; her respect for her subject even when he seems a little silly; her gift for placing the small story of one obsessed individual into the larger setting of postwar Spain. Ross is very much present in the story, but as the passionate observer, eager to hear and see everything that can enrich the story and help make sense of not only Franklin but also the world around him. "El Único Matador" is a model of how to write a Profile. It is so fresh, so humane, and so vivid that it's hard to believe it was written more than sixty years ago. It celebrates, most of all, the exquisiteness of human curiosity. I keep a copy of it on my desk when I work, because like all of these great Profiles, it is not only a lesson in how to write but also a lesson in how to live.

NOTES AND COMMENT

E. B. White

APRIL 21, 1945

WALT WHITMAN TURNED IN THE ABLEST REPORT last week and wrote the perfect account of the President's last journey (and the processions long and winding and the flambeaus of the night). It was quite natural that he should have, and it was ingenious of the *World-Telegram* to give him the space he deserved on the front page. Walt's barbaric yawp, his promulging of democracy, his great sweep and love of the people, had been finding political verification during the past dozen years, and when he wrote of the slow and solemn coffin that passes through lanes and streets, through day and night, with the great cloud darkening the land, with the pomp of the inlooped flags, he was simply filing the continuing story of democracy, shoulder to shoulder with the Associated Press.

For a while after the President's death, our thoughts were cool and amorphous—a private phenomenon which often attends grim public occasions. But a day or so later, in line of duty, we found ourself in the council chambers of those to whom Mr. Roosevelt's death brought a secret sense of relief and the intimations of new life. It was there, by inversion, amid the hopes and yearnings of these people, that we again felt the flame of the President's spirit, for here was the welcoming band, the reception committee, ready to reembrace the status quo, the special privilege, the society of the white Protestant élite, the clipped hedge that guards the inviolate lawn. Here were the conciliators, their hands outstretched to scratch the ears of all the dragons he had tilted with—injustice, compromise, intolerance. It was no wonder, as we walked home, that Walt's old words seemed a perfect fit for the news, no wonder so many millions were at that moment trembling with the tolling bells' perpetual clang and muttering under their breath, "Here, coffin that slowly passes, I give you my sprig of lilac."

. . .

It seems to us that the President's death, instead of weakening the structure at San Francisco, will strengthen it. Death almost always reactivates the household in some curious manner, and the death of Franklin Roosevelt recalls and refurnishes the terrible emotions and the bright meaning of the times he brought us through. By the simple fact of dying, he has again attacked in strength. He now personifies, as no one else could, all the American dead—those whose absence we shall soon attempt to justify. The President was always a lover of strategy: he even died strategically, as though he had chosen the right moment to inherit the great legacy of light that Death leaves to the great. He will arrive in San Francisco quite on schedule, and in hundredfold capacity, to inspire the nations that he named United.

. . .

Today, tomorrow, or some day not far off, the great wish, the long dream, will come true—the end of war in Europe. There may be no surrender, no last laying down of arms, but the victory will be there just the same, the bloody miracle which once seemed hardly possible will have come to pass. "You and eleven million other guys," said the American sergeant to von Papen when he said he wished the war were over. President Roosevelt loved these eleven million other guys very much, and he was well aware that war's end for the soldier in arms would be war's beginning for all the rest of us combined, and for the soldier, too. The President knew this as well as any other man, or better. The guns that spoke in the Hudson Valley last Sunday morning, and Fala's sharp answering bark, were the first salvo of his new fight—for freedom, human rights, peace, and a world under law.

POLLEN MAN

St. Clair McKelway and Harold Ross

NOVEMBER 1, 1941 (ON WALT DISNEY)

HILE MANY OF OUR READERS were seeing Walt Disney's new picture one day last week, we personally were sitting in a hotel room watching Mr. Disney himself imitate a bee. This is the age of journalistic privilege. "In the studio, I'm the bee that carries the pollen," Mr. Disney told us. Rising, in illustration, he held out his two cupped hands, filled with invisible pollen, and walked across the room and stood in front of a chair. "I've got to know whether an idea goes here," he said, dumping some pollen into the chair, "or here," he went on, hurrying to our side of the room and dumping the rest of the pollen on our knees. "Do you draw any more at all?" we asked. "If I do, I don't show my drawings to any of my artists," he said, walking about restlessly. "I've got too many good artists out there. To draw, you've got to get off to yourself. You've got to have nothing else on your mind. I have to talk so much I can't draw. Suppose I'm making a new character like Dumbo. Well, who the hell *is* he? What's he like? What does he feel? Can you make him fly? You've got to keep experimenting, and you've got to keep talking and throwing away a lot of stuff."

Mr. Disney, it developed, has been in South America for the last six weeks or so, gathering pollen for a series of shorts he intends to produce, based on that continent. He took with him, in addition to Mrs. Disney and a sister-in-law, a director and an assistant director, three artists to make sketches of typical South American scenes, three artists to make sketches of typical South American characters, two writers who concentrated on ideas for stories, a composer, and an animator. They flew to Rio and from there to Buenos Aires and on to Santiago, where the Disneys took a ship for New York, leaving the rest of the troupe to fly on independently through Peru, Ecuador, etc. "We were getting lots of stuff," Mr. Disney explained, "but when I saw that boat in Santiago I decided to let the boys finish up by themselves. I've got good men working for me. You know, the hardest thing to get is a good man who has a sense of humor. A man with a dramatic sense but no sense of humor is almost sure to go arty on you. But if he has a really *good* dramatic sense, he'll have a sense of humor along with it. He'll give you a little gag when you need it. Sometimes, right in the middle of a dramatic scene, you've got to have a little gag. I'm going to make these South American pictures simple and not arty. The best way is to work off the cuff. Don't have any script but just go along and nobody knows what's going to happen until it's happened. That was the way we did with *Snow White*. I'd say to a songwriter, 'Look, at this point we got to have a song that expresses love,' and he'd write one. 'What the hell happens next?' the boys would ask me. 'I don't know, but let's try this,' I would say.

"After the South American stuff, I may try to make a picture with live actors in it. I'd like to do that. I'd cut out about half of the dialogue, first of all. Then I'd work animation in, only you wouldn't know it was animation. I don't want any more headaches like the *Nutcracker Suite*. In a thing like that, you got to animate all those flowers, and boy, does that run into dough! All that shading. That damn thing cost two hundred thousand dollars—just the one *Nutcracker Suite*. We're getting back to straight-line stuff, like 'Donald Duck' and the 'Pigs.' But to do that you got to watch out for the boys with the dramatic sense and no sense of humor or they'll go arty on you. You got to keep feeding them pollen."

RUGGED TIMES

Lillian Ross

OCTOBER 23, 1948 (ON NORMAN MAILER)

W E HAD A TALK THE OTHER DAY with Norman Mailer, whose novel *The Naked and the Dead* has been at the top of the best-seller lists for several months now. We met him at Rinehart & Co., his publishers, in a conference room that had, along with other handy editorial equipment, a well-stocked bar. We'd heard rumors that Mailer was a rough-and-ready young man with a strong antipathy to literary gatherings and neckties, but on the occasion of our encounter he was neatly turned out in gray tweeds, with a striped red-and-white necktie and shined shoes, and he assured us that he doesn't really have any deep-seated prejudices concerning dress. "Actually," he said, "I've got all the average middle-class fears." He thinks the assumption that he hasn't got them grew out of his meeting some of the literati last summer when he was wearing sneakers and an old T shirt. He'd just come from a ball game, and it was a very hot day. "I figured anybody with brains would be trying to keep cool," he said.

Mailer is a good-looking fellow of twenty-five, with blue eyes, big ears, a soft voice, and a forthright manner. Locating a bottle of Scotch in the bar, he poured a couple of drinks. "If I'm ever going to be an alcoholic," he said, "I'll be one by November 2nd, thanks to the rigors of the political campaign. I've been making speeches for Wallace. I've made eighteen so far and have another dozen ahead of me. I'm not doing this because I like it. All last year, I kept saying that the intellectuals had to immerse themselves in political movements or else they were only shooting their mouths off. Now I am in this spot as a result of shooting my mouth off." In general, Mailer told us, the success of his novel has caused him to feel uncomfortably like a movie queen. "Whenever I make an appearance," he said, "I have thirty little girls crowding around asking for my autograph. I think it's much better when people who read your book don't know anything about you, even what you look like. I have refused to let *Life* photograph me. Getting your mug in the papers is one of the shameful ways of making a living, but there aren't many ways of making a living that aren't shameful. Everyone keeps asking me if I've ever been psychoanalyzed. The answer is no, but maybe I'll have to be by the end of another five years. These are rough times for little Normie."

Mailer's royalties will net him around thirty thousand this year, after taxes, and he plans to bank most of it. He finds apartments depressing and has a suspicion of possessions, so he and his wife live in a thirty-dollar-a-month furnished room in Brooklyn Heights. He figures that his thirty thousand will last at least five years, giving him plenty of time in which to write another book. He was born in Long Branch, New Jersey, but his family moved to Brooklyn when he was one, and that has since been his home. He attended P.S. 161 and Boys High, and entered Harvard at sixteen, intending to study aeronautical engineering. He took only one course in engineering, however, and spent most of his time reading or in bull sessions. In his sophomore year, he won first prize in *Story*'s college contest with a story entitled "The Greatest Thing in the World." "About a bum," he told us. "In the beginning, there's a whole *tzimes* about how he's very hungry and all he's eating is ketchup. It will probably make a wonderful movie someday." In the Army, Mailer served as a surveyor in the field artillery, an Intelligence clerk in the cavalry, a wireman in a communications platoon, a cook, and a baker, and volunteered, successfully, for action with a reconnaissance platoon on Luzon. He started writing *The Naked and the Dead* in the summer of 1946, in a cottage outside Provincetown, and took sixteen months to finish it. "I'm slowing down," he said. "When I was eighteen, I wrote a novel in two or three months. At twenty-one, I wrote another novel, in seven months. Neither of them ever got published." After turning in the manuscript of *The Naked and the Dead,* he and his wife went off to Paris. "It was wonderful there," he said. "In Paris, you can just lay down your load and look out at the gray sky. Back here, the crowd is always yelling. It's like a Roman arena. You have a headache, and you scurry around like a rat, like a character in a Kafka nightmare, eating scallops with last year's grease on them."

Mailer has an uneasy feeling that Dostoevski and Tolstoy, between them, have written everything worth writing, but he nevertheless means to go on turning out novels. He thinks *The Naked and the Dead* must be a failure, because of the number of misinterpretations of it that he has read. "People say it is a novel without hope," he told us. "Actually, it offers a good deal of hope. I intended it to be a parable about the movement of man through history. I tried to explore the outrageous propositions of cause and effect, of effort and recompense, in a sick society. The book finds man corrupted, confused to the point of helplessness, but it also finds that there are limits beyond which he cannot be pushed, and it finds that even in his corruption and sickness there are yearnings for a better world."

LUGUBRIOUS MAMA

A. J. Liebling

NOVEMBER 15, 1947 (ON EDITH PIAF)

ONE OF OUR MEN, who used to admire Edith Piaf, the tiny French singer, in Paris in 1939, was afraid that she might have brightened up her repertory for her engagement at the Playhouse here, on the theory that Americans demand optimism. He was so concerned that he went over to the Hotel Ambassador to see her before he took a chance on going to the show to hear her—said he wanted to remember her in all her pristine gloom, and not be disillusioned. In Paris, he said, she used to stand up straight and plain in front of a nightclub audience—no makeup, a drab dress—and delight it with a long series of songs ending in a drowning, an arrest, an assassination, or death on a pallet. At the finish of each, the listeners would gulp a couple of quick drinks before the next began. "She was a doleful little soulful," our man remarked sentimentally. He made an engagement with her for one o'clock, and when he called on the hotel phone at that hour, she thanked him in French for being so punctual. "I forgot to set the alarm clock," she explained, "and if you hadn't come, I'd have gone on sleeping." Our man went up to the chanteuse's living room to wait while she dressed, and while waiting there saw some pencilled notes lying on a coffee table beside a book titled *L'Anglais sans Peine,* open to a chapter called "Pronunciation of the English Th," which began, "Some people who lisp pronounce without wishing to do so the two sounds of the th as in English perfectly." The notes were in English and were obviously for introductory speeches for songs that Mlle. Piaf was going to sing in French. Knowing that she had never appeared before an English-speaking audience, prior to her current engagement, he concluded that she had been memorizing the speeches with *L'Anglais sans Peine* as a reference.

"A woman is waiting for a suitor who promised to return to her when he becomes a captain," the first note read. "In the corner a phonograph is playing a popular record it is cold as long as there is life there is hope. She waits for 20 years but he does not come back and the record keeps on playing until it is worn out." The second said, "Perrine—and now the sad story of Perrine, a pretty girl who worked for a priest, but had a secret lover. One night the priest surprises them together and Perrine hides her lover in a large box, but alas forgets about him and leaves him to the mercies of the rats. When he is found a candlestick is made from his leg and a basin for the church from his head, and so ends the sad story of a young man who liked girls too well." Heartened by what he had read, our man greeted Mlle. Piaf, when she appeared, like an old friend upon whom he could depend. She wore gold mules with platform soles about six inches thick, which increased her height to approximately five feet. Her mop of rusty-red hair, a stage trademark, was imprisoned under a tight turban. She looked sleeker offstage than on, our man said. Mlle. Piaf was born in Belleville, a quarter of Paris not generally considered chic, and made her first public appearance at seven, in a circus in which her father was an acrobat. She made her adult début in 1935, and was a hit almost from the start. When our man asked her—disingenuously, it would seem—whether she had any more of those wonderful sad songs she used to sing, she said, "No, I don't feel the old songs any more. I have evolved. I was never really a pessimist. I believe that there is always a little corner of blue sky, nevertheless, somewhere. In those old songs, there arrived invariably, at the end, a catastrophe. But now I have one called 'Mariage,' which is quite different. It begins in the cell of a woman who has *already* murdered her husband. She reviews her life, she hears the wedding bells, she sees herself in the arms of this man whom she has killed, an innocent young bride. It's very beautiful." As for herself, Mlle. Piaf said, she has never married and never killed anybody. "For me, love always goes badly," she said. "It is perhaps because I have a mania of choosing. I don't wait to be chosen. That places me in a position of inferiority. And I always choose badly. So the relationships turn out badly. Sometimes only two or three days. But I'm always optimistic." She is studying English hard, with the assistance of an associate professor at Columbia and of the night clubs of the city. She thinks Ray Bolger is *formidable* and had been to see him three times up to the day our man called.

Reassured, our man went to hear Mlle. Piaf a couple of nights later, and turned up at the office the next morning radiant. "The best number she did," he said, "was where an accordionist goes off to the war and gets killed. His sweetheart listens to the music of another accordion and goes nuts. Then there is one about a woman tourist who has one big night with a sailor in a port where the ship stops, and the sailor goes off on another ship and gets drowned. For an encore, she sang that old honey about the woman who falls in love with a Foreign Legion soldier—she hasn't even had time to learn his name—and he gets killed and they bury him under the warm sand. I haven't had such a good time in years."

GOSSIP WRITER

St. Clair McKelway

JUNE 15, 1940 (ON WALTER WINCHELL)

O N SATURDAY, SEPTEMBER 2, 1939, it seemed certain to Walter Winchell, as it did to the rest of us, that Great Britain was about to go to war with Germany. Unlike the rest of us, Winchell did something about this. After turning it over in his mind, he sent a cablegram early the next morning to Prime Minister Chamberlain, as follows:

> May I respectfully offer the suggestion that if Britain declares war the declaration might be worded not as "War Against Germany" but as "War against Adolf Hitler personally and his personal regime." Stressing the fact that Hitler does not really represent the true will of the vast civilian population of Germany. Such declaration might have the astonishing effect of bringing the German people to their senses especially if such declaration can be made known to the German people and inevitably it would via radio and other channels. This is merely a layman's suggestion offered in hopes of a new era of world peace.

The next day Winchell made public the text of this cablegram by printing it in his daily column, "Walter Winchell on Broadway," which appears in the *Daily Mirror* in New York and in a hundred and sixty-five other newspapers in the United States. He printed it without comment, merely making it clear to his readers that it was he who had sent the cablegram.

The day after that, September 5th, Winchell wrote in his column:

If you read Monday's column, this may interest you. At 2:33 A.M. September 4, the London telegraph agency flashed a dispatch reporting that Prime Minister Chamberlain had just read a proclamation to the German people via a French radio station, in which he stated that Great Britain did not declare war against the German people, but against Adolf Hitler and the Nazi regime. . . . The suggestion was sent to the Prime Minister in a cablegram, acknowledgment of which has arrived.

It is significant that in announcing what is to him an extraordinary personal coup, Winchell simply presents the facts unemotionally, setting them down for history's sake, as it were. The inner conviction that he is actually responsible for Chamberlain's proclamation appears to stir him only intellectually. A tone of almost melancholy aloofness is discernible, as if Winchell no longer enjoys as an adventurer the sweet fruits of triumph but is beginning to see himself with sober detachment as an actor on the stage of current events. There is a telling phrase in the text of his cablegram to Chamberlain. He insists that in what he is saying to the British Prime Minister he is speaking merely as a layman. This is the familiar protestation of the man of consequence. Nobody but a distinguished personage whose eminence is unassailable ever tries to palm himself off as an ordinary, run-of-the-mill citizen.

There are probably critics who would say that it is ridiculous for a mere gossip writer to put his nose into serious international affairs, and that for Winchell to presume that his cablegram actually influenced Chamberlain is patently absurd. This is a narrow view. Winchell has no reason to think that gossip writing is dishonorable or undignified, or that, as a gossip writer, he deserves anything but respectful consideration. Calling Winchell a mere gossip writer is like calling Lindbergh a mere aviator or Gene Tunney a mere prizefighter. The writing of gossip, the setting down of items about the private lives of his fellow-citizens, is responsible for Winchell's enormous success in life, but it would be an understatement to sum him up by saying, "He writes gossip," just as it would be to say of Tunney, "He beat Dempsey," or of Lindbergh, "He flew to Paris."

From the beginning of his career as a gossip writer fifteen years ago, people whom Winchell looks up to have encouraged him in his work. Such celebrities as George Bernard Shaw, Theodore Dreiser, Leopold

Stokowski, James J. Walker, Faith Baldwin, Gypsy Rose Lee, Rupert Hughes, James Montgomery Flagg, Shirley Temple, and Lowell Thomas have written guest columns for him so he could take vacations in the summer. From the start he has been on friendly and sometimes intimate terms with the members of some of the oldest and most respected families of New York. They call him Walter and give him items for his column. He was the favorite columnist of the leading gangsters of New York when they ruled the town; they took him to prizefights and gave him elaborate parties. One of them once sent him a Stutz. About a year ago he was guest of honor at a luncheon tendered in the Capitol Building in Washington by the Vice-President of the United States, and some months before that the President of the United States, in starting off a forty-five-minute tête-à-tête with Winchell, had slapped him affectionately on the knee and said, "Walter, I've got an item for you." The American Legion has given him a gold medal "in recognition of his contribution to Americanism," and Lakewood, New Jersey, has named a thoroughfare Winchell Street in honor of "the first soldier in our land in the cause of democracy." His patriotic writings have been reprinted at the expense of the government and handed out to the public by the Democratic Party. His valuable life, once zealously protected by bodyguards assigned to him by his friends Owney Madden and Lucky Luciano, has in more recent years been watched over by agents on the payroll of the Federal Bureau of Investigation, assigned to him by his friend J. Edgar Hoover.

To a sympathetic follower of Winchell's career it is clear that his gesture in giving advice to Chamberlain was not that of a busybody trying to mind somebody else's business. It was the thoughtful action of a public figure fulfilling a responsibility which had more or less been thrust upon him. While the idea of conducting the second World War against Hitler rather than against the German people may have occurred to England's best minds before Winchell cabled Chamberlain (the Allies having made the same distinction between the Kaiser and the German people at the beginning of the first World War), it does not seem unreasonable to suppose that Winchell's cablegram was shown to the British Prime Minister, that he read it, and that it was respectfully acknowledged.

. . .

At the moment Winchell is unquestionably the country's most easily recognized non-layman, with the exception of Father Divine. The major and minor aspects of his existence are distinctive in almost every detail.

Success and public acclaim have not made him a stuffed shirt. He has a gift for idiosyncrasy and is not self-conscious about it. He has two children and both are named after him; his son is Walter and his daughter is Walda. He goes to sleep around nine or ten in the morning and gets up in time to have breakfast while his children are having their supper. In the inside pocket of his coat he carries a loose-leaf booklet containing as many as twenty photographs of Walter and Walda, and in another pocket of his coat he carries a loaded automatic. In his overcoat pocket he carries a second loaded automatic. Although he has never been shot at and has been beaten up only twice, he is always expecting to be attacked.

The *Mirror* pays him $1,200 a week and 50 percent of the money from the syndication of his column, amounting to some $750 a week, and he makes $5,000 a week more for his weekly radio talk. As Winchell has pointed out in his column, he pays around 50 percent of his earnings to the state and federal governments. This leaves him a net income of approximately $185,000 a year, but he wears shoes until they have holes in the soles. He almost invariably wears a blue suit, a blue shirt, a blue tie, and a snap-brim gray felt hat. He has never played golf or tennis or badminton or ping-pong. He learned to swim only last summer. Until 1932 he had never seen a football game. He took up the rumba a few months ago and is now an enthusiast. Practically the only other form of relaxation his friends have actually seen him engage in is motoring. The New York Police Department has given him special permission to equip his sedan with a short-wave receiving set with which he picks up calls sent from Police Headquarters to police radio patrol cars.

This device forms the centre of Winchell's recreational activities. For hours, late at night, he cruises the streets of Manhattan accompanied by three or four friends and sometimes some celebrity like Brenda Frazier or John Gunther. The radio picks up police messages and Winchell drives hurriedly to the scene of action. The action almost invariably consists of policemen looking for a burglar. Once in a great while the car reaches the scene of a holdup or a murder in time for Winchell to get what he calls "a thrill."

This almost nightly routine is trying to Winchell's friends and the personnel in the sedan is constantly in process of replenishment. The celebrities seldom go more than once. Myrna Loy dropped off to sleep the time she went. It is possible to sleep in Winchell's sedan, for although the Police Department has given him permission to equip it with a siren, he is conscious of the disturbance the siren creates in the early hours of the morning and uses it only when he is going on what looks like a particularly exciting call. One night he was speeding up Central Park West on such a call with the siren on. As he approached the apartment house in which he lives, he shut it off. "I don't want to wake up Walter and Walda," he explained to his friends. He did not turn the siren on again until the car reached 110th Street.

. . .

Winchell has written more words on the subject of friendship than any other modern gossip writer, but the people he calls his friends do not number more than seven or eight and most of these are new rather than old. "The best way to get along," he once wrote, "is never to forgive an enemy or forget a friend," but he has made up with at least one man who denounced him publicly and with another who punched him in the nose. Conversely, he has lost many friends by printing objectionable items about them in his column and, in defending this policy, has said, "I never lost a friend I wanted to keep." On several occasions when friends have remonstrated with Winchell for what they considered a betrayal of friendship, he has said, "I know—I'm just a son of a bitch." Some of his friends have accepted this explanation and have continued the friendship; others have regarded it as an inadequate excuse and have broken off with him.

Friends who have not broken off with Winchell are apt to assume a puzzled expression when asked to describe the subject of their attachment. "He's a remarkable guy!" one of them blurted recently, after considerable thought. "He's not a man—he's a column," said another, effusively. Nearly all seven or eight of Winchell's friends will tell you that they have been injured at one time or another by an item about themselves in Winchell's column. One friend had climbed his way up to a position of intimacy with Winchell which allowed him to dandle young Walter, Jr., on his knee. He was doing this when Winchell informed him that an embarrassing item about him would appear in the column the next day. "I'm just an s.o.b.," Winchell explained, using the abbreviated form, while Walter, Jr., innocently played with the friend's vest buttons. The friend started to protest and then nodded acquiescently. He has not broken off with Winchell. Winchell's journalistic integrity is such that his duty to his public almost always vanquishes whatever impulses of sentimentality he may have toward a friend when what he calls "a good item" is involved.

When a friend Winchell wanted to keep was killed in an automobile accident some years ago, Winchell published a eulogy which expresses his faith in the practical side of friendship, if not the sentimental side. "Shucks!" he wrote. "A guy like me cannot afford to lose a friend like Donald Freeman! He was one of the few fellers who liked me—and the second important magazine editor to hold out his hand and lift me into his heaven. When I was on a rag that the whole town belittled [the *Evening Graphic*] away back in 1927—almost a million years ago! Poor Don—he was motoring to see his mother and sister at Mt. Kisco and his car crashed, and now he's no more. I'll miss Donald Freeman. I'll miss that shrewd counsel he always gave me when I needed it. . . ." The late Mr. Freeman was managing editor of *Vanity Fair*, which published some articles by Winchell in 1927 and 1928.

Even if no tempting bit of gossip develops to endanger a friendship with Winchell, he is apt to think of something which the friend will find objectionable and then print it. A friendship with Winchell rarely cools off gradually and reaches a condition of mutual indifference. If he feels that the relationship is losing its first flush of passionate admiration on both sides, he is inclined to take the initiative and strike while the friendship is warm. His phrase for what he does is "I let him have it." Winchell was once on friendly terms with Lucius Beebe, a fellow-columnist. Mr. Beebe never has found out what happened, but he thinks Winchell decided that some minor criticism of Winchell in another paper (not the *Herald Tribune,* on which Beebe works) and signed "L.B." was the trouble. Beebe doesn't know who this "L.B." was. In any case, Winchell printed a series of passionately unfriendly items about Beebe. Another time Winchell made up his mind that another very close friend, also a fellow-columnist, had become detached in his attitude toward their relationship. He let the friend have it. The friend happened to possess a thick skin as well as a philosophical attitude toward Winchell. He did not retaliate. Months went by and Winchell was mystified. Finally the two met in a night club and Winchell magnanimously offered to patch things up. "You've been swell," he told his friend. "I like the way you didn't knock me when you were sore at me."

The practical realism of Winchell's slant on friendship is present in his attitude toward casual human relationships as well. In conversation he likes either to talk about himself or to listen to something that will be of use to him in his column. Richard Rodgers, the composer, once had an awesome encounter with Winchell in Palm Beach. Rodgers was telling some companions on the beach about an investment he had made in a manufacturing concern when Winchell happened along and joined the group. Rodgers, who had never known Winchell very well, turned to him politely and began to sum up for Winchell's benefit the subject of the interrupted conversation. When Rodgers was halfway through, Winchell held up a hand with the palm close to Rodgers' face and said, "Never mind, never mind." Rodgers was nonplussed. "How do you mean?" he mumbled uncertainly. "It's no good for the column," Winchell explained, and walked on down the beach. Rodgers finished telling his friends about the investment he had made in the manufacturing concern, but, as he has remarked since, his heart wasn't in it.

When Winchell is talking about himself, he demands the unwavering attention of his listeners. James Cannon, a former sportswriter and one of his closest friends, was in a restaurant one night with his girl and was joined by Winchell. Winchell started to talk about himself. He talked for ten minutes without interruption. Cannon began to wonder if his girl would enjoy the evening more if she had another drink. Keeping his eyes fastened on Winchell's face so as to appear to be attentive, he said to his girl rapidly and out of the side of his mouth, "Honey, you want something?" Winchell stopped in the middle of a sentence and grabbed Cannon's arm. "Jimmy!" he said reproachfully. "You're not listening!"

Winchell believes, with some justification, that practically everybody reads his column every day. If, in conversation, he wishes to refer to something he has written, he says, for example, "The item on the Brooklyn spy scare. Well, listen. Thursday night I called up Hoover," etc. A friend of Winchell's once admitted he had not seen the column on a certain Tuesday. Winchell wanted to know with sincere concern if the friend had been ill. Another time another friend returned to New York after a trip abroad. "Jeez, Walter," he said, "I sure did miss the column. I didn't see it for two whole weeks." "That's all right," said Winchell. "You can go over to the *Mirror* office tomorrow and look at the files."

. . .

A great many people, meeting Winchell for the first time in some restaurant or night club, have exclaimed afterward, "Say, he isn't such a bad guy!" This is understandable. Winchell has a peculiarly bewitching personality. He has a lean face, full of alertness, with an expression of questing intelligence like a fox terrier's. His eyes are blue and hard. He is consistently lively and restless; it is impossible to imagine him in repose.

He has an enormous nervous energy, and the experience of watching him burn it up extravagantly is stimulating and sometimes touching. What he says may be uninteresting in itself, but his voice and manner are charged with an inner excitement which is communicable. One of his phrase-making friends calls him "a thrilling bore." When he is not talking, he sits forward with his head raised unnaturally in an attitude of intense awareness. His heel is apt to beat quick time on the floor like a swing musician's, his gaze roves ceaselessly over the room, and his hands go on little fruitless expeditions over the tablecloth, up and down the lapels of his coat, in and out of his pockets. In a gathering of ten or twelve at a place like Lindy's or the Stork Club, he appears to listen to the general conversation with only half an ear, but that is enough. If something is mentioned that will make an item for his column, he will say, "I can use that," and will take out a pencil and notebook and write it down. Having responsibilities which far exceed those of the ordinary journalist, he usually carries a notebook instead of a sheaf of copy paper. He is left-handed, and this makes him look especially intense and painstaking when he is writing something down. At all times he gives the impression of being hungry, of being incessantly in want. In a man of such vitality this is an appealing quality. It is possible for a person to have an entirely unselfish impulse to give Winchell something.

Winchell has a certain integrity, as well as a number of codes all his own. He is as magnificently eccentric in thought as he is in action. He is ashamed of nothing he does. He uses his column at times as an instrument of personal revenge, but he does this as straightforwardly as a cave man would swing a club. "I let him have it three days later," he will say evenly, in recalling what he wrote about some person who had slighted or insulted him. He is naturally aggressive and is always on the offensive. There is nothing apologetic or cringing in his nature. He has a childlike pride in his success and he makes no bones about it. He is fully conscious of the damage a casual item in his column can do to persons he has no wish to hurt. He seems to be mellowing. It is a process like the aging of granite and is perceptible to people who have been acquainted with him for years. Lately he has been known to writhe in honest agony when the painful consequences of one of his own items are pointed out to him. To a small degree he literally suffers with those he wounds. His attitude on this curious state of affairs seems to be based on the belief that the appearance of such items in his column is as inexorable as fate. "What could I do?" he will say passionately. "It was a good item, wasn't it?"

Thus he continues to print gossip about the marital relations of people who have not applied for divorce, he does not hesitate to hint at homosexual tendencies in local male residents, and he reports from time to time attempted suicides which otherwise would not be made public. He believes that if a thing is true, or even half true, it is material for his column, no matter how private or personal it may be. He makes one exception to this rule. He claims that he never knowingly reports on extra-marital relationships if he knows the marriage is a happy one. This is pointed to with pride by Winchell's greatest admirers as being generous and downright decent.

It is true that Winchell has seen married men and women dallying with persons of the opposite sex in night clubs and has withheld this information from the public. In such cases he has known, or has been told, that the marriage of the person concerned seems to be a happy one. If he knows, or has been told, that the marriage is pretty much on the rocks anyway, he feels justified in printing an item about the dallying. There are times, too, of course, when he just doesn't know, or hasn't been told, that the person concerned is married at all. "I can't be expected to know everything," he has said in defending himself when a harmful item of this sort has appeared in his column. Winchell's reason for suppressing items which he knows might upset a happy marriage seems to be purely personal. "I'm a married man," he says. "Where would I be if somebody printed something about my taking a dame out?"

Winchell makes an effort to check some items with certain more or less fortunate people to find out whether the item will do them any particular harm. These people are usually relatively prominent ones whom Winchell has met and has not taken a dislike to. Sometimes they are called to the telephone by Winchell's secretary, who introduces herself with understandable assurance and says something like "We understand you are sort of crazy about So-and-So. Have you any objection to our printing it?" If the celebrity has what seems to him a legitimate objection, he explains what it is to the secretary and the item is usually not published. This gives the person concerned a feeling of gratitude toward Winchell, coupled with a sensation of general insecurity. Sometimes, even if someone has asked that an item be suppressed, Winchell decides that the request is unreasonable and goes ahead and prints it anyway. Under these circumstances he is apt to accuse the person later of having tried to take advantage of his journalistic ethics. Winchell has been disillusioned many times in thus striving for accuracy and fair play. He cites numerous cases in which both parties to a disintegrating marriage have denied that they were going to separate and have persuaded him to withhold an item saying that they were, and then, without warning, have filed suit for divorce. "You try to play square with people like that," he complains bitterly, "and they lie to you. It burns me up."

Although Winchell prides himself on his accuracy, he fears libel suits and refuses to accept the financial responsibility for libellous items in his column or in his radio program. Some years ago an indignant citizen, a carpenter who, Winchell said in one radio talk, had sat on the end of a tree limb and sawed it off, sued him for libel, claiming injury to his professional reputation. Winchell was asked by his sponsors to share the attorneys' fees, court costs, and a small settlement granted the carpenter. Winchell refused to do this. He demanded that a clause be inserted in his radio contract providing that the sponsors defend and if necessary settle all libel suits which might result from his broadcasts. The sponsors gave in. Then Winchell asked the *Mirror* to put a similar clause in its contract with him. The *Mirror* agreed. Only three or four people since then have worked themselves up to the point of indignation achieved by the carpenter.

. . .

Winchell writes his column and prepares the script for his Sunday-night radio broadcast at home. He employs two secretaries, who work in an office at the *Mirror*, which he rarely visits. He keeps in touch with his secretaries mostly by telephone. His column goes to press around six in the evening, soon after he wakes up, and at that time he may make last-minute changes by telephone. Then he starts on the column which will go to press the next evening. His mail, which is stupendous in size and variety of subject matter, is sent to him by a messenger around 6 P.M., and he gets a great part of his material from that. He spends several hours going through it and selecting items which he will use in the column he is preparing. He is practically incommunicado during this period and his secretaries call him only on extremely urgent business. He scribbles replies on letters he wishes to answer, then they are sent back to the *Mirror* office and the secretaries work on them the next day. He does not pay for items.

Winchell does not often go to night clubs any more, except for the Stork Club. The Stork Club serves as an outside office. He arrives there almost every night around eleven o'clock, having prepared the major part of his column from his mail. He is usually at the Stork Club until four or five in the morning. After that he drives around in his car for a while and then goes home, finishes his column, sends it to the *Mirror* office, and goes to sleep around 9 or 10 A.M. While he is asleep, the column is set up in type and proofs are sent to King Features Syndicate, the Hearst syndicate organization, where it is edited for out-of-town papers. Most of the changes are made in possibly libellous items. Winchell accepts this editing without protest. A lawyer employed by the *Mirror* also reads a proof and makes changes or deletions which he thinks may prevent libel suits.

At the Stork Club, Winchell takes telephone calls from persons he wishes to speak to and receives personally some of the many people who are always wanting to see him, ranging from celebrities and politicians to chorus girls with a complaint about labor conditions. Sometimes he sees them in the Stork Club barbershop and sometimes at a table just inside the entrance. While he is there, the barbershop may be reached only by persons whom Winchell wishes to see. It is in a loft building next door and has two entrances—through the front of the loft building and through a passage from the club. In the club he orders captains of waiters about in a proprietary manner, and although there has been a rumor for years that he has a financial interest in the place, he says he hasn't. His friend Sherman Billingsley, proprietor of the Stork Club, says the same thing, adding that Winchell's frequent mentions of the place in his column have had much to do with its success and that he is grateful to Winchell and friendly with him. "That rat!" Mr. Billingsley exclaimed to some table companions recently when Winchell, in spite of their friendship and the fact that Billingsley is still married, linked his name with that of a musical-comedy star. But he managed to conquer his irritation before he saw Winchell later that evening.

When sitting at his table, surrounded by three or four friends, with perhaps one bodyguard in the offing, Winchell may listen to a reformer from Atlantic City who believes his efforts to clean up the resort will be successful only if he has Winchell's support, or to a hysterical admirer who tiptoes up and says, as if making a speech, "I want to shake your hand, Walter. I think you are a great man and America's most valuable citizen." Winchell shakes the hand. Such tributes are frequent. People sit at the Stork Club bar for hours waiting for Winchell to come in so that they may have the opportunity to compliment him. Many of them are sincere, and have no axes to grind. Occasionally the pleasure Winchell receives from the outbursts of enthusiasm is dulled by an afterthought which the admirer expresses as he bows himself away, such as "I'm a tenor. So-and-So's the name," or "I'm at Loew's State this week. Song and dance. So-and-So's the name." Winchell deplores sycophancy of this sort and never rewards such a person with a mention in his column, even a scandalous one. Then there are the bold ones at the Stork Club, such as the débutante who one night slipped over and grabbed Winchell's bread when he was eating his supper. "A bet," she said demurely, and skipped off. Late at night, a literary relationship between Winchell and Leonard Lyons, gossip man for the *Post*, is apt to be revealed. It is comparable to Conrad's paternal friendship for Stephen Crane. Lyons, who is Winchell's protégé, not a rival, the *Post* being an afternoon paper and his "Lyons Den" gossip column being also syndicated by Hearst, appears unobtrusively from somewhere and says, "Walter, may I check a gag?" "O.K.," says the veteran. Lyons then recites an anecdote which he intends to pass on to his readers the next day. If it is old or sour, in Winchell's opinion, he advises Lyons to throw it out. If not, he says "O.K." a second time and Lyons goes happily back to his job of hopping from table to table, looking for gossip and gags.

· · ·

Winchell has been described in the New York press as "Broadway's Greatest Scribe," "Boyfriend of Broadway," "Little Boy Peep," and "The Bard of Broadway." He prefers the last. His friends sometimes refer to him as The Brain and The King. He is unable to decide which of these is his favorite. He is like a king in many ways but not in others. Edmund Burke once asserted that "kings are naturally lovers of low company." His general argument was that the status of a king is so much higher than that of the next greatest dignitary that the difference between the highest and the lowest non-kings is slight, from a king's point of view. A king, according to Burke, is irritated by the more consequential non-kings because they feel a responsibility for his behavior, frown at his vices, and try to make him go straight. He therefore consorts with lowly folk who flatter and amuse him. Although Winchell is sought after by many prominent people, he usually shakes them off an hour or two after midnight and hobnobs with mediocre newspaper reporters and undistinguished theatrical folk. He feels more at ease with them. On the other hand, kings, throughout history, have made a habit of putting aside their public personalities and going around incognito. Presidents have shown a similar weakness. Both Wilson and Coolidge used to slip away from the Secret Service men and take walks by themselves, revelling in anonymity. If Winchell has ever had such impulses, he has suppressed them resolutely. He seems to have no desire to get away from himself. When he goes to Miami Beach in the winter he always stops at the Roney Plaza, where everybody knows him. For years he spent his summer vacations hanging around night clubs and restaurants in town. Two summers ago, his wife having persuaded him to buy a house in Westchester, he discovered and endorsed the country, but in his summer home he sleeps all day in an air-conditioned room kept dark by lightproof blinds and usually comes to town every night whether he has to do so professionally or not. Occasionally, driving around after midnight with friends, he plays a sort of reverse version of the incognito game, the object being to see how soon he will be recognized in a public place off the beaten track. Almost anywhere in town he is recognized by somebody within a few minutes. If he is not, it is his custom to say to a bartender or waiter, "I'm Walter Winchell." In no time the place is in a hubbub, and Winchell leaves.

Once, not long ago, Winchell and a friend stopped for some coffee at an unpretentious roadside restaurant in lower Westchester. Nobody was in the place but a slatternly girl working behind the counter. She did not recognize Winchell and looked at him sourly, as if he were just a man buying a cup of coffee. Halfway through his coffee, Winchell winked at his friend and then drew the girl into conversation.

"Do you read the *Mirror*?" he asked.

"Nah," she said. "I take the *News*."

"Ever listen to the radio?"

"Sometimes."

"Ever listen to Ben Bernie or Walter Winchell?"

"Nah," said the girl. "What I really like is Hawaiian music."

Winchell and his friend left the place without further talk. As they got into the car, Winchell said, "Can you imagine that dumb biddy?" Later, as they drove along, Winchell suddenly said "Huh!" The friend asked him what he meant by this. "I was just thinking about that dumb biddy," Winchell said. "Can you imagine it?"

GOETHE IN HOLLYWOOD

Janet Flanner

DECEMBER 13/20, 1941 (ON THOMAS MANN)

OR FORTY YEARS, Thomas Mann has endured the singular experience of being regularly described, while still alive, in terms usually
reserved for the exceptional dead. In a half-dozen languages he has
been called a genius, a modern classic, Germany's noblest novelist, and,
occasionally, one of the immortal literary figures of all countries, of all
time. In the King's English of the book critics of London, the only literate capital where he has never caught on, he has also been described, less
conventionally, as heavy weather. Before Hitler ordered Mann's political
books to be burned, German spokesmen, with their special racial passion for altitude, had solemnly lifted Mann's major fictional works to the
rank of *Faust, Pilgrim's Progress, The Divine Comedy,* and, as a final tribute, Beethoven's ninth symphony. A couple of months ago a Nazi radio
commentator simply pegged him under the head of "degenerate Western
literature." By his New York publisher, Alfred Knopf, Mann is professionally presented as "the greatest living man of letters," a carefully composed selling slogan with a fine, chiselled touch applicable to a public
statue. By Mann's few friends, less numerous than the members of his
own large family, it has been stated as a natural law that "one speaks of
him with the reverence he deserves." Thus they speak of him reverently,
though they also call him Tommy. His children, of whom there are six,
cheerfully refer to him, beyond his hearing, as the Master.

Thomas Mann, now sixty-six years old and on his thirty-first book,
began being exactly what he is today when he was twenty-five and had
just completed his first novel. Mann's youth and age, gauged by the inte-

rior and the exterior of his impressive head, seem peculiarly interchangeable, because both his work and his physiognomy started by being mature and have remained perfectly preserved. Mann's first opus, *Buddenbrooks*, a quarter-million-word, two-volume biographical account of the melancholy decline of three earlier generations of very rich merchant Manns, was written by the young author as a private performance, to read aloud to his less opulent family to amuse them after dinner. However, it was the Buddenbrook family's sad, sure sense of social insecurity, felt as Europe's newly industrialized eighteen-hundreds ended, which made the novel, when published, Germany's first disturbing national classic of the nineteen-hundreds. Its sales eventually reached 1,300,000 copies, making it the biggest best-seller, next to Remarque's *All Quiet on the Western Front*, of pre-Hitler Europe. "It was fame," as Mann himself commented a few years ago in his privately printed *A Sketch of My Life*, employing that lenslike literary manner he invented as a young man in order to view himself with magnified detachment. "I was snatched up into a whirl of success. My mailbag was swollen, money flowed in streams, my picture appeared in the papers, a hundred pens made copy of the product of my secluded hours, the world embraced me amid congratulations and shouts of praise. . . . Society took me up—in so far as I let it, for in this respect society has never been very successful."

Certainly, Mann is a recluse, though an elegant one. Even his children, when little, rarely saw him. To them he was the invisible smell of glue from the fine bookbindings in his study and the smoke of his expensive light cigars. In the midst of the ample life he was born in, married into, and writes about, he has always remained comfortably cloistered. He has never made an appreciable use of his select social position but has been careful to take it for granted. He was born to the bourgeois purple. In the seventeen-hundreds, the Mann family, prosperous, prolific woolen drapers in Nürnberg, moved to Lübeck, where they eventually became even more flourishing grain merchants. For a precious hundred years they inhabited mansions, ate rich, stately dinners, and became senators and consuls. They finally attained the climax of their commercial disintegration not only by losing their business but also by producing Thomas and his elder brother, Heinrich, a pair of purely literary scions. From this biological break with family precedent, Heinrich, who took after their mother, a lady with Latin blood, has derived less fame but possibly a lot more pleasure than the more Mannlike Thomas has. Thomas Mann, as shocked by his talent as if he were one of his own conservative Hanseatic ancestors, from the very first regarded his or anybody's creative temper-ament as a suspicious, unhealthy crack in the ideal, solid *Bürgertum* norm, and has always thought the perfect artist—Goethe or Wagner or himself, each of whom he has spent years of his life conscientiously analyzing—a singular cross between a social pariah and a savior of civi-lization, with a dash of the charlatan thrown in. To the aesthetic refine-ment of this blend he has devoted his career.

In appearance, Thomas Mann is *démodé* in the grand style. A disre-spectful press photographer once said Mann looks like a well-carved, old-fashioned walking stick. His face has the ligneous angles of a mu-seum woodcut. Beneath his properly tailored tweeds, he moves with the correct, erect, salon stiffness of an older Teutonic generation. His man-ners are a model. Strangers whom his poise alarms consider him a mon-ster of politeness. He presents a kindly yet intimidating supercivilized surface which is partly the product of his native character and partly a deliberate construction of his own. Beneath this lies his air of inner pre-occupation, illuminated by intermittent flashes of outward interest, and enlivened by the occasional, gentle boom of his Nordic baritone voice. In conversation (he doesn't talk much, but at times he discourses) he con-tributes, at rare moments, a tardy, three-toned laugh, like an indulgent, superior spectre who has heard a delayed overtone of humor which the rest of the company's duller ears have missed. For those he knows well, behind his courtly gestures and silences there are festooned affections and loyalties. When necessary, he goes out of his way very handsomely. There appears to be nothing even remotely casual in the whole complex Mann personality. In spirit, he is melancholy, ironic, weighty, and se-rene. He is used to his instinctive pessimism by now and it doesn't upset him. He has no deistic conviction, but lately he has put a veneer of Chris-tianity upon the lectures he has been giving on tour. With his profound interest in the fate of humanity, he might have become a religious writer if he had had any faith. Mentally, he is the perfect man of integrity; he is cautious, conservative, egocentric, and explorative. He moves slowly in a circle, or even consciously sidewise, toward a decision, does not bother to think of anything that he is not going to ponder recurrently, has the past on his mind, and suffers, profitably, from total recall. Socially, both as an upper-class European and a sensitive individual, he is skeptical of but not indifferent to this world's gauds. He'll usually choose the pure-silk peo-ple, a yard wide. As a young intellectual, he saw no reason a poet's trou-sers and coat shouldn't match, disliked bohemianism because he thought it disorderly, and was a daydreamer, idle, vain, irritable, and scornful; he was impressionable and assimilative rather than ardent or generous. Today, no bad qualities show. This gives Mann an awesome psychological shape, like a large, unfamiliar figure seen from a distance.

. . .

Though Mann has spent forty years as a novelist creating characters in print, on the whole he is devoid of interest in flesh-and-blood people. He views them as models rather than as mortals. He forgets both names and faces; he politely asks the dinner guest once again if she is married but will recall a curious ring she wore on her right hand a year before. He himself has noticeably well-sculptured hands; his books contain frequent descriptions of shapely fingernails. Of a handsome young woman, lunching for the first time at his Munich family table, he remarked to one of his daughters, with the abstract detachment of an author discussing a snag in a plot, "Strange. If your friend were a boy, she would be very beautiful." A person's appearance may fill Mann's eye, but the suitable psychology to accompany this appearance he himself supplies, often in a subsequent short story. Like his rich mercantile forebears, he is less an inventor than a wise and thrifty manipulator. As a young author, his skill at borrowing his acquaintances as material for his writings led to his being accused not only of incorporating a certain neighbor in an acid short story called "Tristan" but also of peeking at him from a window with opera glasses. Mann declared that, as usual with his characters, he himself was mostly the Tristan in question, but he admitted using and enjoying the opera glasses. Indubitably, Mann's lack of intimate interest in others has been compensated for by his conscientious and fecund concentration on himself as material for ten or more of his famous and varied characterizations. Whereas the narcissism of most romantic writers leads them to use themselves as heroes, Mann's has led him to use himself as almost everything—as a hunchback, a swindler, a dilettante, as at least two overbred bourgeois youths, named Hanno and Hans, and as a regular bevy of authors, including Dr. Gustave Aschenbach, hero of *Death in Venice,* whom Mann describes as a European writer so great that "his antithetic eloquence led serious critics to rank it" with Schiller's. (This is usually cited as one of Mann's characteristic bits of humor, the joke, of course, being that Mann isn't like Schiller but like Goethe.) Mann has recently even endowed the Biblical character of the young Joseph in *Joseph in Egypt* with some of his own psychology as a Nordic youth. It is no joke to say that the greatest study of Mann is Mann. One of his children has said it is difficult not to see his writings as "a complex of family allusions." Unconsciously, the Mann children speak of their father as if he were an edition.

· · ·

Ever since Thomas Mann began to write, he has written each morning from nine-thirty till noon. To his labors he says he gives "zealous preparation" and writes "with the patience which my native slowness laid upon me, a phlegm perhaps better described as restrained nervousness." He writes about forty lines a day. His concentration is prodigious. He can work anywhere, under any conditions, in any environment. He has done his writing in his summer houses, his winter town homes, in trains, in hotels, on shipboard, in strange cities, in Italian fishing ports, in a beach chair on a Baltic dune, or as a weekend guest in an American garden— a man who will be "writing probably on his way to his own funeral," as one astonished Connecticut host noted in his private correspondence, "and while being very much part of the world around him, in his quiet, courteous ways, writing as if that world did not exist." Only once in Mann's long career of writing has his habit of the daily stint been interrupted. That was in 1933, in Switzerland, when he realized that what had begun as a casual, pleasant holiday from Germany must continue as a painful exile. Here at last, for this deeply racial Teuton, was tragical material for motionless thought and grief rather than for some ever-growing manuscript.

He has no control over his literary mileage. The most popular of his works in America, *The Magic Mountain*, started out to be a *novella* and ended up as an enormous two-volume novel that took twelve years to complete. *The Beloved Returns*, last year's full-length *vie romanciée* about Goethe, started as a short sketch. *Joseph in Egypt*, which has already run into a trilogy of novels and may become a tetralogy, since it is already going backward into the story of Jacob, began as a little preface he was asked to write for a folio of Biblical drawings by an artist friend of Frau Mann's.

Mann writes his works in school notebooks, in longhand. His small, tight script is so difficult to read that he makes it an excuse for never writing anyone letters. His wife is his expert decoder. As part of her métier of devotion, built around his career of writing, she learned typing, and on their travels she carries a portable typewriter in order to keep abreast of his voluminous manuscripts. Frau Mann, the family manager and businessman, is a small, volatile, articulate, personable lady with short gray hair and considerable worldly experience. It is unquestionably a tribute to her that there have been moments when publishers felt that Thomas Mann as a bachelor would have been easier to handle as an author.

Frau Mann was born Katja Pringsheim, of a rich, highly cultivated Jewish family, orginally from Oels in Silesia. Her grandfather built the railroads in the Upper Silesian industrial area and his Wilhelmstrasse mansion was notable as the Haus Pringsheim. Her father, Alfred Pringsheim, assembled a famous collection of Italian trecento and quatrocento majolicas which ranked as the finest in existence outside a museum and ran to four hundred items, supplemented by a two-volume illustrated catalogue. Frau Mann's father was also a member of the Bavarian Academy of Science, a brilliant mathematician and lecturer, an acquaintance of Richard Wagner, a musicologue, a bibliophile, and an art-lover in general. He abandoned the faith of his fathers, married a Christian, Fräulein Hedwig Dohm, of a Berlin literary family, and made of their Munich home in Arcisstrasse a centre of the Bavarian capital's social and artistic life during the reign of Ludwig II and the Regency. As a child, Fräulein Katja, like her four brothers, one of whom was her twin, possessed a private library of beautifully bound books and was brought up in the double luxury of an atmosphere that was both rich and brainy. Though Mann's family had been well educated rather than intellectual, the author and his wife, who first met in Munich when he was in his late twenties, had much in common—mainly an elegance of background that was still traditional in big German mercantile and industrial families. To set against the Pringsheims' gilded Renaissance salons, Mann possessed, at least in memory, the parquetry ballroom of his childhood, where, before the family lost its money, "officers of the garrison," as he later contentedly wrote, "courted the daughters of the patriciate." Against the imposing public funeral of the celebrated Munich artist Lembach, who had painted Fräulein Katja's portrait and whose interment the very cultivated Pringsheims attended almost as though it were an artistic event, Mann could match the funeral of his father, "which in size and pomp," as he later specified in his memoirs, "surpassed anything that had been seen in Lübeck for years," his father having been so important a grandee that the Hanseatic troops dipped their colors to him as he passed them on the street.

Thomas Mann was thirty years old when, as he still sentimentally recorded twenty-five years later, "I exchanged rings with my fairy bride." He had first seen her, and been attracted to her, in a more realistic vein, on a Munich tramcar, while she was having a victorious argument with the conductor. From this highly successful marriage have come six children and about two dozen volumes.

· · ·

Mann's own family, whose decadence he even as a boy proudly accepted as evidence of its aristocracy, did indeed rank as tiptop. His great-grandfather established the clan in Lübeck, which, from the thirteenth through the seventeenth century, was head of the Hanseatic League, that shrewd alliance of rich traders controlling the maritime commerce of northern Europe. The great-grandfather wore powdered wigs and lace frills and was a Voltairian freethinker. Mann's grandfather, who was Consul to the Netherlands, wore leg-o'-mutton sleeves and linen chokers, and ranked as a pillar in the family's strict Protestant Church. He was what was then called, politically, a liberal, which at that moment in German history meant he considered the democratizing of the Lübeck Senate only a piece of bad taste. He spoke French and Low German around the house, where the family motto, "Work, Pray, Save," was carved over the great front door, and he once drove his coach-and-four to south Germany, where he did a nice bit of business in wheat for the Prussian Army, which was just then preparing for Napoleon and Waterloo. Mann's father was a senator of Lübeck and was also twice mayor; he died at an early age of blood poisoning, when his son was fifteen. Thomas's mother, a pure exotic in this northern family, was Julia Da Silva-Bruhns, who was born in Brazil, the daughter of a resident German planter and his South American wife, who was in turn the offspring of a Portuguese-Indian union. This foreign Frau Mann was beautiful and musical. Thomas Mann had two sisters, both of whom died by their own hand. With his startling genius for appreciating every dramatic scrap of family material and also for invariably publishing it, he relates in his autobiography that his sister Clara was an untalented actress, unconventional, macabre, and refined, that she kept a skull and poison in her room, that she was betrothed to an Alsatian industrialist, that a doctor "used his power over her for his own gratification," that the fiancé discovered he had been deceived, and that she then "took her cyanide, enough to kill a whole regiment of soldiers. The last that was heard from her," Mann adds with fraternal clinical accuracy, "was the sound of the gargling with which she tried to cool the burning of her corroded throat." He has not yet set down the subsequent sad case of his other sister, Julia. "Her grave is too new," he has written. "I will leave the story to a later narrative in a larger frame," in all probability to be furnished by his publisher.

As a child, little Thomas had a happy, privileged, sheltered life. As a boy, he loathed school. As a youth in his late teens, upon the sale, after his father's death, of the family mansion and the father's share of the Mann grain business, which had long been running downhill, Mann moved with his mother to Munich, where he became an insurance clerk. Working at his job by day, at night he began to try his hand at short stories and, on having the first accepted, gave up business forever and entered the University of Munich, where he remained briefly. He afterward spent a scant year in Italy with his brother Heinrich, who, though he was later to become an author, was then studying to be a painter. Thomas, the young northerner, didn't like the south; as he said, all that *bellezza* made him nervous. To stabilize himself amid the glories of Rome, he devoured Scandinavian and Russian literature in translation. The brothers spent much of their time playing dominoes in cafés and carefully made no friends.

Back in Munich, Mann, then in his early twenties, was taken on the staff of *Simplicissimus,* the weightiest, wittiest satiric magazine in Europe. When he was a book-loving child, his first literary stimulation had been received from Hans Andersen; when he was a boy, he had devoured Schiller, along with his afternoon plate of bread and butter. In his Munich twenties, he was subjected to two profoundly maturing influences. The first was the works of Nietzsche, from whom Mann, though disdaining the philosopher's blond-beast doctrine, absorbed the dogma of victory over self. The second influence was Schopenhauer, a set of whose works he bought at a sale, for months left uncut, and then suddenly absorbed, reading day and night, as one reads only once in a lifetime. What Mann derived from Schopenhauer was, oddly enough, he has stated, "the element of eroticism and mystic unity" in the great pessimist's philosophy.

In 1899, at the age of twenty-four, Mann sent the manuscript of *Buddenbrooks* to Berlin's most distinguished publishing house, S. Fischer Verlag. It is a wonder that the publishers ever read, let alone accepted, *Buddenbrooks.* It was written in longhand and on both sides of the paper. When Mann mailed it at the post office, he carefully insured it for a thousand marks, because it was the only copy on earth, and the post-office clerk smiled. The serious young author had drastically underestimated himself. In the next twenty-five years, the book went through a hundred and fifty-nine editions, founded his fame, and started his fortune. *Buddenbrooks* was published in 1900. It thus came into the European world two years before Samuel Butler's posthumous novel, *The Way of All Flesh,* had been heard of. In their separate ways, these were the key German and English books about unhappy fathers and sons, about family fights between members of a decadent nineteenth-century class, fights which were in miniature prophetic of the twentieth-century wars between nations, which were to kill a way of life.

. . .

Mann's first visit to America, made in 1934 at the invitation of his publisher, was tied up to the celebration of his fifty-ninth birthday, and was turned into quite a New York literary event, with local literati, including Mayor LaGuardia, attending a dinner in his honor at the Plaza Hotel. Mann, who was trying to learn English, made a speech in which, as a compliment, he meant to call Alfred Knopf a creator and called him a creature. Mann later said that this constituted his début in the English language. After two other visits, one of which was for the purpose of making a lecture tour, Mann returned here, with his wife, in 1938 to be welcomed as his country's leading literary anti-Nazi. Upon his arrival, he announced to the astonished New York ship reporters, "Where I am, there is Germany." The next year he applied for his naturalization papers. At first the Manns lived in Princeton, where the university had invited him to give some public lectures on the humanities. These lectures proved difficult. They had to be written in German and translated, and the English had to be annotated with diacritical markings and little private cabalistic signs to guide his pronunciation. Last year he resigned his post and the family moved to Pacific Palisades, one of Los Angeles' elegant scenic suburbs, near Hollywood. Mann likes living in a small town surrounded by scenery which pleases him on his occasional motor rides. He enjoys few diversions unless they figure in his orderly routine. After his morning's work, he takes a brisk walk with Niko, his poodle, before lunch. There have been a series of dearly loved dogs in his life; indeed, the only story he ever wrote with a happy ending was one about a dog. Mann also cares about eating, in a controlled way. He likes rich and childish dishes. He also likes the beginnings and the ends of his dinners, favoring tasty soups and American ice cream.

. . .

Though Hollywood is now the German intellectual émigrés' accepted centre, Mann's interest in settling there was not altogether social. Apparently he has recently played with the idea of writing a Hollywood novel as a parallel to *The Magic Mountain* and its special theme of sickness. He thinks there is a psychological condition peculiar to Hollywood which makes of it an island not unlike his island of Davos, on its Swiss mountaintop. Mann also has a tiny Achilles' heel; he would love to have a movie made of one of his novels. In the *Times*' critique of his *Joseph in Egypt,* his reviewer, Mrs. Meyer, who often speaks as Mann's Delphic oracle, stated that the book contained drama such as even Hollywood had never approached. Among members of the book trade this was taken to mean that Mann, a master psychologist, hoped that Hollywood, piqued, would say that it could indeed approach anything, even the subject of a contract. A nibble was actually made by one of the film companies, but the scheme fell through, supposedly because the officials felt that only David Wark Griffith in his heyday could have dared tackle such a situation.

. . .

Just two months ago, taking advantage of an international convention forbidding the distribution of propaganda to prisoners of war, the Germans suddenly put a ban on the circulation of Mann's books among German prisoners in England. In the last war, Mann was exempted from military service because the Imperial German Army doctor who examined him was a reverent admirer of his writings. As Mann says in his autobiography, "He laid his hand on my bare shoulder and said, 'You shall be left alone.'"

. . .

The fact that Thomas Mann today is a political refugee and the circumstance that he is living in exile in our democracy constitute a pair of the more illuminating personal paradoxes involved in this present war. When the last war ended, Mann was still ignorant of politics, he disliked the democratic form of government, and he published, in 1918, a much-discussed essay, "The Reflections of a Non-Political Man," to prove both. Mann was still an ivory-tower German aesthete interested in liberty for the artist, not the polloi; he was a humanist concerned with the brain, not the body politic. In his so aptly named essay, Mann blamed Bismarck for teaching romantic Germany about politics in the first place; he further wrote, "Democracy is an empty frame of life," declared his mistrust of the citizen type, whom he dubbed *Herr Omnes* ("Mr. Everybody"), and added, "I want neither parliamentarianism nor party administration. I want no politics at all. I want objectivity, order, and dignity." He also wanted to polish off, with dignity, his novel-writing brother, Heinrich, who was pro-democrat, pro-politics, pro-French, and, what was apparently worse, against the German bourgeoisie. In Heinrich's realistic social novel, *The Poor,* published the year before, he had attacked the Wilhelmenian middle class as a soulless, greedy, ambitious lot. To Thomas, the younger but more famous literary Mann, who was still wrapped elegantly, as in a démodé, brocaded house robe, in the nineteenth-century family glamour of the Mann (or Buddenbrooks) *Bürgertum,* this was doubtless *lèse-majesté.*

This bitter ideological feud between the two Manns led postwar Germany's agitated political circles to nickname them *die feindlichen Brüder* ("the enemy brothers"), a reference to two medieval robber-baron brothers who had built neighboring castles on the Rhine because they hated each other so much they could not let each other out of sight. The feud also led to Heinrich Mann's becoming one of the most beloved leaders of the young German intellectuals, who, impatient with the old bourgeoisie, disgusted by the now-collapsed monarchy, and alarmed by the notion that revolution was brewing, were ardently gathering in support of the democratic ideals of the new Weimar Republic. As little boys, the *feindlichen* brothers Mann shared the same bedroom but often did not talk to each other; when they grew up, they failed to speak even the same language. Heinrich, who took after their Latin mother, was Gallic-minded, in a pinkish, liberal way was still cheering for the French Revolution, held Flaubert and Zola as his gods, had aimed in his half-dozen unappreciated books at being a European rather than a Germanic writer, and liked Bordeaux wine. Thomas drank Rhine wine and, in his own special fashion, Wagner, Martin Luther, and deep drafts of Goethe. In 1918, in his non-political essay, he described Heinrich (without actually naming him, of course, for it was a well-bred feud) as a *Zivilisationslit-*

erat. By this, Thomas, who thought French *Zivilisation* inferior to German *Kultur,* apparently meant that his brother was a Frenchified scribbler.

Thomas Mann, like most proud men of his class, was violently partisan in the last war. In Germany's first victorious year, he published a patriotic polemic extolling Frederick the Great that included a famous preface, which, like "The Reflections of a Non-Political Man," has never been published in English. In this preface, properly called "Thoughts in War" and written in September, 1914, he said:

> That conquering warring principle of today—organization—is the first principle, the very essence of art. . . . The Germans have never been as enamored of the word civilization as their western neighbors. . . . Germans have always preferred *Kultur* . . . because the word has a human content, whereas in the other we sense a political implication that fails to impress us. . . . This is because the Germans, this most inwardly directed of all peoples, this people of metaphysics, pedagogy, and music, is not politically but morally inclined. In Germany's political progress, it has shown itself more hesitant and uninterested in democracy than the other countries. . . . As if Luther and Kant did not more than compensate for the French Revolution! As if the emancipation of the individual before God and as if *The Critique of Pure Reason* were not a far more radical revolution than the proclamation of the rights of man! . . . Our soldiering spirit is related to our morality. Whereas other cultures, even in their art, incline toward a civilian pattern of ethics [*Gesittung*], German militarism remains a matter of German morals. The German soul is too deep to find in civilization its highest conception. . . . And with the same instinctive aversion it approaches the pacifist ideals of civilization, for is not peace the element of civil corruption which the German soul despises? . . . Germany's full virtue and beauty unfold only in wartime. . . . The political form of our civil freedom . . . can only be completed . . . now after certain victory, a victory in tune with the forces of history, and in the German sense, not in the Gallic, revolutionary sense. A defeated Germany would mean demoralization, ours and Europe's. After such a defeat, Europe would never be safe from Germany's militarism; Germany's victory, on the contrary, would assure Europe's peace. . . . It is not easy to be a German, not as

comfortable as being an Englishman or as being a Frenchman and living with brilliance and gaiety. Our race has great trouble with itself . . . it is nauseated by itself. However, those who suffer the most are worth the most. . . . There is something deep and irrational in the German soul which presents it to more superficial people as disturbing, savage, and repulsive. This something is Germany's militarism, its moral conservatism, and soldierly morality, which refuses to acknowledge as the highest human goal the civilian spirit. . . . The Germans are great in the realm of civilian morality but do not want to be submerged by it. . . . Germany is the least known of all European peoples. . . . But it must be recognized. Life and history insist upon it, and the Germans will prove how unfeasible it is to deny, from sheer ignorance, the calling and character of this nation. You expect to isolate, encircle, and exterminate us, but Germany will defend its most hated and innermost "I" like a lion and the result of your attack will be that much to your amazement you will one day be forced to study us.

Thus ends the 1914 "Thoughts in War," perhaps the most extraordinarily accurate exposition of the German racial psychology which Mann, that noted German analyst of men and women, ever penned.

It took Mann exactly twenty-three years, starting from this political attitude, to become the militant liberal and profound hater of the German concept of racial domination that he is today. To his heavy devotion to the past and his scrupulous, weighty, literary slowness, he was gradually forced to add the burden of his long-drawn-out ideological metamorphosis. In 1923, five years after the Weimar Republic had been founded (and his brother Heinrich had successfully started leading German youth), Thomas Mann, in a Goethe Memorial Day speech to the students of the University of Frankfort-am-Main, finally advised the young folk to rally to the Republic idea, to which, with meticulous truthfulness, he admitted he was not yet converted. However, he said, the Republic offered "the climate of humanity," in which soul could speak to soul rather than citizen to citizen. It was this literary mixture of metaphysics, formal non-democracy, and old-fashioned Prussian nationalism that made Mann seem a chauvinist to the French intelligentsia, still nervous in victory across the Rhine, and led the Institut de France in 1924 to describe him as a dangerous pan-Germanist of the *d'après-guerre* variety.

In 1924, Mann's major opus, the 400,000-word novel called *The Magic*

Mountain, which he had taken twelve years to write, was published. Its European success was immense. It was translated into Hungarian, Dutch, and Swedish, and in four years sold over a hundred thousand copies even in an impoverished Germany where the sixteen-mark price of the novel could buy a dozen dinners. Mann seems to have hoped that the educated German classes would be influenced by the book's metaphysical-social European symbolism, in which a character who is a Jew with a Jesuit education represents Communism, plus medievalism, mysticism, and the Catholic Church; an Italian dialectic democrat is satirized as an organ-grinder; and a Russian seductress represents Asia and is unsuccessfully loved by the well-bred German bourgeois hero Hans, "simple-minded though pleasing." Mann was especially confident that the Teutonic reader would recognize himself in this typical German Hans and, as he later wrote in his autobiography, "could and would be guided by him." Unfortunately, it was the Austrian Adolf who soon did the guiding, and after the 1930 elections, which gave the Nazis their first big political victory, Mann made an alarmed speech of intellectual warning in Berlin during which Nazi rowdies rioted. His suddenly taking a stand vaguely disturbed the German nationalists, who ever since his early essay on the non-political man had supposed him safely on the anti-democratic side of the fence. As Germany's leading intellectual, Mann, had he remained complacent, would have been valuable to the Nazis at the moment. Furthermore, the year before, he had won the Nobel Prize for Literature, and for both national and international propaganda reasons the Nazis wanted to muscle in on his honor. In 1932 Mann addressed a lengthier, impassioned appeal to the German intelligentsia and made his first public reference to the working class, whom he praised.

In March, 1933, two weeks after the Reichstag fire and two months after Hitler had assumed power as *Reichskanzler,* Mann and his wife, who were concluding a holiday in Switzerland, received a cryptic warning from their eldest son and daughter, Klaus and Erika, telephoning from the family house in Munich. These modern young Manns, already politically prescient, begged their parents not to come home because the weather was bad. Mann naïvely replied that the weather was bad in Switzerland, too. Erika then alluded to some terrible house-cleaning ahead. It was probably Frau Mann who realized that the weather the young Manns had described was political and that the house-cleaning might be a purging of anti-Nazis. Mann and his wife never set foot in

Germany again. The next day their six sons and daughters made preparations to join them and the voluntary exile of the Mann family began. When, a short time afterward, Mann's passport expired and he asked the local German consulate to have it renewed, he was politely assured this would be done immediately if he returned to Munich. It was his refusal to go back home that made his anti-Nazi attitude official in Nazi eyes.

By the end of the year, Mann's Munich house, library, and bank account had been seized by the Nazis. Late in 1936 the Nazi government deprived Mann and his family, who had remained in Switzerland, of their German nationality. It is characteristic of Mann that only in 1937, after the University of Bonn revoked the honorary degree of Doctor of Philosophy it had conferred upon him, did he break the four-year silence that marked the first stage of his exile. He had thought silence "would enable me to preserve something dear to my heart—the contact with my public in Germany"; that is, the continued circulation of his books there and what he steadfastly hoped would be their influence on German minds. On New Year's Day, 1937, Mann addressed to the dean of the philosophical faculty of the University of Bonn his first public political words of excoriation of the Nazi regime—an indignant three-thousand-word letter, since reprinted in a pamphlet called "An Exchange of Letters," which has been ranked as the noblest of Mann's political statements. His other confessions of democratic faith are *The Coming Victory of Democracy,* hopefully written in the spring of 1938; *This Peace,* which appeared after Munich; and, a tragical third, *This War,* published early in 1940.

When Mann and his family lost their nationality, they were given honorary citizenship, by the Czecho-Slovakian Republic, as an anti-Nazi gesture. Actually, they never lived in Czecho-Slovakia; when they left Switzerland, they lived for a while in Le Lavandou and neighboring towns in the French Midi, and then settled down at Küsnacht, on the Lake of Zurich. Early in 1938, Mann received an offer from an American lecture bureau to visit the United States and go on tour. He accepted the invitation. As he had written to the dean of the University of Bonn, "I am more suited to represent [Germany's cultural] traditions than to become a martyr to them."

In the latest stage of his political evolution, Mann is now discussed in certain foreign diplomatic circles of Washington as the ideal president of the Fourth Reich, once the Nazis are defeated.

As current events have made him feel increasingly remote from life, Mann, since his arrival in America, has gone out little, either to social functions, concerts, the movies (though movies fascinate him as something new under the sun), or the theatre. He was much interested in Robert Sherwood's *There Shall Be No Night* last year and went to see it because he had heard he was the model for the character of the Finnish neurologist. If this were true, he said, he was much honored, but he thought the resemblance slight. He has read some American writers, is especially impressed by John Dos Passos and the early Ernest Hemingway, has recently enjoyed Frederic Prokosch, James M. Cain's *Serenade*, John Steinbeck's *Of Mice and Men*, and was at one time excited by Sinclair Lewis's *It Can't Happen Here*, considered as a document rather than as a literary production. Mann says he is glad his sons and daughters are in an English-speaking country because he thinks that English will be the only literary language that will remain free in the immediate future. Since it was not a language he learned to read with ease when he was young, as he did French, which interests him less, Mann is today driven to revert, for his regular afternoon reading after his nap, to his favorites, the German classics. He reread Goethe's *Faust* five times hand running to get himself into what he considered the correct modern equivalent of the eighteenth-century mood in which to start writing his three novels about Joseph of the Old Testament days.

This trilogy, begun in 1926 and planned as a single book to be called *Joseph and His Brothers*, as time went on overflowed into *Young Joseph* and then into *Joseph in Egypt*, which itself ran into two volumes, and is now spreading into a tetralogy with a volume devoted to Jacob, on which Mann is working in California, where he now lives. The Joseph series (an elaboration, with symbolic commentary, of the familiar Biblical story, plus additional scholarly incidents Mann has culled from the Talmud) has, for the first time in Mann's career, put his American devotees into two frames of mind. Some say it reminds them of Shakespeare's *King Lear* and some merely say they can't read it. The nub of the argument seems to be the lengthy episode involving Potiphar's wife, treated by Mann with a candor which makes of it either the *Three Weeks* of the Old Testament or a remarkable study in Teutonic good-and-evil symbolism, depending on how the reader takes it. Some Mann readers also deplore his characteristic humorous effort in making Potiphar's wife lisp during the major seduction scene, owing to her having symbolically bitten her tongue in a preliminary attempt not to declare her passion. However, most readers, even the uncritical, agree that Potiphar's wife finally saying (in the English translation) "Thleep with me" is definitely funny.

Among European writers of intellectual stature, Mann has outsold the field in America. *Joseph in Egypt* was a Book of the Month Club dividend in 1938, and over 210,000 copies were distributed apart from its bookstore sale of about 47,000. *Buddenbrooks* has sold about 48,000 copies in America and has just been put on phonograph records for the blind and placed in the twenty-seven regional libraries for the blind by the Library of Congress. *The Magic Mountain,* best known of his books among Americans, has sold more than 125,000 copies. *Death in Venice,* possibly the most beloved of his stories in this country, nevertheless had an original sale (accounted for, apparently, by only his most steadfast followers) of less than 20,000. However, it was included in *Stories of Three Decades,* which was also a Book of the Month Club dividend in 1936 and which sold 92,000 altogether. Even before this war, Mann's largest group of readers was, owing to the Nazis' suppression of his work, already concentrated in the United States; the Scandinavians ranked next. He has been alternately admired and suppressed by official Moscow. When the Revolution broke out he was unprintable because he was a bourgeois. After the rise of the Popular Front in France, the Soviet State publishing house brought him out in a handsome cheap edition. Just before the Berlin-Moscow pact was signed, his books began to be attacked again.

It is impossible to estimate how large a fortune Mann had assembled from his writings when the Nazis seized his worldly goods. Before the exile of the Mann family, they lived in a pleasantly prosperous manner (a country summer cottage in Memelland, the town house in Munich, automobiles, travel, six children, and vacations), a state of ease to which few German intellectuals, or even businessmen, could attain. For his American residence, Mann is now building a comfortable California type of house in a section called the Riviera, near Hollywood. His attitude toward his royalties is influenced by the fact that he believes he has a message to give to the world. Thus he has always given the sales of his books the dignified consideration which a prophet, say, would bestow upon his converts. Last year, after his *vie romancieé* about Goethe had been announced to bookshops under the title of *The Beloved Returns,*

Mann became uneasy and decided that he preferred to go back to the original, less sentimental title, "Lotte in Weimar." To this Mann's publisher, Alfred Knopf, agreed, but pointed out that many American Mann readers would lack the courage to ask a clerk for a book whose three-word title contained two words they wouldn't be sure how to pronounce, whereas all would know how to ask for *The Beloved Returns* without embarrassment. After a dignified family parley of several days, Mann announced that he had decided he owed those readers waiting for his new book the courtesy of a title they would be sure of. The book was published under the title *The Beloved Returns,* with the subtitle "Lotte in Weimar." Everyone, presumably including his readers, was happy.

· · ·

Perhaps because of his weighty personality, which, like an old-fashioned, heavily corniced library wall, rises solidly and protectingly behind the unfrivolous print of his thirty carefully written books, Thomas Mann now occupies a unique position in our country, superior to that of all the thousands of other German émigrés, intellectual or once monied, gathered here today. This position, which in three years has become legendary, he acquired partly because he takes his symbolic eminence for granted and partly because his proud racial character has served as a magnet to a company of compatriot refugees who, sick of being ashamed of their nationality, take comfort from the pride of this German gentleman whom they may never have seen, from this German author whose books they may never have read. Mann is also symbolic of those stay-at-home German generations which so carefully, unconsciously, and fatally helped bring about his own logical exile from his fatherland. As he recently wrote to his eldest daughter and son, "German freedom and the Weimar Republic have been destroyed; we, you and I, are not altogether guiltless in that matter." Maybe Weimar's Goethe, Mann's mirror, should also have been included in his roomy *mea culpa*. There is no question but that Mann successfully managed to do what most authors would have tried to avoid—he projected himself backward into history as part of his literary progress in life. Already, by his blood inheritance, bred to look like a medieval portrait of a merchant by Holbein, Mann, because of a nineteenth-century literary affectation, concentrated his young writer's mind on the eighteenth-century Goethe. With the coming of the twentieth century and its hesitant political notions, Mann, as the result of his tardy taste for politics, derived his ideological shape from the bourgeois epoch, the *Grundjahre* of Bismarck, from which the world had just emerged and which the anti-Wilhelmenian young Germans were already trying to shed. Even in his choice of physical residence, Mann, as a domestic character, was equally elegant and démodé, selecting for his marriage and his home the soothing pleasures and academic intellectualities of Munich, capital of delicious old rococo and witty neo-baroque, a city busy with sentimental dreams, devoid of factories, and miles south of the colder industrial atmosphere of brutal Berlin. It is probable that exile alone has finally imposed on Thomas Mann the tragedy of being up to date.

Friends say that Mann suffers deeply from being an émigré, cut off from his country, his people, and his language. Wherever history has moved him, from Munich to Zurich, to Le Lavandou, to Stockton Street in Princeton, to the coast of California, he has tried, with civilized design, to go on living as himself. Some refugees are chameleons, taking their color from what lies around them; Mann is of the snail type, with his self-formed dwelling firm upon his head wherever he may be forced to roam. "I shall always go home," one refugee friend of his has said, "to the house of Thomas Mann in whatever land. There our sadness as aliens is admitted; our homesickness is admitted, our sometimes outbursting love for German language and music—these are admitted. He is our most important, consoling figure. His writing, his art, his wisdom, his life have not been doomed by human circumstances."

Whatever the circumstances, Mann himself, now in his middle sixties, does not think he will endure them long. Accustomed to deciding the destinies of characters in ink, he has decided what will be for him (in the phrase he always places at the end of each of his manuscripts) the *finis operis*. In his autobiographical *Sketch of My Life* he states, without comment, "I have a feeling that I shall die at the same age as my mother, in 1945."

LA FRANCE ET LE VIEUX

Janet Flanner

FEBRUARY 12, 1944 (ON MARSHAL PÉTAIN)

ROM THE BEGINNING, Vichy was a hotel government. One reason Marshal Pétain's capital was set up in this pretty, provincial Allier town was that Vichy, since the time of Julius Caesar France's most populous spa, possessed enough hostelries to accommodate, on short notice, a modern French autocracy. The Ministries moved into establishments formerly occupied by rich invalids with bad livers. The Ministries of Justice and Finance settled down in the Carlton; War was at the Hôtel Thermal. Foreign diplomats were appropriately quartered in the Hôtel des Ambassadeurs. The Marshal established his own headquarters amid the de-luxe imitation period furniture and Lyons hangings indigenous to the third floor of the Hôtel du Parc. The elegant and spacious old Parc was built for service by leisurely chambermaids, not by secretaries, and the Marshal, to speed up government, worked out the system of pounding on his floor with his cane when he wanted Pierre Laval to hurry up from his office below.

Pétain called his government the government of National Revolution, which certainly sounded new to French ears, but the Vichy régime almost immediately took on nostalgic forms. Relics of the dead France of Louis XIV and Richelieu, or indeed from any epoch anterior to the authentic French Revolution, began to turn up in Vichy terminology and even on its money. A portrait of Henri IV appeared on a treasury bond-selling poster; Jacques Cœur, fiscal servant to Charles VII, was commemorated on the new bank notes. The Ministers were renamed Secretaries of State, as they had been known under the monarchies, and they functioned among such dusty nomenclature as *commanderies, intendants,* and even *compagnonnages,* straight out of the good old *moyen âge.* Vichy was marked by leftovers from everything except France's three republics.

It had taken the Third Republic five years, from 1870 to 1875, to get around to writing its Constitution. This Constitution Marshal Pétain wiped out at Vichy in two days, July 10 and 11, 1940. It had probably already been doomed several weeks before by the simple, ominous, generous offer accompanying his announcement that he had asked the Germans for an armistice: "I make to France the gift of my person to lessen her misfortune." The so-called legal arrangements for the receipt of this gift by some twenty million Unoccupied French people were more complicated. On July 9th, those members of the Paris Senate and Chamber of Deputies who had not been stranded on the road as refugees met at Vichy—preliminary to the National Assembly to be held the next day—to cast their first vote on the fate of the Republic. There the supposedly democratic Chamber of Deputies voted three hundred and ninety-five votes for, to three against, the motion that there was need "to amend the constitutional laws." The conservative Senate voted two hundred and twenty-five for, one against. The unique dissenting senatorial vote, registered against what was obviously Pétain's plan for autocracy, was cast by the aged Marquis Pierre de Chambrun, one of the elegant descendants of La Fayette but nevertheless unrelated in political sentiments to his nephew, young Count René de Chambrun, son-in-law to Pierre Laval. The elderly aristocrat, when it came to his vote, shouted *"Je suis un fils de La Fayette. Vive la République toujours!"* and wept.

On July 10th a *Loi Constitutionnelle,* co-signed by Albert Lebrun, the President of the Republic, and Pétain, handed the Republic's powers over to "the authority and signature of Marshal Pétain." The next day he started to use them. In what he bluntly called his *Acte Constitutionnel* No. 1, a brief paragraph of six lines, so stark that the last line consisted only of the date and the first line only of "We, Philippe Pétain, Marshal of France," he plurally declared that he was *chef* of something new called *l'État français* and that Article 2 of the 1875 Constitution was abrogated. Since Article 2 referred solely to the existence of a President, and since the lachrymose Lebrun had refused to resign, Pétain had simply abrogated him along with a piece of the old Constitution. Later that day Pétain issued Act No. 2 and Act No. 3, both of which opened in a more modest titular fashion, "We, Marshal of France," but continued the abrogations. Of these two, Act 3 was the more destructive. In it Pétain paralyzed democracy and made himself an active dictator. This famous Act 3 stated (a) that the Chamber and Senate would continue to exist until the formation of new assemblies as previsioned by Pétain's and Lebrun's original *Loi Constitutionnelle;* (b) that they were adjourned till further order; and (c) that the 1875 Constitution law which established a Chamber and Senate was abrogated. The *Loi Constitutionnelle,* furthermore, specified that it itself had to be "ratified by the nation and applied by the Assemblies it will have created." Since Pétain up to now has never consulted the nation or assembled anything, his authoritarian revolution has been just as illegal as any ever made in the name of liberty.

Act No. 4, issued by Pétain on July 12th, named Pierre Laval to be Vice Premier and the Marshal's dauphin in the governmental succession. The initial Vichy hierarchy of two was now complete.

. . .

It was during this first summer of France's defeat that there sprang up throughout both the Unoccupied and Occupied Zones the widespread, worshipful cult of the Marshal which was known as *la mystique autour de Pétain.* It was only slightly offset by the rarer but more martial emotion in France for General de Gaulle, who on August 2nd was tried—*in absentia,* naturally, since he was busy in London organizing his new Free French to keep up the fight against the Germans—and condemned to death by Vichy as a traitor. To many millions of the French, especially in Vichy France, the Pétain *mystique* became a sort of strange, esoteric state religion. The defeat, the fall, and the cutting up of France had produced in the French people the same sort of profound physical shock that might be experienced by an individual, far from young, who had been cruelly beaten, had had a violent concussion, and had also suffered the agony of amputation. In that shock something French in France came close to dying. Gradually, as they recovered, the people became wracked with penitence and fell into a daze in which the Marshal confusedly figured both as a healer who seemed to have saved life and as a holy man whose intercession with the higher powers had saved the soul. Pétain became a sort of spa saint, an image at a sacred watering place. Vichy turned into a kind of political Lourdes. Iconography and hagiography set in. Just as Napoleon Bonaparte's ardent face had stamped the costly bibelots of his reign, so the Marshal's becalmed features appeared pasted on the cheap brooches and paperweights which were all a conquered nation could afford. On farms, pious peasants hung his photograph in the parlor; shop-keepers placed it among their diminishing wares in the window; men and women to whom the garrulous politicians of the Third Republic now figured as the voice of the tempter began going to mass again to honor the taciturn Hero of Verdun and to meditate on a regenerated France; children prayed that the Marshal might continue to live and marched the streets singing Vichy's favorite juvenile song, "Maréchal, Nous Voilà!" Soldiers wounded in the brief Battle of France kept, in vigil over their cots, postcard portraits of the Marshal who had built his government on their defeat. Pétain's official Vichy biographer, General Auguste Laure, wrote, as if issuing a revelation, "Here, as I see it, is the truth. The Marshal was preserved by God for France during two generations so that he might receive her, expiring, in his arms." On Good Friday of 1941, prayers were read in the churches, as in the old days of kings and emperors, for the country's sovereign, *"pro duce nostro Philippo."*

The more worldly implications of the Pétain *mystique* soon began to show up in certain Teutonic touches as the Nazis, at first at long distance, gave the Vichy propaganda desk the benefit of their experience. The interest in youth movements which Pétain had evidenced before expressed itself in what looked like an imitation of the Hitler *Jugend* movement, called Les Clubs des Amis du Maréchal. One of the organization's tracts told its adolescent members, "If the Marshal said to you, 'Help me,' you would walk in his footsteps to the end of the world." In August, 1940, by Vichy decree, the veterans of both world wars were organized under Pétain's patronage into La Légion Française des Combattants, a French version of Hitler's S.A. In 1942 its youngest zealots were placed in a special group, the counterpart of the S.S., called Les Services d'Ordre Légionnaires, or S.O.L. According to an organization report on a monster S.O.L. meeting in the Rhône district at which forty-five hundred members were enrolled, a legion *Gauleiter,* "after reading the oath of allegiance to the triumph of the National Revolution, ordered the men to kneel as a sign of humility and devotion to the Marshal, then cried, 'Rise, S.O.L.!' As one man the forty-five hundred members rose, stood at attention, and shouted, 'I swear!'" Two of the members' duties were to propagandize for Vichy and to report on "intrigues against Vichy doctrine," which meant to spy. One folksy, rural S.O.L. order from the Vichy Minister of Interior read, "Urgent! . . . Everybody must be gathered round the town square music kiosk at four o'clock. The presence of all section members is compulsory at this protest meeting against Great

Britain. One or two groups of three or four legionaries will be designated who will have to applaud vigorously and shout with all necessary strength, 'Death to the British!' At a certain moment they will also have to approve with clamors the revindication of Canada," this last a queer conquered-French scheme to free French-Canadian Quebec from the yoke of the English.

The selection of members for the S.O.L. was guided by a questionnaire of twenty inquiries, aimed at winnowing the wheat from the chaff. Among them were "What are the political opinions of your family? What were your feelings when the armistice was signed? How do you judge England's attitude toward France since the armistice? What do you think of de Gaulle? Of the role of Stalin? Of Freemasonry and the Jews? If the Marshal were to disappear, what ought we to do? If Germany were to win the war, what would you think of the situation?"

In 1941 an *Almanach de la Légion Française des Combattants,* the bulkiest piece of Pétain propaganda ever published, came out. It was obviously for family consumption, since it contained a brief blessing by the Marshal, who said, "I hope the hearth of each veteran will be enriched with a copy of this work." This book, a hundred-page mélange, was a high propaganda point in masochism, defeatism, and sickly praise of the chill charms of the Marshal. "There is in our present distress a source of joy," the *Almanach's* leading editorial morbidly crowed. "Our misery is great but greater the moral misery we had been living in." The *Almanach's* poetry also twanged the melancholy Vichy note in a verse that declaimed, "*Monsieur le Maréchal,* Your Army is dissolved, Your planes lie dead in the aerodromes." A dubious religious slant was supplied by a sprinkling of anti-Semitic jokes.

One of the strangest portraits of a hero ever drawn by a subordinate was contributed to the *Almanach* by a private who had served in Pétain's Verdun headquarters. He wrote with admiration, "He is *un grand timide;* he knows it and suffers from it. To avoid being taken in by others and to protect his personality, he has created a façade, a shell of ice, and from behind this he attacks. His biting words, sometimes brutal or cruel, stop any interlocutor and make him also timid, and the general finds himself on equal terms. However, if you see him intimately, you see cracks in his façade, revealing a heart profoundly human and a touching sensitivity. But how few have seen those flashes!"

After thirty pages devoted to revivifying the Verdun legend came some remarkable notes on how the Marshal's health in Vichy was holding up (the constant worry about so venerable a leader): "His sight is intact. He is sometimes hard of hearing, but he hears what he wants to. If life is a matter of slow combustion, his lamp must be the best-regulated in the whole world. As a young second lieutenant, he swam the harbor of Villefranche-sur-mer with calm, slow strokes, which is better, *n'est-ce pas,* than to sink from having breathed too quickly?"

The tag-end pages of the *Almanach* were generously given over to the legionnaires' wives and kiddies. A recipe column started with "Ersatz: The word is new for us, the thing also. But"—and here the propagandist showed his teeth—"isn't this the time for new words and new formulas?" A household-hints department finished up with a suggestion for a fuel-less Wednesday dinner menu: "Add salt to raw vegetables, celery, shredded turnips, etc." Then the final, faltering *gourmet* touch: "If one finds them insipid, they may be seasoned with lemon juice."

. . .

From the outset, in his National Revolution, Marshal Pétain shouldered, like a sacred burden, the entire weight of his autocracy. It would seem clear that at least at the start—before disappointments, office-seeking, cabals, intrigues, palace politics, the machinations of Pierre Laval, and the Teutonic Machiavellianism of the seven-year-old Nazi régime had befogged the eighty-four-year-old Marshal's Vichy scene—he had clearly in mind a half-dozen ideas on which to build his Revolution.

His Idea No. I was that France was utterly defeated. "A nation has to be whipped sometimes," he insisted in an early speech, adding later, "The country ought to know we have been beaten. For two years I have been repeating it to myself every morning."

Second, although he had often mistakenly insisted, in the last war, that the Allies were lost, he was sure the Germans were victorious in this one. "The war was practically won by Germany as soon as Italy entered the campaign," he broadcast for historians to mull over. As a loyal French officer, he agreed that a Germany which had swiftly dismembered France would certainly, as someone had said, "wring England's neck like a chicken's." Judging by his experience, Pétain figured that the United States would, as usual, enter the war late, or maybe never.

Third, Pétain, the man who had been a commander in chief in the last war, had come around to accepting the former Corporal Hitler as a militant German phenomenon who, through his unique struggle, had risen so high by 1940 as to be trusted like a brother officer—especially if he had the gentlemanly *Reichswehr* to keep an eye on him. Pétain had asked that the armistice be drawn up "as between soldiers, after the struggle, and in Honor," capitalized. Three days after it was signed, Pétain broadcast, and seemingly believed, that "France will be administered only by Frenchmen."

Fourth, he thought that collaboration was not only unavoidable but astute. "To collaborate is to avoid the worst," he announced, as a maxim, to intimates at Vichy. Of his single meeting with Hitler, in October, 1940, at Montoire, he told the French, "This first meeting between the conqueror and the conquered marks the first step in our country's rehabilitation. . . . Between our two lands a collaboration has been envisaged. I have accepted it in principle." At first, Pétain's collaboration policy, in which he was backed by many brokenhearted or merely ambitious Frenchmen, was based on the assumption that, in the new postwar lineup in Europe, France would be Germany's favored and favorite former enemy. Though busy governing in the summer of 1940, he found time to write a lofty article for the *Revue des Deux Mondes* which wound up, "We should be able to coordinate our thought and action with those which tomorrow will preside over the reorganization of the entire world," or, in simple slang, "We should tie up with the Nazis, who will soon run the whole show."

Fifth, Pétain, a convinced anti-Republican, saw in the defeat of the corrupted, weakened Third Republic a victory for his pre–French Revolution principles of absolutism. In one of his first Vichy broadcasts, he ridiculed the French folly of ever having believed in the ballot.

Sixth, and most important, he regarded himself as a historic savior. Ever since he had figured in the rescue of France at Verdun, he had labored under the dignified obsession that France had not sufficiently appreciated him or harkened to him. Now he was to have the undisputed, and for once undivided, glory of governing what was left of his beloved country, of leading her back, in a bitter penitence for her democracy and her defeat, to a restoration of the autocracy of her great seventeenth-century past, in which he thought her future still lay. "You have suffered. You will suffer more. . . . I permit neither doubts nor murmurs," he warned over the air. "Hitherto I have spoken to you as a father. Today I address you as a chief. Follow me!"

· · ·

In the two-and-a-half-year drama of Unoccupied France, before the Nazis came in and lowered the curtain on November 11, 1942, the Marshal's two most spirited performances were against Pierre Laval, and against a handful of imprisoned statesmen left over from the Third Republic whom and which Pétain put on trial at the court of Riom. Both Laval and Riom were tragic issues in France, yet at moments they afforded the French the only real laughter of their defeat. Certainly the libretto of Laval's opening plot against the Marshal, four months after Pétain had settled on the Vichy chair of state, was as comic, and implausible, as that of any Berlin *opéra bouffe*. Briefly, the idea was this: During November, 1940, the Germans had let the Marshal hope that he and his government might be removed from the purlieus of Vichy and set up in autonomy in the royal precincts of Versailles. Shortly afterward, the Nazis let all France know that on December 15th, a hundred years to the day since the Paris Invalides had received the ashes of Napoleon Bonaparte from his tomb on St. Helena, the Parisian Germans, in a series of parades which would include a magnificent midnight torchlight procession, would finally make to Paris the amazing companion-piece gift of the ashes of Napoleon's son, *l'Aiglon,* to be fetched by brother Austrian Nazis from his crypt in Vienna. (The Nazi newspaper propaganda angle on *l'Aiglon,* devised to impress the French, was a Teutonic, retrospective buildup of Father Bonaparte as a wise, early Hitler who had yearned merely to federate Europe, a good *Führerprinzip* idea in which he had been foiled by British selfishness at Waterloo.) In the weeks of waiting for *l'Aiglon*'s ashes, Laval hatched his *opéra-bouffe* scenario: The Marshal, on the Nazi promise that his government would soon follow, was to be lured to Versailles with the flattering bait that he was the sole legendary French figure worthy of presiding over the December 15th mummery. In the torchlight parade his name was to be evoked in the dark by enthusiastic, rehearsed cries of *"Vive le Maréchal! N'abandonnez pas Paris! C'est Pétain qu'il nous faut!"* If the Marshal, upon his arrival, fell for the setup, he was expected to desert Vichy and remain in Paris. If the Marshal did not fall, he was to be politely imprisoned at Versailles. In either event, Laval would rise to complete power and to a spirit of more complete collaboration with the Germans than the crochety Marshal then seemed willing to give.

The plot thickened when loyal friends tipped Pétain off. On December 13th, as Laval, fresh from Paris and his final stage directions, walked into the Marshal's Vichy office, he was met by the old man's denunciation, insults were exchanged, and Laval was arrested and himself became the prisoner that night in his own nearby château at Châteldon. The next day the Marshal angrily broadcast, "Frenchmen! Monsieur Pierre Laval no longer forms part of the government." On December 16th, Otto Abetz, the Führer's personal delegate, arrived in Vichy, accompanied by what one Vichy propagandist described as collaborators—a Nazi sub-machine-gun outfit. Laval was freed before Christmas. In Pétain's first interview of the New Year, given to an American journalist, he was still in a position to say that Laval filled him with physical revulsion and that he had slept better since getting rid of that "German agent." But that same month Pétain learned that, along with the German O.K. on the cereal and coal he must have if his Unoccupied French were not to starve and freeze, he had also to take Laval, a less desirable life-giving com-modity. As the cultivated Abetz was supposed to have phrased it, "We need Laval until the peace is signed. After that anybody can put a bullet in his belly." Laval was not reinstated; he was merely allowed to continue functioning as a German agent. For Admiral Darlan was reserved the honor of becoming Pétain's new dauphin and of receiving the first bullet on the program.

In order to deafen his Unoccupied Zone to any echoes left over from the Republic, Pétain had replaced the old trumpet call—*Liberté, Egalité, Fraternité*—with a new sober slogan, *Travail, Famille, Patrie*. Unfortu-nately, so far as *le travail* went, his scheme for exchanging a few sick French prisoners in Germany for a multitude of healthy French work-men led to riots of increasing violence in Vichy France. Furthermore, his *Charte du Travail* of October, 1941, aimed at "breaking the old class-war system," was patterned on Mussolini's corporatives and took from French labor its right to organize, to strike, or to function politically. Having eliminated labor unions, Vichy set up, like a cruel ersatz, a Jewish union, the Union Générale des Juifs de France, which every Jew had to join. As for *la famille*, one handsome, healthy octogenarian could no longer con-sole with his famous phrase—"Fathers, those great adventurers of mod-ern times"—a nation of which a million and a half young potential fathers were wasting their manhood as prisoners in the Third Reich. As for *la patrie*, it was hungry.

. . .

Pearl Harbor was no Christmas gift to Vichy. After the United States entered the war, when the Marshal's stately figure made its regular ap-pearance in movie newsreels, young Frenchmen shouted not *"Vive le Maréchal!"* but *"Vive* Roosevelt!" And when little Admiral Darlan was pictured, they yelled, *"Vive l'autre amiral!,"* meaning Admiral Leahy, American Ambassador to Vichy. Nature, as well as history, was unkind to Vichy in its second winter. Unusually cold weather froze the ink on the National Revolution's desks. Short of coal, like everybody else, the government wore its overcoat indoors and wrote with its gloves on. Vichy's propaganda staff's order to Unoccupied Zone newspapers to "kill any story which represents Vichy life as society life in which pleasure plays a great part" was doubtless not needed, but the sharp reminder forbidding publication of "any newspaper column dealing with public discontent" was unquestionably to the point. Fifteen months before, the Marshal, with brisk truthfulness, had told American journalists, "I do not pretend that this government is free. . . . The Germans hold the rope and twist it whenever they consider the accord is not being carried out." In his weak 1942 New Year's broadcast, Pétain, with wearier truth, said that his revolution had not yet "passed from the domain of principles to enter that of facts. . . . Circumstances do not favor enthusiasm. In the partial exile in which I am constrained, in the half liberty left me, I try to do all my duty. Daily I attempt to save this land from the asphyxia which menaces it, from the troubles which lie in wait." The Pétain *mystique* was on the wane. His former worshippers, now divided into two camps, either thought of him as an august, dignified, if defeated, martyr or believed him to be a fine-phrasing old figure with clay feet. Because of Vichy's increasing collaboration with the Germans, millions of those Frenchmen who had never loved him now bitterly regarded him as the country's most aged traitor.

He was also a matter of concern to those who, as part of his régime, were necessarily devoted to him. Even in gerontocratic France, the Marshal, for a chief of state, was becoming old. The Vichy population grew accustomed to seeing the somnolent figure of the elderly man riding through the streets on clement afternoons in his limousine, which flew on its bonnet the official marshal's ensign—a baton, flanked with battle axes, on a tricolor field. To reassure Unoccupied France in general, Dr. Bernard Menetrel, the Marshal's physician, superintended the taking of some newsreels which showed the Marshal in a state of lively health in the garden of his Riviera country place, where a small ditch had been dug expressly in order that the Marshal might be photographed in the act of briskly jumping over it. This Dr. Menetrel had appeared early on the Vichy scene and had become important. He is reported to be the forty-year-old son of an old friend of the Marshal's and has been described as an Action Française Royalist, anti-German, and intelligent. In 1942 the Doctor supposedly diagnosed the patient's condition more or less as follows: The Marshal, who sleeps badly but persists in his lifelong habit of rising at 5 A.M., still has left enough of his phenomenal health to function for about eight hours a day, were his day that of an ordinary idle old man; this exceptional vitality, however, fails to get him through a morning of governing without the aid of a drug (which other Vichy doctors, judging by the way it acts, have deduced must be benzedrine or ephedrine, in carefully controlled doses). The importance of the Doctor's aid to Pétain has been recognized by his being named to the *Secrétariat du Maréchal,* a post which has permitted him to accompany Pétain to Ministerial meetings, where the old man may need all his wits about him.

The latest report on the Marshal's health is this: During his best morning hours, when important visitors see him, his blue eyes are sapphire-clear and his features have the neatness of mere middle age. Flattery acts on him like a tonic; compliments are not enough. In official discussion, he is, while his medicine still upholds him, alert, cynical, hard, realistic, and as pessimistic as ever. For an hour after he has left his doctor, he is a match for anyone, even Laval. The liveliness of the Marshal's luncheons, with eight or ten male guests chosen from among distinguished government officials and visitors, was one of the first legends in Vichy; the Marshal still eats well, or as well as the supplies allow. His discerning, restrained taste in French wines is about all that is left now, however, of his gastronomy. "I beg of you to remain to lunch," he one day urged a visitor, adding, with an old man's courteous candor, "You will give me the added pleasure of an excuse for opening a good bottle of champagne." By afternoon, the Marshal has turned into an old man. When the effect of the drug comes to its end, the transition is swift and startling. While you look at him, he becomes his own old empty shell. Within a few minutes the lights and movements fade from his face, leaving a waxen, uninhabited mask. His blue eyes seem to see nothing, his memory fails to function. His brain closes against any new identifications; he thinks a man he has just met is another man he knew well years ago. Yet from a lifetime of self-control, the habit of dignified wariness still aids him. If forced to receive some visitor—his staff sees to it that only second-string visitors are given afternoon appointments—the Marshal limits himself to rising, bowing, and shaking hands; he will not risk the possible disaster of conversation. Sometimes, though, the Marshal murmurs, as if to himself, small, routine, melancholy phrases such as *"Ah, les bons s'en vont"* or *"Tout est bien changé."* At times these cryptic utterances can daze the caller. More often, since France has indeed lost its good men and since the times are, alas, changed, the Vichy visitor retires impressed by the wise sadness of a weary old statesman.

Once out of his office in the Hôtel du Parc and back home, the Marshal dwells, as he has always done, in complete inaccessibility. Since the first, he and *Madame la Maréchale* have lived in Vichy in a fine old residence known as the Pavillion de Sévigné. Only the few family friends, who can be trusted to take the Marshal as they find him at night, are ever invited to dine with them. In contrast to his notable luncheons, the Marshal's domestic evening meal is light. It is the soft supper of a very old man.

The most visible proof of the Marshal's dwindling popularity was the slump, in 1942, in his fan letters, which had earlier numbered two thousand a day. After the Riom trial, they dropped to nearly nothing (where they have remained), and the propaganda desk, advised by the local police, tactfully advised the Marshal to spare his strength and avoid appearing in public.

· · ·

The Riom trial, by which Pétain meant to shatter the very memory of the Third Republic, succeeded principally in weakening the Vichy régime. The trial, the most hilarious, shameful travesty of French justice and example of Army bigotry since the Dreyfus case, was held in the late winter of 1942, and it apparently began as an alibi for the Germans, who, still smarting from the war-guilt stigma for 1914, wanted to force France to pin on herself the war guilt for 1939. Pétain, in his turn, wished the war guilt to fall not on his beloved France but on the hated Third Republic. Such double-barrelled intentions demanded special preparations. In July, 1940, Pétain issued a decree setting up a supreme court, subsequently established in nearby Riom—the only town in the region which possessed a courthouse big enough for the trial of a dead republic—which should judge those responsible for France's recent "passage from a state of peace to a state of war." In January, 1941, he issued an act, even odder, which was known as the Retroactive Responsibility of Ministers Act. Its tyrannical opening lines must have made the Vichy higher-ups shake in their shoes, since the law stated that all high government officials must "swear allegiance to his person," that as office-holders they "pledged their persons and worldly goods," that if they broke faith with him he could strip them of their political rights, ship them to the colonies, intern them, imprison them in a fortress—everything but hang them up by their thumbs. Less humorously, this law could retroactively apply to "high dignitaries who had held office within the past ten years," which clearly meant the Third Republic's, Popular Front, and Radical-Socialist leaders. In September, Pétain decreed that something to be called a Council of Political Justice be set up with the incredible right to "establish its own rules" and give a preliminary opinion as to the guilt of whoever would be unlucky enough to be tried before the supreme court. On October 13th, Nazi Minister Walther Funk shed considerable light on what was up by broadcasting, from Berlin, that "the French government would soon condemn those guilty of the war." Sure enough, three days later, Pétain himself ordered, on the recommendation of the Council of Justice, that Radical-Socialist Premier Edouard Daladier, Popular Front Premier Léon Blum, and former Generalissimo Maurice Gamelin, principals in the trial to come, be incarcerated in the Pyrenees fortress of Pourtalet on the ground that they were guilty, without having been indicted or tried, of failure in their public duty. Pierre Cot, Popular Front Minister of Air, also on the list of the accused, couldn't be imprisoned, the Council report noted, "as he is a fugitive" in Washington, D.C. Seventeen months after they had been imprisoned as guilty, the three other men blossomed out as defendants in the Riom trial, which opened on February 19, 1942.

Riom is a grim, handsome Auvergnat Renaissance town of black stone fountains and façades carved from the local volcanic rock. To house the trial in style, Riom's famous swarthy Palais de Justice, built in medieval times, was gadgeted with central heating, the walls were decked with priceless Beauvais and Flanders tapestries depicting scenes from the Odyssey, and from the ceilings hung splendid crystal chandeliers which once had twinkled in the Tuileries. To match this stage set, the court officials wore their red robes and white toques and the court president and state's attorney were ringed with ermine collars. The farce, and France's laughter, began when, the first day, Blum's attorney opened by blandly reading aloud the eight secret Vichy orders which, as a preliminary, had been handed to the French press. Order No. 1, which took no cognizance of what the Nazis thought the trial was about, said "Keep in mind that the trial is limited to the unpreparedness for war existing in France from 1936 to May, 1940"—just in case some cub reporter forgot that Pétain had been War Minister in 1934. Order No. 4 instructed the press to make clear that this was a trial of the government of which the French people "had been victims." Order No. 5 said, "Show that this cannot be the trial of the Army." Order No. 7 added, "Especially consider this trust when either the person of the Marshal or his policy is referred to during the trial." That evening, new secret Vichy orders were given to the press, forbidding it to report that Blum's lawyer had disclosed that it had had the secret orders in the first place. As the trial proceeded, other orders forbade reporters to report that Daladier, on the stand, had said that Weygand had said that Pétain had failed to call a Superior War Council from 1934 on, that Pétain had had millions sliced off Daladier's appropriations for training camps, and that Pétain, as War Minister, in 1934 had had the war budget cut by one-third, and that "in 1939 there were strong attacks on Pétain in Parliament." Rather listlessly, Order No. 10 said, "To sum up . . . suppress all that concerns the actions of the Marshal." Order No. 16, with more zest, said, "Do not quote the name of de Gaulle." Once, the state's attorney was driven to admit, "We are not here to decide if [Pétain's] laws are constitutional, but only to enforce them." Once, all that the court president could say, in reply to a Daladier attack on the Marshal, was "Oh! Oh!" After Blum's lawyer had thrown the fat in the fire, the frantic district press censor sent a confidential memorandum to newspaper editors declaring that he no longer dared send them the press instructions "for reasons you can well imagine." He also regretted that he could send no adequate trial report, since by the time he got through censoring he had left "only two or three lines of text per page. Many doubt that the trial can continue much longer." Off the record, he added that Daladier's defense of himself had "produced a very strong impression."

Daladier had opened his defense by boldly prophesying, "We shall see, in the course of this trial, where, by whom, and in what manner France was betrayed," adding, "The hatred of novelty, the hatred of intellectual daring, the hatred of everything modern led the French Army to its ruin." Blum, with logic and wit, pointed out in his opening speech that, because of the trial's peculiar restrictions, "in the debate on the responsibility for the defeat, the war itself will be left out." Gamelin, charged with having let the Army deteriorate, refused to open his mouth in court. This put the prosecution's Army witnesses in a stew and thereafter they threw the court into fits of hilarity; General Mittelhauser, of the Superior War Council, confessed that he got his Army statistics from reading the newspapers; General Lenclud admitted that he had not known an air squadron was attached to his corps during battle; a Colonel Perré kept referring to an aviation program which turned out to be an idea he had once had in mind but never got down in writing. The court president was named Caous, which sounded enough like "chaos" to serve. About a month after the trial began, while the court was still in a state of confusion, the Nazi Party's *Völkischer Beobachter* clarified the issue by pointing out editorially that the trial which had been intended to pin the war guilt on the Third Republic was actually proving the Men of Vichy guilty of the defeat. Soon afterward, the *Frankfurter Zeitung* called Riom "a stupid farce" and Hitler angrily declared in a broadcast that the Riom trial made clear that "the French mentality was really impossible to understand." On March 19th, the German radio announced that M. de Brinon, Vichy Ambassador to Berlin, had notified Marshal Pétain that the Riom trial must be suspended. The tapestries on the Riom Palais de Justice walls were put back into their boxes; the prisoners were put back into their fortress. On April 14th, the *Journal Officiel* announced Pétain's law suspending the hearings of the Supreme Court at Riom. On the same day, without any explanation, Pierre Laval was suddenly moved to the top of the Vichy régime with the titles of Chief of Government and Minister of Foreign Affairs, Interior, and Propaganda, and with the right to pick his subordinates. Before a delegation of legionaries, the Marshal suddenly said, speaking of his relationship with Laval, "There are no longer any clouds between us. When M. Laval speaks, it is in agreement with me, and when I speak myself, it is in accord with him." A few days later, Laval spoke up and said, "I wish for a German victory."

· · ·

During the night of November 7th that year, the American Army invaded French Morocco. To President Roosevelt's last-minute direct appeal to Pétain to respect the traditional friendship between France and the United States and to aid our invading troops, the Marshal answered, in his last show of authority, "I have always declared I would defend our empire if it were attacked; you should know that I would keep my word. . . . We shall defend ourselves: this is the order I am giving." When Admiral Darlan, in North Africa, attempted to excuse the Marshal's vain, tragic order by saying that Pétain spoke under dictation, the Marshal proclaimed, in a crescendo, "To dare say that I speak or act under the menace of duress is an insult to me!" On November 11th, twenty-four years to the day after the armistice of 1918, the Germans, in a race to seize the French fleet before it was scuttled in the waters of Toulon harbor, began to occupy Pétain's Unoccupied France. Pétain, with Dr. Menetrel at his side, dictated to Hitler's delegate, General von Rundstedt, who came to Vichy with the grave news of the occupation and with an adequate number of troops, a spirited, inflammatory protest. The protest was handed to the Vichy press. For an hour, Vichy titillated with excitement while the German soldiers stolidly waited. At the end of an hour, the Marshal, his animation depleted, gave in. Pétain received that day what was, so far as is known, his last personal message from Hitler: "It is well known to me, *Herr Marschall,* that you always have been and still are a faithful partisan of the collaboration of France with National-Socialist Germany." Pétain then disbanded what was left, since the armistice, of the French Army. A week later he announced, in a Vichy radio broadcast, that he was still *chef de l'Etat français* and "the incarnation of France." After that there was silence.

. . .

On November 18, 1943, according to journalists in Switzerland, busiest news centre of unoccupied Europe, Marshal Pétain emerged again as worthy of the European front page. He was reported to have been scheduled to broadcast, on November 13th, an important discourse, which the Germans had called off, and he was said to have refused to deliver a substitute of their own concocting. According to the Swiss papers, the important statements in the Marshal's suppressed speech were "Frenchmen! On July 10, 1940, the National Assembly confided to me the mission of promulgating . . . a new Constitution for the French State. I am now about to finish the drawing up of that constitution. [However] We, Marshal of France, Chief of State, decree . . . that if we die before having been able to attain ratification by the Nation of [our] new Constitution . . . that the power mentioned in the [Third Republic's] Constitutional Law of 1875 will return to the Senate and Chamber."

In setting up his autocracy in Vichy, the Marshal had first named Pierre Laval as his dauphin, then named Admiral Darlan. Apparently Marianne, the battered figurehead of the Third Republic, was to be his third choice. If this was his final wish, no one on this side of the Atlantic knows precisely why. Having been wrong in thinking that the Allies would lose the first World War, having been wrong about his French

Army in the peace between the wars, having been wrong in thinking that the Germans had already won the second World War, perhaps the Marshal wished, now that he could clearly see that the democratic Allies would be victors again, to state that he had also been wrong in believing that an autocracy had been suitable even to a defeated Republic of France.

A year after Marshal Pétain had become the supreme autocrat, he told a Catholic priest, "I wish to be buried in the ossuary at Verdun, among those French and German dead marked as unknown. There is a chapel in the crypt which stands empty. It is for me. Whatever happens to me, it is there that I shall go to take my last rest, at the head of my soldiers." At a moment in Vichy when his faith in himself equalled his power over others, Pétain broadcast to the world the words which might well serve as his epitaph: "It is I alone whom history will judge."

THE HOT BACH

Richard O. Boyer

JUNE 24 AND JULY 1/8, 1944 (ON DUKE ELLINGTON)

UKE ELLINGTON, whose contours have something of the swell and sweep of a large, erect bear and whose color is that of coffee with a strong dash of cream, has been described by European music critics as one of the world's immortals. More explicitly, he is a composer of jazz music and the leader of a jazz band. For over twenty-three years, Duke, christened Edward Kennedy Ellington, has spent his days and nights on trains rattling across the continent with his band on an endless sequence of one-night stands at dances, and playing in movie theatres, where he does up to five shows a day; in the night clubs of Broadway and Harlem and in hotels around the country; in radio stations and Hollywood movie studios; in rehearsal halls and in recording studios, where his band has made some eleven hundred records, which have sold twenty million copies; and even, in recent years, in concert halls such as Carnegie and the Boston Symphony. His music has the virtue of pleasing both the jitterbugs, whose cadenced bouncing often makes an entire building shudder, and the intellectuals, who read into it profound comments on transcendental matters. In 1939, two consecutive engagements Ellington played were a dance in a tobacco warehouse in North Carolina, where his product was greeted with shouts of "Yeah man!," and a concert in Paris, where it was greeted as revealing "the very secret of the cosmos" and as being related to "the rhythm of the atom." On the second occasion, Jacques-Henri Lévesque, a Paris critic, professed to hear all this in the golden bray of trombones and trumpets and in the steady beat of drums, bass, and piano, and Blaise Cendrars, a surrealist poet, said, "Such music is not only a new art form but a new reason for living." A French reporter asked Tricky Sam Nanton, one of Ellington's trombonists, if his boss was a genius. "He's a genius, all right," Sam said, and then he happened to remember that Ellington once ate thirty-two sandwiches during an intermission at a dance in Old Orchard Beach, Maine. "He's a genius, all right," he said, "but Jesus, how he eats!"

Ellington is a calm man of forty-five who laughs easily and hates to hurry. His movements are so deliberate that his steps are usually dogged by his road manager, Jack Boyd, a hard, brisk, red-faced little white man from Texas, whose right index finger was shortened by a planing machine twenty years ago. Boyd, who has been an Ellington employee for some years, yaps and yips at his heels in an effort, for example, to hurry him to a train which in fifteen minutes is leaving a station five miles away. Boyd also lives in fear that Ellington may fall asleep at the wrong time, and since it usually takes an hour of the most ingenious torture to put the slumbering band leader on his feet, the manager's apprehension is not unreasonable. In general, Boyd's life is not a happy one. It is his job to herd about the country a score of highly spirited, highly individual artists, whose colors range from light beige to a deep, blue black, whose tastes range from quiet study to explosive conviviality, and whose one common denominator is a complete disregard of train schedules. Often Duke finishes his breakfast in a taxi. Frequently, driven from the table in his hotel room by the jittery, henlike cluckings of Boyd, he wraps a half-finished chop in a florid handkerchief and tucks it in the pocket of his jacket, from which it protrudes, its nattiness not at all impaired by the fact that it conceals a greasy piece of meat. Not long ago this habit astonished an Icelandic music student who happened to be on a train that Duke had barely caught. The Icelander, after asking for Ellington's autograph, had said, "Mr. Ellington, aren't there marked similarities between you and Bach?" Duke moved his right hand to the handkerchief frothing out of his jacket. "Well, Bach and myself," he said, unwrapping the handkerchief and revealing the chop, "Bach and myself both"—he took a bite from the chop—"write with individual performers in mind."

It is in this jumpy atmosphere that Ellington composes, and some of his best pieces have been written against the glass partitions of offices in recording studios, on darkened overnight buses, with illumination supplied by a companion holding an interminable chain of matches, and in sweltering, clattering day coaches. Sometimes writing a song in no more than fifteen minutes and sometimes finishing concert pieces only a few hours before their performance, he has composed around twelve hundred pieces, many of them of such worth that Stokowski, Grainger, Stravinsky, and Milhaud have called him one of the greatest modern composers. There are many musicians who have even gone as far as to argue that he is the only great living American composer. His career almost spans the life of jazz and has figured prominently in the surge which has brought jazz from the bawdy houses of New Orleans to the Metropolitan Opera House and even to Buckingham Palace. King George, who has one of the world's largest collections of Ellington records, is often found bending over a revolving disc so that he can hear more clearly the characteristically dry, dull thud of the band's bass fiddle pulsing under an Ellington theme or the intricate sinuosity of a tenor saxophone as it curls in and out of the ensemble. To Ellington devotees in Europe, which he toured in 1933 and in 1939, identifying him as a mere writer and player of jazz (his instrument is the piano) is like identifying Einstein as a nice old man. Some notion of their fervor is apparent in the words of a London critic reporting an Ellington concert at the Palladium. "His music has a truly Shakespearean universality," he wrote, "and as he sounded the gamut, girls wept and young chaps sank to their knees." The American counterparts of these European devotees prefer to emphasize the air of gaudy sin that surrounded the birth of jazz instead of likening it to the music of the spheres. They like to dwell on Madam White's Mahogany Hall in New Orleans, a resort which offered its patrons jazz music, and on Buddy Bolden's extravagant love life (Bolden was an early jazz cornettist), and they find pleasure in the belief that most jazz musicians smoke marijuana and die spectacularly in a madhouse. They try to ignore the ugly fact that several of Ellington's musicians learned how to play in Boy Scout bands. In endowing the late Bubber Miley, originator of the growl style on the trumpet and one of the early members of Ellington's band, with an almost legendary aura, although he has been dead less than ten years, they are grateful for the fact that he at least was a very heavy drinker. Anyone who is now forty-five has lived through the entire history of jazz, but this does not prevent the followers of the art from speaking, for example, of the trumpet player King Oliver, who died in 1938, as if he were a Pilgrim Father. In the jazz world, 1910 is the Stone Age and 1923 is medieval. The men in Ellington's band, which was playing when Benny Goodman was in short trousers and when the word "swing" was unknown, have aroused such admiration individually that there are many collectors who spend their time searching for old Ellington records not because they want to listen to the band as a whole but to savor the thirty seconds in which their particular hero takes a solo. As he plays, they mew and whimper in a painful ecstasy or, as they themselves put it, they are sent.

. . .

Ellington has, like most entertainers, a stage self and a real self. On the stage, at least when he supplies the "flesh"—the trade term for personal appearances in movie houses—he presents himself as a smiling, carefree African, tingling to his fingertips with a gay, syncopated throb that he can scarcely control. As the spotlight picks him out of the gloom, the audience sees a wide, irrepressible grin, but when the light moves away, Ellington's face instantly sags into immobility. He has given a lot of thought to achieving serenity and equipoise in a life that gives him neither repose nor privacy. He craves peace. He will not argue with anyone in his band, and his road manager, on whom most of the burdens fall, repeatedly sums up his problem in the phrase "Trouble with this band is it has no boss." The arguments which Duke refuses to have, and which, to Boyd's acute distress, he concedes beforehand, usually involve overtime pay or a request for an advance on next week's salary. When Boyd tries to persuade Duke to take a militant attitude, Ellington usually says, in a tone of wheezy complaint, "I won't let these goddam musicians upset me! Why should I knock myself out in an argument about fifteen dollars when in the same time I can probably write a fifteen-hundred-dollar song?" Besides, Ellington contends that an argument may mean the difference between a musician's giving a remarkable performance and just a performance. Furthermore, doctors will tell you that there is a definite relation between anger and ulcers. "Anyway," he will add, in a final desperate defense of his pacific nature, "why should I pit my puny strength against the great Power that runs the universe?" Ellington wears a gold cross beneath his flamboyant plaids and bold checks, reads the Bible every day, along with Winchell and the comics, and has been known to say, "I'd be afraid to sit in a house with people who don't believe. Afraid the house would fall down." He broods about man's final dissolution, and in an effort to stave his own off he has a complete physical examination every three months.

Part of Duke's character goes well enough with the onstage Ellington who periodically throws back his head and emits a long-drawn-out

"Ah-h-h!" as if the spirit of hot had forced wordless exultation from his lips. He likes to eat to excess and to drink in moderation. He is also fond of what he calls "the chicks," and when they follow him to the station, as they often do, he stands on the back platform of his train and, as it pulls out, throws them big, gusty, smacking kisses. (He is married, but he has been separated from his wife for fifteen years.) He has a passion for color and clothes. He has forty-five suits and more than a thousand ties, the latter collected in forty-seven states of the Union and seven European countries, and his shoes, hats, shirts, and even his toilet water are all custom-made. His usual manner is one of ambassadorial urbanity, but it is occasionally punctuated by deep despair. In explaining his moods, he says, "A Negro can be too low to speak one minute and laughing fit to kill the next, and mean both." Few people know that he is a student of Negro history. He is a member of one of the first families of Virginia, for his ancestors arrived at Jamestown in 1619, a year before the Pilgrims landed on Plymouth Rock. He has written music commemorating Negro heroes such as Crispus Attucks, the first American killed in the American Revolution; Barzillai Lew, one of the men depicted in the painting called *The Spirit of '76;* and Harriet Tubman, Nat Turner, Denmark Vesey, Frederick Douglass, and other Negro fighters for freedom. He has also written an unproduced opera, *Boola,* which tells the story of the American Negro, and a long symphonic work entitled *Black, Brown, and Beige,* which he says is "a tone parallel to the history of the Negro." His concern for his race is not entirely impersonal, since he and his band are constantly faced, even in the North, by the institution of Jim Crow. "You have to try not to think about it," Duke says, "or you'll knock yourself out."

Because Duke likes peace and repose, he tries to avoid the endless controversies that go on in the world of jazz. The followers of jazz cannot even agree on the fundamental point of what it is. To keep out of this dispute in particular, Duke frequently says, when people try to pin him down, "I don't write jazz. I write Negro folk music." There are those who insist that the only "righteous jazz," as they call it, is performed by bands of no more than six or seven men whose music is as spontaneous, unpremeditated, and unrehearsed as that of Shelley's skylark. Yet the very aficionados who insist that all real jazz is improvised and that all the solos must be impromptu often claim that Duke's artistry is the genuine, blown-in-the-bottle stuff, brushing aside his own statement that almost all the music his seventeen-piece band plays has been scored. Partly because of this bickering, Ellington always feels that he has found sanctuary when he boards a train. He says that then peace descends upon him and that the train's metallic rhythm soothes him. He likes to hear the whistle up ahead, particularly at night, when it screeches through the blackness as the train gathers speed. "Specially in the South," he says. "There the firemen play blues on the engine whistle—big, smeary things like a goddam woman singing in the night." He likes, too, to sit next to the window, his chin in his hand, and, in a trancelike state, to stare for hours at the telephone poles flashing by and at the pattern of the curving wires as they alternately drop and ascend. Even at night, particularly if his train is passing through certain sections of Ohio or Indiana, he will remain at the window (shifting to the smoker if the berths are made up), for he likes the flames of the steel furnaces. "I think of music sometimes in terms of color," he says, "and I like to see the flames licking yellow in the dark and then pulsing down to a kind of red glow." Duke has a theory that such sights stimulate composition. "The memory of things gone is important to a jazz musician," he says. "Things like the old folks singing in the moonlight in the back yard on a hot night, or something someone said long ago. I remember I once wrote a sixty-four-bar piece about a memory of when I was a little boy in bed and heard a man whistling on the street outside, his footsteps echoing away. Things like these may be more important to a musician than technique."

Perhaps Duke will still be awake at three in the morning, when his train stops for fifteen minutes at a junction. If there is an all-night lunchroom, he will get off the train, straddle a stool, his Burberry topcoat sagging like a surplice, a pearl-gray fedora on the back of his head, and direct the waitress in the creation of an Ellington dessert. The composition of an Ellington dessert depends upon the materials available. If, as is often the case, there is a stale mess of sliced oranges and grapefruit floating in juice at the bottom of a pan, he will accept it as a base. To this he will have the girl add some applesauce, a whole package of Fig Newtons, a dab of ice cream, and a cup of custard. When Duke is back on the train, Boyd, who has stayed up for the purpose, will beg him to go to bed, if they are on a sleeper, or to take a nap, if the band is travelling by day coach, as is often necessary in wartime. Ellington not infrequently takes out a pad of music-manuscript paper, fishes in his pockets for the stub of a lead pencil, and begins composing, and Boyd departs, complaining to the world that "Ellington is a hard man to get to bed and a harder man to get out of it." Frowning, his hat on the back of his head, swaying from side to side with the motion of the car, occasionally sucking his pencil and trying to write firmly despite the bouncing of the train, humming experimentally, America's latter-day Bach will work the night through.

. . .

Boyd tries to arrange things so that the band will arrive at its destination at about six or seven in the evening, making it possible for Duke to sleep an hour or two before the night's engagement. If the town is in the North, Ellington can occasionally get into a hotel, since his name is well and favorably known, but the other members of the band have to scurry around the Negro section of the town, if there is one, and make their own arrangements for lodgings. Usually they can get rooms in the households of amiable colored citizens, and if they can't do that they often pass the time in some public place like a railway station or a city hall. Most dances begin at nine and run until two in the morning. On dance nights, Boyd has an assignment that almost tears him in two. He is supposed to "stand on the door" and check the number of admissions to the dance, but he is also supposed to have Duke awake and at the dance hall. At about eight-thirty, after a half hour's futile effort to rouse his boss, he is in a frenzy. Then, with the strength of desperation—Boyd is a small man and Duke is six feet tall and weighs two hundred and ten pounds—he props the unconscious band leader in a sitting position on the edge of his bed and, grabbing his arms, pulls him out of bed and onto his feet and walks him across the floor. This usually restores a degree of consciousness, which slowly spreads through the rest of Ellington's system. At this point, Boyd tears off to the dance hall, leaving some hanger-on behind to see that Ellington does not go to sleep again.

. . .

In general, or so its members like to think, the more exhausted the Ellington band is, the better it plays. Ordinarily, the tempo at the beginning of a dance is rather slow; both players and dancers have to warm up to their interdependent climax. By midnight both are in their stride. Then the trumpets screech upward in waves, sometimes providing a background for a solo, soft and sensuous, by tough little Johnny Hodges, alto saxophonist, who advances toward the front of the stage threateningly and who holds his instrument as if it were a machine gun with which he was about to spray the crowd. Johnny is fond of addressing his fans as "Bub" or "Bubber" when they come up to talk to him at a dance. Junior Raglin's bass fiddle beats dully, like a giant pulse. Junior's eyes are closed and his face is screwed up as if he were in pain. Duke's face is dominated by an absorbed, sensual scowl as he plays his piano. Sonny Greer, a cigarette waggling before an impassive face, jounces up and down on his stool so hard that he seems to be on a galloping horse, and Rex Stewart, as the night advances, becomes progressively more cocky and springy as he takes his solos. Sometimes the excitement among the dancers reaches a pitch that threatens literally to bring down the house. Two years ago, a dance in a hall in Arkansas was stopped when the floor began to collapse under the feet of the jitterbugs, and five years ago, in Bluefield, West Virginia, so many people crowded about Duke on the stage that it caved in, fortunately without casualties. Almost always a group of serious thinkers who attend these affairs just for the music and not for the dancing gather before the bandstand in front of Duke and make profound comments. "The guy is really deep here," one will say, over the howling of the jitterbugs. Another will murmur, "Terrific mood, terrific content, terrific musicianship." Prim little colored girls sitting along the wall with their mammas—many of Duke's dances in the North are attended by both Negroes and white people—will get up and really throw it around when they are asked to dance, and then will return demurely to their mammas. The serious thinkers disapprove of the jitterbug and his activities, but Duke says, "If they'd been told it was a Balkan folk dance, they'd think it was wonderful." Every now and then there is a wail from Tricky Sam Nanton's trombone, a sad wa-wa melody which sometimes sounds like an infant crying, sometimes like the bubbly, inane laugh of an idiot, and sometimes like someone calling for help. Sam says, "It's a sad tale with a little mirth. When I play it, I think of a man in a dungeon calling out a cell window." Usually a dance ends peacefully, but more than once, in the Southwest, cowboys have brought the festivities to an abrupt ending by firing their guns at the ceiling. On such occasions, the band gets off the stage in a hurry, which is probably a good idea. Once in a while, in the South, a gentleman draws a gun and insists that the band play only his favorite tunes. Unpleasantness, however, is not confined to regions below the Mason-Dixon line. During prohibition, a group of gangsters tried to shake Duke down when he was in Chicago. They presented their demand to Sam Fleischnick, who was then Duke's road manager. Fleischnick refused. "All our boys carry guns," he told the gangsters. "If you want to shoot it out, we'll shoot it out." Ellington considered getting out of town when he heard of Fleischnick's declaration of war against the gang, but he finally solved the problem in more sensible fashion. He telephoned the influential owner of a New York night club where Duke and his band once had played and the owner arranged for Ellington to have the freedom of Chicago without cost.

· · ·

There are times when Duke Ellington exudes such calm contentment that a colleague, under the influence of the benign radiation, once murmured drowsily, "Duke make me sleepy, like rain on the roof." His nerves and laughter are so loose and easy that members of his jazz band believe that they got that way because of his physical makeup rather than because of the quality of his spirit. "His pulse is so low he can't get excited," they explain. "His heart beat slower than an ordinary man's." Only something in the flow of the blood, they are sure, could explain a calm that has survived twenty-three years in the band business—years in which Duke and his seventeen-piece band have again and again clattered on tour from one end of the country to the other. Duke believes that his calm is an acquired characteristic, attained through practice, but whether acquired or inborn, it is his monumental placidity, which is only occasionally shattered, that enables Duke to compose much of his music in an atmosphere of strident confusion. Most composers, alone with their souls and their grand pianos, regard composition as a private activity. Often, when Duke is working out the details of a composition or an arrangement, the sixteen other members of his band not only are present but may even participate, and the occasion sometimes sounds like a political convention, sometimes like a zoo at feeding time. Ordinarily, Duke completes the melody and the basic arrangement of a composition before he tries it out on the band at a rehearsal; then, as he polishes, or "sets," the arrangement, he is likely to let the men in the band make suggestions in a creative free-for-all that has no counterpart anywhere in the world of jazz or classical music. Perhaps a musician will get up and say, "No, Duke! It just can't be that way!," and demonstrate on his instrument his conception of the phrase or bar under consideration. Often, too, this idea may outrage a colleague, who replies on *his* instrument with *his* conception, and the two players argue back and forth not with words but with blasts from trumpet or trombone. Duke will resolve the debate by sitting down at his piano, perhaps taking something from each suggestion, perhaps modifying and reconciling the ideas of the two men, but always putting the Ellington stamp on the music before passing on to the next part of the work in progress. Duke sometimes quotes Bach. "As Bach says," he may remark, speaking about piano playing, "if you ain't got a left hand, you ain't worth a hoot in hell."

The band rarely works out an entire arrangement collectively, but when it does, the phenomenon is something that makes other musicians marvel. This collective arranging may take place anywhere—in a dance hall in Gary, Indiana, in an empty theatre in Mobile, or in a Broadway night club. It will usually be after a performance, at about three in the morning. Duke, sitting at his piano and facing his band, will play a new melody, perhaps, or possibly just an idea consisting of only eight bars. After playing the eight bars, he may say, "Now this is sad. It's about one guy sitting alone in his room in Harlem. He's waiting for his chick, but she doesn't show. He's got everything fixed for her." Duke sounds intent and absorbed. His tired band begins to sympathize with the waiting man in Harlem. "Two glasses of whiskey are on his little dresser before his bed," Duke says, and again plays the eight bars, which will be full of weird and mournful chords. Then he goes on to eight new bars. "He has one of those blue lights turned on in the gloom of his room," Duke says softly, "and he has a little pot of incense so it will smell nice for the chick." Again he plays the mournful chords, developing his melody. "But she doesn't show," he says, "she doesn't show. The guy just sits there, maybe an hour, hunched over on his bed, all alone." The melody is finished and it is time to work out an arrangement for it. Lawrence Brown rises with his trombone and gives out a compact, warm phrase. Duke shakes his head. "Lawrence, I want something like the treatment you gave in 'Awful Sad,'" he says. Brown amends his suggestion and in turn is amended by Tricky Sam Nanton, also a trombone, who puts a smear and a wa-wa lament on the phrase suggested by Brown. Juan Tizol, a third trombone, says, "I'd like to see a little retard on it." Duke may incorporate some variation of one of the suggestions. Then he'll say, "Come on, you guys. Get sincere. Come on down here, Floor Show"—he is addressing Ray Nance—"and talk to me with your trumpet." In a moment or so the air is hideous as trombone and clarinet, saxophone and trumpet clash, their players simultaneously trying variations on the theme. Johnny Hodges suggests a bar on his alto saxophone, serpentine, firm, and ingratiating, and tied closely to Duke's theme. Harry Carney, baritone sax, may say it is too virtuoso for the whole sax section and clean it up a little, making it simpler. "Come on, you guys. Let's play so far," Duke says. As the band plays in unison, the players stimulate one another and new qualities appear; an experienced ear can hear Rex Stewart, trumpet, take an idea from Brown and embellish it a bit and give it his own twist. Duke raises his hand and the band stops playing. "On that last part—" he says, "trumpets, put a little more top on it, willya?" He turns to Junior Raglin, the scowling bass player, and says, "Tie it way down, Junior, tie it way down." Again they play, and now the bray of the trumpets becomes bolder and more sure, the trombones more liquid and clearer, the saxophones mellower, and at the bottom there is the steady beat, beat, beat, beat, four to a bar, of the drums, bass, and guitar, and the precise, silvery notes of Ellington on the piano, all of it growing, developing, fitting closer together, until Duke suddenly halts them by shouting, "Too much trombone!" Juan Tizol, a glum white man and the only player in the band who likes to play sweet, complains, "I think it's too gutbucket for this kind of piece. I'd like it more legit." He plays a smooth, clear curlicue on his valve trombone. "Well, maybe you're right," Duke says, "but I still think that when Sam gets into that plunger part, he should give it some smear." Again the band begins at the beginning, and as the boys play, Duke calls out directions. "Like old Dusty," he may say (Dusty is a long-dead jazz musician), and even as he says it the emphasis and shaping will change. Or he may lean forward and say to one man, "Like you did in 'The Mooche,'" or he may shout over to Carney, who doubles on the clarinet, "The clarinet is under Tricky too much!" As the music begins to move along, he shouts, "Get sincere! Give your heart! Let go your soul!" His hands flicker over the keyboard, sometimes coming in close together while he hunches his broad, quivering shoulders, one shoulder twisted higher than the other, an absorbed half-smile upon his face. At a signal from Duke, various players, with the theme now solidly in mind, will get up and take solos. He points at the soloist he wants and raises his right index finger, and as long as the player doesn't get too far away from the theme, Duke lets him have his way. Perhaps two hours have gone by. The sky is getting gray, but the boys have the feel of the piece and can't let it alone. They play on and on, their coats off, their hats on the backs of their heads, some with their shoes off, their stocking feet slapping up and down on the floor, their eyes closed, their feet wide apart and braced when they stand for a solo, rearing back as if they could blast farther and better that way. Now Juan Tizol grabs a piece of paper and a pencil and begins to write down the orchestration, while the band is still playing it.

Whenever the band stops for a breather, Duke experiments with rich new chords, perhaps adopts them, perhaps rejects, perhaps works out a piano solo that fits, clear and rippling, into little slots of silence, while the brass and reeds talk back and forth. By the time Tizol has finished getting the orchestration down on paper, it is already out of date. The men begin to play again, and then someone may shout "How about that train?" and there is a rush for a train that will carry the band to another engagement.

. . .

Duke likes trains because, as he says, "Folks can't rush you until you get off." He likes them, too, because dining-car waiters know about his love for food and he is apt to get very special attention. His journeys are punctuated by people who shove bits of paper at him for his autograph. Not long ago, travelling between Cleveland and Pittsburgh on a day coach, a German refugee with sad, weak blue eyes who had once played chamber music in Stuttgart sat down next to Duke and asked him for his autograph, and the two men got into conversation. A friend of Duke's with a historical turn of mind happened to be along on the trip and took notes on what the two men said. The refugee knew little about jazz, but he did know that Stokowski, Stravinsky, and Milhaud had described Ellington as one of the greatest modern composers.

"You can't write music right," Duke said, explaining his methods of composition, "unless you know how the man that'll play it plays poker."

"*Absolut phantastisch!*" the German murmured. Duke seemed startled, then laughed.

"Vot a varm, simple laugh you haf," the refugee said enviously.

Duke laughed again. "No, what I mean is," he said, "you've got to write with certain men in mind. You write just for their abilities and natural tendencies and give them places where they do their best—certain entrances and exits and background stuff. You got to know each man to know what he'll react well to. One guy likes very simple ornamentation; another guy likes ornamentation better than the theme because it gives him a feeling of being a second mind. Every musician has his favorite licks and you gotta write to them."

"His own licks? *Licks?*" asked the refugee.

"His own favorite figures," Duke said. He looked out the window. "I sure hated to leave that chick," he said affably. "I'd just met her. She was all wrapped up for me. All wrapped up in cellophane."

"Please?" asked the German.

"I know what sounds well on a trombone and I know what sounds well on a trumpet and they are not the same," Duke said. "I know what Tricky Sam can play on a trombone and I know what Lawrence Brown can play on a trombone and they are not the same, either."

"Don't you ever write just for inspiration?"

"I write for my band," Duke said. "For instance, I might think of a wonderful thing for an oboe, but I ain't got no oboe and it doesn't interest me. My band is my instrument. My band is my instrument even more than the piano. Tell you about me and music—I'm something like a farmer."

"A farmer that grows things?"

"A farmer that grows things. He plants his seed and I plant mine. He has to wait until spring to see his come up, but I can see mine right after I plant it. That night. I don't have to wait. That's the payoff for me."

"Mr. Ellington, how do you get those lovely melodic passages?"

"If you want to do a mellow cluster with a mixture of trombones and saxes, it will work very well," Duke said. "A real derby, not an aluminum one, will give you a big, round, hollow effect."

"A real derby?"

"A real derby."

"Not an aluminum derby?"

"Not an aluminum derby."

"*Phantastisch!*" the exile said.

Duke laughed. He called to Sonny Greer, his drummer, sitting up ahead, "I sure hated to miss that chick," he said. "She was all wrapped up in cellophane."

The refugee's pale blue eyes stared steadily at Duke. "When inspiration comes, Mr. Ellington," he said finally, "you write, *natürlich?*"

"It's mostly all written down, because it saves time," Duke said. He seemed eager to get away, but the coach was crowded and there wasn't another place to sit. "It's written down if it's only a basis for a change. There's no set system. Most times I write it and arrange it. Sometimes I write it and the band and I collaborate on the arrangement. Sometimes Billy Strayhorn, my staff arranger, does the arrangement. When we're all working together, a guy may have an idea and he plays it on his horn. Another guy may add to it and make something out of it. Someone may play a riff and ask, 'How do you like this?' The trumpets may try something together and say, 'Listen to this.' There may be a difference of opinion on what kind of mute to use. Someone may advocate extending a note or cutting it off. The sax section may want to put an additional smear on it."

"Schmear?"

"Smear," Duke said.

Duke tried a few times to end the discussion, but the exile's questioning kept bringing him back to his exposition, and he was still explaining when the train pulled into Pittsburgh, where he and his band were to give a concert at Carnegie Hall. The hall is a resplendent place. It has tall, gray marble columns with gilt Corinthian capitals, and on its walls are inscribed the names of Schubert, Brahms, Bach, Beethoven, Mozart, and Chopin. As the band trooped through the building to the dressing rooms, Duke glanced at the list of his predecessors and remarked, "Boys, we're in fast company."

FROM WITHIN TO WITHOUT

Geoffrey T. Hellman

APRIL 26, 1947 (ON LE CORBUSIER)

L E CORBUSIER, the Swiss-born French architect who for over twenty-
five years has been the world's most articulate and influential expo-
nent of modern architecture, is rarely satisfied with anything that
happens in building circles, but he was delighted, last December, when
the East River site was accepted by the United Nations for its headquarters. As a member of the United Nations Headquarters Commission, he
delivered a speech to this group's parent body, the General Assembly's
Headquarters Committee, in which he intimated that he had, in a way,
foreseen this decision long before the United Nations came into existence. Le Corbusier, who visited this country on a lecture tour in 1935,
bases his claim to prescience on an article he wrote while he was here.
Under the title "What Is America's Problem?" it appeared, in translation, in the *American Architect*. The passage that he likes to point out
reads:

> Manhattan—great unfilleted sole spread out on a rock—is no good
> except along the backbone; the edges are slums. . . . The edges
> along the East River and the Hudson are inaccessible. The ocean is
> inaccessible, invisible. . . . Yet all that ocean and those great rivers
> are invisible, and the advantages of their beauty, their space, their
> movement, and their lovely light under the sun, all that belongs to
> no one. New York, the immense ocean port, is for its inhabitants as
> inland as Moscow! And those splendid sites along the river, des-
> tined, it would seem, to receive immense apartment houses with

windows opening on space, these sites are desolating—for they are slums. By a well-advised municipal development, it would be easy to rehabilitate these districts and the profit would be sufficient to permit going ahead with rehabilitation of the center of the city, now all violence and anarchy.

Today, a well-advised development—although not a municipal one —is in hand for one of these sites, and Le Corbusier has a good deal to do with it. His conception of what the United Nations Headquarters ought to look like is revealed in the projects, never realized, that he has drawn up for a dozen cities, in Europe, North Africa, and South America, and in a series of buildings that the French government is about to construct, from his plans, in La Rochelle, a war-devastated town in western France, and La Pallice, its port, which during the war was a German submarine base. This conception calls for a group of glass-walled structures perched well above the ground on huge, reinforced-concrete piles, or *pilotis,* and set a few hundred yards apart to provide space in between for parks and athletic fields. Le Corbusier calls a group like this a vertical garden city. Wallace K. Harrison, the eminent American architect who is director of planning for the United Nations headquarters, admires Le Corbusier professionally and selected him as one of ten members of the United Nations Board of Design Consultants, which has been set up to help him design the United Nations buildings. However, Robert Moses, City Construction Coordinator and Mayor O'Dwyer's representative in United Nations negotiations, has little use for him. Moses is the possessor of an intransigence rivalled only by Le Corbusier's. His chauvinism is intense. As one of the chief plumpers for locating the United Nations headquarters in Flushing, he was distressed, last fall, when Le Corbusier, airing his views on that site in a report of the Headquarters Commission, said:

New York is a terrifying city. For us, it is menacing. We are not wrong in keeping it at a distance! . . . Flushing Meadow is not the site for the Headquarters of the United Nations, because Flushing Meadow is inescapably a suburb of New York, a dependency of New York. Now, the United Nations is neither a dependency of New York, nor of the United States of America. Freedom—not constraint—must at every minute be the dominant feeling. In no case must the United Nations become a corollary to America. To implant its Headquarters in the very shadow of the skyscrapers of Manhattan is inadmissible. The Manhattan skyscrapers are by their very nature too precarious; New York is a thrilling city but so questionable that it cannot take the Headquarters of the United Nations into its lap. This is a question of moral proportion. In fact, a question of "respectability."

The Rockefeller offer, paradoxically, seems to have dissipated Le Corbusier's terror of the city, and he now believes that a few East River skyscrapers, especially if designed on vertical-garden-city principles, might not be too precarious after all. Moses is still in favor of keeping Le Corbusier at a distance. "What do these foreign fellows know about our foundations, our hard-rock problems?" he said recently. It is probable that the United Nations buildings will show traces of Le Corbusier's influence, but it is also probable that they will rest on old-fashioned, orthodox foundations rather than on *pilotis*.

Along with the other consultants, Le Corbusier is working on plans in a drafting room on the twenty-seventh floor of the R.K.O. Building. He puts in his mornings on sketches and models. Afternoons, he and his colleagues attend staff meetings with Harrison and others. Harrison knows that Le Corbusier is one of the greatest designers in the world and also one of the most temperamental, and he has been handling him accordingly. Le Corbusier has responded with a great show of sweet reasonableness. "I am in complete calm here," he told a visitor to his working quarters the other day. "I think God has come down to earth. I don't even mind working in a room with other people. An architect shouldn't be alone. He can't do his best work without talking. Talking stimulates you. You develop ideas when you have an audience. And anyway, you don't have to listen to what the other man says." After spending the morning not listening to his colleagues, Le Corbusier usually repairs for lunch to Del Pezzo's, a casual Italian restaurant on West Forty-seventh Street, where he politely ignores the remarks of various friends.

Le Corbusier has spent many years in the study of *urbanisme,* a word that he feels embraces not only living in a city but the sociological and economic problems living in a city creates. His present benign state of mind about New York notwithstanding, this study has strengthened his conviction that he exists in a world of idiots, fools, and paupers who haven't the sense to realize how badly off they are. He is sure that slum dwellers, by and large, are not as unhappy as they ought to be. "I know that a proper plan can make New York the city par excellence of modern times," he wrote in *Quand les Cathédrales Etaient Blanches*, a fairly trenchant book about the United States that was one result of his lecture tour of this country in 1935, "can actively spread daily happiness for these oppressed families—children, women, men stupefied by work, stunned by noise of the rails of the subways or elevateds—who sink down each evening, at the end of their appointed tasks, in the impasse of an inhuman hovel." Nevertheless, he has noted with annoyance that some of the oppressed millions actually seem to perk up toward evening and go bowling or to the movies. His own capacity for moral indignation is boundless.

. . .

Le Corbusier's trip in 1935 seems to have been made under a misapprehension. That summer, Philip L. Goodwin, a trustee of the Museum of Modern Art, and at that time chairman of its Committee on Architecture, visited Le Corbusier in Paris and invited him to come here for a lecture tour. Goodwin said that the Museum would sponsor the tour and pay all expenses, and that the entire favorable difference, if any, between these costs and the lecture fees would go to Le Corbusier. The architect accepted this offer, but upon his arrival in New York he acted as though he hadn't completely understood it and was simply on a sightseeing junket in the course of which he would make a mint of money. His ship was met at Quarantine by Robert A. Jacobs, a young Manhattan architect who had served an apprenticeship with the Parisian architectural firm of Le Corbusier & P. Jeanneret a year before, and whom the Museum had engaged to act as Le Corbusier's interpreter on his American tour. "Jacobs," said Le Corbusier, "where are the photographers?" Jacobs, an obliging man who also admires Le Corbusier intensely, found that the press cameramen on board were busy taking pictures of other celebrities. He slipped a newspaperman five dollars and implored him to take a picture of Le Corbusier. "I've used up all my film," said the photographer, returning the money. Being an obliging fellow himself, however, he snapped his empty camera at Le Corbusier, who looked mollified. The Museum had arranged with the French Institute to put Le Corbusier up in a suite that this organization then maintained on its premises to accommodate visiting French notables, but when Le Corbusier heard about this plan, on his way uptown, he shook his head. *"Je m'en fiche de l'Institut Français,"* he said. *"Je vais au Waldorf."* Jacobs suggested that this might be too expensive, and Le Corbusier, who has always called the Modern Museum the Rockefeller Foundation, said that Mr. Rockefeller would foot the bill. Instead, Jacobs took him and his baggage direct to the Museum, where a press conference had been arranged. Le Corbusier's English is poor, and Joseph Alsop, of the *Herald Tribune*, undertook to help interpret it for the benefit of the less cultured reporters. "Your skyscrapers are too small," Le Corbusier said in the course of the conference, during which it quickly turned out that he knew at least enough English to be able to complain bitterly when he felt that Jacobs or Alsop had translated him inadequately. He also complained when the press photographers started to take pictures of him. According to witnesses, he pulled some studio portraits of himself out of a suitcase and offered to supply them to the newspapermen for five dollars apiece. "My God, you can't do that to the New York *Times*," said Miss Sarah Newmeyer, the Museum's publicity director. Le Corbusier pocketed his pictures and looked injured. (He afterward told Jacobs that he had wanted to help out the French photographers who had taken the pictures.) The interview over, he repeated his refusal to go to the French Institute, although by now he had lost interest in the Waldorf. "I wish to be where I can see Broadway," he said. Fernand Léger, the celebrated French painter, who is a friend of his, was living at the Park Central, so the Museum people got Le Corbusier a room there, on the twenty-fifth floor. His remark about the New York skyscrapers, which was widely repeated in the press, puzzled many readers, and he later said that he had only been joking when he made it; what he had really meant was that the tall buildings here were "little needles all crowded together," whereas "they should be great obelisks, far apart," with space between them for parks and athletic fields—Le Corbusier's ideal for any city.

Accompanied by Jacobs, Le Corbusier started his lecture tour a few days after his arrival. "Jacobs," he said several times, as he riffled through the newspapers of whatever city they happened to be in, "where is the picture they took of me on the boat?" In two months, he delivered twenty-three talks in nearly as many cities. One of them, at Columbia University, was to begin at eight-thirty in the evening, but he arrived half an hour late. Jacobs had delegated his wife to take Le Corbusier up there, and Mrs. Jacobs explained that they had started in time but that he had stopped the cab at a delicatessen on the way. He was finishing off a loaf of French bread as he mounted the platform. During his tour, he was amazed at the vast amounts of silverware that were provided for breakfast in bed at some of the big hotels, and he often enlivened this meal by clapping on his head the silver dome that covered his egg dish. He was also astonished by cellophane toothbrush containers, the ticket slots in the backs of train seats, and the paper wrappers on lump sugar. "In Paris," he said, "food hangs around unsanitarily but appetizingly."

Among the places Le Corbusier lectured at were Yale, Harvard, Princeton, Vassar, Bowdoin, Massachusetts Institute of Technology, the University of Minnesota, and the Philadelphia Art Alliance. During his stay in Philadelphia, George Howe, a famous architect of that city, was introduced, or reintroduced, to him. Howe had been taken to Le Corbusier's Paris apartment by a friend for a drink several years earlier; on this occasion, his host had ignored him for about half an hour and then asked him if he was an architect. Howe nodded. "Oh, I thought you were the naval officer from downstairs," said Le Corbusier. When they met again, in Philadelphia, Howe, who is no man to take umbrage at genius, volunteered to show Le Corbusier around the town. One of the buildings he pointed out was the Philadelphia Saving Fund Society, a notably modern skyscraper, which he and William Lescaze designed. His guest, who until then had been acting as though he still thought Howe was the naval officer from downstairs, gazed at this edifice with approbation. "*Ah, mon vieux,*" he said, "why don't we be partners the next time you have a big job?"

Le Corbusier likes to talk to young people at colleges, and he enjoyed his tour until, toward the end, it dawned on him that he had been put through a pretty heavy schedule and wasn't going to make much money out of it. His expenses came to about twelve hundred dollars. His lecture fees, most of which were seventy-five or a hundred dollars, added up to about eighteen hundred. The Museum gave him a check for the difference. It had also put on a show of his work and sent a couple of his architectural models on a travelling exhibition, from which they had by then returned in a somewhat damaged condition. Le Corbusier felt that the "Rockefeller Foundation" might have treated him more considerately. A few nights later he turned up at a dinner party waving a dollar bill. "This is what the Rockefeller Foundation paid me for my lecture tour," he said. His sorrow was the greater because on earlier lecture tours, in South America, he had been paid higher fees and been received with greater éclat. Mr. Goodwin took this fact, as well as Le Corbusier's astonishment at American hotel silverware and toothbrush containers, into consideration in an urbane letter he wrote to Le Corbusier just after he went back to France:

> I feel that some of your feeling in the matter has been entirely due to a false impression of North America. This is very often the case with foreigners who have been blinded by the money reputation that the country has got, and are absolutely in the dark as regards our methods of doing and living. South America is about as different as the planet Mars, and our actually democratic methods have almost ignored official welcomes to distinguished foreigners. . . . I hope that with time, a more adequate method of dealing with the problem will be possible, but at present it has to come out of the pockets of individuals or organizations interested in, or enthusiastic about, cultural matters and, as a general rule, these have not got large funds to dispose of. . . . I hope that you will come to the United States again and that you, as is often the case with foreigners, will enjoy your second trip much better after having seen the country and understood something more than its mechanical and flashy aspects.

Le Corbusier showed this letter around Paris for some time, advising anyone who would listen that America was the country of the dollar where you never saw the dollar.

Though Le Corbusier loudly expressed his disappointment in the Rockefellers, he actually has no great interest in money. The fusses he kicks up about it are more the result of wounded pride than a desire to get rich. "Intelligent things don't make money," he has said. "Money is the devil and it leads to lies, but it's good to have some in your pocket. I have a *trou de finance* in my head, not the bump. I don't want to be a millionaire or received in the fashionable world. I like friends and a few pleasures—those of the table, and others." He is troubled by moneyed atmosphere, and he thinks that such weather conditions are more oppressive in America than in most places. "Because of its financial control, the United States is the last country to awaken artistically," he says. In *Quand les Cathédrales Etaient Blanches,* he wrote:

> If you are an important businessman . . . you excite yourself with cocktails at five o'clock and are worth nothing afterward; before

the cocktails you were a power in Wall Street or in the midtown skyscrapers—a financial power, with monetary muscles: in that state you buy false Rembrandts. . . . Everyone knows that American millionaires, victims of the unlimited piles of gold which they have heaped up in the vicious circle of their own bank accounts, wish to raise up on the ossuary of their fated victims a socially useful edifice, a work of altruism, thought, instruction, and relief. During the homicidal battles in the Stock Exchange, relations between men are not involved, but rather the law of money. Money saved up by economies, gathered together in mountains, engaged in the channels of the infernal machine, takes on a movement which is all its own; it becomes a Niagara, drowns, breaks whatever is in its path, absorbs what is around it with the exactitude and fatality of a physical law, straightens up as a typhoon on the edge of the abyss which it has hollowed out. In order to set up a trophy, money makes hecatombs. . . . A mechanical, automatic, inhuman, cruel, and indeed a sterile game, since Mr. X or Mr. Y, on top of his mountain of gold, can do no more than sit down to a simple dinner of chicken and spinach—or to put it still more exactly, a bowl of semolina and milk. In this formidable game, in which he was victor, he lost his stomach.

Le Corbusier has rarely accumulated a mountain, or hill, of more than a few thousand francs. He likes to flex his monetary muscles, but only in small ways, and he does not care to be beholden to anyone. Years ago, a friend who had come into a modest legacy and knew that Le Corbusier was hard up mailed him a check. Le Corbusier called on his benefactor the next day and gave him hell. "I can't take your money," he said. "You know I can't stand feeling gratitude to anyone." This speech apparently having acted as a cathartic, he kept the check and cashed it without suffering any ill effects.

Le Corbusier's attitude toward finance, and toward a good many other things, is clearly set forth in "Urbanisme," a series of articles he wrote in his thirties for *L'Esprit Nouveau* (a long-defunct *avant-garde* Paris magazine of which he was co-publisher) and that was later published in book form. After recommending the demolition and reconstruction of the center of Paris, he suggested that part of the reconstructed area be set aside as a sort of colony for foreigners of all nations, "for would they not then take good care that it was not destroyed by long-range guns or bombing airplanes?" Warming to this theme, he came to the conclusion that the presence of this colony of aliens would be an insurance for the entire capital. "If twenty skyscrapers over five hundred feet in length and six hundred feet high were set thus in the center of Paris, Paris would be protected from all barbarian destruction," he wrote. "That should mean something to the War Office," he added hopefully. Having thus demonstrated the value of his project, Le Corbusier proceeded to show that it was economically feasible. "If a decree were passed for the general expropriation of the center of Paris," he began, "the value of the land would stand at a certain figure which we will call A. This figure can easily be ascertained by experts from the contemporary records of sales of land at various points in Paris. The value is thus A." The chapter in which this explicit passage occurred was headed "Finance and Realization."

. . .

The complete reconstruction of urban life is a continuing passion in Le Corbusier. Shortly after returning to Paris from his American lecture tour, he drew up a slum-clearance project, never put into effect, that provided for the conversion of a large section of the city into vertical-garden units. Soon thereafter, he visited Rio de Janeiro, where, at the invitation of the Brazilian government, he gave several lectures and acted as consultant to a group of local architects, who closely followed his recommendations when they designed a new Ministry of National Education and Public Health building. "In 1936," he says, "Brazil awoke after my presence." He went on to Buenos Aires and devised a master plan for that city, which was not used. Two years later, in Algiers, a city he has visited a number of times since 1930 in futile efforts to have it rebuilt according to his ideas, he worked up another unfulfilled project—a skyscraper office building for ten thousand workers, equipped with a novel form of air-admitting but sun-deflecting shutters outside its windows. This building, by concentrating so many people under one roof, would, he thought, centralize the business community and do away with a vast amount of street traffic.

Le Corbusier has an intense curiosity. He likes to explore strange cities at odd hours. In 1938, as he was studying a disreputable part of Algiers after midnight, taking illustrated notes on local *urbanisme* problems, he was so ruthlessly mugged by a gang of thieves that he was unconscious for nearly an hour. "Everything looked golden," he says. "I thought I was in Heaven." He dismissed this idea when he discovered that the bandits had removed not only his money, the loss of which he was philosophical about, but also his notes and sketches, about which he was not. For a while, he toyed with the notion that his attackers might have been partisans of the Ecole des Beaux-Arts, an institution whose architectural devotion to eclecticism he had derided in many articles and books, and of which he had written, two years before:

The distressing [architectural] ugliness of the nineteenth and twentieth centuries comes in a straight line from the schools. Design has killed architecture. Design is what they teach in the schools. The leader of these regrettable practices, the Ecole des Beaux-Arts in Paris, reigns in the midst of equivocation, endowed with a dignity which is only a usurpation of the creative spirit of earlier periods. It is the seat of a most disconcerting paradox, since under the ferrule of extremely conservative methods, everything is good will, hard work, faith. The dilemma is in the heart of the School, an institution which is in excellent health, like mistletoe, that lives on the sap of dignified and lofty trees, like cancer, which establishes itself comfortably around the pylorus of the stomach or around the heart. *The cancer is in excellent health!* Death is in excellent health.

At forty-nine, Le Corbusier is also in excellent health, but he sometimes jeopardizes this by a physical recklessness as immoderate as his literary style. He likes to swim tremendous distances. In the pleasant prewar days in Paris, he would close his architectural office for a month and, accompanied by his wife and his partner, a second cousin named Pierre Jeanneret, go to some seaside resort, generally on the French Riviera. While he was staying at Cap Martin, in the early spring of 1937, he went, on an out-of-season impulse, for a long swim in cold water. The nerves in his neck became inflamed and he was laid up for five months. The next year, at St. Tropez, he was swimming under water when a sizable yacht sailed over him. He saw its hull in time and remained under water until he thought it had passed. As he came up, however, the propeller struck him and one thigh was so badly ripped that it required a foot or so of stitches. One affliction of his, now apparently cured, was the result of a purely aesthetic pursuit. Until he became involved in the United Nations project, he had painted nearly every morning since he was thirty-five, always standing while he worked and resting most of his weight on his right leg. After several years, he developed a painful varicose condition, which he called "the paralysis of the painter."

Le Corbusier prides himself on his will power, and this pride, rather than any apprehensiveness about his health, prompted him, shortly before the last war, to give up smoking. All day long, for two decades, he had smoked cigarettes, cigars, and pipes. He had finally come to own sixty pipes, and he had his suits made with a pocket that would hold a box of two hundred and fifty kitchen matches, of which he used up a box a day. Then, one day, a friend of his, André Jaoul, a prominent French industrialist, told him he had given up smoking. "Very few people could do a thing like that after so many years," he said. "You think I can't?" said Le Corbusier. "I doubt it," said Jaoul. Le Corbusier, who has an idea that big business is inimical to his kind of city planning, is no man to be outdone by an industrialist. He tossed away the cigar he was puffing, put his sixty pipes in a bureau drawer, and telephoned his tailor to omit the special pocket from a suit that was in progress. He hasn't smoked since. "I was profoundly tempted at banquets on site-inspecting tours I made last year," he says. "All those excellent cigars we were offered in Boston, Philadelphia, and San Francisco! But I resisted. It's a joke, in a way, but I don't treat it as such. Discipline is essential." Le Corbusier, who was probably the first architect to state the now famous modernist doctrine that building plans should proceed "from within to without," feels that his renunciation of smoking is in a sense like his lifelong fight against the Beaux-Arts school of architecture. For him to light up a White Owl now would be the equivalent, morally, of putting an Italian Renaissance façade on a building or providing it with a mansard roof instead of a flat one on which to sun-bathe and grow wild flowers.

• • •

Le Corbusier rarely relaxes. His face, mobile and animated when he is speaking, is tense even in repose. He loves to talk to people he feels are responsive. His voice is low, gentle, insistent, and musical; his characteristic expression is one of intelligent observation. He thinks about architecture, or form and color in general, most of the time. Even when he is sitting on a beach, he manages to keep busy. He examines the architectural structure of pebbles, shells, and bits of wood. They often turn up in his paintings, though sometimes in rather abstract form. His interest in food is similarly professional; he especially admires the structure of melons, in which he sees no traces of a regrettable eclecticism. He also approves of bee cells, since bees, like himself, distinguish between the wall as an insulating factor and the wall as a supporting factor.

The war slowed Le Corbusier down as an architect, but it provided him, for a while, with extra time in which to examine pebbles. In June, 1940, when France fell, he and Jeanneret were in Aubusson, working on plans for a cartridge factory there. After the armistice, they decided not to return to Occupied Paris, and, accompanied by Mme. Le Corbusier, drove to the Pyrenees village of Ozon, near an electro-chemical plant for which the two partners had designed buildings. The factory was in need of certain alterations, but the work didn't amount to much and Le Corbusier was soon reduced to bicycling, painting, swimming, and inspecting pebbles. After four months of this idling, Jeanneret went to live with friends in Grenoble. Le Corbusier returned to Paris, and then went to Algiers, where he resumed his studies of the local *urbanisme* problem. In 1942, he returned to France. The Vichy government, perhaps suspecting that it was dealing with a dissident spirit, told him that he would have to have a new license if he wished to resume the practice of architecture in France. "We'll consider your case and act accordingly," an official informed him. "I was not appointed to the Committee to Normalize Building, which the Vichy government set up," Le Corbusier said recently. "I was given no work in France until the Liberation. I was denounced as a Communist and threatened with arrest, but I never became a Communist, although my city-planning philosophy implies capitalist reforms. The Communists asked me to join their party, but I told them it was they who ought to join me. The Pétain government invited me to go on one of those artists' trips to Germany, but I declined. I spent most of my time painting. The Germans never touched Picasso or me. It would have made too much of a scandal. The only time I talked to a German was in 1942, when I went to the chief of artistic propaganda to protest against the banning of a Fernand Léger exhibition. He said that Léger had gone to the United States, so they couldn't show his paintings." During the war, Le Corbusier was lower in funds than usual, and he was helped out by friends. He had so little to eat that he suffered from two hernias, for which he had to have operations. His wife fared just as badly. Coming home one evening, he found her lying on the kitchen floor with a broken leg. A doctor said that malnutrition had caused a bone in the leg to break.

Even before the war, Le Corbusier, although he was better known than any other French architect—and probably than *any* other architect

—had never been given government work in France. He attributes this neglect to the hostility of academicians high in the government. After the Liberation, he began to come into his own, and it was not long before he became a bureaucrat himself. In 1945, he founded a new, cooperative architectural firm, Atelier des Bâtisseurs, or Atbat, but he did not invite his old partner, Jeanneret, to join the firm, apparently because he felt that Jeanneret's decision to leave him to go to live in Grenoble during the war was not the act of a friend. Jeanneret, who eventually became active in the Resistance movement in France, is now designing furniture in Paris. Le Corbusier is president of Atbat, with which twenty-five young architects and engineers are associated. "For thirty years, I'd been a consultant talking in the desert," he has said. "Since 1945, I've led the architectural movement in France. I arrive at a stage where many things in my life flower, like a tree in season." This sense of burgeoning was induced by his assignment to plan the reconstruction of La Rochelle and La Pallice; by his appointment to head a governmental Cultural Relations mission to the United States in 1945 to report on the progress of American architecture since 1939; by his being chosen, in February, 1946, the French delegate to the United Nations Headquarters Commission; and, a year later, by his elevation to membership in the United Nations Board of Design Consultants.

In these last three capacities, Le Corbusier has spent most of the past fifteen months adjusting himself to New York. His wife, who is not in good health, did not accompany him here, and he flies back to Paris every three or four months to visit her. He is living in the Grosvenor, at Fifth Avenue and Tenth Street, where he has converted his bathroom into a painting studio. He sometimes feels lonely, a sensation that he hints at in a passage that occurs in the Headquarters Commission's official report, a section of which he wrote:

Whether his stay be long or short, the [transient United Nations employee] is a traveller; that is, a man snatched from his usual habits, uprooted from his home. The major part of his day is taken up by his mission. But, as all travellers, he will fall upon many empty and often depressing hours. This man must be taken care of, appropriate facilities must provide for his well-being and for proper mental stimulation. The success of his mission will in great part depend on his physical and mental equilibrium. When his daily work is over, he must not be left derelict.

Le Corbusier, who was born Charles Edouard Jeanneret, didn't bother to provide himself with a first name when, some twenty-five years ago, he decided to adopt the name by which he is now famous, so he just signed this report Le Corbusier, but he has permitted himself to be identified as Charles Le Corbusier on the rosters of the Headquarters Commission and the Board of Design Consultants. His pleasure in being a bureaucrat got a big fillip last October, when he received a letter from the *Biographical Encyclopædia of the World,* saying that it would like to include him in the "Who's Important in Government" section of its next edition. The encyclopedia, it appeared, also contained a section on "Who's Important in Art." He was delighted at being tapped for the bureaucratic category of the book and didn't mind being left out of the art section. He filled out the necessary forms with alacrity. His well-being and mental stimulation have been somewhat provided for by a number of friends here—notably José Luis Sert, an architect and city planner who once served an apprenticeship with Le Corbusier & P. Jeanneret, and Constantino Nivola, a young Italian painter who lives on Eighth Street. Sundays, when Le Corbusier gets tired of painting in his bathroom, he sometimes drops in at Nivola's studio and spends several hours painting there. The first time he went around, he examined his host's work and then launched into a thirty-minute exposition of what he thought was wrong with it. He made notes and sketches as he talked, and presented them to Nivola. Nivola decided, after some contemplation, that there was a good deal in what Le Corbusier had said. The Nivolas and the Serts frequently dine with Le Corbusier at the Jumble Shop, an Eighth Street restaurant, or at the Monte, an Italian eating place on Macdougal Street. The Monte is in a dark and windowless basement, a setting as remote from Le Corbusier's favorite architectural concept—a glass-walled structure set above the ground on *pilotis*—as anything could well be. "My God, a cavern!" he exclaimed the first time he was taken there. He felt better after eating a plate of excellent spaghetti. "It's strange," he said. "I should be against this place, but it's really not so bad."

When he is not with close friends, Le Corbusier often displays a lively sense of his own importance. The fact that he is the world's most influential architect is not universally recognized in this country, and last year, while the United Nations Headquarters Commission subcommittee to which he was attached as an expert was making its site-inspecting jaunts about the country, he was always offended when the newspaper photographers asked him to step aside while they took pictures of city officials and subcommittee members. They made this request because a commission delegate was considered to belong to a bureaucratic echelon inferior to that of subcommitteemen and municipal officeholders. "I have never had to deal with such imbeciles in my life," he grumbled after being invited to get out of a photograph in Philadelphia. Dr. Eduardo Zuleta-Angel, a Colombian, who was head of the Headquarters Committee, is a great admirer of Le Corbusier, and he tried to salve his feelings, and also gain some useful advice, by taking him up in a helicopter to inspect the land that Philadelphia was offering the United Nations. On the whole, Le Corbusier was favorably impressed by Philadelphia. He also liked Boston, despite a rather unfortunate incident at a dinner tendered him and his colleagues at the Harvard Club of Boston. According to Le Corbusier, a bishop and a lawyer flanking him at the table persisted in talking across him to each other. He did not consider the fact that his English is poor and that his dinner neighbors' French was worse a mitigating circumstance, and presently he picked up his chair and moved it next to Serge Koussevitzky, a French-speaking guest. Before Rockefeller made his offer of the East River area, Le Corbusier had been inclined to regard San Francisco, where his inspection group spent three days, as the best site. "The receptions there included ladies," he says. "At Boston and Philadelphia, they were stag."

. . .

These days, in addition to working on plans for United Nations buildings and holding conferences with Reynal & Hitchcock, who, having just published a translation of his *Quand les Cathédrales Etaient Blanches,* are planning to bring out another book of his, *Inexpressible Space,* Le Corbusier frequently shows up in Harrison's office with new tables of organization for the United Nations headquarters project, in which his name and the names of his disciples are prominently displayed. Harrison, who admires Le Corbusier more as an architect than as a bureaucrat, tactfully clears his throat. Le Corbusier is also working on plans for a model of a typical Le Corbusier vertical garden city, which he figures can be put on the market as a useful educational toy, and he is promoting a tape measure of his devising, seven and a half feet long, which he calls the Règle d'Or. The Règle d'Or is based on the proportions of the human body, or, at any rate, the human body in the form of a man standing up with his arm raised comfortably high over his head. This measure is bisected by a line running down the middle of its entire length and is ruled off, horizontally, on either side by lines at varying intervals. These intervals, taken in threes, bear the same ratio to each other as the distance between the standing man's fingertips and the top of his head, the distance between the top of his head and his solar plexus, and the distance from there to his heels. The sum of the first two of these distances is equal to the third. Le Corbusier worked this out with his own body as source material, but he says it applies to everyone. According to him, the measure embodies many historically accepted formulas for calculating the rules of proportion and is invaluable in designing windows, doors, walls, formats for books, or anything else in which proportion is a factor. He hopes that it will become a universal instrument, and he believes that, if adopted on a worldwide scale, it would break down nationalism by making all doors and windows in the same proportion, thus setting up a kind of architectural Esperanto of good design. John D. Dale, president of Charles Hardy, Inc., a Manhattan engineering firm, is manufacturing this device, which is to be sold to architects and engineers under the name of Modulor. Each one will bear Le Corbusier's signature and will be accompanied by a thirty-page explanatory booklet Le Corbusier has written.

Last June, Sert's partner in an architectural firm here, Paul Lester Wiener, who is a friend of Einstein's, took Le Corbusier to Einstein's house, in Princeton, so that the architect could get Einstein's opinion of his measure. With Wiener translating Le Corbusier's artistic terms into mathematical terms and Le Corbusier waggling his Règle d'Or at Einstein, the two men had a lengthy technical conversation. Einstein is probably the only man in the world in whose presence Le Corbusier would feel like a disciple instead of a master, but even so his eagerness to explain his ideas about proportion was so acute that he interrupted Einstein in mid-exposition several times. "It's a new language of proportions," Einstein finally said of the Règle d'Or, "which expresses the good easily and the bad only with complications." Le Corbusier, who took this to mean that his baby would eliminate the bad, beamed. He assumed a pleased, almost diffident expression when Wiener, at the end of their visit, produced a camera and took a photograph without asking him to get out of the picture.

The United Nations building plans are supposed to be completed by July, and Le Corbusier expects to return to Paris then. He likes the idea of going back to live in a place where people say *"Bon jour, Corbu"* to him on the street, but he thinks that he will miss New York. "This is a funny country," he told an American friend one night recently. "Your hospitality is Draconian, and your convictions are too tied up with finance. Money is ferocious here. Your brutality turns sensitive people into Surrealists. But the country has an extra cipher in population and money—it is *alive,* and everything is possible in it. All life is poisoned by the disorderliness of your cities; people look like cockroaches from your skyscrapers, and, oh, the loneliness of your large crowds, the anonymity of your cafeterias! No *terrasses de café* here, where three or four friends can talk over an apéritif—not that I ever have time for this in Paris. I was astonished by the fact that Americans never climb stairs. They will lose their legs. I'm the only man here who climbs stairs two at a time. Your escalators are undignified. New York is a turntable where you meet everyone in the world. I often ride the Third Avenue 'L' at two in the morning, looking at all the Negresses and Chinese dead of fatigue. I like the light here. Paris is gray—it used to be white—and Zurich is greenish, but New York is a red city—the color of blood and life. Everything in it arouses both enthusiasm and disgust; it reflects God and the Devil. Its potentiality is terrific. Your sky at night is formidable. It's terrible to soil it with General Motors and Lucky Strike publicity. The beauty of the sky should belong to the people. I like your restaurants, and the great freshness in young people here. And how can one be bored in a city in which the young women wear crowns of flowers and in which the houses are red?"

THE GREAT FOREIGNER

Niccolò Tucci

NOVEMBER 22, 1947 (ON ALBERT EINSTEIN)

THERE IS SUCH A THING as being a foreigner, but not in the sense implied by passports. Foreigners exist, to be sure, but they may be found only in places where it would be impossible to discover a single policeman or a single immigration official—in the field of the intellect. A man who achieves anything great in any province of the mind is, inevitably, a foreigner, and cannot admit others to his province. If you are one of his own people, you will, of course, find him, because you yourself are there, but if you are not, your knowledge of him will be mostly confined to the petty intelligence of the gossip columns. Now, we all know from experience what it means, in this sense, to be refused entry, even as a temporary visitor, into this or that foreigner's domain. We meet a great man and cannot talk to him, because, alas, we happen not to be able to get interested in the thing in which he excels. Silly though it seems, this is humiliating, for it makes us aware of our limitations. Yet that feeling is soon forgotten. There are people today, however, whose foreignness can't be forgotten, and these are the physicists, who have done things to us that keep us wondering, to say the least. They have lessened—in fact, almost destroyed—our hopes of a quiet and happy future. It is true that they have also increased our hopes of surviving discomfort and disease, but, oh, how far away that seems, and how near seems the possibility of extermination! That is why, when my mother-in-law, who flew over from Europe a couple of weeks ago, said that she wanted me to accompany her on a visit to the home of her friend Albert Einstein, in Princeton, I was very reluctant to go.

I had seen Einstein several times in the past eight or nine years, and on the last occasion—in 1942, I believe—I had been bold enough to invite him to come out of his inaccessible territory and into that of all the unscientific people, like myself. Would he, I asked, explain, in words rather than in mathematical symbols, what he and his colleagues actually meant by the fourth dimension? And he did, so simply and so clearly that I left his house with an uncontrollable feeling of pride. Here, I, the living negation of anything even slightly numerical, had been able to understand what Einstein had said—had *really* said, for he had said it not only in his conversation with me but years before in his theories. Obviously, he had explained to me merely what a child would be able to grasp, but it impressed me as much more because my schoolteachers and my father, all of them less great than Einstein, had never forgone a chance to make me feel a perfect fool (and to tell me, lest I should have missed drawing the inference), even when they spoke to me about fractions or equations of the first degree. I consequently realized that Einstein belonged to the extremely rare type of foreigner who can come out of his seclusion and meet aliens on alien ground. Yet, much as I cherished the recollection of that pleasant experience, I did not think it altogether advisable to try my luck again. "This time," I said to my mother-in-law, who is called Bice in the family, "he may easily make me feel like a fool. Besides, in 1942 Einstein's achievements did not keep me awake at night, as they do now. If I saw him now, I would not be moved by the slightest scientific curiosity about his work. I would much rather ask him what he thinks of the responsibility of modern scientists, and so forth. It might be quite unfair to him and unpleasant for me."

Well, mothers-in-law must have secret ways of persuasion, because a few days later I gave in, not only on seeing Einstein but also on taking along Bimba, my six-year-old daughter. "All right," I said resignedly, "but you, Bimba, will be sorry for this. You don't know who Einstein is. He has all the numbers; they *belong* to him. He will ask you how old you are." And I must say here that Bimba, even more than myself, is the mathematical scandal of our family. She tries to count her six years on her fingers, but she forgets how high she has counted and must try again. Upon a guarantee from me that Einstein would not interview her on that delicate subject, we made peace and departed. On our way out of the apartment, we met my eight-year-old son, Vieri, who was playing ball on the sidewalk.

"Vieri," I said, "want to come and see Einstein?"

"Einstein the great mathematician?" he asked.

"Yes," I said.

"Naw," he said. "I have enough arithmetic in school."

. . .

On the train that morning, my mother-in-law and I talked a great deal about Maja, Einstein's younger sister, one of two links Bice has with higher mathematics. But I must say that she is a weak link, because Maja is the opposite of all abstraction. She looks exactly like her brother (one would almost say that she, too, needs a haircut), but she is a Tuscan peasant, like the people who work in the fields near her small estate of Colonnata, just outside Florence. Even her frame of mind is, in spite of her cosmopolitan culture, Tuscan. Whatever in conversation does not make sense to her in plain, human terms she will quickly dismiss with a witty remark. But before becoming a Tuscan peasant, Maja was a brilliant young German student of philosophy in Paris. She interrupted her studies to take a job as governess in charge of young Bice, whose mother had just died, leaving her the only female of the family, surrounded by a number of older brothers and her father. All this happened forty years ago. Soon after her arrival in the family, Maja became Bice's second mother and dearest friend. Even after Maja resumed her studies and got married, they remained very close, and did not lose touch with each other until shortly before the outbreak of the recent war, when Maja left Italy to join her brother in Princeton. And today Bice, accompanied by a somewhat impatient son-in-law and by a pestiferous young angel of a granddaughter, was rushing to Princeton for the great reunion.

On the way, we also talked pleasantly about America (like all Europeans who come here for the first time, Bice was eager to know about everything in the first week), we discussed the fate of the world and the wisdom of those who run it, we quarrelled over theology (Bice is fond of theologies, with a marked preference for her own, the Roman Catholic), and finally I noticed that she wasn't listening to me any more. She frowned, she shook her head, then she smiled and nodded, staring in front of her, but not at me and not at Bimba. I knew that she was making an inventory of her sentimental luggage. All the news of the troubled years, from the death of her eldest son in the war to the latest item of family gossip, from the bombings of towns to the latest method of making a pound of sugar last a year, were being called to mind, so that everything would surely be ready for Maja. I made a sign to Bimba not to interrupt her grandmother, and Bimba sat there and stared, somewhat frightened by this woman who was looking so intently at her own life.

When we arrived in Princeton, it was quite misty, and there was a threat of rain in the Indian summer air. At the station, we took a cab and soon learned that the driver, a young student, was the son of a friend of ours in Florence. He was trying to make enough money driving a cab to finance a trip to South America. Our conversation with him was so interesting that only the sight of open country around us made us realize that we had driven all the way out of town. We drove back and stopped in front of a house on Mercer Street. I had forgotten the exact address, but this house looked like the right one. In her eagerness, Bice ran ahead of me toward the door, but the reunion could not take place, because, as we discovered when we rang the bell, it was the wrong house. Luckily for us, the cab was still there, so we drove along a little, and finally, after ringing the bells of two other families that refused, not without sorrow, to be the Einsteins, we decided upon one more house, which happened to be the right one. Miss Dukas, Einstein's secretary, greeted us at the door; then came Margot, his delicate and silent stepdaughter, who looks so much like a Flemish painting; and Chico, the dog, who tried to snatch Bimba's red ribbons from her pigtails.

"Bimba," I said, "don't get the dog excited. Remember how he ate your doll five years ago. Now, if you are not very quiet today, I am going to ask you in front of Einstein how much makes three and two—understand?"

She nodded, and whispered, "Four?"

We were asked to wait for a moment in the small anteroom that leads to the dining room. Maja was upstairs; she was being helped out of bed and into the chair in which she spends most of her day. She is recovering from a long illness, which has delayed her return to Italy, so it was only natural that this reunion should be delayed until she was ready and comfortable. And yet this addition of even a few minutes to years of separation created an effect of absurdity. One always imagines that the crossing of the last span of a trip bridging years will be something impulsive: when all the *real* impediments, such as continents, oceans, and passports, have been overcome, friends should run into each other's arms as fast as they can. Still, it is never quite that way. We become so used to living at a distance that we slowly begin to live *with* it, too; we lean on it, we share it, in equal parts, with our faraway friends, and when it's gone and we are again there, corporeally present, we feel lost, as if a faithful servant had abandoned us.

To fill in those extra minutes, we began to look at the furniture in the anteroom and dining room, and I noticed again what I had noticed five years ago in those same rooms: everything suggested the house of a faculty member of a German university. I could not trace this impression to any particular object. The large dining-room table in the center, with the white tablecloth on it, was not particularly German, nor was the furniture in the anteroom, but there was the same quiet atmosphere of culture that had impressed me so deeply in the houses of university professors, in Freiburg, Leipzig, and Berlin, to which my parents had taken me when I was a boy and spent my summers travelling over Europe. It is something that remains suspended in the air almost as stubbornly as the smell of tobacco; one might say that the furniture had been seasoned with serious conversation. Curiously, it is an atmosphere that can never be found in the apartment of a diplomat, even if he is the son of a professor and has inherited his father's furniture.

· · ·

We were finally called upstairs by Margot, who then disappeared into her study. Bice's impatience was such that, not finding Maja in the first room we entered, she said disappointedly, "Not here," and ran toward a closed door to open it, like a child playing hide-and-go-seek. This search lasted only a matter of seconds, because the house isn't large enough for a long search. But by the time we reached Maja, Bice seemed almost to have lost hope that she would ever get there. Maja was standing near her chair waiting, quiet, dignified, almost ironical, under a cloud of white hair. She never shows any emotion, never speaks louder than a whisper, and never more than a few appropriate words—just like the Tuscan peasants, with the difference that when *they* whisper, they might as well be addressing a crowd across a five-acre field.

The "How well you look!" and "How unchanged you are!" were soon over, and then the Great Foreigner arrived, pipe in hand and smiling gently. He complimented Bice on looking just the same as ever, and received the same compliment with grace, then inquired about Michele, Bice's eldest brother and her second link with higher mathematics. Uncle Michele is a gentle little man who sits in Bern, Switzerland, and looks out into the world, leaning on a white beard that descends from almost under his blue eyes to the end of his necktie. Every night for twenty years, in the company of a friend, he has looked into *The Divine Comedy*, taking time off to look into his soul with a fierce, puritanical spirit tempered by a great deal of natural goodness; he has also looked into the field of economics, trying to find mathematical formulae to solve the crisis of the world; and for a long time, in the company of Einstein, he looked into the mysteries of higher mathematics. We had just finished hearing all about Uncle Michele's health and his many grandchildren when Bice seemed suddenly to recall an extremely urgent matter—as if, indeed, it were the very reason she had flown all the way over here from Europe. "Herr Professor," she asked, in German (the whole conversation, in fact, was in German), "this I really meant to ask you for a long time—why hasn't Michele made some important discovery in mathematics?"

"*Aber, Frau Bice,*" said Einstein, laughing, "this is a very good sign. Michele is a humanist, a universal spirit, too interested in too many things to become a monomaniac. Only a monomaniac gets what we commonly refer to as *results.*" And he giggled happily to himself.

Then we spoke about dreams. Bice told us two symbolic dreams she had had years ago; I told the dream that the grandfather of a friend of mine had had the day before he died; Einstein told an absurd dream of his. He seemed the only one to find the conversation interesting, which it was not. Bice was now sleepy (the emotion had been too great for her); Maja sat silent and ate her lunch, which a nurse had brought in on a tray; and I nodded to Einstein's words, searching impatiently for a way out of dreams to the subject of the responsibility of modern scientists. But the atmosphere somehow weighed on me. The mist was getting thicker, and it had begun to rain, with that quick, fingertip drumming on the leaves, on the roof, on some pail outside, that makes you go to sleep. It was dark in the room now. The only points of light were the white of the bed, the white of the nurse's uniform, and the white of Maja's hair and of Einstein's head against the window—and his laughing eyes, his voice, and the joy that sprang from him. "Damn the responsibility of modern scientists on a damp day like this," I thought. It made me both envious and angry to see this man in front of me who laughed so heartily at the most trivial things, who listened with such concentration to our nonsense, who was so full of life while I could see no reason even for breathing in that damp, misty air. "Why is he so young," I asked myself, "and what makes him laugh so? Is he making fun of us, or what is this?" Then I began to understand. He had just come from the other room; he was stretching his mind; he was "abroad." All these words were only formally addressed to us; actually they were references to some demonstration he must have received, in the heart of his own secret country, that something was exactly as he had suspected it would be. Yes, it could be nothing but this: he had done fruitful work that morning. I saw it now because I recognized myself in him—not as a scientist, alas, but as a child of seven, at which age it was my hobby to make locomotives with tin cans and old shaving brushes (the smokestack with the smoke). The *situation* was the same. When the joy of toymaking became too great, I had to interrupt my work and run to the living room, where the grownups were boring themselves to death. And I laughed at their words without bothering to inquire what they meant; I found them interesting, new, exciting; I was praised for being such good company while in actuality I was still playing with my locomotive—I was deciding in my mind what colors I would paint it, what I would use for wheels and lanterns—and it was good to know that no one shared my secret. "You and your toys," I thought, looking at Einstein with the envy that an ailing old man has for a young athlete.

· · ·

Lunch was announced, and we went downstairs, leaving Maja alone. The smell of food consoled me for my humiliation. I began to eat. Einstein asked Bice for her impression of America, and she expressed her disappointment at the bad manners of children in this country. This led to a family argument, in which Einstein was asked to act as arbiter. Bice claimed that American children (she meant mine, of course) have no respect for the authority of their parents, or for that of such people as park attendants. To prove her point, she said that, on the day before, Vieri and his friend Herbert had laughed in the face of a park attendant when he told them not to play ball. Yes, they had obeyed him in the end, but not without making strange noises in his honor. (She didn't know the name for this Bronx ceremony.) I conceded that this was frightful, but I reminded her that a park attendant in Europe was a sort of Commander-in-Chief of Leaves and Flowers and First Admiral of Public Fountains and of the paper boats in them. Even a smile addressed to him without proper authorization was considered daring. "When I was a boy in Italy, we never questioned anyone's authority," I said, "and thus we passed, with the most perfect manners, from the hands of our nurses to those of our tyrants."

As moderator, Einstein asked me how I had managed to lose authority over my children.

"I didn't have to work much," I replied. "It was rather simple. I just told them, 'Look at the kind of world in which we live. See what we, the grownups, are able to invent, from passports to radioactive clouds.'"

Bice contended that nothing is gained by embittering the lives of children with remarks of that nature, but Einstein was in full agreement with me when I answered that less than nothing is gained—in other words, that much is lost—by lulling them into the illusion that all is as it should be in the world. "You, as a scientist," I said to Einstein, "know that the world is round and not divided naturally by cow fences into holy, restricted fatherlands. When you were young, there was still a semblance of good in governments and institutions, but today—see where we are today."

He became very serious, as if he were seeing where we are today, but suddenly a smile lit up in his eyes, and it quickly spread all over his face and beyond it. He laughed happily, then said, "Let me tell you what happened to me years ago, before the other war, when there were no passports. The only two countries that required them were Russia and Rumania. Now, I was in Hungary and had to go to Rumania. I didn't know where and how to apply for a passport, but I was told that it wasn't necessary. There was a man who had a passport of his own, and he was kind enough to let anybody use it to cross the border. I accepted the offer, but when they asked me at the frontier what my name was, I said, 'Wait a moment,' took out the passport from my pocket, and had a great deal of trouble trying to find out who I was. Now, to go back to your point, I agree with you that those who exercise any kind of authority, be it the authority of a father or that of a government, have a definite obligation to show that they deserve respect, but the trouble with grownups in our day is that they have lost the habit of disobedience, and they should quickly learn it again, especially when it comes to the infringement of their individual rights." He laughed again, this time like a bad boy, then, shaking his head, said, "These grownups. Isn't it terrible how readily *they* will obey?"

"Take the loyalty test for federal employees, against which so few have protested," I said.

"That is a case in point," he answered. "People are asked to be loyal to their jobs. But who wouldn't be loyal to his job? Too many people, indeed. Also in Italy and in Germany they used to test people's loyalty to their jobs, and they found a far greater loyalty to jobs than to democracy. But now tell me another thing. What do you give to your children in the way of *good* news about the world?"

"Plenty," I said. "For example, I tell them about Socrates, who was killed by the greatest democracy on earth for standing at the corner drugstore and asking questions that made the politicians feel uncomfortable."

"That's not a cheerful story, either," he said, "but if they were able to absorb some of the spirit of the Greeks, that would serve them a great deal later on in life. The more I read the Greeks, the more I realize that nothing like them has ever appeared in the world since."

"You read the Greeks?" I said.

"But of course," he replied, slightly surprised at my amazement. And so I heard, partly from him and partly from Miss Dukas, that he reads the Greeks to Maja every night for an hour or so, even if he has had a very tiring day. Empedocles, Sophocles, Aeschylus, and Thucydides receive the tribute of the most advanced and abstract modern science every night, in the calm voice of this affectionate brother who keeps his sister company.

"You know," I said, "that is great news. Young Americans, who have an idea of the pure scientist worthy of the comics, should be told that Einstein reads the Greeks. All those who relish the idiotic and dangerous myth of the scientist as a kind of Superman, free from all bonds of responsibility, should know this and draw their conclusions from it. Many people in our day go back to the Greeks out of sheer despair. So you too, Herr Professor, have gone back to the Greeks."

He seemed a little hurt. "But I have never gone away from them," he said. "How can an educated person stay away from the Greeks? I have always been far more interested in them than in science."

Lunch was over, and Einstein announced that he was going to go upstairs for his nap. Bice was assigned, for hers, a couch under a red-nosed portrait of Schopenhauer in the library-and-music room. The sun was shining again, so Bimba was told that she could go out to the garden to play, and I went for a walk around the town.

. . .

When, after an hour or so, I came back to the house, I found Bimba still in the garden. I was quite disappointed to hear that I had missed an extraordinary event. Just after I had left and just as Einstein started to go upstairs, Bimba had asked him to play the violin for her. He had not touched his instrument for almost a year, but he took it out and played Bimba a few bars from a Mozart minuet.

I saw Einstein on the porch, waving to me. I joined him there and sat down next to him while he stretched his legs on a deck chair and leaned back, one hand behind his head, the other holding his pipe in mid-air. I had a volume of the German translation of Plato by Preisendanz in my briefcase and asked his permission to read aloud a passage from *Gorgias*. He listened patiently and was very amused by Socrates' wit. When I was through, he said, "Beautiful. But your friend Plato"—and he extended his pipe in such a way that it became Plato—"is too much of an aristocrat for my taste."

"But you would agree," I said, "that all the qualities that make for a democratic attitude *are* noble qualities?"

"I would never deny that," he said. "Only a noble soul can attain true independence of judgment and exercise respect for other people's rights, while any so-called nobleman prefers to conceal his vulgarity behind such cheap shields as an illustrious name and a coat of arms. But, you see, in Plato's time and even later, in Jefferson's time, it was still possible to reconcile democracy with a moral and intellectual aristocracy, while today democracy is based on a different principle—namely, that the other fellow is no better than I am. You will admit that this attitude doesn't altogether facilitate emulation."

There was a silence, and he interrupted it, almost talking to himself. "I lived for a while in Italy," he said, "and I think that the Italians are among the most humane people in the world. When I want to find an example of a naturally noble creature, I must think of the Italian peasants, the artisans, the very simple people, while the higher you go in Italian society . . ." and as he lifted his pipe a little, it became a contemptible specimen of a class of Italians he does not admire.

A small airplane was appearing and disappearing between treetops, and gargling noisily right into our conversation.

"In the past," said Einstein, "when man travelled by horse, he was never alone, never away from the measure of man, because"—he laughed—"well, the horse, you might say, is a human being; it *belongs* to man. And you could never take a horse apart, see how it works, then put it together again, while you can do this with automobiles, trains, airplanes, bicycles. Modern man is besieged by mechanics. And even more ominous than this invasion of our lives is the rise of a class of people born of the machine, so to speak—people to whom certain powers must be delegated without the moral screening of a democratic process. I mean the technicians. You can't elect them, you can't control them from below; their work is not of the type that may be improved by public criticism."

"Yes," I said, "and they are born Fascists. What can you do against them?"

"Only one thing," he said. "Try to prevent them from becoming a closed society, as they have become in Russia."

"This is why," I said, "now that we have lost the company of the horse, we may get something out of the company of men such as the Greeks were."

"It may be an antidote to conformism," he said.

"Don't you think that American youth is becoming more and more conformist?" I asked.

"Modern conformism," he said, "is alarming everywhere, and naturally here it is growing worse every day, but, you see, American conformism has always existed to some extent, because American society, being based on the community itself and not on the authority of a strong central state, needs the cooperation of every individual to function well. Therefore, the individual has always considered it his duty to act as a kind of spiritual policeman for himself and his neighbor. The lack of tolerance is also connected with this, but much more with the fact that American communities were religious in their origin, and religion is by its very nature intolerant. This will also help you understand another seemingly strange contradiction. For example, you will find a far greater amount of tolerance in England than over here, where to be 'different' is almost a disgrace, for everyone, starting with schoolboys and up to the inhabitants of small towns. But you will find far more democracy over here than in England. That, also, is a fact."

"Tell me, Herr Professor," I said. "This has nothing to do with what we were discussing, but what are the chances that a chain reaction may destroy the planet?"

He looked at me with sincere sympathy, took his pipe slowly out of his mouth, stretched out his arm in my direction, and explained why his pipe (now the planet) was not likely to be blown to bits by a chain reaction. And I was so pleased by his answer that I didn't bother to understand the reasons.

"Tell me," I now asked, "why is it that most scientists are so cynical with regard to the issues of war and peace today? I know many physicists who worked on nuclear reactions, and I am struck by their complete indifference to what goes on outside their field. Some of them are as conspicuous for their silence as they are for their scientific achievements."

"So much more credit for those who talk," said he. "But, believe me, my friend, it's not only the scientists who are cynical. Everyone is. Some people sit in heated offices and talk for years and write reports and draw their livelihood from the fact that there exist displaced persons who cannot afford to wait. Wouldn't you call this cynicism? I know that you were going to ask me about the responsibility of the scientists. Well, it is exactly the same as that of any other man. If you think that they are more responsible because in the course of their research they found things that are dangerous, such as the atomic bomb, then also Newton is responsible, because he discovered the law of gravitation. Or the philologists who contributed to the development of languages should be considered responsible for Hitler's speeches. And for his actions. If scientists were to refrain from investigation for fear of what bad people might do with the results, then all of us might as well refrain from living altogether."

"In other words," I said, "it would amount to a form of censorship on all our actions and thoughts."

"A rather useless censorship," he said, "for you can trust man to find other channels of evil." Then he laughed heartily and added, "You may underestimate man's ability to do evil."

. . .

It was time to go. I ran upstairs to say goodbye to Maja and call Bice. "We heard you laugh a good deal," said Maja. "You must have had a good time downstairs."

"Indeed," I said. "And it was a great honor to have Professor Einstein spend such a long time chatting with me."

"Macchè onore d'Egitto," said Maja, which means, in colloquial Italian, "Honor, hell."

Einstein went slowly back into his study. I caught a glimpse of his face; he was miles away from everybody, back in his foreign land.

As Bice, Bimba, and I were walking to the station, Bimba began to cry because she had lost the hat of a paper doll Miss Dukas had given her. She wanted to run back to look for it, but there was no time for that. To console her, Bice said, "Think, Bimba, when you grow up, you will be able to say that Einstein played the violin for you."

"Oh, come," said Bimba, "it isn't true."

"Why?" I asked. *"Didn't* he play for you?"

"Call that play?" she said, making a sour face. "He had to use a stick to play it."

THE YEARS ALONE

E. J. Kahn, Jr.

JUNE 12, 1948 (ON ELEANOR ROOSEVELT)

O N APRIL 12, 1945, Mrs. Franklin Delano Roosevelt became the most celebrated widow on earth. Since that date, she has spiritedly, and characteristically, upset the long-standing American tradition that the widows of Presidents should be rarely seen and practically never heard. Some observers of the contemporary scene credit her with having involuntarily jeopardized another tradition. "God knows I'm not the kind of guy who would want to sound the least bit disrespectful toward Bess Truman," an old-school Democratic Party leader told a friend not long ago, "but there's no getting around the fact that Eleanor Roosevelt is still the first lady of this country." This unofficial ranking has been bestowed on Mrs. Roosevelt, in public as well as in private, by many other people, quite a few of whom have argued that she can be even more aptly termed the first lady of the world. She was thus hailed, early this winter, by Bernard Baruch, a man bristling with distinctions himself, among them the fact that he is the only admirer of Mrs. Roosevelt who has been bold enough to demonstrate his affection for her by gallantly kissing her while she was standing in the receiving line at a formal diplomatic function.

Mrs. Roosevelt is the only representative in the United Nations General Assembly in whose honor all the other representatives have spontaneously risen to their feet, this demonstration having taken place as she walked through their ranks on her way to the speakers' platform. Last December, when she went to Geneva, Switzerland, to attend a meeting of the United Nations Commission on Human Rights, of which she is chairman, she was received like a visiting head of state, and on at least one occasion while she was in that notably peaceful land its constabulary had to be called out to maintain order, owing to the eagerness of the Swiss—who by now might be expected to be blasé about the high-caste folk who turn up there for international debates—to get a glimpse of her. Even among Americans, except in certain die-hard quarters, Mrs. Roosevelt has attained a stature far surpassing that which she automatically had by virtue of her residence in the White House. Early in 1946, she went to London—along with the then Secretary of State James Byrnes, ex-Secretary Stettinius, Senators Vandenberg and Connally, John Foster Dulles, and many other very important people—to represent the United States at the first meeting of the General Assembly. At the end of the session, Vandenberg confessed to a friend that he had been disturbed when he heard that she was to be one of his associates but that he had certainly changed his mind about her, and Dulles told Mrs. Roosevelt that after working with her in London he considered it an honor to be one of her fans. Mrs. Roosevelt's popularity in this country is scarcely confined, however, to elder Republican statesmen. A recent poll by the *Woman's Home Companion* indicates that, at least in the minds of the readers of that magazine, she is the most popular living American of either sex, an accolade that is doubly impressive considering that for the past seven years she has been a regular contributor to the *Ladies' Home Journal*.

The esteem in which Mrs. Roosevelt is currently held undoubtedly derives in part from the circumstance that she bears her husband's still influential name, but it is merely in part. When he died, it seemed not unlikely that his widow—though she had already acquired an immense celebrity in her own right—would gradually become less of a public figure. Three years after his death, the reverse appears to be the case. "We in the family can perhaps sense better than most people how Mother's status has changed," her son Franklin said a while ago. "She always used to be good for a joke, you know. Well, you hardly ever run into that sort of thing any more. People don't kid her much now. They've begun to realize, little by little, that she's an honest, serious, straightforward person who does what she does because she's acutely conscious of the evils in the world and is anxious to help try to relieve them. When Father died, she was worried at first about having to make decisions on her own, and about assuming responsibilities, because, before, he had always been there to advise her and, if she flew off on a tangent, to check her. It's clear now that she didn't have to fret. Recent history has proved that she has the intelligence and the integrity not only to carry the ball but to carry it brilliantly."

Mrs. Roosevelt's present eminence is hardly due to any concrete achievements. In the field of national affairs, she has maintained an aggressively liberal stand that has inspired few noteworthy acts by the legislative and executive branches of the government. In the field of international affairs, she has worked ardently for the welfare of the United Nations, an organization that has not gained much ground during her association with it. The principal reason for her popularity may be that in an era conspicuous for the self-interest of both nations and individuals, she has become more and more widely recognized as a person of towering unselfishness. "As far as Europe is concerned," a man with impressive overseas connections said recently, "Mrs. Roosevelt is an outstanding figure today because she doesn't represent a faction. There are plenty of people over there who admire, for instance, Churchill, and plenty who admire Stalin, but even the staunchest supporters of both will admit that their boys have personal motives for nearly everything they say or do. Mrs. Roosevelt never cares if there's nothing in it for herself. She has absolutely no pride of station and no personal ambition. What's more, many Americans who have neither the time, the energy, the contacts, nor the ability that she has look upon her efforts to improve the lives of her fellow-men as the kind of thing they would like to do themselves if only they were capable of it and could get around to it. To them—and I suspect there are an awful lot of them—she is the personification of the American conscience."

Mrs. Roosevelt realizes that she occupies an unusual niche in domestic and world affairs, but she doesn't seem to be fully aware of the scope of her eminence. This was as true during the twelve years she presided over the White House as it is today. Early in the war, for example, she thought that her husband was making a needless fuss when he put in a couple of transatlantic phone calls to Churchill and the late John Winant, then our Ambassador to the Court of St. James, and asked them not to permit her to fly home by way of Lisbon on her return from a trip to England to inspect the war activities of British women. The President believed that German agents in Portugal would probably find out about her itinerary if she showed up there, and that the Nazi high command would deem her a first-rate military objective and make vigorous efforts to have her plane shot down. Her husband persuaded her to change her plans only when he pointed out, in a phone call direct to her, that if anything untoward happened to a plane she was in, its other occupants would undoubtedly be affected, too. She consented to be sneaked to an Army air base in Scotland at night and flown home from there. She was identified in preflight communications as a general. Mrs. Roosevelt said later that the crew of the plane were terribly astonished when they realized that the general was a woman. It seemed not to have occurred to her that the crew might have been surprised at discovering who the woman was. Eighteen months ago, in "My Day," the syndicated column that Mrs. Roosevelt writes for about ninety newspapers, she furnished added evidence of her tendency to underestimate her position. She said that she must be getting old indeed, because an elderly, white-haired lady had risen and offered her a seat on a bus. It apparently had not struck Mrs. Roosevelt, whose hair is a light gray, that this courtesy might have been prompted not by her age but by her identity.

Mrs. Roosevelt will be sixty-four on October 11th. Aside from partial deafness in the right ear, she is in excellent physical condition, but of late she has had the notion that she is getting old and infirm. The life she leads provides no proof of this. She still puts in the kind of bruising day that most women twenty years younger would find excessive. A year ago, she declined to take to her bed when suffering what she judged to be a mild indisposition. It was not until after she was feeling tiptop again that a more scientific diagnosis revealed that she had had bronchial pneumonia. Around the same time, she did make a concession to the passing years by giving up ice-cold showers and by modifying a violent schedule of daily calisthenics with which she had been torturing herself. Recently, talking about a walk she had taken with somebody, she matter-of-factly said that her companion was "trotting after me." Her companion undoubtedly did just that, since Mrs. Roosevelt's normal pace is a brisk lope. At Hyde Park, where she lives most of the time in a comfortable twelve-room house that she calls a cottage (not so many years ago, it was a furniture factory, and that is what she called it), she takes two or three vigorous walks a day. She walks with her body sloping forward, like a skier's, and her legs and her stride are long. Few human beings can keep up with her, and she has little patience with laggards, so she generally elects to walk with dogs. Her favorite companions are Fala, who is now eight and graying but still spry, and Tamas McFala, a year-old, coal-black, and frisky grandson of the President's renowned pet. Once, a weekend guest, a man troubled with insomnia, who had never seen her in sustained motion and who had heard her say she was getting old, saw her starting off with the dogs for a stroll before breakfast on Sunday morning, and asked if he might go along. Mrs. Roosevelt tried to dissuade him, on the ground that he wouldn't enjoy it, but he insisted, and set out determinedly at her side. An hour or so later, as the rest of the household was coming down to breakfast, he slouched back, alone. He reported that he had done all right for the first mile but that Mrs. Roosevelt had gradually outdistanced him and that finally, when he rounded a bend in desperate pursuit, he found that she had disappeared, as he put it, "over the horizon." During the big storm of last December, two and a half feet of snow fell at Hyde Park. Mrs. Roosevelt was to make a broadcast from a Poughkeepsie radio station, some five miles from her home, the next day. None of the roads on her place had been plowed out, and a studio executive phoned her that he'd send a sleigh to her house to pick her up. She said she wouldn't hear of putting him to that trouble, and that she'd get to the station somehow. She did, by wading through the snow two miles to a cleared highway, and from there hitching a ride. After the broadcast, she was driven back to her jumping-off place and walked the two miles home. The return trip, she said, was easier, since she just followed the track she had broken on her way out.

· · ·

Last winter was Mrs. Roosevelt's first in residence at Hyde Park. (In the pre–White House days, the Roosevelts spent the winter months in their town house on East Sixty-fifth Street, which they sold six years ago.) She stays there as much as possible nowadays, but a heavy calendar of engagements in the city obliges her to make frequent use of a six-room apartment at 29 Washington Square West that she has maintained since 1942. Both her homes are littered with bric-a-brac. She collects odds and ends almost as feverishly as her husband did. She is especially partial to photographs, and the walls of both places are cluttered with them. When she gets hold of a picture of someone she is particularly fond of, she often has a duplicate made, so that she can put it on both urban and rural display. Wherever she is, she is usually in the company of Miss Malvina Thompson, the amiable, efficient, and hardboiled woman, now in her fifties, who has served as her secretary for twenty-six years. Mrs. Roosevelt once said that Miss Thompson was one of her two best friends. The other, she said, was Fala. Mrs. Roosevelt calls her older best friend Tommy (as, by now, do several hundred government officials, political bosses, foreign dignitaries, and heads of organizations whose axes Mrs. Roosevelt has ground), and she tries to get Miss Thompson to call her Eleanor, as does Westbrook Pegler. The secretary, like many other people who have been close to Mrs. Roosevelt, finds it impossible not to temper intimacy with awe, and she has always addressed her employer as Mrs. R., a deferential form that has been adopted—not only in talking about Mrs. Roosevelt but in talking to her—by many government officials, political bosses, foreign dignitaries, heads of organizations, and plain acquaintances. Almost no one calls her Eleanor. Royalty excepted, modern history affords no parallel of a woman who is referred to by her first name frequently by her detractors and sparingly by her friends.

Shortly after her husband's death, Mrs. Roosevelt announced that she intended to lead a "private and inconspicuous existence." It was her idea to devote her working hours merely to her newspaper column, her *Ladies' Home Journal* articles, and the writing of a book of memoirs that would be a sequel to an autobiographical volume, *This Is My Story*, which was published in 1937. Thus far, her private existence has been so limited that she has been able to get only halfway through the book. A man who has seen some of the early chapters says that it looks like a promising entry in the sweepstakes for reminiscences that depend for their appeal mainly on the authors' relationship to President Roosevelt. "There won't be anything sensational in Mrs. R.'s book," he said. "It'll just probably be the definitive one of the lot." Her hopes of enjoying a tranquil life ended in December, 1945, when President Truman appointed her a representative in the United Nations General Assembly. He did this on the recommendation of the State Department, which was eager to have a woman on the United States team and decided, despite the demurrers of some of its more conservative officials, that Mrs. Roosevelt was the ideal choice for this distaff role. She took the job gladly, having often expressed high hopes for the United Nations and for the idea of having an American woman in its General Assembly. She got along amicably with the State Department until it did a back flip on Palestine this March. Since then, her disagreement with parts of the Middle East aspect of our foreign policy has been sharp and outspoken. A high-ranking statesman was overheard to observe after a recent conference with her, "That was the most effective 'damn' I ever heard."

Mrs. Roosevelt's language is usually impeccable, but her performance as a United Nations delegate has not been notable for the ladylike decorum that the State Department may have had in mind. She is often thought to be a dreamy, idealistic type of woman, incapable of the practical, down-to-earth wrangling expected of male statesmen. She *is* idealistic, and, as she has admitted, she is vague, but at the United Nations she has demonstrated many times that she can be exceedingly practical, and even tough, though in an outwardly dreamy and idealistic way. Every now and then, she will retort as quickly as possible to a statement by another delegate, as if motivated only by a righteous, womanly instinct to get in a word fast. Actually, her haste is apt to be prompted by her familiarity with newspaper deadlines and by her extremely practical realization that a rebuttal attains widest notice if published coincidentally with the remarks that provoked it. This knowledgeable trick is referred to admiringly in the State Department as the "smother technique." Mrs. Roosevelt has, moreover, polished to a high degree an effective method of debating that comes naturally to her but of the value of which experience has made her thoroughly aware—a shy, Socratic approach to the matter at hand. In an arena dominated by men who seem to have made up their minds, she goes out of her way not to appear opinionated, even though her own mind may be pretty well made up, too. "Now, of course, I'm a woman and I don't understand all these things," she will remark softly, almost maternally, "and I'm sure there's a great deal to be said for your arguments, but don't you think it would be a good idea if . . ." Stating her position hesitantly, interrogatively, and above all sensibly, she sometimes manages to elicit a "Yes" or a "Maybe" from someone who a moment before had seemed in immutable opposition. This might be called the mother technique. A State Department career man, after watching her artfully maneuver her way through a delicate discussion, once murmured, "Never have I seen naïveté and cunning so gracefully blended." On the whole, Mrs. Roosevelt gets along better with the men accredited to the United Nations than with the women. Occasionally, to be sure, her outlook seems conventionally feminine. "No one can ever tell me that women like to talk longer than men," she wrote in her column after one session, and "I'm frank to say it is always a surprise to me to find how passionately men can feel about rules of procedure" after another. All in all, however, she takes a dispassionate view of feminism, and at times she apparently regards herself as not typical of her sex. Reflecting in "My Day" on a conversation about current events with three of her four sons and their wives, she intimated that in such discussions women perhaps belong in the background but that the rules of the game do not apply to her. "Now here we were again," she wrote, "all of us arguing passionately on ideas, all of us trying to talk at once, even the wives becoming so interested that they could not help but join in!"

. . .

Until Mrs. Roosevelt got into the United Nations, she had had very little experience in dealing with public affairs at the diplomatic or conference level. She made no bones about the fact that the tactical intricacies of international negotiation were largely unknown to her, and, shortly before the Assembly convened in London, she wrote in her column, "Some things I can take to the first meeting—a sincere desire to understand the problems of the rest of the world and our relationship to them; a real good-will for all the peoples throughout the world; a hope that I shall be able to build a sense of personal trust and friendship with my co-workers, for without that type of understanding our work would be doubly difficult." The United States delegation sailed on the Queen Elizabeth. It was a fairly historic occasion—the beginning of this country's participation in a fellowship of nations—and some of our departing standard-bearers understandably made the most of the event, turning up at the pier in glittering limousines with a retinue of well-wishers and intoning solemn prepared farewell statements while floodlights warmed them and newsreel cameras purred flatteringly. Mrs. Roosevelt arrived alone in a taxi and proceeded along the pier unobserved until a Customs man spotted her and escorted her on board. The following day, a statement *she* had prepared in advance was published in her column. "The day is here at last when I am to set sail, apparently with quite a number of others, for London Town!" she said. "I am told we will be 'briefed,' whatever this may mean, during the trip. . . . I need it in the worst possible way."

Whether an American spokesman at an official international gathering has been thoroughly briefed or not depends pretty much on his inclinations and durability. Not far from the portals of all major conference chambers there are obscure State Department career experts on one aspect of foreign policy or another to whom briefing comes as easily as breathing. They stand ready to provide our delegates with up-to-the-minute, authoritative counsel, and they, or even more shadowy aides, prepare thoughtful essays setting forth the official United States position on all foreseeable points of contention. These documents are called "position papers." As a rule, they come to the delegates bound in folders and are then called "position books." The delegates are not, of course, supposed merely to parrot the sentiments expressed in these treatises. Our representatives on United Nations committees and commissions are counted upon to use their own knowledge, intelligence, initiative, instinct, skill, and viewpoints in reconciling the United States position to that of other nations—without, however, straying in any important respect from Department policy—in order to arrive, if possible, at a multilaterally satisfactory solution of the issue under discussion. The delegates, who are expected to read the position books, along with many supplementary texts, between the conclusion of one long-drawn-out meeting and the beginning of the next, informally call this literature "homework." Its unsung authors know that much of it is not read or, at best, is hastily skimmed, so they were flabbergasted, in London, when Mrs. Roosevelt accepted her homework gratefully and did all of it, an unorthodox practice to which she has heroically adhered ever since. She showed further signs of eccentricity in London by remarking that her hotel accommodations seemed unnecessarily elegant, by making an effort to attend every session she was supposed to attend, and by being on time. So unflagging was her devotion to duty that when the King and Queen of England invited her to a private luncheon one day, she replied, to the astonishment of several State Department protocol men, that she would be delighted to come but that she'd have to leave early, to make a subcommittee meeting.

Our delegates to each session of the General Assembly are picked by the President, and their assignments lapse upon adjournment. Mrs. Roosevelt is the only American who has been an official representative at every regular Assembly session. Her appointment to the Human Rights Commission, in April, 1946, was a separate one, for the duration (four years) of the United States' current term of service in that group. She was immediately elected chairman by its other members. The commission has been engaged principally in framing an International Bill of Rights. Some United Nations officials do not consider this as urgent a piece of business as, say, the control of atomic energy, but Mrs. Roosevelt feels that it is time the United Nations stated clearly and ringingly what rights it thinks its member nations should guarantee the individuals residing in them. Our State Department, and Mrs. Roosevelt, originally had in mind simply a brief declaration of fundamental rights, possibly to be followed later on by one or more covenants setting forth basic civil rights, along the lines of the American Bill of Rights. The Soviet Union was agreeable, but whenever anybody brought up the subject of the exact contents, the U.S.S.R. delegate and his cohorts insisted on putting all the emphasis on economic rights—like the right to work, the right to be housed, the right to free medical care, and so on. The majority of the other nations represented on the commission were not satisfied with the idea of beginning merely with a declaration. They wanted a formal covenant to be drawn up at the same time, and they won their point at Geneva. "We often make the mistake of thinking, when we go into an international meeting," Mrs. Roosevelt said afterward, "that our views will naturally please everyone else. Besides, you really couldn't blame the small nations for feeling the way they did. Many of the things that happened to some of them during the war might not have happened if there had been existing and binding international agreement on what human rights could not be violated." The project is still in draft form—a declaration, a covenant, and a section dealing with proposals for implementing the covenant. The Commission is now revising these at Lake Success, on the basis of recommendations by the United Nations' fifty-eight member states. By the end of this month Mrs. Roosevelt hopes to have a final draft ready for the Economic and Social Council, which, if it endorses this version, will pass it along to the General Assembly for consideration at its next regular session, in September. If the Assembly approves the bill, the covenant will be submitted to the member nations for ratification, and if ratified (locally, if it were regarded as a treaty, the United States Senate would have to approve it by a two-thirds vote), it will become binding—if, that is, it can be enforced.

Mrs. Roosevelt approached her work on the Human Rights Commission with the skittish self-deprecation that has characterized her sorties into other fields. "The writing of a preliminary draft of the bill of rights," she confessed in her column, "may not seem so terrifying to my colleagues in the drafting group . . . all of whom are learned gentlemen. But to me it seems a task for which I am ill-equipped. However, I may be able to help them put into words the high thoughts which they can gather from past history and from the actuality of the contemporary situation, so that the average human being can understand and strive for the objectives set forth. I used to tell my husband that, if he could make *me* understand something, it would be clear to all the other people in the country—and perhaps that will be my real value to the drafting commission!" Mrs. Roosevelt has since admitted that she is surer of herself than that, and while it would be impossible to credit any one person with sole responsibility for a statute so often rephrased as the bill already has been, in United Nations circles it is generally conceded to be her baby.

Mrs. Roosevelt has run her commission as firmly and efficiently as she has run her private life. Two and a half years ago, she was an indifferent parliamentarian, and it still seems to bother her a bit when she has to cut off a speaker in mid-flourish, but nowadays she can chairman a meeting as expertly as if she had been born with an "Out of order" on her lips. When the Geneva meeting was convened, last December, some of the delegates muttered gloomily that, because of the inevitable tendency of such conferences to drag on, they wouldn't get home for Christmas. Mrs. Roosevelt had sixteen grandchildren (she now has one more), and she likes to spend Christmas with her family. On December 3rd, she announced from the chair that she expected the delegates to attend to all the items on their agenda in the next two weeks. The commission wound up its business at eleven-thirty on the night of December 17th. Later, Mrs. Roosevelt was asked by the envious chairman of another commission how she had managed this minor miracle. "There was nothing to it," she replied. "I simply made them work from the beginning exactly as people at conferences usually do at the very end." As the delegates were bidding each other farewell, the Soviet representative complained good-humoredly to her that Madam Chairman had driven everybody too hard, and that while she didn't appear terribly tired, his wife, who had served him as secretary and interpreter, was exhausted. Mrs. Roosevelt was not feeling good-humored about her colleague—who, she thought, had been needlessly severe toward the delegates of several small nations who had disagreed with him at the meeting—and in saying goodbye to the Russian she emphatically indicated her devotion to the human right of freedom of expression by murmuring that she was sorry to hear about his wife but glad that he had learned that even in the decadent democracies some people knew how to work.

As a rule, Mrs. Roosevelt sternly forbids herself the luxury of any overt show of exasperation. Her patience is formidable, but once or twice she has, if not quite lost it, at least mislaid it momentarily. Last fall, she delivered a sharp impromptu lecture to the General Assembly's Social, Humanitarian, and Cultural Committee, which had just been treated to a statement on war-mongering and slander by a Yugoslav humanitarian. "The longer I listen to this committee and I hear what happens in other committees," Mrs. Roosevelt said, "the more I think the time has come for some very straight thinking among us all. The ultimate objective that we have is to create better understanding among us, and I well acknowledge that this is going to be difficult. And I will give you the reasons why. I have never yet heard a representative of any of the U.S.S.R. group acknowledge that in any way their government can be wrong. They may say it at home—I do not know—and they may think it is wrong to do it outside. They are very young, and the young rarely do acknowledge anything which they may have done that may not be quite right. With maturity we grow much more humble, and we know that we have to acknowledge very often that things are not quite perfect. [At this point, two listening officials of the State Department, which traditionally takes an unkindly view of acknowledging American imperfections, looked at each other and gulped.] Because we acknowledge it does not mean that we love our country any less, that we do not basically believe in the rightness of the things that exist in our country. What it does mean is that we know that human nature is not perfect and that we hope that all of us can contribute to something better." She concluded with, "Now, I don't expect the millennium immediately, but I do expect and hope and pray that we are going to see a gradual increase in good will rather than a continual backwards and forwards of telling us what dogs we are and how bad we are. I see no use in that at all. I am weary of it all, and all I can say to my colleagues is that I hope we can work with good will."

. . .

Mrs. Roosevelt is pessimistic about the prospect of effecting an immediate East-West rapprochement through United Nations councils or by any other method, but her relations with her colleagues from Eastern Europe have been, on the whole, extremely cordial. "A lot of diplomats play that part of the game correctly," one State Department man has observed, "but in Mrs. R's case it's obvious that she does so not only because it's the proper thing to do but because she has a real sincerity of feeling." Mrs. Roosevelt's relations with domestic Communists have of late been less friendly. She is a leading example of an American who has become disillusioned with our Communist Party, not because of the editorial page of the *Journal-American* but through association with its members. She does not try to hide the fact that in past years she often supported organizations in which Communists were prominent, and, before her first appointment to the United Nations, Miss Thompson cheerfully compiled, for the benefit of any federal character investigators who might drop around, a list of all the groups, among the hundreds with which her employer had been involved, that Miss Thompson thought the government might deem subversive. Mrs. Roosevelt cut herself adrift from the extreme Left three years ago. Shortly before that, she had allowed a youth organization to hold a meeting at the White House. She knew that some of the members present were Communists and she told her guests that she knew it. She added that, in order to let everyone there know who stood where, she would appreciate it if the Communists in the room would rise and identify themselves. Nobody got up. Mrs. Roosevelt regards deception as an unforgivable sin. Not long thereafter, in "My Day," she said that the members of the Communist Party of the United States "taught the philosophy of the lie" and added that "I happen to believe that anyone has a right to be a Communist, to advocate his beliefs peacefully and accept the consequences. A Communist here will be—quite rightly, it seems to me—under certain disadvantages. He will not be put into positions of leadership. I do not believe that he should be prevented from holding his views and earning a livelihood. But because I have experienced the deception of the American Communists, I will not trust them." Since then, Mrs. Roosevelt has been wary about permitting her name to be used by any organization. As a result of her experiences, she is perhaps better equipped than most Americans to understand the nature of Communist negotiating tactics. After one particularly harrowing meeting of a United Nations committee, another American, who had never been mixed up with a Communist front in his life, came up to her and, mopping his brow, said, "Well, at least we had *that* argument out today." "We'll have it again tomorrow," she replied placidly, and so they did.

Mrs. Roosevelt does not think that this country's chances of ultimately attaining peaceful relations with Russia are hopeless. She has become convinced, after many months of reflection on the world situation, that the surest way of attaining them is through economics, and that the two powers might get along better if we were to offer to send an economic mission to the U.S.S.R.—chiefly, to begin with, to help it develop its vast natural resources, some of which the United States, now pressed for many raw materials, could make profitable use of. "I've learned that the Politburo admires toughness," Mrs. Roosevelt said not long ago, "and therefore I would have put on the mission, along with others, the very toughest, best group of industrialists we could get—people like Ernest Weir and Tom Girdler and Alfred Sloan—because theirs has been the kind of success that the Russians appreciate. These men could say to the Russians, 'Now, look, we didn't come over here only for your good; we came to get something mutually advantageous.' If we were to do that, and it convinced the Russians that we were willing to co-operate with them and didn't want to monopolize all the economic processes—as I think it might—then maybe we could start moving in a sensible direction." She has not sounded out the Messrs. Weir, Girdler, and Sloan, but she has presented the idea to a number of our highest government officials, who are presumably mulling it over.

Some of Mrs. Roosevelt's fellow-citizens think that the best mission this country could send to Russia would be Mrs. Roosevelt herself. She recently returned from a trip to Europe, which she made principally to attend the unveiling of the statue of her husband that the British put up in London. Her itinerary included brief excursions to Belgium, where she spoke to an assembly of women's clubs; to Switzerland, where she called on a sick friend; and to Holland. She was invited to the Netherlands by Princess Juliana, an old acquaintance, and in her note of acceptance she said that she would be glad to run over to pay her respects to Queen Wilhelmina and the children. The Princess wrote back that she appreciated Mrs. Roosevelt's interest in the family but that the main reason for the invitation was the belief that the morale of the Dutch people would be immeasurably buoyed up if Mrs. Roosevelt were to appear in person among them. Since the end of the war, nearly all the nations of Europe, including some within the Soviet orbit, have repeatedly asked Mrs. Roosevelt, either formally or informally, to pay them visits, in many cases indicating to her that they regard her as an incomparable morale builder.

Busy as Mrs. Roosevelt was in Switzerland, she did take time out to meet with some Swiss national officials in Berne and some canton officials in Geneva and talk over a few of their problems with them. In Geneva one night, at her instigation, she had a three-hour conversation with the local men in charge of commerce, welfare, agriculture, and labor. She asked them a great many questions and took careful notes on their answers. The Swiss were delighted and flattered by her interest, and told her so. "You know," she said later to a friend, "for the first time I realized that I can really create good will abroad for the United States." Her admirers believe that even in Russia she could create good will. When her son Elliott saw Stalin in Moscow, a year and a half ago, the Premier's first words of greeting indicated that in at least one respect he is not as different from the heads of Western European governments as is commonly thought. "When is your mother coming?" he asked.

EL ÚNICO MATADOR

Lillian Ross

MARCH 26, 1949 (ON SIDNEY FRANKLIN)

THE BEST BULLFIGHTERS IN THE WORLD have come, traditionally, from Spain or Mexico. The old Spanish province of Andalusia has contributed more bulls and more bullfighters to the bull ring than all the rest of Spain. Manolete, probably history's top-ranking matador, who, at the age of thirty, was fatally gored in the summer of 1947, was an Andalusian. Carlos Arruza, who retired last year, at twenty-eight, with a two-million-dollar fortune and the reputation of fighting closer to the bull than any other matador had ever done, was born in Mexico, of Spanish-born parents. Belmonte, an Andalusian, and Joselito, a Spanish gypsy, were the leading figures in what is known in bullfight countries as the Golden Age of Bullfighting, which ended with Belmonte's retirement to breed bulls, in 1921, a year after Joselito's death in the arena. The only Mexican who ranked close to Belmonte and Joselito in their time was Rodolfo Gaona, an Indian, who, in 1925, retired a millionaire with large real-estate interests in Mexico City. Some years ago a Chinese bullfighter named Wong, who wore a natural pigtail, turned up in Mexico as El Torero Chino, and a Peruvian lady bullfighter, Conchita Cintrón, is active today. Only one citizen of the United States has ever been recognized as a full-fledged matador. He is Sidney Franklin, who was born and raised in the Park Slope section of Brooklyn.

Franklin, who is now forty-five, estimates that he has killed two thousand bulls so far. Last winter, in Mexico, he killed thirteen. He is planning to go to Spain this summer to kill as many bulls as he can get contracts to fight, although he is much older than the usual bullfighter is at his peak. "Age has nothing to do with art," he says. "It's all a matter of what's in your mind." He hopes someday to introduce bullfighting to this country, and, if he succeeds, expects it to become more popular than baseball. Ernest Hemingway, who became an authority on bullfighting, as well as on Franklin, while preparing to write *Death in the Afternoon*, maintains that to take to bullfighting a country must have an interest in the breeding of fighting bulls and an interest in death, both of which Hemingway feels are lacking in the United States. "Death, shmeath, so long as I keep healthy," Franklin says. When aficionados, or bullfight fans, charge that Americans born north of the border are incapable of the passion necessary for bullfighting, Franklin replies passionately that coldness in the presence of danger is the loftiest aspect of his art. "If you've got guts, you can do anything," he says. "Anglo-Saxons can become the greatest bullfighters, the greatest ballet dancers, the greatest anything." When, in 1929, Franklin made his Spanish début, in Seville, the aficionados were impressed by the coldness of his art. "Franklin is neither an improviser nor an accident nor a joker," wrote the bullfight critic for *La Unión*, a Seville newspaper. "He is a born bullfighter, with plenty of ambition, which he has had since birth, and for the bulls he has an ultimate quality—serene valor. Coldness, borrowed from the English, if you please. . . . He parries and holds back with a serene magnificence that grandly masks the danger, and he doesn't lose his head before the fierce onslaughts of the enemy." "Franklin fought as though born in Spain; the others fought as though born in Chicago," another critic observed a year later, in comparing Franklin's manner of dispatching two bulls with the work of the Spanish matadors who appeared on the same bill in a Madrid bull ring. One day early in his career, Franklin killed the two bulls that had been allotted to him, then, taking the place of two other matadors, who had been gored, killed four more. This set off such an emotional chain reaction in the ring that another bullfighter dropped dead of excitement. Today, many aficionados, both Spanish and Mexican, disparage Franklin's artistry. "Manolete made you feel inside like crying, but Franklin does not engrave anything on your soul," a Spanish aficionado of thirty years' standing complained not long ago. "Franklin has no class," another Spaniard has said. "He is to a matador of Spanish blood what a Mexican baseball player is to Ba-bee Ruth." "I am A Number One," Franklin says. "I am the best in the business, bar none."

Franklin was nineteen when he saw his first bullfight. He was in Mexico, having recently run away from home after a quarrel with his father. As he recalls this particular bullfight, he was bored. In Brooklyn, he had belonged, as a charter member, to the *Eagle*'s Aunt Jean's Humane Club and to the old New York *Globe*'s Bedtime Stories Club, which devoted itself to the glorification of Peter Rabbit. "At that time, the life to me of both man and beast was the most precious thing on this planet," he says. "I failed to grasp the point." The following year, he fought his first bull—a twelve-hundred-pound, four-year-old beast with horns a foot and a half long—and was on his way to becoming a professional. In the quarter of a century since then, Franklin has come to feel that the act of dominating and killing a bull is the most important and satisfying act a human being can perform. "It gives me a feeling of sensual well-being," he has said. "It's so deep it catches my breath. It fills me so completely I tingle all over. It's something I want to do morning, noon, and night. It's something food can't give me. It's something rest can't give me. It's something money can't buy." He is certain that bullfighting is the noblest and most rewarding of all pursuits. He often delivers eloquent discourses on his art to men who are more interested in power, money, love, sex, marriage, dollar diplomacy, atomic energy, animal breeding, religion, Marxism, capitalism, or the Marshall Plan. When his listener has been reduced to acquiescence, or at least bewilderment, Franklin will smile tolerantly and give him a pat on the back. "It's all a matter of first things first," he will say. "I was destined to taste the first, and the best, on the list of walks of life." The triumph of man over bull is not just the first walk on Franklin's own list; it is the only one. There are no other walks to clutter him up. "I was destined to shine," he adds. "It was a matter of noblesse oblige."

The expression "noblesse oblige" is one Franklin is fond of using to describe his attitude toward most of his activities in and out of the bull ring, including the giving of advice to people. He is an unbridled advice-giver. He likes to counsel friends, acquaintances, and even strangers to live in a sensible, homespun, conventional, well-tested manner, in line with the principles of saving nine by a stitch in time, of finding life great if one does not weaken, of gathering moss by not rolling, of trying and trying again if success is slow in arriving, and of distinguishing between what is gold and what merely glitters. He is convinced that he thought up all these adages himself. In order to show how seriously he takes them, he often pitches in and helps a friend follow them. He takes credit for having helped at least a half-dozen other bullfighters make hay while the sun shone; for having proved to habitués of saloons and night clubs that there is no place like home; for having taught a number of ladies how to drive automobiles, after telling them emphatically that anything a man can do a woman can do; for having encouraged young lovers to get married, because the longer they waited, the more difficult their adjustment to each other would be; and for having persuaded couples to have babies while they were still young, so that they might be pals with their children while they were growing up. "I was destined to lead," Franklin states. "It was always noblesse oblige with me." Some Americans who have watched Franklin dispose of bulls on hot Sunday afternoons in Spain believe that he is right. "Sidney is part of a race of strange, fated men," says Gerald Murphy, head of Mark Cross and a lover of the arts. Franklin has a special category of advice for himself. "I never let myself get obese or slow," he says. "I make it a point never to imbibe before a fight. I never take more than a snifter, even when socializing with the select of all the professions. I am always able to explain to myself the whys and wherefores. I believe in earning a penny by saving it. By following the straight and narrow path, I became the toast of two continents. My horizon is my own creation."

• • •

Franklin, who has never married, is tall—five feet, eleven and a half inches—thin, fair-skinned, and bald except for a few wavy bits of sandy-colored hair at the base of his skull. The backs of his hands and the top of his head are spotted with large tan freckles. His eyebrows are heavy and the color of straw. His ears are long. His eyes are brown, narrow, and lacking in depth, and there are a good many lines around them. There is a small scar at the tip of his nose. His build is considered good for bull-fighting, because a tall bullfighter can more easily reach over a bull's horns with his sword for the kill. Franklin's only physical handicap is his posterior, which sticks out. "Sidney has no grace because he has a terrific behind," Hemingway says. "I used to make him do special exercises to reduce his behind." When Franklin walks down a street, he seems to dance along on his toes, and he has a harsh, fast way of talking. He sounds like a boxing promoter or a cop, but he has many of the gestures and mannerisms of the Spanish bullfighter. "Americans are taught to speak with their mouths," he likes to say. "We speak with our bodies." When the parade preceding the bullfight comes to a halt, he stands, as do the Mexicans and Spaniards, with the waist pushed forward and the shoulders back. When he becomes angry, he rages, but he can transform himself in a moment into a jolly companion again. In the company of other bullfighters or of aficionados, he glows and bubbles. Last winter, at a hotel in Acapulco, he discovered that the headwaiter, D'Amaso Lopez, had been a matador in Seville between 1905 and 1910. "Ah, Maestro!" cried Franklin, embracing Lopez, who grabbed a tablecloth and started doing *verónicas*. "He is overjoyed to see me," Franklin told his host at dinner. "I'm a kindred spirit." At parties, he likes to replace small talk or other pastimes with parlor bullfighting, using a guest as the bull. (Rita Hayworth is considered by some experts to make his best bull.) Claude Bowers, former United States Ambassador to Spain, used to invite Franklin to his soirées in Madrid. "Sidney loved to perform," an Embassy man who was usually Franklin's onrushing bull has said. "He'd give the most fascinating running commentary as he demonstrated with the cape, and then he'd spend hours answering the silliest questions, as long as they were about bullfighting. He was like a preacher spreading the gospel."

Franklin gets along well with Mexicans and Spaniards. "On the streets of Seville, everybody talks to him," a friend who has seen a good deal of him there says. "He knows all the taxi-drivers and lottery venders, and even the mayor bows to him." Franklin claims that he has made himself over into an entirely Spanish bullfighter. "I know Spain like I know the palm of my hand," he says. "I happen to be much more lucid in Spanish than in English. I even *think* in Spanish." Franklin's lucidity in Spanish has been a help to other Americans. Rex Smith, former chief of the Associated Press bureau in Madrid, occasionally used him as a reporter. During a rebellion in 1932, he commissioned Franklin to look into a riot near his office. "Suddenly, I heard a great hullabaloo outside my window," Smith says in describing the incident. "I looked out, and there was Sidney telling the crowd, in Spanish, where to get off." "Sidney is fabulous on language," Hemingway has said. "He speaks Spanish so grammatically good and so classically perfect and so complete, with all the slang and damn accents and twenty-seven dialects, nobody would believe he is an American. He is as good in Spanish as T. E. Lawrence was in Arabic." Franklin speaks Castilian, *caló* (or gypsy talk), and Andalusian. The favorite conversational medium of bullfighters in Spain is a mixture of *caló* and Andalusian. Instead of saying "*nada*" for "nothing" to other bullfighters, he says "*na', na', na',*" and he says "*leña,*" which is bullfight slang, instead of the classical "*cuerno,*" in talking of an especially large horn of a bull. In conversing with a lisping Spanish duke, Franklin assumes a lisp that is far better than his companion's, and he is equally at home in the earthy language of the cafés frequented by bullfighters. The Spanish maintain that Franklin never makes a mistake in their tongue. One day, he went sailing in a two-masted schooner. A Spanish companion called a sail yard a *palo*. "You ought to know better than that," Franklin told him, and went on to explain that the sail yard he had spoken of was a *verga*, that *palo* meant mast, and that there were three terms for mast—one used by fishermen, another by yachtsmen, and the third by landlubbers.

When Franklin first went to Mexico, in 1922, he did not know any Spanish. A few years later, while he was training for bullfighting on a ranch north of Mexico City, he started a class in reading and writing for forty illiterate peons, of all ages. After three months, sixteen of Franklin's pupils could read and write. "They idolized me for it," he says. In any restaurant—even a Schrafft's, back home—he follows the Spanish custom of calling a waiter by saying "Psst!" or clapping the hands. His Christmas cards say, *"Feliz Navidad y Próspero Año Nuevo."* Conversation with bulls being customary during a fight, he speaks to them in Spanish. *"Toma, toro! Toma, toro!"* he says, when urging a bull to charge. *"Ah-ah, toro! Ah-ah-ah, toro!"* he mutters, telling a bull to come closer.

In putting on his coat, Franklin handles it as though it were a bullfighter's cape, and his entire wardrobe is designed to express his idea of a bullfighter's personality. "Sidney always took a long time to dress in the morning," says Hemingway, who often sleeps in his underwear and takes a half minute to put on his trousers and shirt. "I always had to wait for him. I don't like a man who takes a long time to dress in the morning." Most of Franklin's suits were tailored in Seville. "Genuine English stuff—nothing but the best," he tells people. His wardrobe includes a transparent white raincoat, several turtleneck sweaters, some Basque berets, a number of sombreros, and a purple gabardine jacket without lapels. His bullfighting costumes are more elegant and more expensive than those of any other matador in the business. He has three wigs—two parted on the left side, one parted on the right—which are the envy of bald bullfighters who have never been to Hollywood or heard of Max Factor. A bullfighter's looks have a lot to do with his popularity, especially in Mexico, where a bald bullfighter is not esteemed. A Spanish matador named Cayetano Ordóñez, professionally called Niño de la Palma, who was the prototype of Hemingway's young bullfighter in *The Sun Also Rises,* lost a good part of his Mexican public when he lost his hair. In 1927, when he appeared in Mexico City and dedicated one of the bulls he was about to kill to Charles A. Lindbergh, he was young, slender, and graceful, with dark, curly hair. "An Adonis," Franklin says. "Niño had a marvellous figure. All the sexes were wild about him." Eight years later, Niño, who had been fighting in Spain, returned to Mexico heavier and partially bald. The moment he took off his matador's hat in the ring, the ladies in the audience transferred their affections to a slimmer and handsomer matador, and the men turned to the bulls. One day, Franklin showed his wigs to Niño. "Poor Niño was flabbergasted," says a witness. "He put on a wig and stood in front of the mirror for an hour, tears in his eyes. My God, what a scene when Sidney tried to take the wig away from him!" Franklin used to wear his wigs whenever he appeared in public, but lately he has worn them only in the bull ring, at the theatre, and when having his picture taken. He says that someday, if the action in the ring gets dull, he is going to hang his wig on the horn of a bull.

In accordance with his belief in noblesse oblige, Franklin feels that he can afford to be generous toward his fellow-man. "Sidney doesn't envy his neighbors a thing," says a friend. "He is the extreme of what most men like to think of themselves, so much so that he never thinks about it. He doesn't want things. He thinks he has everything." Although Franklin does not carry noblesse oblige so far as to forgive enemies, he is tolerant of those whose friendship for him has cooled. He has rarely seen Hemingway, whom he had come to know in 1929, since leaving him in Madrid in 1937, in the middle of the civil war. Franklin had been doing odd jobs for Hemingway, then a war correspondent.

"I weighed Ernest in the balance and found him wanting," Franklin remarks. "When he began coloring his dispatches about the war, I felt it was time for me to back out on the deal."

"Obscenity!" says Hemingway in reply.

"Ernest got to the point where I knew his mind better than he did himself. It began to annoy him," Franklin says.

"Obscenity!" says Hemingway.

"I may disagree with Ernest, but I'll always give him the benefit of the doubt, because he is a genius," Franklin says.

"Obscenity obscenity!" says Hemingway.

Franklin is highly critical of most of his confreres, but there are a few he praises when he feels they deserve it. After a bullfight in Mexico City a year ago, a friend commented to him that one of the matadors looked good only because he had been given a good bull to kill—a good bull being one that has perfect vision and is aggressive, high-spirited, and, from a human point of view, brave. Franklin said no—that the bull was a bad bull. "The fellow had the guts to stand there and take it and make a good bull out of a lemon," he said. "You can't understand that, because you have no grasp of noblesse oblige." Because of his own grasp of noblesse oblige, Franklin is determined to go on fighting bulls as long as his legs hold out, and he would like to see Brooklyn continue to be represented in the bull ring after he retires. To this end, he took under his wing for a while a twenty-six-year-old Brooklyn neighbor of his named Julian Faria, nicknamed Chaval, meaning "the Kid." Chaval, whose parents are of English, Spanish, and Portuguese descent and whose face resembles a gentle, sad-eyed calf's, made his début as a matador in Mexico in the fall of 1947, fighting with Franklin in some of the smaller rings. On the posters announcing the fights, Chaval's name appeared in letters an inch high, beneath Franklin's name in letters two inches high, along with the proclamation that Franklin was "El Único Matador Norteamericano."

· · ·

"There are two kinds of people," Franklin repeatedly says. "Those who live for themselves and those who live for others. I'm the kind that likes to serve mankind." He believes that he would have made a wonderful doctor, and he acts as a general practitioner whenever he gets a chance. One afternoon, a bull ripped open one of his ankles. "I took a tea saucer and put some sand in it and mixed it up with tea leaves and manure and applied it to the injured member," Franklin says, with a look of sublime satisfaction. "I was then ready to get right back in the ring, functioning perfectly to a T." Once, when he was working on the ranch in Mexico, a peon accidentally chopped off two of his, the peon's, toes. Franklin claims that he sewed them back on with an ordinary needle and thread. "I put a splint underneath the foot, bandaged it, and told him to stay off it for a few days," he says. "In no time at all, the man was as good as new." In Mexico a few years ago, Franklin stood by as an appendectomy was performed upon his protégé, Chaval, advising Chaval, who had been given a local anesthetic, not to show any fear or sign of pain, not even to grunt, because other bullfighters would hear about it. Chaval didn't make a sound. "I saw to it that the appendectomy was performed according to Hoyle," Franklin says.

Franklin considers himself an expert on mental as well as physical health. At a bullfight in Mexico City, last winter, he sat next to a British psychiatrist, a mannerly fellow who was attending the Unesco conference. While a dead bull was being dragged out of the ring, Franklin turned to the psychiatrist. "Say, Doc, did you ever go into the immortality of the crab?" he asked. The psychiatrist admitted that he had not, and Franklin said that nobody knew the answer to that one. He then asked the psychiatrist what kind of doctor he was. Mental and physiological, the psychiatrist said.

"I say the brain directs everything in the body," Franklin said. "It's all a matter of what's in your mind."

"You're something of a psychosomaticist," said the psychiatrist.

"Nah, all I say is if you control your brain, your brain controls the whole works," said Franklin.

The psychiatrist asked if the theory applied to bullfighting.

"You've got something there, Doc," said Franklin. "Bullfighting is basic. It's a matter of life and death. People come to see you take long chances. It's life's biggest gambling game. Tragedy and comedy are so close together they're part of each other. It's all a matter of noblesse oblige."

The psychiatrist looked solemn. Another bull came into the ring, and a matador executed a *verónica*. It was not a good one. The matador should hold the cape directly before the bull's face, one hand close to his own body, the other away from his body, stretching the cape, then pull it away from the bull's face in such a manner that when the animal follows it, he passes directly in front of him. This matador held both hands far away from his body, and the bull passed at some distance from him. The crowd whistled and shouted insults. "Look at that, Doc," said Franklin. "There's a guy who doesn't have the faintest grasp of noblesse oblige."

The psychiatrist cleared his throat. The bullfight, he said, might be looked upon as a plastic model of Freud's concept of the mind and its three divisions: the id, the uncivilized brute in man; the ego, a combination of environment, which has tamed the id, and of the id itself; and the super-ego, the conscience, often represented by the father or the mother, who approves or disapproves. He suggested that the id might be represented by the bull, the ego by the bullfighter, and the super-ego by the whistling and hooting crowd. "Many things you do in life," he added, "are a projection, or model, of what is going on in your mind. For instance, you might be fighting bulls because internally you have a conflict between your id and ego, id and super-ego, or ego and super-ego, or possibly a conflict between your combined id and ego and your super-ego. The bullfight, then, might be a good model of your state of mind."

"Nah," said Franklin. "If I had my life to live all over again, I'd do exactly the same thing. Do you grasp my point?"

The psychiatrist thought it over for a while, then said yes, he believed he did.

After the bullfight, Franklin, in saying goodbye to the British psychiatrist, advised him to take care of himself. "If you can't be good, be careful, Doc," he said.

. . .

In general, Franklin says, he likes the life of a bullfighter because of the number of things he can pack into it. "You come into a town, and the moment you arrive, be it by plane, ship, train, or car, everybody is there to receive you," he says. "You barely have time to change your clothes before it's a high old round of banquets and dinners. You don't pay for a thing; others consider it a privilege to pay for you. You're yanked out to go swimming, hunting, fishing, and riding, and if you don't know how to do those things, others consider it a privilege to teach you, to satisfy your every whim and desire. The select of all the professions like to be seen with you." "They're never alone," Hemingway says morosely of bullfighters. "What Ernest has in mind when he says that is that all the sexes throw themselves at you," Franklin explains. "I never went in for that night-owl stuff. I never let myself become detoured. Many of them allow themselves to become so detoured they never get back on the main highway."

Chaval's attitude toward the bullfighter's life is rather different. "I just like to scare girls," he says. "Boy, I bring the bull so close to me, the girls, they scream. Boy, I get a kick out of making girls scream."

Franklin used to lecture Chaval on the significance of noblesse oblige in bullfighting to help the young man stay on the main highway. "I am alive today only because I was in *perfect* condition when I had my accidents in the ring," he sternly told Chaval, who had night-owl inclinations.

"Jeez, Sidney, all you gotta do in the ring is show you're brave," said Chaval. "That's what girls like, when you're brave."

Most bullfighters agree with Chaval, but they state their case with more dignity. A young woman who once met Carlos Arruza at a party in

Mexico City complimented him on his bravery in fighting so close to a bull. "You think I am going to be killed, but for you I am courageous in the face of death," Arruza replied gallantly. "This is manliness. I fight to make money, but I like very much to bring the bull to his knees before me." The fearlessness of Manolete is legendary. He specialized in the most difficult and dangerous maneuver in bullfighting—the *pase natural*, which, properly executed, requires the bull to pass perilously close to the body. He had no worthy competitors, but he always tried to outdo himself. "Manolete was a tremendous personality," a Mexican aficionado said recently. "He never smiled." He was gored several times before he received his fatal wound. On more than one occasion, he might have saved himself by moving an inch or two. "Why didn't you move, Manolo?" he was asked after suffering a leg wound one afternoon. "Because I am Manolete," he replied sombrely. Lack of fear has been attributed by some people simply to lack of imagination. Franklin disagrees with this theory. "I believe in facing facts," he says. "If you're a superman, you're a superman, and that's all there is to it." Few of the critics who hold to the opinion that Franklin lacks artistry believe that he lacks *valentía*, or bravery. "Nobody ever lives his life all the way up except bullfighters," Franklin says, quoting from *The Sun Also Rises*.

In giving advice to Chaval on how to live his life all the way up, Franklin once said, "You've got to be the sun, moon, and stars to yourself, and results will follow as logically as night follows day."

"Jeez, Sidney! I don't get it," Chaval replied. "All I know is I gotta kill the bull or the bull kills me."

"Bullfighting taught me how to be the master of myself," Franklin said. "It taught me how to discard all that was unimportant."

"Jeez, Sidney!" said Chaval.

Franklin began to make history in the bull ring at his Spanish début, on June 9, 1929, in Seville. Aficionados who saw him fight that day wept and shouted, and talked about it for weeks afterward. "On that day, I declared, 'Bullfighting will never again be the same,'" Manuel Mejías, the bullfighting father of five bullfighting sons, has said. "Sidney Franklin introduced a revolutionary style in the bull ring." "Sidney was a glowing Golden Boy," recalls an American lady who was at the fight. "He was absolutely without fear. He was absolutely beautiful."

"I was carried out on the shoulders of the crowd through the gates reserved for royalty," Franklin told Chaval ecstatically not long ago. "The history of the ring was then a hundred and ninety-nine years old. All that time, only four fellows had ever been carried out of the ring on the shoulders of the crowd. I was the fifth. Traffic in the streets of Seville was wrecked. The next day, they passed a law prohibiting the carrying of bullfighters through the public streets. I was taken out of the ring at seven and deposited at my hotel at twelve-twenty that night. I didn't know what I was doing or what had happened to me. I was so excited I took all my money out of a dresser drawer and threw it to the crowds on the street. The die was cast that day. I was riding on the highest cloud in this or any other world. I felt so far above anything mundane that nothing mattered. I didn't hear anything. I didn't see anything. I looked, but I didn't see. I heard, but nothing registered. I didn't care about food. I didn't care about drink. I was perfectly satisfied to lay my head on the pillow and pass out."

PART FIVE
THE CRITICS

NOTES AND COMMENT

E. B. White

DECEMBER 12, 1948

BEFORE A BOOK CAN BE PUBLISHED in Czechoslovakia, the publisher must submit an outline of it to the government for approval. Accompanying the outline must be written opinions of "responsible literary critics, scientists, or writers." (We are quoting from a dispatch to the *Times*.) The question of who is a responsible critic or writer comes up in every country, of course. It must have come up here when the Algonquin Hotel advertised special weekend rates for "accredited writers." We often used to wonder just how the Algonquin arrived at the answer to the fascinating question of who is an accredited writer, and whether the desk clerk required of an applicant a rough draft of an impending novel. It seems to us that the Czech government is going to be in a spot, too. No true critic or writer is "responsible" in the political sense which this smelly edict implies, and in order to get the kind of censorship the government obviously wants, the government will need to go a step further and require that the critic himself be certified by a responsible party, and then a step beyond that and require that the responsible party be vouched for. This leads to infinity, and to no books. Which is probably the goal of the Czech government.

The matter of who is, and who isn't, a responsible writer or scientist reminds us of the famous phrase in Marxist doctrine—the phrase that is often quoted and that has won many people to Communism as a theory of life: "From each according to his ability; to each according to his needs." Even after you have contemplated the sheer beauty of this concept, you are left holding the sheer problem of accreditation: who is needy, who is able? Again the desk clerk looms—a shadowy man. And behind the clerk another clerk, for an accreditation checkup. And so it goes. Who shall be the man who has the authority to establish our innermost need, who shall be the one to approve the standard of achievement of which we are capable? Perhaps, as democracy assumes, every man is a writer, every man wholly needy, every man capable of unimaginable deeds. It isn't as beautiful to the ear as the Marxian phrase, maybe, but there's an idea there somewhere.

BOOKS

A NOTE BY JOAN ACOCELLA

THE SECOND WORLD WAR WAS A CATASTROPHE for most of the people in the East and the West, including *The New Yorker*'s book critics. Hence the leading characteristics of this collection of reviews from the 1940s. Nine essays culled from ten years do not an average make. The editors have of course pulled up the most interesting pieces. The table of contents reads like a short list of mid-century masters: Edmund Wilson on Jean-Paul Sartre, Lionel Trilling on George Orwell, Orwell on Graham Greene, W. H. Auden on T. S. Eliot—a wide gamut. Nevertheless, most of the reviews share one striking trait: an unashamed quest for objective truth. Modernism, with its claim that perception is relative to the perceiver, had been around for nearly a half century, but the writers of the forties, looking out over the wreckage of Dresden and Hiroshima, decided that the events leading up to this were not relative to the perceiver. Trilling, in his review of *Nineteen Eighty-Four*, speaks of Orwell's "old-fashioned faith that the truth can be got at, that we can, if we actually want to, see the object as it really is." The same might be said of most of the writers in this group.

They want seriousness. Not one of them fails to discuss politics, or something close. They fear ideologies, and not just those that underlay the war. They also inspect the belief systems, seemingly benign, that rose up out of the rubble. Wilson, always Johnny-on-the-spot, voices his mixed feelings about Existentialism, the new French philosophy. Other critics mull over the religious orthodoxy embraced by many intellectuals of the pre- and postwar period. Orwell, in his review of Greene's *Heart of the Matter*, casts a cold eye on the author's adopted Roman Catholicism, and on what he saw as the new Catholics' habit of exalting vice as well as virtue, at least in their co-religionists: "This cult of the sanctified sinner seems to me to be frivolous, and underneath it there probably lies a weakening of belief, for when people really believed in Hell, they were not so fond of striking graceful attitudes on its brink." On the other side, Louise Bogan thinks that neo-Catholicism may have exacerbated Robert Lowell's tortured introspection, and thereby unsettled his mind.

Communism, of course, comes under discussion. After Stalin's show trials, some writers frankly denounce the Soviet Union. (It is certainly the foremost model for the dystopia in which *Nineteen Eighty-Four* is set.) Others still embrace a diluted Communism—for example, that of the Loyalists in the Spanish Civil War, as portrayed by Hemingway in *For Whom the Bell Tolls.* Clifton Fadiman, in his review of that book, quotes the hero's farewell to his young mistress as he goes off to blow up a bridge, and die: "I love thee as I love all that we have fought for. I love thee as I love liberty and dignity and the rights of all men to work and not be hungry." Today's readers may find this rather gassy, but I think that they will still grant the man's convictions some honor. The point is not which program for living the reviewers recommended or condemned, but that they regarded such endorsements as part of their job. Even in the one frankly comic essay in this collection, Wilson's "Why Do People Read Detective Stories?," the basic complaint is that detective fiction has no moral content. Reading such novels, Wilson says, "I finally felt that I was unpacking large crates by swallowing the excelsior in order to find at the bottom a few bent and rusty nails."

These critics feared the loss of their world: their allegiances, the books they lived by, the emotions born of those books. In *Notes Towards the Definition of Culture,* T. S. Eliot, by then a declared Tory, voiced his worry that the dominant culture of the West was going to be tossed out by arrivistes. Auden, in his review of that book, has some fun imagining the howls of rage that such views, coming from the most honored poet and critic of the period, were going to provoke. They did. But it is worth noting that Eliot, and also Auden, were taking on the gravest questions of their time. Their difference from other critics of the period was only that they tried to figure out, and say, what the problem was. Before the Second World War book criticism in *The New Yorker* was, in general, a casual business. Reviews tended to be short—relaxed, genial, as if the critic were sitting down and lighting a pipe and recording his thoughts in an hour or two after dinner. In the forties, because of the war—and also, I believe, because of the example of Edmund Wilson, who arrived at the magazine as a weekly book reviewer in 1944 and stayed for about twenty-five years, raising the bar—the treatment of books became more searching. In a 1946 review of Robert Lowell's second collection of poems, *Lord Weary's Castle,* Louise Bogan says that Lowell "may be the first of that postwar generation which will write in dead earnest." This was a prescient judgment. Lowell was indeed one of the first representatives of the new seriousness, but he was also the most personal and hair-tearing. Soon after him, as people became used to postwar blues, we get comedy, and not just in Wilson's piece on detective stories (he also has a sterling essay on horror stories) but also in the glints of wit between the lines of Orwell's view of the apocalyptic Greene, and Auden's view of Eliot's Toryism. Still, they were all writing in dead earnest.

CLIFTON FADIMAN

ERNEST HEMINGWAY CROSSES THE BRIDGE

OCTOBER 26, 1940 (ON *FOR WHOM THE BELL TOLLS*)

IT'S NOT INACCURATE TO SAY that Hemingway's *For Whom the Bell Tolls* is *A Farewell to Arms* with the background, instead, the Spanish Civil War. The hero, Robert Jordan, a young American Loyalist sympathizer, recalls to mind Frederic Henry. Like Henry, he is anti-heroically heroic, anti-romantically romantic, very male, passionate, an artist of action, Mercutio modernized. Though the heroine, Maria, reminds one rather less of Catherine Barkley, the two women have much in common. Also, in both books the mounting interplay of death and sex is a major theme, the body's intense aliveness as it senses its own destruction.

But there, I think, the resemblance ends. For this book is not merely an advance on *A Farewell to Arms.* It touches a deeper level than any sounded in the author's other books. It expresses and releases the adult

Hemingway, whose voice was first heard in the groping *To Have and Have Not*. It is by a better man, a man in whom works the principle of growth, so rare among American writers.

The story opens and closes with Robert Jordan lying flat on the pine-needle floor of a Spanish forest. When we first meet him he is very much alive and planning the details of his job, which is to join forces with a band of Spanish guerrillas and with their aid blow up an important bridge at the precise instant that will most help the Loyalist advance on Segovia. When we last see him he has fulfilled his mission and is facing certain death. Between the opening and closing pass three days and three nights. Between the opening and closing pass a lifetime for Robert and Maria and something very much like a lifetime for the reader. "I suppose," thinks Robert, "it is possible to live as full a life in seventy hours as in seventy years." The full life lived by Robert and Maria spills over into your own mind as you read, so the three days and three nights are added to your life, and you are larger and more of a person on page 471 than you were on page 1. That is one test of a first-rate work of fiction.

For Whom the Bell Tolls is about serious people engaged in serious actions. The word "serious" (a favorite among Spaniards) occurs again and again. The thoughts of Robert, even at his most sardonic, are serious thoughts. "There are necessary orders that are no fault of yours and there is a bridge and that bridge can be the point on which the future of the human race can turn. As it can turn on everything that happens in this war." It is a stern and grave reflection, sterner, graver than anything in *A Farewell to Arms*. The title itself is part of a grave reflection, from the sermons of John Donne. That we may see on what a new and different level of emotion Hemingway now works, I quote the sentence from which the title is taken: "No man is an Iland, intire of it selfe; every man is a peece of the Continent, a part of the maine; if a Clod bee washed away by the Sea, Europe is the lesse, as well as if a Promontorie were, as well as if a Mannor of thy friends or of thine owne were; any mans death diminishes me, because I am involved in Mankinde; And therefore never send to know for whom the bell tolls; It tolls for thee."

This utterance (I suppose it is one of the greatest sentences in English) is about death and says yes to life. That men confer value on life by feeling deeply each other's mortality is the underlying theme of the novel. Here is something other than Hemingway's old romantic absorption in death, though growing out of it. Remember that *For Whom the Bell Tolls* is an anti-Fascist novel. "Any mans death diminishes me, because I am involved in Mankinde." All of what the dictator most profoundly and religiously disbelieves is in that sentence. Hemingway is no fool. He portrays many of the Loyalists as cowards, brutes, and politicians—as they undoubtedly were. He portrays some of the Fascists as men of twisted nobility—as they undoubtedly were. But he knows that the war, at its deepest level (the first battle of the war now on your front pages), is a war between those who deny life and those who affirm it. And if it is not yet such a war, it must become so, or it will, no matter who wins, have been fought in vain. I take that to be the central feeling of *For Whom the Bell Tolls*, and that is why the book is more than a thrilling novel about love and death and battle and a finer work than *A Farewell to Arms*.

It is interesting to watch in this new book a certain process of etherealization. Just as the Wagnerian death fascination of *Death in the Afternoon* changes here into something purer, so the small-boy Spartanism and the parade of masculinity which weakened the earlier books are transformed into something less gross, something—Hemingway would despise the word—spiritual. And yet this is by far the most sensual of all his books, the most truly passionate. This process of purification extends even to minor matters. In the other books, for example, drinking is described as a pleasure, as a springboard for wit, as a help to love, as fun, as madness. There is much drinking in *For Whom the Bell Tolls*, and none of it is solemn, but it becomes at times a serious thing. Liquor, drunk by these Spanish guerrillas before a battle, is a noble and necessary pleasure. Drinking has dignity.

Dignity also is what each of the characters possesses, from Fernando, who wears it like another skin, down to Augustin, whose every third word is an obscenity. Each has his own dignity, which means worth, and that dignity is gradually lifted to the surface by the harsh touch of death, as the grain of a fine wood reveals itself with polishing. Anselmo, the Shakespearean old man who fears his own cowardice ("I remember that I had a great tendency to run at Segovia") and comes through at the end to a good and sound death; Rafael, the gypsy, unreliable, gluttonous, wild; El Sordo, the deaf guerrilla leader; Andrés, the Bulldog of Villaconejos; Pablo, the sad-faced revolutionary with the spayed spirit, the treacherous heart, and the subtle, ingrown mind; Pilar, the greatest character in the book, with her ugliness, her rages, her terrible memories, her vast love for the Republic, her understanding and envy of the young Robert and Maria; Maria herself, knitting her spirit together after her rape by the Falangists, finding the purpose of her young life in the three days and nights with her American lover—each of these (all of them flawed, some of them brutal, one of them treacherous) has a value, a personal weight that Hemingway makes us feel almost tangibly, so that their lives and deaths are not incidents in a story but matters of moment to us who are "involved in Mankinde."

For Whom the Bell Tolls rises above *A Farewell to Arms* in still another way. The love story in *A Farewell to Arms is* the book. Chapters like that describing the retreat from Caporetto or that beautiful scene of the conversation with the old man at the billiard table are mere set pieces and might conceivably have been used in some other book. But the love of Robert and Maria is a structural part of *For Whom the Bell Tolls*. It is not "love interest," nor is it the whole story, either; it is an integral portion of three days and three nights of life lived by two young people facing death. Furthermore, though this love does not rise above passion, it endows passion with an end and a meaning. In the great scene just before Robert goes out to blow up the bridge, knowing that he will almost surely die, when he makes love to Maria, describing, his heart breaking, the fine life he knows they will never lead, he arrives at an identification of which Hemingway's other heroes were incapable: "I love thee as I love all that we have fought for. I love thee as I love liberty and dignity and the rights of all men to work and not be hungry."

Fine as the Italians were in *A Farewell to Arms*, these Spaniards are finer. "There is no people," thinks Robert, "like them when they are good and when they go bad there is no people that is worse." And here they are, good and bad. They are in some ways like Russians, the pre-Soviet Russians, very philosophic and confessional and poetical. But they are not soft; indeed, the Spanish fury to kill, to kill as a pure act of faith, is one of the dominating emotions of the book. And their language is superb, translated literally out of its elegant and formal original, a trick which sounds as if it might be atrocious and turns out 100 percent effective. As a matter of fact, I would imagine *For Whom the Bell Tolls* to be as excellent a Spanish novel as it is an American one.

I have no idea whether this is a "great" book, for I have read it only once, and too quickly. But I know there are great things in it and that the man who wrote it is a bigger man than he was five years ago. There are some technical flaws. For example, I think the chapters describing the disorganization and political chicanery of the Loyalist command impede the story. But the faults are far outweighed by a dozen episodes that invade the memory and settle there: El Sordo's last fight on the hilltop; any of the love scenes; the struggle at the bridge; Pilar's dreadful story of Pablo's killing of the Fascists; Maria's recital of the noble death of her mother and father; Pilar's memories of her life among the bullfighters; the astounding conversation—this is a set piece, but it's forgivable— about "the smell of death;" and the final scene, in which Robert, his left leg smashed, alone and on the threshold of delirium, trains his machine gun on the advancing Fascists and prepares himself, knowing at last why he is doing so, to die.

So I do not much care whether or not this is a "great" book. I feel that it is what Hemingway wanted it to be: a true book. It is written with only one prejudice—a prejudice in favor of the common human being. But that is a prejudice not easy to arrive at and which only major writers can movingly express.

Robert's mission is to blow up a bridge, and he does so. Oddly, it is by the blowing up of just such bridges that Robert Jordan and Ernest Hemingway and all of us may be able to cross over into the future.

EDMUND WILSON

WHY DO PEOPLE READ DETECTIVE *STORIES?*

OCTOBER 14, 1944

FOR YEARS I HAVE BEEN HEARING about detective stories. Almost everybody I know seems to read them, and they have long conversations about them in which I am unable to take part. I am always being reminded that the most serious public figures of our time, from Woodrow Wilson to W. B. Yeats, have been addicts of this form of fiction. Now, except for a few of the Father Brown stories by Chesterton, for which I did not much care, I have not read any detective stories since one of the earliest, if not the earliest, of the imitators of Sherlock Holmes—a writer named Jacques Futrelle, now dead, who invented a character called the Thinking Machine and published his first volume of stories about him in 1907. Enchanted though I had been with Sherlock Holmes, I got bored with the Thinking Machine and dropped him, beginning to feel, at the age of twelve, that I was outgrowing that form of literature.

In my present line of duty, however, I have decided that I ought to take a look at some specimens of this school of writing, which has grown so prodigiously popular and of which the output is now so immense that this department has to have a special editor to deal with its weekly production. To be sure of getting something above the average, I waited for new novels by writers who are particularly esteemed by connoisseurs, and started in with the recent volume of Nero Wolfe stories by Rex Stout: *Not Quite Dead Enough* (Farrar & Rinehart).

What I found rather surprised me and let me down. Here was simply the old Sherlock Holmes formula reproduced with a fidelity even more complete than it had been by Jacques Futrelle almost forty years ago. Here was the incomparable private detective, ironic and ceremonious, with a superior mind and eccentric habits, keen on money, and regarding himself as an artist, given to lapsing into apathetic phases of gluttony and orchid-raising as Holmes had his enervated indulgence in his cocaine and his violin, but always dramatically reviving himself to perform prodigies of intellectual alertness; and here were the admiring stooge, adoring and slightly dense, and Inspector Lestrade of Scotland Yard, energetic but completely at sea, under the new name of Inspector Cramer of Police Headquarters. Almost the only difference was that Nero Wolfe was fat and lethargic instead of lean and active like Holmes, and that he liked to make the villains commit suicide instead of handing them over to justice. But I rather enjoyed Nero Wolfe, with his rich dinners and quiet evenings in his house in farthest West Thirty-fifth Street, where he savors an armchair sadism that is always accompanied by beer. I was somewhat disappointed in the stories that made up this most recent book—*Not Quite Dead Enough* and *Booby Trap*—but, as they were both under the usual length and presented Nero Wolfe partly distracted from his regular profession by a rigorous course of training for the Army, I concluded that they might not be first-rate examples of what the author could do in this line and read also *The Nero Wolfe Omnibus* (World), which contains two earlier book-length stories: *The Red Box* and *The League of Frightened Men*. But neither did these supply the excitement I had hoped for. If the later stories seemed sketchy and skimpy, these seemed to have been somewhat padded, for they were full of long episodes that led nowhere and had no real business to be in the story. It was only when I looked up Sherlock Holmes that I realized how much Nero Wolfe was a dim and distant copy of an original. The old stories of Conan Doyle had a wit and a fairy-tale poetry of hansom cabs, gloomy London lodgings, and lonely country estates that Rex Stout could hardly duplicate with his backgrounds of modern New York; and the surprises were much more entertaining: you at least got a room with a descending ceiling or a snake trained to climb down the bellrope, whereas in Nero Wolfe—though *The League of Frightened Men* does make use of rather a clever psychological idea—the solution of the mystery was not usually either fanciful or unexpected. I finally felt that I was unpacking large crates by swallowing the excelsior in order to find at the bottom a few bent and rusty nails, and I began to nurse a rankling conviction that detective stories in general profit by an unfair advantage in the code which forbids the reviewer to give away the secret to the public—a custom which results in the concealment of the pointlessness of a good deal of this fiction and affords a protection to the authors which no other department of writing enjoys. It is not difficult to create suspense by making people await a revelation, but it demands a certain originality to come through with a criminal device which is ingenious or picturesque or amusing enough to make the reader feel the waiting has been worthwhile. I even began to mutter that the real secret that Rex Stout had been screening by his false scents and interminable divagations was a meagreness of imagination of which one only came to realize the full horror when the last chapter had left one blank.

· · ·

I have been told by the experts, however, that this endless carrying on of the Doyle tradition does not represent all or the best that the detective story has been able to do during the decades of its proliferation; there has been also the puzzle mystery, and this has been brought to a high pitch of ingenuity in the stories of Agatha Christie. So I have read also the new Agatha Christie, *Death Comes as the End* (Dodd, Mead), and I confess that I have been had by Mrs. Christie. I did not guess who the murderer was, I was incited to keep on and find out, and when I did finally find out, I was surprised. Yet I did not care for Agatha Christie and I never expect to read another of her books. I ought, I suppose, to discount the fact that *Death Comes as the End* is supposed to take place in Egypt two thousand years before Christ, so that the book has a flavor of Lloyd

C. Douglas not, I understand, quite typical of Mrs. Christie ("No more Khay in this world to sail on the Nile and catch fish and laugh up into the sun whilst she, stretched out in the boat with little Teti on her lap, laughed back at him"); but her writing is of a mawkishness and banality which seem to me literally impossible to read. You cannot read such a book, you run through it to see the problem worked out; and you cannot become interested in the characters because they never can be allowed an existence of their own even in a flat two dimensions but have always to be contrived so that they can seem either reliable or sinister, depending on which quarter, at the moment, is to be baited for the reader's suspicion. This I had found also a source of annoyance in the case of Mr. Stout, who, however, has created, after a fashion, Nero Wolfe and Archie Goodwin and has made some attempt at characterization of the people that figure in the crimes; but Mrs. Christie, in proportion as she is more expert and concentrates more narrowly on the puzzle, has to eliminate human interest completely, or rather fill in the picture with what seems to me a distasteful parody of it. In this new novel she has to provide herself with puppets who will be good for three stages of suspense: you must first wonder who is going to be murdered, you must then wonder who is committing the murders, and you must finally be unable to foresee which of two men the heroine will marry. It is all like a sleight-of-hand trick, in which the magician diverts your attention from the awkward or irrelevant movements that conceal the manipulation of the cards, and it may mildly amuse and amaze you, as such a sleight-of-hand performance may. But here the patter is a constant bore and the properties lack the elegance of playing cards. Still fearing that I might be unjust to a department of literature that seemed to be found so absorbing by many, I went back and read *The Maltese Falcon*, which I assumed to be a classic in the field, since it had been called by Alexander Woollcott "the best detective story America has yet produced" and, at the time of its publication, had immediately caused Mr. Hammett to become what Jimmy Durante, speaking of himself, has called "duh toast of duh intellectuals." But it was hard for me to understand what they had thought—in 1930—they were toasting. Mr. Hammett did have the advantage of real experience as a Pinkerton detective, and he recharged the old formula of Sherlock Holmes with a certain cold underworld brutality which gave readers a new shudder in the days when it was fashionable to be interested in gangsters; but, beyond this, he lacked the ability to bring the story to imaginative life. As a writer—despite the praise of him one has heard—he is surely almost as far below Rex Stout as Rex Stout is below James M. Cain. *The Maltese Falcon* today seems not much above those newspaper picture strips in which you follow from day to day the ups and downs of a strong-jawed hero and a hardboiled but beautiful adventuress.

What, then, is the spell of the detective story that has been felt by T. S. Eliot and Paul Elmer More but which I seem to be unable to feel? As a department of imaginative writing, it looks to me completely dead. The spy story may only now be realizing its poetic possibilities, as the admirers of Graham Greene contend; and the murder story that exploits psychological horror is an entirely different matter. But the detective story proper bore its really fine fruit in the middle of the nineteenth century, when Poe communicated to M. Dupin something of his own ratiocinative intensity and when Dickens invested his plots with a social and moral significance that made the final solution of the mystery a revelatory symbol of something that the author wanted seriously to say. Yet the detective story has kept its hold; had even, in the two decades between the great wars, become more popular than ever before; and there is, I believe, a deep reason for this. The world during those years was ridden by an all-pervasive feeling of guilt and by a fear of impending disaster which it seemed hopeless to try to avert because it never seemed conclusively possible to pin down the responsibility. Who had committed the original crime and who was going to commit the next one?—that murder which always, in the novels, occurs at an unexpected moment, when the investigation is well under way, which may happen, as in one of the Nero Wolfe stories, right in the great detective's office. Everybody is suspected in turn, and the streets are full of lurking agents whose allegiances we cannot know. Nobody seems guiltless, nobody seems safe; and then, suddenly, the murderer is spotted, and—relief!—he is not, after all, a person like you or me. He is a villain—known to the trade as George Gruesome—and he has been caught by an infallible Power, the supercilious and omniscient detective, who knows exactly how to fix the guilt.

JEAN-PAUL SARTRE: THE NOVELIST AND THE EXISTENTIALIST

AUGUST 2, 1947 (ON *THE AGE OF REASON*)

THE AGE OF REASON is the first novel of Jean-Paul Sartre's to be translated into English. It is the first installment of a trilogy under the general title *The Roads to Freedom,* of which the second installment in translation has been announced for the fall. *The Age of Reason* deals with a group of young people in Paris—*lycée* teachers and students, Bohemians and night-club entertainers—in the summer of 1938. The second novel, *The Reprieve,* which has already appeared in French, carries the same characters along but works them into a more populous picture of what was going on in France during the days of the Munich Conference. The third volume, *The Last Chance,* has not yet been published in French, so it is impossible at the present time to judge the work as a whole or even to know precisely what the author is aiming at.

The Age of Reason, however, stands by itself as a story. Sartre displays here the same skill at creating suspense and at manipulating the interactions of characters that we have already seen in his plays. His main theme is simply the odyssey of an ill-paid *lycée* teacher who does not want to marry his pregnant mistress and who is trying to raise the relatively large fee required for a competent abortion; but though the author makes this provide a long narrative, in which we follow the hero's every move and in which every conversation is reported in its banal entirety, he stimulates considerable excitement, holds our attention from beginning to end, and engineers an unexpected dénouement which has both moral point and dramatic effectiveness. The incidents are mostly sordid, but, if you don't mind this, entertaining. The characters are well observed and conscientiously and intelligently studied, so that the book makes an interesting document on the quality and morale of the French just before their great capitulation. An American reader is struck by the close similarity of these young people, with their irresponsible love affairs, their half-hearted intellectual allegiances, and their long drinking conversations, to the same kind of men and girls at the same period in the United

States—just as the novel has itself much in common with certain novels that these young people produced. I do not believe, however, that this is the result of imitation by Sartre of the contemporary American novelists whom he is known to admire so much. It is rather that such young people everywhere have come to be more alike, so that the originals for Sartre's Parisians must have been far less specifically Parisian than the Parisians of Balzac or Flaubert or Anatole France or Proust.

It is true also that the writing of the book shows few of the traditional traits that we have been used to in French fiction. It tells the story with a "functional" efficiency, but it is colorless, relaxed, rather flat. It loses little in the English translation, not merely because the translator knows his business, but because Sartre's style does not put upon him any very severe strain. The conversation is mainly conducted in a monotonous colloquialism of catchwords, where some expression like *"C'est marrant"* does duty for as many emotions as our own ever-recurring "terrific"; and for this Mr. Eric Sutton has been able to find a ready equivalent in a jargon basically British with a liberal admixture of Americanisms. (In only one important respect has Mr. Sutton departed from Sartre's text. The reader should be warned that Daniel, in the third chapter from the end, has decided to castrate himself, not, as the translation seems to suggest, to commit suicide by cutting his throat.)

Of Sartre's imaginative work, I have read, besides this novel, only his plays and a few of his short stories. On this showing, I get the impression of a talent rather like that of John Steinbeck. Like Steinbeck, Sartre is a writer of undeniably exceptional gifts: on the one hand, a fluent inventor, who can always make something interesting happen, and, on the other, a serious student of life, with a good deal of public spirit. Yet he somehow does not seem quite first-rate. A play of Sartre's, for example, such as his recent *The Unburied Dead*—which is, I suppose, his best play—affects me rather like *The Grapes of Wrath*. Here he has exploited with both cleverness and conviction the ordeal of the French Resistance, as Steinbeck has done that of the sharecroppers; but what you get are a virtuosity of realism and a rhetoric of moral passion which make you feel not merely that the fiction is a dramatic heightening of life but that the literary fantasy takes place on a plane which does not have any real connection with the actual human experience which it is pretending to represent.

. . .

I have approached *The Age of Reason* purposely from the point of view of its merits as a novel without reference to the Existentialist philosophy of which Sartre is one of the principal exponents and which the story is supposed to embody. But, with the publication, also, of a translation of a lecture of Sartre's called "Existentialism" (Philosophical Library) and a pamphlet called "What Is Existentialism?," by William Barrett (Partisan Review), this demands consideration, too. It should, however, be said that neither of these discussions of the subject provides for the ordinary person the best possible key to Sartre's ideas. The Barrett essay, though very able, is mainly an exposition of the ideas of Martin Heidegger, a contemporary German philosopher, from whom Sartre took some of his prime assumptions, and it presupposes on the part of the reader a certain familiarity with the technical language of philosophy. The Sartre lecture has the special object of defending Existentialism against charges which have been brought against it by the Communists, so that it emphasizes certain aspects of the theory without attempting to state its fundamental principles. It would have been well if the publisher had included a translation of the article called "Présentation," in which Sartre explained his position in the first number of his magazine, *Les Temps Modernes* (October 1, 1945), and which gives the best popular account I have seen of what this literary school is up to. I can also recommend especially a short summary of the history of Existentialist thought and of its political and social implications—"Existentialism: A New Trend in Philosophy"—contributed by Paul Kecskemeti, a former U.P. foreign correspondent who is also a trained philosopher, to the March, 1947, issue of a magazine called *Modern Review* (published in New York by the American Labor Conference on International Affairs). This study has the unusual merit of not getting so deeply enmeshed in the metaphysical background of Existentialism that it fails to focus clearly on the picture of mankind on the earth which is the most important thing to grasp in a doctrine which is nothing if not realistic.

What is this picture, then? In Sartre's version—to skip altogether the structure of philosophical reasoning on which it is made to rest and which Sartre has set forth at length in a book called *L'Etre et le Néant*—it places man in a world without God (thought not all Existentialists are atheists), in which all the moral values are developed by man himself. Human nature is not permanent and invariable: it is whatever man himself makes it, and it changes from age to age. Man is free, beyond certain limits, to choose what he is to be and do. His life has significance solely in its relation to the lives of others—in his actions or refrainings from action: to use a favorite phrase of Sartre's, the individual must "engage himself."

Now, this conception of man's situation may appear to the non-religious reader, if he has also the "historical" point of view, precisely what he has always assumed, and may cause him to conclude with surprise that he has been an Existentialist without knowing it. To a Marxist, when he has further discovered that Sartre assigns human beings to the categories of the social classes almost as relentlessly as Marx, it will be evident that Sartre has borrowed from Marxism, and he may ask in what way Existentialism is an improvement over Marxism. In a debate between Sartre and a Marxist, a record of which follows the printed lecture, the Marxist actually scores rather heavily. The one advantage, it seems to me, that the doctrine of Sartre has is that it does away with Dialectical Materialism and its disguised theological content. There is for Sartre no dialectical process which will carry you straight to salvation if you get on the proletarian train. He sides with the proletariat, but intellectual or proletarian has to put up his own battle, with the odds looking rather against him. Yet Sartre does insist like a Marxist that every member of modern society belongs to a social class, and that "every one of his feelings, as well as every other form of his psychological life, is revelatory of his social situation." This molding of the individual by class—and Sartre allows also for the effects of "origin," "milieu," nationality, and sexual constitution—produces the limitation on freedom which I mentioned in passing above. One finds oneself in a situation which one did not make for oneself, but, given that situation, one can choose various ways of behaving in it. The bourgeois—with whom Sartre is particularly concerned—can either go along with his class or rebel against it and try to get away from it. The Marxist may inquire how this differs from the classical Marxist formulation that "men make their own history, but ... do not choose the circumstances for themselves," and how Sartre's practical doctrine of man realizing himself through action differs from Marx's conception of testing our ideas through action. To the reviewer, the conception of a wholly free will seems as naïve as the contrary conception of a wholly mechanistic determinism, and it is surely hardly less naïve to declare, as Sartre appears to do, that we are determined up to a certain point, but that beyond that we can exercise choice. If Marx and Engels, in exploring these problems, are somewhat less schoolmasterishly clear, they seem to me, in their tentative way, to give a more recognizable picture of what happens when what we take for the will tries to act on what we take for the world, and of the relation between man and his environment.

But the Existentialist philosophy of Sartre is the reflection of a different age from that which stimulated the activist materialism of Marx, and it has the immense advantages of sincerity and human sympathy over the very peculiar version of Marxism, totalitarian and imperialistic, now exported by the Soviet Union. Let us see it in its historical setting. Mr. Kecskemeti has shown in his essay how the neo-Kantian idealism of the pre-1914 period in Germany, which "admirably expressed the average German's awe in the presence of every kind of expert and official," had to give way, after the first German defeat, which shook this faith in specialized authority, to an effort to find principles of morality in the study of human conduct itself. So, eventually, the Germans got Heidegger. In the same way, Kecskemeti says, the defeat of the French in 1940 deprived them of all they had leaned on: they had at one stroke lost both their great traditions—the tradition of the French Revolution, which collapsed with the Third Republic, and the monarchist-Catholic tradition, which, through Pétain, had sold them out to the invaders. It is characteristic of the French that the destruction of French institutions should have seemed to them a catastrophe as complete as the Flood and caused them to evolve a philosophy which assumes that the predicament of the patriotic Frenchmen oppressed by the German occupation represented the situation of all mankind. They felt imperatively the duty to resist, with no certainty of proving effective, and they had, as Albert Camus has said, to formulate for themselves a doctrine which would "reconcile negative thought and the possibility of affirmative action." Hence the emphasis on the individual—since the Resistance was always an effort of scattered men and women—so different from the emphasis of Marx on the importance of collective action at a time when a great working-class movement was looming and gathering strength. Hence, also, the suffocating atmosphere of corruption, degradation, and depression which is a feature of Sartre's work and for which the French Communists, hopped up by the Kremlin to the cocksureness of propaganda, are in the habit of showering him with scorn. But such reproaches have no real validity, either artistic or moral: this atmosphere is Sartre's subject, and he has not allowed it to drug his intelligence or his conscience. This is the climate of the Occupation, and it is, in my opinion, his principal distinction that he has conveyed to us the moral poisoning of a France humiliated and helpless, in which people, brooding guiltily or blaming someone else, squabbled horribly, betrayed one another, or performed acts of desperate heroism. For, says Sartre, though you cannot appeal to God, you have always a margin of freedom: you can submit, you can kill yourself, or you can sell your life dear by resisting. Where this freedom is now to lead Frenchmen since the Germans have been driven out, I do not think that Sartre has yet made clear. Though anti-bourgeois and pro-working-class, he is evidently not an orthodox Communist of the kind who takes his directives from Moscow. One has a little the feeling about him that his basic point of view has been forged, as his material has been supplied, so completely under pressure of the pain and constraint of the collapse and the Occupation that he may never readapt himself to the temper of any new period.

. . .

And now how does *The Age of Reason* point the morals of Existentialist principles? Well, if you already know something of the subject, you will recognize some of its concepts turning up in the reflections of the hero as he walks drearily through the streets of Paris. And the conflict of classes is there: a seceder from the bourgeoisie, we see him revolving in a lonely orbit but experiencing gravitational pulls from a successful lawyer brother who represents the bourgeoisie, an old friend who has become a Communist and represents the proletariat, and a young girl of Russian émigré parents who represents the old nobility. It is not, however, this central character, so far as this volume takes him, who "engages himself" by a choice: his choices are all of the negative kind. It is the sexual invert Daniel, a neurotic and disconcerting personality, who, exercising his free will, resists his suicidal impulses and performs, unexpectedly and for devious reasons, a responsible and morally positive act. Here the difficult "situation" is a matter not of social class but of biological dislocation; and the triumph of Daniel's decision is to be measured by the gravity of his handicap.

Yet it is difficult to see how this story can have been very profoundly affected by Sartre's Existentialist theory. In such a production of his as his play *The Flies,* the dramatist turns academic and rather destroys the illusion by making the characters argue his doctrine; but this novel might perfectly have been written if Sartre had never worked up Existentialism. It differs from the picture of life presented by the embittered French Naturalists after the French defeat of 1871, whose characters were invariably seen as caught in traps of heredity and circumstance and rarely allowed to escape—though Sartre's mood, as in his play *No Exit,* is sometimes quite close to theirs. But this book does not essentially differ from the novels of other post-Naturalistic writers such as Malraux, Dos Passos, and Hemingway, for whom the international socialist movement has opened a door to hope and provided a stimulus to action that were unknown to such a Frenchman as Maupassant or to the Americans who paralleled his pessimism. In Sartre, as in these other writers, you have a study of the mixture in man's nature of moral strength and weakness, and a conviction that, though the individual may not win the stakes he is playing for, his effort will not be lost.

. . .

Since *Partisan Review* has published, also, in the same series as Mr. Barrett's pamphlet a translation of one of Sartre's long articles, "Portrait of the Anti-Semite," one should say something about his activity as a journalist. These essays which he contributes to his *Temps Modernes* seem to me among the most interesting work of their kind that has appeared during the current slump in serious periodical writing. In this field, Sartre can be compared only with George Orwell in England; we have nobody so good over here. Mr. Barrett, in an article on Sartre, has complained that he ignores, in his "Portrait," the Freudian springs of anti-Semitism. It is true that he makes no attempt to explain this phenomenon historically in its political and social connections; but he does pursue with merciless insight at least one of the psychological factors involved: the need of small, frustrated people to fake up some inalienable warrant for considering themselves superior to somebody. Sartre's whole essay, in fact, pretends to be nothing else than an elaborate development of this theme. It is no scientific inquiry but an exercise in classical irony, which might almost have been written, we reflect, by one of the more mordant eighteenth-century Encyclopedists. *The Age of Reason* of Sartre's novel is the intellectual maturity of the hero, but the phrase recalls also a period with which Sartre has a good deal in common. In these enormous and solid editorials that mix comment on current affairs with a philosophy which, whatever its deficiencies, is always clearly and firmly expressed, we are surprised and reassured to find ourselves chewing on something which we might have feared the French had lost. For it is Sartre's great strength in his time that he is quite free from the Parisian chichi of the interval between the wars. If Existentialism has become, like Surrealism, something of a *mouvement à exporter,* no one has probed so shrewdly as Sartre, in one of his articles in *Les Temps Modernes,* the recent attempts of the French to distract the attention of the world from their political and military discredit by exploiting the glory of their writers, or pointed out so boldly the abuses to which this practice may lead. If he sometimes has the air of pontificating, it is probably always difficult for a French literary man to resist becoming a *chef d'école.* And Sartre, bourgeois and provincial, has succeeded in preserving for the French qualities which they very much need and which it is cheering to see still flourish: an industry, an outspokenness, and a common sense which are the virtues of a prosaic intelligence and a canny and practical character. This does not, perhaps, necessarily make him a top-flight writer, but, in these articles of *Les Temps Modernes,* it does provide some very satisfactory reading.

LOUISE BOGAN

REVIEW OF
LORD WEARY'S CASTLE

NOVEMBER 30, 1946 (ON ROBERT LOWELL)

R ELIGIOUS CONVERSION, in the case of two modern poets writing in English—T. S. Eliot and W. H. Auden—brought an atmosphere of peace and relief from tension into their work. But Robert Lowell, a young American who has forsaken his New England Calvinist tradition for the tenets of the Roman Catholic Church, exhibits no great joy and radiance in the forty-odd poems now published under the title *Lord Weary's Castle* (Harcourt, Brace). A tremendous struggle is still going on in Lowell's difficult and harsh writings, and nothing is resolved. These poems bring to mind the crucial seventeenth-century battle between two kinds of religious faith, or, in fact, the battle between the human will and any sort of faith at all. They are often at what might be called a high pitch of baroque intensity. They do not have the sweetness of the later

English "metaphysical" writers; Lowell faces the facts of modern materialism more with the uncompromising tone and temper of the Jacobean dramatists, Webster and Tourneur, or of Donne, who (to quote Professor Grierson), "concluding that the world, physical and moral, was dissolving in corruptions which human reason could not cure, took refuge in the ark of the Church." (Lowell, it is clear, has not taken refuge anywhere.) He also bears some relationship to Herman Melville, the American with Puritan hellfire in his bones. The more timid reader would do well to remember these forerunners, and the conditions that fostered them, when confronted with young Lowell's fierce indignation.

Lowell's technical competence is remarkable, and this book shows a definite advance over the rather stiff and crusty style of his first volume, *Land of Unlikeness,* published in 1944 by the Cummington Press. This competence shows most clearly in his "imitations" and arrangements of the work of others, which he hesitates to call direct translations. "The Ghost" (after Sextus Propertius), "The Fens" (after Cobbett), and the poems derived from Valéry, Rimbaud, and Rilke reveal a new flexibility and directness. These poems might well be read first, since they show the poet's control of both matter and manner. The impact of the other poems in the book is often so shocking and overwhelming, because of the violent, tightly packed, and allusive style and the frequent effects of nightmare horror, that his control may seem dubious. The extraordinary evocation of the sea's relentlessness and the terror of death at sea, in "The Quaker Graveyard in Nantucket" (an elegy to a drowned merchant seaman), is equalled in dreadfulness by the grisly emblems of "At the Indian Killer's Grave," a poem wherein successive layers of spiritual and social decomposition in the Massachusetts Bay Colony come to light through a descent into the King's Chapel Burying Ground in Boston. Lowell, again in the seventeenth-century way, continually dwells upon scenes of death and burial. He is at his best when he mingles factual detail with imaginative symbol; his facts are always closely observed, down to every last glass-tiered factory and every dingy suburban tree. To Lowell, man is clearly evil and a descendant of Cain, and Abel is the eternal forgotten victim, hustled away from sight and consciousness. And the modern world cannot reward its servants; no worthy pay is received by the good mason who built "Lord Wearie's castle." (The old ballad from which the book's title is taken runs: "It's Lambkin was a mason good As ever built wi' stane: He built Lord Wearie's castle But payment gat he nane.") These are the themes that run through this grim collection. Lowell does not state them so much as present himself in the act of experiencing their weight. It is impossible to read his poems without sharing his desperation. Lowell may be the first of that postwar generation which will write in dead earnest, not content with providing merely a slick superficiality but attempting to find a basis for a working faith, in spite of secretive Nature and in defiance of the frivolous concepts of a gross and complacent society. Or he may simply remain a solitary figure. Certainly his gifts are of a special kind.

GEORGE ORWELL

THE *SANCTIFIED SINNER*

JULY 17, 1948 (ON *THE HEART OF THE MATTER* BY GRAHAM GREENE)

A FAIRLY LARGE PROPORTION of the distinguished novels of the last few decades have been written by Catholics and have even been describable as Catholic novels. One reason for this is that the conflict not only between this world and the next world but between sanctity and goodness is a fruitful theme of which the ordinary, unbelieving writer cannot make use. Graham Greene used it once successfully, in *The Power and the Glory,* and once, with very much more doubtful success, in *Brighton Rock.* His latest book, *The Heart of the Matter* (Viking), is, to put it as politely as possible, not one of his best, and gives the impression of having been mechanically constructed, the familiar conflict being set out like an algebraic equation, with no attempt at psychological probability.

Here is the outline of the story: The time is 1942 and the place is a West African British colony, unnamed but probably the Gold Coast. A certain Major Scobie, Deputy Commissioner of Police and a Catholic convert, finds a letter bearing a German address hidden in the cabin of the captain of a Portuguese ship. The letter turns out to be a private one and completely harmless, but it is, of course, Scobie's duty to hand it over to higher authority. However, the pity he feels for the Portuguese captain is too much for him, and he destroys the letter and says nothing about it.

Scobie, it is explained to us, is a man of almost excessive conscientiousness. He does not drink, take bribes, keep Negro mistresses, or indulge in bureaucratic intrigue, and he is, in fact, disliked on all sides because of his uprightness, like Aristides the Just. His leniency toward the Portuguese captain is his first lapse. After it, his life becomes a sort of fable on the theme of "Oh, what a tangled web we weave," and in every single instance it is the goodness of his heart that leads him astray. Actuated at the start by pity, he has a love affair with a girl who has been rescued from a torpedoed ship. He continues with the affair largely out of a sense of duty, since the girl will go to pieces morally if abandoned; he also lies about her to his wife, so as to spare her the pangs of jealousy. Since he intends to persist in his adultery, he does not go to confession, and in order to lull his wife's suspicions he tells her that he has gone. This involves him in the truly fearful act of taking the Sacrament while in a state of mortal sin. By this time, there are other complications, all caused in the same manner, and Scobie finally decides that the only way out is through the unforgivable sin of suicide. Nobody else must be allowed to suffer through his death; it will be so arranged as to look like an accident. As it happens, he bungles one detail, and the fact that he has committed suicide becomes known. The book ends with a Catholic priest's hinting, with doubtful orthodoxy, that Scobie is perhaps not damned. Scobie, however, had not entertained any such hope. White all through, with a stiff upper lip, he had gone to what he believed to be certain damnation out of pure gentlemanliness.

I have not parodied the plot of the book. Even when dressed up in realistic details, it is just as ridiculous as I have indicated. The thing most obviously wrong with it is that Scobie's motives, assuming one could believe in them, do not adequately explain his actions. Another question that comes up is: Why should this novel have its setting in West Africa? Except that one of the characters is a Syrian trader, the whole thing might as well be happening in a London suburb. The Africans exist only as an occasionally mentioned background, and the thing that would actually be in Scobie's mind the whole time—the hostility between black and white, and the struggle against the local nationalist movement—is not mentioned at all. Indeed, although we are shown his thoughts in considerable detail, he seldom appears to think about his work, and then only of trivial aspects of it, and never about the war, although the date is 1942. All he is interested in is his own progress toward damnation. The improbability of this shows up against the colonial setting, but it is an improbability that is present in *Brighton Rock* as well, and that is bound to result from foisting theological preoccupations upon simple people anywhere.

The central idea of the book is that it is better, spiritually higher, to be an erring Catholic than a virtuous pagan. Graham Greene would probably subscribe to the statement of Maritain, made apropos of Léon Bloy, that "there is but one sadness—not to be a saint." A saying of Péguy's is quoted on the title page of the book to the effect that the sinner is "at the very heart of Christianity" and knows more of Christianity than anyone else does, except the saint. All such sayings contain, or can be made to contain, the fairly sinister suggestion that ordinary human decency is of no value and that any one sin is no worse than any other sin. In addition, it is impossible not to feel a sort of snobbishness in Mr. Greene's attitude, both here and in his other books written from an explicitly Catholic standpoint. He appears to share the idea, which has been floating around ever since Baudelaire, that there is something rather distingué in being damned; Hell is a sort of high-class night club, entry to which is reserved for Catholics only, since the others, the non-Catholics, are too ignorant to be held guilty, like the beasts that perish. We are carefully informed that Catholics are no better than anybody else; they even, perhaps, have a tendency to be worse, since their temptations are greater. In modern Catholic novels, in both France and England, it is, indeed, the fashion to include bad priests, or at least inadequate priests, as a change from Father Brown. (I imagine that one major objective of young English Catholic writers is not to resemble Chesterton.) But all the while—drunken, lecherous, criminal, or damned outright—the Catholics retain their superiority, since they alone know the meaning of good and evil. Incidentally, it is assumed in *The Heart of the Matter,* and in most of Mr. Greene's other books, that no one outside the Catholic Church has the most elementary knowledge of Christian doctrine.

This cult of the sanctified sinner seems to me to be frivolous, and underneath it there probably lies a weakening of belief, for when people really believed in Hell, they were not so fond of striking graceful attitudes on its brink. More to the point, by trying to clothe theological speculations in flesh and blood, it produces psychological absurdities. In *The Power and the Glory,* the struggle between this-worldly and other-worldly values is convincing because it is not occurring inside one person. On the one side, there is the priest, a poor creature in some ways but made heroic by his belief in his own thaumaturgic powers; on the other side, there is the lieutenant, representing human justice and material progress, and also a heroic figure after his fashion. They can respect each other, perhaps, but not understand each other. The priest, at any rate, is not credited with any very complex thoughts. In *Brighton Rock,* on the other hand, the central situation is incredible, since it presupposes that the most brutishly stupid person can, merely by having been brought up a Catholic, be capable of great intellectual subtlety. Pinkie, the racecourse gangster, is a species of satanist, while his still more limited girl friend understands and even states the difference between the categories "right and wrong" and "good and evil." In, for example, Mauriac's "Thérèse" sequence, the spiritual conflict does not outrage probability, because it is not pretended that Thérèse is a normal person. She is a chosen spirit, pursuing her salvation over a long period and by a difficult route, like a patient stretched out on the psychiatrist's sofa. To take an opposite instance, Evelyn Waugh's *Brideshead Revisited,* in spite of improbabilities, which are traceable partly to the book's being written in the first person, succeeds because the situation is itself a normal one. The Catholic characters bump up against problems they would meet with in real life; they do not suddenly move onto a different intellectual plane as soon as their religious beliefs are involved. Scobie is incredible because the two halves of him do not fit together. If he were capable of getting into the kind of mess that is described, he would have got into it years earlier. If he really felt that adultery is mortal sin, he would stop committing it; if he persisted in it, his sense of sin would weaken. If he believed in Hell, he would not risk going there merely to spare the feelings of a couple of neurotic women. And one might add that if he were the kind of man we are told he is—that is, a man whose chief characteristic is a horror of causing pain—he would not be an officer in a colonial police force.

There are other improbabilities, some of which arise out of Mr. Greene's method of handling a love affair. Every novelist has his own conventions, and, just as in an E. M. Forster novel there is a strong tendency for the characters to die suddenly without sufficient cause, so in a Graham Greene novel there is a tendency for people to go to bed together almost at sight and with no apparent pleasure to either party. Often this is credible enough, but in *The Heart of the Matter* its effect is to weaken a motive that, for the purposes of the story, ought to be a very strong one. Again, there is the usual, perhaps unavoidable, mistake of making everyone too highbrow. It is not only that Major Scobie is a theologian. His wife, who is represented as an almost complete fool, reads poetry, while the detective who is sent by the Field Security Corps to spy on Scobie even writes poetry. Here one is up against the fact that it is not easy for most modern writers to imagine the mental processes of anyone who is not a writer.

It seems a pity, when one remembers how admirably he has written of Africa elsewhere, that Mr. Greene should have made just this book out of his wartime African experiences. The fact that the book is set in Africa while the action takes place almost entirely inside a tiny white community gives it an air of triviality. However, one must not carp too much. It is pleasant to see Mr. Greene starting up again after so long a silence, and in postwar England it is a remarkable feat for a novelist to write a novel at all. At any rate, Mr. Greene has not been permanently demoralized by the habits acquired during the war, like so many others. But one may hope that his next book will have a different theme, or, if not, that he will at least remember that a perception of the vanity of earthly things, though it may be enough to get one into Heaven, is not sufficient equipment for the writing of a novel.

W. H. AUDEN

PORT AND NUTS WITH THE ELIOTS

JULY 17, 1948 (ON "NOTES TOWARDS THE DEFINITION OF CULTURE" BY T. S. ELIOT)

LIKE MOST IMPORTANT WRITERS, Mr. T. S. Eliot is not a single figure but a household. This household has, I think, at least three permanent residents. First, there is the archdeacon, who believes in and practices order, discipline, and good manners, social and intellectual, with a thoroughly Anglican distaste for evangelical excess:

> . . . his conversation, so nicely
> Restricted to What Precisely
> And If and Perhaps and But.

And no wonder, for the poor gentleman is condemned to be domiciled with a figure of a very different stamp, a violent and passionate old peasant grandmother, who has witnessed murder, rape, pogroms, famine, flood, fire, everything; who has looked into the abyss and, unless restrained, would scream the house down:

> Reflected in my golden eye
> The dullard knows that he is mad.
> Tell me if I am not glad!

Last, as if this state of affairs were not difficult enough, there is a young boy who likes to play slightly malicious practical jokes. The too earnest guest, who has come to interview the Reverend, is startled and bewildered by finding an apple-pie bed or being handed an explosive cigar.

From its rather formidable title, it is evident that Mr. Eliot's latest essay, "Notes Towards the Definition of Culture" (Harcourt, Brace), is officially from the pen of the archdeacon, who is diffident about his powers but determined to do his social duty even under very unpropitious circumstances:

> In a society of smaller size (a society, therefore, which was less feverishly *busy*) there might be more conversation and fewer books; and we should not find the tendency—of which this essay provides one example—for those who have acquired some reputation, to write books outside the subject on which they have made that reputation.

With a proper caution and a schoolmaster's conscientiousness, the archdeacon begins by defining the various senses in which the word "culture" is used: to mean (1) the conscious self-cultivation of the individual, his attempt to raise himself out of the average mass to the level of the élite; (2) the ways of believing, thinking, and feeling of the particular group within society to which an individual belongs; and (3) the still less conscious way of life of society as a whole.

There are always two cultural problems: cultural innovation, i.e., how to change a culture for the better, however "good" may be defined; and cultural transmission, i.e., how to transmit what is valuable in a culture from one generation to the next. It is to the second problem that Mr. Eliot addresses himself—and rightly, most people, I think, will agree, for in the unstatic and unstable societies of our age, transmission, or cultural memory, is the major problem. Starting from the premise that no culture has appeared or evolved except together with a religion, whichever may be the agent that produces the other, he states and develops the thesis that the transmission of any culture depends on three conditions: (1) the persistence of social classes; (2) the diversity of local or regional cultures within a larger cultural unit; (3) the diversity of religious cult and devotion within a large universality of religious doctrine. The premise is, I think, undeniable, even by the most violent atheist, for the word "religion" simply means that which is binding, the beliefs or habits of conduct that the conscience of an individual or a society tells him he should affirm, even at the cost of his life (and nobody has a personal identity without such). For example, a Logical Positivist is a person who is prepared to be shot rather than say that metaphysical statements about value are real statements. If he is not so prepared, or if, recanting under pressure, he is not ashamed, then he is not a Logical Positivist. Nor will anyone quarrel, I think, with Mr. Eliot's contention that in a civilized society religion and culture, though interdependent—"bishops are a part of English culture, and horses and dogs are a part of English religion"—are not and should not be identical; e.g., it is only in a barbarous society that to drive on the right or to eat boiled cabbage or to listen to the music of Elgar would be regarded not as matters of habit or convenience or taste but as matters of ultimate significance. This, however, involves the conclusion that the religion of a civilized society is distinguished by the existence of dogma as separate from mythology and cult, and at this word "dogma" the hackles of the liberal are apt to rise. He immediately has visions of Torquemada and the stake, and, like Dr. Humdrum, in Macaulay's poem, begins to wonder:

> . . . how we should dress for the show,
> And where we should fasten the powder,
> And if we should bellow or no.

Yet his experiences of the last twenty years have perhaps made him less likely to be alarmed by that word, for the all too successful anti-liberal

heresies have compelled him to recognize that there is a liberal orthodoxy, of which he was unaware only because for so long it was never seriously challenged; he is forced to admit that there are beliefs from
which, if he can, he must convert and which, if he cannot, he must, in
however genteel a manner, persecute.

Nobody has ever really believed in freedom of religion. Where religion is concerned, the hardest virtue is tolerance, and to find out what a
person's religion is one has only to discover what he becomes violent
about. If one has never heard of a riot in the streets of New York between
Greeks and Italians over the Filioque Clause, or of an elder from the
Fifth Avenue Presbyterian Church defending Predestination with an
umbrella against the Arminian onslaughts of a vestryman from Trinity,
Wall Street, this means merely that to the majority of Americans today
Christianity is not religion but only culture, and not an important aspect
of that. In a revolutionary age like the present, the greatest threat to
freedom is not dogmas but the reluctance to define them precisely, for in
times of danger, if nobody knows what is essential and what is unessential, the unessential is vested with religious importance (to dislike ice
cream becomes a proof of heresy), so the liberal who is so frightened by
the idea of dogma that he blindly opposes any kind, instead of seeing
that nothing is made an article of faith that need not be so, is promoting
the very state of tyranny and witch-hunting that he desires to prevent.
However, it is not Mr. Eliot's views on religion that are going to get him
into hot water with a great many people but his approval of hereditary
classes and his doubts about universal education, for here the archdeacon
is from time to time replaced by the boyish practical joker, whose favorite
sport is teasing the Whigs, particularly if they happen to be Americans:

> In a healthily *stratified* society, public affairs would be a responsi-
> bility not equally borne: a greater responsibility would be inherited
> by those who inherited special advantages and in whom self-
> interest, and interest for the sake of their families ("a stake in the
> country"), should cohere with public spirit.

> A high average of general education is perhaps less necessary for
> a civil society than is a respect for learning.

> In justice to Thomas Gray, we should remind ourselves of the
> last and finest line of the quatrain, and remember that we may also

have escaped some Cromwell *guilty* of his country's blood. The proposition that we have lost a number of Miltons and Cromwells through our tardiness in providing a comprehensive state system of education cannot be either proved or disproved: it has a strong attraction for many ardent reforming spirits.

This is the hotfoot treatment, and the howls of anguish and rage that have already begun to go up are not altogether displeasing to at least one listener's ear, for one of the more unattractive characteristics of the Enlightened is their almost total lack of a sense of humor. The archdeacon in me, however, must regret them, because an enraged audience will not listen, even to refute. The value of Mr. Eliot's book is not the conclusions he reaches, most of which are debatable, but the questions he raises. For instance, how has culture been transmitted in the past? If the methods of the past are no longer possible, how can it be transmitted now? Mr. Eliot is only partly right, I think, in asserting that in the past the role of transmission was played by a class or by classes. For many centuries, it was transmitted by the Church; i.e., by an institution with a hereditary status whose members could be drawn from any social class. In England, it was only during the last two centuries or so that the responsibility for culture passed to social classes, first to the landed aristocracy, and then, when they became stockholders without responsibility, to the professional classes—the clergy, the doctors, the lawyers, etc. And even then it was certain institutions—the greater universities, the cathedral closes— that were really responsible. In Scotland, moreover, it was not only, or mainly, the rich who attended the universities.

The American problem has been unique. Jefferson and Hamilton read no different from Europeans; then, between 1830 and 1870, say, there emerged a culture that was definitely non-European but also entirely Anglo-Saxon; after that, in a sense, America had to begin all over again. It was perhaps unfortunate that, with the exception of the Germans of '48 and the Jews who came to escape persecution, the stimulus to immigration from Europe during the nineteenth century was so simply poverty, for this meant that of, for instance, the Irish and Italians who came, few were conscious bearers of their native culture and few had many memories they wished to preserve. This, and the absence of any one dominant church, has placed almost the whole cultural burden on the school, which has had to struggle along as best it could, with all too little help from even the family. It is a very encouraging sign that social groups within American society—the labor unions, for instance—are beginning to go into education instead of leaving it all to the state. I have never understood how a liberal, of all people, can regard state education as anything but a necessary and—it is to be hoped—temporary evil. The only ground for approval that I can see is the authoritarian ground that Plato gives—that it is the only way to insure orthodoxy. Well, if it comes to that, the gospel according to Teachers' Training College is not mine. Further, the more the total task of education can be shared among different groups, the smaller the educational unit can be. It is almost impossible for education organized on a mass scale not to imitate the methods that work so well in the mass production of goods.

The greatest blessing that could descend on higher education in this country would be not the erection of more class barriers but the removal of one; namely, the distinction drawn between those who have attended college and those who have not. As long as employers demand a degree for jobs to which a degree is irrelevant, the colleges will be swamped by students who have no disinterested love of knowledge, and teachers, particularly in the humanities, aware of the students' economic need to pass examinations, will lower their standards to let them.

. . .

So one could go on chatting and wrangling with the archdeacon all evening. If, from time to time, a small head has popped around the door and shouted "Boo to Jefferson!" or "Excuse me, are you out of the top drawer?," it could be politely ignored. The talk has been stimulating, the port excellent. Do go on. I am not questioning the usefulness . . .

Ichabod! Ichabod!

(Heavens! *What* was that extraordinary noise?) You were saying, sir, that the zealots of World Government seem to assume . . .

Mene, Mene, Tekel, Upharsin.

(There it goes again.)

The conversation trails off into silence. Whig? Tory? All flesh is grass. Culture? The grass withereth. One realizes that one is no longer reading lucid prose or following an argument; one has ceased trying to understand or explain anything; one is listening to the song of the third Eliot, a voice in Ramah, weeping, that will not be comforted.

LIONEL TRILLING

ORWELL ON THE FUTURE

JUNE 18, 1949 (ON *NINETEEN EIGHTY-FOUR*)

GEORGE ORWELL'S NEW NOVEL, *Nineteen Eighty-Four* (Harcourt, Brace), confirms its author in the special, honorable place he holds in our intellectual life. Orwell's native gifts are perhaps not of a transcendent kind; they have their roots in a quality of mind that ought to be as frequent as it is modest. This quality may be described as a sort of moral centrality, a directness of relation to moral—and political—fact, and it is so far from being frequent in our time that Orwell's possession of it seems nearly unique. Orwell is an intellectual to his fingertips, but he is far removed from both the Continental and the American type of intellectual. The turn of his mind is what used to be thought of as peculiarly "English." He is indifferent to the allurements of elaborate theory and of extreme sensibility. The medium of his thought is common sense, and his commitment to intellect is fortified by an old-fashioned faith that the truth can be got at, that we can, if we actually want to, see the object as it really is. This faith in the power of mind rests in part on Orwell's willingness, rare among contemporary intellectuals, to admit his connection with his own cultural past. He no longer identifies himself with the British upper middle class in which he was reared, yet it is interesting to see how often his sense of fact derives from some ideal of that class, how he finds his way through a problem by means of an unabashed certainty of the worth of some old, simple, belittled virtue. Fairness, decency, and responsibility do not make up a shining or comprehensive morality, but in a disordered world they serve Orwell as an invaluable base of intellectual operations.

Radical in his politics and in his artistic tastes, Orwell is wholly free of the cant of radicalism. His criticism of the old order is cogent, but he is chiefly notable for his flexible and modulated examination of the political and aesthetic ideas that oppose those of the old order. Two years of service in the Spanish Loyalist Army convinced him that he must reject the line of the Communist Party and, presumably, gave him a large portion of his knowledge of the nature of human freedom. He did not become—as Leftist opponents of Communism are so often and so comfortably said to become—"embittered" or "cynical"; his passion for freedom simply took account of yet another of freedom's enemies, and his intellectual verve was the more stimulated by what he had learned of the ambiguous nature of the newly identified foe, which so perplexingly uses the language and theory of light for ends that are not enlightened. His distinctive work as a radical intellectual became the criticism of liberal and radical thought wherever it deteriorated to shibboleth and dogma. No one knows better than he how willing is the intellectual Left to enter the prison of its own mass mind, nor does anyone believe more directly than he in the practical consequences of thought, or understand more clearly the enormous power, for good or bad, that ideology exerts in an unstable world.

Nineteen Eighty-Four is a profound, terrifying, and wholly fascinating book. It is a fantasy of the political future, and, like any such fantasy, serves its author as a magnifying device for an examination of the present. Despite the impression it may give at first, it is not an attack on the Labour Government. The shabby London of the Super-State of the future, the bad food, the dull clothing, the fusty housing, the infinite ennui—all these certainly reflect the English life of today, but they are not meant to represent the outcome of the utopian pretensions of Labourism or of any socialism. Indeed, it is exactly one of the cruel essential points of the book that utopianism is no longer a living issue. For Orwell, the day has gone by when we could afford the luxury of making our flesh creep with the spiritual horrors of a successful hedonistic society; grim years have intervened since Aldous Huxley, in *Brave New World,* rigged out the welfare state of Ivan Karamazov's Grand Inquisitor in the knickknacks of modern science and amusement, and said what Dostoevski and all the other critics of the utopian ideal had said before— that men might actually gain a life of security, adjustment, and fun, but only at the cost of their spiritual freedom, which is to say, of their humanity. Orwell agrees that the State of the future will establish its power by destroying souls. But he believes that men will be coerced, not cosseted, into soullessness. They will be dehumanized not by sex, massage, and private helicopters but by a marginal life of deprivation, dullness, and fear of pain.

This, in fact, is the very center of Orwell's vision of the future. In 1984, nationalism as we know it has at last been overcome, and the world is organized into three great political entities. All profess the same philosophy, yet despite their agreement, or because of it, the three Super-States are always at war with each other, two always allied against one, but all seeing to it that the balance of power is kept, by means of sudden, treacherous shifts of alliance. This arrangement is established as if by the understanding of all, for although it is the ultimate aim of each to dominate the world, the immediate aim is the perpetuation of war without victory and without defeat. It has at last been truly understood that war is the health of the State; as an official slogan has it, "War Is Peace." Perpetual war is the best assurance of perpetual absolute rule. It is also the most efficient method of consuming the production of the factories on which the economy of the State is based. The only alternative method is to distribute the goods among the population. But this has its clear danger. The life of pleasure is inimical to the health of the State. It stimulates the senses and thus encourages the illusion of individuality; it creates personal desires, thus potential personal thought and action.

But the life of pleasure has another, and even more significant, disadvantage in the political future that Orwell projects from his observation of certain developments of political practice in the last two decades. The rulers he envisages are men who, in seizing rule, have grasped the innermost principles of power. All other oligarchs have included some general good in their impulse to rule and have played at being philosopher-kings or priest-kings or scientist-kings, with an announced program of beneficence. The rulers of Orwell's State know that power in its pure form has for its true end nothing but itself, and they know that the nature of power is defined by the pain it can inflict on others. They know, too, that just as wealth exists only in relation to the poverty of others, so power in its pure aspect exists only in relation to the weakness of others, and that any power of the ruled, even the power to experience happiness, is by that much a diminution of the power of the rulers.

The exposition of the *mystique* of power is the heart and essence of Orwell's book. It is implicit throughout the narrative, explicit in excerpts from the remarkable *Theory and Practice of Oligarchical Collectivism*, a subversive work by one Emmanuel Goldstein, formerly the most gifted leader of the Party, now the legendary foe of the State. It is brought to a climax in the last section of the novel, in the terrible scenes in which Winston Smith, the sad hero of the story, having lost his hold on the reality decreed by the State, having come to believe that sexuality is a pleasure, that personal loyalty is a good, and that two plus two always and not merely under certain circumstances equals four, is brought back to health by torture and discourse in a hideous parody on psychotherapy and the Platonic dialogues.

Orwell's theory of power is developed brilliantly, at considerable length. And the social system that it postulates is described with magnificent circumstantiality: the three orders of the population—Inner Party, Outer Party, and proletarians; the complete surveillance of the citizenry by the Thought Police, the only really efficient arm of the government; the total negation of the personal life; the directed emotions of hatred and patriotism; the deified Leader, omnipresent but invisible, wonderfully named Big Brother; the children who spy on their parents; and the total destruction of culture. Orwell is particularly successful in his exposition of the official mode of thought, Doublethink, which gives one "the power of holding two contradictory beliefs in one's mind simultaneously, and accepting both of them." This intellectual safeguard of the State is reinforced by a language, Newspeak, the goal of which is to purge itself of all words in which a free thought might be formulated. The systematic obliteration of the past further protects the citizen from Crimethink, and nothing could be more touching, or more suggestive of what history means to the mind, than the efforts of poor Winston Smith to think about the condition of man without knowledge of what others have thought before him.

By now, it must be clear that *Nineteen Eighty-Four* is, in large part, an attack on Soviet Communism. Yet to read it as this and as nothing else would be to misunderstand the book's aim. The settled and reasoned opposition to Communism that Orwell expresses is not to be minimized; but he is not undertaking to give us the delusive comfort of moral superiority to an antagonist. He does not separate Russia from the general tendency of the world today. He is saying, indeed, something no less comprehensive than this: that Russia, with its idealistic social revolution now developed into a police state, is but the image of the impending future and that the ultimate threat to human freedom may well come from a similar and even more massive development of the social idealism of our democratic culture. To many liberals, this idea will be incomprehensible, or, if it is understood at all, it will be condemned by them as both foolish and dangerous. We have dutifully learned to think that tyranny manifests itself chiefly, even solely, in the defense of private property and that the profit motive is the source of all evil. And certainly Orwell does not deny that property is powerful or that it may be ruthless in self-defense. But he sees that, as the tendency of recent history goes, property is no longer in anything like the strong position it once was, and that will and intellect are playing a greater and greater part in human history. To many, this can look only like a clear gain. We naturally identify ourselves with will and intellect; they are the very stuff of humanity, and we prefer not to think of their exercise in any except an ideal way. But Orwell tells us that the final oligarchical revolution of the future, which, once established, could never be escaped or countered, will be made not by men who have property to defend but by men of will and intellect, by "the new aristocracy . . . of bureaucrats, scientists, trade-union organizers, publicity experts, sociologists, teachers, journalists, and professional politicians."

> These people [says the authoritative Goldstein, in his account of the revolution], whose origins lay in the salaried middle class and the upper grades of the working class, had been shaped and brought together by the barren world of monopoly industry and centralized government. As compared with their opposite numbers in past ages, they were less avaricious, less tempted by luxury, hungrier for pure power, and, above all, more conscious of what they were doing and more intent on crushing opposition. This last difference was cardinal.

The whole effort of the culture of the last hundred years has been directed toward teaching us to understand the economic motive as the irrational road to death, and to seek salvation in the rational and the planned. Orwell marks a turn in thought; he asks us to consider whether the triumph of certain forces of the mind, in their naked pride and excess, may not produce a state of things far worse than any we have ever known. He is not the first to raise the question, but he is the first to raise it on truly liberal or radical grounds, with no intention of abating the demand for a just society, and with an overwhelming intensity and passion. This priority makes his book a momentous one.

THE CURRENT
CINEMA

A NOTE BY DAVID DENBY

FOR THE OVERWHELMING MAJORITY OF AMERICANS, "the movies,"
in the 1940s, meant the films that issued forth from the Hollywood
studios in satisfying numbers and played at the local theatres built
right in the middle of town. The movies belonged to everyone, and they
fitted into weekly life all over the country. Some successful films had
long runs, of course, but many theatres (which were owned by the studios) changed their shows every week. Most Americans didn't read critics, or wait to hear what their friends said; they thought of movies, as the
critic Robert Warshow put it, as a "pure" culture, like fishing or baseball,
and they went to films without much thought or planning. After the war,
weekly attendance peaked at more than eighty million (it's now around
thirty million). There wasn't, after all, much competition to speak of,
apart from dance bands, newspapers, magazines, radio, bowling, bingo,
and fornication.

The studio system, still firmly in place at the beginning of the decade,
generated genres and stars. Family pictures opened every other week,
and also Westerns, women's pictures, high-kilowatt Technicolor musi-
cals, dark-shadowed crime films, and psychological dramas—indeed,
dreams and traumas of varying sorts, accompanied by portentously
equivocal music, took over many serious films, and sympathetic doctors,
some of them played by Claude Rains, performed miracle cures, something that now seems inconceivable (Freud's reputation was running
high in the forties). The movie theatre was a place of moral comfort and,

frequently, reassurance, though the studios produced infinite and intriguing variations on formula stories for moviegoers who valued style. It was definitely a time for classicists and connoisseurs in the audience. In later decades, the auteur critics discovered thematic patterns in the work of individual directors, but few people recognized such things at the time or cared. The artists among the directors put up with many frustrations: the demand to stay on schedule as each studio turned out fifty or so movies a year; the revisions of many screenwriters, often guided by producers; the frequent reediting of a movie after a tepid preview. Despite all this, the system worked well for such creators as Alfred Hitchcock, Howard Hawks, George Cukor, Preston Sturges, Vincente Minnelli, Raoul Walsh, William Wyler, Billy Wilder, and many others. It did not work well for Orson Welles, a man too original and restless to mesh with semi-authoritarians in suits. It was a rich, sinful, corrupt, and productive decade.

It has been said that Brahms was the first composer to possess the same sense of music history (periods, influences, shifts in harmonic inventiveness) that we do. I'm not sure there were many directors or critics who had a comparable sense of movie history in the forties (the way that Scorsese and Tarantino do now). U.S.C. began its film program early, in 1929, and by 1932 was offering a degree in film studies, and U.C.L.A. followed in 1947, but film study was rare or nonexistent at most universities. During the silent period, there had been an enormous flow of euphoric writing about movies as an art form in little magazines devoted to experimental work (*Hound & Horn*) or left-wing politics (*New Masses*). But the coming of sound, and the greater psychological plausibility and realism that came with it, tended, at the serious level, to chase away the aestheticians and to encourage the sociological critics who harped on important themes and the social responsibility of the medium. In the forties, magazine and newspaper criticism was mostly what it had always been, plot summary garlanded with a grade, though there was one great critic, James Agee, at *The Nation*, who wrote enduring American prose about movies.

When *The New Yorker* began, in 1925, the magazine was much more New York–centric than it is now, and the prime local industry in the arts was theatre, not movies. Some of the magazine's staff wrote for the theatre, or mixed happily with theatre people and wits who lived and breathed plays, productions, actors, and actresses. Hollywood, the place of disillusion, was "out there," as Dorothy Parker later put it, though, of course, many *New Yorker* writers, including Parker, went to Hollywood (Pauline Kael has immortalized this coastal transfer in *The Citizen Kane Book*). The general attitude was that Hollywood was a place to make money and have a hell of a good time (when you weren't having a hell of a bad time).

Movies were omnipresent, familiar, loved, but rather taken for granted. The magazine demanded brevity and wit in its movie reviews and no more than a glancing touch of seriousness, and the writing, from our viewpoint, lacks sensuous evocation and physicality—the commanding impress of image, landscape, atmosphere, eros. Throughout the forties, however, the critics wrestled with the apprehension that something complicated and subtle might be going on in at least some of the films. I admire John Mosher's way of capturing the bewildering tonal shifts in Chaplin's *The Great Dictator*. And Mosher's impressive piece on *The Grapes of Wrath* does indeed work as evocation. I'm surprised that Mosher writes off, with a witticism, the resemblance of Charles Foster Kane to William Randolph Hearst, since that resemblance was, of course, part of what made *Citizen Kane* exciting, but Mosher understood that Welles was creating an entirely new form in his great film. John Lardner, in his appreciation of the noirish *Double Indemnity*, edges toward a recognition of perversity; the movie, he says, is "a smooth account of sordid minds at work, and compromises with sweetness and light only at well-spaced intervals." And John McCarten, in his lovely review of Vittorio De Sica's *The Bicycle Thief*, attempts to describe an entirely new mode of feeling: "By now I imagine you will have gathered," he says at the end, "that I think the thing is a masterpiece."

JOHN MOSHER

THE GREAT HILDY

JANUARY 13, 1940 (ON *HIS GIRL FRIDAY*)

S INCE 1931, every movie of newspaper people and their lives has been
in one way or another just a repeat of *The Front Page.* No young
actor dressed up as a cub reporter and waiting his turn on the set
has failed to make his little prayer to the shades of Hildy Johnson, and
perhaps each pavilion for the care of the mentally unbalanced has its crop
of youngsters who happened to see the movie, or the Hecht-MacArthur
play it came from, just before they landed a job in some city room. Looking back through my line-a-day book, with marginalia, for '31, I discover
I thought then *The Front Page* was the funniest movie in town, and I
evidently had a very good time with its ribald and hilarious comedy.
Now, after all these years and after God knows how many feeble, wispy,
sad imitations of the original, I find the new and authentic adaptation—
which is what *His Girl Friday,* titled from Walter Winchell's weekly val-
entine, turns out to be—as fresh and undated and bright a film as you
could want.

Mysterious things, to be sure, have happened to the original, as you
can imagine when you hear that the role which brought Pat O'Brien to
the screen has been revamped for Rosalind Russell. And that role, you
may remember, is the Hildy Johnson part itself. Miss Russell is Hildy
and is unabashed at her own audacity, and even Lee Tracy, the first of all
the Hildys, should appreciate her verve. With Cary Grant as her editor—
that was Menjou once, you know—there's a shift in the plot, with some
new scenes and a ludicrously innocent part for Ralph Bellamy, but the
big central scene of the police reporters' room in the city jail, the jail
break of the condemned man—no longer an anarchist, for that would
date the piece, as one now doesn't seem to hear much about anarchists for
some reason or other—and all the give and take of the old pretty dialogue remain. It's not ladyfied a moment just because the beautiful Miss
Russell is planted right in the midst of the rumpus. The idea seems ominous, yet perhaps we had best face the prospect: she may do for the ladies what Lee Tracy and Pat O'Brien did for the young men. The
women's wards in those hospitals had better lay in some new cots.

ZANUCK'S JOADS

FEBRUARY 3, 1940 (ON *THE GRAPES OF WRATH*)

OUT FROM CALIFORNIA now comes *The Grapes of Wrath*, the epic of starvation. With a majesty never before so constantly sustained on any screen, the film never for an instant falters. Its beauty is of the sort found in the art of Burchfield, Benton, and Curry, as the landscape and people involved belong to the world of these painters. Its visual qualities, too, can be traced back through the history of the movies; the best of the past has been used, every lesson learned. Thus there are moments when we see a lone figure silhouetted against the horizon as in the old films which aspired to impress. It was a stunt that was impressive then, and it is still impressive. Again, there are moments in *The Grapes of Wrath* so direct and simple that they are like excerpts from a fine newsreel. That, too, is right. Or again, the camera seems to pause in the style of the Russian films, and we are given what is almost a series of stills. Faces are brought forward, out from the huge panorama, and held a moment, close and enlarged—the faces of hungry children, work-racked old men and women—silent and unmoving before us. Such a method, as here employed, does not slow down the film as it has often done in Soviet pictures. John Ford has kept his pace swift, and when familiar approaches to his subject have been essential, he has made them as fresh as though he had been the first to note the dramatic value of that man placed against the sky. He showed what he could do in *The Informer,* and he has gone beyond that in *The Grapes of Wrath.*

The script he had to work from is in itself a tremendous success. Nunnally Johnson must have found the Steinbeck novel no kindergarten job to adapt for the movies. It was long, outspoken, and, being a best-seller, something sacred. Its scandalized, delighted, and authoritative readers, many of whom refused to find even any monotony in the original discursive and iterative chronicle, were loyally ready to jump on a digression. From the moment it was heard that the book was to be screened, appreciative admirers wondered how the true force of the dialogue could be handled with the propriety requisite for screen delicacy, and, above all, how the odd dietary incident which Steinbeck devised as the shock of his conclusion could be managed. The hegira of the Joads has been abbreviated, of course, but the story of it is fully given. From the first glimpse we have of Tom coming down the dusty Oklahoma road, we are moved straight to the world of the Okies; though without reference to either digestive or procreative processes, the language manages to be virile; Mr. Johnson keeps his characters buttoned up but human. And, perhaps with more force than the book, the film closes on Ma Joad's words: "We're the people that live. Can't nobody wipe us out. Can't nobody lick us. We'll go on forever. We're the people."

Ma was the great characterization in the book. Holding together her whole family in their desperate effort to survive, she was most definitely a clarified personality—not a mere type, not, so to speak, a social problem. She alone might be called Steinbeck's creation in the novel. Jane Darwell, who plays Ma, has been long in the theatre and in pictures, and now she suffers from the very experience she has had. Here her expertness does not stand her in good stead. Competent she is, yet she never quite frees her performance from the suggestion of the theatre. Actually this does not matter in an appraisal of the film as much as might be thought. This is no scenario for stars. Individuals are lost against the grandeur of the landscape or in the huge mass movements of many people. The extras count as much as the featured players.

Henry Fonda's Tom Joad stands out at times in the vast assemblage, and occasional specific gestures or exclamations draw our eyes and ears to the Grampa and Granma of Charley Grapewin and Zeffie Tilbury, to the Rosasharn of Dorris Bowdon, the Connie of Eddie Quinlan, the Casy of John Carradine, the Pa Joad of Russell Simpson, and the Muley of John Qualen. Mostly, though, we think of the film in terms of groups, the family on the truck, the family gathered around Grampa's grave, the children in the store in front of the candy, the other children staring at food—something to eat—in the camp. It is a great film of the dust plains, the highways, the camps, of the sky above, and of a nameless, evicted people.

CHARLIE'S HITLER

OCTOBER 26, 1940 (ON *THE GREAT DICTATOR*)

THERE'S A GENERAL FEELING, I discover, prevalent around the town that *The Great Dictator* is a very curious affair indeed, something distinctly odd, and certainly unique. People aren't sure that they like it, or anyhow they aren't very eloquent about why they do, or, on the other hand, why they don't. Reports and small talk aren't apparently going to send crowds to see it, though I think the baffled and inarticulate discussions may sustain that curiosity which was so coyly nourished during all the five years of the film's making. The truth probably is that too much has happened in these five years for the film's own good. I don't mean that too much has happened in Hollywood. I refer to occurrences in other portions of the globe.

There were never any very good Hitler jokes, and now, I should say, there are none anywhere near being good. Photographs suggested that Hitler looks somewhat like Charlie Chaplin, which had perhaps once some comic aspect, but it happens to be an aspect not largely relevant at this moment. The resemblance evidently did amuse Charlie Chaplin himself, and it is the cornerstone of this whole picture. That it should turn out to be even as sturdy material for laughter as it does is one of the amazing and baffling factors of this truly singular production. It is by no means so amazing, though, as that we should find ourselves titillated by hilarious burlesques of ghettos, Nazi troopers, and concentration camps. Charlie Chaplin alone could have dreamed of such an approach to the events of the day, and surely only Charlie Chaplin could somehow have swung the whole fantastic conglomeration into anything nearly successful or even endurable.

Where he is successful, which is throughout a considerable length of the picture, he is just being his old self, Hitler or no Hitler. If anything, he has grown younger with the years. As a Jewish barber, he again and again is that familiar figure of his great days, though this time it's the Nazis he's dodging and not the cops. The dictator role is newer stuff for him, but here, too, he is best when he can be overwhelmed or crushed down, or at least abandoned to the wildest phantasmagoria, as in the famous scene with the balloon. I would say that the scene of the balloon (a balloon with the world painted upon it), the dance of the dictator at play with the world itself, is just about as delightful a bit as Charlie Chaplin has ever given us anywhere. It is sheerest fantasy, child's fantasy, and I think this childlike naïveté saves the picture. Like Hitler or not, like Mussolini or not (and Jack Oakie's mimicry is very apt also), the people of this picture, until near the very end, belong to another sphere. There's a child's humor in the names, names such as Bacteria, Garbitsch, Herring, and Hynkel, and much kindergarten tomfoolery in the business of the barber chairs and in a great deal of the hearty slapstick of the ghetto. Ghetto scenes and palace scenes have this young gusto about them, which is surely sustained through the first half but begins to abate from then on, until, all of a sudden, without any warning, Charlie Chaplin grows old. In the last speech, commenced in a scene of characteristic comedy, he launches into direct exhortation straight from the screen. I fear the wrench is too great. The power of the film is its detachment, its use of current matters as though surveyed from another planet, and we can't be jolted in a jiffy back to real life like this. Nor, on the same grounds, are we prepared to see the little Jewish girl (Paulette Goddard), whom we have watched so merrily smack the Storm Troopers over their noddles with a frying pan, exalted in a final closeup as the symbol of all Jewish womankind in the lands of the dictators. Mr. Chaplin might have been wiser to have played his stunt for its full worth, making perhaps, after all, a good Hitler joke; he should have stayed on that other planet and never for a moment have touched this one.

CHILDE ORSON

MAY 3, 1941 (ON *CITIZEN KANE*)

THE NOISE AND THE NONSENSE that have attended the release of *Citizen Kane* may for the time being befog the merit of this extraordinary film. Too many people may have too ready an inclination to seek out some fancied key in it, after the silly flurry in our press, and to read into the biography of its leading character extraneous resemblances to persons in actual life. There is a special kind of pleasure to be found in such research, and the success of the most commonplace movie often lies in the simple fact that it suggests one's neighbors, or the scandalous people who took the house on the corner one year, or the handsome bootlegger who used to call every week. *Citizen Kane* can hardly suggest the ways and habits of neighbors, at least to most householders, but it may remind some of revelations in Sunday supplements. To others, I suppose, it will all seem more like Mars—just Mr. Orson Welles and his Mars again.

Since movies hitherto have commenced with a cast list and a vast directory of credits, we are promptly jolted out of our seats when *Citizen Kane* ignores this convention and slides at once into its story. For introduction, there is only a stylized and atmospheric hint of background, of shut high gates and formidable fencing, and this formal difference seems revolutionary enough to establish Mr. Welles' independence of the conventions. This independence, like fresh air, sweeps on and on throughout the movie, and in spite of bringing to mind, by elaborately fashioned decoration, a picture as old in movie history as *Caligari,* the irregularity of the opening sets a seal of original craftsmanship on what follows. Something new has come to the movie world at last.

Mr. Welles is not merely being smart, clever, or different. By the elliptical method he employs, he can trace a man's life from childhood to death, presenting essential details in such brief flashes that we follow a complex narrative simply and clearly and find an involved and specialized character fully depicted, an important man revealed to us. With a few breakfast scenes, the progress of a marriage is shown as specifically as though we had read the wife's diary. By a look and a gesture, electricians high above a stage describe the sad squawks an opera singer is giving below them. The use of an imaginary "March of Time" provides an outline which allows us to escape long exposition. Scenes in the great man's Xanadu never drag, never oppress one with useless trimmings, yet we get an immediate comprehension of the unique, absurd establishment, with its echoes and its art collection, and the one gag allowed ("Don't talk so loud. We're not at home") becomes just a reasonable statement.

Sometimes I thought there was too much shadow, that the film seemed to be performed in the dark. Mr. Welles likes a gloom. He blots out the faces of speakers and voices come from a limbo when it is what is being said and not how people look that is important. Only once or twice, at times like these, does the film seem mannered. For the most part we are too absorbed in the story and its characters to observe any tricks, too swiftly carried on by its intense, athletic scenes.

Dorothy Comingore, George Coulouris, and Joseph Cotten are on the list of the fine players, but clearly it is Orson Welles himself, as Mr. Kane, the great millionaire publisher, the owner of Xanadu, the frustrated politician, the bejowled autocrat, the colossus of an earlier American era, who is the centre and focus of all the interest of the film. By a novelist's device, we learn of this man through the comments of the few who have been close to him, the second wife's being the most sensational— that second wife whom he drives into the grotesque mortification of an operatic career for which she has no talent. The total impression, though, is not of something entirely monstrous. Mr. Kane does not come out of all this a melodrama villain. I think it is a triumph of the film, and proof of its solid value and of the sense of its director and all concerned, that a human touch is not lost. Sympathy for the preposterous Mr. Kane survives. Indeed, there is something about him which seems admirable. I can imagine that various rich gentlemen who own newspapers may find the characterization only right and proper, and claim that their sensitivity, like Mr. Kane's, has been misunderstood by their intimates, and others may recognize many a Mr. Kane among their competitors.

DAVID LARDNER

PRE-EISENHOWER

NOVEMBER 28, 1941 (ON *CASABLANCA*)

EVEN THOUGH THE ARMED FORCES might be said to have taken some of the play away from them, Warner Brothers have gone right ahead and released a film called *Casablanca*. They may feel that General Eisenhower has merely served them well as an advance agent. The Casablanca on the screen is the old Casablanca of three or four weeks ago, and much of the heavy intrigue indulged in by Humphrey Bogart, Ingrid Bergman, Claude Rains, Sydney Greenstreet, and Paul Henreid has presumably been cleaned up by the army of occupation by now, but there is probably enough topical truth left in the picture to suit the topical-minded. Not to speak of the eternal truths always to be found in the better screen plays.

The centre of intrigue in old Casablanca, we learn, was Rick's, a night spot where forged passports flowed like water. Into this dive, operated by Bogart, come Henreid, as the leader of an underground movement in Europe, and Miss Bergman, as Europe's most beautiful woman. Henreid has escaped from a concentration camp and is trying to get to America. The Germans would like to stop him by fair means or unwholesome. Claude Rains, as the local police chief, sits cheerfully on the fence and won't do much for anybody. Bogart and Miss Bergman have met before in Paris, it turns out, and they become particularly melancholy whenever the song "As Time Goes By" is played. It's as good a tune as any to attach sentiment to, and a good one to attach to this picture, which, although not quite up to *Across the Pacific,* Bogart's last spyfest, is nevertheless pretty tolerable and deserves attractive accessories.

BLOOD AND PREMIUMS

SEPTEMBER 16, 1944 (ON *DOUBLE INDEMNITY*)

A PRETTY GOOD MURDER MELODRAMA has come to town, named *Double Indemnity.* I have an idea that Paramount, which launched it, takes a certain artistic pride in the fact that the two leading characters, played by Fred MacMurray and Barbara Stanwyck, are heels who behave antisocially throughout and die violent deaths at the finish. This, you understand, is not the kind of thing fan clubs are accustomed to, and a producer who runs such a chance with the public's sweet tooth is no doubt entitled to bask at his desk in a glow of prestige while assistants wring his hand in shifts and say "Chief, you are game as a pebble."

Be that as it may, there is another point about *Double Indemnity* which strikes me as even more unusual. That is the nature of its treatment of the insurance industry and those predatory types among us who buy insurance. Taking up the message of the James Cain novel on which it was based, the picture, without so much as blinking, shows insurance as a deadly war between beneficiaries, felonious to a man, and the company, which fights tooth and nail in defense of its capital holdings. The true giant of the battle, and therefore of the film, is Edward G. Robinson, the company's claims inspector, a gentleman tortured by the thought that a client may get away with something but practically infallible in forestalling such a calamity. When Mr. Robinson, told that the police are giving up their investigation of the death of a policyholder, says scornfully, "Sure, it's not their money," he sounds the keynote of the struggle. He is very entertaining, I should add, and not a little convincing.

It appears that sentinels as keen as this can be duped only by someone on the inside, who knows all the angles—by choice, an insurance salesman. Personally, I have done business with three or four salesmen who were, like Mr. MacMurray in the picture, genial and fair-spoken and absolute mother lodes of human knowledge and special information. It now occurs to me that if I had wanted to commit a perfect crime, and I won't say I didn't, I should have consulted one of them on the spot. That is what Miss Stanwyck does with Mr. MacMurray. She is anxious to dispose of her husband, at a profit, and Mr. MacMurray puts his unique resources at her service with a readiness which weakens the picture somewhat, for, though Miss Stanwyck's beauty is great and the temptation to outwit one's employer may be equally so, the salesman's character, as written and acted, does not make his crime wholly credible. Apart from this fault, *Double Indemnity* is a smooth account of sordid minds at work, and compromises with sweetness and light only at well-spaced intervals. There are one or two especially good moments, as when Mr. Robinson, sharing Mr. Cain's relish for this sort of detail, intones as he would a hymn the statutory variations of suicide.

JOHN McCARTEN

VERY RARE VINTAGE

DECEMBER 1, 1945 (ON *THE LOST WEEKEND*)

THE FILM VERSION of *The Lost Weekend* is every bit as impressive a tour de force as the Charles Jackson novel from which it was adapted. The suspense that Mr. Jackson managed to instill into his study of an alcoholic is tautly evident throughout the picture, and as its protagonist, Ray Milland conveys, with a realism often overwhelming, the anguish of a man trying to find in drink a narcotic to ease the ache of failure. The problem posed by *The Lost Weekend* is a lot more important than any that Hollywood has tackled in a long, long time, and it is presented in thoroughly adult fashion, with dialogue pitched for sensible ears and photography designed for discerning eyes. Most of the outstanding episodes of Mr. Jackson's book are here, from the sordid, drunken bout that the hero of the piece finances by withholding ten dollars from a cleaning woman to the nerve-racking night he spends in the alcoholic ward of Bellevue. In his role of a frustrated, dipsomaniac writer, Mr. Milland shows a nice appreciation of the terrors a sheet of blank paper can hold for an author, and in a scene in which he plods brokenly for miles along Third Avenue in an attempt to hock his typewriter, only to discover in the end that every pawnshop is closed for Yom Kippur, he gets hold of all the tragic irony of the situation.

While the burden of carrying *The Lost Weekend* along devolves mainly upon Mr. Milland, he receives some sturdy assistance from the rest of the cast. As a tough-tongued bartender, Howard da Silva is as convincing as anybody I've run across behind a beer pump, and as a spiteful, supercilious male nurse, Frank Faylen will make your hackles rise. There are excellent performances, too, by Jane Wyman, Philip Terry, Doris Dowling, and, for that matter, everybody else in the cast. While I'm scattering compliments around this way, I wouldn't want to overlook Billy Wilder and Charles Brackett, who fashioned the screen play and served, respectively, as director and producer. They can congratulate themselves on having made one of the best films of the past decade.

NONE BETTER

DECEMBER 10, 1949 (ON *THE BICYCLE THIEF*)

VITTORIO DE SICA, who directed the remarkable Italian film *Shoe-Shine*, has come along with another offering, called *The Bicycle Thief*, which should establish him forthwith as the peer of any moviemaker in the world. In this one, De Sica, starting with a slender theme, winds up with a drama that is at once funny, appealing, exciting, and sad. The picture is set in Rome, and chronicles the agitated weekend of a workman who, after holding down a new job as billposter for only part of a day, sees a crook make off with his bicycle, a necessary tool of his trade. De Sica has previously established the importance of this bicycle by showing the workman's wife pawning the family sheets to get it out of hock, and it seems a very real catastrophe when the vehicle is stolen. The pursuit of the thief makes up the rest of the picture, and the chase leads the workman into all kinds of strange situations. Following right behind him is his small son, and the pair of them, as played by Lamberto Maggiorani and Enzo Staiola, are totally persuasive.

De Sica never slips in his direction, whether he is taking his hero and the boy through the corridors of a wonderfully realistic mission, full of battered derelicts and starchly prim workers in the Lord's vineyard, or plunging them into the dangerous midst of the thieves and black-marketeers of Rome. No matter how tense the movement of the film becomes, he always has time to find a touch of humor in such things as the small boy's bewilderment when, during a rainstorm, he takes cover against a wall, along with half a dozen young seminarians, all of whom are jabbering away in German, and the child's confusion at the mission when, on peering into a confessional, he is rapped sharply on the head by the attendant cleric. And another funny scene is a glimpse of the youngster's irritation at being compelled to wait outside a brothel while his father is inside looking around for the thief. Throughout the picture, the emotional interdependence of father and son is studied compassionately, and when, in an access of frustration, the workman denounces the boy as a nuisance and slaps him, it makes for as poignant a moment as I've ever experienced at the movies. Since the acting is altogether superior, it is worth remarking that there is only one professional in the cast. The man who plays the hero is a metalworker, his supposed wife is a journalist, and the boy is a seven-year-old whom De Sica happened upon while shooting a street scene. A good many of those in the supporting cast are just what they are made out to be. The photography is endlessly varied, and there is some fine visual irony in the views of the workman and his son making their way through crowds of fashionable and sporting cyclists in the hope of recovering the worn-out bicycle on which their livelihood depends. By now I imagine you will have gathered that I think the thing is a masterpiece.

THE THEATRE

A NOTE BY HILTON ALS

THE BEST, MOST INTERESTING CRITICISM is produced by those writers who are willing to risk being artists themselves. Between 1940 and his death eighteen years later, Wolcott Gibbs was *The New Yorker*'s first-string theatre critic, a role he assumed after Robert Benchley hung up his visor following eleven years on the job. But Benchley, with his schnauzer eyes and commonsense wit, had a second career, as a sometime monologist or character actor in films ranging from the 1935 Oscar-winning short *How to Sleep* to Alfred Hitchcock's 1940 film *Foreign Correspondent*. Unlike Benchley, however, Gibbs—bespectacled, more tall than square—was temperamentally unsuited for the job of critic as public figure; his writing was his defense against a world that both entranced and bugged him.

Gibbs felt outside life's party from the first. He was born in 1902 into a prosperous family with ties to science, industry, and politics; his father died early, when Wolcott was six. Gibbs's alcoholic mother was incapable of taking care of the future writer and his siblings, so Wolcott was sent off to live with an uncle. Gibbs's education was spotty; he was expelled from one boarding school and never attended college. In 1927, after a stint as a reporter at a Long Island newspaper, he joined the staff of Harold Ross's *New Yorker*, where he worked in various capacities—editor, Talk of the Town reporter, short-story and Profile writer—for the next thirty years. (His very sweet and funny 1950 play, *Season in the Sun*, about a sort of Gibbs-like writer's life on Fire Island, is not least among his accomplishments, and is ripe for revival.)

But Gibbs wrote about theatre more consistently than he did any other subject for the magazine; rereading his *New Yorker* theatre pieces now is like looking at an ongoing journal about a cultural world where some things lasted and other things did not. (It is difficult to recall, for instance, how significant Elmer Rice's politically motivated work was to the theatre landscape of the 1930s and '40s, before Arthur Miller took his spot.) But what is consistent throughout is Gibbs's voice. It was the voice of New York—always on the verge of giving up without forgoing optimism entirely. Take this moment from his first review as *The New Yorker*'s lead theatre critic, published February 3, 1940:

> On the night when most of my fortunate and sporty friends were watching Henry Armstrong beat the ears off a fighter called Pedro Montanez, I found myself imbedded in the play known as *Young Couple Wanted*. . . . If I were asked to furnish a description of it to ornament the marquee of the Maxine Elliott, I think "winsomely inept" are the words I would choose. Jed and Catherine want to get married, but, because the capitalist system makes no provision for the basically unemployable, they can't. Instead they live together in Greenwich Village, planning to manufacture a product made out of grapes and peanuts. In the end . . . but for some reason I find that I am disinclined to go on with all this. Armstrong won by technical knockout in the ninth. Or so they told me, later that night.

Nothing is more tedious than describing the plot of a play that one finds tedious. Gibbs was one of the first to make a game of it; indeed, it became a hallmark of his style. But when it came to the "new" theatre of the 1940s, ushered in by Tennessee Williams and Oscar Hammerstein II, among others, Gibbs acknowledged how his earlier critical style—with its Deco-like sheen and New York provincialism—would have to change in accordance with the America these and other artists were bringing to realistic, often lyrical light. In short, Gibbs would have to be more open and go deeper as a writer himself. Writing about Eugene O'Neill's 1946 masterwork, *The Iceman Cometh*—he didn't love it as much as the previous decade's *Mourning Becomes Electra*—he acknowledged how the entire enterprise "was certainly enough to intimidate the most frivolous critic." Never content with his facility, Gibbs, during the 1940s, threw it in the rumble seat of his past, and began producing some of the best work of his career, in any genre—without sacrificing any of his caricaturist's love of the small or big gesture. In his review of the 1946 Broadway musical *Annie Get Your Gun*, he praises Ethel Merman for her gift of suggesting a wide range of emotion without perceptibly altering her expression—her leer is wonderfully suggestive but practically immobile; laughter disturbs her face only for an instant and then usually in only a rather chilly parody of amusement; and love for her, at least in *Annie,* is expressed by a look of really terrible vacancy.

This is as beautiful and true as anything the poet Edwin Denby wrote about the dance and dancers. Like Denby, Gibbs wrote criticism that was the synthesis of everything he produced outside it, including "Eden, with Serpents," his sad, hard short story about a clinic where people with names like Mrs. Charlie Goodenough lounge while drying out, or any number of other stories in which drinking and recovery play a part. You cannot be funny without knowing not only that great sadness is at the bottom of the precipice, but that it is actually holding up the earth you stand on. Criticism suited Gibbs because he could be alone in a crowd, immersed in the world of someone else's vulnerability and imagination, which called on his own. That's where he lived. And where his words continue to live, too.

WOLCOTT GIBBS

THE BOYS IN THE BACK ROOM

OCTOBER 19, 1946 (ON *THE ICEMAN COMETH* BY EUGENE O'NEILL)

THE CIRCUMSTANCES ATTENDING the appearance last week of Eugene O'Neill's *The Iceman Cometh* were certainly enough to intimidate the most frivolous critic. There was the illustrious author—except for Shaw, perhaps the only living Olympian—returning from years of mysterious silence with a play that was vaguely reported to be just a part of a far vaster project; there was the knowledge that this work, though possibly only a fragment, was still of such dimensions that the acting of it could not be accomplished in anything less than four and a half hours; there was the impression, somehow confirmed by the cryptic title and by the fact that the reviewers were furnished with the text in advance, that the visible play offered but a very small percentage of its author's total meaning and would therefore require a concentration on everybody's part at least adequate for deciphering the hieroglyphs on the Rosetta stone. Under these conditions, it was a little disconcerting to find that *The Iceman Cometh*, while an interesting play, was by no means comparable to its author's best efforts in the past, either in style or substance, and furthermore that, except for some possible ambiguity at the end, it was no harder to understand than any work that attempts to convey large general ideas in terms of specific and circumscribed action. Mr. O'Neill's idea in this case is no more original or abstruse than the discovery, not unknown to melancholy sophomores, that life is insupportable without illusions; his treatment of it, however, is so monumental, so clearly designed to merit words like "Greek" and "symphonic," that it is no wonder that elaborate interpretations are already being provided by the metaphysicians in the parish. For the moment, we will stick to the facts.

The curtain at the Martin Beck goes up on the bar of a Raines Law hotel in the summer of 1912. It is six o'clock in the morning and a dozen or so of the inmates are sprawled asleep over the tables. They are thus disposed, rather than being upstairs in their beds, because they are waiting for the arrival of Hickey, a sporty travelling salesman who turns up once a year on the proprietor's birthday to buy them drinks and to relieve the tedium of their lives with the horsy humors of the road. It is a scene of appalling squalor, though Robert Edmond Jones has made it tremendously effective theatrically, and it is not improved as, one by one, the lost men wake up and we are allowed to inspect them in more detail. Inevitably, since Mr. O'Neill is dealing with the fate of all mankind, the personnel is extensive, ranging from cheap whores and mad Nihilists to scarecrow remittance men and Harvard graduates sunk without a trace. All they have in common, except for chronic alcoholism and filth, are their sorry lies about the past and their boozy dreams of an impossible tomorrow, but these still are enough to distinguish them as living men, capable of at least some dim parody of the emotions of human beings, even including a kind of desperate gaiety.

Hickey turns up at last, but it is soon obvious that he is not the companion they have known in the past. It is bad enough for them to discover that he is on the wagon but far worse to learn that he is preaching a curious salvation. Peace can come to them, he says, as it has come to him, only when they have abandoned all their empty dreams. Before these illusions can be given up, however, it is necessary to put them to the test, and, one by one—sober, terrified, and dressed with pathetic care—the bums leave the shelter of the bar to make their doomed attempts to take up life again. When they come back, they are finally without hope, but peace has escaped them, too. Faced with the tragic truth about themselves, some wearily accept the idea of death, some are roused to a savage hatred of their companions, all begin to lose their last resemblance to men. In their extremity, however, they learn that Hickey has murdered his wife, whose illusions about his behavior had given him an intolerable sense of guilt, and that the peace he offered them was only a spiritual counterpart of the physical death he had already accepted for himself. At the last moment, stricken with remorse at the terrible effect of his compassionately meant interference with their lives, he allows them to think that he has been insane, and with enormous relief they go back to their bottles and their hollow, happy dreams.

This, of course, is only a bare summary of Mr. O'Neill's theme. There is also an almost intolerable mass of supporting detail, for each derelict in the bar is relentlessly determined to give his own personal history, often as many as three or four times. Obviously, there isn't room for all of these here, but a few may help to indicate the play's impressive range and, incidentally, since this review is necessarily a work of drastic compression, give a partial listing of the cast that supports James Barton in the tremendous central role. Harry Hope (Dudley Digges), the owner of the bar, has never stepped out of it for twenty years. It is his pipe dream, his special evasion of the fact of lost will, to imagine that he has sequestered himself because of his grief over his wife's death and that any day now he will go out and resume his old career as a wardheeling politician. Piet Wetjoen (Frank Tweddell) and Cecil Lewis (Nicholas Joy) fought on opposite sides in the Boer War, and it is their delusion that presently they will go back across the sea to an honorable old age. Willie Oban (E. G. Marshall), a law-school graduate, is the son of a convicted bucket-shop operator. The most hopeless alcoholic of them all, he dreams of straightening up and getting a brilliant job in the district attorney's office. Rocky Pioggi (Tom Pedi) is Harry's night bartender, and his illusion is of a peculiar and negative character. He is under the impression that although two agreeable girls turn over their earnings to him, he is not a pimp, for the excellent reason that he holds a regular job and prostitution is only a casual sideline in his life. Unlike the rest, Larry Slade (Carl Benton Reid), a disenchanted radical, appears to be without any hope whatever. He is, he says, through with the Cause and only waiting around to die. In spite of the fact that he is able to identify the real nature of Hickey's peace and to fight it for the others, he is finally obliged to accept it for himself, since, if I am not mistaken, he is the symbol of tragic omniscience (or the author) on the stage. Of them all, only Dan Parritt (Paul Crabtree), who has betrayed his Anarchist mother to the police out of motives very similar to those that led Hickey to shoot his wife, dies in the end. All through the play, he and the metaphysical drummer have had a curious sense of identity with each other, and when the truth about Hickey is revealed and he is taken off to the electric chair, the other man finds his parallel solution in suicide.

There are many more in the cast, but these characters—all superlatively acted, by the way—should be enough to establish Mr. O'Neill firmly in the company of William Saroyan as a wonderfully prolific inventor of damned and fascinating people. His other qualifications for the position of America's leading playwright, however, I'm afraid remain just about what they were before. The construction, the ponderous building up, over three acts, of a situation that is to be resolved by a much too abrupt theatrical trick at the end of the fourth, is at least questionable, especially when the trick is so executed that it can be interpreted in two ways by the audience. If, that is, my own impression is right and Hickey's insanity is feigned for the purpose of giving his companions back their drunken hopes, he is simply a misguided philanthropist who has sincerely believed right up to the last that peace can be found only in the final, absolute acceptance of defeat. If, on the other hand, he is really insane, he is only a figure of crazy malevolence and the point of the play is hard to imagine. This alternate explanation, while it can hardly be justified on reflection, is nevertheless one that seems to have been subscribed to by a great many reasonably attentive people, including at least one critic, after the opening night, so it is hard to credit Mr. O'Neill with wholly satisfactory craftsmanship from a sheerly theatrical point of view. He has erred even further, I think, in a certain obscurity of intention that seems to mark several members of the cast. The demented Nihilist, for instance, undoubtedly keys in with Hickey's own spiritual Nihilism, but the analogy is never clearly developed and all that appears on the stage is a sort of irrelevant, comic-supplement bomb-thrower. The same thing applies to a lot of the others—they are obviously meant to be essential pieces of the total design, but their exact relation to it is not sufficiently defined and they become merely atmospheric "characters," present for a scenic effect rather than for comprehensible artistic purposes. I'm sure, of course, that Mr. O'Neill could readily explain how each actor is vital to the pattern and the forward movement of his play, but it is certainly by no means apparent in the theatre, where, unfortunately, the playwright's secret mind is not on view.

In regard, finally, to the style in which *The Iceman* has been written, I can only say that there is little evidence of the lofty eloquence that distinguished *Mourning Becomes Electra* or even, indeed, some of Mr. O'Neill's lesser works. As several critics have pointed out, the locale of the play and the prototypes of the bums who appear in it have been taken from the author's own remote past. The assumption, however, that he has exactly recaptured the sound of their speech may be open to question, and it is my opinion that, while Mr. O'Neill is a superb reporter of behavior and even of processes of thought, the language he uses to convey them is actually non-realistic, being of the conventional dese-dem-dose school of dialect, which a certain kind of abstracted literary intelligence, from Richard Harding Davis to Thomas Wolfe, has somewhat arbitrarily decided is the language of the lower depths. It is odd but nevertheless a fact that a writer can often understand perfectly what is being said around him without really hearing the accent of the voice or the structure of the sentence, and I'm afraid that this is particularly true of Mr. O'Neill.

Inaccurate as his bums may be, however, I'm not sure that they are as painful as some of his more articulate types. Slade, the radical, who serves more or less as his author's spokesman, is naturally given some rather towering sentiments to express and perhaps he may be forgiven a certain grandiloquence, but there can be no such excuse in the case of the burlesque old-school-tie locutions employed by the British captain, the elaborate, pedantic witticisms of the fallen Harvard man; or the laborious Babbittries and really stupefying repetitions of Hickey himself. On the whole, in fact, I suspect that Hickey is the worst of all, and there were times during the now famous sixteen-minute speech when I felt a deep sympathy with the old saloonkeeper and his guests, who could only murmur hopelessly, "For God's sake, Hickey, give us a rest! All we want to do is pass out in peace."

WELL WORTH WAITING FOR

FEBRUARY 19, 1949 (ON *DEATH OF A SALESMAN* BY ARTHUR MILLER)

THOUGH IT SEEMS TO ME that Arthur Miller still has a tendency to overwrite now and then, his *Death of a Salesman*, at the Morosco, is a tremendously affecting work, head and shoulders above any other serious play we have seen this season. It is the story of Willy Loman, a man at the end of his rope, told with a mixture of compassion, imagination, and hard technical competence you don't often find in the theatre today, and probably the highest compliment I can pay it is to say that I don't see how it can possibly be made into a moving picture, though I have very little doubt that somehow or other eventually it will. The acting, especially that of Lee J. Cobb, as the tragic central figure, Mildred Dunnock, as his loyal wife, and Arthur Kennedy, as a son whose character he has lovingly and unconsciously destroyed, is honest, restrained, and singularly moving; Jo Mielziner's set, centering on the interior of a crumbling house somewhere in Brooklyn but permitting the action to shift as far away as a shoddy hotel room in Boston, is as brilliant and resourceful as the one he did for *A Streetcar Named Desire;* Elia Kazan, also, of course, an important collaborator on *Streetcar,* has directed the cast with the greatest possible intelligence, getting the most out of a script that must have presented its difficulties; and an incidental score, by Alex North, serves admirably to introduce the stretches of memory and hallucination that alternate with the actual contemporary scenes on the stage. Kermit Bloomgarden and Walter Fried, to round out this catalogue of applause, are the fortunate producers of *Death of a Salesman,* and I think the whole town ought to be very grateful to them.

The happenings in Mr. Miller's play can hardly be called dramatic in any conventional sense. Willy is sixty-three years old, and he has spent most of his life as the New England representative of a company that I gathered sells stockings, though this point was never exactly specified.

Recently the firm has cut off his salary and put him on straight commission, and the income from that is obviously not enough for him to get along on, what with a mortgage, and insurance, and the recurring payments on an electric icebox, an ancient contraption about which he remarks bitterly, "God, for once I'd like to own something before it's broken down!" In addition to his financial troubles, his health and his mind are failing (he has been having a series of automobile accidents, basically suicidal in intent), and his two sons aren't much comfort to him. Long ago, he had had muddled, childish dreams for them both—the elder, in particular, was to be a famous football star, greater than Red Grange—but things didn't work out, and now one is a stock clerk, not interested in much except women, and the other, when he works at all, is just an itinerant farmhand. Willy's deep, hopeless recognition of what has become of him, of the fact that, mysteriously, society has no further use for him, has reduced him to a strange borderland of sanity, in which fantasy is barely distinguishable from reality. The only remaining hope he has, in fact, lies in some crackbrained scheme the two boys have for making a fortune selling sport goods in Florida, and when that collapses, too, there is clearly nothing left for him but to kill himself, knowing that at least his family will manage somehow to survive on the money from his insurance.

That is the rough outline of Mr. Miller's play, and it doesn't, I'm afraid, give you much idea of the quality of his work, of how unerringly he has drawn the portrait of a failure, a man who has finally broken under the pressures of an economic system that he is fatally incapable of understanding. There are unforgettable scenes: the interview in which he is fired by the head of the firm, a brassy young man, who plays a hideous private recording in which his little boy names the capitals of all the states, in alphabetical order; a sequence in the Boston hotel, when his son finds him with a tart and his love turns to hatred and contempt; a dream meeting with his brother Ben, who has made a fortune in diamonds in the Kimberley mines and stands, in his mind, as the savage, piratical symbol of success; and, near the end of the play, a truly heartbreaking moment when Willy at last comes to realize that he is "a dollar-an-hour man" who could never, conceivably, have been anything more.

Death of a Salesman is written throughout with an accurate feeling for speech and behavior that few current playwrights can equal. It may not be a great play, whatever that means, but it is certainly a very eloquent and touching one. The cast, besides Mr. Cobb, Miss Dunnock, and Mr.

Kennedy, includes Cameron Mitchell, Thomas Chalmers, Howard Smith, Don Keefer, and Alan Hewitt. They are all just what I'm sure the author hoped they'd be.

WHAT A WONDERFUL WAR

APRIL 16, 1949 (ON RODGERS & HAMMERSTEIN'S *SOUTH PACIFIC*)

WHILE *SOUTH PACIFIC*, the only musical, as far as I know, ever to be based on a Pulitzer Prize book, lacks the special quality of *Oklahoma!*, a sort of continuous sunny gaiety, it has about everything else. Richard Rodgers' score, if not his best, certainly isn't far from it, and Oscar Hammerstein's lyrics, with one or two exceptions, are just as successful; the plot, a difficult combination of sentimental love, tragic passion, and the rowdy behavior of our armed forces, is admirably handled on all three levels; the performances, especially those of Ezio Pinza and Mary Martin, are practically flawless; and Jo Mielziner's sets, ranging from the cockeyed disorder of a naval base to the strange beauty of a tropical island, are executed with extraordinary humor and charm. Altogether, it is a fine show, and I wouldn't be surprised if it were still at the Majestic when another Presidential election rolls around.

I don't remember James Michener's stories very clearly (somehow I have a feeling that they weren't really especially memorable) but I do know that it never occurred to me that they might furnish material for a musical comedy, since, like most honest pieces about war, they hadn't much in the way of orderly design and an acceptable love interest was conspicuously missing. However, Mr. Hammerstein and Joshua Logan, who collaborated with him on the libretto in addition to serving as director, have taken care of all that with the greatest possible ingenuity. The principal theme now is the romance between an exiled French planter, who didn't, as I recall, appear at all in Mr. Michener's book, and a jaunty nurse from Little Rock, Arkansas, who did turn up in one of the stories, though in a rather different context. The only obstacle to their marriage is the fact that he is the father of two children by a Polynesian wife, and though she has died, it is a circumstance that would probably make any young woman think twice.

The secondary plot has to do with a lieutenant of Marines and his affair with a beautiful native girl. This is doomed from the outset, partly because her mother is a disreputable old baggage, dealing in grass skirts and shrunken human heads, but mostly because he is a native of Philadelphia and a graduate of Princeton and, naturally, somewhat conscious of his glorious heritage. These two separate but parallel stories are firmly joined together in the end, when the two men undertake a suicidal mission against the Japanese (an English remittance man was the hero of this episode in Mr. Michener's version), in the course of which the Marine is killed but from which the planter comes back to the nurse, who by now has realized the error of her ways. As you can see, this is a fairly weighty narrative sequence, calling for a liberal administration of comic relief. I'm glad to say that the authors have been generously and happily inspired about that, too, creating any number of fine, tough characters and providing them with some wonderfully funny material, including a vaudeville number, featuring Miss Martin in an outsize sailor suit and Myron McCormick with a full-rigged vessel tattooed on his heaving stomach, that may be the best show-inside-a-show you ever saw.

Some time ago, in an interview, Cole Porter remarked that he wished to hell theatre critics would refrain from discussing music, on the ground that even the most educated of them wouldn't recognize the national anthem unless the people around them stood up. Having taken this advice to heart, I will confine my comment on Mr. Rodgers' score to saying that "Some Enchanted Evening," magnificently delivered by Mr. Pinza, seems to me a tremendously moving song; that "I'm Gonna Wash That Guy Right Outa My Hair" and "I'm in Love with a Wonderful Guy," as rendered by Miss Martin, and "There Is Nothing Like a Dame," as sung, or bellowed, by the naval personnel, strike me as being among the liveliest of Mr. Rodgers' and Mr. Hammerstein's joint efforts; and, to intrude one dissenting note in this rhapsody, that I wasn't particularly impressed by "Bali Ha'i," which sounded to me a good deal like any number of other songs celebrating exotic place names, or by something called "You've Got to Be Taught," a poem in praise of tolerance that somehow I found just a little embarrassing.

There is nothing, of course, to say about Mr. Pinza's voice, beyond the fact that no greater one has been heard on the musical-comedy stage. Since he is also an intelligent and imposing actor, his appearance in *South Pacific* is one of the pleasantest things that have happened to the theatre this season. Miss Martin, whose talents as a comedienne haven't had much scope, at least in New York, since she first enchanted us all with "My Heart Belongs to Daddy," has just what she wants this time, and I think her performance is a delight from beginning to end. Of the others, Mr. McCormick gives perhaps the funniest and most hideous female impersonation in history; Betta St. John is astonishingly lovely as a kind of Tonkinese Madame Butterfly; Juanita Hall, as her unspeakable mother, is not only an accomplished comedienne but also the possessor of another notable voice; and there are sound, attractive contributions by William Tabbert, as the faithless Princetonian, and by Martin Wolfson and Harvey Stephens, as a couple of irascible officers. The nine young ladies who represent Navy nurses didn't look very medical to me.

ART &
ARCHITECTURE

A NOTE BY PETER SCHJELDAHL

"**M**ANHATTAN—great unfilleted sole spread out on a rock—is no good except along the backbone; the edges are slums," Le Corbusier had written in 1935. The words appear in the majestic Profile of the architect, published in three issues of *The New Yorker* in 1947, by Geoffrey T. Hellman, who was the magazine's extravagantly sophisticated reporter on New York institutional culture and high society. The quote is germane to a furious debate about where to put the United Nations buildings, which ranged Le Corbusier, who endorsed the East River site, against Robert Moses, who—grumping, "What do these foreign fellows know about our foundations, our hard-rock problems?"—plumped for Flushing Meadows. Those were dramatic days in the edifice game. Having added nothing much to the skyline for more than a decade, New York suddenly found itself the capital city of planet Earth, with wealth and bursting ambition to match. Dynamite thumped, bulldozers howled, and cranes bristled. No one knew that the first major International Style skyscrapers would remain, for all time, the best. Briefly, power could seem at one with poetry, in stanzas of steel and glass.

The New Yorker responded handsomely. Its architecture critic was Lewis Mumford, the philosopher of urbanism whose concern for humane values shaded the epochal triumph of modernist styles, which he well understood, with prophetic compunctions. Imagine Rockefeller Center's towers reduced from seventy to thirty-two stories. On a revisit to the complex, Mumford declared that that would have made a good project great by bringing it into overall harmony with pedestrian experience. Think about this the next time you're there. (I have, and I get it.) Think also, at any of the city's postwar housing projects, of the baleful legacy of Le Corbusier's beau ideal, the "vertical garden city." (When genius blunders, the future weeps.) *The New Yorker*'s architecture coverage in the forties spelled out ideas and broached issues that resound to this day.

Meanwhile, a handful of mostly impoverished painters downtown were revolutionizing the aesthetics of modern art and would soon wrench world leadership from the war-groggy School of Paris. The magazine's art critic at the time, Robert M. Coates, gave the movement its name. In his regular column, The Galleries, in the issue of March 30, 1946, Coates called the German-émigré painter and teacher of painters Hans Hofmann "one of the most uncompromising representatives of what some people call the spatter-and-daub school of painting and I, more politely, have christened abstract Expressionism." (He must have performed the baptism in conversation; no earlier printed citation has been found.) But the critic fretted, adding that he would have been willing "to dismiss [Hofmann's paintings] as sheer nonsense" but for certain formal qualities that marked Hofmann as a fairly, truth be told, compromising member of the avant-garde. To his credit, Coates had noted the volcanic talent of Jackson Pollock from the start, but, as late as 1949, he found the artist "curiously baffling." And he maintained a mysterious hostility to the all-around best New York painter, ever: Willem de Kooning.

Still, Coates is an intriguing figure. A Yale man, he became a fixture of the Lost Generation of expatriates in Paris in the twenties. He may have introduced his friends Ernest Hemingway and Gertrude Stein to each other, on a stroll in the Luxembourg Gardens. (Accounts differ.) Coates wrote novels tinged with the influences of Dada and Surrealism. His *The Eater of Darkness* (1926) remains a tangy read. Simply, he couldn't, or wouldn't, shake off his deference to European culture. He accurately detects Abstract Expressionism's trace elements of Symbolism, Expressionism, Cubism, and Surrealism, but misses its transcendence of them. Meanwhile, he reflects the provincial crouch of a local art world, still insular and crabby, in which intellectual boldness could blow up your social life. In column after column, Coates gingerly pats the heads of not entirely bad artists whose names today glow dimly, if at all.

The crown jewel of the magazine's arts coverage in the forties, for me, is a breathtaking epic of reportage: the three-part "The Beautiful Spoils," detailing the wartime German looting—a "scramble for beauty"—of Europe's art treasures and the campaign of a ragtag U.S. Army unit to recover them. By Janet Flanner, the magazine's luminous Paris correspondent for nearly fifty years, it reads like a thriller, indelibly, and it anatomizes the aesthetic passions that so weirdly attended Nazism's monstrousness. Flanner zeroes in on the pillager-in-chief, Hermann Göring, whose "easy, vulpine smile" at his Nuremberg trial may come to haunt you, Cheshire fashion, as it now does me. The Reichsmarschall's ravening connoisseurship—often in sneaking competition with that of Hitler, who was likewise smitten but otherwise distracted—made him probably the most prodigious art collector of all time, though with merciful brevity. We meet, in his company, a rogue's gallery of silky crooks and fawning collaborators. And we all but smell the grunge on the ill-provisioned dozen soldiers of the U.S. Monuments, Fine Arts, and Archives group as they rushed around France and Germany to save a continent's patrimony, not least from souvenir-craving G.I.s.

Flanner puts us in the boots of thunderstruck young Americans a mile deep in the gleaming caverns of a salt mine near Salzburg, which was packed with art, including well over five thousand Old Masters, intended for a museum in Hitler's hometown of Linz. They noticed particular crates labeled "Marble, Don't Move." These contained explosives which, but for a last-minute disobedience of S.S. orders, would have destroyed everything. By the reckoning of certain Nazis, likely including the jovial Göring before he cheated the hangman with a cyanide capsule, we were barbarians undeserving of joys so high and pure.

ROBERT M. COATES

ASSORTED MODERNS

DECEMBER 23, 1944

THERE'S A SCATTERING of one-man and group shows this week— Kurt Seligmann at Durlacher, David Burliuk at the A.C.A., a modern French collection at Pierre Matisse, and an American one at the 67 Gallery—and although they are all pleasant enough to see, they're as difficult to describe, consecutively, as a patchwork quilt. I was a little disappointed in the new Seligmanns, to begin with him, and I think the color he employs in his current set of paintings is at the root of the difficulty. To be sure, he has never been particularly noteworthy as a colorist. It's that queer half-Surrealist, half-medieval mythology he has created, with its tatter-demalion knights, bony and distorted, cavorting against backgrounds of ruins, that chiefly arouses the interest, and I have frequently felt that he does rather better in his etchings and other black-and-whites than he does in his paintings.

Until now, his color has never seemed greatly to interfere with his artistic intentions, but in the group of paintings at Durlacher there is a kind of candy-coated brilliance, a gaudy mingling of reds and greens and yellows, that just gets in the way all the time. Seligmann's philosophy always has been essentially a sombre one. What he paints is the poetry of decay, of a world going tortuously downhill, and the trouble is that the bright coloration he applies to his pattern irresistibly suggests quite another mythology, that of the child's story book, in which knights and other medieval characters are also depicted but in which the whole line of thought is on a lighter, more cheerful plane. Mr. Seligmann may have some deliberate plan behind this incongruity. Looking at his *Quattuor* and *Full Daylight,* I almost thought so, for in both these there is a cold glare about the color that enhances the design. But in a number of others, such as *Isis, Acteon, Alaska,* and *Apparition,* the conflict between pigment and portent produces only confusion. In effect, you don't know whether to laugh or to cry, to clap your hands childishly or think deeply, and the effort to decide detracts a good deal from the power of his painting. Perhaps the most important requirement set upon any artist, abstract, representational, or otherwise, is that he must control the emotional response of his audience.

• • •

By contrast, David Burliuk, at the A.C.A., goes on in the same delightful fashion, as always, of just being Burliuk. He still paints in at least four styles at once—naïve, Dutch realist, Expressionist, and Surrealist—and in spite of this wild disparity in techniques he still manages to give each picture a quality that stamps it as unmistakably his. This is not as easy a trick as it sounds. I can think of at least a dozen other artists, though I name no names, as well known as or even better known than Burliuk, artists who, if they varied an inch from their established methods and content, would almost certainly drop instantly into anonymity.

Burliuk's identity, however, shows through all his work, and although it is difficult to say straight off why, I think the reason is to be found in the quality of innocent earnestness that runs through it. In that sense, no matter what style he uses, he is always naïve. Whether he offers you Surrealism, as in his portrait of Nicolai Cikovsky, or switches to primitivism, as in his meticulously detailed *Village on the Sea,* whether he paints realistically, as in his jolly, bucolic little *Montauk Bar,* or expressionistically, as in his big, swirling *Two Flowers,* he is always trying to tell you something. And though it may seem at first glance paradoxical, Burliuk, with his four styles, is no different from naïve painters who have only one or none; there is the same reaching-out quality about them all. It's a lovely quality to have, and I for one hope that Burliuk goes on and on having it.

. . .

The group show at the Pierre Matisse is called Hommage au Salon de la Libération, by which is meant the 1944 Salon d'Automne, held in Paris hardly more than a month after the freeing of the city from the Germans and in which the outpouring of art (most of it, by its very nature, detestable to the Fascists) was an even realler symbol of the independent spirit of the French than the outcropping of flags, equally long-hidden, which greeted the entering Allied troops. There are twenty-eight painters and sculptors in the show. One, Chaim Soutine, is dead, nine are in France, and the remainder are in this country, and the total effect is at once an indication of the dispersion of French artists because of the war and a testimonial to the strength of the tradition behind them. I found it an unexpectedly moving exhibition, and I think you may find it so too. At any rate, disentangling the artistic from the political, let me recommend the Soutine study of a red-vested valet de chambre called *Peinture,* the brilliant *Ma Vie Blanche et Noire* by Yves Tanguy, the slightly precious but still touching memento of the flight from Paris, by Eugene Berman, called *Les Enfants Perdus sur la Route,* and the solidly painted, securely Impressionist still life by Bonnard, also called *Peinture.* . . . There's a style of painting gaining ground in this country which is neither Abstract nor Surrealist, though it has suggestions of both, while the way the paint is applied—usually in a pretty free-swinging, spattery fashion, with only vague hints at subject matter—is suggestive of the methods of

Expressionism. I feel some new name will have to be coined for it, but at the moment I can't think of any. Jackson Pollock, Lee Hersch, and William Baziotes are of this school, and you will find all three in the show at the 67 Gallery, in addition to some forty other contemporaries, all of them in the by now hallowed Abstract or Surrealist manner. Except for Pollock's work, which frequently shows real power, I can't say that I am quite up to this new school yet; it still seems too aggressively undisciplined to me. But there it is, and it has to be taken into account. In addition, there are a nice Mark Rothko abstraction (listed simply as "Untitled" in the catalogue), as well as an extremely delicate painting on glass by I. Rice Pereira, called "Interpenetrating Planes," and a pleasant little "Dancers" by David Smith.

GEORGES BRAQUE, AND THE AMERICAN ABSTRACT ARTISTS

APRIL 9, 1949

G EORGES BRAQUE, the subject of a really massive retrospective exhibition at the Museum of Modern Art, and Pablo Picasso—who, between them, are generally recognized as the founders of the Cubist movement—were practically inseparable almost from the time they first met, in 1907, in Paris, through the six or seven years that their friendship lasted. It is unlikely that in the history of art any other two such dissimilar personalities were ever brought into such an intimate, productive relationship. The stocky, swarthy Picasso—passionate, volatile, aggressive, brilliantly imaginative and creative—was very nearly the exact opposite of Braque, who was tall, slow, sparely built, elegant, and rather retiring. They quarrelled, over some minor matter, just before the First World War, and after that saw little of each other. It is significant that the period of their friendship was that of Cubism's greatest development, and the pair of them, working together, did far more to formulate, express, and expound that theory than they possibly could have done apart. Their association not only covered but defined an era, and I have always believed that one reason for its dissolution was that they no longer had any artistic need for each other.

Braque, at the beginning of their friendship, was twenty-five, having been born in 1882, in Argenteuil, down the Seine from Paris, and as the earliest canvases in the exhibition reveal, he was still a bit insecure in his style. *The Port* and *Port at Antwerp,* for instance, done in 1904 and 1906, respectively, are both rather Fauve in manner (the latter, a charming little painting, is extremely reminiscent of the early Dufy), while *Landscape at l'Estaque,* also of 1906, shows an equally strong Cézanne influence. It is the *Large Nude,* of 1907, that marks the change. This was, incidentally, the year Picasso completed his *Demoiselles d'Avignon,* often called the first Cubist picture, and the similarity of approach in the two canvases is startling. In this case, I feel that although Braque was undoubtedly influenced by Picasso's design, no plagiarism was involved, and that it is simply an early evidence of the curious capacity the two men were to develop for thinking and painting alike.

Braque, like Picasso, had only partly awakened to the possibilities of Cubism, and for a while (see *Houses at l'Estaque* and *Port in Normandy*) he vacillated between it and his old styles. *Guitar and Compote Dish,* dated 1909, seems to me the first picture in the show in which Cubist principles are fully realized—in which a group of small objects, chosen for their pictorial opportunities rather than for any literal affinity, have been set down together and really studied, in an attempt to break up and then recombine their forms in a firmer and more durable relationship.

Braque, again like Picasso, did a great deal of such studying from then on, and this large show (which includes oils, drawings, prints, and sculptures) gives a comprehensive account of his progress and achievements. The first definite development of the movement was "facet" Cubism, and there is a roomful of pictures in that style, the most noteworthy being the oval *Battleship, Still Life with Playing Cards, Glass and Violin, Still Life on Table,* and the beautifully organized *Man with a Guitar.* These are dated from 1910 to 1913, in the period of Braque's close relation with Picasso. After that ended, their paths diverged, in Braque's case toward a looser, gentler, and at the same time more elegant abstract style, of rugged outlines and simple forms and subdued though richly harmonious colors, in which textures, too, played an increasingly effective part, so that now they have become as important as the forms delineated.

Still-lifes predominate, and there are some excellent pieces in this section of the show, covering the years from 1914 to 1930—the fine, angular *The Musician*, the small *Still Life with Grapes*, the slightly Juan Gris-ish *Café-Bar*, the handsome *On the Table*, *The Mantelpiece*, and *Still Life: The Table*. One of the handicaps of the Cubist style had been that it tended to limit itself to "arranged" subjects, such as still-lifes and portraits, and, beginning with "Nude with Basket of Fruit," of 1924, Braque has tried occasionally to break these bonds, by attacking less static material. He has not always been successful, and among the few real failures in the show must be listed *Painter and Model* and *Woman with a Mandolin*, as well as his formalized landscapes (*Cliffs and Fishing Boat*, *The Cliffs*, and so on), which are basically inept. Unquestionably, it is chiefly as a painter of still-lifes that Braque will survive, and of these the show contains a rich assortment. I was especially interested in some of the latest examples, in which again, though he's now nearly sixty-seven, he appears to be seeking new modes of expression. Note, for instance, the rather realistically handled *The Stove*, of 1944, as contrasted with the practically Expressionistic *The Sunflowers* and *The Chair*, of 1946 and 1947, respectively—a final fillip to show that the Old Master can still throw his weight around.

. . .

The complaints about abstract and non-objective painting have ranged from the perennial "Let them learn how to draw" to statements that the artists involved are obviously subversive. But almost the only complaint that ever held water is that they model their styles too closely and unimaginatively on those of the great originators, such as Braque, Picasso, Mondrian, and Kandinsky. Even this tendency is dying out, if the current annual exhibition of the American Abstract Artists, at the Riverside Museum, can be taken as evidence. Some influences are apparent, to be sure. Mondrian appears here and there, as in Ilya Bolotowsky's very fine *Prairie Window*, and Kandinsky in Joseph Meierhans' cheerful *Sun Bow*, among others. But classic French Cubism, slavishly applied to American subjects, is happily absent, and the emphasis instead is on that new type of "abstract Expressionism" that seems, on the whole, to be better rooted in this country. All this makes for a lively showing, and the fact that this year a number of guest artists have been included gives extra breadth to the collection. I liked particularly Eleanor de Laittre's gray-and-white *Steel and Plastic*, Fannie Hillsmith's large, fluently designed *Table with Object*, Charles Shaw's *Composition*, and Serge Chermayeff's colorful

Barn Dance. Among the sculptures, Peter Gripp's *Symbolic Figure* and Ward Bennett's gracefully handled *Fish* are the most notable.

LEWIS MUMFORD

ROCKEFELLER CENTER REVISITED

MAY 4, 1940

N INE YEARS AGO, Rockefeller Center was still on the drafting board. Mr. Rockefeller was referring hopefully to the possibility of giving the buildings an Egyptian touch. Some directors of the Metropolitan Opera House were talking hopefully about a new home. The Center's publicity men, dreaming of larger and more magnificent headlines, had collaborated with the late Raymond Hood to concoct one of the most insipid ideas the project has been afflicted with: hanging gardens. More romantic than anyone else, Mr. Rockefeller's financial advisers were talking hopefully about producing even more rentable space than would be required to create an income on which Columbia University could live in the style to which it was accustomed. About the last thought that occurred to anyone was that a group of office buildings ought to be efficiently designed as offices.

In spite of all these handicaps, Rockefeller Center has turned into an impressive collection of structures; they form a composition in which unity and coherence have to a considerable degree diminished the fault of overemphasis. In other words, they get by. Now, when the project is complete, one can see that the worst mistakes were made at the beginning and that as the decade wore on, the architects, at least, gradually achieved a more rational conception of their problem. But the most gigantic blunders had already been made. Among those blunders one must include the seventy-story R.C.A. Building, because of its seventy stories, the sunken plaza, the hanging gardens, and the—alas!—superfluous motion-picture theatre.

. . .

So much has happened since 1931 that most people have probably forgotten the modifications that have been made in the original design, such as the elimination of the oval-shaped building, looking in the renderings exactly like a hatbox, which was originally intended as the central mass for Fifth Avenue. They may also have forgotten that nine years ago the architects were still pondering the idea of using brick and that there was still a chance some "interpretation" of Egypt or the Renaissance might be inflicted on the façades.

One can see that the choice of rough-faced limestone for the façades of the buildings was on the whole a happy one, for the stone has been steadily absorbing soot, so by now both the stone face and the metal plaques are about the same tone and color. Certainly the limestone, combined with the blue of the windowshades, was a safe choice. But now that there is a striking contrast in color between the new and the old façades, one can also see how the architects, by clinging to a single material and color, lost a jolly opportunity. Eventually all the buildings will have the same hue, whereas a positive contrast in color between the central mass and the supporting buildings would have made permanent what is only a temporary effect.

Because the architects went in for façades that were severe and uniform, they doubtless felt doubly bound to relieve this severity with ornament. It only remains to be said that never were so much money and pains spent with so little effect. The hanging gardens were, of course, hardly architectural devices. But even the ornamental sculpture that was used about the entrances is overpowered by the tremendous masses above them. Michelangelo could not have prevailed against this handicap. Furthermore, the most conspicuous murals, those of Sert and Ezra Winter, are aesthetically the worst flops.

The most blatant misuse of sculpture occurs in front of the Fifth Avenue entrance to the International Building. By itself, that entrance, with its absolutely severe rectangular columns framing rectangular glass openings, without a frill, without a fluting, is beyond doubt the finest single architectural element in the whole Center—traditional but fresh, superb in proportion and scale, complete. The beauty of that entrance was marred when the idiotic form of Atlas was placed in front of it.

The architects, too, made a serious muff of the one conspicuous piece of decoration that lay within their direct control: the vertical signs and the marquees which identify the Center Theatre and the Music Hall. This is an art form in which architectural effort has been lacking, yet it is one of the most important features of any modern urban street composition, both by day and by night. The Rockefeller Center signs are, I regret to say, failures. They attempt monumentality and merely look elephantine; moreover, the lettering is clumsy and the use of script for "The" and "Theatre" is indefensible. Once the architect breaks away from the old-fashioned street layout, in which the buildings are consecutively numbered, it is important to have distinguishable signs to number and identify the buildings at a distance. It is only when one is close to these buildings—and not always then—that one is told, by lettering or decoration, where one is. This was a chance for organic ornament, so ably used on the office building at 417 Fifth Avenue, at Thirty-eighth. By going in for traditional embellishments, the architects of Rockefeller Center diverted themselves from their real task. (This same failure to identify irregularly placed buildings plagues one on university campuses and in modern housing projects, too, and it drives the casual visitor crazy.)

But the most serious aesthetic error in Rockefeller Center was the original mistake in scale. Except at a distance, one cannot see the top of the R.C.A. Building without tilting one's chin at an uncomfortable angle. At a distance, it is no more impressive than twenty other buildings in the city; not nearly so good, in fact, as the Daily News Building or the Insurance Company of North America's Building. What makes the Center architecturally the most exciting mass of buildings in the city is the nearby view of the play of mass against mass, of low structures against high ones, of the blank walls of the theatres against the vast, checkered slabs of glass in the new garage. All this is effective up to a height of thirty stories. Above that, the added stories only increase the burdens on the elevator system and inflate the egos of great executives.

Employing a unit like the sixteen-story office building that has been put up on Forty-eighth Street, a more compact and economic and efficient use might have been made of the whole site. Like the R.C.A. Building, this latest structure has a broad, low base of two or three stories for exhibition space and shops; and running through the middle of the block, insulated from the streets, set back from its neighbors across the way, is the main mass. This is definitely a new type of building, a substantial innovation and an excellent one. This unit is Rockefeller Center's most conspicuous contribution to the city of the future, unlike the wasteful towers and the dark, overgrown masses of earlier days. It corresponds in plan to the type arrived at in the new Memorial Hospital on East Sixty-eighth Street, and it is not merely a good unit but it makes possible, through the provision of a garage on the lower floors, adequate parking facilities. This structure has not got half the publicity the hanging gardens and the skating rink have received. But it is the real architectural justification of Rockefeller Center.

With a limit of thirty-two stories on the R.C.A. Building, and with units of eight and sixteen stories and theatres flanking this structure, the results would have been stunning, and what is more, every part of the project would have been easy to see. As it is, only from two points—from Forty-seventh Street and Sixth Avenue, and from a third of the way east along the block on Fiftieth Street—can one see the Center at its best. Of course, many of the camera views of the buildings are striking, but then a camera doesn't mind being tilted at a forty-five-degree angle for as much as five minutes, while the human neck does object. Good architecture is designed for the human beings who use or view the buildings, not for publicity men or photographers.

. . .

Rockefeller Center is still to be seen as our descendants may see it in another generation. Once we lay out parks and ribbons of open space around such units—the Medical Center is another—they will form a new kind of urban organism. Don't think that the future opening up of the city is just a pipe dream. The parking lots of today, like that on the site of the old Hippodrome, will be the gay playgrounds and squares of tomorrow. Rockefeller Center will look pretty old-fashioned by 1970, but then the Pyramids look old-fashioned now. Seen from quarter of a mile away, the Center group will knock one romantically cold. Even the R.C.A. Building.

THE ARCHITECTURE OF
POWER

JUNE 7, 1941

"A NEW ARCHITECTURE, bold as the engineering from which it springs, is rising in the valley. . . . Look at it, and be proud that you are an American." Those fine words by Stuart Chase stand at the entrance of the exhibition of TVA architecture at the Museum of Modern Art (it closes this Sunday), and they sum up admirably my feeling about the work that is on view. In these dams and power stations the largely unconscious precedents of our grain elevators and storage warehouses and coalbins reach the final mark of a conscious aesthetic expression. The photographs and models are excellent, but the actual buildings, as I saw them recently in their natural setting of hill and woodland and quarry and boat basin and river, are even more breathtaking than the photographs indicate. These structures are as close to perfection as our age has come.

There is something in the mere cant of a dam, when seen from below, that makes one think of the Pyramids of Egypt. Both pyramid and dam represent an architecture of power. But the difference is notable, too, and should make one prouder of being an American. The first grew out of slavery and celebrated death. Ours was produced by free labor to create energy and life for the people of the United States. Thanks to these dams, the colossal forces of the Tennessee River are held back or released almost as easily as one turns the water on and off at one's private faucet, and instead of wasted water, there is an abundance of electricity. Aren't we entitled to a little collective strutting and crowing? Though the whole staff of the TVA gets credit for the architectural success of these buildings, Mr. Roland Wank, the chief architect, deserves to be hauled out of his seat to take a bow. He would deserve it if only for the masterful way in which he has used concrete.

Engineers and architects have used concrete for a long time without thinking of anything better to do with it than to sheathe it in stone, as the Romans did, or else to rub away every last vestige of texture in the surface. Wank strove for a new effect; instead of obliterating the delicate pattern impressed in the concrete by the grain of the wood in the rectangular forms into which the concrete was poured, he made the effect all the bolder by contrasting horizontal with vertical patterns. The result is handsome, comparable to what Eliel and Ero Saarinen achieved in the new Buffalo Music Hall by using a facing of stone, and, needless to say, it is the most economic treatment possible.

While the Hiwassee Dam is perhaps the most striking work of pure engineering that the TVA has done, the generator building at Guntersville, Alabama, looks extremely good. The interior is finished in tile, both walls and floor, and the outside of the main structure is done in brick, with a great rectangular panel of glass set off in a simple brick frame, above which the name "Guntersville" appears in bold letters. There is not a superfluous touch in this whole structure, and the architect's high achievement with tile and brick shows that the success of the other buildings is no mere fluke of engineering and is not due only to a happy trick in employing certain materials.

The only criticism I have to make of this show is that it was too modestly conceived. Lack of space, if nothing else, confined it to the main structures in the Tennessee Valley and made it impossible sufficiently to indicate the architectonic treatment of the whole landscape. In modern architecture, not merely are the interior and the exterior equally important but the individual unit and the plan of the whole must be conceived as one. I can think of no better example of this partnership than the structures of the TVA. Here is modern architecture at its mightiest and its best. The Pharaohs did not do any better.

. . .

The most important things that have happened in American architecture during the last month or so are three books. This is an event even rarer than the building of a skyscraper, for our architectural history and criticism have lagged a long way behind practice. Because of that, our practice has been more smug and provincial than it need have been.

Siegfried Giedion's *Space, Time, and Architecture: The Growth of a New Tradition* has been put out in a most sumptuous format, and it is a very exciting piece of work. The book derives from the Norton lectures this Zurich critic and historian gave at Harvard in 1938 and 1939. Many of its illustrations and some exceedingly interesting data, however, came out of research in the history of American architecture which Giedion did after he came over here, and there is no one, no matter how well informed about the modern movement, who will not be stimulated and occasionally made rather starry-eyed by the pictures of a developing world, creating new symbols for a new consciousness of nature and man, that Giedion presents.

The weakest part of Giedion's book is his handling of modern city development, particularly his failure to understand the historic significance or the future importance of Ebenezer Howard's conception of the garden city. In a book that stresses the social side of modern architecture, this is a serious blind spot. But apart from this, Giedion has done a good job. His emphasis on the social, the personal, and the human makes it as decisive a departure from the standpoint of Le Corbusier's *Vers une Architecture* as that in turn was a departure from the commonplaces of the traditionalists. Giedion sees that our main problem is "to humanize— that is, to reabsorb emotionally—what has been created by the spirit. All talk about organizing and planning is vain when it is not possible to create again the whole man, unfractured in his methods of thinking and feeling."

. . .

The doctrine that underlies Giedion's book is one that Frank Lloyd Wright has been preaching and practicing his entire life, and never more vocally, never more visibly, than during the last decade. But Wright's pronouncements on architecture had never been brought together and many of them have long been inaccessible, so we owe a special debt to Frederick Gutheim for collecting and collating them in an admirable book, *Frank Lloyd Wright on Architecture: Selected Writings, 1894–1940*.

The book begins with a speech by Wright on architecture and the machine given in 1894 and ends with a dinner talk at Hull House. The very first words are characteristic and could not be improved: "The more true culture a man has, the more significant his environment becomes to him." The color of Wright's personality, the wide range of his mind, his healthy aplomb, his deeply moral feeling about life and art are all visible in these pages. These pronouncements and challenges, these reports and jottings and memoranda are an indispensable part of America's cultural history. One learns, for example, that Wright's houses were first called "dress reform houses"—a precious sidelight which indicates that the removal of the bustle and the corset and the manifold petticoat went logically along with his opening up of window space, the breaking down of partitions, and the removal of the triple layer of curtaining that once screened the American home from light.

When he is talking about nature, when he is finding a new beauty in the rocks or the vegetation of some little-known region, interpreting its values for architectural form, Wright is at his supreme best. To read Wright on Arizona and South Dakota is to find a fresh reason for being an American. Enough if I say that this book is of the same order as Whitman's *Democratic Vistas*, the fruition of a brilliant individual life and the seed of a better life to come.

· · ·

After remaining on the high level of Giedion's historical criticism and Wright's contemporary challenges, you may like to climb down to earth again by reading *Architecture in Old Chicago*, by the late Thomas E. Tallmadge. Even so, you will not be very far away from Wright or Giedion, for the Chicago Tallmadge tells about was the capital city of the New American architecture, and though Tallmadge was not an acute critic, he was familiar with the personalities and the material remains of the great days of Chicago architecture. By now even a New Yorker should know that all the fundamental experiments in both the aesthetics and the technics of the skyscraper were worked out in Chicago between 1883 and 1893. If he doesn't, it is high time that he learned. When the history of American architecture comes finally to be written, the material in Tallmadge's little book—left unfinished, alas, at his death—will be important.

MUSICAL EVENTS

A NOTE BY ALEX ROSS

FOR DECADES, classical-music criticism in *The New Yorker*, like much other writing in the magazine, struck an urbane, irreverent, studiously off-the-cuff tone. The first custodian of the Musical Events column, Robert A. Simon, zigzagged between classical and popular music, dabbling in Broadway work in his spare time. (He wrote lyrics for "Ups-a-Daisy," "The Gang's All Here," "Hold Your Horses," and "Champagne, Sec.") One of Simon's early reviews, from 1926, begins thus: "Enter into the conductorial arena Otto Klemperer, the seven foot dynamo from Wiesbaden, the terror of second trombonists, the cave man who yanks 'em by the collar and shakes sweet music from their quivering instruments, the wild bull of the symphony, Brann the Iconoclast, and all the rest of it." The *New Yorker* fact-checking department was not quite the colossus it eventually became: Klemperer was, in fact, six feet four.

Such was the tenor of the musical conversation in the twenties, thirties, and forties. Classical music had not yet been fenced off in the public mind as an elite, effete pursuit; it held a prominent position in mainstream culture, inspiring Hollywood biopics and occupying prime slots on the radio schedule. Up to ten million people tuned in for Arturo Toscanini's broadcasts with the NBC Symphony. Classical performers and even a few composers appeared on the cover of *Time.* In the chic 1944 thriller *Laura*, the hard-boiled detective played by Dana Andrews catches Vincent Price in a philharmonic fib: "Why did you say they played Brahms's First and Beethoven's Ninth at the concert Friday night? They changed the program at the last minute and played nothing but

Sibelius." A red-blooded American male didn't throw his masculinity into question if he showed a taste for opera.

The embattled heroism of the symphonic literature matched the mood of a nation reeling from the Depression and war. The *New Yorker* writer Philip Hamburger, visiting wounded soldiers at the Halloran General Hospital, on Staten Island, in 1943, reported that the young men were listening as avidly to Wagner and Shostakovich as they were to popular fare. Leonard Bernstein became a sleek matinee idol, his 1943 debut at the New York Philharmonic covered in the same cheeky tones as the discovery of a starlet at Schwab's Pharmacy. The civil-rights movement came alive with the tremendous spectacle of Marian Anderson performing on the steps of the Lincoln Memorial, in 1939. Aaron Copland created the sound of the American heartland, notwithstanding his leftist politics. There was, in fact, no contradiction between the leftist slant of Roosevelt's America and the bent toward classical sounds: Clifford Odets, among others, saw Beethoven as the herald of an egalitarian future, one in which contentious individual voices would unite in a major-key consensus.

The populist streak in classical culture coincided with a significant, though short-lived, effort on the part of the federal government to give employment to musicians and other Depression-battered artists. In 1935, the Federal Music Project was launched, under the auspices of the Works Progress Administration; across the country, orchestras and opera companies offered high-quality events on the cheap. The arts projects were largely shut down in 1939, as a result of anti–New Deal agitation, but W.P.A. orchestras lingered on in a few places, notably in New York. "You can't lose at the New York City W.P.A. Symphony concerts," Simon writes in 1942. With the purchase of War Savings Stamps—ranging in price from fifty cents to five dollars—attendees got to see Nathan Milstein and Gregor Piatigorsky in the Brahms Double Concerto. How were they? "Immense."

Simon remained on the beat until 1948, when he ceded his position to Hamburger, who, despite the fact that he had not studied music, turned out to be a keen, deft observer. ("Just listen and write," Harold Ross sensibly told him.) After a year, Hamburger moved on to the brave new world of television, and Douglas Watt, best remembered for his theatre reviews, wrote the column for a few years. Winthrop Sargeant also contributed a few notices, and, in 1953, he took over for a two-decade stint at

Musical Events. A professional violinist who had played under Toscanini in the New York Philharmonic, Sargeant knew the core repertory, but he showed little sympathy for contemporary music. Only with the arrival of the formidable London critic Andrew Porter, in 1972, did *The New Yorker* acquire a classical commentator comparable in influence to the likes of Edmund Wilson, Pauline Kael, and Whitney Balliett. Still, it's permissible to feel a bit of nostalgia for the days when almost any generally cultured person on the staff seemed prepared to write the music page. It was a sign of the times.

ROBERT A. SIMON

COPLAND AND SHOSTAKOVICH

OCTOBER 24, 1942

THIS *RODEO* that the Ballet Russe de Monte Carlo brought to the Metropolitan Opera House last week turned out to be a bright little offering that will please plenty of customers. The scenario, in the language of the program, "deals with the problem that has confronted every American woman, from earliest pioneer times, and which has never ceased to occupy them throughout the history of the building of our country: how to get a suitable man." This is not presented abstractly, there being no spirit of woman struggling to reach the ideal man, or anything like that. There's a cowgirl on a ranch competing with visitors from Kansas City for the attentions of the gents. You follow her adventures from a rodeo to a Saturday-night dance at the ranch house—and that's the story. The rodeo, as a terpsichorean job, is pretty good, a square-dance interlude (without music) is better, and the Saturday-night dance is something of a triumph. The audience doted on the production, and even after the doting tendencies of ballet visitors are discounted, *Rodeo* goes into the books as a hit.

Miss Agnes de Mille devised the show and Aaron Copland wrote the music. At the première, Miss de Mille danced the suitable-man-seeking heroine charmingly, and her associates went along enthusiastically. There was some ironing-out left for future rehearsals and performances, but the show, taken all in all, was right. Mr. Copland's music was good theatre and, like as not, will acquire considerable circulation when a concert suite is fashioned from it. The scenery and costumes, by Oliver Smith and Kermit Love, respectively, were excellent, and the orchestral playing, under the alert direction of Franz Allers, was properly energetic.

. . .

Last week was a Shostakovich week, with performances of three of the composer's symphonies in four days. The Philadelphia Orchestra played the fifth, the Philharmonic-Symphony the seventh, and the Ballet Russe the first, which is the music for *Rouge et Noir*. Of course, all this didn't furnish so unified a view of the three works as the forthcoming performances by Artur Rodzinski and the Philharmonic-Symphony will. Eugene Ormandy's version of the fifth, with the Philadelphia, was a beautifully polished performance, Arturo Toscanini's of the seventh was persuasively intense, and the ballet presentation of the first, under the direction of Gregory Fittelberg, was orchestrally spotty, although Mr. Fittelberg conducted the music firmly and sympathetically.

There were various points of view in the conducting and a difference in the playing of the orchestras, but there still was the Shostakovich music, and it was obvious that all three symphonies, covering sixteen years of the composer's career, had the same musical personality behind them. All three were written by a man who is a natural at writing for orchestra; all three contain power and many ingenuities set off against winning and restrained slow movements; all three—even the seventh, composed in a Leningrad at war—have touches of humor, which, in the fifth, range from amusing kidding to heavy waggishness; and all three demonstrate unevenness in ideas and mastery in workmanship. Naturally, this isn't any attempt to analyze Shostakovich's music as a whole. It's simply one reaction to three symphonies, two of which have had many performances and the third of which probably will be heard frequently. By the way, I find that the first symphony has become more impressive since its first local hearings, and the fifth less so. Of course, other listeners may feel quite the other way.

CURRENT AND RECURRENT

FEBRUARY 22, 1947 (ON BERNSTEIN, TOSCANINI, AND ARMSTRONG)

THE FIRST PARAGRAPH OF MUSIC COMMENT in the first issue of this magazine, twenty-two years ago, concerned a guest conductor— Igor Stravinsky, who was then directing the Philharmonic orchestra as a visiting maestro. Guest conductors have made first-paragraph items for me on many occasions since then, and this is another of them. The guest conductor under discussion is Leonard Bernstein, who was not quite seven years old in February, 1925. Mr. Bernstein appeared in Carnegie Hall as transient director of the Boston Symphony last week, when he conducted one of the most famous of that other guest conductor's compositions, "Le Sacre du Printemps." In the twenties, "Le Sacre" was still something of a chore for a good many listeners. Today, it's an accepted and popular part of the standard orchestral repertory. It makes exacting demands on the instrumentalists and their leader (I doubt that "Le Sacre" ever will play the high-school-orchestra circuit), demands that were met brilliantly by the Boston orchestra and Mr. Bernstein. Everything was clear, logical, and cleanly rhythmic.

Before "Le Sacre," Mr. Bernstein offered Schubert's Seventh Symphony, sometimes known as "the symphony of heavenly length." Actually, it is no longer than a good many other symphonies, and it probably would lose none of its heavenliness if it were shorter by a few measures. Mr. Bernstein led it with directness, crispness, and restraint. The directness and crispness were admirable, but a little less restraint would have benefited the more fanciful episodes of the charming music.

· · ·

In 1925, Berlioz's dramatic symphony "Romeo and Juliet" was an item in the reference catalogues rather than a work for public performance, but it was subsequently brought to life, at least temporarily, by Arturo Toscanini. Recently, Mr. Toscanini revived it again, this time on two Sunday-afternoon broadcasts by the N.B.C. Symphony, a chorus, and vocal soloists. It's a large composition and even now, more than a century since it was written, it is unconventional. In it, one hears music that is at various times exciting, eloquent, good theatre, and meandering. Mr. Toscanini's powerful projection of the score was one of the many great achievements of his career, and his associates responded impressively. Among the attractions of "Romeo and Juliet" is a poetic mezzo-soprano solo, sung in this case by Gladys Swarthout. Not many Berlioz vocal excerpts are apt to be heard at concerts, but this is one that deserves more general circulation, especially when it's sung with the vocal beauty and textual expressiveness that Miss Swarthout gave it.

. . .

There was a deal of chatter about the propriety of jazz music in concert halls twenty-two years ago. Even the mild forms of symphonic and classical jazz were considered by some people as unfit for exhibition in any auditorium where you would expect to hear Beethoven. That's all changed now, of course, and you're likely to encounter jazz in any concert hall, not only at regular concert hours but around midnight as well. When Louis Armstrong brought his band to Carnegie Hall a couple of Saturdays ago, and alternated his remarkable vocals with his wonderful trumpet playing, the concert was regarded as an event to be debated on its own musical merits. In fact, the most serious and furious arguments about music nowadays all seem to involve jazz. The classic eighteenth-century imbroglios between the Handel and Buononcini factions and the Gluck and Piccini enthusiasts have a parallel in the current clashes between various brands of hepcat.

PHILIP HAMBURGER

IN THE HILLS

AUGUST 13, 1949 (ON TANGLEWOOD)

WENT UP TO TANGLEWOOD LAST WEEK, to the Berkshire Festival, to listen to the music. The music was consistently pretty wonderful, often quite exalted, but music was not, by a long shot, the only feature of the festival. I am convinced that future historians of the phenomenon of Tanglewood will devote as much attention to its non-musical as to its musical aspects. Take, for instance, cameras. Everybody seems to be carrying a camera. The throngs that attend these concerts are music lovers, no doubt, but they are camera-happy, too. They appear desperately, almost poignantly, anxious not only to absorb the music in a flamboyantly emotional manner but to record on film every instant of their experience there. They wander up, down, and across the spacious grounds snapping pictures. They snap everything and anything. They take pictures of the gracious postcard scenery, with its rolling lawns, formal gardens, and made-to-order backdrop of lake and misty mountains. They take pictures of their families and friends. They take pictures of total strangers and they ask total strangers to take pictures of them. Mostly, though, they take pictures of Dr. Serge Koussevitzky and the Boston Symphony Orchestra.

I attended a public rehearsal of the orchestra last Saturday morning in the big music shed, and I do not see how Dr. Koussevitzky and his men got through it. An audience of some four thousand persons turned up, everybody having contributed one dollar to the orchestra's pension fund for the privilege. Four-fifths of the audience carried cameras, or so it seemed to me, and they spent four-fifths of their time standing on their seats or ducking in and out of the aisles clicking their shutters. In the moments when they were not taking pictures, they were engaged in the second most evident non-musical aspect of the festival—hero worship. Around Tanglewood, Dr. Koussevitzky has become a legend in his lifetime. The other morning, he could not make a move on the podium, he could not lift or drop his baton, he could not signal to an oboe player or whistle at a flutist without evoking a chorus of "Oh"s and "Ah"s from the audience. Every ordinary, workmanlike gesture was greeted with adulation and open-eyed surprise. I must confess that I found this slightly frightening, and I would wager that Dr. Koussevitzky—who has every right to expect any honor—is a bit disturbed, too. The tangent down which these audiences now seem to be racing is leading in a distinctly non-musical direction. One can well imagine their ohing and ahing with equal fervor at a crooner or some Hollywood celebrity.

Dr. Koussevitzky is, of course, an iron man, and he continues to present programs of the highest merit. The program of a week ago Thursday evening was of magnificent stature. Jascha Heifetz was on hand for a flawless rendition of Tchaikovsky's Violin Concerto. He played with incredible skill and a controlled passion that was quite overwhelming. On Saturday evening, Dr. Koussevitzky, who—for me, at least—is always somewhat inspired, was more inspired than usual. He gave us first a delightful reading of Roussel's Suite in F, and then Milhaud's Concerto for Cello and Orchestra No. 1, with Gregor Piatigorsky as soloist. The Milhaud is at once twinkly and profound, and in the hands of Piatigorsky it became a prize of lasting beauty. Dr. Koussevitzky closed the program with a truly monumental presentation of Mahler's "Das Lied von der Erde." Nothing that Mahler wished to say in this musical poem of life and death was left unsaid by the orchestra or by David Lloyd, the tenor, or by Janice Moudry, the contralto. Miss Moudry's voice that evening was a voice possessed, and there was in it an unforgettable quality of time past and time to come. Even the camera fiends listened to her, and held off taking their pictures until she was finished.

MAY DAY AT LOXFORD

AUGUST 20, 1949 (ON BENJAMIN BRITTEN)

A S IT HAPPENS, I do not hold a membership card in the Benjamin Britten cult, but I am about to apply for one as a result of hearing Britten's opera *Albert Herring*, presented for the first time in this country a week ago Monday by the Opera Department of the Berkshire Music Center, at Tanglewood. Britten and his librettist, Eric Crozier, deserve some sort of words-and-music Croix de Guerre. For one thing, we are confronted with a believable story, involving believable people. There isn't an entombed and lovesick Egyptian princess, a tubercular bohemian, or a down-at-the-heels and hairy demigod on the premises. The story, as simple and lovely as a nursery tale, takes place in the East Suffolk village of Loxford at the turn of the century. Loxford has always been a happy, easygoing place, where the boys go out with the girls and occasionally get home a little late and slightly rumpled, but in the eyes of the town's better element—the local aristocratic dowager, the mayor, the vicar, the leading merchant, the superintendent of police—it is rapidly becoming more wicked than Sodom, Gomorrah, Marseille, and Los Angeles combined. "Something must be done!" cries the mayor. "Strong measures are essential *now*!" shouts the vicar. "Shocking business! I won't have it!" shrieks the dowager. The town worthies, who are about to choose a May Queen, find themselves completely stumped. No local girl is considered sufficiently pure. For example, one candidate, Winifred Brown, "went with her cousin from Kent for a trip in a dogcart one Sunday in Lent." Edith Chase? "Much too flighty. When the postman called one day, she opened the door in her nightie!" And so it goes, through every girl in town. In desperation, the committee decides to choose a May King, and for this dubious honor they select one Albert Herring, a twenty-two-year-old sissy greengrocer, who works for his mama, minds his parsnips, and never, never goes out with the girls. The committee offers him twenty-five pounds, a banquet, and a wreath of orange blossoms. Albert has natural misgivings, but Mama, a harridan, is thrilled beyond calculation and forces him to accept the role. To make a short story even shorter (Crozier, by the way, adapted his plot from de Maupassant's "Le Rosier de Mme. Husson"), Albert gets quietly potted at the banquet when a rakish butcher puts rum in his lemonade, and subsequently disappears on a stolen bicycle, headed for nearby pubs. Next morning, his orange-blossom wreath is found on the road, covered with mud and crushed, apparently by a cart. It is generally assumed that the dear boy has passed to his virtuous reward, and there is wide-spread lamentation. Albert turns up, of course, quite hung over and uncommonly surly, and tells his mother off. He has become, in the common phrase, a man.

Well, there's the plot. I have laid stress upon it because Britten, in his most sardonic, witty, and felicitous manner, has laid stress upon it. His score is devotedly attached to the story. He has written, truly, an opera. He has created musically a strikingly engaging village, and he has musically delineated each character with astonishing clarity. In *Albert Herring*, words and music are as one, and the result is triumphant. The night I heard the opera (there were a number of different singers the following night), practically all hands seemed eminently suited to their parts. I was particularly impressed with David Lloyd, the Herring; Janet Southwick, a proper schoolteacher; Eleanor Davis, the dreadful mama; and James Pease, the vicar. Mr. Pease maintained throughout the evening an air of pained piety that was a complete delight, and his voice struck me as being nothing short of extraordinary. My only quarrel would be with Ellen Faull, as Lady Billows, the dowager; she demonstrated a tendency to overshadow her excellent singing with some rather poor acting. Boris Goldovsky conducted the orchestra and, with Sarah Caldwell, directed the enterprise, and he should be given several echoing cheers.

WINTHROP SARGEANT

THE VIOLIN AND *SZIGETI*

DECEMBER 24, 1949

A S A MUSICAL INSTRUMENT, the violin has its limitations. To begin with, it is incomplete. Except in a handful of musical works, like the Bach solo-violin sonatas, it needs an orchestra or, at the very least, a piano to back it up. The number of great concertos written for it hardly exceeds a dozen, and the number of great sonatas in which it shares honors with the piano or the harpsichord is not very much bigger. It is, moreover, one of the most awkward of all musical instruments, in that its bow is an unevenly balanced affair that, unless firmly controlled, plays louder at the heel than it does at the point, and hence has a tendency to distort, with all sorts of inappropriate swoops and swells, the niceties of musical phrasing. A good violinist (and by this I mean a musical violinist) should be judged to a large extent, I believe, by the skill with which he defeats this tendency and forces his instrument to conform to the principles of fine melodic style. Unfortunately, there are very few good violinists.

In general, our particular generation of violin playing has been dominated by what might be called the glamour violinist. I use this term because to me it conveys the quality of surface finish (comparable to the faultless makeup of the female movie star) that is characteristic of the type. Mr. Heifetz, Mr. Elman, and Mr. Milstein, for example, have developed luscious tone and accurate agility of the left hand to a point of perfection probably unmatched in the history of the instrument. Yet I do not find them interesting violinists. The reason is that, for all their cosmetic glitter, they almost never interpret music with a real understanding of its deeper dramatic and emotional content. They shine magnificently in showy concertos by such composers as Tchaikovsky and Glazunov, but the purity and subtlety of style required in a simple Mozart sonata seem to be beyond them. There exist, of course, plenty of unglamorous but musically sensitive violinists, many of whom are members of string quartets, concertmasters of symphony orchestras, and so on. The trouble with these men is that they lack the individuality, dash, and brilliance of the true virtuoso. In surveying the subject of contemporary performance on stringed instruments, one is led to the conclusion that the only entirely satisfying artist in the field is not a violinist but the cellist Pablo Casals.

All this is by way of a preamble to a discussion of Joseph Szigeti's performance, with the New York Philharmonic-Symphony last Thursday night, of the Alban Berg Concerto for Violin and Orchestra and the Bach G-Minor Concerto. Mr. Szigeti is not a glamour violinist. He is a large man who crouches over his violin, and he occasionally draws from it sounds that scratch and whistle. He lacks the formidable and immaculate polish of Mr. Heifetz. But he is, despite his mechanical faults, my favorite violinist. He never allows the unwieldiness of the bow to interfere with the justness of his phrasing. He never wallows in beautiful tone for the sake of beautiful tone. He is always intent on communicating the inner substance of the music he interprets, and he accomplishes this task with the most scrupulous regard for emphasis and other subtleties of melodic contour. When listening to him, one can forget that one is listening to a violin and listen to the music.

Nothing could have offered a more convincing test of Mr. Szigeti's qualities than the juxtaposition on the program of Bach's serenely classical concerto and Berg's modern, expressionist score. Mr. Szigeti's playing in the first work was here and there a little thin in tone, but he gave both pieces performances of great musical insight, providing each with its own spectrum of musical coloring and making evident the two centuries of change in violin style that separate them. Dimitri Mitropoulos, who conducted, kept the Philharmonic players in unusually intimate rapport with Mr. Szigeti, and the result of this collaboration was, in the case of the Berg concerto, among the most memorable events the musical season has thus far offered.

The Berg violin concerto is, I think, one of the few important symphonic compositions written since the First World War. Finished in 1935, just before Berg's death in Vienna, it has most of the technical features of the atonal style that was popular there at the time, but, unlike most atonal music, it seems to have a sense of poetry that lies beyond its interest as a mere collection of notes. The lack of propulsion that is characteristic of atonality has been compensated for here by a gloomy and intensely dramatic atmosphere that gives the work continuous momentum and excitement. A good deal of this atmosphere is created by Berg's uncanny artistry as an orchestrator and by a stream of dour romantic passion that breaks through the abstract formality of the idiom and brings it to life. Berg has proved in this work that a composer of sufficient genius can make even atonality convey a human message.

. . .

Last week, two symphonies by the contemporary British composer Ralph Vaughan Williams were presented here. One of them, the Fourth, was included on the Philharmonic program I have been discussing; the other, the Sixth, was played earlier in the week by the Philadelphia Orchestra, under Eugene Ormandy. To me, both symphonies are respectable, dignified, and slightly dull compositions, written with obvious sincerity but exhibiting the outward gestures of tragic emotion rather than the true substance. Mr. Ormandy also brought along the well-known violinist Erica Morini, who played the Brahms Concerto for Violin with great sturdiness, fine tone, and impeccable technique but without that understanding of purely musical values that I found in the performances of Mr. Szigeti.

FEMININE
FASHIONS

A NOTE BY JUDITH THURMAN

U NTIL THE 1940S, American fashion was as much of a colonial
backwater, in relation to France, as Gaul was under the Romans.
Seventh Avenue took its marching orders from the Paris couture
houses, whose hegemony was nearly absolute. Even a socialist-feminist-
Yankee patriot like Margaret Fuller—America's first female public
intellectual—couldn't resist, when she got to France, in 1846, going on a
spree for some chic clothes. And this was the dress pattern for a century
to come: the grandes dames of the Gilded Age bought their ball gowns
at Worth; the bohemian rebels of the Belle Époque wore Poiret's harem
pants; the Daisy Buchanans got their madcap shimmer at Patou.

But when the Second World War began, and women of fashion were
confined to North America by German U-boats, a new generation of
designers, many of them female upstarts (Claire McCardell and Bonnie
Cashin, to name two), suddenly had the field to themselves. McCardell
produced inventive leisure wear for a youthful client with a sense of
humor who may even have held down a job. Charles James proved that
an American couturier could design evening wear that rivaled the French
in refinement. Adrian, out in Hollywood, made a specialty of Amazon
queens. At the other end of the social spectrum, Elizabeth Hawes, a
Paris-trained couturier turned champion of fashion for the people, was
designing uniforms for Red Cross volunteers and writing about "girls in
slacks" for the left-wing daily PM. By the end of the decade, when commerce with Europe resumed, France did reassert its dominance (first

with Dior's New Look, of 1947, and later with Courrèges, Cardin, and Yves Saint Laurent.) But by then two iconoclasts from New York, Richard Avedon and Irving Penn, had forever transformed the way that clothes were modeled and photographed.

Lois Long's *New Yorker* columns on "Feminine Fashions" hardly seem to register the decade's seismic shifts. Fashion criticism as we know it did not yet exist, and rather than looking at the big picture, or the emerging picture, of an enterprise in flux, Long approached her work as a pointillist. Her tightly focused columns surveyed the clothes of a new season shop by shop and garment by garment, in meticulous detail. Seventy years before the advent of smartphones, Long pioneered the fashion app: a consummately savvy, user-friendly tool that helped her readers navigate a daunting environment. "I am more concerned about the fate of the poor, bedraggled, bewildered retail customer (which is every one of us)," Long wrote, "than about any other breed of forgotten man—or woman."

Long spent her professional life indefatigably pounding the pavement in a few square blocks of Manhattan around Fifty-seventh Street and Fifth Avenue (she never seems to have visited the Garment District) and rattling the hangers in a handful of emporia with genteel cachet. But, at that treacherous intersection of price and value, she had a keen sense of the absurd; she couldn't be seduced by luxury for its own sake, and she prided herself on being a bargain scout. Her taste, like her prose, was wary of fantasy, if not always of improbability. One of the outfits she recommends is "a black-and-green plaid wool jumper dress ($25), accompanied by a long-sleeved tangerine wool jersey blouse ($9.95) and tangerine knickerbockers." You never discover—perhaps mercifully—the name of the hack who designed them.

No one who writes about fashion year after year is immune from ennui, and Long seems to have fought it by becoming a consumer advocate for the hapless Everyshopper, whose ordeals impassioned her. These included being "ritzed" by snooty salesgirls and run ragged by haphazard merchandising. Why, she fumed, should a parasol be sold on a different floor from the outfit that it accessorizes? (Here, though, her innocence of a common subterfuge speaks to her own high-mindedness. She seems not to have suspected shopkeepers of purposely drawing their customers into a labyrinth of temptation.) Long was, above all, a valiant trooper, reporting tirelessly from the front lines of a consumer revolution. Occasionally, though, her battle fatigue wears through. Rather than fighting "a mob in a big store," she recommends "joining other harassed women in an air-cooled apartment and playing Canasta." (There was no need to mention the frosted martini shaker; *New Yorker* readers took it for granted.)

Long knew her way around a martini. In the 1920s, under the pseudonym Lipstick, the wild and worldly young Lois (born in 1901) had covered Manhattan nightlife for the newly founded magazine, and had cut a racy figure in New York café society as the quintessential flapper. She had sometimes turned up at the office the worse for wear, at five in the morning, still in her scanty evening togs. Harold Ross, the editor-in-chief, was often scandalized by Long's outré wardrobe and behavior. One of the pleasures of Long's writing is a suppressed energy—something caged and seething—which suggests that, in middle age, she both bowed to and bristled at a misogynist prejudice that has still not quite been transcended in certain quarters of the media: that fashion is a beat not worthy of a "real" journalist.

This is not to say that Long's writing lacked wit and authority, or her opinions bite. She always had an impious little riff on fashion and society in her opening paragraphs. The former party girl could smile with benign disdain at a generation of bobby-soxers in burlap and denim, trying to shock mothers who had "survived the Scott Fitzgerald era" by dressing like "serfs under the Hapsburgs." And she always came to life on the subject of hats.

The greatest irony of these columns is that the life they conjure, of literate women condemned to wifely or filial conformity, was alien to the experience of their author. Long, who was married to the *New Yorker* cartoonist Peter Arno (they divorced in 1931, after four years of marriage), was a self-supporting single mother, serial monogamist, social maverick, and modern woman ahead of her time. Yet, when one reads between the lines, her columns also evoke the modern woman's struggle with conflicting imperatives—to self and others. In her last column, on the fad for novelty furs, written in 1969, Long gives her readers some parting advice: "Marry well."

ON THE RETAIL CUSTOMER

APRIL 13, 1940

IT IS QUITE POSSIBLY TRUE, since so many fiery Hearst editorials have said it is, that the lot of the modern businessman is a sorry one. However, I am more concerned about the fate of the poor, bedraggled, bewildered retail customer (which is every one of us) than about any other breed of forgotten man—or woman. Incessant polls, surveys, and other spurious means of consulting our wishes have all but made it impossible to buy the simple things we want. In offices all over the country, high-priced, alert people keep on deciding what we humble souls should be made to buy, which is usually something entirely different from what we yearn for. Despite the writing on the wall proclaiming that the great American public has grown up, the legend persists that it is moronic and incapable of making a decision.

The movies, though still far from perfect, have shown signs now and then of realizing that the average citizen likes good things and isn't flattered by having his lowest tastes condescended to. The studios used to turn out pictures tailored exclusively to the taste of the muggs; now occasionally they go out and hire a Raymond Massey to act his best in a picture, and, to their amazement, the public flocks to see the result. The radio has hardly caught on at all, as anyone who has ever listened to daytime serials will tell you, and its sturdy right arm, the advertising industry, can be equally dense at times. Both have surveyed the human being until he has become, in their minds, simply a piece of machinery, dangerous if not kept under control. Everywhere bright young men sit at their desks and shudder as they try to outwit that mysterious ogre, the American Housewife; hundreds of underlings sort out questionnaires and charts, compiled at vast expense, from which to prepare copy that can sizzle across billboards and into magazines and over the air and supposedly lull American women into docility. In vain, a young lady pleads that she'd like to know how to make last year's evening dress look new for a special occasion. The survey experts chorus that she's crazy and that what she really wants, if she hopes to haunt a reluctant man, is a bottle of perfume that costs ten dollars. It is all most constructive and efficient.

In vain, dear old ladies plead that they would prefer a bottle of My Sin to the nicest gray shawl ever knitted. They don't know what they want, say the boys back of the surveys, rustling around in their statistics to prove that old ladies want shawls and think perfume is a criminal waste of money. I often wonder how much longer women, who for years have been deferred to as a potent factor in our national economy, will take these insults to their intelligence and good nature.

ON READY-TO-WEAR CLOTHES

OCTOBER 27, 1945

THE WAR MUST BE OVER. Arrogance is beginning to strut again among the shoppes. The customer is again being ritzed by sales-ladies and a lot of well-heeled but timid customers are apparently buying whatever is thrown at them. And it looks as if the average woman, the one with a mind of her own and a pocketbook to consider, is going to be kicked around. In other words, the postwar world is just more of the same. None of this, happily, applies to the great veterans of the trade. No initiative, I guess.

For instance, Bergdorf Goodman's third floor, as well behaved as ever, houses a comprehensive collection of ready-to-wear clothes, priced at from $40 to $70 and with lines so suave that Bergdorf must have shopped around quite a bit to find them. The late-afternoon and informal dinner dresses are particularly notable. There is an invaluable black or brown rayon-crêpe one, with a V neck that can be fastened right up to the throat and front drapery that looks like a huge bow, one loop of which makes a deep pocket. This drapery also gives a rounded-hipline effect. At least, that's the way it looks to me. Other black dresses, these with square necks, have long, tight sleeves and a bow on the left shoulder; darts and drapery give that same rounded-hipline effect in the back. A black matelassé dress is cut with deep armholes, long, tight sleeves, and drapery in the skirt that makes it look like a tunic. A long-bodiced dress has a cap-sleeved, round-necked, black jersey top and a gathered black rayon satin skirt; superb, and $40. Next, there's a black moiré two-piece number with a high, keyhole neck, a basque top descending in back, folds over the shoulders, and an easy, swinging skirt. Mustard-yellow rayon crêpe is used to make a top with a turnover collar; this goes with a gathered skirt of black rayon velvet, with black bengaline edging the high, notched waist and the hemline. And if you want lamés, there are lacquer-red, bronze, or green-and-gold affairs with high necks that tie at the throat, cap sleeves, and drapery at the hip that looks like a pocket. All of these are lovely even if you haven't a mink coat to wear over them.

ON AMERICAN MILLINERS

JULY 27, 1946

AMERICAN MILLINERS, who are sometimes referred to as "mad geniuses" in their lush little world, are notoriously perverse folk and unpredictable in direct ratio to their prosperity. The custom hats they have devised for this fall and winter are a challenge to psychiatrists. John-Frederics solemnly speak of fashions that stem from the "landscape of America." But to judge by their offerings, John and Fred think that we slaves to steam heat plan to shake off our bonds and spend the winter on the plains of North Dakota, and they're afraid we'll freeze. So they have put in a lot of time on hats that may start as turbans, cloches, derbies, or whatever, and end up with vast scarf appendages which you wrap tight under your nose (they don't tell you what to do when you want to smoke, have a drink, or kiss somebody—even just a mild goodbye). These flowing businesses, having thus forced your chin deep into your chest, either pin up into casual drapery at the back of the head or, more often, descend over the back of the neck to produce a silhouette that a turtle would consider an infringement on his patent. When the idea turns up in Technicolor white, an ivory shade that I would just as soon not try to describe, the effect is of a person with bandaged facial burns; in dark colors, it suggests, to go on with the boys' elaborate conceit, Oriental rather than Grant Wood landscapes. Then, Lilly Daché, a specialist in the spun-sugar, or wedding-cake, sort of frivolity, has come forth with some of the simplest, most youthful silhouettes to be seen in town.

And Sally Victor, idol of the night-life set, has shown up with striking untrimmed shapes and with felts cunningly draped, in a very suave way, like turbans. It is all most inconsistent and surprising.

The milliners, of course, are subjected to terrific temptations this season. Because they have been short of luxurious fabrics for years, it is understandable that they should go wild now that they again have at hand all the aigrette-type feathers, ostrich plumes, birds' wings, velvets, and other gaudy ingredients they want. Some of the results make me beg you to proceed with caution. It should also be noted, in all fairness, that the temptation of fine felts and French ribbon has not been resisted, either, and usually the results of this are happier.

As for line, the shops show a leaning toward hats with tiny brims that either shoot forward or are turned back, with high, narrow, squarish crowns that slant toward the rear. (You had better see how your profile looks in one of them before you take any definite steps.) There are wonderful adaptations of derbies and what are called "rollers" at Bergdorf Goodman, bonnets at Sally Victor, enchanting tilted contraptions at Daché and Florell. Most of them show the forehead and a bit of hairline, but there is an ominous tendency in some of them to ripple low over the forehead in the style of the twenties. That period is also hinted at in John-Frederics' circlets for evening, that go straight around the head like the band of a wedding veil, and I must admit that they are charming affairs. One is made of brown glycerined ostrich, which trails down the back; others start with diamond (not real, of course) circlets and have soft, spangled scarves coming down over the shoulders. A definite and fearfully elaborate trend is evening hats in the Gaby Deslys style—toques or big velvet hats adorned with ostrich feathers, birds, or velvet ribbon, and sometimes all of them. John-Frederics, who always like to stun their public, have lots of these, often accompanied by boas of curly ostrich or of frail glycerined feathers of the aigrette type. Other examples are simpler; Sally Victor makes vast inverted saucers in felt, absolutely unadorned, and Lilly Daché has a lovely big-brimmed felt with glycerined ostrich clouding the severity of the brim and giving a misty look to the whole thing.

ON FRENCH FASHION

APRIL 19, 1947

IT IS ALWAYS INTERESTING to see which way the wind is blowing in Paris. This year, as always, American buyers over there have been cautious about abandoning veteran designers, but they also have suffered their usual schoolgirl crushes on talented newcomers. The hero of one season can be the dullard of the next in this uncertain world, but no one can say fashion designers hold a franchise on *that* particular complaint. At Bergdorf (to get this discussion down to cases), where a lot of new French clothes are being shown to the custom trade, Balenciaga is the old tried-and-true party and the new darling is Christian Dior, who has got away to such a fine start that he must tremble at the thought of what will be expected of him next season. Balenciaga leads off with a black wool day dress that has sloping shoulders, long, slender sleeves, a deep tuck around the bodice to give the effect of a bolero, and a jabot down the front of the longish, slender skirt. He follows that up with a greenish-blue wool topcoat that is extraordinary—the draped back falls in deep folds and then curves in behind the knees, and the wrapped front has a much shorter hemline. Next, he tosses in a more conventional suit of navy wool, which has a straight skirt and a rather long, fitted jacket, made slightly hippy by three tiered flaps on each side at the waist. And so forth.

Dior ripostes with a nice black wool afternoon dress that has folds over the shoulders and a big black velvet bow across the base of the square neck; the skirt, which comes to within ten inches of the floor, achieves fullness with a pleated back panel. For daytime, he takes a navy wool dress, adds a conventional belt and a tiny white piqué collar with ends that knot at the throat, and uses very full pleating below the hips. Another excellent day dress by Dior is a slickly fitted black crêpe affair that buttons down the back almost to the hem and has a high, round neck. A little mustard shantung gilet, tying in back, can be worn over it; taken straight, it's our old friend the "good, basic black." When Dior gets eccentric, however, he does it thoroughly. Listen carefully; this won't take long. An evening dress of a purplish tie silk has a black sash wrapped a little above the waist of a top that is all loose folds, and the skirt is wide at the hips but looks hobbled at the ankles in front. The back of the skirt, which is floor-length, has a free-swinging panel that begins fairly far up. The model walks, the panel sways, the legs are revealed to a truly startling extent. No comment.

The Bergdorf show, as a whole, provides healthy competition for American designers, but not enough to make them despairingly turn tail and abandon the delights of custom designing for the safe-and-sane refuge of ready-to-wear.

ON COLLEGE CLOTHES
AUGUST 21, 1948

CUSTOM HAS ESTABLISHED the right of every generation to shock the one preceding it, if possible, but this is not always as easy as it looks. The plight of the current college girl, attempting to startle parents who survived the Scott Fitzgerald era, is a case in point, and pitiable indeed. In recent years, the young things have been trying to assert themselves by running around in attire resembling that of underprivileged serfs under the Hapsburgs, but their elders have taken it all with discouraging calm, and present indications are that the whole act has therefore lost its savor. Certainly the college clothes being shown right now are considerably less bulky and bedraggled than they have been for some time.

Not that there aren't still some eccentricities. These occur, mostly, where you'd least expect them—in pants. Knickerbockers, gone underground these several years, are with us again, presumably to the delight of girls who have to find comfort in the notion that *any* leg is enhanced by wearing them. Macy has some that are only moderately full, and come in green, red, or gray corduroy, with notched waistbands and zippers down the backs; $9.34. The same shop has plaid wool plus fours, with elastic across the back of the waist and a fastening down one hip; $8.94. Bonwit Teller show Calfeze, which are slacks that end a few inches above the ankle, cost $14.95, and are made of corduroy in colors like cinnamon, sage, cypress green, and deep mauve. Altman, even more unorthodox, is presenting Spat-slacks—tapering slacks of rainbow tweed that wind up looking like spats over the instep and are held there by a strap under the arch; $22.95. Believing that most women should stick to skirts and that even the rare ones with Hepburn figures shouldn't venture beyond conventional slacks, I can't say that I thrill to such innovations, but on the other hand my readers can't say that they are not kept informed on vital issues.

As to other vital issues, the news is good. Skirts tend to be flat over the hips, with fullness front and back; collars are cut to be worn either very high or thrown open so that they lie wide on the shoulders; Victorian styles continue. Lots of calico and quilting are to be found, and also fabrics that resemble baranduki (Russian for chipmunk) and ocelot fur. Ensembles are everywhere, and the beloved classic gray flannels and sweaters are on hand as usual. The highlights that follow are generally on the gay side and should suit gadabout working girls as well as campus belles.

PART SIX
POETRY

A NOTE BY DAN CHIASSON

THE POEMS IN *THE NEW YORKER* have a relationship to the page something like that of the cartoons, breaking the even, downward drift of the prose and suggesting, as the cartoons do, a distinct set of conventions for capturing reality. In the first part of the twentieth century, those conventions were completely overhauled, in ways that we are still sorting out. By around 1940, the modernism of Pound and Eliot had been mostly absorbed, though both of them very arguably had their best work before them: Pound's *Pisan Cantos* of 1948 and Eliot's *Four Quartets*, first published as a book in 1943. Yeats had died in 1939 after an astounding late period. The branch modernisms, exemplified by Wallace Stevens, Robert Frost, Marianne Moore, and others, were misunderstood, if they were known at all (Frost was considered a lightweight; it would be years before his tragic vision was acknowledged); W. H. Auden, who called the decade "the age of anxiety," though deeply impressed by Eliot, had struck the new tone of engaged sophistication with a Marxist edge. Various homegrown avant-gardes were devised, all of them cool to the touch, each one isolating this or that strain of modernism; George Oppen, Louis Zukofsky, and others founded the Objectivist Press in the early thirties, taking the innovations of William Carlos Williams ("No ideas but in things!") to their farthest frontier. Upstarts had begun to stir: Robert Lowell and Elizabeth Bishop were writing the poems that went into their first books, to be published in 1944 and 1946, respectively.

That's a lot of activity to keep track of, but readers of *The New Yorker* were spared the trouble for most of the thirties, when light and occasional verse by the likes of Phyllis McGinley and Virginia Woods Bellamy filled its pages. Ogden Nash and E. B. White, whose later work appears in our selections here, were frequent standouts among the legions of wags whose poems appealed to *The New Yorker* reader's taste and refinement, like the ads that ran alongside them for gin or haberdashery.

Serious poems had no friend in Harold Ross, who had fought Katherine White for years over whether poetry, as opposed to verse, ought to run in his magazine. It was always an uphill battle, as Ben Yagoda writes in *About Town: The New Yorker and the World It Made,* and Ross nearly cut poetry entirely in 1937. He backed down in response to a memo from White, but he effectively washed his hands of poetry by delegating it to others, first to William Maxwell and then, in 1939, to Charles A. (Cap) Pierce, who became the magazine's first designated poetry editor, serving until Howard Moss took over in 1950.

The poems we include here were all published under Pierce, who did three crucial things: he made it right with great poets the magazine had neglected or ignored, like William Carlos Williams, Marianne Moore, and Langston Hughes; he found poems that had something to say about the war; and he made discoveries, Elizabeth Bishop foremost among them. Bishop contributed eight poems in the forties, half of them before she had published a book. That fact alone locates *The New Yorker* near the center of American poetry in the decade.

By 1940, the war was an incontrovertible fact, and, surprisingly, as Yagoda argues, the poems in the magazine took the lead in facing it. The war crops up even in poems nominally about other things. In a piece of old-fashioned embroidery, E. B. White's "Home Song," we come suddenly upon "the soldier's destination / The sick man's ward, the wife's plantation." The poem deepens in ways that its significant surface charm belies. In Randall Jarrell's little verse fable, "The Blind Sheep," the sheep, when he hears from the surgeon owl that the world "goes as it went ere you were blinded," decides he'd rather stay blind than "witness that enormity" of worldly strife and suffering. Almost a year before Pearl Harbor, *The New Yorker* ran Louis MacNeice's "Barroom Matins," whose final stanzas shatter us by their untelegraphed directness. The poem concludes:

> Die the soldiers, die the Jews,
> And all the breadless homeless queues.
> Give us this day our daily news.

Auden's "The Unknown Citizen" mentions "the war" only once, but the entire poem (among Auden's most famous and most anthologized) functions as a protest against the forces that make "Modern Man" just a number, his death, as MacNeice puts it, "a drop of water in the sea / A journalist's commodity." Poetry, Pound once wrote, is "news that stays news"; as such, it casts a skeptical eye on "our daily news." (That rhyme with "Jews" is astounding: MacNeice seems to have divined, before the magazine's political columnists, where the persecution of Jews was headed.)

These poems measure their own power against the sham claims and rhetoric of institutions, a comparison that is always implicit in poems but breaks to the surface in times of conflict. Langston Hughes's "Sunday-Morning Prophecy" undermines that thieving preacher by its own setting up of his sermon like a piece of theatre. Howard Nemerov pits poetry's means of education against "The Triumph of Education," which, bursting one bubble after another, makes reasonable, modern robots out of the young. Everywhere in these poems we find attacks on the dulling, abstracting, and standardizing forces of modern life, which signals (in Malcolm Cowley's poem) "The End of the World" not by bombing cities but by stifling romantic love:

> Not havoc from the skies, death underfoot,
> The farmhouse gutted, or the massacred city,
> But the very nice couple retired on their savings,
> The weeded garden, the loveless bed.

Against this backdrop, poems that take pains with observation or measure precisely the fluctuations of mood seem anything but slight. They offer what Frost said all poems offer: "small stays against confusion." This is precisely what Richard Wilbur gives in an early poem, "Year's End," when he describes "the death of ferns" and other flora and sounds of winter: "Barrages of applause / Come muffled from a buried radio." Cowley's "The End of the World" has become, in Wilbur's elegant poem, plural and renewable: "the sudden ends of time" brought annually by wind and snow.

Wilbur was a great describer at a time when precise description played a role in proving anew what John Keats called "the holiness of the Heart's affections." *The New Yorker* began, in the forties, a relationship with another great describer that lasted her entire life: Elizabeth Bishop. Bishop's poems are, it would seem, all description; readers of the magazine could find in her the same kind of demonstrably "good writing" they found in the prose. Meticulous, apt, vivid, Bishop would seem to suggest that to be great, poems needed to exemplify only these traits. Who can forget the "big fish tubs . . . lined with layers of beautiful herring scales" in "At the Fishhouses" or, in "The Bight," the water "the color of the gas flame turned as low as possible." But in these poems the details always give way to humor, to tenderness, to wonder. Her poems calmly wait for the enchantment to strike, as when, in "At the Fishhouses," the old fisherman first "accepts a Lucky Strike," then delivers one, disclosing, between the lines, that "He was a friend of my grandfather." Or the way that, in "The Bight" (to which Bishop appended the subtitle "On My Birthday"), the envelopes on her writing desk magically turn into "little white boats . . . piled up / against each other," resembling, amazingly, "torn-open, unanswered letters." It is as though things have to be laundered in the imagination to become fully real. This is precisely the trade practiced in her own "Bight," the sublime "activity" that Bishop, staring down another year, labels, unforgettably, "awful but cheerful." Bishop's birthday gift to herself was also a sublime gift to the magazine and its readers.

HOME SONG

Home is the place where the queer things are:
Hope and compassion and objets d'art.
Home is the centre of mind and of liver,
Under the hill and beside the river.
Home is the strangest of common places,
Drenched with the light of familiar faces.
Here are the leavings of last night's table,
Gloom and gaiety, stoop and gable.

Home is the proving ground of sanity,
Brick and ember, love and vanity,
Paper and string and the carpet sweeper,
And the still form of the late sleeper.
Book and clock, and a plant to water,
Mother of Jesus, son and daughter.
Home is the ink and the dream and the well;
Home is the incompatibles' hell.

Home is the depot of coming and going,
The last kiss, the first snowing.
Home is the soldier's destination,
The sick man's ward, the wife's plantation.
Home is the place where the queer things are:
Hope and compassion and objets d'art.
Home is the pattern and shell of slumber,
Home is a gleam and a telephone number.

Ever at home are the mice in hiding,
Dust and trash, and the truth abiding.
Dark is the secret of home's hall closet—
Home's a disorderly safe deposit.

Home is the part of our life that's arable,
Home is a pledge, a plan, and a parable.
Ever before us is home's immensity,
Always within us its sheer intensity.

—E. B. White
February 5, 1944

THE UNKNOWN CITIZEN

TO

SOCIAL SECURITY ACCOUNT NUMBER 067–01–9818
THIS MARBLE MONUMENT IS ERECTED BY THE STATE

He was found by the Bureau of Statistics to be
One against whom there was no official complaint,
And all the reports on his conduct agree
That, in the modern sense of an old-fashioned word, he was a saint,
For in everything he did he served the Greater Community.
Except for the war, till the day he retired
He worked in one factory and never got fired,
But satisfied his employers, Fudge Motors, Inc.,
Yet was neither a scab nor odd in his views,
For his Union reports that he paid his dues
(Our report on his Union says it was sound),
And our Social Psychology workers found
He was popular with his mates and liked a drink.
The Press are convinced that he bought a paper every day,
And that his reactions to advertisements were normal in every way.
Policies taken out in his name prove that he was fully insured,
And a certificate shows that he was once in hospital but left it cured.
Both *Producer's Research* and *High Grade Living* declare
He was fully sensible to the advantage of the Installment Plan,
And had everything necessary to the Modern Man—
A victrola, a radio, a car, and a frigidaire.
Our investigators into Public Opinion are content
That he held the proper opinions for the time of year;
When there was peace, he was for peace; when there was war, he went.
He was married and added five children to the population,

Which, our eugenist says, was the right number for a parent of his
    generation,
And our teachers report that he never interfered with their education.
Was he free? Was he happy? The question is absurd;
Had anything been wrong, we should certainly have heard.

—*W. H. Auden*
January 6, 1940

THE RITUALISTS

In May, approaching the city, I
saw men fishing in the backwash
between the slips, where at the time
no ship lay. But though I stood

watching long enough, I didn't see
one of them catch anything
more than quietness, to the formal
rhythms of casting—that slow dance.

—*William Carlos Williams*
May 18, 1940

NIGHT JOURNEY

Now as the train bears west,
Its rhythm rocks the earth,
And from my Pullman berth
I stare into the night
While others take their rest.
Bridges of iron lace,
A suddenness of trees,
A lap of mountain mist
All cross my line of sight,
Then a bleak wasted place,
And a lake below my knees.
Full on my neck I feel
The straining at a curve;

My muscles move with steel,
I wake in every nerve.
I watch a beacon swing
From dark to blazing bright;
We thunder through ravines
And gullies washed with light.
Beyond the mountain pass
Mist deepens on the pane;
We rush into a rain
That rattles double glass.
Wheels shake the roadbed stone,
The pistons jerk and shove,
I stay up half the night
To see the land I love.

—Theodore Roethke
June 8, 1940

BARROOM MATINS

Popcorn, peanuts, clams, and gum—
We whose Kingdom has not come
Have mouths like men but still are dumb,

Who only deal with Here and Now
As circumstances may allow;
The sponsored program tells us how.

And yet the preachers tell the pews
What man misuses God can use:
Give us this day our daily news

That we may hear behind the brain
And through the sullen heat's migraine
The atavistic voice of Cain:

"Who entitled you to spy
From your easy heaven? Am I
My brother's keeper? Let him die."

And God, in words we soon forget,
Answers through the radio set,
"The curse is on his forehead yet."

Mass destruction, mass disease—
We thank thee, Lord, upon our knees
That we were born in times like these,

When, with doom tumbling from the sky,
Each of us has an alibi
For doing nothing. Let him die.

Let him die, his death will be
A drop of water in the sea,
A journalist's commodity.

Pretzels, crackers, chips, and beer—
Death is something that we fear,
But it titillates the ear.

Anchovy, almond, ice, and gin—
All shall die though none can win;
Let the *Untergang* begin.

  Die the soldiers, die the Jews,
  And all the breadless, homeless queues.
  Give us this day our daily news.

—Louis MacNeice
January 4, 1941

THE END OF THE WORLD

Not the harsh voice in the microphone,
Not broken covenants or hate in armor,
  But the smile like a cocktail gone flat,
  The stifled yawn.

Not havoc from the skies, death underfoot,
The farmhouse gutted, or the massacred city,
   But the very nice couple retired on their savings,
   The weeded garden, the loveless bed.

House warm in winter, city free of vice,
Tree that outstood the equinoctial gales:
   Dry at the heart, they crashed
   On a windless day.

—Malcolm Cowley
November 22, 1941

THE BLIND SHEEP

The Sheep is blind; a passing Owl,
A surgeon of some local skill,
Has undertaken, for a fee,
The cure. A stump, his surgery,
Is licked clean by a Cat; his tools—
A tooth, a thorn, some battered nails—
He ranges by a shred of sponge,
And he is ready to begin.
Pushed forward through the gaping crowd,
"Wait," bleats the Sheep. "Is all prepared?"
The Owl lists forceps, scalpel, lancet—
The old Sheep interrupts his answer:
"These lesser things may all be well,
But tell me, friend, how goes the world?"
The Owl says blankly, "You will find it
Goes as it went ere you were blinded."
"What?" cries the Sheep. "Then take your fee,
But cure some other fool, not me.
To witness that enormity
I would not give a blade of grass.
I am a Sheep, and not an Ass."

—Randall Jarrell
December 13, 1941

THE LOVERS

In this glass palace are flowers in golden baskets;
in that grim brownstone mansion are silver caskets;
the caskets watch and wait, and the baskets wait,
for a certain day, and hour, and a certain gate.

Wonderfully glow the colors in that bright palace!
Superb the flora, in pyx, and vase, and chalice!
The glass is steamed with a stifling tuberose breath;
and lilies, too, of the valley of the shadow of death.

The caskets are satin-lined, with silver handles,
and the janitor sings, "They'll soon be lighting candles";
he sweeps the sidewalk, and as he sweeps he sings
in praise of a hearse with completely noiseless springs.

Hush—the conspiracy works! It has crossed the street!
Someday, and it's not far off, these lovers will meet!
Casket and basket at last set forth together
for the joyful journey, no matter how bleak the weather;

in a beautiful beetle-black hearse with noiseless tread,
basket and casket together will get to bed,
and start on a Pullman journey to a certain gate,
punctually, at a certain hour, on a certain date.

—Conrad Aiken
March 28, 1942

SUNDAY-MORNING PROPHECY

An old Negro minister concludes his sermon in his
loudest voice, having previously pointed out the
sins of this world.

. . . Now,
When the rumble of death
Rushes down the drainpipe of eternity,
And hell breaks out

The minister switches
his hips like a volup-
tuous woman. He takes
two steps backward and
one forward.

Into a thousand smiles,
And the devil licks his chops,
Preparing to feast on life,
And all the little devils
Get out their bibs
To devour the corrupt bones
Of this world—

His knees sway beneath him.

Oh-ooo-oo-o! Then, my friends!
Oh, then! Oh, then!
What will you do?

He comes up in a crouch.

You will turn back and look toward
The mountains.

He rears back and rocks
and he
rears back and sways.
His knees give way again.
They go way down, but
he rises tall
and smiles
at the triumph of God.

You will turn back and grasp
For a straw.
You will holler, "Lord-d-d-d-d-ah!
Save me, Lord!
Save me!"
And the Lord will say,
"In the days of your greatness
I did not hear your voice!"

He turns,
smiles,
and steps forward.
He crouches and comes up.
Screams.
Frowns terribly.

The Lord will say,
"In the days of your richness
I did not see your face!"
The Lord will say,
"No-oooo-ooo-oo-o!
I will not save you now!"

His voice falls
ten octaves.

And your soul
Will be lost!

Softly.	Come into the church this morning,
	Brothers and sisters,
	And be saved.

Afterthought.	And give freely
	In the collection basket
	That I, who am thy shepherd,
	Might live.
Organ music.	Amen!

—*Langston Hughes*
June 20, 1942

A POET SPEAKS FROM THE VISITORS' GALLERY

Have Gentlemen perhaps forgotten this?—
We write the histories.

Do Gentlemen who snigger at the poets,
Who speak the word professor with guffaws—
Do Gentlemen expect their fame to flourish
When we, not they, distribute the applause?

Or do they trust their hope of long remembrance
To those they name with such respectful care—
To those who write the tittle in the papers,
To those who tell the tattle on the air?

Do Gentlemen expect the generation
That counts the losers out when tolls the bell
To take some gossip-caster's estimation,
Some junior voice of fame with fish to sell?

Do Gentlemen believe time's hard-boiled jury,
Judging the sober truth, will trust again
The words some copperhead who owned a paper
Ordered one Friday from the hired men?

Have Gentlemen forgotten Mr. Lincoln?

A poet wrote that story, not a newspaper,
Not the New Yorker of the nameless name
Who spat with hatred like some others later
And left, as they will, in his hate his shame.

History's not written in the kind of ink
The richest man of most ambitious mind
Who hates a president enough to print
A daily paper can afford or find.

Gentlemen have power now and know it,
But even the greatest and most famous kings
Feared and with reason to offend the poets
Whose songs are marble
                and whose marble sings.
                           —Archibald MacLeish
                              September 11, 1943

A HUNDRED MINNOWS

A hundred minnows, little-finger length,
Own the slim pond. In sets they make
Maneuver: all one way
Change-minded, yet of one mind where clear water
Clouds with their speed an instant;
 All one speed, one purpose, as they veer
And suddenly close circle; and some leap—
There! at an unseen fly,
There! at nothing at all.
Brown minnows, darkening daily
Since the thin time, the spring,
Since nothingness gave birth to such small bones,
Beat the soft water, fill
The wet world; as one,
Occupy movement, owning all August,
Proud minnows.

                          —Mark Van Doren
                            August 11, 1945

THE TRIUMPH OF EDUCATION

The children's eyes, like shadows on the sea,
Were baffling with a false serenity
When they were told, and given all the cause,
"There is no Santa Claus."

The children's eyes did not become more bright
Or curious of sexual delight
When someone said, "Man couples like the beast.
The stork does not exist."

The children's eyes, like smoke or drifted snow,
White shifted over white, refused to show
They suffered loss: "At first it may seem odd—
There isn't any God."

The children, not perturbed or comforted,
Heard silently the news of their last bed:
"For moral care you need not stint your breath,
There's no life after death."

The children's eyes grew hot, they glowed like stoves.
Ambitious, and equipped with all our proofs,
They ran forth little women, little men,
And were not children then.

—Howard Nemerov
October 26, 1946

AT THE FISHHOUSES

Although it is a cold evening,
down by one of the fishhouses
an old man sits netting,
his net, in the gloaming almost invisible,
a dark purple-brown,
and his shuttle worn and polished.
The air smells so strong of codfish

it makes one's nose run and one's eyes water.
The five fishhouses have steeply peaked roofs
and narrow, cleated gangplanks slant up
to storerooms in the gables
for the wheelbarrows to be pushed up and down on.
All is silver: the heavy surface of the sea,
swelling slowly as if considering spilling over,
is opaque, but the silver of the benches,
the lobster pots, and masts, scattered
among the wild jagged rocks,
is of an apparent translucence
like the small old buildings with an emerald moss
growing on their shoreward walls.
The big fish tubs are completely lined
with layers of beautiful herring scales
and the wheelbarrows are similarly plastered
with creamy iridescent coats of mail,
with small iridescent flies crawling on them.
Up on the little slope behind the houses,
set in the sparse bright sprinkle of grass,
is an ancient wooden capstan,
cracked, with two long bleached handles
and some melancholy stains, like dried blood,
where the ironwork has rusted.

The old man accepts a Lucky Strike.
He was a friend of my grandfather.
We talk of the decline in the population
and of codfish and herring
while he waits for a herring boat to come in.
There are sequins on his vest and on his thumb.
He has scraped the scales, the principal beauty,
from unnumbered fish with that black old knife,
the blade of which is almost worn away.

Down at the water's edge, at the place
where they haul up the boats, up the long ramp
descending into the water, thin silver

tree trunks are laid horizontally
across the gray stones, down and down
at intervals of four or five feet.

Cold dark deep and absolutely clear,
element bearable to no mortal,
to fish and to seals . . . One seal particularly
I have seen here evening after evening.
He was curious about me. He was interested in music;
like me a believer in total immersion,
so I used to sing him Baptist hymns.
I sang him "A mighty fortress is our God."
He stood up in the water and regarded me
steadily, moving his head a little.
Then he would disappear, then suddenly emerge
almost in the same spot, with a sort of shrug
as if it were against his better judgment.
Cold dark deep and absolutely clear,
the clear gray icy water . . . Back, behind us,
the dignified tall firs begin.
Bluish, associating with their shadows,
a million Christmas trees stand
waiting for Christmas. The water seems suspended
above the rounded gray and blue-gray stones.
I have seen it over and over, the same sea, the same,
slightly, indifferently swinging above the stones,
icily free above the stones,
above the stones and then the world.
If you should dip your hand in,
your wrist would ache immediately,
your bones would begin to ache and your hand would burn
as if the water were a transmutation of fire
that feeds on stones and burns with a dark-gray flame.
If you tasted it, it would first taste bitter,
then briny, then surely burn your tongue.
It is like what we imagine knowledge to be:
dark, salt, clear, moving, utterly free,
drawn from the cold hard mouth

of the world, derived from the rocky breasts
forever, flowing and drawn, and since
our knowledge is historical, flowing, and flown.

—*Elizabeth Bishop*
August 9, 1947

ASPECTS OF ROBINSON

Robinson at cards at the Algonquin; a thin
Blue light comes down once more outside the blinds.
Gray men in overcoats are ghosts blown past the door.
The taxis streak the avenues with yellow, orange, and red.
This is Grand Central, Mr. Robinson.

Robinson on a roof above the Heights; the boats
Mourn like the lost. Water is slate, far down.
Through sounds of ice cubes dropped in glass, an osteopath,
Dressed for the links, recounts an old Intourist tour.
—Here's where old Gibbons jumped from, Robinson.

Robinson walking in the Park, admiring the elephant.
Robinson buying the *Tribune*, Robinson buying the *Times*. Robinson
Saying, "Hello. Yes, this is Robinson. Sunday
At five? I'd love to. Pretty well. And you?"
Robinson alone at Longchamps, staring at the wall.

Robinson afraid, drunk, sobbing. Robinson
In bed with a Mrs. Morse. Robinson at home;
Decisions: Toynbee or luminal? Where the sun
Shines, Robinson in flowered trunks, eyes toward
The breakers. Where the night ends, Robinson in East Side bars.

Robinson in Glen-plaid jacket, Scotch-grain shoes,
Black four-in-hand, and oxford button-down,
The jewelled and silent watch that winds itself, the brief-
Case, covert topcoat, clothes for spring, all covering
His sad and usual heart, dry as a winter leaf.

—*Weldon Kees*
April 24, 1948

AWAKING

After night, the waking knowledge—
The gravel path searching the Way;
The cobweb crystal on the hedge,
The empty station of the day.

So I remember each new morning
From childhood, when pebbles amaze.
Outside my window, with each dawning,
The whiteness of those days.

The sense felt behind darkened walls
Of a sun-drenched world; a lake
Of light, through which light falls—
It is this to which I wake.

Then the sun shifts the trees around,
And overtops the sky, and throws
House, horse, and rider to the ground,
With knock-out shadows.

The whole day opens to an O,
The cobweb dries, the petals spread,
The clocks grow long, the people go
Walking over themselves, the dead.

The world's a circle, where all moves
Before after, after before,
And my aware awaking loves
The day—until I start to care.

—*Stephen Spender*
May 15, 1948

AT YEARSEND

Now winter downs the dying of the year,
And night is all a settlement of snow;

From the soft street the rooms of houses show
A gathered light, a shapen atmosphere,
Like frozen-over lakes whose ice is thin
And still allows some stirring down within.

I've known the wind by waterbanks to shake
The late leaves down, which frozen where they fell
And held in ice as dancers in a spell
Fluttered all winter long into a lake;
Graved on the dark in gestures of descent,
They seemed their own most perfect monument.

There was perfection in the death of ferns
Which laid their fragile cheeks against the stone
A million years. Great mammoths overthrown
Composedly have made their long sojourns,
Like palaces of patience, in the gray
And changeless lands of ice. And at Pompeii

The little dog lay curled and did not rise
But slept the deeper as the ashes rose
And found the people incomplete, and froze
The random hands, the loose unready eyes
Of men expecting yet another sun
To do the shapely thing they had not done.

These sudden ends of time must give us pause.
We fray into the future, rarely wrought
Save in the tapestries of afterthought.
More time, more time. Barrages of applause
Come muffled from a buried radio.
The Newyear bells are wrangling with the snow.

—*Richard Wilbur*
January 1, 1949

WHAT I KNOW ABOUT LIFE

I have recently been pondering the life expectancy that the Bible allots
to man,

And at this point I figure I have worked my way through nine-
fourteenths of my hypothetical span.
I have been around a bit and met many interesting people and made
and lost some money and acquired, in reverse order, a family and a
wife,
And by now I should have drawn some valuable conclusions about life.
Well, I have learned that life is something about which you can't
conclude anything except that it is full of vicissitudes.
And where you expect logic you only come across eccentricitudes.
Life has a tendency to obfuscate and bewilder,
Such as fating us to spend the first part of our lives being embarrassed
by our parents and the last part being embarrassed by our childer.
Life is constantly presenting us with experiences that are unprecedented
and depleting,
Such as the friend who starts drinking at three in the afternoon and
explains it's only to develop a hearty appetite for dinner because it's
unhealthy to drink without eating.
Life being what it is, I don't see why everybody doesn't develop an
ulcer,
Particularly Mrs. Martingale, the wife of a prominent pastry cook from
Tulsa.
He had risen to fame and fortune after starting as a humble purveyor of
noodles,
So he asked her what she wanted for her birthday and she said a new
Studebaker and he thought she said a new strudel baker and she
hated strudels.
So all I know about life is that it has been well said
That such things can't happen to a person when they are dead.

—*Ogden Nash*
January 15, 1949

THE BIGHT

ON MY BIRTHDAY

At low tide like this how sheer the water is.
White crumbling ribs of marl protrude and glare
and the boats are dry, the pilings dry as matches.

Absorbing, rather than being absorbed,
the water in the bight doesn't wet anything,
the color of the gas flame turned as low as possible.
One can smell it turning to gas; if one were Baudelaire
one could probably hear it turning to marimba music.
The little ochre dredge at work off the end of the dock
already plays the dry perfectly off-beat *claves*.
The birds are outsize. Pelicans crash
into this peculiar gas unnecessarily hard,
it seems to me, like pickaxes,
rarely coming up with anything to show for it,
and going off with humorous elbowings.
Black-and-white man-of-war birds soar
on impalpable drafts
and open their tails like scissors on the curves
or tense them like wishbones, till they tremble.
The frowsy sponge boats keep coming in
with the obliging air of retrievers,
bristling with jackstraw gaffs and hooks
and decorated with bobbles of sponges.
There is a fence of chicken wire along the dock
where, glinting like little plowshares,
the blue-gray shark tails are hung up to dry
for the Chinese-restaurant trade.
Some of the little white boats are still piled up
against each other, or lie on their sides, stove in,
and not yet salvaged, if they ever will be, from the last bad storm,
like torn-open, unanswered letters.
The bight is littered with old correspondences.
Click. Click. Goes the dredge,
and brings up a dripping jawful of marl.
All the untidy activity continues,
awful but cheerful.

—Elizabeth Bishop
February 19, 1949

SONG FOR THE LAST ACT

Now that I have your face by heart, I look
Less at its features than its darkening frame
Where quince and melon, yellow as young flame,
Lie with quilled dahlias and the shepherd's crook.
Beyond, a garden. There, in insolent ease
The lead and marble figures watch the show
Of yet another summer loath to go
Although the scythes hang in the apple trees.

Now that I have your face by heart, I look.

Now that I have your voice by heart, I read
In the black chords upon a dulling page
Music that is not meant for music's cage,
Whose emblems mix with words that shake and bleed.
The staves are shuttled over with a stark
Unprinted silence. In a double dream
I must spell out the storm, the running stream.
The beat's too swift. The notes shift in the dark.

Now that I have your voice by heart, I read.

Now that I have your heart by heart, I see
The wharves with their great ships and architraves;
The rigging and the cargo and the slaves
On a strange beach under a broken sky.
O not departure, but a voyage done!
The bales stand on the stone; the anchor weeps
Its red rust downward, and the long vine creeps
Beside the salt herb, in the lengthening sun.

Now that I have your heart by heart, I see.

—Louise Bogan
October 15, 1949

PART SEVEN

FICTION

A NOTE BY ZADIE SMITH

WRITERS ARE CONFLICTED about "Zeitgeist." Sharing a sensibility with your literary generation is, to a working writer, pretty much an annoyance: vanity demands you sound like no one but yourself. Yet, as the decades pass, having sounded like your peers—having channeled, however unconsciously, the spirit of the age—is what will tend to secure your spot in anthologies like this one. And being remembered, placed, and ranked, these are things that all but the most independent writers come to worry about, eventually—perhaps a little more than they should. Even the great individualist Vladimir Nabokov was glad when publishers sent him anthologies ("homing pigeons really, for all of them contain samples of the recipient's writings"). Although, when called upon—by no one but himself—to rate the stories in *55 Short Stories from The New Yorker, 1940–1950*, he gave only two an A+: his own and Salinger's "A Perfect Day for Bananafish" (which was not available for inclusion here). Nabokov had a theory that you could only ever expect, from any anthology, "two or three first-rate stories." I think that honest readers, writers, and publishers would probably agree with that strike rate. But most of us derive a lot of enjoyment from stories in the B+ to A grade range and, if we are students of the craft, learn something from them, too. Personally I find it hard to learn a lot from A+ stories, much as I love and admire them. Not easy to glean tips on construction when gazing upon a thing so perfect, with no visible joins, like a naturally occurring crystal.

Nabokov is Nabokov and Salinger Salinger. Let's leave them for a moment at the top of the class. Now, what about everybody else? Is there a voice of the forties? Well, how the hell am *I* meant to know? Isn't that something a fella oughta, well, consider for himself? I mean, if he really wants to *understand* anything? Oh, I'm not saying you can't hear a certain rhythm in the dialogue, a self-conscious snap and crackle in the way some of these stiffs speak. I suppose I've got ears just like anybody. And I guess if you really *wanted* you could sure as hell chalk it up to the beloved memory of a half-dozen movie idols of the period, like Spencer Tracy, say, or good old Jimmy Stewart; but it might just as well be the intimate echo of soldiers wisecracking in some abandoned hay barn not far from Omaha Beach, or—if you want to get really *smart* about it—the long shadow of the newly imported Dr. Freud, interpreting everybody's private dreams and poking all around in a fella's private business like a *goddam sneak.* . . .

Dialogue was the thing, in the forties. Many of the writers in this anthology did some work in Hollywood, and almost all of them found their work adapted for film, sooner or later, though the results rarely satisfied. It's one thing to have gabbing fools safely embedded in the adamantine marvel of your prose, but take away the adamantine and what's left? A lot of fools, gabbing. I find I want to say "holy fools." A robust sense of morality hangs over these stories. They are almost all engaged with—to steal the title of another Shirley Jackson story, not included here—the possibility of evil. The demented young man in Nabokov's "Signs and Symbols" would surely find biblical connections throughout, starting with the titles ("Graven Image," "Act of Faith"), and proceeding to the various Old Testament parallels within the stories themselves. Let he who is without sin cast the first stone at Shirley Jackson's "The Lottery." Let he who fears the Babelian hordes listen in on John Cheever's "The Enormous Radio." Meanwhile, over in England, V. S. Pritchett takes Jacob's ladder and turns it into a domestic incident: resentful stepdaughter removes stepmother's staircase to Heaven.

Of course, there was a war on, and devilish behavior was everywhere. When you see that righteous little man in Carson McCullers's "The Jockey," calling out a bookie, a trainer, and "a rich man" as they sit down to an elaborate meal in a hotel restaurant ("You libertines"), the incident, small as it seems, takes on a peculiar magnitude. Here is the jockey, angry for his crippled jockey friend. And here are all the little men of this world sent off to risk life and limb at the behest of the rich and powerful. It's the same controlled ethical disgust you find in Shirley Jackson's notorious vision of small-town ritual murder. *The evil that men do.* But registered in an oblique style, and all the more forceful for it. Those "Patterns of Love" admired by William Maxwell (and published two months to the day after victory in Europe)—are we to take them as the first, uncertain steps toward a peaceful, humane future? In that sweet and subtle story, a lonely man, Arnold, is visiting a happy family, the Talbots, who in turn are always "visiting" him in his guest house, along with the family dog, a Great Dane, name of Satan. The two younger sons often fight. But not always:

> Once Satan was admitted to the little house, it became quite full and rather noisy, but John Talbot appeared and sent the dog out and made the children leave Arnold in peace. They left as they had come, by the window. Arnold watched them and was touched by the way Duncan turned and helped George, who was too small to jump. Also by the way George accepted this help. It was as if their hostility had two faces and one of them was the face of love. Cain and Abel, Arnold thought . . .

Only one of these stories, Irwin Shaw's, looks directly at the face of Cain, but in it we join the noncommissioned officers Seeger, Welch, and Olson after the action, at the end of the war, Shaw being interested in what we would these days call "post-conflict trauma." Trauma itself—now such a familiar tool in the writer's arsenal—was, in the forties, still something to be wrangled with, fresh theory rather than (generally) accepted fact. For E. B. White the talking cure is not to be taken too seriously ("'Ever have any bizarre thoughts?' asked the doctor. . . . Ever have any bizarre thoughts? What kind of thoughts *except* bizarre had he had since the age of two?"). Nabokov's opinions on the subject, meanwhile, are well known, and his perfect gem of a story, "Signs and Symbols," is another repudiation of the Freudian habit of placing, as Jessamyn West puts it elsewhere in this book, the mysteries of life in an orderly manner:

> She thought of the recurrent waves of pain that for some reason or other she and her husband had had to endure; of the invisible giants hurting her boy in some unimaginable fashion; of the incalculable amount of tenderness contained in the world; of the fate of this tenderness, which is either crushed or wasted, or transformed into madness; of neglected children humming to themselves in unswept corners; of *beautiful weeds that cannot hide from the farmer.*

My italics. If I could gather these writers of the forties under one banner it would be their shared desire to protect faulty, small, vulnerable, and yet beautiful phenomena from the forces of destruction. E. B. White wants to save the second tree on the corner—"saturated with the evening, each gilt-edged leaf perfectly drunk with excellence and delicacy"— from the deadening theories of his therapist. Elizabeth Taylor wants to protect the first shoots of new love as they grow out of somebody else's grave. Cheever, like all writers, wants to preserve the voices of passing strangers. And Frank O'Connor—despite his present reputation as a writer of neat little tales that all end in epiphany—wants to tell a shaggy-dog story that allows for the possibility that an "insignificant little gnat" like Freddie or Stevie Leary can yet continue to exist, if only because they have been remembered, by the narrator, "with extraordinary vividness." People forget, and time is violent, and sometimes the "times" are violent, too, in the nonmetaphorical sense. In the forties, the left-hand column of the human ledger was long, longer than seemed possible. Still, these writers found a few luminous things to put down for us on the other side, and we have not yet forgotten the favor.

THE *SECOND* TREE FROM THE CORNER

E. B. White

"EVER HAVE ANY BIZARRE THOUGHTS?" asked the doctor.

Mr. Trexler failed to catch the word. "What kind?" he said.

"Bizarre," repeated the doctor, his voice steady. He watched his patient for any slight change of expression, any wince. It seemed to Trexler that the doctor was not only watching him closely but was creeping slowly toward him, like a lizard toward a bug. Trexler shoved his chair back an inch and gathered himself for a reply. He was about to say "Yes" when he realized that if he said yes the next question would be unanswerable. Bizarre thoughts, bizarre thoughts? Ever have any bizarre thoughts? What kind of thoughts *except* bizarre had he had since the age of two?

Trexler felt the time passing, the necessity for an answer. These psychiatrists were busy men, overloaded, not to be kept waiting. The next patient was probably already perched out there in the waiting room, lonely, worried, shifting around on the sofa, his mind stuffed with bizarre thoughts and amorphous fears. Poor bastard, thought Trexler. Out there all alone in that misshapen antechamber, staring at the filing cabinet and wondering whether to tell the doctor about that day on the Madison Avenue bus.

Let's see, bizarre thoughts. Trexler dodged back along the dreadful corridor of the years to see what he could find. He felt the doctor's eyes upon him and knew that time was running out. Don't be so conscientious, he said to himself. If a bizarre thought is indicated here, just reach into the bag and pick anything at all. A man as well supplied with bizarre thoughts as you are should have no difficulty producing one for the record. Trexler darted into the bag, hung for a moment before one of his thoughts, as a hummingbird pauses in the delphinium. No, he said, not that one. He darted to another (the one about the rhesus monkey), paused, considered. No, he said, not that.

Trexler knew he must hurry. He had already used up pretty nearly four seconds since the question had been put. But it was an impossible situation—just one more lousy, impossible situation such as he was always getting himself into. When, he asked himself, are you going to quit maneuvering yourself into a pocket? He made one more effort. This time he stopped at the asylum, only the bars were lucite—fluted, retractable. Not here, he said. Not this one.

He looked straight at the doctor. "No," he said quietly. "I never have any bizarre thoughts."

The doctor sucked in on his pipe, blew a plume of smoke toward the rows of medical books. Trexler's gaze followed the smoke. He managed to make out one of the titles, *The Genito-Urinary System*. A bright wave of fear swept cleanly over him, and he winced under the first pain of kidney stones. He remembered when he was a child, the first time he ever entered a doctor's office, sneaking a look at the titles of the books—and the flush of fear, the shirt wet under the arms, the book on t.b., the sudden knowledge that he was in the advanced stages of consumption, the quick vision of the hemorrhage. Trexler sighed wearily. Forty years, he thought, and I still get thrown by the title of a medical book. Forty years and I still can't stay on life's little bucky horse. No wonder I'm sitting here in this dreary joint at the end of this woebegone afternoon, lying about my bizarre thoughts to a doctor who looks, come to think of it, rather tired.

The session dragged on. After about twenty minutes, the doctor rose and knocked his pipe out. Trexler got up, knocked the ashes out of his brain, and waited. The doctor smiled warmly and stuck out his hand. "There's nothing the matter with you—you're just scared. Want to know how I know you're scared?"

"How?" asked Trexler.

"Look at the chair you've been sitting in! See how it has moved back away from my desk? You kept inching away from me while I asked you questions. That means you're scared."

"Does it?" said Trexler, faking a grin. "Yeah, I suppose it does."

They finished shaking hands. Trexler turned and walked out uncertainly along the passage, then into the waiting room and out past the next patient, a ruddy pin-striped man who was seated on the sofa twirling his hat nervously and staring straight ahead at the files. Poor, frightened guy, thought Trexler, he's probably read in the *Times* that one American male out of every two is going to die of heart disease by twelve o'clock next Thursday. It says that in the paper almost every morning. And he's also probably thinking about that day on the Madison Avenue bus.

· · ·

A week later, Trexler was back in the patient's chair. And for several weeks thereafter he continued to visit the doctor, always toward the end of the afternoon, when the vapors hung thick above the pool of the mind and darkened the whole region of the East Seventies. He felt no better as time went on, and he found it impossible to work. He discovered that the visits were becoming routine and that although the routine was one to which he certainly did not look forward, at least he could accept it with cool resignation, as once, years ago, he had accepted a long spell with a dentist who had settled down to a steady fooling with a couple of dead teeth. The visits, moreover, were now assuming a pattern recognizable to the patient.

Each session would begin with a résumé of symptoms—the dizziness in the streets, the constricting pain in the back of the neck, the apprehensions, the tightness of the scalp, the inability to concentrate, the despondency and the melancholy times, the feeling of pressure and tension, the anger at not being able to work, the anxiety over work not done, the gas on the stomach. Dullest set of neurotic symptoms in the world, Trexler would think, as he obediently trudged back over them for the doctor's benefit. And then, having listened attentively to the recital, the doctor would spring his question: "Have you ever found anything that gives you relief?" And Trexler would answer, "Yes. A drink." And the doctor would nod his head knowingly.

As he became familiar with the pattern Trexler found that he increasingly tended to identify himself with the doctor, transferring himself into the doctor's seat—probably (he thought) some rather slick form of escapism. At any rate, it was nothing new for Trexler to identify himself with other people. Whenever he got into a cab, he instantly became the driver, saw everything from the hackman's angle (and the reaching over with the right hand, the nudging of the flag, the pushing it down, all the way down along the side of the meter), saw everything—traffic, fare, everything—through the eyes of Anthony Rocco, or Isidore Freedman, or Matthew Scott. In a barbershop, Trexler was the barber, his fingers curled around the comb, his hand on the tonic. Perfectly natural, then, that Trexler should soon be occupying the doctor's chair, asking the questions, waiting for the answers. He got quite interested in the doctor, in this way. He liked him, and he found him a not too difficult patient.

It was on the fifth visit, about halfway through, that the doctor turned to Trexler and said, suddenly, "What do you want?" He gave the word "want" special emphasis.

"I d'know," replied Trexler uneasily. "I guess nobody knows the answer to that one."

"Sure they do," replied the doctor.

"Do *you* know what *you* want?" asked Trexler narrowly.

"Certainly," said the doctor. Trexler noticed that at this point the doctor's chair slid slightly backward, away from him. Trexler stifled a small, internal smile. Scared as a rabbit, he said to himself. Look at him scoot!

"What *do* you want?" continued Trexler, pressing his advantage, pressing it hard.

The doctor glided back another inch away from his inquisitor. "I want a wing on the small house I own in Westport. I want more money, and more leisure to do the things I want to do."

Trexler was just about to say, "And what are those things you want to do, Doctor?" when he caught himself. Better not go too far, he mused. Better not lose possession of the ball. And besides, he thought, what the hell goes on here, anyway—me paying fifteen bucks a throw for these séances and then doing the work myself, asking the questions, weighing the answers. So he wants a new wing! There's a fine piece of theatrical gauze for you! A new wing.

Trexler settled down again and resumed the role of patient for the rest of the visit. It ended on a kindly, friendly note. The doctor reassured him that his fears were the cause of his sickness, and that his fears were unsubstantial. They shook hands, smiling.

Trexler walked dizzily through the empty waiting room and the doctor followed along to let him out. It was late; the secretary had shut up shop and gone home. Another day over the dam. "Goodbye," said Trexler. He stepped into the street, turned west toward Madison, and thought of the doctor all alone there, after hours, in that desolate hole—a man who worked longer hours than his secretary. Poor, scared, overworked bastard, thought Trexler. And that new wing!

It was an evening of clearing weather, the Park showing green and desirable in the distance, the last daylight applying a high lacquer to the brick and brownstone walls and giving the street scene a luminous and intoxicating splendor. Trexler meditated, as he walked, on what he wanted. "What do you want?" he heard again. Trexler knew what he wanted, and what, in general, all men wanted; and he was glad, in a way, that it was both inexpressible and unattainable, and that it wasn't a wing. He was satisfied to remember that it was deep, formless, enduring, and impossible of fulfillment, and that it made men sick, and that when you sauntered along Third Avenue and looked through the doorways into the dim saloons, you could sometimes pick out from the unregenerate ranks the ones who had not forgotten, gazing steadily into the bottoms of the glasses on the long chance that they could get another little peek at it. Trexler found himself renewed by the remembrance that what he wanted was at once great and microscopic, and that although it borrowed from the nature of large deeds and of youthful love and of old songs and early intimations, it was not any one of these things, and that it had not been isolated or pinned down, and that a man who attempted to define it in the privacy of a doctor's office would fall flat on his face.

Trexler felt invigorated. Suddenly his sickness seemed health, his dizziness stability. A small tree, rising between him and the light, stood there saturated with the evening, each gilt-edged leaf perfectly drunk with excellence and delicacy. Trexler's spine registered an ever so slight tremor as it picked up this natural disturbance in the lovely scene. "I want the second tree from the corner, just as it stands," he said, answering an imaginary question from an imaginary physician. And he felt a slow pride in realizing that what he wanted none could bestow, and that what he had none could take away. He felt content to be sick, unembarrassed at being afraid; and in the jungle of his fear he glimpsed (as he had so often glimpsed them before) the flashy tail feathers of the bird courage.

Then he thought once again of the doctor, and of his being left there all alone, tired, frightened. (The poor, scared guy, thought Trexler.) Trexler began humming "Moonshine Lullaby," his spirit reacting instantly to the hypodermic of Merman's healthy voice. He crossed Madison, boarded a downtown bus, and rode all the way to Fifty-second Street before he had a thought that could rightly have been called bizarre.

May 31, 1947

THE JOCKEY

Carson McCullers

THE JOCKEY CAME TO THE DOORWAY of the dining room, then after a moment stepped to one side and stood motionless, with his back to the wall. The room was crowded, as this was the third day of the season and all the hotels in the town were full. In the dining room bouquets of August roses scattered their petals on the white table linen and from the adjoining bar came a warm, drunken wash of voices. The jockey waited with his back to the wall and scrutinized the room with pinched, crêpy eyes. He examined the room until at last his eyes reached a table in a corner diagonally across from him, at which three men were sitting. As he watched, the jockey raised his chin and tilted his head back to one side, his dwarfed body grew rigid, and his hands stiffened so that the fingers curled inward like gray claws. Tense against the wall of the dining room, he watched and waited in this way.

He was wearing a suit of green Chinese silk that evening, tailored precisely and the size of a costume outfit for a child. The shirt was yellow, the tie striped with pastel colors. He had no hat with him and wore his hair brushed down in a stiff, wet bang on his forehead. His face was drawn, ageless, and gray. There were shadowed hollows at his temples and his mouth was set in a wiry smile. After a time he was aware that he had been seen by one of the three men he had been watching. But the jockey did not nod; he only raised his chin still higher and hooked the thumb of his tense hand in the pocket of his coat.

The three men at the corner table were a trainer, a bookie, and a rich man. The trainer was Sylvester—a large, loosely built fellow with a flushed nose and slow blue eyes. The bookie was Simmons. The rich man was the owner of a horse named Seltzer, which the jockey had ridden that afternoon. The three of them drank whiskey with soda, and a white-coated waiter had just brought on the main course of the dinner.

It was Sylvester who first saw the jockey. He looked away quickly, put down his whiskey glass, and nervously mashed the tip of his red nose with his thumb. "It's Bitsy Barlow," he said. "Standing over there across the room. Just watching us."

"Oh, the jockey," said the rich man. He was facing the wall and he half turned his head to look behind him. "Ask him over."

"God no," Sylvester said.

"He's crazy," Simmons said. The bookie's voice was flat and without inflection. He had the face of a born gambler, carefully adjusted, the expression a permanent deadlock between fear and greed.

"Well, I wouldn't call him that exactly," said Sylvester. "I've known him a long time. He was O.K. until about six months ago. But if he goes on like this, I can't see him lasting out another year. I just can't."

"It was what happened in Miami," said Simmons.

"What?" asked the rich man.

Sylvester glanced across the room at the jockey and wet the corner of his mouth with his red, fleshy tongue. "A accident. A kid got hurt on the track. Broke a leg and a hip. He was a particular pal of Bitsy's. A Irish kid. Not a bad rider, either."

"That's a pity," said the rich man.

"Yeah. They were particular friends," Sylvester said. "You would always find him up in Bitsy's hotel room. They would be playing rummy or else lying on the floor reading the sports page together."

"Well, those things happen," said the rich man.

Simmons cut into his beefsteak. He held his fork prongs downward on the plate and carefully piled on mushrooms with the blade of his knife. "He's crazy," he repeated. "He gives me the creeps."

All the tables in the dining room were occupied. There was a party at the banquet table in the centre, and green-white August moths had found their way in from the night and fluttered about the clear candle flames. Two girls wearing flannel slacks and blazers walked arm in arm across the room into the bar. From the main street outside came the echoes of holiday hysteria.

"They claim that in August Saratoga is the wealthiest town per capita in the world." Sylvester turned to the rich man. "What do you think?"

"I wouldn't know," said the rich man. "It may very well be so."

Daintily, Simmons wiped his greasy mouth with the tip of his forefinger. "How about Hollywood? And Wall Street—"

"Wait," said Sylvester. "He's decided to come over here."

The jockey had left the wall and was approaching the table in the corner. He walked with a prim strut, swinging out his legs in a half-circle with each step, his heels biting smartly into the red velvet carpet on the floor. On the way over he brushed against the elbow of a fat woman in white satin at the banquet table; he stepped back and bowed with dandified courtesy, his eyes quite closed. When he had crossed the room he drew up a chair and sat at a corner of the table, between Sylvester and the rich man, without a nod of greeting or a change in his set, gray face.

"Had dinner?" Sylvester asked.

"Some people might call it that." The jockey's voice was high, bitter, clear.

Sylvester put his knife and fork down carefully on his plate. The rich man shifted his position, turning sidewise in his chair and crossing his legs. He was dressed in twill riding pants, unpolished boots, and a shabby brown jacket—this was his outfit day and night in the racing season, although he was never seen on a horse. Simmons went on with his dinner.

"Like a spot of seltzer water?" asked Sylvester. "Or something like that?"

The jockey didn't answer. He drew a gold cigarette case from his pocket and snapped it open. Inside were a few cigarettes and a tiny gold penknife. He used the knife to cut a cigarette in half. When he had lighted his smoke he held up his hand to a waiter passing by the table. "Kentucky bourbon, please."

"Now, listen, Kid," said Sylvester.

"Don't Kid me."

"Be reasonable. You know you got to behave reasonable."

The jockey drew up the left corner of his mouth in a stiff jeer. His eyes lowered to the food spread out on the table, but instantly he looked up again. Before the rich man was a fish casserole, baked in a cream sauce and garnished with parsley. Sylvester had ordered eggs Benedict. There was asparagus, fresh buttered corn, and a side dish of wet black olives. A plate of French-fried potatoes was in the corner of the table before the jockey. He didn't look at the food again, but kept his pinched eyes on the centrepiece of full-blown lavender roses. "I don't suppose you remember a certain person by the name of McGuire," he said.

"Now, listen," said Sylvester.

The waiter brought the whiskey, and the jockey sat fondling the glass with his small, strong, callused hands. On his wrist was a gold link bracelet that clinked against the table edge. After turning the glass between his palms, the jockey suddenly drank the whiskey neat in two hard swallows. He set down the glass sharply. "No, I don't suppose your memory is that long and extensive," he said.

"Sure enough, Bitsy," said Sylvester. "What makes you act like this? You hear from the kid today?"

"I received a letter," the jockey said. "The certain person we were speaking about was taken out from the cast on Wednesday. One leg is two inches shorter than the other one. That's all."

Sylvester clucked his tongue and shook his head. "I realize how you feel."

"Do you?" The jockey was looking at the dishes on the table. His gaze passed from the fish casserole to the corn, and finally fixed on the plate of fried potatoes. His face tightened and quickly he looked up again. A rose shattered and he picked up one of the petals, bruised it between his thumb and forefinger, and put it in his mouth.

"Well, those things happen," said the rich man.

The trainer and the bookie had finished eating, but there was food left on the serving dishes before their plates. The rich man dipped his buttery fingers in his water glass and wiped them with his napkin.

"Well," said the jockey. "Doesn't somebody want me to pass them something? Or maybe perhaps you desire to reorder. Another hunk of beefsteak, gentlemen, or—"

"Please," said Sylvester. "Be reasonable. Why don't you go on upstairs?"

"Yes, why don't I?" the jockey said.

His prim voice had risen higher and there was about it the sharp whine of hysteria.

"Why don't I go up to my god-damn room and walk around and write some letters and go to bed like a good boy? Why don't I just—" He pushed his chair back and got up. "Oh, foo," he said. "Foo to you. I want a drink."

"All I can say is it's your funeral," said Sylvester. "You know what it does to you. You know well enough."

The jockey crossed the dining room and went into the bar. He ordered a Manhattan, and Sylvester watched him stand with his heels pressed tight together, his body hard as a lead soldier's, holding his little finger out from the cocktail glass and sipping the drink slowly.

"He's crazy," said Simmons. "Like I said."

Sylvester turned to the rich man. "If he eats a lamb chop, you can see the shape of it in his stomach a hour afterward. He can't sweat things out of him any more. He's a hundred and twelve and a half. He's gained three pounds since we left Miami."

"A jockey shouldn't drink," said the rich man.

"The food don't satisfy him like it used to and he can't sweat it out. If he eats a lamb chop, you can watch it tooching out in his stomach and it don't go down."

The jockey finished his Manhattan. He swallowed, crushed the cherry in the bottom of the glass with his thumb, then pushed the glass away from him. The two girls in blazers were standing at his left, their faces turned toward each other, and at the other end of the bar two touts had started an argument about which was the highest mountain in the world. Everyone was with somebody else; there was no other person drinking alone that night. The jockey paid with a brand-new fifty-dollar bill and didn't count the change.

He walked back to the dining room and to the table at which the three men were sitting, but he did not sit down. "No, I wouldn't presume to think your memory is that extensive," he said. He was so small that the edge of the table top reached almost to his belt, and when he gripped the corner with his wiry hands he didn't have to stoop. "No, you're too busy gobbling up dinners in dining rooms. You're too—"

"Honestly," begged Sylvester. "You got to behave reasonable."

"Reasonable! Reasonable!" The jockey's gray face quivered, then set in a mean, frozen grin. He shook the table so that the plates rattled, and for a moment it seemed that he would push it over. But suddenly he stopped. His hand reached out toward the plate nearest to him and deliberately he put a few of the French-fried potatoes in his mouth. He chewed slowly, his upper lip raised, then he turned and spat out the pulpy mouthful on the smooth red carpet which covered the floor. "Libertines," he said, and his voice was thin and broken. He rolled the word in his mouth, as though it had a flavor and a substance that gratified him.

"You libertines," he said again, and turned and walked with his rigid swagger out of the dining room.

Sylvester shrugged one of his loose, heavy shoulders. The rich man sopped up some water that had been spilled on the tablecloth, and they didn't speak until the waiter came to clear away.

August 23, 1941

GRAVEN IMAGE

John O'Hara

THE CAR TURNED IN at the brief, crescent-shaped drive and waited until the two cabs ahead had pulled away. The car pulled up, the doorman opened the rear door, a little man got out. The little man nodded pleasantly enough to the doorman and said "Wait" to the chauffeur. "Will the Under Secretary be here long?" asked the doorman.

"Why?" said the little man.

"Because if you were going to be here, sir, only a short while, I'd let your man leave the car here, at the head of the rank."

"Leave it there *anyway*," said the Under Secretary.

"Very good, sir," said the doorman. He saluted and frowned only a little as he watched the Under Secretary enter the hotel. "Well," the doorman said to himself, "it was a long time coming. It took him longer than most, but sooner or later all of them—" He opened the door of the next car, addressed a colonel and a major by their titles, and never did anything about the Under Secretary's car, which pulled ahead and parked in the drive.

The Under Secretary was spoken to many times in his progress to the main dining room. One man said, "What's your hurry, Joe?," to which the Under Secretary smiled and nodded. He was called Mr. Secretary most often, in some cases easily, by the old Washington hands, but more frequently with that embarrassment which Americans feel in using titles. As he passed through the lobby, the Under Secretary himself addressed by their White House nicknames two gentlemen whom he had to acknowledge to be closer to The Boss. And, bustling all the while, he made his way to the dining room, which was already packed. At the entrance he stopped short and frowned. The man he was to meet, Charles Browning, was chatting, in French, very amiably with the maître d'hôtel. Browning and the Under Secretary had been at Harvard at the same time.

The Under Secretary went up to him. "Sorry if I'm a little late," he said, and held out his hand, at the same time looking at his pocket watch. "Not so very, though. How are you, Charles? Fred, you got my message?"

"Yes, sir," said the maître d'hôtel. "I put you at a nice table all the way back to the right." He meanwhile had wig-wagged a captain, who stood by to lead the Under Secretary and his guest to Table 12. "Nice to have seen you again, Mr. Browning. Hope you come see us again while you are in Washington. Always a pleasure, sir."

"Always a pleasure, Fred," said Browning. He turned to the Under Secretary. "Well, shall we?"

"Yeah, let's sit down," said the Under Secretary.

· · ·

The captain led the way, followed by the Under Secretary, walking slightly sideways. Browning, making one step to two of the Under Secretary's, brought up the rear. When they were seated, the Under Secretary took the menu out of the captain's hands. "Let's order right away so I don't have to look up and talk to those two son of a bitches. I guess you know which two I mean." Browning looked from right to left, as anyone does on just sitting down in a restaurant. He nodded and said, "Yes, I think I know. You mean the senators."

"That's right," said the Under Secretary. "I'm not gonna have a cocktail, but you can. . . . I'll have the lobster. Peas. Shoestring potatoes. . . . You want a cocktail?"

"I don't think so. I'll take whatever you're having."

"O.K., waiter?" said the Under Secretary.

"Yes, sir," said the captain, and went away.

"Well, Charles, I was pretty surprised to hear from you."

"Yes," Browning said, "I should imagine so, and by the way, I want to thank you for answering my letter so promptly. I know how rushed you fellows must be, and I thought, as I said in my letter, at your convenience."

"Mm. Well, frankly, there wasn't any use in putting you off. I mean till next week or two weeks from now or anything like that. I could just as easily see you today as a month from now. Maybe easier. I don't know where I'll be likely to be a month from now. In more ways than one. I may be taking the Clipper to London, and then of course I may be out on my can! Coming to New York and asking *you* for a job. I take it that's what you wanted to see me about."

"Yes, and with hat in hand."

"Oh, no. I can't see you waiting with hat in hand, not for anybody. Not even for The Boss."

Browning laughed.

"What are you laughing at?" asked the Under Secretary.

"Well, you know how I feel about him, so I'd say least of all The Boss."

"Well, you've got plenty of company in this goddam town. But why'd you come to me, then? Why didn't you go to one of your Union League or Junior League or whatever-the-hell-it-is pals? There, that big jerk over there with the blue suit and the striped tie, for instance?"

Browning looked over at the big jerk with the blue suit and striped tie, and at that moment their eyes met and the two men nodded.

"You *know* him?" said the Under Secretary.

"Sure, I know him, but that doesn't say I *approve* of him."

"Well, at least that's something. And I notice he knows you."

"I've been to his house. I think he's been to our house when my father was alive, and naturally I've seen him around New York all my life."

"Naturally. Naturally. Then why didn't you go to *him*?"

"That's easy. I wouldn't like to ask him for anything. I don't approve of the man, at least as a politician, so I couldn't go to him and ask him a favor."

"But, on the other hand, you're not one of our team, but yet you'd ask me a favor. I don't get it."

"Oh, yes you do, Joe. You didn't get where you are by not being able to understand a simple thing like that."

Reluctantly—and quite obviously it was reluctantly—the Under Secretary grinned. "All right. I was baiting you."

"I know you were, but I expected it. I have it coming to me. I've always been against you fellows. I wasn't even for you in 1932, and that's a hell of an admission, but it's the truth. But that's water under the bridge—or isn't it?" The waiter interrupted with the food, and they did not speak until he had gone away.

"You were asking me if it isn't water under the bridge. Why should it be?"

"The obvious reason," said Browning.

"'My country, 'tis of thee'?"

"Exactly. Isn't that enough?"

"It isn't for your Racquet Club pal over there."

"You keep track of things like that?"

"Certainly," said the Under Secretary. "I know every goddam club in this country, beginning back about twenty-three years ago. I had ample time to study them all then, you recall, objectively, from the outside. By the way, I notice you wear a wristwatch. What happens to the little animal?"

Browning put his hand in his pocket and brought out a small bunch of keys. He held the chain so that the Under Secretary could see, suspended from it, a small golden pig. "I still carry it," he said.

"They tell me a lot of you fellows put them back in your pockets about five years ago, when one of the illustrious brethren closed his downtown office and moved up to Ossining."

"Oh, probably," Browning said, "but quite a few fellows, I believe, that hadn't been wearing them took to wearing them again out of simple loyalty. Listen, Joe, are we talking like grown men? Are you sore at the Pork? Do you think you'd have enjoyed being a member of it? If being sore at it was even partly responsible for getting you where you are, then I think you ought to be a little grateful to it. You'd show the bastards. O.K. You showed them. Us. If you hadn't been so sore at the Porcellian so-and-so's, you might have turned into just another lawyer."

"My wife gives me that sometimes."

"There, do you see?" Browning said. "Now then, how about the job?"

The Under Secretary smiled. "There's no getting away from it, you guys have got something. O.K., what are you interested in? Of course, I make no promises, and I don't even know if what you're interested in is something I can help you with."

"That's a chance I'll take. That's why I came to Washington, on just that chance, but it's my guess you can help me." Browning went on to tell the Under Secretary about the job he wanted. He told him why he thought he was qualified for it, and the Under Secretary nodded. Browning told him everything he knew about the job, and the Under Secretary continued to nod silently. By the end of Browning's recital the Under Secretary had become thoughtful. He told Browning that he thought there might be some little trouble with a certain character but that that character could be handled, because the real say-so, the green light, was controlled by a man who was a friend of the Under Secretary's, and the

Under Secretary could almost say at this moment that the matter could be arranged.

At this, Browning grinned. "By God, Joe, we've got to have a drink on this. This is the best news since—" He summoned the waiter. The Under Secretary yielded and ordered a cordial. Browning ordered a Scotch. The drinks were brought. Browning said, "About the job. I'm not going to say another word but just keep my fingers crossed. But as to you, Joe, you're the best. I drink to you." The two men drank, the Under Secretary sipping at his, Browning taking half of his. Browning looked at the drink in his hand. "You know, I was a little afraid. That other stuff, the club stuff."

"Yes," said the Under Secretary.

"I don't know why fellows like you—you never would have made it in a thousand years, but"—then, without looking up, he knew everything had collapsed—"but I've said exactly the wrong thing, haven't I?"

"That's right, Browning," said the Under Secretary. "You've said exactly the wrong thing. I've got to be going." He stood up and turned and went out, all dignity.

March 13, 1943

THE PATTERNS OF LOVE

William Maxwell

K ATE TALBOT'S BANTAM ROOSTER, awakened by the sudden appearance of the moon from behind a cloud on a white June night, began to crow. There were three bantams—a cock and two hens—and their roost was in a tree just outside the guest-room windows. The guest room was on the first floor and the Talbots' guest that weekend was a young man by the name of Arnold, a rather light sleeper. He got up and closed the windows and went back to bed. In the sealed room he slept, but was awakened at frequent intervals until daylight Saturday morning.

Arnold had been coming to the Talbots' place in Wilton sometime during the spring or early summer for a number of years. His visits were, for the children, one of a thousand seasonal events that could be counted on, less exciting than the appearance of the first robin or the arrival of violets in the marsh at the foot of the Talbots' hill but akin to them. Sometimes Duncan, the Talbots' older boy, who for a long time was under the impression that Arnold came to see *him*, slept in the guest room when Arnold was there. Last year, George, Duncan's younger brother, had been given that privilege. This time, Mrs. Talbot, knowing how talkative the boys were when they awoke in the morning, had left Arnold to himself.

When he came out of his room, Mrs. Talbot and George, the apple of her eye, were still at breakfast. George was six, small and delicate and very blond, not really interested in food at any time, and certainly not now, when there was a guest in the house. He was in his pajamas and a pink quilted bathrobe. He smiled at Arnold with his large and very gentle eyes and said, "Did you miss me?"

"Yes, of course," Arnold said. "I woke up and there was the other bed, flat and empty. Nobody to talk to while I looked at the ceiling. Nobody to watch me shave."

George was very pleased that his absence had been felt. "What is your favorite color?" he asked.

"Red," Arnold said, without having to consider.

"Mine, too," George said, and his face became so illuminated with pleasure at this coincidence that for a moment he looked angelic.

"No matter how much we disagree about other things," Arnold said, "we'll always have that in common, won't we?"

"Yes," George said.

"You'd both better eat your cereal," Mrs. Talbot said.

Arnold looked at her while she was pouring his coffee and wondered if there wasn't something back of her remark—jealousy, perhaps. Mrs. Talbot was a very soft-hearted woman, but for some reason she seemed to be ashamed—or perhaps afraid—to let other people know it. She took refuge continually behind a dry humor. There was probably very little likelihood that George would be as fond of anyone else as he was of his mother, Arnold decided, for many years to come. There was no real reason for her to be jealous.

"Did the bantams keep you awake?" she asked.

Arnold shook his head.

"Something tells me you're lying," Mrs. Talbot said. "John didn't wake up, but he felt his responsibilities as a host even so. He cried 'Oh!' in his sleep every time a bantam crowed. You'll have to put up with them on Kate's account. She loves them more than her life."

Excluded from the conversation of the grownups, George finished his cereal and ate part of a soft-boiled egg. Then he asked to be excused and, with pillows and pads which had been brought in from the garden furniture the night before, he made a train right across the dining-room floor. The cook had to step over it when she brought a fresh pot of coffee, and Mrs. Talbot and Arnold had to do likewise when they went out through the dining-room door to look at the bantams. There were only two—the cock and one hen—walking around under the Japanese cherry tree on the terrace. Kate was leaning out of an upstairs window, watching them fondly.

"Have you made your bed?" Mrs. Talbot asked.

The head withdrew.

"Kate is going to a houseparty," Mrs. Talbot said, looking at the bantams. "A sort of houseparty. She's going to stay all night at Mary Sherman's house and there are going to be some boys and they're going to dance to the victrola."

"How old is she, for heaven's sake?" Arnold asked.

"Thirteen," Mrs. Talbot said. "She had her hair cut yesterday and it's too short. It doesn't look right, so I have to do something about it."

"White of egg?" Arnold asked.

"How did you know that?" Mrs. Talbot asked in surprise.

"I remembered it from the last time," Arnold said. "I remembered it because it sounded so drastic."

"It only works with blonds," Mrs. Talbot said. "Will you be able to entertain yourself for a while?"

"Easily," Arnold said. "I saw *Anna Karenina* in the library and I think I'll take that and go up to the little house."

"Maybe I'd better come with you," Mrs. Talbot said.

The little house was a one-room studio halfway up the hill, about a hundred feet from the big house, with casement windows on two sides and a Franklin stove. It had been built several years before, after Mrs. Talbot had read *A Room of One's Own*, and by now it had a slightly musty odor which included lingering traces of wood smoke.

"Hear the wood thrush?" Arnold asked, as Mrs. Talbot threw open the windows for him. They both listened.

"No," she said. "All birds sound alike to me."

"Listen," he said.

This time there was no mistaking it—the liquid notes up and then down the same scale.

"Oh, that," she said. "Yes, I love that," and went off to wash Kate's hair.

. . .

From time to time Arnold raised his head from the book he was reading and heard not only the wood thrush but also Duncan and George, quarrelling in the meadow. George's voice was shrill and unhappy and sounded as if he were on the verge of tears. Both boys appeared at the window eventually and asked for permission to come in. The little house was out of bounds to them. Arnold nodded. Duncan, who was nine, crawled in without much difficulty, but George had to be hoisted. No sooner were they inside than they began to fight over a wooden gun which had been broken and mended and was rightly George's, it seemed, though Duncan had it and refused to give it up. He refused to give it up one moment, and the next moment, after a sudden change of heart, pressed it upon George—*forced* George to take it, actually, for by that time George was more concerned about the Talbots' dog, who also wanted to come in.

The dog was a Great Dane, very mild but also very enormous. He answered to the name of Satan. Once Satan was admitted to the little house, it became quite full and rather noisy, but John Talbot appeared and sent the dog out and made the children leave Arnold in peace. They left as they had come, by the window. Arnold watched them and was touched by the way Duncan turned and helped George, who was too small to jump. Also by the way George accepted this help. It was as if their hostility had two faces and one of them was the face of love. Cain and Abel, Arnold thought, and the wood thrush. All immortal.

John Talbot lingered outside the little house. Something had been burrowing in the lily-of-the-valley bed, he said, and had also uprooted several lady slippers. Arnold suggested that it might be moles.

"More likely a rat," John Talbot said, and his eyes wandered to a two-foot espaliered pear tree. "That pear tree," he said, "we put in over a year ago."

Mrs. Talbot joined them. She had shampooed not only Kate's hair but her own as well.

"It's still alive," John Talbot said, staring at the pear tree, "but it doesn't put out any leaves."

"I should think it would be a shock to a pear tree to be espaliered," Mrs. Talbot said. "Kate's ready to go."

They all piled into the station wagon and took Kate to her party. Her too-short blond hair looked quite satisfactory after the egg shampoo, and Mrs. Talbot had made a boutonnière out of a pink geranium and some little blue and white flowers for Kate to wear on her coat. She got out of the car with her suitcase and waved at them from the front steps of the house.

"I hope she has a good time," John Talbot said uneasily as he shifted gears. "It's her first dance with boys. It would be terrible if she didn't have any partners." In his eyes there was a vague threat toward the boys who, in their young callowness, might not appreciate his daughter.

"Kate always has a good time," Mrs. Talbot said. "By the way, have you seen both of the bantam hens today?"

"No," John Talbot said.

"One of them is missing," Mrs. Talbot said.

· · ·

One of the things that impressed Arnold whenever he stayed with the Talbots was the number and variety of animals they had. Their place was not a farm, after all, but merely a big white brick house in the country, and yet they usually had a dog and a cat, kittens, rabbits, and chickens, all actively involved in the family life. This summer the Talbots weren't able to go in and out by the front door, because a phoebe had built a nest in the porch light. They used the dining-room door instead, and were careful not to leave the porch light on more than a minute or two, lest the eggs be cooked. Arnold came upon some turtle food in his room, and when he asked about it, Mrs. Talbot informed him that there were turtles in the guest room, too. He never came upon the turtles.

The bantams were new this year, and so were the two very small ducklings that at night were put in a paper carton in the sewing room, with an electric-light bulb to keep them warm. In the daytime they hopped in and out of a saucer of milk on the terrace. One of them was called Mr. Rochester because of his distinguished air. The other had no name.

All the while that Mrs. Talbot was making conversation with Arnold, after lunch, she kept her eyes on the dog, who, she explained, was jealous of the ducklings. Once his great head swooped down and he pretended to take a nip at them. A nip would have been enough. Mrs. Talbot spoke to him sharply and he turned his head away in shame.

"They probably smell the way George did when he first came home from the hospital," she said.

"What did George smell like?" Arnold asked.

"Sweetish, actually. Actually awful."

"Was Satan jealous of George when he was a baby?"

"Frightfully," Mrs. Talbot said. "Call Satan!" she shouted to her husband, who was up by the little house. He had found a rat hole near the ravaged lady slippers and was setting a trap. He called the dog, and the dog went bounding off, devotion in every leap.

While Mrs. Talbot was telling Arnold how they found Satan at the baby's crib one night, Duncan, who was playing only a few yards away with George, suddenly, and for no apparent reason, made his younger brother cry. Mrs. Talbot got up and separated them.

"I wouldn't be surprised if it wasn't time for your nap, George," she said, but he was not willing to let go of even a small part of the day. He wiped his tears away with his fist and ran from her. She ran after him, laughing, and caught him at the foot of the terrace.

Duncan wandered off into a solitary world of his own, and Arnold, after yawning twice, got up and went into the house. Stretched out on the bed in his room, with the Venetian blinds closed, he began to compare the life of the Talbots with his own well-ordered but childless and animalless life in town. Everywhere they go, he thought, they leave tracks behind them, like people walking in the snow. Paths crisscrossing, lines that are perpetually meeting: the mother's loving pursuit of her youngest, the man's love for his daughter, the dog's love for the man, the two boys' preoccupation with each other. Wheels and diagrams, Arnold said to himself. The patterns of love.

. . .

That night Arnold was much less bothered by the crowing, which came to him dimly, through dreams. When he awoke finally and was fully awake, he was conscious of the silence and the sun shining in his eyes. His watch had stopped and it was later than he thought. The Talbots had finished breakfast and the Sunday *Times* was waiting beside his place at the table. While he was eating, John Talbot came in and sat down for a minute, across the table. He had been out early that morning, he said, and had found a chipmunk in the rat trap and also a nest with three bantam eggs in it. The eggs were cold.

He was usually a very quiet, self-contained man. This was the first time Arnold had ever seen him disturbed about anything. "I don't know how we're going to tell Kate," he said. "She'll be very upset."

Kate came home sooner than they expected her, on the bus. She came up the driveway, lugging her suitcase.

"Did you have a good time?" Mrs. Talbot called to her from the terrace.

"Yes," she said, "I had a beautiful time."

Arnold looked at the two boys, expecting them to blurt out the tragedy as soon as Kate put down her suitcase, but they didn't. It was her father who told her, in such a roundabout way that she didn't seem to understand at all what he was saying. Mrs. Talbot interrupted him with the flat facts; the bantam hen was not on her nest and therefore, in all probability, had been killed, maybe by the rat.

Kate went into the house. The others remained on the terrace. The dog didn't snap at the ducklings, though his mind was on them still, and the two boys didn't quarrel. In spite of the patterns on which they seem so intent, Arnold thought, what happens to one of them happens to all. They are helplessly involved in Kate's loss.

At noon other guests arrived, two families with children. There was a picnic, with hot dogs and bowls of salad, cake, and wine, out under the grape arbor. When the guests departed, toward the end of the afternoon, the family came together again on the terrace. Kate was lying on the ground, on her stomach, with her face resting on her arms, her head practically in the ducklings' saucer of milk. Mrs. Talbot, who had stretched out on the garden chaise longue, discovered suddenly that Mr. Rochester was missing. She sat up in alarm and cried, "Where is he?"

"Down my neck," Kate said.

The duck emerged from her crossed arms. He crawled around them and climbed up on the back of her neck. Kate smiled. The sight of the duck's tiny downy head among her pale ash-blond curls made them all burst out laughing. The cloud that had been hanging over the household evaporated into bright sunshine, and Arnold seized that moment to glance surreptitiously at his watch.

They all went to the train with him, including the dog. At the last moment Mrs. Talbot, out of a sudden perception of his lonely life, tried to give him some radishes, but he refused them. When he stepped out of the car at the station, the boys were arguing and were with difficulty persuaded to say goodbye to him. He watched the station wagon drive away and then stood listening for the sound of the wood thrush. But, of course, in the center of South Norwalk there was no such sound.

July 7, 1945

ACT OF FAITH

Irwin Shaw

"PRESENT IT TO HIM in a pitiful light," Olson was saying as they picked their way through the almost frozen mud toward the orderly-room tent. "Three combat-scarred veterans, who fought their way from Omaha Beach to . . . What was the name of the town we fought our way to?"

"Königstein," Seeger said.

"Königstein." Olson lifted his right foot heavily out of a puddle and stared admiringly at the three pounds of mud clinging to his overshoe. "The backbone of the Army. The noncommissioned officer. We deserve better of our country. Mention our decorations, in passing."

"What decorations should I mention?" Seeger asked. "The Marksman's Medal?"

"Never quite made it," Olson said. "I had a cross-eyed scorer at the butts. Mention the Bronze Star, the Silver Star, the Croix de Guerre with palms, the Unit Citation, the Congressional Medal of Honor."

"I'll mention them all." Seeger grinned. "You don't think the C.O.'ll notice that we haven't won most of them, do you?"

"Gad, sir," Olson said with dignity, "do you think that one Southern military gentleman will dare doubt the word of another Southern military gentleman in the hour of victory?"

"I come from Ohio," Seeger said.

"Welch comes from Kansas," Olson said, coolly staring down a second lieutenant who was passing. The lieutenant made a nervous little jerk with his hand, as though he expected a salute, then kept it rigid, as a slight, superior smile of scorn twisted at the corner of Olson's mouth. The lieutenant dropped his eyes and splashed on through the mud. "You've heard of Kansas," Olson said. "Magnolia-scented Kansas."

"Of course," said Seeger. "I'm no fool."

"Do your duty by your men, Sergeant." Olson stopped to wipe the cold rain off his face and lectured him. "Highest-ranking noncom present took the initiative and saved his comrades, at great personal risk, above and beyond the call of you-know-what, in the best traditions of the American Army."

"I will throw myself in the breach," Seeger said.

"Welch and I can't ask more," said Olson.

They walked heavily through the mud on the streets between the rows of tents. The camp stretched drearily over the Reims plain, with the rain beating on the sagging tents. The division had been there over three weeks, waiting to be shipped home, and all the meagre diversions of the neighborhood had been sampled and exhausted, and there was an air of watchful suspicion and impatience with the military life hanging over the camp now, and there was even reputed to be a staff sergeant in C Company who was laying odds they would not get back to America before July 4th.

"I'm redeployable," Olson sang. "It's so enjoyable." It was a jingle he had composed, to no recognizable melody, in the early days after the victory in Europe, when he had added up his points and found they came to only sixty-three, but he persisted in singing it. He was a short, round boy who had been flunked out of air cadets' school and transferred to the infantry but whose spirits had not been damaged in the process. He had a high, childish voice and a pretty, baby face. He was very good-natured, and had a girl waiting for him at the University of California, where he intended to finish his course at government expense when he got out of the Army, and he was just the type who is killed off early and predictably and sadly in moving pictures about the war, but he had gone through four campaigns and six major battles without a scratch.

Seeger was a large, lanky boy, with a big nose, who had been wounded at St.-Lô but had come back to his outfit in the Siegfried Line quite unchanged. He was cheerful and dependable and he knew his business. He had broken in five or six second lieutenants, who had later been killed or wounded, and the C.O. had tried to get him commissioned in the field, but the war had ended while the paperwork was being fumbled over at headquarters.

They reached the door of the orderly tent and stopped. "Be brave, Sergeant," Olson said. "Welch and I are depending on you."

"O.K.," Seeger said, and went in.

. . .

The tent had the dank, Army-canvas smell that had been so much a part of Seeger's life in the past three years. The company clerk was reading an October, 1945, issue of the Buffalo *Courier-Express*, which had just reached him, and Captain Taney, the company C.O., was seated at a sawbuck table which he used as a desk, writing a letter to his wife, his lips pursed with effort. He was a small, fussy man, with sandy hair that was falling out. While the fighting had been going on, he had been lean and tense and his small voice had been cold and full of authority. But now he had relaxed, and a little pot belly was creeping up under his belt and he kept the top button of his trousers open when he could do it without too public loss of dignity. During the war, Seeger had thought of him as a natural soldier—tireless, fanatic about detail, aggressive, severely anxious to kill Germans. But in the last few months, Seeger had seen him relapsing gradually and pleasantly into the small-town hardware merchant he had been before the war, sedentary and a little shy, and, as he had once told Seeger, worried, here in the bleak champagne fields of France, about his daughter, who had just turned twelve and had a tendency to go after the boys and had been caught by her mother kissing a fifteen-year-old neighbor in the hammock after school.

"Hello, Seeger," he said, returning the salute with a mild, offhand gesture. "What's on your mind?"

"Am I disturbing you, sir?"

"Oh, no. Just writing a letter to my wife. You married, Seeger?" He peered at the tall boy standing before him.

"No, sir."

"It's very difficult." Taney sighed, pushing dissatisfiedly at the letter before him. "My wife complains I don't tell her I love her often enough. Been married fifteen years. You'd think she'd know by now." He smiled at Seeger. "I thought you were going to Paris," he said. "I signed the passes yesterday."

"That's what I came to see you about, sir."

"I suppose something's wrong with the passes." Taney spoke resignedly, like a man who has never quite got the hang of Army regulations and has had requisitions, furloughs, and requests for courts-martial returned for correction in a baffling flood.

"No, sir," Seeger said. "The passes're fine. They start tomorrow. Well, it's just—" He looked around at the company clerk, who was on the sports page.

"This confidential?" Taney asked.

"If you don't mind, sir."

"Johnny," Taney said to the clerk, "go stand in the rain someplace."

"Yes, sir," the clerk said, and slowly got up and walked out.

Taney looked shrewdly at Seeger and spoke in a secret whisper. "You pick up anything?" he asked.

Seeger grinned. "No, sir, haven't had my hands on a girl since Strasbourg."

"Ah, that's good." Taney leaned back, relieved, happy that he didn't have to cope with the disapproval of the Medical Corps.

"It's—well," said Seeger, embarrassed, "it's hard to say—but it's money."

Taney shook his head sadly. "I know."

"We haven't been paid for three months, sir, and—"

"Damn it!" Taney stood up and shouted furiously. "I would like to take every bloody, chair-warming old lady in the Finance Department and wring their necks."

The clerk stuck his head into the tent. "Anything wrong? You call for me, sir?"

"No!" Taney shouted. "Get out of here!"

The clerk ducked out.

Taney sat down again. "I suppose," he said, in a more normal voice, "they have their problems. Outfits being broken up, being moved all over the place. But it's rugged."

"It wouldn't be so bad," Seeger said, "but we're going to Paris tomorrow. Olson, Welch, and myself. And you need money in Paris."

"Don't I know it?" Taney wagged his head. "Do you know what I paid for a bottle of champagne on the Place Pigalle in September?" He paused significantly. "I won't tell you. You wouldn't have any respect for me the rest of your life."

Seeger laughed. "Hanging is too good for the guy who thought up the rate of exchange," he said.

"I don't care if I never see another franc as long as I live." Taney waved his letter in the air, although it had been dry for a long time.

There was silence in the tent, and Seeger swallowed a little embarrassedly. "Sir," he said, "the truth is, I've come to borrow some money for

Welch, Olson, and myself. We'll pay it back out of the first pay we get, and that can't be too long from now. If you don't want to give it to us, just tell me and I'll understand and get the hell out of here. We don't like to ask, but you might just as well be dead as be in Paris broke."

Taney stopped waving his letter and put it down thoughtfully. He peered at it, wrinkling his brow, looking like an aged bookkeeper in the single, gloomy light that hung in the middle of the tent.

"Just say the word, Captain," Seeger said, "and I'll blow."

"Stay where you are, son," said Taney. He dug in his shirt pocket and took out a worn, sweat-stained wallet. He looked at it for a moment. "Alligator," he said, with automatic, absent pride. "My wife sent it to me when we were in England. Pounds don't fit in it. However . . ." He opened it and took out all the contents. There was a small pile of francs on the table in front of him when he finished. He counted them. "Four hundred francs," he said. "Eight bucks."

"Excuse me," Seeger said humbly. "I shouldn't've asked."

"Delighted," Taney said vigorously. "Absolutely delighted." He started dividing the francs into two piles. "Truth is, Seeger, most of my money goes home in allotments. And the truth is, I lost eleven hundred francs in a poker game three nights ago, and I ought to be ashamed of myself. Here." He shoved one pile toward Seeger. "Two hundred francs."

Seeger looked down at the frayed, meretricious paper, which always seemed to him like stage money anyway. "No, sir," he said. "I can't take it."

"Take it," Taney said. "That's a direct order."

Seeger slowly picked up the money, not looking at Taney. "Sometime, sir," he said, "after we get out, you have to come over to my house, and you and my father and my brother and I'll go on a real drunk."

"I regard that," Taney said gravely, "as a solemn commitment."

They smiled at each other, and Seeger started out.

"Have a drink for me," said Taney, "at the Café de la Paix. A small drink." He was sitting down to tell his wife he loved her when Seeger went out of the tent.

Olson fell into step with Seeger and they walked silently through the mud between the tents.

"Well, *mon vieux*?" Olson said finally.

"Two hundred francs," said Seeger.

Olson groaned. "Two hundred francs! We won't be able to pinch a whore's behind on the Boulevard des Capucines for two hundred francs. That miserable, penny-loving Yankee!"

"He only had four hundred," Seeger said.

"I revise my opinion," said Olson.

They walked disconsolately and heavily back toward their tent.

Olson spoke only once before they got there. "These raincoats," he said, patting his. "Most ingenious invention of the war. Highest saturation point of any modern fabric. Collect more water per square inch, and hold it, than any material known to man. All hail the quartermaster!"

. . .

Welch was waiting at the entrance of their tent. He was standing there peering excitedly and shortsightedly out at the rain through his glasses, looking angry and tough, like a big-city hack driver, individual and incorruptible even in the ten-million colored uniform. Every time Seeger came upon Welch unexpectedly, he couldn't help smiling at the belligerent stance, the harsh stare through the steel-rimmed G.I. glasses, which had nothing at all to do with the way Welch really was. "It's a family inheritance," Welch had once explained. "My whole family stands as though we were getting ready to rap a drunk with a beer glass. Even my old lady." Welch had six brothers, all devout, according to Welch, and Seeger from time to time idly pictured them standing in a row, on Sunday mornings in church, seemingly on the verge of general violence, amid the hushed Latin and the Sabbath millinery.

"How much?" Welch asked loudly.

"Don't make us laugh," Olson said, pushing past him into the tent.

"What do you think I could get from the French for my combat jacket?" Seeger said. He went into the tent and lay down on his cot.

Welch followed them in and stood between the two of them. "Boys," he said, "on a man's errand."

"I can just see us now," Olson murmured, lying on his cot with his hands clasped behind his head, "painting Montmartre red. Please bring on the naked dancing girls. Four bucks' worth."

"I am not worried," Welch announced.

"Get out of here." Olson turned over on his stomach.

"I know where we can put our hands on sixty-five bucks." Welch looked triumphantly first at Olson, then at Seeger.

Olson turned over slowly and sat up. "I'll kill you," he said, "if you're kidding."

"While you guys are wasting your time fooling around with the infantry," Welch said, "I used my head. I went into Reems and used my head."

"Rance," Olson said automatically. He had had two years of French in college and he felt, now that the war was over, that he had to introduce his friends to some of his culture.

"I got to talking to a captain in the Air Force," Welch said eagerly. "A little, fat old paddle-footed captain that never got higher off the ground than the second floor of Com Z headquarters, and he told me that what he would admire to do more than anything else is take home a nice shiny German Luger pistol with him to show to the boys back in Pacific Grove, California."

Silence fell on the tent, and Welch and Olson looked at Seeger.

"Sixty-five bucks for a Luger, these days," Olson said, "is a very good figure."

"They've been sellin' for as low as thirty-five," said Welch hesitantly. "I'll bet," he said to Seeger, "you could sell yours now and buy another one back when you got some dough, and make a clear twenty-five on the deal."

Seeger didn't say anything. He had killed the owner of the Luger, an enormous S.S. major, in Coblenz, behind some bales of paper in a warehouse, and the major had fired at Seeger three times with it, once nicking his helmet, before Seeger hit him in the face at twenty feet. Seeger had kept the Luger, a heavy, well-balanced gun, lugging it with him, hiding it at the bottom of his bedroll, oiling it three times a week, avoiding all opportunities of selling it, although he had once been offered a hundred dollars for it and several times eighty and ninety, while the war was still on, before German weapons became a glut on the market.

"Well," said Welch, "there's no hurry. I told the captain I'd see him tonight around eight o'clock in front of the Lion d'Or Hotel. You got five hours to make up your mind. Plenty of time."

"Me," said Olson, after a pause, "I won't say anything."

Seeger looked reflectively at his feet, and the two other men avoided looking at him.

Welch dug in his pocket. "I forgot," he said. "I picked up a letter for you." He handed it to Seeger.

"Thanks," Seeger said. He opened it absently, thinking about the Luger.

"Me," said Olson, "I won't say a bloody word. I'm just going to lie here and think about that nice, fat Air Force captain."

. . .

Seeger grinned a little at him and went to the tent opening to read the letter in the light. The letter was from his father, and even from one glance at the handwriting, scrawly and hurried and spotted, so different from his father's usual steady, handsome, professorial script, he knew that something was wrong.

"Dear Norman," it read, "sometime in the future, you must forgive me for writing this letter. But I have been holding this in so long, and there is no one here I can talk to, and because of your brother's condition I must pretend to be cheerful and optimistic all the time at home, both with him and your mother, who has never been the same since Leonard was killed. You're the oldest now, and although I know we've never talked very seriously about anything before, you have been through a great deal by now, and I imagine you must have matured considerably, and you've seen so many different places and people. Norman, I need help. While the war was on and you were fighting, I kept this to myself. It wouldn't have been fair to burden you with this. But now the war is over, and I no longer feel I can stand up under this alone. And you will have to face it sometime when you get home, if you haven't faced it already, and perhaps we can help each other by facing it together."

"I'm redeployable. It's so enjoyable," Olson was singing softly, on his cot. He fell silent after his burst of song.

Seeger blinked his eyes in the gray, wintry, rainy light, and went on reading his father's letter, on the stiff white stationery with the university letterhead in polite engraving at the top of each page.

"I've been feeling this coming on for a long time," the letter continued, "but it wasn't until last Sunday morning that something happened to make me feel it in its full force. I don't know how much you've guessed about the reason for Jacob's discharge from the Army. It's true he was pretty badly wounded in the leg at Metz, but I've asked around, and I know that men with worse wounds were returned to duty after hospitalization. Jacob got a medical discharge, but I don't think it was for the shrapnel wound in his thigh. He is suffering now from what I suppose you call combat fatigue, and he is subject to fits of depression and hallucinations. Your mother and I thought that as time went by and the war and the Army receded, he would grow better. Instead, he is growing worse. Last Sunday morning when I came down into the living room from upstairs he was crouched in his old uniform, next to the window, peering out."

"What the hell," Olson was saying. "If we don't get the sixty-five bucks we can always go to the Louvre. I understand the Mona Lisa is back."

"I asked Jacob what he was doing," the letter went on. "He didn't turn around. 'I'm observing,' he said. 'V-1s and V-2s. Buzz bombs and rockets. They're coming in by the hundred.' I tried to reason with him and he told me to crouch and save myself from flying glass. To humor him I got down on the floor beside him and tried to tell him the war was over, that we were in Ohio, 4,000 miles away from the nearest spot where bombs had fallen, that America had never been touched. He wouldn't listen. 'These're the new rocket bombs,' he said, 'for the Jews.'"

"Did you ever hear of the Panthéon?" Olson asked loudly.

"No," said Welch.

"It's free."

"I'll go," said Welch.

Seeger shook his head a little and blinked his eyes before he went back to the letter.

"After that," his father went on, "Jacob seemed to forget about the bombs from time to time, but he kept saying that the mobs were coming up the street armed with bazookas and Browning automatic rifles. He mumbled incoherently a good deal of the time and kept walking back and forth saying, 'What's the situation? Do you know what the situation is?' And once he told me he wasn't worried about himself, he was a soldier and he expected to be killed, but he was worried about Mother and myself and Leonard and you. He seemed to forget that Leonard was dead. I tried to calm him and get him back to bed before your mother came down, but he refused and wanted to set out immediately to rejoin his division. It was all terribly disjointed, and at one time he took the ribbon he got for winning the Bronze Star and threw it in the fireplace, then he got down on his hands and knees and picked it out of the ashes and made me pin it on him again, and he kept repeating, 'This is when they are coming for the Jews.'"

"The next war I'm in," said Olson, "they don't get me under the rank of colonel."

It had stopped raining by now, and Seeger folded the unfinished letter and went outside. He walked slowly down to the end of the company street, and, facing out across the empty, soaked French fields, scarred and neglected by various armies, he stopped and opened the letter again.

"I don't know what Jacob went through in the Army," his father wrote, "that has done this to him. He never talks to me about the war and he refuses to go to a psychoanalyst, and from time to time he is his own bouncing, cheerful self, playing handball in the afternoons and going around with a large group of girls. But he has devoured all the concentration-camp reports, and I found him weeping when the newspapers reported that a hundred Jews were killed in Tripoli some time ago.

"The terrible thing is, Norman, that I find myself coming to believe that it is not neurotic for a Jew to behave like this today. Perhaps Jacob is the normal one, and I, going about my business, teaching economics in a quiet classroom, pretending to understand that the world is comprehensible and orderly, am really the mad one. I ask you once more to forgive me for writing you a letter like this, so different from any letter or any conversation I've ever had with you. But it is crowding me, too. I do not see rockets and bombs, but I see other things.

"Wherever you go these days—restaurants, hotels, clubs, trains—you seem to hear talk about the Jews, mean, hateful, murderous talk. Whatever page you turn to in the newspapers, you seem to find an article about Jews being killed somewhere on the face of the globe. And there are large, influential newspapers and well-known columnists who each day are growing more and more outspoken and more popular. The day that Roosevelt died I heard a drunken man yelling outside a bar, 'Finally they got the Jew out of the White House.' And some of the people who heard him merely laughed, and nobody stopped him. And on V-J Day, in celebration, hoodlums in Los Angeles savagely beat a Jewish writer. It's difficult to know what to do, whom to fight, where to look for allies.

"Three months ago, for example, I stopped my Thursday-night poker game, after playing with the same men for over ten years. John Reilly happened to say that the Jews got rich out of the war, and when I demanded an apology, he refused, and when I looked around at the faces of the men who had been my friends for so long, I could see they were not with me. And when I left the house, no one said good night to me. I know the poison was spreading from Germany before the war and during it, but I had not realized it had come so close.

"And in my economics class, I find myself idiotically hedging in my lectures. I discover that I am loath to praise any liberal writer or any liberal act, and find myself somehow annoyed and frightened to see an article of criticism of existing abuses signed by a Jewish name. And I hate to see Jewish names on important committees, and hate to read of Jews fighting for the poor, the oppressed, the cheated and hungry. Somehow, even in a country where my family has lived a hundred years, the enemy has won this subtle victory over me—he has made me disfranchise myself from honest causes by calling them foreign, Communist, using Jewish names connected with them as ammunition against them.

"Most hateful of all, I found myself looking for Jewish names in the casualty lists and secretly being glad when I saw them there, to prove that there, at least, among the dead and wounded, we belonged. Three times, thanks to you and your brothers, I found our name there, and, may God forgive me, at the expense of your blood and your brother's life, through my tears, I felt that same twitch of satisfaction.

"When I read the newspapers and see another story that Jews are still being killed in Poland, or Jews are requesting that they be given back their homes in France or that they be allowed to enter some country where they will not be murdered, I am annoyed with them. I feel that they are boring the rest of the world with their problems, that they are making demands upon the rest of the world by being killed, that they are disturbing everyone by being hungry and asking for the return of their property. If we could all fall in through the crust of the earth and vanish in one hour, with our heroes and poets and prophets and martyrs, perhaps we would be doing the memory of the Jewish race a service.

"This is how I feel today, son. I need some help. You've been to the war, you've fought and killed men, you've seen the people of other countries. Maybe you understand things that I don't understand. Maybe you see some hope somewhere. Help me. Your loving Father."

. . .

Seeger folded the letter slowly, not seeing what he was doing, because the tears were burning his eyes. He walked slowly and aimlessly across the dead, sodden grass of the empty field, away from the camp. He tried to wipe away his tears, because, with his eyes full and dark, he kept seeing his father and brother crouched in the old-fashioned living room in Ohio, and hearing his brother, dressed in the old, discarded uniform, saying, "These're the new rocket bombs. For the Jews."

He sighed, looking out over the bleak, wasted land. Now, he thought, now I have to think about it. He felt a slight, unreasonable twinge of anger at his father for presenting him with the necessity of thinking about it. The Army was good about serious problems. While you were fighting, you were too busy and frightened and weary to think about anything, and at other times you were relaxing, putting your brain on a shelf, postponing everything to that impossible time of clarity and beauty after the war. Well, now, here was the impossible, clear, beautiful time, and here was his father, demanding that he think. There are all sorts of Jews, he thought: there are the sort whose every waking moment is ridden by the knowledge of Jewishness; who see signs against the Jew in every smile on a streetcar, every whisper; who see pogroms in every newspaper article, threats in every change of the weather, scorn in every handshake, death behind each closed door. He had not been like that. He was young, he was big and healthy and easygoing, and people of all kinds had liked him all his life, in the Army and out. In America, especially, what was going on in Europe had been remote, unreal, unrelated to him. The chanting, bearded old men burning in the Nazi furnaces, and the dark-eyed women screaming prayers in Polish and Russian and German as they were pushed naked into the gas chambers, had seemed as shadowy and almost as unrelated to him, as he trotted out onto the stadium field for a football game, as they must have been to the men named O'Dwyer and Wickersham and Poole who played in the line beside him.

These tortured people had seemed more related to him in Europe. Again and again, in the towns that had been taken back from the Germans, gaunt, gray-faced men had stopped him humbly, looking searchingly at him, and had asked, peering at his long, lined, grimy face under the anonymous helmet, "Are you a Jew?" Sometimes they asked it in English, sometimes French, sometimes Yiddish. He didn't know French or Yiddish, but he learned to recognize that question. He had never understood exactly why they asked the question, since they never demanded anything of him, rarely even could speak to him. Then, one day in Strasbourg, a little, bent old man and a small, shapeless woman had stopped him and asked, in English, if he was Jewish. "Yes," he'd said, smiling at them. The two old people had smiled widely, like children. "Look," the old man had said to his wife. "A young American soldier. A Jew. And so large and strong." He had touched Seeger's arm reverently with the tips of his fingers, then had touched the Garand Seeger was carrying. "And such a beautiful rifle."

And there, for a moment, although he was not particularly sensitive, Seeger had got an inkling of why he had been stopped and questioned by so many before. Here, to these bent, exhausted old people, ravaged of their families, familiar with flight and death for so many years, was a symbol of continuing life. A large young man in the uniform of the liberator, blood, as they thought, of their blood, but not in hiding, not quivering in fear and helplessness, but striding secure and victorious down the street, armed and capable of inflicting terrible destruction on his enemies.

Seeger had kissed the old lady on the cheek and she had wept, and the old man had scolded her for it while shaking Seeger's hand fervently and thankfully before saying goodbye.

Thinking back on it, he knew that it was silly to pretend that, even before his father's letter, he had been like any other American soldier going through the war. When he had stood over the huge, dead S.S. major with the face blown in by his bullets in the warehouse in Coblenz, and taken the pistol from the dead hand, he had tasted a strange little extra flavor of triumph. How many Jews, he'd thought, has this man killed? How fitting it is that I've killed him. Neither Olson nor Welch, who were like his brothers, would have felt that in picking up the Luger, its barrel still hot from the last shots its owner had fired before dying. And he had resolved that he was going to make sure to take this gun back with him to America, and plug it and keep it on his desk at home, as a kind of vague, half-understood sign to himself that justice had once been done and he had been its instrument.

Maybe, he thought, maybe I'd better take it back with me, but not as a memento. Not plugged, but loaded. America by now was a strange country for him. He had been away a long time and he wasn't sure what was waiting for him when he got home. If the mobs were coming down the street toward his house, he was not going to die singing and praying.

When he had been taking basic training, he'd heard a scrawny, clerkish soldier from Boston talking at the other end of the PX bar, over the watered beer. "The boys at the office," the scratchy voice was saying, "gave me a party before I left. And they told me one thing. 'Charlie,' they said, 'hold onto your bayonet. We're going to be able to use it when you get back. On the Yids.'"

He hadn't said anything then, because he'd felt it was neither possible nor desirable to fight against every random overheard voice raised against the Jews from one end of the world to the other. But again and again, at odd moments, lying on a barracks cot, or stretched out trying to sleep on the floor of a ruined French farmhouse, he had heard that voice, harsh, satisfied, heavy with hate and ignorance, saying above the beery grumble of apprentice soldiers at the bar, "Hold onto your bayonet."

And the other stories. Jews collected stories of hatred and injustice and inklings of doom like a special, lunatic kind of miser. The story of the Navy officer, commander of a small vessel off the Aleutians, who in the officers' wardroom had complained that he hated the Jews because it was the Jews who had demanded that the Germans be beaten first, and the forces in the Pacific had been starved in consequence. And when one of his junior officers, who had just come aboard, had objected and told the commander that he was a Jew, the commander had risen from the table and said, "Mister, the Constitution of the United States says I have to serve in the same Navy with Jews, but it doesn't say I have to eat at the same table with them." In the fogs and the cold, swelling Arctic seas off the Aleutians, in a small boat, subject to sudden, mortal attack at any moment. . . . And the million other stories. Jews, even the most normal and best adjusted, became living treasuries of them, scraps of malice and bloodthirstiness, clever and confusing and cunningly twisted so that every act by every Jew became suspect and blameworthy and hateful. Seeger had heard the stories and had made an almost conscious effort to forget them. Now, holding his father's letter in his hand, he remembered them all.

He stared unseeingly out in front of him. Maybe, he thought, maybe it would've been better to have been killed in the war, like Leonard. Simpler. Leonard would never have to face a crowd coming for his mother and father. Leonard would not have to listen and collect these hideous, fascinating little stories that made of every Jew a stranger in any town, on any field, on the face of the earth. He had come so close to being killed so many times; it would have been so easy, so neat and final. Seeger shook his head. It was ridiculous to feel like that, and he was ashamed of himself for the weak moment. At the age of twenty-one, death was not an answer.

. . .

"Seeger!" It was Olson's voice. He and Welch had sloshed silently up behind Seeger, standing in the open field. "Seeger, *mon vieux*, what're you doing—grazing?"

Seeger turned slowly to them. "I wanted to read my letter," he said.

Olson looked closely at him. They had been together so long, through so many things, that flickers and hints of expression on each other's faces were recognized and acted upon. "Anything wrong?" Olson asked.

"No," said Seeger. "Nothing much."

"Norman," Welch said, his voice young and solemn. "Norman, we've been talking, Olson and me. We decided—you're pretty attached to that Luger, and maybe, if you—well—"

"What he's trying to say," said Olson, "is we withdraw the request. If you want to sell it, O.K. If you don't, don't do it for our sake. Honest."

Seeger looked at them standing there, disreputable and tough and familiar. "I haven't made up my mind yet," he said.

"Anything you decide," Welch said oratorically, "is perfectly all right with us. Perfectly."

The three of them walked aimlessly and silently across the field, away from camp. As they walked, their shoes making a wet, sliding sound in the damp, dead grass, Seeger thought of the time Olson had covered him in the little town outside Cherbourg, when Seeger had been caught, going down the side of a street, by four Germans with a machine gun in the second story of a house on the corner and Olson had had to stand out in the middle of the street with no cover at all for more than a minute, firing continuously, so that Seeger could get away alive. And he thought of the time outside St.-Lô when he had been wounded and had lain in a minefield for three hours and Welch and Captain Taney had come looking for him in the darkness and had found him and picked him up and run for it, all of them expecting to get blown up any second. And he thought of all the drinks they'd had together, and the long marches and the cold winter together, and all the girls they'd gone out with together, and he thought of his father and brother crouching behind the window in Ohio waiting for the rockets and the crowds armed with Browning automatic rifles.

"Say." He stopped and stood facing them. "Say, what do you guys think of the Jews?"

Welch and Olson looked at each other, and Olson glanced down at the letter in Seeger's hand.

"Jews?" Olson said finally. "What're they? Welch, you ever hear of the Jews?"

Welch looked thoughtfully at the gray sky. "No," he said. "But remember, I'm an uneducated fellow."

"Sorry, bud," Olson said, turning to Seeger. "We can't help you. Ask us another question. Maybe we'll do better."

Seeger peered at the faces of his friends. He would have to rely upon them, later on, out of uniform, on their native streets, more than he had ever relied on them on the bullet-swept street and in the dark minefield in France. Welch and Olson stared back at him, troubled, their faces candid and tough and dependable.

"What time," Seeger asked, "did you tell that captain you'd meet him?"

"Eight o'clock," Welch said. "But we don't have to go. If you have any feeling about that gun—"

"We'll meet him," Seeger said. "We can use that sixty-five bucks."

"Listen," Olson said, "I know how much you like that gun, and I'll feel like a heel if you sell it."

"Forget it," Seeger said, starting to walk again. "What could I use it for in America?"

February 2, 1946

THE ENORMOUS RADIO

John Cheever

JIM AND IRENE WESTCOTT were the kind of people who seem to strike that satisfactory average of income, endeavor, and respectability that is reached by the statistical reports in college alumni bulletins. They were the parents of two young children, they had been married nine years, they lived on the twelfth floor of an apartment house in the East Seventies between Fifth and Madison Avenues, they went to the theatre on an average of 10.3 times a year, and they hoped someday to live in Westchester. Irene Westcott was a pleasant, rather plain girl with soft brown hair and a wide, fine forehead upon which nothing at all had been written, and in the cold weather she wore a coat of fitch skins dyed to resemble mink. You could not say that Jim Westcott, at thirty-seven, looked younger than he was, but you could at least say of him that he seemed to feel younger. He wore his graying hair cut very short, he dressed in the kind of clothes his class had worn at Andover, and his manner was earnest, vehement, and intentionally naïve. The Westcotts differed from their friends, their classmates, and their neighbors only in an interest they shared in serious music. They went to a great many concerts—although they seldom mentioned this to anyone—and they spent a good deal of time listening to music on the radio.

Their radio was an old instrument, sensitive, unpredictable, and beyond repair. Neither of them understood the mechanics of radio—or of any of the other appliances that surrounded them—and when the instrument faltered, Jim would strike the side of the cabinet with his hand. This sometimes helped. One Sunday afternoon, in the middle of a Schubert quartet, the music faded away altogether. Jim struck the cabinet repeatedly, but there was no response; the Schubert was lost to them forever. He promised to buy Irene a new radio, and on Monday when he came home from work he told her that he had got one. He refused to describe it, and said it would be a surprise for her when it came.

The radio was delivered at the kitchen door the following afternoon, and with the assistance of her maid and the handyman Irene uncrated it and brought it into the living room. She was struck at once with the physical ugliness of the large gumwood cabinet. Irene was proud of her living room, she had chosen its furnishings and colors as carefully as she chose her clothes, and now it seemed to her that the new radio stood among her intimate possessions like an aggressive intruder. She was confounded by the number of dials and switches on the instrument panel, and she studied them thoroughly before she put the plug into a wall socket and turned the radio on. The dials flooded with a malevolent green light, and in the distance she heard the music of a piano quintet. The quintet was in the distance for only an instant; it bore down upon her with a speed greater than light and filled the apartment with the noise of music amplified so mightily that it knocked a china ornament from a table to the floor. She rushed to the instrument and reduced the volume. The violent forces that were snared in the ugly gumwood cabinet made her uneasy. Her children came home from school then, and she took them to the Park. It was not until later in the afternoon that she was able to return to the radio.

The maid had given the children their suppers and was supervising their baths when Irene turned on the radio, reduced the volume, and sat down to listen to a Mozart quintet that she knew and enjoyed. The music came through clearly. The new instrument had a much purer tone, she thought, than the old one. She decided that tone was most important and that she could conceal the cabinet behind a sofa. But as soon as she had made her peace with the radio, the interference began. A crackling sound like the noise of a burning powder fuse began to accompany the singing of the strings. Beyond the music, there was a rustling that reminded Irene unpleasantly of the sea, and as the quintet progressed, these noises were joined by many others. She tried all the dials and switches but nothing dimmed the interference, and she sat down, disappointed and bewildered, and tried to trace the flight of the melody. The elevator shaft in her building ran beside the living-room wall, and it was the noise of the elevator that gave her a clue to the character of the static. The rattling of the elevator cables and the opening and closing of the elevator doors were reproduced in her loudspeaker, and, realizing that the radio was sensitive to electrical currents of all sorts, she began to discern through the Mozart the ringing of telephone bells, the dialling of phones, and the lamentation of a vacuum cleaner. By listening more carefully, she was able to distinguish doorbells, elevator bells, electric razors, and Waring mixers, whose sounds had been picked up from the apartments that surrounded hers and transmitted through her loud-speaker. The powerful and ugly instrument, with its mistaken sensitivity to discord, was more than she could hope to master, so she turned the thing off and went into the nursery to see her children.

. . .

When Jim Westcott came home that night, he went to the radio confidently and worked the controls. He had the same sort of experience Irene had had. A man was speaking on the station Jim had chosen, and his voice swung instantly from the distance into a force so powerful that it shook the apartment. Jim turned the volume control and reduced the voice. Then, a minute or two later, the interference began. The ringing of telephones and doorbells set in, joined by the rasp of the elevator doors and the whir of cooking appliances. The character of the noise had changed since Irene had tried the radio earlier; the last of the electric razors was being unplugged, the vacuum cleaners had all been returned to their closets, and the static reflected that change in pace that overtakes the city after the sun goes down. He fiddled with the knobs but couldn't get rid of the noises, so he turned the radio off and told Irene that in the morning he'd call the people who had sold it to him and give them hell.

. . .

The following afternoon, when Irene returned to the apartment from a luncheon date, the maid told her that a man had come and fixed the radio. Irene went into the living room before she took off her hat or her furs and tried the instrument. From the loudspeaker came a recording of the "Missouri Waltz." It reminded her of the thin, scratchy music from an old-fashioned phonograph that she sometimes heard across the lake where she spent her summers. She waited until the waltz had finished, expecting an explanation of the recording, but there was none. The music was followed by silence, and then the plaintive and scratchy record was repeated. She turned the dial and got a satisfactory burst of Caucasian music—the thump of bare feet in the dust and the rattle of coin jewelry—but in the background she could hear the ringing of bells and a confusion of voices. Her children came home from school then, and she turned off the radio and went to the nursery.

When Jim came home that night, he was tired, and he took a bath and changed his clothes. Then he joined Irene in the living room. He had just turned on the radio when the maid announced dinner, so he left it on, and he and Irene went to the table.

Jim was too tired to make even a pretense of sociability, and there was nothing about the dinner to hold Irene's interest, so her attention wandered from the food to the deposits of silver polish on the candlesticks and from there to the music in the other room. She listened for a few moments to a Chopin prelude and then was surprised to hear a man's voice break in. "For Christ's sake, Kathy," he said, "do you always have to play the piano when I get home?" The music stopped abruptly. "It's the only chance I have," a woman said. "I'm at the office all day." "So am I," the man said. He added something obscene about an upright piano, and slammed a door. The passionate and melancholy music began again.

"Did you hear that?" Irene asked.

"What?" Jim was eating his dessert.

"The radio. A man said something while the music was still going on—something dirty."

"It's probably a play."

"I don't think it *is* a play," Irene said.

They left the table and took their coffee into the living room. Irene asked Jim to try another station. He turned the knob. "Have you seen my garters?" a man asked. "Button me up," a woman said. "Have you seen my garters?" the man said again. "Just button me up and I'll find your garters," the woman said. Jim shifted to another station. "I wish you wouldn't leave apple cores in the ashtrays," a man said. "I hate the smell."

"This is strange," Jim said.

"Isn't it?" Irene said.

Jim turned the knob again. "'On the coast of Coromandel where the early pumpkins blow,'" a woman with a pronounced English accent said, "'in the middle of the woods lived the Yonghy-Bonghy-Bò. Two old chairs, and half a candle, one old jug without a handle . . .'"

"My God!" Irene cried. "That's the Sweeneys' nurse."

"'These were all his worldly goods,'" the British voice continued.

"Turn that thing off," Irene said. "Maybe they can hear *us*." Jim switched the radio off. "That was Miss Armstrong, the Sweeneys' nurse," Irene said. "She must be reading to the little girl. They live in 17-B. I've talked with Miss Armstrong in the Park. I know her voice very well. We must be getting other people's apartments."

"That's impossible," Jim said.

"Well, that was the Sweeneys' nurse," Irene said hotly. "I know her voice. I know it very well. I'm wondering if they can hear us."

Jim turned the switch. First from a distance and then nearer, nearer, as if borne on the wind, came the pure accents of the Sweeneys' nurse again: ""Lady Jingly! Lady Jingly!"" she said, ""Sitting where the pumpkins blow, will you come and be my wife," said the Yonghy-Bonghy-Bò . . .""

Jim went over to the radio and said "Hello" loudly into the speaker.

""I am tired of living singly,"" the nurse went on, ""on this coast so wild and shingly, I'm a-weary of my life; if you'll come and be my wife, quite serene would be my life . . .""

"I guess she can't hear us," Irene said. "Try something else."

Jim turned to another station, and the living room was filled with the uproar of a cocktail party that had overshot its mark. Someone was playing the piano and singing the Whiffenpoof Song, and the voices that surrounded the piano were vehement and happy. "Eat some more sandwiches," a woman shrieked. There were screams of laughter and a dish of some sort crashed to the floor.

"Those must be the Hutchinsons, in 15-B," Irene said. "I knew they were giving a party this afternoon. I saw her in the liquor store. Isn't this too divine? Try something else. See if you can get those people in 18-C."

The Westcotts overheard that evening a monologue on salmon fishing in Canada, a bridge game, running comments on home movies of what had apparently been a fortnight at Sea Island, and a bitter family quarrel about an overdraft at the bank. They turned off their radio at midnight and went to bed, weak with laughter. Sometime in the night, their son began to call for a glass of water and Irene got one and took it to his room. It was very early. All the lights in the neighborhood were extinguished, and from the boy's window she could see the empty street. She went into the living room and tried the radio. There was some faint coughing, a moan, and then a man spoke. "Are you all right, darling?" he asked. "Yes," a woman said wearily. "Yes, I'm all right, I guess," and then she added with great feeling, "But, you know, Charlie, I don't feel like myself any more. Sometimes there are about fifteen or twenty minutes in the week when I feel like myself. I don't like to go to another doctor, because the doctor's bills are so awful already, but I just don't feel like myself, Charlie. I just never feel like myself." They were not young, Irene thought. She guessed from the timbre of their voices that they were middle-aged. The restrained melancholy of the dialogue and the draft from the bedroom window made her shiver, and she went back to bed.

• • •

The following morning, Irene cooked breakfast for the family—the maid didn't come up from her room in the basement until ten—braided her daughter's hair, and waited at the door until her children and her husband had been carried away in the elevator. Then she went into the living room and tried the radio. "I don't want to go to school," a child screamed. "I hate school. I won't go to school. I hate school." "You will go to school," an enraged woman said. "We paid eight hundred dollars to get you into that school and you'll go if it kills you." The next number on the dial produced the worn record of the "Missouri Waltz." Irene shifted the control and invaded the privacy of several breakfast tables. She overheard demonstrations of indigestion, carnal love, abysmal vanity, faith, and despair. Irene's life was nearly as simple and sheltered as it appeared to be, and the forthright and sometimes brutal language that came from the loudspeaker that morning astonished and troubled her. She continued to listen until her maid came in. Then she turned off the radio quickly, since this insight, she realized, was a furtive one.

Irene had a luncheon date with a friend that day, and she left her apartment at a little after twelve. There were a number of women in the elevator when it stopped at her floor. She stared at their handsome and impassive faces, their furs, and the cloth flowers in their hats. Which one of them had been to Sea Island, she wondered. Which one had overdrawn her bank account? The elevator stopped at the tenth floor and a woman with a pair of Skye terriers joined them. Her hair was rigged high on her head and she wore a mink cape. She was humming the "Missouri Waltz."

Irene had two Martinis at lunch, and she looked searchingly at her friend and wondered what her secrets were. They had intended to go shopping after lunch, but Irene excused herself and went home. She told the maid that she was not to be disturbed; then she went into the living room, closed the doors, and switched on the radio. She heard, in the course of the afternoon, the halting conversation of a woman entertaining her aunt, the hysterical conclusion of a luncheon party, and a hostess briefing her maid about some cocktail guests. "Don't give the best Scotch to anyone who hasn't white hair," the hostess said. "See if you can get rid of that liver paste before you pass those hot things, and could you lend me five dollars? I want to tip the elevator man."

As the afternoon waned, the conversations increased in intensity. From where Irene sat, she could see the open sky above Central Park. There were hundreds of clouds in the sky, as though the south wind had broken the winter into pieces and were blowing it north, and on her radio she could hear the arrival of cocktail guests and the return of children and businessmen from their schools and offices. "I found a good-sized diamond on the bathroom floor this morning," a woman said. "It must have fallen out of that bracelet Mrs. Dunston was wearing last night." "We'll sell it," a man said. "Take it down to the jeweller on Madison Avenue and sell it. Mrs. Dunston won't know the difference, and we could use a couple of hundred bucks . . ." "'Oranges and lemons, say the bells of St. Clement's,'" the Sweeneys' nurse sang. "'Half-pence and far-things, say the bells of St. Martin's. When will you pay me? say the bells at old Bailey . . .'" "It's not a hat," a woman cried, and at her back roared a cocktail party. "It's not a hat, it's a love affair. That's what Walter Flo-rell said. He said it's not a hat, it's a love affair," and then, in a lower voice, the same woman added, "Talk to somebody, for Christ's sake, honey, talk to somebody. If she catches you standing here not talking to anybody, she'll take us off her invitation list, and I love these parties."

The Westcotts were going out for dinner that night, and when Jim came home, Irene was dressing. She seemed sad and vague, and he brought her a drink. They were dining with friends in the neighborhood, and they walked to where they were going. The sky was broad and filled with light. It was one of those splendid spring evenings that excite mem-ory and desire, and the air that touched their hands and faces felt very soft. A Salvation Army band was on the corner playing "Jesus Is Sweeter." Irene drew on her husband's arm and held him there for a minute, to hear the music. "They're really such nice people, aren't they?" she said. "They have such nice faces. Actually, they're so much nicer than a lot of the people we know." She took a bill from her purse and walked over and dropped it into the tambourine. There was in her face, when she re-turned to her husband, a look of radiant melancholy that he was not fa-miliar with. And her conduct at the dinner party that night seemed strange to him, too. She interrupted her hostess rudely and stared at the people across the table from her with an intensity for which she would have punished her children.

It was still mild when they walked home from the party, and Irene looked up at the spring stars. "'How far that little candle throws its beams,'" she exclaimed. "'So shines a good deed in a naughty world.'" She waited that night until Jim had fallen asleep, and then went into the living room and turned on the radio.

. . .

Jim came home at about six the next night. Emma, the maid, let him in, and he had taken off his hat and was taking off his coat when Irene ran into the hall. Her face was shining with tears and her hair was disordered. "Go up to 16-C, Jim!" she screamed. "Don't take off your coat. Go up to 16-C. Mr. Osborn's beating his wife. They've been quarrelling since four o'clock, and now he's hitting her. Go up there and stop him."

From the radio in the living room, Jim heard screams, obscenities, and thuds. "You know you don't have to listen to this sort of thing," he said. He strode into the living room and turned the switch. "It's indecent," he said. "It's like looking in windows. You know you don't have to listen to this sort of thing. You can turn it off."

"Oh, it's so horrible, it's so dreadful," Irene was sobbing. "I've been listening all day, and it's so depressing."

"Well, if it's so depressing, why do you listen to it? I bought this damned radio to give you some pleasure," he said. "I paid a great deal of money for it. I thought it might make you happy. I wanted to make you happy."

"Don't, don't, don't, don't quarrel with me," she moaned, and laid her head on his shoulder. "All the others have been quarrelling all day. Everybody's been quarrelling. They're all worried about money. Mrs. Hutchinson's mother is dying of cancer in Florida and they don't have enough money to send her to the Mayo Clinic. At least, Mr. Hutchinson says they don't have enough money. And some woman in this building is having an affair with the superintendent—with that hideous superintendent. It's too disgusting. And Mrs. Melville has heart trouble and Mr. Hendricks is going to lose his job in April and Mrs. Hendricks is horrid about the whole thing and that girl who plays the 'Missouri Waltz' is a whore, a common whore, and the elevator man has tuberculosis and Mr. Osborn has been beating Mrs. Osborn." She wailed, she trembled with grief and checked the stream of tears down her face with the heel of her palm.

"Well, why do you have to listen?" Jim asked again. "Why do you have to listen to this stuff if it makes you so miserable?"

"Oh, don't, don't, don't," she cried. "Life is too terrible, too sordid and awful. But we've never been like that, have we, darling? Have we? I mean we've always been good and decent and loving to one another, haven't we? And we have two children, two beautiful children. Our lives aren't sordid, are they, darling? Are they?" She flung her arms around his neck and drew his face down to hers. "We're happy, aren't we, darling? We are happy, aren't we?"

"Of course we're happy," he said tiredly. He began to surrender his resentment. "Of course we're happy. I'll have that damned radio fixed or taken away tomorrow." He stroked her soft hair. "My poor girl," he said.

"You love me, don't you?" she asked. "And we're not hypercritical or worried about money or dishonest, are we?"

"No, darling," he said.

. . .

A man came in the morning and fixed the radio. Irene turned it on cautiously and was happy to hear a California-wine commercial and a recording of Beethoven's Ninth Symphony, including Schiller's "Ode to Joy." She kept the radio on all day and nothing untoward came from the speaker.

A Spanish suite was being played when Jim came home. "Is everything all right?" he asked. His face was pale, she thought. They had some cocktails and went in to dinner to the "Anvil Chorus" from "Il Trovatore." This was followed by Debussy's "La Mer."

"I paid the bill for the radio today," Jim said. "It cost four hundred dollars. I hope you'll get some enjoyment out of it."

"Oh, I'm sure I will," Irene said.

"Four hundred dollars is a good deal more than I can afford," he went on. "I wanted to get something that you'd enjoy. It's the last extravagance we'll be able to indulge in this year. I see that you haven't paid your clothing bills yet. I saw them on your dressing table." He looked directly at her. "Why did you tell me you'd paid them? Why did you lie to me?"

"I just didn't want you to worry, Jim," she said. She drank some water. "I'll be able to pay my bills out of this month's allowance. There were the slipcovers last month, and that party."

"You've got to learn to handle the money I give you a little more intelligently, Irene," he said. "You've got to understand that we won't have as much money this year as we had last. I had a very sobering talk with Mitchell today. No one is buying anything. We're spending all our time promoting new issues, and you know how long that takes. I'm not getting any younger, you know. I'm thirty-seven. My hair will be gray next year. I haven't done as well as I'd hoped to do. And I don't suppose things will get any better."

"Yes, dear," she said.

"We've got to start cutting down," Jim said. "We've got to think of the children. To be perfectly frank with you, I worry about money a great deal. I'm not at all sure of the future. No one is. If anything should happen to me, there's the insurance, but that wouldn't go very far today. I've worked awfully hard to give you and the children a comfortable life," he said bitterly. "I don't like to see all of my energies, all of my youth, wasted in fur coats and radios and slipcovers and—"

"Please, Jim," she said. "Please. They'll hear us."

"*Who'll* hear us? Emma can't hear us."

"The radio."

"Oh, I'm sick!" he shouted. "I'm sick to death of your apprehensiveness. The radio can't hear us. Nobody can hear us. And what if they can hear us? Who cares?"

Irene got up from the table and went into the living room. Jim went to the door and shouted at her from there. "Why are you so Christly all of a sudden? What's turned you overnight into a convent girl? You stole your mother's jewelry before they probated her will. You never gave your sister a cent of that money that was intended for her—not even when she needed it. You made Grace Howland's life miserable, and where was all your piety and your virtue when you went to that abortionist? I'll never forget how cool you were. You packed your bag and went off to have that child murdered as if you were going to Nassau. If you'd had any reasons, if you'd had any good reasons—"

Irene stood for a minute before the hideous cabinet, disgraced and sickened, but she held her hand on the switch before she extinguished the music and the voices, hoping that the instrument might speak to her kindly, that she might hear the Sweeneys' nurse. Jim continued to shout at her from the door. The voice on the radio was suave and noncommittal. "An early-morning railroad disaster in Tokyo," the loudspeaker said, "killed twenty-nine people. A fire in a Catholic hospital near Buffalo for the care of blind children was extinguished early this morning by nuns. The temperature is forty-seven. The humidity is eighty-nine."

May 17, 1947

MY DA

Frank O'Connor

STEVIE LEARY IS A BOY I remember with extraordinary vividness, so I suppose that even from the first there must have been something outstanding in him. The Learys lived next door to us, and Stevie's mother was a great friend of my mother's. Mrs. Leary was a big, buxom woman with a rich, husky voice, and she made her living as a charwoman. In her younger days she had left Ireland and spent a couple of years in America.

"It was love sent me there, Ma'am," she would say to my mother, in a rich, wheezy, humorous voice. "Love was always the ruination of me. If I might have stuck on there, I could have chummed up with some old, sickly geezer of seventy that would think the world of me and leave me his money when he'd die. I was a fine-looking girl in those days. Frankie Leary used to say I was like the picture of the Colleen Bawn."

I often studied the picture of the Colleen Bawn in her kitchen to see could I detect some resemblance between herself and Mrs. Leary, but I failed. The Colleen Bawn was a glorious-looking creature, plump and modest and all aglow, as if she had a lamp inside her.

"Why then indeed," my mother would say loyally, "you're a fine woman to this day, Mrs. Leary."

"Ah, I'm not, Ma'am, I'm not," Mrs. Leary would say with resignation. "I had great feeling, and nothing ages a woman like the feelings. But I was mad in love with Frankie Leary, and lovers can never agree. I had great pride. If he so much as lay a hand on me, I'd fight in a bag tied up."

"Ah, 'tis a wonder you'd put up with it from him," my mother would say. She had strong ideas about the dignity of womanhood.

"Ah, wisha, you would, Ma'am, you would," Mrs. Leary would say with a sigh for my mother's lack of experience. "A man would never love you properly till he'd give you a clout. I could die for that man when he beat me."

Then, with a tear in her eye, she'd take out the snuffbox she kept in her enormous bosom and tell again the sad story of herself and Frankie. Frankie, it seemed, had even greater pride than herself. He had always been too big for his boots. America, he had said, was the only country for a man of spirit. Now, Mrs. Leary had a weakness for the little drop, and several times Frankie had warned her that if she didn't give it up he'd leave her and go to America. One night when she was on a bat, she came home and found that he had been as good as his word. But she had a spirit as great as his own. Leaving Stevie, still a baby, with her mother-in-law, she had followed her husband to America. True, she had never succeeded in finding him. America was a big place, and Frankie Leary wasn't the sort to leave traces. All the same, she'd had the experience, and she never let you forget it. Even Mrs. Delury, whom she mostly worked for, didn't succeed in keeping her in her place. Mrs. Delury owned a shop and had a son in Maynooth going for the priesthood, but Mrs. Leary dismissed both of these sources of pride with a sarcastic "We have a priest in the family and a pump in the yard." As Mrs. Delury said, you couldn't expect better of anyone who had spent years in that horrible country.

Stevie was twelve, the same age I was, with a big, round, almost idiotic face and a rosy complexion, a slovenly, hasty stride that was almost a scamper, and a shrill, scolding, old woman's voice. He was always in a hurry, and when someone called to him and he stopped, it was just as if some invisible hand had tightened the reins on him; he slithered and skidded to a halt with his beaming face over his shoulder. He was never a kid like the rest of us. He took life too seriously. His mother had told him the story of an American millionaire who had made his way up from rags to riches, and Stevie hoped to do the same thing. He collected swill for the Mahoneys, carried messages for the Delurys, and for a penny would do anything for you, from minding the baby to buying the dinner. He had a frightfully crabbed air, and would talk in that high-pitched voice of his about what was the cheapest sort of meat to make soup of. "You should try Reilly's, Ma'am," he would tell my mother. "Reilly's keeps grand stewing beef." My mother thought he wasn't quite right in the head. "Ah, he's a good poor slob," she would say doubtfully when politeness required her to praise him to his mother. Mrs. Leary would sigh and take a pinch of snuff and say, "Ah, he'll never be the man his father was, Ma'am." I more or less knew Stevie's father as the man Stevie would never be.

Occasionally, Mrs. Leary's feelings would get too much for her. We'd be playing some boys' game and Stevie would be sitting on the wall outside their little cottage, looking at us with a smile that was half superciliousness and half envy. A kid coming up the road would say, "Stevie, I seen your old one on a bat again." "Oh, japers!" Stevie would groan. "That woman will be the death of me. Where is she now, Jerry?" "I seen her down by the Cross." "Clancy's or Mooney's?" Stevie would ask, and away he would go. Sometimes I would go along after him and watch him darting into each pub as he passed, the very image of an up-to-date businessman, and shouting to the barmaid, "You didn't see my ma today, Miss O.? . . . You didn't? I'll try Riordan's." Eventually he would discover her in some snug with a couple of cronies. Mrs. Leary was the warm sort of drunkard who attracts hangers-on.

"Ah, come on home now, Ma," Stevie would cry coaxingly.

"Jasus help us!" the cronies would say in pretended admiration. "Isn't he a lovely little boy, God bless him!"

"Ah, he'll never be the man his father was, Ma'am," Mrs. Leary would say, beaming at him regretfully. "There was a man for you, Ma'am! A fine, educated, independent man!"

It might be nightfall before Stevie got her home—a mountain of a woman, who would have stunned him if she'd collapsed on him. He would make her a cup of tea, undress her, and put her to bed. If my mother were by, she would lend a hand and, furious at any woman's making such an exhibition of herself and before a child, she would rate Mrs. Leary soundly.

Sometimes, late at night, we'd hear Stevie crying, "Ah, stay here, Ma, and I'll get it for you!" and his mother roaring, "Gimme the money!" Stevie would groan and steal away to whatever hiding hole he was then keeping his savings in. "That's all I have now," he would say hopefully. "Will tuppence do you?" With the cunning of all drunkards, Mrs. Leary seemed to know to a farthing how much he had. Night after night she shuffled down to Miss O.'s with nothing showing through the hood of the shawl but one sinister, bloodshot eye, and tuppence by tuppence Stevie's capital vanished, till he started life again with all the bounce gone out of him, as poor as any of us who had never heard the life story of an American millionaire.

Then one night Frankie Leary came back from the States. My mother was at Mrs. Leary's when Frankie strolled up the road one summer evening, without even a bag, and stood in the doorway with an impassive air. "Hallo," he said lightly. Mrs. Leary rose from her stool by the fire, gaping at him; then she tottered, and finally she ran and enveloped him in her arms. "Oh, Frankie!" she sobbed. "After all the years!" This apparently wasn't at all the sort of conduct that the independent Frankie approved of. "Here, here," he said roughly. "There's time enough for that later. Now I want something to eat." He pushed her away and looked at Stevie, who was staring at him, enraptured by the touching scene. "Is this the boy?" he asked, and then all at once he smiled pleasantly and held out his hand. "How're ye, Son?" he asked heartily. "Oh, grand, Father," said Stevie, who was equal to any occasion. "Did you have a nice journey?"

Frankie didn't even reply to that. Maybe he hadn't had a nice journey. Unlike the American Stevie had been told of, Frankie came home as poor as he left, and next day he had to go to work on the railway. It seemed America wasn't all it was cracked up to be.

· · ·

For a week or two, Stevie was in a state of real hysteria over his father's arrival. For the first time he had, like the rest of us, a da of his own, and as our das generally flaked hell out of us, Stevie felt it was up to him to go in fear and trembling of what "my da" might do to him. Of course, it was all showing off, for his da did nothing whatever to him. On the contrary, Frankie was painfully and anxiously correct with him, as though he were trying to make up for any slight he might have inflicted on the boy by his eleven-year absence. He found that Stevie was interested in America, and talked to him patiently for hours on end about it while Stevie, in an appalling imitation of some old man he had seen in a pub, sat back in his chair with his hands in his trousers pockets.

Frankie spoke to him one day about keeping his hands in his pockets, and even this mild criticism, delivered in a low, reasonable tone, was enough to make Stevie jump. He tried in other ways to please Frankie. He tried to moderate his intense, fancy-haunted shamble so that he wouldn't have to pull himself up on the rein, to break his voice of its squeak, and to imitate his father.

Stevie trying to be tough like Frankie was one of the funniest of his phases, for undoubtedly Frankie was the man Stevie would never be. He was a lean, leathery sort of man, with a long face, cold eyes, and a fish's mouth. No doubt he had his good points. He made Mrs. Leary give up the daily work and wear a hat and coat instead of the shawl. He made Stevie give up the swill and the messages and learn to read and write, an accomplishment that had apparently been omitted from the education of whatever American millionaire he had been modelling himself on. Frankie had few friends on the road; he was a quiet, self-centered, scornful man. But with his coming the years seemed to drop from Mrs. Leary. I understood at last what she meant when she said that Frankie in their courting days had compared her to the Colleen Bawn. She seemed to become all schoolgirlish and lit up inside, as though, but for modesty, she'd love to take you aside and tell you what Frankie did to her.

You wouldn't believe the change that came over their little cottage. Of course, a couple of times there were scenes when Mrs. Leary came home with the signs of drink on her. They weren't scenes as we understood them. Frankie didn't make smithereens of the house, as my da did when domesticity became too much for him. But for all that, the scenes frightened Stevie. Each time there was one, he burst into tears and begged his father and mother to agree.

And then one night a terrible thing happened. Mrs. Leary came in a bit more expansive than usual. She wasn't drunk, she told my mother afterward—just friendly. Frankie had been reading the evening paper and he looked up.

"Where were you?" he asked.

"Ah, I ran into Lizzie Desmond at the Cross and we started to talk," Mrs. Leary said good-humoredly.

"Then ye started to drink, you mean."

"We had two small ones," said Mrs. Leary with a shrug of her shoulders. "What harm was there in that? Have you the kettle boiling, Stevie?"

"You know better than anyone what harm is in it," Frankie said. "I hope you're not forgetting what it cost you last time?"

"And if it did, wasn't I well able to get along without you? 'Tisn't many would be able for what I did, with my child to bring up, and no one to advise me or help me."

"Whisht now, Ma! Whisht!" Stevie cried in an agony of fear. "You know my da is only speaking for your good."

"Speaking for my good?" she shouted. With great dignity she drew herself up and addressed Frankie. "How dare you? Is that my thanks after all I did for you—crossing the briny ocean after you, you insignificant little gnat!"

"What's that you said?" Frankie asked quietly. Without waiting for an answer, he threw down his paper and went up to her with his fists clenched.

"Gnat!" she repeated scornfully, looking him up and down. "Insignificant little gnat, that wouldn't make a bolt for a back door! How dare you?"

Even before Stevie could guess what he was up to, Frankie had drawn back his fist and given it to her fair in the mouth. He didn't pull his punch, either. Stevie nearly got sick at the sound. Mrs. Leary gave a shriek that was heard in our house, and then went in a heap on the floor. Stevie shrieked, too, and rushed to her assistance. He lifted her head on his knee. Her mouth was bleeding and her eyes were closed.

"Oh, Ma, look at me, look at me!" he bawled distractedly. "'Tis all right. I'm Stevie, your own little boy."

She opened one red-rimmed eye and looked at him for a moment. Then she closed it carefully, with a moan of pain, as though the sight of him distressed her too much. Stevie looked up at his father, who seemed to be hardly aware of his presence.

"Will I get the priest for her, Da?" asked Stevie. "She's dying."

"Get to bed out of this," Frankie replied in a tone that put the fear of God into Stevie. He crept into bed, leaving his mother still lying on the floor. A little later he heard his father close the bedroom door on himself. His mother still lay there. He was quite certain she was dead until an hour later he heard her pick herself up and make herself a cup of tea. But never before had Stevie allowed his mother to remain like that without assistance. It couldn't have happened except for Frankie. He was afraid of Frankie.

Stevie woke next morning with all the troubles of the world on his young shoulders. Things were desperate in the home. All the light he had on the subject was contained in a sermon he had once heard in which the preacher said children were a great bond between the parents. Stevie felt it was up to him to be a bond. Purposefully cheerful, he gave Frankie his breakfast and took his mother a cup of tea. After that she insisted on getting up and going out. He begged her to stay in bed, and offered to bring the porter to her, but she wouldn't. He knew she was going out to get drunk, and at the same time that she was far more frightened than he was. That was what she meant when she said that lovers could never agree. It was her terrible pride that wouldn't allow her to give in to his father.

In the afternoon, Stevie found her in a pub in town and brought her home. He did everything he could to make her presentable; he made her tea, washed her face, combed her hair, and finally even tried to induce her to hide in our house. At six, Frankie came in, and Stevie bustled around him eagerly and clumsily, laying the table for his supper. In his capacity of bond, he had reverted to type. "You'd like a couple of buttered eggs?" he squeaked. "You would, to be sure. Dwyer's keeps grand eggs."

After supper, Frankie grimly got up and took his cap. "You won't be late, Da?" Stevie asked appealingly. Frankie didn't answer. Stevie went to the door and watched him all the way down the road. Then he returned and sat opposite his mother by the fire.

"Ah," he said, "I don't suppose he'll come back at all."

"Let him go," his mother muttered scornfully. "We did without him before and we can do without him again. Insignificant little gnat!"

"Ah, I dunno," Stevie said. "'Twas nice having him, all the same."

The dusk fell and they sat there, not speaking.

"You ought to see is he at your Uncle John's," Mrs. Leary said suddenly, and Stevie knew the panic was rising again through the drink.

"I'll try," he said, "but I wouldn't have much hope."

His doubts were fully justified. Whatever way Frankie had of losing himself, he had disappeared again.

. . .

Little by little the old air of fecklessness and neglect descended on the Learys' cottage. Mrs. Leary, no longer looking like the Colleen Bawn, went back to the shawl and the daily work for the Delurys, and Stevie to the swill and the messages. Everything was exactly as though Frankie had never returned. Yet in one way it wasn't. After a year or two, Stevie started to go to night school. That caused us all considerable amusement. It was the daftest of Stevie's metamorphoses.

But then a really incredible thing happened—Stevie began to study for the priesthood. It seemed that the teacher in the Technical School had spoken to the parish priest, and the parish priest was arranging for Mrs. Leary to have regular work in the presbytery, so that Stevie could attend the seminary. This wasn't a matter for laughter. In a way, it was a public scandal. Of course, it wouldn't be like Mrs. Delury's son who had been to Maynooth; it would only be for the Foreign Mission, but you'd think that even the Foreign Mission would draw the line somewhere. Even my mother, who had great pity for Stevie, was troubled. I was causing her concern enough as it was, for I had lost my faith for the first time. She was an exceedingly pious woman, and I don't think she ever put it in so many words, but I fancy she felt that if the Catholic Church was having to fall back on people like Stevie, there might be some grounds for a young fellow losing his faith. I remember the incredulity with which I spoke to Stevie myself when for the first time I met him on the road in his black suit and black soft hat. I could see he knew about my losing my faith. He might even have tried to help me with it, but, of course, being Stevie, he was in a hurry to get back to his Latin roots.

When he said his first Mass in the parish church, we all turned up, a few—like my mother—from piety, the rest from curiosity. Mrs. Delury, her two sons, and her daughter were there. Mrs. Delury, of course, was boiling at the thought of her charwoman's son being a priest like her own Jeremiah, and she blamed it all on America. Stevie preached on the Good Shepherd, and whether it was just the excitement or the faces of the Delurys all looking up at him from one pew—a sight to daunt the boldest heart—he got mixed up between the ninety-nine and the one. What else could you expect of Stevie? My mother and I went around to the sacristy afterward to get his blessing. (By this time I had got back my faith again and I didn't lose it a second time till two years afterward.) As we knelt, I could hardly keep my face straight, for at every moment I expected Stevie to say, "Wouldn't a few pounds of stewing beef be better, Ma'am?"

When we came out of the church, I saw that the Opposition, headed by Mrs. Delury, was holding an overflow meeting on the road down from the chapel. "Poor Father Stephen got a bit mixed in his sums," said Mrs. Delury in her pleasant way as we passed.

"Ah, the dear knows, wouldn't anyone get excited on an occasion like that?" said my mother, flushed and angry at this insult to the cloth.

"Ah, well," said Mrs. Delury comfortably, "I don't suppose in America they'll know the difference."

"Why?" I asked in surprise. "Is he going to America?"

"So it seems," she replied with a giggle. "I wonder why."

. . .

But I knew why, and for days it haunted my mind. I called the night before Stevie went away, and had a cup of tea with Mrs. Leary and him.

I cursed myself for not noticing before what a nice, intelligent, sensitive fellow Stevie was. He was nervous and excited by the prospect before him. "Ah, he'll love it," his mother said in her deep, snug, husky voice. "'Twill be like a new life to him. The dear knows, I might go out to him myself, one of these days."

"How bad 'twould be now to have you keeping house for him!" I said.

"Japers," said Father Stephen shyly, "that'd be grand."

Of course, all three of us knew it was impossible. There are certain luxuries that a young priest must deny himself and one is a mother whose feelings become too much for her. The whole time Stevie was at home, Mrs. Leary was irreproachable, a perfect lady. But next evening, after she had seen him off, a sympathetic policeman brought her home, and my mother put her to bed. "Ah, indeed," my mother kept saying reproachfully, "what would Father Stephen say if he saw you now?" During the night we heard her shouting, but there was no Stevie to say, "Stay here and I'll get it for you, Ma." Stevie at last had become the man his father was, and left us all far away behind him.

October 25, 1947

THE MYSTERIES OF LIFE IN
AN ORDERLY MANNER

Jessamyn West

I<small>T WAS INITIATION NIGHT</small>, a candle-lighting ceremony, a big night in the lodge, and through the spring twilight of the California hill town, past the parking meters and the street-corner loungers, the matrons carrying their candles unlit drifted like moths. Not mothlike certainly in their plumpness but varicolored, fluttering, and pleasure-bent.

Emily Cooper (Mrs. W. H. Cooper—William H. Cooper, Inc., Insurance—"See Us B 4 U Burn") sat with her husband in their car, parked at the curb. Across the street from them, and a little way down, was the Vasconi Building, where the initiation was being held. Emily was herself to be initiated that night, but she didn't know the Pocahontas women very well and she was sitting for a time with her husband, gathering up courage from his matter-of-factness and checking the suitability of her dress against what she could see of the evening dresses of the other initiates, passing in the fading light. Only the initiates wore evening dresses (formals, formals, Emily reminded herself to say). The established lodge members, the Pocahontases in good standing, went to their meetings in Indian regalia. Emily watched them go by in the twilight, coats thrown back, because the evening was warm, fringes swaying, beaded headbands gleaming, moccasined feet silent on the sidewalk. Emily was proud to recognize some of them.

"There's Mrs. Asta Bell," she said to her husband. "She's Keeper of the Wampum."

"Keeper of what?" asked Mr. Cooper, himself no lodge man. Emily got into Pocahontas because of her father, Clement McCarthy, a long-time Redman, though not a resident of the state. "Join, join," her father had always urged her, but Emily would not so long as the children were little.

"Wampum," said Emily. "Indian for money. She's treasurer."

Mrs. Edna Purvis went by, black-haired and straight, most Indianlike of all, and Mrs. Wanda Turner, married to the county sheriff, and Zula Throne, married to no one at all, the only unmarried Pocahontas in the lodge. When Emily had remarked on this to some of the other lodge members, she had been told, "Most single girls are too frivolous for lodge work. Can't concentrate on ritual and memorizing, let alone beadwork. Spend their time mooning about, thinking of . . ."

Emily, anxious to appear quick-witted before her sisters-to-be, had suggested in this pause "Men," and her informer had repeated the word, but it had seemed not quite to fill the bill. "Yes and no," she had told Emily. "Yes and no." But Zula Throne was an exception—no mooner, they said, and, though maiden, as brisk in ritual and beadwork as any married lady.

More officers, some of the most important, passed by on the sidewalk. "Look, look," said Emily, whispering, "but not right away. Now, that's the Grand Prophetess."

Mr. Cooper looked. "Couldn't tell her from an ordinary prophetess," he said calmly.

"Oh, she's full of authority," said Emily. "A power in the lodge, believe me."

. . .

It was exciting for Emily to sit in the car with her husband, pointing out to him the town's leading ladies. It was a novelty, too, for it was he who had usually known everyone and done the pointing. But they were new in Midvale, the insurance office had been open only a couple of months, and Mr. Cooper's work in opening it had kept him too busy for getting acquainted with the Pocahontas ladies.

"That's Mrs. Pleasant Jones," said Emily. "She's First Scout, and the one with her, the tall one with the red headband, I can't remember her name but I know she's the Second Runner."

Following the Second Runner were the Guards of Tepee and Forest, and Pocahontas, herself—Mrs. Vigila Smiley—with feathers in her headband. Emily knew all three of them and pointed them out as they went by carrying their candles and squares or oblongs of home-baked cake. They passed on foot, by twos and threes, or alighted, singly, from cars driven by their husbands. They were laughing and talking, but their voices were low; an initiation by candlelight was solemn and secret; it was spring, it was almost night.

"They shouldn't have candles, really," Emily explained to her husband.

"No candles?" said Mr. Cooper, who had been watching the Second Runner. "Why not?"

"It's not in the Ritual. But the Grand Prophetess says we're so far off the beaten track here in the hills that we can plead ignorance in case of criticism."

"Why, sure," said Mr. Cooper. "Sure you can. Why not?"

"We shouldn't be hit-or-miss," explained Emily. "The lodge treats of the mysteries of life in an orderly manner."

Mr. Cooper looked at his wife inquiringly.

"That's what I was told," she said. "And the candles aren't part of that order."

"Maybe they're part of the mystery," suggested Mr. Cooper.

Emily supposed that her husband was smiling, but no, he was serious, looking intently into the creamy blooms of the laurel trees that lined the sidewalk, and listening to the birds that were singing on into the night because of the springtime.

"It's the second spring," said Emily.

In California, the first spring is in November. March only echoes it. In November the first spring is brief and sharp after the early rains. Then the grass flares up like fire; dry stream beds, as dead to the eye as old snakeskins, revive, all their bends and shallows filled with the curve of bright water; quail call; mushrooms push their blunt heads through the sodden leaves under the valley oaks; and at the end of the town's short streets, early sunsets and winter barley, alike green, meet. Spring is sharp in November—a slap, a blow, a kiss, soon over, soon forgotten, colder weather to follow. In March it is easy, gentle, nothing to wonder at, it will last a long time. Summer will come, the hills be brown and faded, no one able to say just when the rains stopped or the grass withered.

"Counting November, it's the second spring," said Mr. Cooper.

"I *was* counting November," said Emily, dangling a hand out the car window to test the air. It was still warm, though the sun was down, no color left behind, the sky as drab as a cast-iron skillet. Emily pushed her feet, slim in pointed satin slippers, up the incline of the floor boards until they cleared her full, white marquisette skirt. She reset the white daphne she had pinned in her hair and redampened her handkerchief from the bottle of Hoyt's perfume she had in her purse.

"Do I look all right?" she inquired anxiously of her husband.

"Fine, fine," said he. "Couldn't look better."

"Do I smell too strong of cologne?"

"Look fine, smell fine."

With sudden energy, Emily gathered her coat about her shoulders, grasped her candle, prepared to depart. "I always look fine," she said irritably. "I always look fine and I always smell fine to you. You don't give me any confidence."

Mr. Cooper leaned over, detained her with his hand on her arm. "But you do," he said. "You always do. What do you want me to say? Want me to be a liar?"

"No," said Emily, "but if I knew you were critical, it would give me more confidence."

"Oh, critical!" said Mr. Cooper, surprised. "Why, I'm critical, critical as all getout. That Second Runner, now. She's bandy-legged. I criticized it in her first thing. They'd ought to have given her the wampum job. Something she could do sitting down, not put her to running."

. . .

Emily opened the car door, jumped out, and banged it behind her. It was dark enough for the first stars to show, not distinctly, a little blurred in their outlines, as if the moist spring air had caused them to run a bit. The birds were still rustling and chirping in the laurel trees, unwilling for this day to end. Down the street the neon signs said "Eat," said "Drink," said "Short Orders," said "Church of the Open Door." There were no Pocahontases in sight and Emily felt a little strange, on the street after dark in her long white dress. A man paused under the "Drink" sign to look at her before pushing the swinging doors apart. She lingered at the car side.

"Don't joke about serious things," she said fiercely. "It makes me nervous. And I'm already nervous to begin with."

"Don't be nervous," said Mr. Cooper. "I'm critical and you look fine and smell fine and you are going to see the marvels of life in an orderly manner."

"Mysteries," said Emily, "*mysteries*," and she turned away without so much as a goodbye and started toward the Vasconi Building. But before she had taken two angry steps, Mr. Cooper had caught up with her.

"Mysteries was what I meant," he said contritely, and they walked on together arm in arm, past the birds and the trees and the plate-glass windows and the men going in for a drink. "The mysteries of life in an orderly manner," he said, "was what I fully intended to say."

March 27, 1948

SYMBOLS AND SIGNS

Vladimir Nabokov

OR THE FOURTH TIME in as many years, they were confronted with
the problem of what birthday present to take to a young man who
was incurably deranged in his mind. Desires he had none. Man-
made objects were to him either hives of evil, vibrant with a malignant
activity that he alone could perceive, or gross comforts for which no use
could be found in his abstract world. After eliminating a number of articles that might offend him or frighten him (anything in the gadget
line, for instance, was taboo), his parents chose a dainty and innocent
trifle—a basket with ten different fruit jellies in ten little jars.

At the time of his birth, they had already been married for a long
time; a score of years had elapsed, and now they were quite old. Her drab
gray hair was pinned up carelessly. She wore cheap black dresses. Unlike
other women of her age (such as Mrs. Sol, their next-door neighbor,
whose face was all pink and mauve with paint and whose hat was a cluster of brookside flowers), she presented a naked white countenance to the
faultfinding light of spring. Her husband, who in the old country had
been a fairly successful businessman, was now, in New York, wholly dependent on his brother Isaac, a real American of almost forty years'
standing. They seldom saw Isaac and had nicknamed him the Prince.

That Friday, their son's birthday, everything went wrong. The subway
train lost its life current between two stations and for a quarter of an
hour they could hear nothing but the dutiful beating of their hearts and
the rustling of newspapers. The bus they had to take next was late and
kept them waiting a long time on a street corner, and when it did come,
it was crammed with garrulous high-school children. It began to rain as
they walked up the brown path leading to the sanitarium. There they
waited again, and instead of their boy, shuffling into the room, as he

usually did (his poor face sullen, confused, ill-shaven, and blotched with acne), a nurse they knew and did not care for appeared at last and brightly explained that he had again attempted to take his life. He was all right, she said, but a visit from his parents might disturb him. The place was so miserably understaffed, and things got mislaid or mixed up so easily, that they decided not to leave their present in the office but to bring it to him next time they came.

Outside the building, she waited for her husband to open his umbrella and then took his arm. He kept clearing his throat, as he always did when he was upset. They reached the bus-stop shelter on the other side of the street and he closed his umbrella. A few feet away, under a swaying and dripping tree, a tiny unfledged bird was helplessly twitching in a puddle.

During the long ride to the subway station, she and her husband did not exchange a word, and every time she glanced at his old hands, clasped and twitching upon the handle of his umbrella, and saw their swollen veins and brown-spotted skin, she felt the mounting pressure of tears. As she looked around, trying to hook her mind onto something, it gave her a kind of soft shock, a mixture of compassion and wonder, to notice that one of the passengers—a girl with dark hair and grubby red toenails—was weeping on the shoulder of an older woman. Whom did that woman resemble? She resembled Rebecca Borisovna, whose daughter had married one of the Soloveichiks—in Minsk, years ago.

The last time the boy had tried to do it, his method had been, in the doctor's words, a masterpiece of inventiveness; he would have succeeded had not an envious fellow-patient thought he was learning to fly and stopped him just in time. What he had really wanted to do was to tear a hole in his world and escape.

The system of his delusions had been the subject of an elaborate paper in a scientific monthly, which the doctor at the sanitarium had given to them to read. But long before that, she and her husband had puzzled it out for themselves. "Referential mania," the article had called it. In these very rare cases, the patient imagines that everything happening around him is a veiled reference to his personality and existence. He excludes real people from the conspiracy, because he considers himself to be so much more intelligent than other men. Phenomenal nature shadows him wherever he goes. Clouds in the staring sky transmit to each other, by means of slow signs, incredibly detailed information regarding him. His inmost thoughts are discussed at nightfall, in manual alphabet, by darkly gesticulating trees. Pebbles or stains or sun flecks form patterns representing, in some awful way, messages that he must intercept. Everything is a cipher and of everything he is the theme. All around him, there are spies. Some of them are detached observers, like glass surfaces and still pools; others, such as coats in store windows, are prejudiced witnesses, lynchers at heart; others, again (running water, storms), are hysterical to the point of insanity, have a distorted opinion of him, and grotesquely misinterpret his actions. He must be always on his guard and devote every minute and module of life to the decoding of the undulation of things. The very air he exhales is indexed and filed away. If only the interest he provokes were limited to his immediate surroundings, but, alas, it is not! With distance, the torrents of wild scandal increase in volume and volubility. The silhouettes of his blood corpuscles, magnified a million times, flit over vast plains; and still farther away, great mountains of unbearable solidity and height sum up, in terms of granite and groaning firs, the ultimate truth of his being.

· · ·

When they emerged from the thunder and foul air of the subway, the last dregs of the day were mixed with the street lights. She wanted to buy some fish for supper, so she handed him the basket of jelly jars, telling him to go home. Accordingly, he returned to their tenement house, walked up to the third landing, and then remembered he had given her his keys earlier in the day.

In silence he sat down on the steps and in silence rose when, some ten minutes later, she came trudging heavily up the stairs, smiling wanly and shaking her head in deprecation of her silliness. They entered their two-room flat and he at once went to the mirror. Straining the corners of his mouth apart by means of his thumbs, with a horrible, mask-like grimace, he removed his new, hopelessly uncomfortable dental plate. He read his Russian-language newspaper while she laid the table. Still reading, he ate the pale victuals that needed no teeth. She knew his moods and was also silent.

When he had gone to bed, she remained in the living room with her pack of soiled playing cards and her old photograph albums. Across the narrow courtyard, where the rain tinkled in the dark against some ash cans, windows were blandly alight, and in one of them a black-trousered man, with his hands clasped under his head and his elbows raised, could be seen lying supine on an untidy bed. She pulled the blind down and examined the photographs. As a baby, he looked more surprised than most babies. A photograph of a German maid they had had in Leipzig and her fat-faced fiancé fell out of a fold of the album. She turned the pages of the book: Minsk, the Revolution, Leipzig, Berlin, Leipzig again, a slanting house front, badly out of focus. Here was the boy when he was four years old, in a park, shyly, with puckered forehead, looking away from an eager squirrel, as he would have from any other stranger. Here was Aunt Rosa, a fussy, angular, wild-eyed old lady, who had lived in a tremulous world of bad news, bankruptcies, train accidents, and cancerous growths until the Germans put her to death, together with all the people she had worried about. The boy, aged six—that was when he drew wonderful birds with human hands and feet, and suffered from insomnia like a grown-up man. His cousin, now a famous chess player. The boy again, aged about eight, already hard to understand, afraid of the wallpaper in the passage, afraid of a certain picture in a book, which merely showed an idyllic landscape with rocks on a hillside and an old cart wheel hanging from the one branch of a leafless tree. Here he was at ten—the year they left Europe. She remembered the shame, the pity, the humiliating difficulties of the journey, and the ugly, vicious, backward children he was with in the special school where he had been placed after they arrived in America. And then came a time in his life, coinciding with a long convalescence after pneumonia, when those little phobias of his, which his parents had stubbornly regarded as the eccentricities of a prodigiously gifted child, hardened, as it were, into a dense tangle of logically interacting illusions, making them totally inaccessible to normal minds.

All this, and much more, she had accepted, for, after all, living does mean accepting the loss of one joy after another, not even joys in her case, mere possibilities of improvement. She thought of the recurrent waves of pain that for some reason or other she and her husband had had to endure; of the invisible giants hurting her boy in some unimaginable fashion; of the incalculable amount of tenderness contained in the world; of the fate of this tenderness, which is either crushed or wasted, or transformed into madness; of neglected children humming to themselves in unswept corners; of beautiful weeds that cannot hide from the farmer.

· · ·

It was nearly midnight when, from the living room, she heard her husband moan, and presently he staggered in, wearing over his nightgown the old overcoat with the astrakhan collar that he much preferred to his nice blue bathrobe.

"I can't sleep!" he cried.

"Why can't you sleep?" she asked. "You were so tired."

"I can't sleep because I am dying," he said, and lay down on the couch.

"Is it your stomach? Do you want me to call Dr. Solov?"

"No doctors, no doctors," he moaned. "To the devil with doctors! We must get him out of there quick. Otherwise, we'll be responsible. . . . Responsible!" He hurled himself into a sitting position, both feet on the floor, thumping his forehead with his clenched fist.

"All right," she said quietly. "We will bring him home tomorrow morning."

"I would like some tea," said her husband, and went out to the bathroom.

Bending with difficulty, she retrieved some playing cards and a photograph or two that had slipped to the floor—the knave of hearts, the nine of spades, the ace of spades, the maid Elsa and her bestial beau.

He returned in high spirits, saying in a loud voice, "I have it all figured out. We will give him the bedroom. Each of us will spend part of the night near him and the other part on this couch. We will have the doctor see him at least twice a week. It does not matter what the Prince says. He won't have much to say anyway, because it will come out cheaper."

The telephone rang. It was an unusual hour for it to ring. He stood in the middle of the room, groping with his foot for one slipper that had come off, and childishly, toothlessly, gaped at his wife. Since she knew more English than he, she always attended to the calls.

"Can I speak to Charlie?" a girl's dull little voice said to her now.

"What number do you want? . . . No. You have the wrong number."

She put the receiver down gently and her hand went to her heart. "It frightened me," she said.

He smiled a quick smile and immediately resumed his excited monologue. They would fetch him as soon as it was day. For his own protection, they would keep all the knives in a locked drawer. Even at his worst, he presented no danger to other people.

The telephone rang a second time. The same toneless, anxious young voice asked for Charlie.

"You have the incorrect number. I will tell you what you are doing. You are turning the letter 'o' instead of the zero." She hung up again.

They sat down to their unexpected, festive midnight tea. He sipped noisily; his face was flushed; every now and then he raised his glass with a circular motion, so as to make the sugar dissolve more thoroughly. The vein on the side of his bald head stood out conspicuously, and silvery bristles showed on his chin. The birthday present stood on the table. While she poured him another glass of tea, he put on his spectacles and reexamined with pleasure the luminous yellow, green, and red little jars. His clumsy, moist lips spelled out their eloquent labels—apricot, grape, beach plum, quince. He had got to crab apple when the telephone rang again.

May 15, 1948

THE LOTTERY

Shirley Jackson

THE MORNING OF JUNE 27TH was clear and sunny, with the fresh warmth of a full-summer day; the flowers were blossoming profusely and the grass was richly green. The people of the village began to gather in the square, between the post office and the bank, around ten o'clock; in some towns there were so many people that the lottery took two days and had to be started on June 26th, but in this village, where there were only about three hundred people, the whole lottery took only about two hours, so it could begin at ten o'clock in the morning and still be through in time to allow the villagers to get home for noon dinner.

The children assembled first, of course. School was recently over for the summer, and the feeling of liberty sat uneasily on most of them; they tended to gather together quietly for a while before they broke into boisterous play, and their talk was still of the classroom and the teacher, of books and reprimands. Bobby Martin had already stuffed his pockets full of stones, and the other boys soon followed his example, selecting the smoothest and roundest stones; Bobby and Harry Jones and Dickie Delacroix—the villagers pronounced this name "Dellacroy"—eventually made a great pile of stones in one corner of the square and guarded it against the raids of the other boys. The girls stood aside, talking among themselves, looking over their shoulders at the boys, and the very small children rolled in the dust or clung to the hands of their older brothers or sisters.

Soon the men began to gather, surveying their own children, speaking of planting and rain, tractors and taxes. They stood together, away from the pile of stones in the corner, and their jokes were quiet and they smiled rather than laughed. The women, wearing faded house dresses and sweaters, came shortly after their menfolk. They greeted one another and exchanged bits of gossip as they went to join their husbands. Soon the women, standing by their husbands, began to call to their children, and the children came reluctantly, having to be called four or five times. Bobby Martin ducked under his mother's grasping hand and ran, laughing, back to the pile of stones. His father spoke up sharply, and Bobby came quickly and took his place between his father and his oldest brother.

The lottery was conducted—as were the square dances, the teen-age club, the Halloween program—by Mr. Summers, who had time and energy to devote to civic activities. He was a round-faced, jovial man and he ran the coal business, and people were sorry for him, because he had no children and his wife was a scold. When he arrived in the square, carrying the black wooden box, there was a murmur of conversation among the villagers, and he waved and called, "Little late today, folks." The postmaster, Mr. Graves, followed him, carrying a three-legged stool, and the stool was put in the center of the square and Mr. Summers set the black box down on it. The villagers kept their distance, leaving a space between themselves and the stool, and when Mr. Summers said, "Some of you fellows want to give me a hand?," there was a hesitation before two men, Mr. Martin and his oldest son, Baxter, came forward to hold the box steady on the stool while Mr. Summers stirred up the papers inside it.

The original paraphernalia for the lottery had been lost long ago, and the black box now resting on the stool had been put into use even before Old Man Warner, the oldest man in town, was born. Mr. Summers spoke frequently to the villagers about making a new box, but no one liked to upset even as much tradition as was represented by the black box. There was a story that the present box had been made with some pieces of the box that had preceded it, the one that had been constructed when the first people settled down to make a village here. Every year, after the lottery, Mr. Summers began talking again about a new box, but every year the subject was allowed to fade off without anything's being done. The black box grew shabbier each year; by now it was no longer completely black but splintered badly along one side to show the original wood color, and in some places faded or stained.

Mr. Martin and his oldest son, Baxter, held the black box securely on the stool until Mr. Summers had stirred the papers thoroughly with his hand. Because so much of the ritual had been forgotten or discarded,

Mr. Summers had been successful in having slips of paper substituted for the chips of wood that had been used for generations. Chips of wood, Mr. Summers had argued, had been all very well when the village was tiny, but now that the population was more than three hundred and likely to keep on growing, it was necessary to use something that would fit more easily into the black box. The night before the lottery, Mr. Summers and Mr. Graves made up the slips of paper and put them into the box, and it was then taken to the safe of Mr. Summers' coal company and locked up until Mr. Summers was ready to take it to the square next morning. The rest of the year, the box was put away, sometimes one place, sometimes another; it had spent one year in Mr. Graves' barn and another year underfoot in the post office, and sometimes it was set on a shelf in the Martin grocery and left there.

There was a great deal of fussing to be done before Mr. Summers declared the lottery open. There were the lists to make up—of heads of families, heads of households in each family, members of each household in each family. There was the proper swearing-in of Mr. Summers by the postmaster, as the official of the lottery; at one time, some people remembered, there had been a recital of some sort, performed by the official of the lottery, a perfunctory, tuneless chant that had been rattled off duly each year; some people believed that the official of the lottery used to stand just so when he said or sang it, others believed that he was supposed to walk among the people, but years and years ago this part of the ritual had been allowed to lapse. There had been, also, a ritual salute, which the official of the lottery had had to use in addressing each person who came up to draw from the box, but this also had changed with time, until now it was felt necessary only for the official to speak to each person approaching. Mr. Summers was very good at all this; in his clean white shirt and blue jeans, with one hand resting carelessly on the black box, he seemed very proper and important as he talked interminably to Mr. Graves and the Martins.

Just as Mr. Summers finally left off talking and turned to the assembled villagers, Mrs. Hutchinson came hurriedly along the path to the square, her sweater thrown over her shoulders, and slid into place in the back of the crowd. "Clean forgot what day it was," she said to Mrs. Delacroix, who stood next to her, and they both laughed softly. "Thought my old man was out back stacking wood," Mrs. Hutchinson went on, "and then I looked out the window and the kids was gone, and then I remembered it was the twenty-seventh and came a-running." She dried her hands on her apron, and Mrs. Delacroix said, "You're in time, though. They're still talking away up there."

Mrs. Hutchinson craned her neck to see through the crowd and found her husband and children standing near the front. She tapped Mrs. Delacroix on the arm as a farewell and began to make her way through the crowd. The people separated good-humoredly to let her through; two or three people said, in voices just loud enough to be heard across the crowd, "Here comes your Mrs., Hutchinson," and "Bill, she made it after all." Mrs. Hutchinson reached her husband, and Mr. Summers, who had been waiting, said cheerfully, "Thought we were going to have to get on without you, Tessie." Mrs. Hutchinson said, grinning, "Wouldn't have me leave m'dishes in the sink, now, would you, Joe?," and soft laughter ran through the crowd as the people stirred back into position after Mrs. Hutchinson's arrival.

"Well, now," Mr. Summers said soberly, "guess we better get started, get this over with, so's we can go back to work. Anybody ain't here?"

"Dunbar," several people said. "Dunbar, Dunbar."

Mr. Summers consulted his list. "Clyde Dunbar," he said. "That's right. He's broke his leg, hasn't he? Who's drawing for him?"

"Me, I guess," a woman said, and Mr. Summers turned to look at her. "Wife draws for her husband," Mr. Summers said. "Don't you have a grown boy to do it for you, Janey?" Although Mr. Summers and everyone else in the village knew the answer perfectly well, it was the business of the official of the lottery to ask such questions formally. Mr. Summers waited with an expression of polite interest while Mrs. Dunbar answered.

"Horace's not but sixteen yet," Mrs. Dunbar said regretfully. "Guess I gotta fill in for the old man this year."

"Right," Mr. Summers said. He made a note on the list he was holding. Then he asked, "Watson boy drawing this year?"

A tall boy in the crowd raised his hand. "Here," he said. "I'm drawing for m'mother and me." He blinked his eyes nervously and ducked his head as several voices in the crowd said things like "Good fellow, Jack," and "Glad to see your mother's got a man to do it."

"Well," Mr. Summers said, "guess that's everyone. Old Man Warner make it?"

"Here," a voice said, and Mr. Summers nodded.

· · ·

A sudden hush fell on the crowd as Mr. Summers cleared his throat and looked at the list. "All ready?" he called. "Now, I'll read the names—heads of families first—and the men come up and take a paper out of the box. Keep the paper folded in your hand without looking at it until everyone has had a turn. Everything clear?"

The people had done it so many times that they only half listened to the directions; most of them were quiet, wetting their lips, not looking around. Then Mr. Summers raised one hand high and said, "Adams." A man disengaged himself from the crowd and came forward. "Hi, Steve," Mr. Summers said, and Mr. Adams said, "Hi, Joe." They grinned at one another humorlessly and nervously. Then Mr. Adams reached into the black box and took out a folded paper. He held it firmly by one corner as he turned and went hastily back to his place in the crowd, where he stood a little apart from his family, not looking down at his hand.

"Allen," Mr. Summers said. "Anderson. . . . Bentham."

"Seems like there's no time at all between lotteries any more," Mrs. Delacroix said to Mrs. Graves in the back row. "Seems like we got through with the last one only last week."

"Time sure goes fast," Mrs. Graves said.

"Clark. . . . Delacroix."

"There goes my old man," Mrs. Delacroix said. She held her breath while her husband went forward.

"Dunbar," Mr. Summers said, and Mrs. Dunbar went steadily to the box while one of the women said, "Go on, Janey," and another said, "There she goes."

"We're next," Mrs. Graves said. She watched while Mr. Graves came around from the side of the box, greeted Mr. Summers gravely, and selected a slip of paper from the box. By now, all through the crowd there were men holding the small folded papers in their large hands, turning them over and over nervously. Mrs. Dunbar and her two sons stood together, Mrs. Dunbar holding the slip of paper.

"Harburt. . . . Hutchinson."

"Get up there, Bill," Mrs. Hutchinson said, and the people near her laughed.

"Jones."

"They do say," Mr. Adams said to Old Man Warner, who stood next to him, "that over in the north village they're talking of giving up the lottery."

Old Man Warner snorted. "Pack of crazy fools," he said. "Listening to the young folks, nothing's good enough for *them*. Next thing you know, they'll be wanting to go back to living in caves, nobody work any more, live *that* way for a while. Used to be a saying about 'Lottery in June, corn be heavy soon.' First thing you know, we'd all be eating stewed chickweed and acorns. There's *always* been a lottery," he added petulantly. "Bad enough to see young Joe Summers up there joking with everybody."

"Some places have already quit lotteries," Mrs. Adams said.

"Nothing but trouble in *that*," Old Man Warner said stoutly. "Pack of young fools."

"Martin." And Bobby Martin watched his father go forward. "Overdyke. . . . Percy."

"I wish they'd hurry," Mrs. Dunbar said to her older son. "I wish they'd hurry."

"They're almost through," her son said.

"You get ready to run tell Dad," Mrs. Dunbar said.

Mr. Summers called his own name and then stepped forward precisely and selected a slip from the box. Then he called, "Warner."

"Seventy-seventh year I been in the lottery," Old Man Warner said as he went through the crowd. "Seventy-seventh time."

"Watson." The tall boy came awkwardly through the crowd. Someone said, "Don't be nervous, Jack," and Mr. Summers said, "Take your time, son."

"Zanini."

· · ·

After that, there was a long pause, a breathless pause, until Mr. Summers, holding his slip of paper in the air, said, "All right, fellows." For a minute, no one moved, and then all the slips of paper were opened. Suddenly, all the women began to speak at once, saying, "Who is it?," "Who's got it?," "Is it the Dunbars?," "Is it the Watsons?" Then the voices began to say, "It's Hutchinson. It's Bill," "Bill Hutchinson's got it."

"Go tell your father," Mrs. Dunbar said to her older son.

People began to look around to see the Hutchinsons. Bill Hutchinson was standing quiet, staring down at the paper in his hand. Suddenly, Tessie Hutchinson shouted to Mr. Summers, "You didn't give him time enough to take any paper he wanted. I saw you. It wasn't fair!"

"Be a good sport, Tessie," Mrs. Delacroix called, and Mrs. Graves said, "All of us took the same chance."

"Shut up, Tessie," Bill Hutchinson said.

"Well, everyone," Mr. Summers said, "that was done pretty fast, and now we've got to be hurrying a little more to get done in time." He consulted his next list. "Bill," he said, "you draw for the Hutchinson family. You got any other households in the Hutchinsons?"

"There's Don and Eva," Mrs. Hutchinson yelled. "Make *them* take their chance!"

"Daughters draw with their husbands' families, Tessie," Mr. Summers said gently. "You know that as well as anyone else."

"It wasn't *fair*," Tessie said.

"I guess not, Joe," Bill Hutchinson said regretfully. "My daughter draws with her husband's family, that's only fair. And I've got no other family except the kids."

"Then, as far as drawing for families is concerned, it's you," Mr. Summers said in explanation, "and as far as drawing for households is concerned, that's you, too. Right?"

"Right," Bill Hutchinson said.

"How many kids, Bill?" Mr. Summers asked formally.

"Three," Bill Hutchinson said. "There's Bill, Jr., and Nancy, and little Dave. And Tessie and me."

"All right, then," Mr. Summers said. "Harry, you got their tickets back?"

Mr. Graves nodded and held up the slips of paper. "Put them in the box, then," Mr. Summers directed. "Take Bill's and put it in."

"I think we ought to start over," Mrs. Hutchinson said, as quietly as she could. "I tell you it wasn't *fair*. You didn't give him time enough to choose. *Every*body saw that."

Mr. Graves had selected the five slips and put them in the box, and he dropped all the papers but those onto the ground, where the breeze caught them and lifted them off.

"Listen, everybody," Mrs. Hutchinson was saying to the people around her.

"Ready, Bill?" Mr. Summers asked, and Bill Hutchinson, with one quick glance around at his wife and children, nodded.

"Remember," Mr. Summers said, "take the slips and keep them folded until each person has taken one. Harry, you help little Dave." Mr. Graves took the hand of the little boy, who came willingly with him up to the box. "Take a paper out of the box, Davy," Mr. Summers said. Davy put his hand into the box and laughed. "Take just *one* paper," Mr. Summers said. "Harry, you hold it for him." Mr. Graves took the child's hand and removed the folded paper from the tight fist and held it while little Dave stood next to him and looked up at him wonderingly.

"Nancy next," Mr. Summers said. Nancy was twelve, and her school friends breathed heavily as she went forward, switching her skirt, and took a slip daintily from the box. "Bill, Jr.," Mr. Summers said, and Billy, his face red and his feet overlarge, nearly knocked the box over as he got a paper out. "Tessie," Mr. Summers said. She hesitated for a minute, looking around defiantly, and then set her lips and went up to the box. She snatched a paper out and held it behind her.

"Bill," Mr. Summers said, and Bill Hutchinson reached into the box and felt around, bringing his hand out at last with the slip of paper in it.

The crowd was quiet. A girl whispered, "I hope it's not Nancy," and the sound of the whisper reached the edges of the crowd.

"It's not the way it used to be," Old Man Warner said clearly. "People ain't the way they used to be."

"All right," Mr. Summers said. "Open the papers. Harry, you open little Dave's."

Mr. Graves opened the slip of paper and there was a general sigh through the crowd as he held it up and everyone could see that it was blank. Nancy and Bill, Jr., opened theirs at the same time, and both beamed and laughed, turning around to the crowd and holding their slips of paper above their heads.

"Tessie," Mr. Summers said. There was a pause, and then Mr. Summers looked at Bill Hutchinson, and Bill unfolded his paper and showed it. It was blank.

"It's Tessie," Mr. Summers said, and his voice was hushed. "Show us her paper, Bill."

Bill Hutchinson went over to his wife and forced the slip of paper out of her hand. It had a black spot on it, the black spot Mr. Summers had made the night before with the heavy pencil in the coal-company office. Bill Hutchinson held it up, and there was a stir in the crowd.

"All right, folks," Mr. Summers said. "Let's finish quickly."

Although the villagers had forgotten the ritual and lost the original black box, they still remembered to use stones. The pile of stones the boys had made earlier was ready; there were stones on the ground with the blowing scraps of paper that had come out of the box. Mrs. Delacroix selected a stone so large she had to pick it up with both hands and turned to Mrs. Dunbar. "Come on," she said. "Hurry up."

Mrs. Dunbar had small stones in both hands, and she said, gasping for breath, "I can't run at all. You'll have to go ahead and I'll catch up with you."

The children had stones already, and someone gave little Davy Hutchinson a few pebbles.

Tessie Hutchinson was in the center of a cleared space by now, and she held her hands out desperately as the villagers moved in on her. "It isn't fair," she said. A stone hit her on the side of the head.

Old Man Warner was saying, "Come on, come on, everyone." Steve Adams was in the front of the crowd of villagers, with Mrs. Graves beside him.

"It isn't fair, it isn't right," Mrs. Hutchinson screamed, and then they were upon her.

June 26, 1948

THE BEGINNING OF A STORY

Elizabeth Taylor

THEY COULD HEAR THE BREATHING through the wall. Ronny sat watching Marian, who had her fingers in her ears as she read. Sometimes he leaned forward and reached for a log and put it on the fire, and for a second her eyes would dwell on his movements, on his young, bony wrist shot out of his sleeve, and then, like a lighthouse swinging its beam away, she would withdraw her attention and go back to her book.

A long pause in the breathing would make them glance at one another questioningly, and then, as it was hoarsely resumed, they would fall away from one another again, he to his silent building of the fire and she to her solemn reading of *Lady Audley's Secret.*

He thought of his mother, Enid, in the next room, sitting at her own mother's deathbed, and he tried to imagine her feelings, but her behavior had been so calm all through his grandmother's illness that he could not. It is different for the older ones, he thought, for they are used to people dying. More readily, he could picture his father at the pub, accepting drinks and easy sympathy. "Nothing I can do," he would be saying. "You only feel in the way." Tomorrow night, perhaps, "a happy release" would be his comfortable refrain, and solemnly, over their beer, they would all agree.

Once, Marian said to Ronny, "Why don't you get something to do?"

"Such as what?"

"Oh, don't ask me. It's not my affair." These last few days, Marian liked, as often as she could, to disassociate herself from the family. As soon as the grandmother became ill, the other lodger, a girl from the same factory as Marian, had left. Marian had stayed on, but with her fingers stuck in her ears, or going about with a blank immunity, polite and distant to Enid. They were landlady and lodger to one another, no more, Marian constantly implied.

"Well, you could make some tea," she said at last to Ronny, feeling exasperation at his silent contemplation of her. He moved obediently and began to unhook cups from the dresser without a sound, setting them carefully in their saucers on a tray—the pink-and-gilt one with the moss rose for Marian, a large white one with a gold clover leaf for his mother.

"You take it in to her," he said when the tea was ready. He had a reason for asking her, wishing to test his belief that Marian was afraid to go into that other room. She guessed this, and snapped her book shut.

"Lazy little swine," she said, and took up his mother's cup.

. . .

Enid rose as Marian opened the door. The room was bright and warm. It was the front room, and the Sunday furniture had been moved to make space for the bed. The old woman was half sitting up, but her head was thrown back upon a heap of pillows. Her arms were stretched out over the counterpane, just as her daughter had arranged them. Her mouth, without teeth, was a gray cavern. Except for the breathing, she might have been dead.

Enid had been sitting up with her for nights, and she stood stiffly now, holding the cup of tea, her eyes dark with fatigue. I ought to offer, thought Marian, but I'd be terrified to be left alone in here.

She went back to Ronny, who looked at her now with respect added to all the other expressions on his face. His father had come back from the pub and was spreading his hairy hands over the fire to get warm. He was beery and lugubrious. They were all afraid of Enid. At any sound from the other room, they flicked glances at one another.

"Poor old gel," said Ronny's father over and over again. "Might as well get to bed, Marian. No need for you to make yourself ill."

Ronny found his father's way of speaking and his look at the girl intolerable.

Marian had been waiting for someone to make the suggestion. "Well . . ." She hesitated. "No sense, I suppose . . ."

"That's right," said the older man.

She went out to the sink in the scullery and slipped her shoulders out of her blouse. She soaped a flannel under the icy water and passed it quickly over her throat, gathering up her hair at the back to wash her neck, curving one arm, then the other, over her head as she soaped her armpits.

Ronny and his father sat beside the fire, listening to the water splashing into the bowl. When they heard the wooden sound as Marian pulled at the roller towel, the older man glanced at the door and moved, stirred by the thought of the young girl.

It was one of the moments of hatred that the son often felt for him, but it seemed to make no impression on his father.

Marian came in, fresh, her face shiny, her blouse carelessly buttoned. "Well, good night," she said, and opened the door behind which stairs led up to the little bedrooms. "If you want me, you know where I am."

There was no sophistication in either man to see the ambiguity of her words; they simply took them to mean what she intended.

The door closed, and they heard her creak upstairs and overhead. They went on sitting by the fire and neither spoke. Occasional faint beer smells came from the father. It did not occur to him to go into the other room to his wife. Ronny took the tea things into the scullery and washed up. It was dark out there and lit by a very small oil lamp. He remained there for as long as he thought he could without being questioned. The tap dripped into the sink. He smelled the soap she had used. He could no longer hear the breathing.

Marian lay between the rough twill sheets, shivering. Her feet were like ice, although she had rolled them in her cardigan. The only hot-water bottle was in the bed downstairs. She hated this house but had no energy to move from it. Or had she stayed because of that sickened curiosity that always forced her to linger by hearses while coffins were carried out? Ron, too, she thought—it isn't right for us. We're young. In the mornings, I'm not fit for work. If only Enid knew how the girls at the factory went on: "What's happening now?" "The blinds down yet?" "How awful for you!" She drew up her knees, yawned, and crossed her arms on her breast. The young slip into the first attitude with beautiful ease and relaxation.

. . .

Because the house had been so quiet for days, the sound of a door bursting open, a chair scraped hurriedly back, shocked Marian out of sleep, and she lay trembling, her feet still entangled in the cardigan. She felt that it was about halfway through the night, but could not be sure. She heard Ron stumbling upstairs, tapping on her door. She put on her rain-coat over her nightgown and went out to him.

"It's Gran," he said. "She's gone."

"What had I better do?" she asked in panic, with no example before her of how she should behave. He had wakened her but did not know why.

"Ron!" Enid came to the bottom of the stairs and called up. The light from the room behind her threw a faint nimbus around her head.

"Yes, Mother," he said, looking down at her.

"Did you wake Marian?"

"Yes." He answered guiltily, but evidently she thought his action right and proper.

"You will have to go for Mrs. Turner," his mother said.

"Why?"

"She—she's expecting you."

"In the middle of the night?"

"Yes. Right away—now." She turned away from the bottom of the stairs.

"Who is Mrs. Turner?" Marian whispered.

"I think— She lays people out." Ronny felt shame and uneasiness at his words, which seemed to him crude, obscene.

The girl covered her face with her hands. "Oh, life's horrible."

"No, it's death, not life."

"Don't leave me."

"Come with me, then."

"Is it far?"

"No, not far. Hurry."

"Stand there by the door while I get ready."

Marian moved into the dark bedroom, and he stood leaning against the doorframe, waiting, with his arms folded across his chest. She came back quickly, wearing the raincoat, a scarf tied over her head.

They went downstairs into the bright kitchen, where Enid stood fix-ing candles into brass holders while her husband poured some brandy from an almost empty bottle into a glass. Enid drowned the brandy with warm water from the kettle and drank it off swiftly, her dark eyes ex-pressionless.

"Give some to the children," she said, without thinking. They stiffened at the word "children" but took their brandy-and-water and sipped it.

"It's a cold night," said Enid. "Now, go quickly."

"Marian's coming with me."

"So I see," said Enid. Her husband drank the last spoonful from the bottle, neat. "The end house, Lorne Street, right-hand side, by the Rose and Crown," she said, turning back to the other room.

The fumes of the brandy kindled in Ron's and Marian's breasts. "Remember that," he said. "The end house." He unlatched the back door.

"Next the Rose and Crown," she added. They slipped out into the beautiful, shocking air of the night.

. . .

When Ronny shone his torch down, they could see the yellow hands of the leaves lying on the dark, wet pavements. Now there was only a flick of moisture in the air. He had taken her arm, and they walked alone in the streets, which flowed like black rivers. She wished that they might go on forever and never turn back toward that house. Or she would like it to be broad daylight, so that she could be at work, giggling about it all with the girls. ("Go on, Marian!" "How awful for you!")

His arm was pressed against her ribs. Sometimes she shivered from the cold and squeezed him to her. Down streets and around corners they went. Not far away, goods trains shunted up and down. Once, she stumbled over a curb, and in saving her he felt the sweet curve of her breast against his arm and walked gaily and with elation, filled with excitement and delight, swinging the beam of the torch from side to side, thinking it was the happiest evening of his life, seeing the future opening out suddenly, like a fan, revealing all at once the wonder of human relationships.

"The Rose and Crown," she whispered. The building was shuttered for the night, the beer smells all washed away by the rain, the signboard creaking in the wind.

"The next house then." She felt tensed up, but he was relaxed and confident.

"I've forgotten the name," she said.

"Turner."

They went up a short path onto a dark porch and knocked at the door. After a moment, a window at the front of the house was thrown up and a woman's voice called out. They stepped back into the garden and looked up.

"Who is it?" the voice asked.

"We're from Mrs. Baker's," Ron said.

"Poor soul! She's gone, then, at last. How's your mother?"

Ronny considered this and then said, "She's tired."

"She will be. Wait there, and I'll come along with you." She disappeared and the window was slammed down.

"She seemed an ordinary sort of woman," whispered Marian.

They drew back into the shelter of the porch and waited. No sounds came from the house, but a smell of stuffiness seemed to drift out through the letter slot in the door.

"Suppose she goes back to bed and leaves us here?" Marian asked, and began to giggle. She put her mouth against his shoulder to stifle the little giggles, and he put his arm around her. She lifted her papery-white face in the darkness and they kissed. The word "bliss" came into his mind, and he tasted it slowly on his tongue, as if it were a sweet food. Platitudes began to come true for them, but they could not consider them as such.

Suddenly, a step sounded on the other side of the door, bolts were slid back with difficulty, a chain rattled.

"Here we are!" said the brisk voice. The woman stepped out onto the porch, putting on a pair of fur gloves and looking up at the night sky and the flocks of curdy, scudding clouds. "It's a sad time," she said. "A very sad time for your poor mum and dad. Come on, then, lad, you lead the way. Quick, sharp!"

And now the footsteps of the three of them rang out metallically upon the paving stones as they walked between the dark and eyeless cliffs of the houses.

October 29, 1949

THE LADDER

V. S. Pritchett

"WE HAD THE BUILDERS IN AT THE TIME," my father says in his accurate way, if he ever mentions his second marriage, the one that so quickly went wrong. "And," he says, clearing a small apology from his throat, as though preparing to say something immodest, "we happened to be without stairs."

It is true. I remember that summer. I was fifteen years old. I came home from Miss Compton's School at the end of the term, and when I got to our place in Devonshire not only had my mother gone but the stairs had gone, too. There was no staircase in the house.

We lived in an old crab-colored cottage, with long windows under the eaves that looked like eyes half closed against the sun. Now, when I got out of the car, I saw scaffolding over the front door and two heaps of sand and mortar on the crazy paving, which my father asked me not to tread in, because it would "make work for Janey." (This was the name he called his second wife.) I went inside. Imagine my astonishment. The little hall had vanished, the ceiling had gone; you could see up to the roof; the wall on one side had been stripped to the brick, and on the other hung a long curtain of builder's sheets. "Where are the stairs?" I said. "What have you done with the stairs?" I was at the laughing age.

A mild, trim voice spoke above our heads. "Ah, I know that laugh," the voice said sweetly and archly. There was Miss Richards, or, I should say, my father's second wife, standing behind a builder's rope on what used to be the landing, which now stuck out precariously without banisters, like the portion of a ship's deck. The floor appeared to have been sawed off. She used to be my father's secretary before the divorce, and I had often seen her in my father's office, but now she had changed. Her fair hair was now fluffed out, and she wore a fussed and shiny brown dress that was quite unsuitable for the country. The only definite idea of what marriage would be like must have come to her from magazines; my father was a successful man, and she supposed she would always be going to cocktail parties, and at twelve in the morning on went the dress.

I remember how odd they both looked, she up above and my father down below, and both apologizing to me. The builders had taken the old staircase out two days before, they said, and had promised to put the new one in against the far wall of the room, behind the dust sheets, before I got back from school. But they had not kept their promise.

"We go up by the ladder," said my father, cutting his wife short, for she was apologizing too much, as if she were speaking to one of his customers.

He pointed. At that moment, his wife was stepping to the end of the landing, where a short ladder, with a post to hold on to at the top as one stepped on the first rung, sloped to the ground.

"It's horrible!" called my stepmother.

My father and I watched her come down. She came to the post and turned round, not sure whether she ought to come down the ladder frontward or backward.

"Backward!" called my father . . . "No, the other hand on the post!" My stepmother blushed fondly and gave him a look of fear. She put one foot on the top rung and then took her foot back and put the other one there, and then pouted. It was only eight feet from the ground; at school, we climbed halfway up the gym walls on the bars. I remembered her as a quick and practical woman at the office; she was now, I was sure, playing at being weak and dependent.

"My hands," she said a moment later, looking at the dust on her hands as she grasped the top rung.

My father and I stopped where we were and watched her. She put one leg out too high, as if, artlessly, she were showing us the leg first. And she was; she was a plain woman, and her legs (she used to say) were her "nicest thing." This was the only coquetry she had. She looked like one of those insects that try the air around them with their feelers before they move. I was surprised that my father (who had always been formally attentive to my mother, especially when he was angry, and had almost bowed to me when he met me at the station and helped me in and out of the car) did not go to help her. I saw an expression of obstinacy on his face.

"You're at the bottom," he said at last. "Only two more steps."

"Oh dear," said my stepmother, getting off the last rung onto the floor, and she turned with her small chin raised, offering us her helplessness for admiration. She came to me and kissed me and said, "Doesn't she look lovely? You are growing into a woman."

"Nonsense," said my father.

And, in fear of being a woman and yet pleased by what she said, I took my father's arm. "Is that what we have to do? Is that how we get to bed?" I said.

"It's only until Monday," my father said.

They both of them looked ashamed, as though by having the stairs removed they had done something foolish. My father tried to conceal this by an air of modest importance. They seemed a very modest couple. Both of them looked shorter to me since their marriage; I was rather shocked by this. *She* seemed to have made him shorter. I had always thought of my father as a dark, vain, terse man, very logical and never giving in to anyone. He seemed much less important now his secretary was in the house.

"It is easy," I said, and I went to the ladder and was up it in a moment.

"Mind!" called my stepmother.

But in a moment I was down again, laughing. While I was coming down, I heard my stepmother say quietly to my father, "What legs. She is growing."

My legs and my laugh! I did not think that my father's secretary had the right to say anything about me. She was not my mother.

. . .

After this, my father took me around the house. I looked behind me once or twice as I walked. On one of my shoes was some of the sand he had warned me about. I don't know how it got on my shoe. It was rather funny seeing this one sandy footmark making work for Janey wherever I went.

My father took me through the dust curtains into the dining room and then to the far wall, where the staircase was going to be.

"Why have you done it?" I asked. He and I were alone.

"The house has wanted it for years," he said. "It ought to have been done years ago."

I did not say anything. When my mother was there, she was always complaining about the house, saying it was poky, barbarous—I can hear her voice now saying "Barbarous," as if it were the name of some terrifying and savage queen—and my father had always refused to alter any-thing. Barbarous—I used to think of that word as my mother's name.

"Does Janey like it?" I asked.

My father hardened at this question. He seemed to be saying, "What has it got to do with Janey?" But what he said was—and he spoke with amusement, with a look of quiet scorn—"She liked it as it was."

"I did, too," I said.

I then saw—but, no, I did not really understand this at the time; it is something I understand now I am older—that my father was not altering the house for Janey's sake. She hated the whole place, because my mother had been there, but was too tired by her earlier life in his office, fifteen years of it, too unsure of herself, to say anything. It was an act of amends to my mother. He was punishing Janey by getting in builders and mak-ing everyone uncomfortable and miserable; he was creating an emotional scene with himself. He was annoying Janey with what my mother had so maddeningly wanted and he would not give her.

. . .

After my father had shown me the house, I said I would go and see Janey getting lunch ready.

"I shouldn't do that," he said. "It will delay her. Lunch is just ready. Or should be." He looked at his watch.

We went to the sitting room, and while we waited, I sat in the green chair and he asked me questions about school and we went on to talk about the holidays. But when I answered, I could see he was not listening to me but trying to catch sounds of Janey moving in the kitchen. Occa-sionally there were sounds; something gave an explosive fizz in a hot pan, and a saucepan lid fell. This made a loud noise and the lid spun a long time on the stone floor. The sound stopped our talk.

"Janey is not used to the kitchen," said my father. I smiled very close to my lips. I did not want my father to see it, but he looked at me and he smiled by accident, too. There was a sudden understanding between us.

"I will go and see," I said.

He raised his hand to stop me, but I went.

It was natural. For fifteen years, Janey had been my father's secretary. She had worked in an office. I remember when I went there when I was young she used to come into the room with an earnest and hushed air, leaning her head a little sidewise and turning three-quarter face toward my father, at his desk, leaning forward to guess at what he wanted. I admired the great knowledge she had of his affairs, the way she carried letters, how quickly she picked up the telephone when it rang, the authority of her voice. Her strength had been that she was impersonal. She had lost that in her marriage. As his wife, she had no behavior. When we were talking, she raised her low bosom, which had become round and ducklike, with a sigh and smiled at my father with a tentative, expectant fondness. After fifteen years, a life had ended; she was resting.

But Janey had not lost her office behavior; that she now kept for the kitchen. The moment I went to the kitchen, I saw her walking to the stove, where the saucepans were throbbing too hard. She was walking exactly as she had walked toward my father at his desk. The stove had taken my father's place. She went up to it with impersonal inquiry, as if to anticipate what it wanted; she appeared to be offering a pile of plates to be warmed as if they were a pile of letters. She seemed baffled because it could not speak. When one of the saucepans boiled over, she ran to it and lifted it off, suddenly and too high, in her telephone movement; the water spilled at once. On the table beside the stove were basins and pans she was using, and she had them all spread out in an orderly way, like typing; she went from one to the other with the careful look of inquiry she used to give to the things she was filing. It was not a method suitable to a kitchen.

When I came in, she put down the pan she was holding and stopped everything—as she would have done in the office—to talk to me about what she was doing. She was very nice about my hair, which I had had cut; it made me look older and I liked it better. But blue smoke rose behind her as we talked. She did not notice it.

No, it was not the way to cook a meal.

I went back to my father.

"I didn't want to be in the way," I said.

"Extraordinary," he said, looking at his watch. "I must just go and hurry Janey up."

He was astonished that a woman so brisk in an office should be languid and dependent in a house.

"She is just bringing it in," I said. "The potatoes are ready. They are on the table. I saw them."

"On the table?" he said. "Getting cold?"

"On the kitchen table," I said.

"That doesn't prevent them getting cold," he said. My father was a sarcastic man.

I walked about the room humming. My father's exasperation did not last. It gave way to a new thing in his voice—resignation.

"We will wait, if you do not mind," he said to me. "Janey is slow. And by the way," he said, lowering his voice a little, "I shouldn't mention we passed the Leonards in the road when I brought you up from the station."

I was surprised. "Not the Leonards?" I said.

"They were friends of your mother's," he said. "You are old enough to understand. One has to be sometimes a little tactful. Janey sometimes feels . . ."

I looked at my father. He had altered in many ways. Giving me this secret, his small, brown eyes gave a brilliant flash, and I opened my blue eyes very wide and gravely to receive it. He had changed. His rough, black hair was clipped closer at the ears, and he had that too-young look that middle-aged men sometimes have, for by certain lines it can be seen that they are not as young as their faces. Marks like minutes on the face of a clock showed at the corners of his eyes, his nose, his mouth; he was much thinner; his face had hardened. He had often been angry and sarcastic, sulking and abrupt, when my mother was with us, but I had never seen him before, as he was now, blank-faced, ironical, and set in impatient boredom. After he spoke, he had actually been hissing a tune privately through his teeth at the corner of his mouth.

At this moment, Janey came in smiling too much and said lunch was ready.

"Oh," I laughed when we got into the dining room, "it is like—it is like France." Miss Richards—how she would sit in the house in her best clothes, like a visitor, expectant, forgetful, stunned by leisure, watchful, wronged and jealous to the point of tears.

. . .

Perhaps if the builders had come, as they had promised, on the Monday, my stepmother's story would have been different.

"I am so sorry we are in such a mess," she said to me that morning at breakfast. She had said it many times, as if she thought I regarded the ladder as her failure.

"It's fun," I said. "It's like being on a ship."

"You keep on saying that," my stepmother said, looking at me in a very worried way, as if trying to work out the hidden meaning of my remark. "You've never been on a ship."

"To France," I said. "When I was a child."

"Oh, yes," said my stepmother.

"I hate mess," said my stepmother to both of us, getting up. In a prosaic person emotion looks grotesque, like clothes suddenly become too large.

"Do leave us alone," my father said.

There was a small scene after this. My father did not mean by "us" himself and me, as she chose to think; he was simply speaking of himself and he had spoken very mildly. My stepmother marched out of the room. Presently, we heard her upstairs. She must have been very upset to have faced going up the ladder.

"Come on," said my father. "I suppose there's nothing for it. I'll get the car out. We will go to the builders'."

He called up to her that we were going and asked if she'd like to go with us.

Oh, it was a terrible holiday. When I grew up and was myself married, my father said, "It was a very difficult summer. You didn't realize. You were only a schoolgirl. It was a mistake." And then he corrected himself. I mean that. My father was always making himself more correct; it was his chief vanity that he understood his own behavior.

"I happened," he said—this was the correction—"to make a very foolish mistake." Whenever he used the phrase "I happened," my father's face seemed to dry up and become distant; he was congratulating himself. Not on the mistake, of course, but on being the first to put his finger on it. "I happen to know," "I happen to have seen"—it was this incidental rightness, the footnote of inside knowledge on innumerable minor issues, and his fatal wrongness, in a large, obstinate, principled way, about anything important, that, I think, made my beautiful and dishonest mother leave him. She was a tall woman, taller than he, with the eyes of a cat, shrugging her shoulders, curving her long, graceful back to be stroked, and with a wide, champagne laugh.

My father had a clipped-back, monkeyish appearance and that faint grin of the bounder one sees in the harder-looking monkeys that are without melancholy or sensibility; this had attracted my mother, but very soon his youthful bounce gave place to a kind of meddling honesty and she found him dull. And, of course, ruthless. The promptness of his second marriage, perhaps, was to teach her a lesson. I imagine him putting his divorce papers away one evening at his office and realizing, when Miss Richards came in to ask if "there is anything more tonight," that here was a woman who was reliable, trained, and, like himself, "happened" to have a lot of inside knowledge.

To get out of the house with my father, to be alone with him! My heart came alive. It seemed to me that this house was not my home any more. If only we could go away, he and I; the country outside seemed to me far more like home than this grotesque divorced house. I stood longing for her not to answer, dreading that she would come down.

My father was not a man to beg her to change her mind. He went out to the garage. My fear of her coming made me stay for a moment. And then (I do not know how the thought came into my head) I went to the ladder and I lifted it away. It was easy to move a short distance, but it began to swing when I tried to lay it down, and I was afraid it would crash. I could not put it on the floor, so I turned it over and over against the other wall, out of reach. Breathlessly, I left the house.

"You've got white on your tunic," said my father as we drove off. "What have you been doing?"

"I rubbed against something," I said.

"Oh, how I love motoring." I laughed beside my father.

"Oh, look at those lovely little rabbits," I said.

"Their little white tails." I laughed.

We passed some hurdles in a field.

"Jumps." I laughed. "I wish I had a pony."

"What would you do?" asked my father.

"Jump," I said to my father.

And then my terrible dreams came back to me. I was frightened. I tried to think of something else, but I could not. I could only see my stepmother on the edge of the landing. I could only hear her giving a scream and going over headfirst. We got into the town and I felt sick. We arrived at the builders' and my father stopped there. Only a girl was in the office, and I heard my father say in his coldest voice, "I happen to have an appointment."

My father came out and we drove off. He was cross.

"Where are we going?" I said when I saw we were not going home.

"To Longwood," he said. "They're working over there."

I thought I would faint. "I—I—" I began.

"What?" my father said.

I could not speak. I began to get red and hot. And then I remembered. I could pray.

It is seven miles to Longwood. My father was a man who enjoyed talking to builders; he planned and replanned with them, built imaginary houses, talked about people. Builders have a large acquaintance with the way people live; my father liked inside knowledge, as I have said. Well, I thought, she is over. She is dead by now. I saw visits to the hospital. I saw my trial.

"She is like you," said the builder, nodding to me. All my life I shall remember his mustache.

"She is like my wife," said my father. "My first wife. I happen to have married twice." He liked puzzling and embarrassing people. "Do you happen to know a tea place near here?" he asked.

"Oh, no," I said. "I don't feel hungry."

But we had tea at Gilling. The river is across the road from the teashop and we stood afterward on the bridge. I surprised my father by climbing the parapet.

"If you jumped," I said to my father, "would you hurt?"

"You'd break your legs," said my father.

Her "nicest thing"!

I shall not describe our drive back to the house, but my father did say, "Janey will be worried. We've been nearly three hours. I'll put the car in afterward."

. . .

When we got back, my father jumped out and went down the path. I got out slowly. I could hardly walk down the path. It is a long path leading across a small lawn, then between two lime trees; there are a few steps down into where the roses are, and across another piece of grass you are at the door. I stopped to listen to the bees in the limes, but I could not wait any longer. I went into the house.

There was my stepmother standing on the landing above the hall. Her face was dark red, her eyes were long and violent, her dress was dusty, and her hands were black with dust. She had just finished screaming something at my father, and her mouth had stayed open after her scream. I thought I could *smell* her anger and her fear the moment I came into the house, but it was really the smell of a burned-out saucepan coming from the kitchen.

"You moved the ladder! Six hours I've been up here. The telephone has been ringing, something has burned on the stove. I might have burned to death. Get me down, get me down! I might have killed my-self. Get me down!" She came to the gap where the ladder ought to have been.

"Don't be silly, Janey," said my father. "I didn't move the ladder. Don't be such a fool. You're still alive."

"Get me down!" Janey cried out. "You liar, you liar, you liar! You did move it!"

My father lifted the ladder, and as he did so, he said, "The builder must have been."

"No one has been!" screamed my stepmother. "I've been alone! Up here!"

"Daddy *isn't* a liar," I said, taking my father's arm.

"Come down," said my father when he had got the ladder in place. "I'm holding it."

And he went up a step or two toward her.

"No!" shrieked Janey.

"Now, come on. Calm yourself," said my father.

"No, no, I tell you!" said Janey.

"All right, you must stay," said my father, and stepped down.

That brought her, of course.

"*I* moved the ladder," I said when she had come down.

"Oh," said Janey, swinging her arm to hit me, but she fainted instead.

. . .

That night, my father came to my room when I was in bed. I had moved my mother's photograph to the bedside table. He was not angry. He was tired out.

"Why did you do it?" he asked.

I did not answer.

"Did you know she was upstairs?" he asked.

I did not reply.

"Stop playing with the sheet," he said. "Look at me. Did you know she was upstairs?"

"Yes," I said.

"You little cat!" he said.

I smiled.

"It was very wrong," he said.

I smiled. Presently he smiled. I laughed.

"It is nothing to laugh at," he said. And suddenly he could not stop himself; he laughed. The door opened and my stepmother looked in while we were both shaking with laughter. My father laughed as if he were laughing for the first time in many years; his bounderish look, sly and bumptious and so delicious, came back to him. The door closed.

He stopped laughing.

"She might have been killed," he said, severe again. And then he remembered what I had asked him on the bridge at Gilling.

I lowered my head.

"You wanted—" he said.

"No, no, no!" I cried, and tears came to my eyes. He put his arm around me.

My mother was a cat, they said, a wicked woman, leaving us like that. I longed for my mother.

Three days later, I went to camp. I apologized to my stepmother and she forgave me. I never saw her again.

November 5, 1949

June. 26, 1948

Editor;

I will never buy the New Yorker again. I resent being tricked into reading perverted stories like "the lottery."

Nathan Koffman

36 Maple St.

Dorchester 21

Mass.

ACKNOWLEDGMENTS

All hands were on deck for this volume. Good thing, too. It was some deck—and those were some hands. They represented a wide span of generations and sensibilities. Some lived through the forties; others were happy to live through the ones who lived through the forties. Special thanks go to Roger Angell, Katia Bachko, Robert P. Baird, Madeleine Baverstam, Pete Canby, Chris Curry, Noah Eaker, Rob Fischer, Sameen Gauhar, Hannah Goldfield, Ann Goldstein, Mary Hawthorne, Neima Jahromi, Susan Kamil, Carolyn Korman, Taylor Lewis, Ruth Margalit, Pam McCarthy, Caitlin McKenna, Wyatt Mitchell, Lynn Oberlander, Erin Overby, Beth Pearson, Tom Perry, Joshua Rothman, Eric Simonoff, Simon M. Sullivan, and Susan Turner. And, of course, to all the worthies whose bylines appear in these pages.

CONTRIBUTORS

JOAN ACOCELLA has written for *The New Yorker* since 1992 and became the magazine's dance critic in 1998. Her books include *Mark Morris* (1993), *Willa Cather and the Politics of Criticism* (2000), and *Twenty-eight Artists and Two Saints* (2007).

CONRAD AIKEN (1889–1973) was a London correspondent for *The New Yorker* in the 1930s. He won a Pulitzer Prize in 1930 for his *Selected Poems* and a National Book Award in 1954 for his *Collected Poems*.

HILTON ALS became a staff writer at *The New Yorker* in 1994 and a theatre critic in 2002. He is the author of *The Women* (1996) and *White Girls* (2013).

W. H. AUDEN (1907–1973) was born in York, England, was educated at Oxford University, and achieved fame as a poet in the 1930s. In 1939 he immigrated to the United States and published his first poem in *The New Yorker*. He won a Pulitzer Prize in 1948 for *The Age of Anxiety* and a National Book Award in 1956 for *The Shield of Achilles*.

S. N. BEHRMAN (1893–1973), a playwright, screenwriter, and biographer, first appeared in *The New Yorker* in 1929 and continued to contribute to the magazine for nearly half a century.

ELIZABETH BISHOP (1911–1979) published her first poem in *The New Yorker* in 1940. She won a Pulitzer Prize in 1956 for *Poems: North & South—A Cold Spring* and was elected to the American Academy of Arts and Letters in 1976.

LOUISE BOGAN (1897–1970) was the poetry editor of *The New Yorker* for nearly forty years. In 1945, she became the first woman to serve as the United States poet laureate. Her books include *Body of This Death* (1923), *Dark Summer* (1929), and *The Sleeping Fury* (1937).

RICHARD O. BOYER (1903–1973) was an American journalist who began contributing to *The New Yorker* in 1931. His books include *Labor's Untold Story* (1955) and *The Legend of John Brown* (1973).

JOHN CHEEVER (1912–1982) sold his first story to *The New Yorker* in 1935 and was a regular contributor of fiction to the magazine until his death. His books include *The Wapshot Chronicle* (1957), *The Wapshot Scandal* (1964), and *Falconer* (1977).

DAN CHIASSON is an associate professor of English at Wellesley College and has written about poetry for *The New Yorker* since 2008. His books include the poetry collections *Where's the Moon, There's the Moon* (2010) and *Bicentennial* (2014), and a book of essays, *One Kind of Everything* (2007).

ROBERT M. COATES (1897–1973) joined the staff of *The New Yorker* in 1929. He coined the term "Abstract Expressionism," in a piece for the magazine in 1946. His books include *The Eater of Darkness* (1926) and *The Outlaw Years* (1930).

MALCOLM COWLEY (1898–1989) was a novelist, poet, and literary critic. He published his first poem in *The New Yorker* in 1941. His books include *Blue Juniata* (1929) and *Exile's Return* (1934).

DAVID DENBY has been a staff writer and film critic at *The New Yorker* since 1998. He is the author of *Great Books* (1996), *American Sucker* (2004), *Snark* (2009), and *Do the Movies Have a Future?* (2012).

CLIFTON FADIMAN (1904–1999) joined *The New Yorker* in 1933 as a books editor. He was a judge for the Book of the Month Club and hosted *Information Please*, a popular radio quiz show. His books include *Party of One* (1955), *Any Number Can Play* (1957), and *Enter Conversing* (1962).

JANET FLANNER (1892–1978) became *The New Yorker*'s Paris correspondent in 1925 and wrote the Letter from Paris column until she retired in 1975. She is the author of *The Cubical City* (1926), *Conversation Pieces* (1942), and *Paris Was Yesterday* (1972).

WOLCOTT GIBBS (1902–1958) joined *The New Yorker* in 1927 as a writer and editor. In 1940, he became the magazine's drama critic, and in 1950 his play *Season in the Sun* (adapted from his earlier book about Fire Island bohemianism) became a Broadway hit.

PHILIP HAMBURGER (1914–2004) was a staff writer at *The New Yorker* from 1939 until his death. He published eight collections of his work, including *Friends Talking in the Night* (1999) and *Matters of State* (2000), and was one of the few staff writers to work for all five of the magazine's editors.

GEOFFREY T. HELLMAN (1907–1977) began reporting for The Talk of the Town in 1929. His books include *How to Disappear for an Hour* (1947), *Mrs. de Peyster's Parties* (1963), *The Smithsonian: Octopus on the Mall* (1966), and *Bankers, Bones and Beetles* (1969).

JOHN HERSEY (1914–1993) sold his first article to *The New Yorker* in 1944 and published some two dozen nonfiction pieces over the next half century. "Hiroshima," his account of six people during the first atomic attack, was the sole article to ever fill the entire editorial space of a single issue. In 1945 he won a Pulitzer Prize for his novel *A Bell for Adano*.

LANGSTON HUGHES (1902–1967) was an American poet and novelist, and a leader of the Harlem Renaissance. He published his first short story in *The New Yorker* in 1934. His books include *Fine Clothes to the Jew* (1927), *Not Without Laughter* (1930), and *Montage of a Dream Deferred* (1951).

SHIRLEY JACKSON (1916–1965) contributed her first story to *The New Yorker* in 1944. She wrote six novels, including *The Haunting of Hill House* (1959), which was nominated for the National Book Award, as well as four short-story collections, two memoirs, and four children's books.

RANDALL JARRELL (1914–1965) was a poet and novelist who served as the United States poet laureate from 1956 to 1958. His books include *Pictures from an Institution* (1954) and *The Woman at the Washington Zoo* (1960), which won a National Book Award.

E. J. KAHN, JR. (1916–1994), became a staff writer at *The New Yorker* in 1937 and remained at the magazine for five decades. He wrote twenty-seven books, including *The Separated People* (1968), *The American People* (1974), and *About The New Yorker and Me* (1979).

WELDON KEES (1914–1955) was a poet, novelist, and painter whose books include *The Last Man* (1943) and *The Fall of the Magicians* (1947).

DAVID LARDNER (1919–1944) wrote about theatre, film, and sports for *The New Yorker.* He was killed in Germany during the Second World War while reporting for the magazine.

JOHN LARDNER (1912–1960), the brother of David Lardner, wrote a television-and-radio column, The Air, for the magazine for many years.

JILL LEPORE, a staff writer and a professor of history at Harvard, has been contributing to *The New Yorker* since 2005. Her books include *The Name of War*, which won the Bancroft Prize in 1999, *New York Burning* (2005), and *Book of Ages* (2013).

A. J. LIEBLING (1904–1963) joined the staff of *The New Yorker* in 1935. During the Second World War he was a correspondent in Europe and Africa. After the war he wrote the magazine's Wayward Press column for many years. His books include *The Sweet Science* (1956), *The Earl of Louisiana* (1961), and *Between Meals* (1962).

LOIS LONG (1901–1974) joined *The New Yorker* in 1925. She wrote the Feminine Fashions column from 1927 until 1968.

ARCHIBALD MACLEISH (1892–1982) was a poet, playwright, and essayist and the Librarian of Congress between 1939 and 1944. His *Collected Poems: 1917–1952* won a Pulitzer Prize and a National Book Award in 1953.

LOUIS MACNEICE (1907–1963) was a poet, playwright, and essayist whose books include *The Last Ditch* (1940), *Holes in the Sky* (1948), and *The Burning Perch* (1963).

WILLIAM MAXWELL (1908–2000) was a novelist, short-story writer, essayist, and children's author who served as the fiction editor for *The New Yorker* from 1936 to 1975. His books include *So Long, See You Tomorrow*, which won a National Book Award in 1982, and *All the Days and Nights: The Collected Stories* (1995).

JOHN MCCARTEN (1911–1974) joined the staff of *The New Yorker* in 1934 and began reviewing films for the magazine in 1945.

CARSON MCCULLERS (1917–1967) was a novelist and short-story writer. Her books include *The Heart Is a Lonely Hunter* (1940) and *The Member of the Wedding* (1946).

ST. CLAIR MCKELWAY (1905–1980) joined the staff of *The New Yorker* in 1933. He was the magazine's managing editor between 1936 and 1939, and he contributed numerous pieces throughout his long career. His books include *True Tales from the Annals of Crime & Rascality* (1950) and a posthumous collection, *Reporting at Wit's End* (2010).

LOUIS MENAND, a professor of English at Harvard, has contributed to *The New Yorker* since 1991, and has been a staff writer since 2001. His books include *The Metaphysical Club* (2001), which won a Pulitzer Prize and a Francis Parkman Prize from the Society of American Historians, *American Studies* (2002), and *The Marketplace of Ideas* (2010).

JOSEPH MITCHELL (1908–1996) began writing for the magazine in 1933. His books include *McSorley's Wonderful Saloon* (1943), *Joe Gould's Secret* (1965), and *Up in the Old Hotel and Other Stories* (1992).

JOHN MOSHER (1892–1942) wrote for *The New Yorker* from 1926 to 1942.

LEWIS MUMFORD (1895–1990), a philosopher, literary critic, historian, and city planner, wrote the magazine's architecture column, The Sky

Line, from 1931 to 1963. He wrote numerous books, including *The City in History* (1961), which won a National Book Award.

VLADIMIR NABOKOV (1899–1977) was a Russian-born writer who immigrated to the United States in 1940. He began contributing to *The New Yorker* in 1942, and his fiction, poetry, and memoirs appeared in the magazine throughout the rest of his life. His novels include *Lolita* (1955), *Pnin* (1957), and *Pale Fire* (1962).

OGDEN NASH (1902–1971) was a poet renowned for his light verse. He began contributing to *The New Yorker* in 1930, and he spent three months working on the magazine's editorial staff the following year. His books include *I'm a Stranger Here Myself* (1938), *Good Intentions* (1942), and *Bed Riddance* (1969).

HOWARD NEMEROV (1920–1991) was the United States poet laureate from 1963 to 1964 and again from 1988 to 1990. "The Triumph of Education," reprinted here, was his first contribution to *The New Yorker*. His *Collected Poems* (1977) won a National Book Award, a Pulitzer Prize, and a Bollingen Prize.

FRANK O'CONNOR (1903–1966) was an Irish writer best known for his short stories. He began contributing to *The New Yorker* in 1945. His books include *Guests of the Nation* (1931), *Traveller's Samples* (1951), and *Domestic Relations* (1957).

JOHN O'HARA (1905–1970) was a novelist and short-story writer. He first contributed to *The New Yorker* in 1928, and he went on to publish more than two hundred short stories in the magazine, more than any other writer. His novels include *Appointment in Samarra* (1934), *BUtterfield 8* (1935), and *Ten North Frederick* (1955), which won a National Book Award.

SUSAN ORLEAN began contributing articles and Talk of the Town pieces to *The New Yorker* in 1987 and became a staff writer in 1992. She is the author of *The Orchid Thief* (1998), *The Bullfighter Checks Her Makeup* (2001), and *Rin Tin Tin* (2011).

GEORGE ORWELL (1903–1950) was the pen name of Eric Arthur Blair, a novelist, essayist, journalist, and critic. His books include *Homage* *to Catalonia* (1938), *Animal Farm* (1945), and *Nineteen Eighty-Four* (1949).

GEORGE PACKER became a staff writer for *The New Yorker* in 2003 and covered the Iraq War for the magazine. His books include *The Assassins' Gate,* which was named one of the ten best books of 2005 by *The New York Times* and won the New York Public Library's Helen Bernstein Book Award for Excellence in Journalism and an Overseas Press Club's book award, and *The Unwinding,* which won a 2013 National Book Award.

MOLLIE PANTER-DOWNES (1906–1997) became a bestselling author at the age of sixteen, with her début novel, *The Shoreless Sea* (1923). Her other novels include *The Chase* (1925), *My Husband Simon* (1931), and *One Fine Day* (1947). She wrote the magazine's Letter from London column for five decades, starting in 1939.

V. S. PRITCHETT (1900–1997) was a writer best known for his short stories, and a book critic for *The New Yorker* for many years. "The Ladder," reprinted here, was his first story for the magazine. His books include *The Complete Short Stories* (1990) and *Complete Collected Essays* (1991).

DAVID REMNICK has been the editor of *The New Yorker* since 1998. He became a staff writer in 1992 and has written more than a hundred pieces for the magazine. He is the author of *Lenin's Tomb* (1993), for which he received a Pulitzer Prize, *The Devil Problem* (1996), *Resurrection* (1997), *King of the World* (1998), *Reporting* (2006), and *The Bridge* (2010).

THEODORE ROETHKE (1908–1963) was a poet whose books include *Words for the Wind* (1957) and *The Far Field* (1964), both of which won a National Book Award. He began contributing to *The New Yorker* in 1937.

ALEX ROSS has been contributing to *The New Yorker* since 1993 and became the magazine's music critic in 1996. He is the author of *The Rest Is Noise* (2007), which won a National Book Critics Circle Award and a Guardian First Book Award, and *Listen to This* (2010).

HAROLD ROSS (1892–1951) founded *The New Yorker* in 1925 and served as its editor from the first issue until his death.

LILLIAN ROSS became a staff writer at *The New Yorker* in 1945. She is the author of several books, including *Picture* (1952), *Portrait of Hemingway* (1961), and *Here but Not Here* (1998).

RICHARD ROVERE (1915–1979) joined *The New Yorker* in 1944 and wrote the magazine's Letter from Washington column from 1948 until his death. His books include *The American Establishment and Other Reports, Opinions, and Speculations* (1962) and *Waist Deep in the Big Muddy* (1968).

WINTHROP SARGEANT (1903–1986) was a writer, critic, and violinist. In 1930, after stints playing with the New York Symphony and the New York Philharmonic, he abandoned his musical career to become a writer. From 1949 to 1972 he wrote the Musical Events column for *The New Yorker*, and he continued to contribute to the magazine until his death.

PETER SCHJELDAHL joined *The New Yorker* in 1998 as the magazine's art critic. He is the author of four books, including *The Hydrogen Jukebox* (1991) and *Let's See* (2008).

IRWIN SHAW (1913–1984) was a playwright, screenwriter, novelist, and short-story writer whose books include *The Young Lions* (1948), *Rich Man, Poor Man* (1970), and *God Was Here, but He Left Early* (1973).

ROBERT A. SIMON (1897–1981) was a writer and translator. He was *The New Yorker*'s music critic from its first issue in 1925 until 1948. His books include *Our Little Girl* (1923) and *Sweet & Low* (1926).

ZADIE SMITH is the author of four novels, *White Teeth* (2000), *The Autograph Man* (2002), *On Beauty* (2005), and *NW* (2012), and a collection of essays, *Changing My Mind* (2009).

STEPHEN SPENDER (1909–1995) was a poet, novelist, and essayist. His books include *The Still Centre* (1939), *Ruins and Visions* (1942), and *The Edge of Being* (1949).

ELIZABETH TAYLOR (1912–1975) was a novelist and short-story writer. Her books include *A Game of Hide and Seek* (1951) and *The Real Life of Angel Deverell* (1957).

JUDITH THURMAN began contributing to *The New Yorker* in 1987, and became a staff writer in 2000. She is the author of *Isak Dinesen: The Life of a Storyteller* (1982), which won a National Book Award; *Secrets of the Flesh: A Life of Colette* (1999), which won a Los Angeles Times Book Award; and *Cleopatra's Nose* (2007), a collection of her pieces from the magazine.

LIONEL TRILLING (1905–1975) was a professor of English at Columbia whose books include *The Liberal Imagination* (1950), *The Opposing Self* (1955), and *Beyond Culture* (1965).

NICCOLÒ TUCCI (1908–1999) was an Italian-born novelist and short-story writer who immigrated to the United States in 1938. "The Evolution of Knowledge," reprinted here, was his first contribution to *The New Yorker*.

MARK VAN DOREN (1894–1972) was a poet, critic, and scholar. His *Collected Poems: 1922–1938* won a Pulitzer Prize.

JESSAMYN WEST (1902–1984) was a novelist and short-story writer. Her books include *The Friendly Persuasion* (1945), *Love Is Not What You Think* (1959), and *Except for Me and Thee* (1969).

REBECCA WEST (1892–1983) was an English journalist, literary critic, and travel writer. Her books include *Black Lamb and Grey Falcon* (1941), *The Meaning of Treason* (1949), and *A Train of Powder* (1955), based on her articles about the Nuremberg trials, originally published in *The New Yorker*.

E. B. WHITE (1899–1985) joined the staff of *The New Yorker* in 1927. He contributed humor pieces, poems, short stories, newsbreak captions, and even one cover illustration, but he was most associated with the Notes and Comment essays, which he wrote for thirty years. His books include the children's classics *Stuart Little* (1945), *Charlotte's Web* (1952), and *The Trumpet of the Swan* (1970). He received the Presidential Medal of Freedom in 1963 and an honorary Pulitzer Prize in 1978 for his work as a whole.

RICHARD WILBUR is a poet and translator. He was the United States poet laureate from 1987 to 1988. His books include *Things of This World*

(1956), which won a Pulitzer Prize and a National Book Award, and *New and Collected Poems* (1988), which also won a Pulitzer Prize.

WILLIAM CARLOS WILLIAMS (1883–1963) was a poet and doctor. His books include *Spring and All* (1923), *The Desert Music and Other Poems* (1954), *Pictures from Brueghel and Other Poems* (1962), which won a Pulitzer Prize, and *Paterson* (1963).

EDMUND WILSON (1895–1972) was a critic, novelist, and poet. He became *The New Yorker*'s book critic in 1944, a position he held for many years. His numerous books include *Axel's Castle* (1931), *To the Finland Station* (1940), and *The Shores of Light* (1952).

ABOUT THE TYPE

This book was set in Caslon, a typeface first designed in 1722 by William Caslon (1692–1766). Its widespread use by most English printers in the early eighteenth century soon supplanted the Dutch typefaces that had formerly prevailed. The roman is considered a "workhorse" typeface due to its pleasant, open appearance, while the italic is exceedingly decorative.